The Wars of the Romans

ALBERICO GENTILI

The Wars of the Romans

A Critical Edition and Translation of *De armis Romanis*

Edited by
BENEDICT KINGSBURY
and
BENJAMIN STRAUMANN

Translated by
DAVID LUPHER

A project of the Institute for International Law and Justice at New York University School of Law

OXFORD
UNIVERSITY PRESS

OXFORD
UNIVERSITY PRESS

Great Clarendon Street, Oxford OX2 6DP

Oxford University Press is a department of the University of Oxford.
It furthers the University's objective of excellence in research, scholarship,
and education by publishing worldwide in

Oxford New York

Auckland Cape Town Dar es Salaam Hong Kong Karachi
Kuala Lumpur Madrid Melbourne Mexico City Nairobi
New Delhi Shanghai Taipei Toronto

With offices in

Argentina Austria Brazil Chile Czech Republic France Greece
Guatemala Hungary Italy Japan Poland Portugal Singapore
South Korea Switzerland Thailand Turkey Ukraine Vietnam

Published in the United States
by Oxford University Press Inc., New York

First published 2011

British Library Cataloguing in Publication Data
Data available

Library of Congress Cataloging in Publication Data
Data available

Typeset by SPI Publisher Services, Pondicherry, India
Printed in Great Britain
on acid-free paper by
CPI Antony Rowe

ISBN 978–0–19–960051–9

1 3 5 7 9 10 8 6 4 2

Editors' Note and Acknowledgments

This edition of Alberico Gentili's *De armis Romanis* (1599) represents both the first translation of this book into English or any other language, and its first publication in Latin since it was reprinted in the (uncompleted) Naples edition of Gentili's collected works in 1770. As editors we are deeply indebted to Professor David Lupher, a classical scholar who has made a major contribution also to the field of the early modern reception of the classics with his book *Romans in a New World: Classical Models in Sixteenth-Century Spanish America* (2003). In undertaking this translation and entering upon the field of Gentili studies, he has brought to the project his wide erudition and exceptional gifts as a translator and scholar. This edition would not have been conceivable without David's imagination, thoroughness, and dry wit.

The modern study of Alberico Gentili (1552–1608) owes a great deal to the pioneering work and continued leadership of Professor Diego Panizza, Professor Emeritus of the History of Political Thought at the University of Padua. His innovative book *Alberico Gentili, giurista ideologo nell'Inghilterra elisabettiana* (1981), which remains a leading contribution to scholarship on Gentili, has been followed by a rich series of papers illuminating many aspects of Gentili's work, including a seminal essay on *De armis Romanis* prepared for the volume we have edited as a companion to the present text and translation, *The Roman Foundations of the Law of Nations: Alberico Gentili and the Justice of Empire* (Oxford University Press). That essay, together with the learned essay on *De armis Romanis* by David Lupher in the same volume, are to the best of our knowledge among the first critical studies of *De armis Romanis*. Our aim in editing the companion volume has been to provide readers who become interested in this and related works of Gentili with a set of contemporary essays by leading scholars placing that work in its wider contexts.

Much of the more recent scholarly work on Gentili has been undertaken with the Centro Internazionale Studi Gentiliani (CISG). The founding of the CISG in Gentili's birthplace, San Ginesio, in 1981 began a new phase in the recrudescence of studies of Gentili launched by Thomas Erskine Holland's 1874 Oxford inaugural lecture on Gentili and Grotius. Led with much success in 1991–8 by the late Alessandro Taccari, the CISG's very substantial recent academic and programmatic work has been orchestrated through to publication of the present volume under the indefatigable leadership of Pepe Ragoni of San Ginesio. She has organized conferences, raised funds, identified possible speakers, and provided newly clarified information on Gentili's biography, some of which is incorporated into our short

chronological compilation of principal events in Gentili's life. The regular publications of the CISG in the series issued by Giuffré in Milan have given an important impetus to modern Gentili studies. We are deeply indebted to Pepe Ragoni, Diego Panizza, and all involved in the CISG for their support.

Support for this translation came from the Comitato Nazionale Alberico Gentili in Italy, whose members are listed below, as well as four associated sponsors from the private sector in Italy, also listed below. We are grateful to them, and to New York University School of Law, particularly Dean Richard Revesz, the Institute for International Law and Justice, the Hauser Global Law School Program, the Straus Institute for the Advanced Study of Law and Justice, and the Greenberg and D'Agostino Research Fund. This is a publication of the Program in the History and Theory of International Law at NYU Law School.

John Louth and Alex Flach at Oxford University Press have given this project their steadfast encouragement from the outset. We are grateful also to Fiona Stables and Natasha Knight for supervising the production process, Bonnie Blackburn for her exceptional copy-editing, Leofranc Holford-Strevens for the proofreading, and Yvonne Dixon for compiling the indices.

In identifying and tracking down Gentili's marginal references, we have received generous assistance from Professor Kenneth Pennington (Catholic University of America), who gave much help on legal sources, Christian Zendri and Giuliano Marchetto (Università di Trento), Katherine Eggert (University of Colorado), Daniel Kinney (University of Virginia), and Professor Jan Waszink (Erasmus University Rotterdam). Professor Ann Blair (Harvard University) provided help on early modern *Problemata* literature. Needless to say, any remaining errors are our own.

We thank also Dr. Meredith Shedd-Driskel and the staff of the Madison Law Library of the Library of Congress, the staff of the Sonderlesesaal of the Universitätsbibliothek Basel, the staff of the Rare Book and Manuscript Library at Columbia University's Butler Library, and Sabrina Sondhi and the other librarians at the Arthur W. Diamond Law Library at Columbia University School of Law.

Benjamin Straumann extends special thanks to Ossai Miazad and Andreas Gyr for enduring so much of Gentili and the darkness of some of his marginalia, and to Patrick Straumann for help with the cover design.

Benedict Kingsbury expresses his deep appreciation to Benjamin Straumann, whose expertise in classical languages and sources has led to his taking on the entire burden of the more recondite scholarly work required to produce this edition, in close and fruitful collaboration with David Lupher.

The Comitato Nazionale Alberico Gentili, which has supported preparation of this volume, is organized under the patronage of the Ministero per i Beni e le Attività Culturali, Direzione Generale per i beni librari, gli istituti culturali e il diritto d'autore, and consists of: Ministro per i beni e le attività

culturali; Ministro degli affari esteri; Ministro della pubblica istruzione; Ministro dell'università e della ricerca; Ambasciatore d'Italia Giuseppe Balboni Acqua; Presidente della Regione Marche; Presidente della Provincia di Macerata; Sindaco del Comune di San Ginesio; Università degli studi di Macerata; Università degli studi di Camerino; Università degli studi di Perugia; Università degli studi di Padova; Università degli studi di Napoli 'L'Orientale'; Università degli studi di Roma 'La Sapienza'; Associazione Italiana storici delle dottrine politiche; Società Italiana diritto internazionale; Istituto studi giuridici internazionali del CNR; Consiglio nazionale forense; Centro internazionale studi Gentiliani; Giorgio Badiali; Giuseppe Cataldi; Peter Haggenmacher; Tony Honoré; Benedict Kingsbury; Luigi Lacchè; Anna Maria Lazzarino Del Grosso; Vaughan Lowe; Sergio Marchisio; Filippo Mignini; Giovanni Minnucci; Massimo Montella; Diego Panizza; Diego Quaglioni; Pepe Ragoni; Boudewijn Sirks; Ferdinando Treggiari; Alain Wijffels. Further financial support was kindly provided by: Fondazione Cassa di Risparmio della Provincia di Macerata; Camera di Commercio Industria Artigianato e Agricoltura di Macerata; Silvano Lattanzi; Fondazione Cassa di Risparmio di Fermo.

B.K., B.S.

New York
June 2010

Benedict Kingsbury is Murry and Ida Becker Professor of Law at New York University. He specializes in the history and theory of international law and his publications include *Hugo Grotius and International Relations* (Oxford University Press, 1990, with Hedley Bull and Adam Roberts) and *Alberico Gentili e il Mondo Extra-Europeo* (Giuffrè, 2001).

Benjamin Straumann is Alberico Gentili Fellow at New York University. He is the author of *Hugo Grotius und die Antike: Römisches Recht und römische Ethik im frühneuzeitlichen Naturrecht* (Nomos Verlagsgesellschaft, 2007) and co-editor (with Benedict Kingsbury) of *The Roman Foundations of the Law of Nations: Alberico Gentili and the Justice of Empire* (Oxford University Press, 2010).

Professor David Lupher is Professor of Classics at the University of Puget Sound. He is the author of *Romans in a New World: Classical Models in Sixteenth-Century Spanish America* (University of Michigan Press, 2003).

Contents

Introduction: Roman Wars and Roman Laws

How can questions concerning imperial expansion be addressed from the perspective of justice? To what extent does law provide a satisfactory way of making assessments of the justice or rectitude of imperial wars, imperial conquests, and governance within a far-flung empire? How does the law concerning relations within and between empires overlap or differ from the law concerning interstate relations? To what extent are specific practices and legal principles of the Roman empire instantiations of arguments about universal moral principles of justice in imperial and interstate relations applicable also to other contexts?

In *The Wars of the Romans*, first published in its complete form by Wilhelm Anton in Hanau-am-Main in 1599, the Italian jurist Alberico Gentili explicitly deals with the military expansion of the Roman empire from the perspectives of law and justice. The publication of *De armis Romanis* followed the publication in 1598, by the same publisher, of Gentili's most widely known and influential work, *The Law of War (De iure belli libri tres). De armis Romanis* appeared as a single volume, comprising two books. The first book, under the title "Indictment of the Injustice of the Romans in Warfare," constitutes an attack on Roman imperialism in thirteen chapters, accusing the Romans of unjust warfare and culminating in a chapter on "The Tyranny of the Romans." The second book, titled "Defense of the Justice of the Romans in Warfare," aims at rebutting chapter by chapter the accusations of injustice made in the first book, concluding with a eulogy of Roman imperialism in the final chapter, "The Good Fortune of the Roman Empire."

The prosecution of Roman imperialism in the first book is entrusted to "Picenus," while the defense has as its voice that of "a Roman," a Roman, however, familiar with many of Gentili's contemporary authors and thus clearly not of the classical era. "Picenus" means someone hailing from ancient Picenum, the modern Marche d'Ancona in Italy, which is Alberico Gentili's native region; moreover, the Picenus in question is clearly identified as being from San Ginesio,[1] Gentili's place of birth, and as a civil lawyer by education. This poses a puzzle for the reader—the critic of Roman imperialism is given the trappings and vestments of Alberico Gentili, yet Gentili himself as author of the two books seems rather more sympathetic to the point of view expressed in Book 2 by the Roman. This may be simply a literary device to maintain the tension of the debate. A further explanation, suggested by

[1] *The Wars of the Romans* 2. 5, p. 203: "you men of San Ginesio, you San Ginesians."

David Lupher,[2] is connected to the history of the development of *The Wars of the Romans*. The work had developed out of a pair of speeches originally devised as public speeches (*actiones*) to be delivered at ceremonial occasions at the faculty of law at the University of Oxford. The first version of the first speech had originally been published by the printer of Oxford University, Joseph Barnes, under the title *De iniustitia bellica Romanorum actio*, accompanied by a dedicatory epistle to the Earl of Essex, Robert Devereux (reprinted, with English translation, as an Appendix to the present volume). The dedication mentions that Gentili had "ready a defense of the Romans and a disputation directly opposed to this one on their justice in making wars,"[3] but the second speech was never published in its original form. Lupher suggests that when Gentili revised, and considerably expanded, the speeches for publication as *The Wars of the Romans* in the late 1590s, calling the prosecutor of Book 1 "Picenus" was an ironic way of acknowledging the printed earlier version of the "indictment," which had appeared under Gentili's name. When writing in the voice of the Roman defender of imperialism of Book 2, Gentili dismisses ironically the stance of the prosecutor in Book 1 as that of a narrow-minded provincial from San Ginesio.

As the titles of its two books suggest, *The Wars of the Romans* affirms and indeed presupposes that considerations of justice are relevant to international relations and to proper assessment of the behavior and norms of imperial Rome. In writing the arguments for both sides in the debate about the justice of the Roman empire, Gentili does not attribute to either side the claim that there are no moral norms that govern and constrain the external or internal actions of states. To the contrary, both the indictment of Roman imperialism in Book 1 of *The Wars of the Romans* and its defense in Book 2 are predicated on the assumption that it is apposite to judge the expansion of the Roman empire by way of warfare according to certain moral normative criteria—indeed, denying or affirming the justice of the Roman empire is precisely what *The Wars of the Romans* is all about. The accusation against the Roman empire is not framed principally in terms of the prudential considerations that inform much thought in the realist tradition of politics, but instead focuses on criteria of justice; and the defense in Book 2 maintains, not that making claims of justice in the international realm is essentially impossible or undesirable, but that Roman imperialism was *just*. There are nonetheless strands in Book 2 of arguments that attribute some justificatory force to self-interest and *raison d'état*. Gentili's early interest in Machiavelli's thought, evident, for example, in his *De legationibus* (1585), can be traced to these aspects of *De armis Romanis*.

---

[2] See Lupher's contribution in B. Kingsbury and B. Straumann (eds.), *The Roman Foundations of the Law of Nations: Alberico Gentili and the Justice of Empire* (Oxford: Oxford University Press, 2010).

[3] *quoniam Defensionem Romanorum et disputationem huic adversariam de ipsorum iustitia bellica paratam habeo.*

The contentions between the prosecutor of Book 1 and the defender of Book 2 are frequently framed not as disagreements about what norms apply; rather, the disagreement is often empirical, about historical events and the trustworthiness of certain historians and other authors. While the prosecutor favors such authors as the second-century AD historian Florus and the Fathers of the Church, the defender emphasizes the accuracy and trustworthiness of Polybius, Livy, and Dionysius of Halicarnassus. For example, adducing Florus, the epitomator of Livy who is one of his favorite sources, the prosecutor in Book 1 accuses Romulus of having "seized upon an excuse for war against the inhabitants of Fidenae—as if those men drove off booty from your Roman territory."[4] Countering the accusation, the defender of Book 2 first notes that the accusator fails to make mention of a great many of Rome's expansionary wars, presuming that the historical facts do not bear out the prosecutor's claims: "[A]s for the very many wars of the Romans, the accuser's silent admission stands to my account, for despite the vast number of the wars he dared to discuss only a very few."[5] He then goes on to undermine the historical credibility of the prosecutor's source, instead putting forward his own favorite historian, namely Livy. The issue at hand is still Romulus' conflict with the inhabitants of Fidenae:

> But what is the man thinking when he begins with the Fidenates? For did not the Fidenates themselves stir up the war through their depredations and ravaging? But that reliable and careful writer, the esteemed Livy, writes about this—a writer incomparably preferable to Florus. Who is Florus here, that he be trusted against Livy and Dionysius [of Halicarnassus]?[6]

In arguing the case against or for the justice of the Roman empire in terms of contending views of the empirical-historical record,[7] both Picenus, the prosecutor of Book 1, and the Roman defending his city in Book 2 seem implicitly to agree on the normative criteria to be applied, including moral criteria.[8]

The shared criteria for determining whether a particular war that expanded the Roman empire was just or unjust are grounded in the standards of Roman fetial law and ultimately of natural law, in a way strongly reminiscent of the so-called Carneadean dialogue in book 3 of Cicero's *Republic*.[9] Gentili's framing of the question of the justice or injustice of empire and imperial

---

[4] *The Wars of the Romans* 1. 2, p. 31.

[5] *The Wars of the Romans* 2. 2, p. 161.

[6] Ibid.

[7] See e.g. the discussion of the respective weight and authority of various historical sources in *The Wars of the Romans* 2. 8, p. 232–235. Note also how Gentili motivates his undertaking in the dedicatory epistle to Essex to his earlier *De iniustitia bellica Romanorum actio* (see Appendix to this volume).

[8] See Diego Panizza's remark in his *Alberico Gentili, giurista ideologo nell'Inghilterra elisabettiana* (Padua, 1981), 127 n. 56. See also David Lupher's contribution in Kingsbury and Straumann (eds.), *The Roman Foundations*, 85–100.

[9] See for this argument David Lupher's contribution in Kingsbury and Straumann (eds.), *The Roman Foundations*.

wars in terms of Roman law and Roman just-war theory is a fundamental feature of *De armis Romanis*. Cicero's text cannot have been known to Gentili directly, but was familiar to him through its partial transmission in Lactantius' and Augustine's works. In Cicero's version (which also had an important impact on the thought of Hugo Grotius), the Carneadean dialogue concerning imperialism and international justice takes place between Lucius Furius Philus, standing in (albeit unwillingly) for the Greek skeptic Carneades and attacking the possibility of justice in international affairs, and the learned Gaius Laelius, who defends the applicability of moral, justice-based arguments in international relations.[10]

Carneades' skeptical, "realist" argument, which is reproduced (without being embraced) in Book 1 of Gentili's *Wars of the Romans*, maintains that international affairs are governed only by self-interest and criteria of expedience, not by justice. There simply are no standards of justice to be had in international affairs, according to Carneades, or if there were any, no one could be motivated to adhere to them. The argument is then applied to Roman imperialism, where it is presented as a *reductio*; if the Romans wanted to be just, they would have to give up the gains resulting from their imperialism, a course of action quite obviously lacking in motivational force. In *The Wars of the Romans*, Picenus, the prosecutor in Book 1, cites Cicero's *Republic* in the following passage:

> And thus Carneades quite properly told you, Romans, that if you wished to be just, you ought to return to those huts from which you first set forth, and you ought to surrender this empire of the world.[11] Was it not from huts you set forth? "Had Rome not moved forth its power into the vast world, she would even now be filled with straw huts."[12]

The Roman imperialist of Book 2 in his direct answer does not have any patience for the *reductio*, but nor does he embrace Carneades. Instead he purports to direct the debate toward empirical evidence: "[I]t is enough and more than enough if we win through some real arguments. Throw away those empty words: . . . the huts, . . . and the straw. Direct your contention over here at the real issues."[13] However, the whole structure of the argument of Book 2 can be understood as being based on Carneades' challenge, and on Laelius' answer to it in Cicero's *Republic*. It takes seriously the need to defend Rome's expansion in terms of justice, rather than as a prudential, expedient course of action based on successful pursuit of self-interest. Moreover, Book 2 of *The*

---

[10] For Cicero's treatment of the original Carneadean debate, see J. E. G. Zetzel, "Natural Law and Poetic Justice: A Carneadean Debate in Cicero and Virgil," *Classical Philology*, 91 (1996), 297–319.

[11] From Cicero, *De republica* 3. 21, which Gentili can only have known from a passage in Lactantius, *Divinae institutiones* 5. 16. 2–5, the end of which is: *omnibus populis qui florerent imperio, et Romanis quoque ipsis qui totius orbis potirentur, si iusti velint esse, hoc est si aliena restituant, ad casas esse redeundum et in egestate ac miseriis iacendum*. The point is made in the context of Carneades' argument that justice consists in stupidity.

[12] *The Wars of the Romans* 1. 8, p. 69. The last quotation is from Ovid, *Amores* 2. 9. 17–18.

[13] *The Wars of the Romans* 2. 8, p. 249.

Wars of the Romans also borrows from Cicero's rendering of the Carneadean debate the idea that the international norms of justice to which the Roman empire is held answerable should be couched in terms of a universal natural law and the Roman doctrine of just war.

In Cicero's *Republic*, the standard of justice is natural law, which is put forward in its traditional Stoic form at the beginning of Laelius' defense of Rome's justice thus: "True law is right reason, consonant with nature, spread through all people. It is constant and eternal; it summons to duty by its orders, deters from crime by its prohibitions.... [A]ll nations at all times will be bound by this one eternal and unchangeable law."[14] When applied in Cicero to the specific question of the justice of Roman imperialism, the natural law argument for Rome's empire rests on two central claims. First is the claim that the empire had been gained by virtue of just wars.[15] Second is what might be called the "civilizational" claim, that Rome's conquest and rule had made the conquered better off by taking away the right to do injury "from wicked people."[16]

This is the background tradition within which *The Wars of the Romans* is to be situated.[17] The two claims on behalf of Roman imperialism as put forward in Cicero's *Republic* by Laelius constitute the foundation on which the Roman defender of Book 2 of *The Wars of the Romans* builds his argument, an argument provoked by a self-conscious invocation of Philus' Carneadean challenge to those claims. The following passage from the accusation in Book 1 illustrates this with regard to the first claim. Adducing Lactantius, who in turn is giving a summary of Philus' speech in Cicero's *Republic*, the accuser, Picenus, asserts that Roman just-war doctrine was void of any moral content. Accusing the Roman people of being "passionate with love for wars and ready to inflict war upon peoples when there was often no just reason," Picenus goes on to discuss the adoption of the fetial laws and the legal formalities of just-war doctrine by the Romans:

> But are we to call it [i.e. just-war doctrine] a remedy—or rather a sticking plaster and rouge? Rouge would be the better term. Look what... Firmianus Lactantius tells us: "Just how far utility stands from justice the Roman people itself teaches us, for by declaring wars through the fetial priests and imposing wrongs under cover of law and by always craving and plundering other peoples' things they acquired for themselves possession of the entire world."[18]

---

[14] Cicero, *De republica* 3. 33: *Est quidem vera lex recta ratio, naturae congruens, diffusa in omnis, constans, sempiterna, quae vocet ad officium iubendo, vetando a fraude deterreat... et omnes gentes et omni tempore una lex et sempiterna et inmutabilis continebit....* This passage from the *Republic* was known to Gentili through the Christian apologist Lactantius. For Cicero's formulation of Stoic natural law doctrine, see also Cicero, *De legibus* 1. 22 ff.

[15] Cicero, *De republica* 3. 34–5.

[16] Ibid. 3. 36. Translations from the *Republic* are from *Cicero, On the Commonwealth and On the Laws*, ed. J. E. G. Zetzel (Cambridge: Cambridge University Press, 1999).

[17] See David Lupher's contribution in Kingsbury and Straumann (eds.), *The Roman Foundations.*

[18] *The Wars of the Romans* 1. 3, p. 35. The Lactantius passage is from *Divinae institutiones* 6. 9. 3–4 (= Cicero, *De republica* 3. 20).

Against this accusation, Gentili has Rome's defender in Book 2 of *The Wars of the Romans* use the language of Roman just-war theory, stressing those elements in the fetial law concerning the waging of a just war that carry some moral weight and are not mere legal formalities; defending the record of King Tullus, the Roman says: "Tullus also declares war against the Sabines because there were wrongs done (*iniuriae factae*) on both sides, and things seized were sought back (*res repetitae*) in vain."[19] The seeking of redress (*rerum repetitio*) after an injury (*iniuria*) has been done is, according to the fetial law, one of the necessary conditions for the waging of a just war. It is described, along with the other conditions, by Laelius in Cicero's *Republic*: "No war is considered just unless it is announced and declared and unless it involves recovery of property."[20] This can also mean the recovery of property on behalf of allies; the Roman empire is thus said to have "gained control of the entire world through defending its allies."[21] This doctrine is invoked by Gentili's Roman defender, who argues that the Samnite War had been undertaken not on behalf of the Romans themselves, but—"something much more respectable"—on behalf of their allies, the Campanians.[22] Against the charge that it was "cheating, perfidy, avarice, audacity, cruelty that brought forth" Roman rule and the empire,[23] Rome's defender in Book 2 asserts that all of Rome's wars had been waged as just wars according to the criteria of the Roman just-war doctrine; relying on Livy and Dionysius of Halicarnassus, he states that "it is fitting to affirm the testimony of the most serious men, who record that the Romans never took up arms except in just causes."[24]

As in Cicero, there is a strong sense in *The Wars of the Romans* that the specifically Roman institution of fetial law, with its just-war procedure, has the source of its validity in natural law—or at least that natural law is the source of the morally relevant parts of Roman just-war doctrine, particularly those concerned with the recovery of property. This normative kernel is acknowledged by Picenus in the first book and by Rome's defender in the second,[25] as in the following claim: "But our activity was not solely directed at acquiring an empire, but also at acquiring it honestly, through just causes."[26]

---

[19] *The Wars of the Romans* 2. 3, p. 168f: *Bellum et Sabinis indicit Tullus: quod utrinque factæ essent injuriæ: et res nequidquam repetitæ essent.* See for Tullus' war against the Sabines, Livy 1. 30. 4 ff.

[20] *De republica* 3. 35: *Nullum bellum iustum habetur nisi denuntiatum, nisi dictum, nisi de repetitis rebus.* Gentili knows this passage from Isidore of Seville, *Etymologiae* 18. 1. 2–3; cf. Cicero, *De officiis* 1. 36. See also Cicero, *De republica* 2. 31 (a passage Gentili could not have known).

[21] *De republica* 3. 35: *Noster autem populus sociis defendendis terrarum iam omnium potitus est.*

[22] *The Wars of the Romans* 2. 7, p. 227. This argument was subsequently made by Grotius in *De iure praedae* (1604–8) in defending Dutch actions against Portuguese vessels in the East Indies on the grounds that the Dutch were coming to the aid of their ally, the Sultan of Johore, who had been a victim of Portuguese depredations.

[23] *The Wars of the Romans* 1. 1, p. 17.

[24] *The Wars of the Romans* 2. 7, p. 215.

[25] Cf. *The Wars of the Romans* 1. 7, p. 57: "Or is there no justification in nature for the principle that profits acquired by others not be taken away from them?"

[26] *The Wars of the Romans* 2. 12, p. 331.

The second, civilizational, claim made by Laelius in the *Republic*, namely that Rome's conquest and rule had made the conquered better off by taking away the right to do injury "from wicked people," has equally important reverberations in Gentili's late sixteenth-century framing of the debate on *The Wars of the Romans*. In the following passage, Picenus makes the case that, compared to the Roman empire, the Ottoman empire of his own day hardly qualifies as barbarian, then cites from Tacitus' *Agricola* the Caledonian chieftain Calgacus' famous anti-Roman speech:

> Go off and tell me about Turkish barbarity! You hear of provinces conquered with the blood of provinces. Where they have made a solitude, there they used to allege that they had established peace, as the Briton [Calgacus] complained.[27] Robbers of the whole world, whom neither the East nor the West will have satisfied, and who, although they have shut up the whole world in that city of theirs, nonetheless coveted the little huts of the Britons—as the Briton [Calgacus] cries out in the same place.[28] "Like a stomach that can't be filled is Rome, consuming everything and always hungry still, since into its lap are gathered the riches scraped away from all the overthrown cities and the denuded lands"—and so on. (The pious and religious witness Orosius writes these things.[29]) "The one and only state born for the destruction of the human race," says Arnobius,[30] a holy man.[31]

To answer this hyperbole, the defender in Book 2 asserts the civilizing effect of Roman rule. Far from making a solitude and calling it peace, the Romans had pacified the territories of the subjugated peoples by eliminating "kings and chieftans, who were the sources of internal wars there," and, what is more, Rome thus established "public tranquility and, so to speak, the health of a single well-joined body." The peoples of Italy, the defender maintains, "before the time of the Roman Empire . . . were considered barbarians not only by the Greeks but even by the barbarians themselves, but soon emerged as the most cultivated people and rulers of everything." To the Germans Roman rule had bestowed "all the arts of civilization," turning them "from rude and rustic men into the most polished."[32] As for the criticism, leveled by Calgacus, that Roman imperialism was motivated by nothing but material greed, epitomized by the excessive levying of tributes, the defender cites the famous speech by the Roman general Petilius Cerialis as put forward in Tacitus' *Histories*:

---

[27] Tacitus, *Agricola* 30. 6 Gentili offers a cumbersome version of Calgacus' terse *atque ubi solitudinem faciunt, pacem appellant*.

[28] A free paraphrase of Tacitus, *Agricola* 30. 4–5.

[29] Orosius, *Historiae adversus paganos* 5. 18.

[30] Arnobius, *Disputationes adversus gentes*.

[31] *The Wars of the Romans* 1. 13, p. 117. For Gentili's criticism of Roman imperialism and his use of the Roman tradition and Tacitus, see Kaius Tuori, "Alberico Gentili and the Criticism of Expansion in the Roman Empire: The Invader's Remorse," *Journal of the History of International Law*, 11 (2009), 205–19.

[32] *The Wars of the Romans* 2. 1, p. 129.

As for tributes and levies, Cerialis has answered: "By the right of victory we have imposed upon the defeated only that amount by which we might be able to maintain peace. For it is impossible to have peace among peoples without arms, or arms without soldiers' pay, or soldiers' pay without tributes. Everything else has been placed in common between us. The defeated themselves have for the most part been appointed as commanders over the legions and as magistrates over the provinces. Nothing is set apart or put off limits."[33] It is in *this* way that the provinces were conquered by the blood of provinces.[34]

A further important argument Gentili presents for Roman imperial rule is its incorporation of members of conquered groups into the ranks of Roman citizens. Roman rule thereby ceased to be foreign rule for the new citizens. Access to power is open to those under Roman rule as well and not exclusive to the conquerors—everything "has been placed in common between us," nothing is "set apart or put off limits." This is articulated by Gentili's Roman defender: "We have wished our enemies to be friends, allies, citizens. Behold, gradually the citizenship was given to all who lived in the Roman world. Behold: Rome, the common fatherland."[35] This argument of Roman inclusivity reinforces the claims relating to its civilizing and pacifying effects as arguments for the overall benignity of Roman imperial rule.

The alternative to civilized Roman rule is a state of nature, which Gentili conceives, anticipating Thomas Hobbes in an original manner, as a war of all against all. The underlying anthropology is Hobbesian, or rather Tacitean; as Cerialis in the same speech has it: "There will be vices as long as there are men."[36] Therefore, "should the Romans be driven out . . . what can result but wars between all these nations?"[37] This is echoed at the very end of Gentili's *Wars of the Romans*, in the defender's final pleadings:

But at last the empire was overthrown, and along with all other mortal affairs it had its end. But what had been predicted so long before by wise men, behold, when the Romans had been driven away. . . . But behold, . . . behold now the wars of all, of all peoples among themselves. "Neighboring cities, the laws among them burst asunder, take arms; impious Mars rages throughout the globe; as when chariots pour out from the starting pens, they go faster each lap; nor does anyone hold the halter; the chariot is carried along by the horses, and no one guides the reins."[38] And are you laughing here, Picenus? Is the world laughing? And do you still laugh when the world's peoples differ in customs, laws, languages, sacred rites, and thoughts? But if the look of the globe and the faces of all mortal men are saying anything to me, then we have triumphed over you, and all lament the now sundered unity of hearts and sigh for Roman piety, liberality, trustworthiness, magnanimity, peace, security, justice—and for the Roman Empire,

---

[33] Tacitus, *Historiae* 4. 74. [34] *The Wars of the Romans* 2. 13, p. 347.
[35] *The Wars of the Romans* 2. 13, p. 347. [36] Tacitus, *Historiae* 4. 74. [37] Ibid.
[38] Vergil, *Georgica* 1. 510–14. Gentili was apparently quoting from memory, for the last lines should read "and vainly pulling on the halter, the charioteer is borne along by the horses, and the chariot doesn't heed the reins"—*et frustra retinacula tendens / fertur equis auriga neque audit currus habenas.*

from which, in all of its justice, fairness, and goodness, they lament that they have been withdrawn.[39]

The civilizing effect is not confined to the material advantages and the prosperity resulting from pacification, security, and a certain unification of legal and customary norms. It also finds expression in, paradoxically, a larger amount of *liberty* for those newly subject to Roman rule. The Kingdoms of Macedonia and Illyrium are said by Rome's defender to have been "*ordered* to live under their own laws and be free."[40] And the "blessedness (*felicitas*) of those regions" is "that, upon being conquered, they were twice as well off—nay, incomparably better off (if liberty is a thing that cannot be measured)—under the power of their enemy than under the power of their own citizens."[41]

These elements of Gentili's approach to evaluating the Roman Empire bear also on the question, posed in the essays of Diego Panizza and David Lupher:[42] what is the relationship between *The Wars of the Romans* and Alberico Gentili's central treatise on the law of war and of nations, the *De iure belli*? Panizza makes the case that the two works are very closely related as part of a single humanist project, with *The Wars of the Romans* (especially the second book) constituting in some respects a "satellite treatise of historical criticism gravitating towards the core of Gentili's system of jurisprudence" as elaborated in the grand system of *De iure belli*?[43] David Lupher suggests that differences between the two works are both considerable and significant.[44]

A feature of both works is that Gentili endeavors in them to give a specifically *legal* answer to the problems of the content, applicability, and validity of norms in intra-imperial and international relations.[45] A key element in Gentili's defense of the Roman empire in Book 2 of *The Wars of the Romans* is that the Roman empire provided not only civilizing peace but, most importantly, the advantages of a high-quality and durable system of law. The people of Spain, for example, are said by Rome's defender to have been "brought over by our laws to a more cultivated way of life,"[46] and earlier King Tullus had "transferred" the city of Alba "to the Roman state with much honor and equality before the law (*iuris aequalitas*)."[47] While the defender of

---

[39] *The Wars of the Romans* 2. 13, p. 355.

[40] *The Wars of the Romans* 2. 13, p. 337 (our italics).

[41] Ibid.

[42] See their respective contributions in Kingsbury and Straumann (eds.), *The Roman Foundations*. See also our Introduction to that volume.

[43] Panizza, "Alberico Gentili's *De armis Romanis*: The Roman Model of the Just Empire," in *The Roman Foundations*, 81.

[44] Lupher, "The *De armis Romanis* and the Exemplum of Roman Imperialism," in *The Roman Foundations*, 85–100.

[45] See on this also our Introduction in *The Roman Foundations*, and B. Straumann, "The *Corpus iuris* as a Source of Law between Sovereigns in Gentili's Thought," in *The Roman Foundations*, 101–23.

[46] *The Wars of the Romans* 2. 13, p. 349.

[47] Ibid. 2. 3, p. 169.

Book 2 takes pride that the Romans had as a matter of policy left many particular laws and customs of the conquered populations untouched,[48] the unifying role of Roman law is praised both in a Christian and in a pagan register. God is said to have given Rome the "scepter of the world" so that "the customs, the reverence, the languages, the minds, and the sacred rites of diverse peoples" could be brought under "one set of laws."[49] Similarly, citing the Greek pagan Claudian's panegyric of Stilicho, Rome, the "parent of arms and law," is said to have "offered the cradle of the beginnings of law."[50]

It is this, the diffusion of the Roman law, that provides both justification for Roman imperialism in *The Wars of the Romans* and a fundamental connection of that work with Gentili's treatise *De iure belli*.[51] In the last chapter of the pro-Roman second book of *The Wars of the Romans*, Rome's defender conjures up the most important remnant of Roman rule—the Roman law:

> That is the law code of our state, which . . . persists to the present day even now that the empire has been extinguished and penetrates into all parts of the world, even those parts to which Roman arms did not reach.[52] Picenus, you possess what the world longs for, you possess what the world delights in—the world which, though deprived of that blessed good luck of our empire, nevertheless tenaciously hangs onto and thirstily gulps down Roman laws, with which it renews for itself the sweet memory of its ancient happiness under Roman rule and alleviates the sadness of these times by this little bit of pleasure that has been mixed in.[53]

The Roman law, then, is the pivotal legacy of Roman imperialism. In the *De iure belli*, Gentili gives some reasons why this is so—not simply because the *Corpus iuris* provides rules suitable for the complexities of life in urban settings and for cross-border trade, but also, and more essentially for Gentili, because the Roman law is also a source for the operational norms of the law of nations and the law of nature. And this in turn means that it is a source for norms that hold, not only between the private citizens of any given polity, but even between sovereign states. Although Gentili first states that "our own Justinian," "who made laws for his countrymen, did not go beyond the boundaries of the state which he desired to furnish with those laws,"[54] he

---

[48] See e.g. *The Wars of the Romans* 2. 13, p. 337: "And the city-states of Sicily we received into our friendship and protection in such a way that, after they were subjugated in war, they lived under the same law code as they had before."

[49] *The Wars of the Romans* 2. 13, p. 349. Gentili here cites an account by Prudentius of what allegedly are the martyr Lawrence's words.

[50] *The Wars of the Romans* 2. 13, p. 351. The citation is from Claudian, *De consulatu Stilichonis* 3. 136–7.

[51] For more on this, see Straumann, "The *Corpus iuris* as a Source of Law," 101–23.

[52] Cf. Gentili's *De iure belli libri tres* (Hanau, 1612), 1. 3, p. 26 in vol. 16, pt. 1 of The Classics of International Law series, ed. James Brown Scott (Oxford, 1933).

[53] *The Wars of the Romans* 2. 13, p. 351.

[54] *De iure belli* 1. 1, p. 3: *Iustinianus quoque noster, qui leges tulit suis, pari ratione egressus non est rempublicam, quam legibus illis voluit adornare.* Translations are taken from vol. 16, pt. 1 of The Classics of International Law series, ed. Scott, and are occasionally modified.

then goes on to make a powerful argument in favor of using the *Corpus iuris* as a source of legal norms between sovereigns. This argument connects Gentili's interest in the justice of the ancient Roman empire in *The Wars of the Romans* with his concerns about the basis for, and content of, the law of war and peace in *De iure belli*:

> [T]he law which is written in those books of Justinian is not merely that of the state [*civitas*], but also that of the nations [*gentes*] and of nature; and with this last it is all so in accord, that if the empire were destroyed, the law itself, although long buried, would yet rise again and diffuse itself among all the peoples [*gentes*] of mankind. This law therefore holds for sovereigns [*principes*] also, although it was established by Justinian for private individuals.[55]

This establishes a parallel that is also a fundamental unity of law: the rules that hold for and between sovereigns are the very rules that held for private individuals before the establishment of political power (that is, in a natural state), and for private individuals in established commonwealths, to the extent that these natural rules have not been modified by arrangements of the civil law. The parallel between individuals and states conceived by Gentili is in fact much more rigid than the one later devised by Hobbes, while Hugo Grotius' view was to be strikingly similar to Gentili's. Justifying his use of private Roman law in an international context, Grotius argued that it "is true that Ulpian was referring . . . to private law; but the same principle is equally applicable to the present discussion concerning the territories and laws of peoples, since peoples in relation to the whole of mankind occupy the position of private individuals."[56] In *De iure belli*, the epistemic criterion Gentili uses in order to determine whether any established legal norm is actually part of the law of nature and of nations (*ius naturae et gentium*) is the following: Whenever a norm cannot be shown to be specific to any state, it should be included in the set of norms belonging to the *ius naturae et gentium*, the norms, that is, which are an expression of natural justice and thus hold for and between sovereigns as well. Gentili in *De iure belli* then goes on to give examples of Roman law principles that presumably are principles of natural law and thus applicable to sovereigns:

---

[55] Ibid. 26: *Ius etiam, illis perscriptum libris Iustiniani, non civitatis est tantum, sed & gentium, & naturae. & aptatum sic est ad naturam universum, ut imperio extincto, & ipsum ius diu sepultum surrexerit tamen, & in omnes se effuderit gentes humanas. Ergo & Principibus stat: etsi est privatis conditum a Iustiniano*. See also Gentili, *Hispanicae advocationis libri duo* (Amsterdam, 1661), ch. 25, pp. 114–15: "Add that between princes and also—and this is our case—between a prince and the subject of another nation it is the practice that the civil law should not apply but rather the law of nations alone."

[56] Grotius, *De iure praedae* 12, fol. 105 (= *Mare liberum* 5, p. 36). Hugo Grotius, *De iure praedae commentarius: A Collotype Reproduction of the Original Manuscript of 1604*, ed. J. B. Scott (The Classics of International Law, 22, vol. 2; Oxford, 1950). For the translation we have used Hugo Grotius, *De Iure Praedae: Commentary on the Law of Prize and Booty*, trans. G. L. Williams, with W. H. Zeydel, ed. J. B. Scott (The Classics of International Law, 22, vol. 1; Oxford, 1950). Hugo Grotius, *Mare liberum, The Freedom of the Seas*, trans. R. van Deman Magoffin, ed. and intro. J. B. Scott (New York, 1916).

But if anything of this sort is not shown to be peculiar to a given state, to remove it from these discussions of public matters would be more than ridiculous, more than silly. Again, are not the following principles from the books of Justinian applicable to sovereigns:[57] to live honourably; not to wrong another; to give every man his due; to protect one's children; to defend oneself against injury; to recognize kinship with all men; to maintain commercial relations; along with other similar and cognate matters *which make up almost the whole of those books*? These belong to the law of nations and to the laws of war.[58]

The universality of the *Corpus iuris* is thus explained by, and its validity based on, the idea that it is an expression of natural law.[59] As some of the passages cited above indicate, Gentili does not distinguish sharply between the law of nature (*ius naturae*) and the law of nations (*ius gentium*). Anticipating in that regard Thomas Hobbes and Samuel Pufendorf, Gentili holds that the law of nations does not derive its validity merely from human agreement and, ultimately, human will, but that it is rather an expression of natural law, deriving its validity from natural reason (*ratio naturalis*) in the way articulated by the Roman jurist Gaius.[60] Similarly, in *The Wars of the Romans*, no systematic distinction is drawn between natural law and the law of nations, and both are integrated with core arguments based on natural justice in the defense of Roman imperialism mounted in the second book. The "original source of the law of nations," Gentili says here in an utterly Stoic vein, is "that of human fellowship."[61] This Stoic explanation of the source of the *ius gentium* and for its binding force has, apart from Gaius, other important Roman precursors, most notably Cicero, and Gentili's ideas on the topic seem to build directly on this Roman tradition.[62]

The fact that Gentili does not draw a systematic distinction between the law of nations and the law of nature and declares the Roman law of the *Corpus iuris* to be, at least to a large extent, declaratory of the rules of the law of nations, could have provided a foundation for a kind of positivism in the law of nations, but Gentili did not pursue such an approach. To the contrary, in his arguments about issues of international justice, the last word remains

[57] This is a reference to *Institutes* I. I. 1–3; *Digest* II. I. 10.

[58] *De iure belli* I. I, pp. 27 f. Our italics.

[59] See also e.g. *De iure belli* I. I, pp. 27–8: "[T]he edicts of the praetors are new and follow nature and natural justice more closely than the old laws. Justinian, as he often declares, not only adapted his laws to the simplicity of nature, but also restored the old laws to harmony with nature, from which they had strayed."

[60] See *Institutes* I. 2. I = *Digest* I. I. 9; *Digest* 41. I. 1–3. Gaius himself of course built on a Stoic tradition.

[61] *The Wars of the Romans* 2. 2, p. 146f: *Primum iuris gentium caput everterint: quod humanae est societatis, et conjunctionis?*

[62] See e.g. Cic. *De officiis* I. 50, where Cicero deduces "natural principles" from the "human community and society" (*communitas et societas humana*) which is taken to be a "natural society"; Grotius was later to use this idea, ultimately based on the Stoic doctrine of *oikeiosis*, in the Prolegomena to his *De iure belli ac pacis*; see *prol.* 8: "This maintenance of the social order (*societatis custodia*), which we have roughly sketched, and which is consonant with human reason, is the source of law (*fons iuris*) properly so called." For a discussion of the view that Gentili's legal theory was influenced by Lutheran legal theory, see Straumann, "The *Corpus iuris* as a Source of Law," 116–18.

with natural reason. It is not sufficient that a rule is observed in practice and is one that cannot "be shown to be peculiar to a given state." Gentili does not make clear whether he adheres to a voluntarist view of the basis of the obligation that is owed to the law of nature, or to a rationalist one; are the laws of nature binding because they are commands of God, or is any obligation to the authority of God derived from the law of nature? A remark in *The Wars of the Romans* leans rather toward a rationalist stance. In this remark Gentili of course does not deny that genealogically, the law of nature has its origin in God, but the source of its *validity* (as opposed to its origin) seems to lie in natural reason: "Thus God wished to bring us all together and to place this necessity upon human affairs: that one person's profit might be bound up with that of his neighbor; and the entire world is thus constituted; for men would not otherwise pay attention to what profits his neighbor—and yet it was not so much God who wished this as it is by virtue of the reason of our shared humanity that we might be well-wishers and benefactors of all."[63] The *Corpus iuris* is taken to be valid for relations between sovereigns only to the extent that it is *declaratory* of natural law. The significance of the *Corpus iuris* is that it is an expression of natural reason. For international relations, it is not a source of law that could in any straightforward way be built into a positivist theory of law.[64] The relationship between natural law and custom (*consuetudo*) is conceived analogously: "[t]hat which is true by nature acquires force also through custom."[65]

If the prominent role of natural justice and of the law of nature as the basis of normativity places Gentili and *The Wars of the Romans* in a fairly orthodox tradition of natural law, Gentili's views on the role of self-interest, necessity, and preemptive defense as expressed in the second book of *The Wars of the Romans* make him an important outlier from traditional just-war theory. Self-interest, preemptive defense, and necessity as criteria for just wars bring into Gentili's legal thought some elements of *ragion di stato*. What is the significance of Gentili's engagement with these ideas? We have elsewhere expressed doubts that it is of great value to treat Gentili's use of these concepts mainly as placing him in what Richard Tuck and others have called a "humanist" tradition of international political and legal thought,[66] as

---

63 *The Wars of the Romans* 2. 8, p. 231. The position is close to Grotius' and Hobbes'.

64 See our Introduction in *The Roman Foundations*; and Straumann, "The *Corpus iuris* as a Source of Law," 101–23. For a different view, see Jeremy Waldron, "*Ius Gentium*: A Defense of Gentili's Equation of the Law of Nations and the Law of Nature," in *The Roman Foundations*, 283–96.

65 *The Wars of the Romans* 2. 2, p. 137.

66 For more on this, see our Introduction in *The Roman Foundations* and the literature referred to there; and the nuanced contribution by Noel Malcolm, "Alberico Gentili and the Ottomans," in *The Roman Foundations*, 127–45, which first appeared in Alberico Gentili, *La salvaguardia dei beni culturali nel diritto internazionale* (Milan, 2008), 63–89. See also B. Kingsbury and B. Straumann, "State of Nature versus Commercial Sociability as the Basis of International Law: Reflections on the Roman Foundations and Current Interpretations of the International Political and Legal Thought of Grotius, Hobbes and Pufendorf," in S. Besson and J. Tasioulas (eds.), *The Philosophy of International Law* (Oxford: Oxford University Press, 2010), 33–51.

opposed to a "scholastic" tradition of authors who rely on the Christian Fathers and on medieval philosophers and canon lawyers.[67] To give one example, Gentili, when developing his view on necessity in *The Wars of the Romans*, quotes two celebrated maxims: "That which is not allowable according to the law necessity makes allowable. Necessity has no law, but it itself makes law."[68] These are quotations, not from classical authors favored by "humanists," but from canon law sources—the first maxim is taken from the *Liber Extra* of Gregory IX, and the second from Gratian's *Decretum*.[69]

While Gentili thus cannot be situated in any simple way in a "humanist" camp, his views, especially on preemptive warfare and the bilateral justice of war, were original and strained the framework of traditional just-war doctrine.

Gentili's right of preemption, although premised on a very permissive interpretation of self-defense, is not simply the normative outcome of a state of nature conceived as a mere Hobbesian condition of war of all against all and with a *ius in omnia et omnes*, devoid of any mutual duties and wanting any grounds of obligation except for prudential ones. Preemptive warfare is constrained by the principle of self-defense; the Roman defender in Book 2 treats it as a principle of natural justice, and, defending Rome's destruction of Corinth, berates Picenus thus for not acknowledging it:

> But are you, Picenus, unaware—such a great teacher of law as you wish to appear—that it is permitted to look out for one's own state and security? Are you unaware that it is permitted to make away with all things which, while not perhaps actually to be feared, offer even some slight hint of danger? It is even fitting to look ahead into the distant future and not to wait until danger beats on one's doors, one's bedchamber, and one's very bedposts.[70]

Addressing one of the major Roman cases, Gentili suggests that the ultimate concern of the Romans in destroying Corinth is said to lie with Greek liberty, not Roman self-defense, although in Gentili's thought both seem to qualify as just causes for war independently: "For the Romans' concern was that condition and liberty of Greece, whose founders they themselves were."[71]

Preemptive warfare construed as self-defense is in Gentili's view a normative concept and constrained by (modest) objective qualifications, as explained in the *De iure belli*: "a just cause of fear is required; suspicion is not enough."[72] That preemption is meant not to provide a mere license, but is

---

[67] See Richard Tuck, *The Rights of War and Peace: Political Thought and the International Order from Grotius to Kant* (Oxford: Oxford University Press, 1999), 9 ff., 51.

[68] *The Wars of the Romans* 2. 2, p. 151. See on the concept of necessity in international realist thought Jonathan Haslam, *No Virtue like Necessity: Realist Thought in International Relations since Machiavelli* (New Haven: Yale University Press, 2002).

[69] *Liber Extra* [Decretals of Gregory IX] 5. 41. 4; *Decretum Gratiani* C.1 q.1 d.p.c.39.

[70] *The Wars of the Romans* 2. 9, p. 253.

[71] Ibid. 255.

[72] *De iure belli* 1. 14, p. 99: *Iusta caussa metus requiritur: suspicio non est satis.*

instead to be governed by objective criteria applicable to all, is reinforced by Gentili's statement in *De iure belli* that Perseus and Mithridates had cause to invoke it *against* the Romans, siding here with the prosecutor of Book 1 of *The Wars of the Romans* rather than with the Roman defender.[73] While the latter work, polemical in character, almost never—in its second book—admits any injustices and moral lapses committed by the Romans, the former at times argues for the very normative principles advocated by the Roman in the second book, turning them against the Roman empire.

While preemptive warfare is thus conceived as a special case of self-defense—expansive though the criteria may be—there are indications in *The Wars of the Romans* that mere unconstrained imperial self-interest could amount to a justifying principle. Such a prudential principle, devoid of any moral constraint of natural law, would situate that work quite obviously in a prudential, Machiavellian tradition of *ragion di stato*. The closest Gentili—or rather the Roman of Book 2—comes to acknowledging such a principle is when he asks Picenus: "Have you not learned from your teachers that war for glory and empire is just by the law of nations? And that the empire of the Romans was thus just because it grew in that way?"[74] However, Rome's defender then adds what amounts to a qualification, namely that "[y]ou would also have learned that a war directed at just and upright domination is just," and comments that the territory in question, Sicily, needed to be "freed from so many monsters and disasters" and should be rejoined "to its ancient head."[75] Reading on, it becomes clear that none of these arguments is crucial to Rome's case, which formally rests on self-defense by Rome on behalf of its ally, the Mamertines, against Carthage—a just war according to traditional criteria. Defending allies is an extension of the general justification for Rome's expansion put forward by the defender when he cites Augustine's *City of God*: "It constitutes a just defense of the Romans for so many wars undertaken and waged that it was the necessity of protecting their safety and liberty, not greed for acquiring human glory, that forced them to resist enemies who attacked them violently."[76]

That Gentili's relatively rich natural legal order is not exclusively based on prudential norms of utility but depends on a more substantive moral vision is further attested by his arguments for subjective natural rights,[77] including a natural right to punish. Gentili's treatment of punishment as a just cause for

---

[73] See *De iure belli* 1. 14, p. 103. See on this Lupher, "The *De armis Romanis* and the Exemplum of Roman Imperialism," in *The Roman Foundations*, 9.

[74] *The Wars of the Romans* 2. 8, p. 229.

[75] Ibid., p. 231.

[76] *The Wars of the Romans* 2. 2, p. 163, citing Augustine, *De civitate Dei* 3. 10. On the use of Augustine and the Roman model of empire in the 16th-c. debate on the justice of the Spanish empire, see David Lupher, *Romans in a New World: Classical Models in Sixteenth-Century Spanish America* (Ann Arbor: University of Michigan Press, 2003).

[77] For a strong formulation of a subjective natural right, see *The Wars of the Romans* 2. 6, p. 210: *ius suum naturæ*.

war—present in *De iure belli* and further affirmed in *The Wars of the Romans*—necessarily presupposes an objective natural-law framework of norms against which the claims of punishment can be measured and justified. The argument for the right to punish is not merely a self-interested prudential argument such as self defense, nor does it depend on the same grounds as self-defense. But the right to punish presupposes an offence against natural law, a violation of duties under some natural legal order—something unthinkable in a state of nature conceived along Hobbesian lines, where there are no moral duties whatsoever, just prudential grounds of obligation, and where there is consequently no natural right to punish either. Such a right implies a more substantive natural legal order, and Gentili in this regard belongs to a tradition stretching ahead to Grotius and Pufendorf, who, not surprisingly, also acknowledge a right to punish in the state of nature.[78]

The Wars of the Romans can thus be seen as an attempt to justify a legal order, introduced by Roman imperialism into a situation in which only an under-specified body of natural law applied. Rather than lending support to the empires of Gentili's own day, *The Wars of the Romans* focuses on the Roman empire of classical antiquity, its justification, and its legal legacy. The rules and norms developed by the Romans were apt, in Gentili's analysis, to guide and justify some imperial conduct, but also to constrain early modern empires and emerging sovereign states. Indeed, Gentili is critical of the Spanish and Ottoman empires of the late sixteenth century, and far from enthusiastic about the Holy Roman Empire. While he does not deny a certain continuity between the latter and the ancient Roman empire, his argument in *The Wars of the Romans* clearly does not rest on an analogy between the two. Rather, the Holy Roman Empire of his own day appears in his thought as but one polity among many, all of which are susceptible to being judged according to the principles of law established in the ancient and enduring Roman legal order.

Benedict Kingsbury
Benjamin Straumann

[78] See on this our "State of Nature versus Commercial Sociability"; and A. Blane and B. Kingsbury, "Punishment and the *ius post bellum*", in *The Roman Foundations*, 241–65.

Principal Events in Gentili's Life

1552 Alberico Gentili born on 14 January 1552 in San Ginesio in the Marche d'Ancona region of Italy, the eldest of six children of Matteo Gentili and Lucrezia Petrelli.

1569 Gentili enters the faculty of law at the University of Perugia, a stronghold of the *mos Italicus*.

1572 Gentili receives his doctoral degree in law on 23 September.

1572–4 He proceeds to become Praetor (*podestà*), a municipal function with civil as well as criminal jurisdiction, in the town of Ascoli, where his father practices medicine.

1574 Alberico returns to San Ginesio and assumes a position in the political hierarchy of the city appropriate to his family's standing, notwithstanding that his father had been banished on the ground of heresy.

1576 He is confirmed in the post of lawyer to the municipality in San Ginesio and charged with the reform of the municipal statute books.

1577 After finishing the reform, Gentili steps back from his post and dedicates his time to scholarly activities and research.

1578 The Gentili family is (rightly) suspected by the Roman Inquisition of Protestant leanings; Alberico, soon to be joined by his youngest brother Scipio, leaves Italy first for Laibach, which belongs to the House of Austria. In the same year he is imprisoned in Padua by the Inquisition but is able to escape.

1580 Alberico Gentili travels to London, where he arrives on 1 August 1580, via Heidelberg, Neustadt, and Cologne. Scipio is left in Tübingen to study law.

1581 Alberico's doctorate is acknowledged by the University of Oxford, after he was introduced and recommended to the University by the Earl of Leicester; in March he is appointed Professor of Roman law at St. John's College. Matteo Gentili joins his son in England; he practices as a physician in London, where he dies in 1602.

1582 Alberico Gentili's first publication, *De iuris interpretibus dialogi sex*, appears in London, dedicated to the Earl of Leicester; the dialogues defend the traditional *mos Italicus* against the new humanist *mos Gallicus*.

1583–4 Gentili publishes a collection of letters and lectures under the title *Lectionum et epistolarum quae ad ius civile pertinent*, a polemical work directed, again, against the humanism of the new French school (*mos Gallicus*).

1584 The Spanish ambassador Bernardino de Mendoza is accused of conspiring to overthrow Queen Elizabeth; Gentili, consulted by the Privy Council, which tried the case, opined that Mendoza enjoyed criminal immunity as an ambassador. The Council decided Mendoza should be allowed to leave England.

1585 Gentili's *De legationibus libri tres*, originating from a lecture, appear in London, dedicated to his friend and benefactor Sir Philip Sidney.

1586 Sidney falls in a campaign against Spain in the Netherlands; Gentili leaves England for Wittenberg, Germany, as Latin secretary to the banker Horatio Palavicino, who is entrusted with a special mission to the Elector of Saxony by Queen Elizabeth.

1587 Gentili is recalled to England by Queen Elizabeth in June and appointed Regius Professor of Civil Law at the University of Oxford.

1588–9 Gentili publishes a set of three lectures, originally held before the comitia in Oxford on the occasion of the graduation of his students, *De iure belli commentationes tres*, dedicated to a new friend, Robert Devereux, Earl of Essex.

1590 The *De iniustitia bellica Romanorum actio*, the nucleus of the first book of what was to become *De armis Romanis*, is published with a dedication to the Earl of Essex (the dedication is reproduced and translated as an Appendix to the present volume).

1598 The *De iure belli libri tres*, developed from the three earlier *commentationes* on the law of war, appear.

1599 The *De armis Romanis libri duo* appear.

1600 Gentili is admitted as a member of Gray's Inn and starts practicing law in London.

1601 His *Disputationum de nuptiis libri VII* appears.

1603 Queen Elizabeth dies, and James VI of Scotland accedes to the throne as James I. Gentili's works are placed on the *Index librorum prohibitorum*.

1605 Gentili is appointed counsel to the Spanish legation to England; much of his work in this capacity, advocacy on behalf of Spain before the Admiralty Court, is reflected in the *Hispanicae advocationis libri duo*.

1605 The *Regales disputationes tres* appear in London, consisting of *De potestate regis absoluta*, *De unione regnorum Britanniae*, and *De vi civium in regem semper iniusta*. Also, Gentili publishes his *Disputationes tres* in London, consisting of *De libris iuris canonici*, *De libris iuris civilis*, and *De Latinitate veteris Bibliorum versionis male accusata*.

1608 Alberico Gentili dies on 19 June in London.

1613 Scipio Gentili publishes his brother's *Hispanicae advocationis libri duo* posthumously.

Translator's Note on the Text and Translation with Acknowledgments

In producing this first English translation of *De armis Romanis*, I have worked from photocopies of two editions of the work: the first edition of 1599, published by Wilhelm Anton in Hanau-am-Main, and the edition published in the first volume of Giovanni Gravier's edition of Gentili's *Opera juridica selectiora* (Naples, 1770). I am grateful to the Centro Internazionale Studi Gentiliani of San Ginesio for the former, and to the Biblioteca Comunale "Scipione Gentili" of the Comune di San Ginesio for the latter. I have not consulted the 1612 second printing of the work by the heirs of Wilhelm Anton nor the 1737 edition edited by Giovanni Poleni and published in Venice by Giovanni Battista Pasquali.

This edition is based on the 1599 edition. The Latin transcription has eliminated accent marks and has written "&" as "et." Paragraphing has been added (corresponding to that of the English translation), but the 1599 punctuation (largely reproduced in the 1770 edition) has been retained. Where both editions concur in what seem to me clearly faulty readings, I have indicated my own emendations in the notes and have translated the emended text. (See the table of errata on pp. 362–3.) Throughout "quum" has been replaced by "cum".

I have done my best to honor the desire of Benedict Kingsbury and Benjamin Straumann for a reasonably literal and straightforward translation of Gentili's Latin. Two factors, however, have colluded to force me at times to insist upon a freer translation. One of these factors is Gentili's tendency to employ an extreme spareness of style, necessitating a certain amount of latitude in the translation in order to maintain general clarity in the English version. For example, Gentili's often vague use of pronouns—and his lack of an explicit subject for certain verbs—has often led me to supply nouns as an act of mercy to the reader. In addition, Gentili had a fondness for irony and even sarcasm that he frequently neglected to make sufficiently explicit through the normally requisite stylistic devices (abundant though such devices are in Latin). Accordingly, I have sometimes taken the liberty of bringing out the tone of passages that would be stylistically confusing if translated literally. In general, though, I have resisted—or been persuaded by my colleagues to resist—the temptation to be unduly free in rendering Gentili's often obscure text.

Where Gentili misunderstood or misquoted passages from other authors, I have translated the quoted text as he appears to have understood it, drawing

attention to the textual problems in the notes. Also, I have attempted to supply more precise information about his sources than he himself tended to offer in his marginal notes. For example, the fourth marginal citation in chapter 1 of Book 1 reads "Vop. Prob. Diod. 1. Herodia. 1." I have expanded this as "Flavius Vopiscus (*Scriptores historiae Augustae*), *Probus* 1. 1–2; Diodorus Siculus 1. 2. 7; Herodian 1. 1. 1–2." I have also corrected mistaken references. For instance, the tenth marginal reference of the work reads "Cic. *Pro Sext.*" where I have noted that the correct reference is to *Pro Flacco* 4. 9–10. I have also attempted to identify allusions and quotations not noted in Gentili's marginal notes. I should add that, unless otherwise noted, all translations of quoted passages are my own.

I need to declare that I am a classical scholar with no particular expertise in Roman or canon law, much less the fairly extensive medieval and early modern legal authorities cited by Gentili. Fuller identifications of these sources in the notes are the work of Benjamin Straumann.

I have been greatly assisted at every stage of this project by the expert knowledge, keen eye, and sound judgment of Benjamin Straumann. Not only has his wide knowledge of Roman law often helped me understand the true meaning of many passages whose import originally escaped me, but his ear for both Latin and English style has consistently been of great assistance. While there may have been a few occasions when I resisted or modified his suggestions, his editorial work on this translation has been of a very impressive order indeed. I should note also that he has also improved and expanded many of the explanatory notes to the text.

I am grateful to the Comitato Nazionale Alberico Gentili for providing the University of Puget Sound the funding for a course release from my teaching schedule in the spring of 2008. I wish also to thank Elizabeth Vandiver for her acute advice on how to interpret and render many of the most challenging passages in Gentili's text.

David Lupher

Note on Gentili's Marginal References

Conscious of the importance of Gentili's sources for his thought, we have spent considerable effort trying to identify and verify as many of Gentili's marginal references as possible. In this rather thorny task we were able to build upon the efforts of previous editors and translators of other works of Gentili; the Italian edition of *De iure belli* (Milan: Giuffrè editore, 2008) has been especially helpful in this regard, in particular the *apparatus criticus* by Giuliano Marchetto and Christian Zendri. The degree of precision reached depended to a certain degree on Gentili's own precision; sometimes his paraphrase proved too loose to track down a particular passage; sometimes the citation seems to be referring consciously to a whole book or chapter. Whenever Gentili's citations proved too loose, or simply wrong, we have supplied what we deem to be the correct citation—to the extent this was possible—in our notes; since Gentili's marginal references in Latin are also reproduced in the notes, the reader will be able to compare our attributions with the original citations. Alternative references, or doubts as to whether a citation is correct, are noted in square brackets.

In referring to authors we use what we believe is the most common form of the author's name encountered in (English language) scholarship, without aiming at consistency in styles of nomenclature. Classical authors are cited according to prevailing scholarly standards, and medieval and early modern authors are cited fully the first time their works are referenced; thereafter, we provide authors' names and the titles of the works in question. With regard to classical authors as well as legal sources such as the medieval canon law compilations, we have used standard editions and methods of citation. With regard to early modern treatises and writers closer to Gentili's own time we aim—whenever possible and sensible—to cite editions Gentili himself could have used; in this, electronic reproductions of such editions available in Google Books and the collection of Early English Books Online (EEBO) proved very useful.

Benedict Kingsbury
David Lupher
Benjamin Straumann

TEXT AND TRANSLATION

ALBERICI
GENTILIS
I. C. CLARISSIMI
PROFESSORIS
Regii,
DE ARMIS ROMANIS
Libri duo,
Nunc primum in lucem editi.
AD ILLVSTRISSIMVM
COMITEM ESSEXIAE, ARCHIMARE-
schallum Angliæ

HANOVIÆ
Apud Guilielmum Antonium
MDXCIX

ALBERICO

GENTILI

DISTINGUISHED JURIST

Regius Professor

Two books on

THE WARS OF THE ROMANS

Now for the first time published.

Dedicated to the Most Illustrious Earl of Essex and Earl Marshal of England

HANAU

By Wilhelm Anton

1599

ILLVSSTRISS. ET EXCELLENTISS.
ROB. DEVREVXO
COMITI
DE ESSEX, ET EV.
VICECOMITI
DE HEREFORD ET BOVRGCHER.
BARONI

DE FERRERS ET LOVAIN, &C.
Regio consiliario fideliss.
EQVITI GARTERIÆ
MAGISTRO EQVOR.
PRÆF. MACHIN. MILIT.
Archimareschallo Angliæ fortiss.
Supremo gub. Hiberniæ providentiss. &c.
ARM. ET BEL. PRÆSTANTISS.
LIT. ET PAC. ART. ORNATISS.
Reip. regendæ sapientiss.
Suus refert hæc sua,
ET DD. BM.

ALBERICVS GENTILIS

TO THE MOST ILLUSTRIOUS
AND EXCELLENT
ROBERT DEVEREUX
EARL OF ESSEX AND EWE
VISCOUNT
OF HEREFORD AND BOURCHIER
BARON

OF FERRERS AND LOUVAIN, ETC.
Most Loyal Member of the Royal Council
KNIGHT OF THE GARTER
MASTER OF THE HORSE
MASTER-GENERAL OF THE ORDNANCE
Most Puissant Earl Marshal of England
Most Provident Lord Lieutenant of Ireland
MOST DISTINGUISHED IN ARMS AND WAR
MOST GIFTED IN THE ARTS
OF LETTERS AND PEACE
MOST WISE IN THE GOVERNING
OF THE STATE
HIS DEVOTED ALBERICO GENTILI
HANDS OVER
AND GIVES AND DEDICATES THIS WORK
TO ONE DESERVING

INDEX CAPITVM
IN HIS DVOBVS LIBRIS
DE ARMIS ROMANIS
CONTENTORVM

LIBRI SECVNDI

INDEX OF CHAPTERS

IN THESE TWO BOOKS

ON THE WARS OF THE ROMANS

CONTENTS

OF THE SECOND BOOK

p. 1 ALBERICI GENTILIS

DE ARMIS ROMANIS

LIBER I
VEL
De iniustitia bellica Romanorum
ACTIO.

Rerum Romanarum veritatem vitiatam.
CAP. I

Est M. Ciceronis illa vox, in controversia militaris rei, et Sapientiæ civilis, [a]*Virtus militaris populo Romano nomen, urbi æternam gloriam peperit, orbem terrarum parere huic imperio coegit.* et a nobis existimata semper verissima est vox: cum veritas oppressa malis malorum scriptorum artibus iacuit aut submersa, aut demersa profundissime: de quibus populum Romanum sanctum, populum Romanum pulchrum, populum Romanum invictum, populum Romanum omni laudis genere sic florentem, tantum inter alios caput ext-
p. 2 ollentem, [b]*quantum lenta solent inter viburna cu | pressi*: ut de eo alter ocellus Virgilius cecinit: et id genus alia oculis hausimus attentissimis: et specie ducti eruditionis auctorum summæ, et blandiloquenti oratione perducti eorum, credidimus, et decepti sumus. Evaluit persuasionis vultus, et oratio gratiosa nos a tramite transverso rapuit veritatis. [c] Hæ scilicet res duæ non hic solum turbant, sed passim inferunt veritati cladem. [d] Ut tanta sit sæpe res, non quanta est ipsa per se, at quanta dicentis virtus fuerit, et eloquentia: et omnes omnium virtutes tantæ sint, quantas videri voluerunt illorum ingenia, qui descripserunt. [e] *Nemo rem veritate ponderat, sed ornatu*: rectissime Lactantius. [f] Et ergo exclamavit ad Achillis tumulum Alexander, exclamavit Scipio, *Felix Æacide, cui tali contigit ore Gentibus ostendi: crevit tua carmine virtus.* Crevit? Immo credita virtus: quæ longissime abfuit a virtute. Longissime abfuit: si res respicimus laudati herois, quas ipsi habent laudatores, non obstupefacti, et

[a] *Cic. pro Muræ.* [b] *Virg. ecl.* 1. [c] *Plut. de Hero. mali.* [d] *Vop. Prob. Diod.* 1. *Herodia.* 1.
[e] *Lact.* 5. *Inst.* 1. [f] *Cic. pro Arch. et* 5. *fam.* 12.

---

[1] Cicero, *Pro Murena* 22. [2] Vergil, *Eclogae* 1. 25.
[3] **Translator's note:** The phrase "face of persuasion" (*persuasionis vultus)* is from a fragment of Sophocles, quoted in Plutarch's *On the Malice of Herodotus*, 854 F.
[4] Flavius Vopiscus (*Scriptores historiae Augustae*), *Probus* 1. 1–2; Diodorus Siculus 1. 2. 7; Herodian 1. 1. 1–2.
[5] Lactantius, *Divinae institutiones* 5. 1. 17. [6] Cicero, *Pro Archia* 24; *Epistulae ad familiares* 5. 12. 7.

ALBERICO GENTILI p. 1

ON THE WARS OF THE ROMANS

BOOK 1

OR

Indictment of the Injustice of the Romans in Warfare

CHAPTER 1

The Truth of Roman History is Tainted

There is a famous utterance of Cicero in a dispute about military affairs and political wisdom: "Military excellence has engendered fame for the Roman people and eternal glory for the city; it has forced the whole world to obey this rule."[1] And this utterance has always been deemed very true by us, while the real truth, overpowered by the base arts of bad writers, has been cast down, oppressed, overwhelmed, and sunk to the depths. That the Roman people was holy, that the Roman people was beautiful, that the Roman people was invincible, and that the Roman people flourished with every sort of excellence, raising its head among other peoples "as much as cypresses are wont to do among the pliant wayfaring-trees," as the darling [*alter ocellus*] Virgil has p. 2
sung about it[2]—this, and other stuff of that sort, we have imbibed with the most attentive eyes and, drawn by the semblance of the authors' consummate erudition and seduced by their soothing speech, we have taken it on trust and been deceived by it. The fair face of persuasion has prevailed, and pleasant style has snatched us off-course from the truth.[3] These two things, indeed, cause trouble not only in this instance, but everywhere bring disaster upon truth.[4] The result is that often a thing would be not as great as it actually is in itself, but as great as was the power and eloquence of the speaker, and all the virtues of all things would be as great as the talents of those who describe them have wished them to appear.

"No one weighs a matter by the truth, but by its embellishment," says Lactantius, very correctly.[5] And therefore Alexander exclaimed at the tomb of Achilles, just as Scipio too exclaimed, "Lucky descendant of Aeacus, whose luck it was to be shown forth to the nations by such a voice. Your excellence grew through a poem."[6] Grew? Rather, through a poem an excellence became believed in that in fact lay far from true excellence—very far indeed, for if we pay attention to the praised hero's actual doings, which the encomiasts

attoniti ad laudes stamus. Adeamus ad Platonis libros de republica et ex ipso Homero vitia exprimemus Achillis, quæ laudes legeramus.

[a] *O fides alma, apta pinnis ius iurandum Iovis*: huc, huc pro gemina tibi veritate contra mendacia turpissima, et calumnias iniquissimas adsis. Veritatem alis in altum sublatam tuis, et Iovis patris magni assertam manu iam
p. 3 tandem conspicere fas sit: orbemque | terrarum nunc demum, tot respublicas, tot imperia urbi uni virtute non concessisse intelligamus. Age, exponantur omnia simpliciter: quando fucum illum, et illam fallaciam orationis vituperamus in aliis non immerito. Age, producantur res ipsæ nude: ut sine omni periculo, faciliusque iudicium fieri rerum possit. Eripiatur nostris illis Hortensiis artificium omne, quo Romani populi iniusta facta, et aliena a virtute bellica tegere, et contrario veluti velamento ornare solent. Advocentur illico testes: [b] et testimonia singulorum expendantur. Testibus, non testimoniis credatur: ut providum Adriani Imperatoris consilium est: et relatum in leges est. Sed et in persona testium exploretur, quod eædem iubent leges, an quis inimicus ei sit, adversus quem tulerit testimonium: vel amicus ei sit, pro quo testimonium dederit. [c] Cetera in personis, et in testimoniis expendantur: quæ considerat sapiens iudex, et religiosus, et qui fidem testium dictis credulus non adcommodat. Iudex religiosus Græculis testibus, servis illis Romanorum, fidem non adcommodaverit. Romani contemnunt, M. Tullius de omni deiicit fide. [d] *Testimoniorum religionem et fidem nunquam ista natio colit: totiusque huiusce rei quæ sit vis, quæ auctoritas, quod pondus ignorant: unde*
p. 4 *illud est, Da mihi testimonium mutuum? Num Gallorum, num Hispanorum pu-| tatur? Totum istud Græcorum est: ut, etiam qui Græce nesciunt, hoc quibus verbis a Græcis dici soleat, sciant*: et cetera quæ Cicero contra Græcos testes detonat: et cetera, quæ alii de Græca fide, [e] ipsi etiam Græci tradidere. Aut sic sunt Græcorum testimonia levia, historiæ non sunt leves? Quasi, qui iurati nesciunt dicere verum, ubi et redargui in os possunt ab offensis, et puniri a iudicibus, iidem iniurati, nec arguendi forte, nec puniendi certe, verum amabunt? Quasi pater historiæ Græcæ Herodotus non audiat mendacissi-

[a] *Cic. 3. de off.* [b] *l. 3. de testi.* [c] *Cic. pro Font.*
[d] *Cic. pro Sext.* [e] *Polyb. lib.* 6.

[7] Cicero, *De officiis* 3. 104. **Translator's note:** Cicero was citing a passage from a tragedy of Ennius. The Latin text ("O fides alma, apta pinnis iurandum Iovis") should supply *et ius* before *iurandum*.

[8] **Translator's note:** By Hortensii here Gentili means deceptive defense lawyers of unworthy clients. The reference is to Quintus Hortensius, the clever but ultimately unsuccessful defense lawyer of Gaius Verres, corrupt ex-governor of Sicily prosecuted by Cicero in the speeches *In Verrem*.

[9] *Digest* 22. 5. 3.

[10] Cicero, *Pro Fonteio* 23.

[11] **Translator's note:** Gentili's note cites *Pro Sexto Roscio Amerino*, but in fact it is *Pro Flacco* 9–10. The common Greek phrase to which Cicero refers is δάνεισόν μοι μαρτυρίαν.

[12] Polybius 6. 56. 13.

themselves record, we do not stand stupefied and amazed at the praises. Let us go to Plato's *Republic* and elicit from Homer's own words the vices of Achilles, which we had once read as praises.

"O kindly trustworthiness, fitted with wings, and the oath of Jupiter"[7]—may you come here, here, and be present on behalf of your twofold truth against the basest lies and the most unjust slanders. May it at long last be fitting and proper for us to catch sight of truth, raised aloft by your wings, set free by the hand of Jupiter, the great father, and let us understand now at last that the entire globe, so many republics, so many empires have not yielded to p. 3
one city because of virtue. Come, let everything be laid out straightforwardly, while we find fault—not without due cause—with egregious pretense and deceitfulness of speech in others. Come, let the facts themselves be brought forth without adornment, so that a reasoned judgment may come about more easily and without any risk. Let us snatch away from those Hortensii[8] of ours every artifice by which they are accustomed to cover and adorn as with a concealing screen the Roman people's unjust deeds and actions devoid of martial excellence. Let witnesses be summoned at once, and let the testimonies of individuals be weighed.[9] Let faith be put in the witnesses, not in the testimonies, as is the provident advice of the emperor Hadrian and as it is noted down in the laws. But let us also, as the same laws bid, look into the part played by a witness, to determine whether he might be a personal enemy of the one against whom he has offered testimony, or might be a friend to the one on whose behalf he has given testimony. With regard to witnesses and testimonies let other things be weighed which a wise and scrupulous judge examines, one who does not naively place his trust in the words of witnesses.[10]

A scrupulous judge will not have put his faith in Greekling witnesses, those slaves of the Romans. The Romans themselves scorn them; Cicero has robbed them of all credibility: "That nation has never practiced the sanctity and trustworthiness of testimony. They don't know what the power or authority or importance of this whole matter is. What is the origin of the phrase 'Bear me testimony, and I'll do the same for you'? Is it thought to come from the Gauls? From the Spaniards? No, that whole business comes p. 4
from the Greeks, so that even those who don't know the Greek language know with what words this thing would normally be expressed by the Greeks."[11] And other things that Cicero thunders against Greek witnesses—and that others say about "Greek faith"—even the Greeks themselves have handed down.[12] If the legal testimonies of Greeks are so unreliable, are not their histories unreliable as well? As if those who are unable to tell the truth under oath, even when they can be refuted in person by those they have injured and punished by judges, are going to love the truth when they are not under oath, are perhaps not going to be refuted, and are certainly not going to be punished! As if Herodotus, father of Greek history, did not

mus? Quasi Græcia mendax non audiat in historiis, veluti multum propriumque vitium suum? Hispanis sane, M. Tulli, Gallisque credemus magis. Ego Hispanum Orosium, Gallum Trogum adducam testes, te iudice, M. Tulli, meliores. Etiam illi Græci, viri exteri, nec versati satis in re Romana. Hæc mihi attendantur; hæc discutiantur. [a]*Quicquid non discutitur, iustitia non putatur.*

Equidem alios dum audio, et Livium Romanæ eius historiæ primum, qui nominant hostes omnes, contra quos gererent Romani bellum, suspectas habeam ipsorum historias, necesse est: nam profitentur palam, inimicos se esse omnibus, qui inimici Romanis exstitissent. Amici Romanorum fuere omnino: et itaque gratiæ (an dubitamus?) dederit plurimum. Visus idem
p. 5 Livius est plurimum Pompeianus: | et non æquo tractasse calamo Iulianas partes. Et non fuerit plurimum, atque plurimum Romanus: hostibus Romanorum iniquus plurimum, atque plurimum? Quid cum historiam eius, et aliorum testium Romanorum in narrationibus rerum falsam, atque mendacem; in iudicationibus temerariam, variam, vanam certissimis argumentis deprehendimus sæpe, et sæpe rationibus vincimus indubitatis?

[b] Instrumentum, falsum in uno, censetur falsum in omnibus: ut est recepta iurisconsultorum sententia: et est ratio, quia deficiat fides, quæ individua est. Et testis, falsus in uno, falsus in omnibus intelligitur. [c] Vel si in uno admittatur aut scripturæ sacræ quodlibet mendacium, tota scripturæ sacræ fides vacillat, et nulla fit auctoritas: ut sanctissime scribitur ab Augustino. Quid cum libris hominum fiet: quorum est proprium, esse mendaces? [d]*Omnis homo mendax.* [e]Contendit magnus auctor Cardanus, non Tacito, non Tranquillo oportere contra Neronem credere: quoniam essent viri illi senatoriæ factionis, principi adversæ. Etiam contra Neronem. [f] Non ipse Tacitus testatur, odiis recentibus multa adversum defunctos principes scripta? [g] Non contestatur Iosephus, etiam contra Neronem et impudentia, et aperta exstitisse mendacia? Nos
p. 6 vero viris Romanis credemus adversum Romanorum hostes loquen|tibus? et eos non sane Nerones, sed principes fortissimos, aut civitates, et gentes præstantissimas. [h] Et non cognoscimus, quod Orosius ait in hac ipsa caussa, separata hostis esse, et victoris iudicia? [i] Et non ille ingeniose, qui sæpe hoc inquit, aliter proculdubio scripturum fuisse Gothum, quam Romanus fecerit?

[a] *Cassiod.* 7. *Var.* 8. [b] *Alciat.* 5. *cons.* 139. 7. 4. et 9. 79. [c] *c.* 7. *dist.* 9.
[d] *Rom.* 3. [e] *Card. enco. Nero.* [f] *Tac.* 1. *hist.* [g] *Iose.* 20. *antiq.*
[h] *Oros. lib.* 2. *cap.* 20. [i] *Krantz. Suec.* 2.

---

[13] Cassiodorus, *Variae* 7. 8.

[14] Alciatus [Andrea Alciati], *Consilia* 5. 139, col. 729; 7. 4, col. 938; 9. 79, col. 1582 [*Responsa libris novem digesta*, Basileae, Apud Thomam Guarinum, 1582].

[15] Augustine, *Confessiones* 7. 6. 9. **Translator's note:** It is not quite clear what Gentili is aiming at here.

[16] Romans 3: 4.

[17] Hieronymus Cardanus [Girolamo Cardano], *Encomium Neronis* 1. 3 [Nikolaus Eberl, *Cardanos Encomium Neronis*, Edition, Übersetzung und Kommentar (Frankfurt a. M.: Peter Lang, 1994), 24].

[18] Tacitus, *Historiae* 1. 1. [19] Josephus, *Antiquitates Judaicae* 20. [20] Orosius 2. 20.

[21] Albertus Krantzius, *Regnorum Aquilonarium, Daniae, Suecíae, Norvagiae chronica*, Francoforti ad Moenum, 1575. [The section on Sweden must be meant.]

have the reputation of being the most consummate liar! As if Greece were not called mendacious in the history books, that being its great and characteristic vice! Yes, Cicero, we shall sooner trust the Spaniards and the Gauls! With you serving as judge, Cicero, I shall bring in as better witnesses the Spaniard Orosius and the Gaul Pompeius Trogus. Furthermore, those Greeks, as foreigners, were not sufficiently versed in Roman affairs. Let me consider these things, let me discuss them. "Whatever is not discussed is not considered an act of justice."[13]

Indeed, while I listen to others—and first and foremost Livy in his Roman history—who designate as enemies all those against whom the Romans waged war, it is necessary that I consider their own histories suspect. For they openly admit that they were hostile to all those who stood forth as enemies to the Romans. They were in every respect friends of the Romans, and thus (how can we doubt it?) they would give the greatest weight to partisan feelings. This same Livy seemed for the most part a partisan of Pompey, and did not treat Caesar's side with an impartial pen. And would he p. 5
not have been far and away thoroughly Roman and far and away thoroughly unjust to the enemies of the Romans? What of the fact that we have often discovered by the surest proofs and often triumphantly demonstrated by the most irrefutable arguments that his history and those of other Roman witnesses are false and lying in their narratives and hasty, inconsistent, and empty in their judgments?

A document that is false in one thing is judged to be false in everything, as is the received opinion of the jurist—and there is good reason why its trustworthiness would be lacking, for trustworthiness is indivisible.[14] Similarly, a witness who is false in one thing is taken to be false in all things. If in one matter any lie at all be allowed to sacred scripture, then the whole trustworthiness of sacred scripture totters, and its authority becomes null, as was written in the most holy way by Augustine.[15] What, then, is to happen with the books of mere mortal men, whose character it is to be mendacious? "Every man is a liar."[16] That great authority Cardanus has asserted that we ought not trust Tacitus or Suetonius against Nero, for those men were of the senatorial party, which was hostile to the emperor.[17] Not even against Nero! Doesn't Tacitus himself testify that many things were written against dead emperors on account of still fresh hatred?[18] Does not Josephus add his testimony that there were shameless and open lies told even against Nero?[19] Are we, forsooth, to trust Romans who speak out against the enemies of the Romans—and those p. 6
enemies not at all Neroes but very brave leaders or very outstanding states and peoples? And do we not acknowledge what Orosius said in this very matter: that the judgments of enemy and victor are quite different?[20] And did not that man make a clever point who often declared that without any doubt a Goth would be apt to write far differently from a Roman?[21]

Sunt autem hic genera rerum duo, de quibus disputetur, narrationes nudæ factorum, et adiectæ sententiæ. Et quamquam est in censendis narrationibus maior, quam in diiudicandis sententiis difficultas: si tamen aut non conveniunt testimonia, aut verisimilia non sunt, aut quid eorum aliud patiuntur, propter quæ fidem elevari testimoniorum tradunt late auctores iuris: iam superest et in genere isto nobis facultas non minima ad refellendos scriptores, in quibus vitia notare isthæc valemus. Non mihi excitatus ab inferis Philenius est, aut Sosilus, aut Eumacus, aut alius, qui partium Romanarum non studiosus suggerat argumenta, per quæ vanissimas illas reliquorum narrationes, et testimonia levissima arguam. [a] Nihil de Carthaginensium habeo rebus gestis, nisi quod scripserunt hostes eorum: nihil de aliis, cum quibus contentiones, et bella Romanorum fuerunt. Sed sunt vel in his ipsis hostibus plura, et disiecta passim, et quasi in amplo quodam naufragio dissipata, quæ
p. 7 per sedulam operam collecta | vincere vulgi opinionem, consensum hominum inveteratum superare, persuasionem de virtute Romanorum bellica tollere possunt. Et verum hoc est, verum, etsi credibile, aut verisimile non videtur: [b]quemadmodum credibilia existimantur multa, ac similia veris, quæ falsa sunt.

Nam in altero, quod est de censendis sententiis, si dico, deferri nobis oportere aliquid amplius, quam adversariis scriptoribus, id arrogantiæ nullius nomine condemnari potest. Ut enim non moveam, quod gravem habet virorum eruditorum litem, si non perperam, et præter historici munus faciant, qui non modo facta, dicta narrant, verum etiam de his iudicium apponunt suum: hoc certe controversiam habere non debet; quod, cum eodem nos, atque illi fuerint, simus loco, aut etiam meliori, qui studio partium non imbuti, et seculis succedentibus magis instructi, artibusque nonnullis rei isti necessariis subornati fortasse magis, accedimus ad iudicandum: et nobis esse oportet facultatem disputandi, et, quæ illis fuit, censendi, etiam contra illos. Quamquam non illis fuit, non sane ista facultas. Non est testi iudicandi facultas. [c] Et testem, qui iudicat, non audiendum, prudentes iam dudum docent. Scilicet is ostendit affectum se, et propensum ad partem alteram
p. 8 omnino hominem levem, et itaque levis fidei, qui officii sui fines transiliit. | [d]Valebit autem in utroque genere Socratis sapientis eius documentum sapientissimum, ut rationi uni magis, quam mille credamus testibus. Ratio est vera regula: testimonium est illa flexilis Lesbia, quod sic est, ut persona est

[a] *Vict. ep. an. pol. Arist.* [b] *Arist. Quinct.* [c] *Dec. cons.* 83. [d] *Pla. Gorg.*

22 **Translator's note:** Sosylus and Eumachus were Greek historians of Hannibal. "Philenius" seems a mistake for Silenus, another historian of Hannibal.

23 Petrus Victorius [Pietro Vettori], *Commentarii in VIII libros Aristotelis de optimo statu civitatis*, Florentiae, In officina Iuntarum, Bernardi Filiorum, 1576. [The passage can be found on the fourth page of the unpaginated preface, Petrus Victorius Lectori: "ac quidquid de ipsis memoriae proditum est, id omne ab hostibus, adversarijsque laudis ac gloriae ipsorum narratum fuit."].

24 Aristotle, *Rhetorica* 2. 23. 22; Quintilian, *Institutio oratoria* 4. 2. 34 ("Sunt enim plurima vera quidem, sed parum credibilia, sicut falsa quoque frequenter veri similia").

25 Philippus Decius [Filippo Decio], *Consilia* 83 [*Consiliorum pars prima*, Lugduni, 1550; Gentili here probably has Consilium 82 in mind, fols. 70^{v} f.].

26 Plato, *Gorgias* [471 D–472 D].

Moreover, there are two kinds of things about which one may take issue: bare narrations of deeds, and opinions that are added on. And although there is a greater difficulty in judging narrations than in judging the merits of opinions, nonetheless if testimonies are not in agreement, or if they are not plausible, or if they have any of the features on account of which legal authorities far and wide declare that the trustworthiness of testimonies is diminished, then it follows that in this genre also we have a very considerable ability to reject writers in whom we are able to note those sorts of faults. I have not stirred up from the shades Philenius or Sosylus or Eumachus or any of the other writers who chose not to industriously pile up the arguments of the Roman party to help me prove those other [i.e. pro-Roman] accounts quite empty and their testimonies utterly worthless.[22] I do not have access to anything about the deeds of the Carthaginians except what their enemies have written, nor do I have access to anything of the other peoples with whom the Romans had their disputes and wars.[23] But there are even in the writings of these enemies of theirs very many things scattered throughout, as though strewn about over some large shipwreck, which, when gathered with painstaking toil, can defeat the opinion of the common people, overcome the p. 7 long ingrained consensus of men, and do away with the standard view of the Romans' virtuous war-making. And this is true, true I say, even though it does not seem credible or likely, in just the same way that many things are judged to be credible and likely which are in fact false.[24]

Now, in that other matter—that is, the judging of opinions—if I say that greater latitude ought to be granted to us than to writers who are our enemies, that cannot be condemned under the charge of mere conceitedness. I wouldn't want to raise the question (about which there is a serious dispute among learned men) as to whether those who do not just narrate actions and speeches but also add their own judgment about these things are acting wrongly and beyond a historian's duty. But this at least ought not be a matter of dispute: that, since we are in the same position as they were, or even better, for we come to the making of judgments untainted with party zeal, better instructed by succeeding ages, and perhaps better furnished with various arts necessary for this task, then we too ought to have the right they had to dispute and judge—even against them. And yet they themselves didn't have this right—absolutely not. For a witness doesn't have the authority to make judgments. And wise men have been teaching for a long time that one shouldn't listen to a witness who offers judgments.[25] Indeed that man who leaps over the boundaries of his task shows himself to be impaired, leaning to one side of the question, and an utterly inconsequential fellow and thus of trifling trustworthiness. Rather, the very wise utterance of the philosopher p. 8 Socrates will prove valid in either genre [narrative and judgments]: that we should trust reason alone over a thousand witnesses.[26] Reason is the true yardstick; while testimony is that supple "Lesbian rule," which is as the

testis, inimicum inimici, improbum improbi, ineptum inepti. Sed ratio est natura altera, consilium prudentiæ, lux veritatis.

Agite, mortalium acerrimi Europæi, Lybes prudentissimi, potentissimi magnæ Asiæ reges, agite, huc convenite: et mecum una genti Romuleæ coronam trahite; quam gerit, et de nobis omnibus partam triumphat. Huc mihi fortis conveniat Italus, durus Germanus, bellicosus Gallus, indomitus Hispanus, [a]*invictus Romano Marte Britannus*: et triumphantem per dolos malos de nobis, et per malitias malas Romuli populum vincant. Quid tu Græcia nobilis? Quid gentium domitrix Macedonia? Quid tu Africæ tuæ perfectissimum columen Carthago? Quid Persæ, Medi, Assyrii, vetustissima, et latissima regna? An illam audire, et ferre vocem potestis. *Virtus militaris populo Romano nomen, urbi Romæ æternam gloriam peperit, orbem terrarum parere imperio Romano coegit.* Immo, ut pro orbis reliqui dignitate iam tandem contendere incipiamus, immo non ita est, M. Tulli. Sed fraus, perfidia, avaritia, audacia, crudelitas, illud nobis imperium pepererunt: orbem terræ
p. 9 ali|quem, et orbis punctum, ut nominas [b] alibi, simpliciorem, iustiorem, humaniorem, faciliorem, moderatiorem subegerunt: nam gloriam, quam fingis tibi æternam, et nomen laudatum falsiloqui homines effecerunt.

[a] *Tib.* 4. *eleg.* 1. [b] *Cic. Somn.*

[27] **Translator's note:** For the "Lesbian rule," see Aristotle, *Ethica Nicomachea* 1137^{b}30–1. Unlike Gentili's, Aristotle's appeal to the "Lesbian rule" is approving. The realities of complicated cases often preclude the application of a strict standard of justice.

[28] Pseudo-Tibullus, *Panegyricus Messallae* 149.

[29] **Translator's note:** The phrase *per dolos malos* alludes to the category of *dolus malus* (fraud or bad faith) in Roman law. See Labeo in *Digest* 4. 3. 1. 2.

[30] Cicero, *De republica* 6. 16 (*Somnium Scipionis*).

character of the witness is: hostile for a hostile man, base for a base man, stupid for a stupid man.[27] But reason is a second nature, the counsel of prudence, the light of truth.

Come, Europeans, shrewdest of mortals, most prudent Libyans, most powerful kings of great Asia, come, gather together here, and join me in snatching away from the people of Romulus the crown which it wears and glories in, having acquired it from all of us. Let the brave Italian come, the tough German, the warlike Gaul, the untamable Spaniard, "the Briton unconquered by Roman warfare,"[28] and let them defeat the people of Romulus who triumph over us through intentional fraud[29] and wicked acts of malice. What of you, noble Greece? And you, Macedonian, subduer of peoples? What of you, most perfect pillar of your Africa, Carthage? What of the most ancient and extensive kingdoms of the Persian, the Mede, the Assyrian? Can you hear and endure that utterance: "Military excellence has engendered fame for the Roman people and eternal glory for the city; it has forced the whole world to obey this rule." On the contrary, Cicero, on the contrary—so may we begin at long last to struggle for the dignity of the rest of the world—it is not as you would have it. Rather, it was cheating, perfidy, avarice, audacity, cruelty that brought forth that empire over us. They have subjugated a certain area of the world and a single point of the globe, as you p. 9
put it elsewhere,[30] that was more honest, more just, more humane, more good-natured, more moderate than they were themselves. For it was men who speak falsehoods who have created that glory you pretend to yourself is eternal—and that lauded name.

De varia Romuli iniustitia.
CAP. II

Atque fraus quæ est, et perfidia maior, quam ut sacrilego incestu nati Deum sibi patrem vindicarent? [a] Fabulam tu quidem Cicero dicis: sed exsecrabili imposturæ nomen suum non imponis: et ludos hæc nobis crimina fuisse significas. Educti illi sub fornice, latronum coacta manu, et seminario futurorum sato bellorum iniustissimorum, agrum occupant alienum: ubi novam, sed tetriorem, Caci cavernam, aperto asylo, aliis quibusque perditissimis futuram receptui, exædificarunt. [b] Quam tu aliam, Philippe rex, πονηρόπολιν appellasti? [c] Aut quæ alia est ἀσελγής dicta vulgo? Hæc civitas iniustorum, vitiosorum. Hæc una improborum colluvies improba barbarorum: [d] si barbaros recte notavit Plato eos esse, qui nulla inter se morum, sermonisque communione devincti sunt. Huc enim Troia profugi, ex Etruria, ex Opicis, ex Latio, ex Græcia, undique transfugæ, linguis diversi, institutis discordes convenerunt. [e]*Populus de sceleratis, et nocentibus congregatur*: ait Cyprianus: et Augustinus itidem facinorosorum asylum constitutum scribit: p. 10 et collectam, et arma|tam manum contra suas civitates: quæ videlicet leges, et magistratus timeret. [f] Omnes recipiebat in asylum Romulus: nec servum domino, nec creditoribus nexum, nec magistratibus criminosum reddebat: ita Plutarchus: non soli Ætoli, non solus Mithridates dicebat, Etruscorum vernas esse Romanos. [g]*Romulus infami complevit mœnia lucu*: Lucanus, historicus verius, quam poeta. [h] Et poeta, si aut Iuvenalis poeta, qui mentiri nescius, *Et tamen ut longe repetas, longeque revolvas Nomen, ab infami gentem deducis asylo. Maiorum primus quisquis fuit ille tuorum, Aut pastor fuit, aut illud, quod dicere nolo*. Latronem dicere noluit, aliumve facinorosum, et improbum.

[a] *Cic.* [b] *Plut. de curios.* [c] *Lib. dem. adv. Mid. Iun. Tert. de pa.* 3. [d] *Pla. polit.*
[e] *Cypr.* 4. *de ido. na. Aug.* 1. *de co. ev.* 12. [f] *Plut. Rom. Iust.* 28. 38. [g] *Luca.* 7. [h] *Iuv. saty.* 8. 3.

---

[31] **Translator's note:** Gentili simply cites Cicero by name in the margin here, without mentioning a work. Cicero implicitly classifies Romulus' divine paternity as a *fabula* in *De republica* 2. 4 ("ut iam a fabulis ad facta veniamus"), but Gentili did not have access to this passage. At *De civitate Dei* 3. 15, Augustine appeals to Cicero's words from *De republica* to support the notion that the story of Romulus' apotheosis was simply "adulatio fabulosa." ("Satis et Cicero illam inter deos Romuli receptionem putatam magis significat esse quam factam . . .")

[32] **Translator's note:** The cavern of Cacus is a reference to the robber giant killed by Hercules at the site of future Rome (Vergil, *Aeneis* 8. 184–279).

[33] Plutarch, *De curiositate* 520 A. [Philip gathered the refuse of his kingdom into a town he called "Poneropolis."]

[34] Demosthenes, *In Meidiam*; Junius on Tertullian *De pallio* 3. **Translator's note:** The passage in Tertullian refers to the city of Selge in Pisidia. Junius presumably noted the ancient notion that the city's name was either derived from or was the source of the adjective ἀσελγής, "wanton, licentious." See, for example, the entry on Selge in the Suda: "A city of Pisidia, where the people used to lead bad lives and have [incestuous] sexual intercourse with each other. Hence, by extension, ἀσέλγεια ['licentiousness'] and ἀσελγαίνειν ['to be licentious']," translated by David Whitehead, from the Suda On Line. See *Suda*, s.v. Selge, ed. Ada Adler, *Suidae Lexicon* (Stuttgart, 1928–1938), sigma, 197. Demosthenes' speech against Meidias does not refer to Selge, but it does often invoke against Meidias the adjective and its cognates in the sense of "wantonly violent." The noun ἀσέλγεια occurs in the speech's first sentence.

CHAPTER 2

On the Multiple Injustice of Romulus

But what could be greater trickery or perfidy than that those who were born of sacrilegious incest should lay claim to a god as their father? True, Cicero, you do call it a "tale."[31] But you don't put the proper name on the abominable hoax, and you call "games" those things that are crimes to us. After having been brought up in a brothel, and having assembled a band of robbers and planted a seed-bed of most unjust wars for the future, those men seize other people's land, where they build a new but even more disgusting cavern of Cacus, destined to serve as a wide-open asylum and refuge for any and all of the most desperate men.[32] What other city was it, King Philip, that you called "Rogueville"?[33] Or what other city was it that was commonly given the name ἀσελγής "wanton" [Selge]?[34] *This* is the sole base dregs of base barbarians, if Plato was right when he observed that barbarians are those who are united by no commonality of customs and language.[35] For to this place there assembled refugees from Troy and deserters from Etruria, from Oscan territory, from Latium, and from Greece, men diverse in languages and discordant in customs. "A people gathered together from criminals and dangerous men," says Cyprian.[36] And Augustine in like manner writes that a refuge of base men was set up and a band assembled and armed against their p. 10
own states, a band which obviously was afraid of laws and magistrates.[37] Romulus used to receive everyone in sanctuary. He wouldn't give a slave back to a master, a debtor [*nexus*[38]] to a creditor, a guilty man to magistrates. All this is recorded by Plutarch.[39] Not only the Aetolians, not only Mithridates used to say that the Romans were domestic slaves of the Etruscans. "Romulus filled the walls with the disreputable grove" as Lucan, a truer historian than a poet, wrote.[40] And a poet—if Juvenal, who doesn't know how to lie, is really a poet—wrote: "Yet, for all that, if you trace and unscroll your name way back, you derive your race from a base asylum. The first of your ancestors, whoever he was, was either a shepherd or something I'd rather not name."[41] He didn't want to say "robber" or some other criminal and wicked type.

---

[35] Plato, *Politicus* 262 D. **Translator's note:** Plato here explains the use of the name "barbarian" to refer collectively to a set of non-Greek peoples which have no relation in blood or language to each other.

[36] *De idolorum vanitate* 4.

[37] *De consensu evangelistarum* 1. 12.

[38] **Translator's note:** A kind of debtor reduced to debt bondage, a sort of slavery, in the early Republic; see Cicero, *De republica* 2. 59 for a discussion of the abolition of debt bondage (*nexum*) by the Poetelian law; cf. Livy 8. 28 on the occasion for the law. The historicity of *nexi* and *nexum* is contested.

[39] *Romulus* 9. 3 and Justin 28. 38.

[40] Lucan, *De bello civili* 7. 438 [The grove was the site of the original asylum.]

[41] Juvenal, *Satirae* 8. 272–5. [On Juvenal as "mentiri nescius," see *Sat.* 3. 41: "quid Romae faciam? mentiri nescio."]

Hæc improborum civitas improba: in qua primum facinus parricidium nepote scilicet Dardani parricidæ patratum a conditore. [a]*Parricidio Roma dedicata*: ait Hieronymus. *Prima certe, victima Remus munitionem urbis novæ sanguine suo consecravit*: ita Florus. Id Augustinus, id Cyprianus, id omnes exprobrant [b] fratricidæ: ut inquit Tertullianus. *Fraterno maduerunt sanguine muri.* [c] Et qui Remum occidit, in gratiæ facti vicem meruit a fratricida tribunus equitum fieri. Et Romulum tamen aliquis historicorum, vel poetarum dixit, aut finxit, nec occidisse fratrem, nec aliquod perpetrasse flagi-
p. 11 tium: ut id Augustinus notat valde. Et nos habemus notare valde, | et validam ex eo capere coniecturam, quemadmodum nihil sit a Romanis unquam, et maximum, et clara luce factum turpe, quod scriptores mendaciis suis non invertant, et omni machinatione non pervertant. Ceterum parricidii huius memoria certa manet, et perpetuis consignata monumentis perdurat.

Quæ igitur, Iliæ fili, quæ causa tibi parricidii fuit? Nam facinus tibi defendendum est, quod admissum negare non potes. [d] At vero audias maximum iurisconsultum prius, qui parricidium patrari facilius, quam excusari Cæsari Bassiano, itidem parricidæ respondit. [e]*In parricidio nulla satis iusta caussa ad sceleris patrocinium prætexi potest.* Ludibrio, ais tu, mea habuit mœnia et per ludibrium traiecit. Tua, Romule? in quibus condendis æque ac tu laboravit frater: qui itaque consors audit, [f]*Mœnia consorti non habitanda Remo.* Ludibrio habuit? [g] Qui immo te monuit, et docuit saltu illo, ad tutelam urbis non fuisse vallum satis: ut id quoque est in historia: Immo; immo fratrem, nihil in te mali perpetrantem occidisti nulla iustitiæ vindicta, sed cupidine principatus: quod illi iidem theologi magni probant. [h] Ast pronunciet hic ipse Romulus Arpinas, *Muri species honestatis nec probabilis, nec sane idonea: peccasti Quirine.* [i] Tu ante iuniorem Dionysium, illum Siciliæ tyran-
p. 12 num, huic cui debebas regni consortium, ne spiritus quidem consor|tium

[a] *Hier. ep.* 4. et *c.* 41. 7. *q.* 1. *Flor.* 1. [b] *Tert. de Spect.* [c] *Servius* 11. *Æneid.*
[d] *Spart. Carac.* [e] *Iusti. lib.* 16. *Pla.* 9. *de legi.* [f] *Tib.* 2. *eleg.* 5. [g] *P. Diac.* 1.
[h] *Cic.* 3. *de off.* [i] *Iustin.* 21.

---

[42] **Translator's note:** Gentili seems to confuse the Trojan ancestor Dardanus with the Scythian king Dardanus who killed his own daughter.

[43] Jerome, *Epistulae* 125. 15 [J.-P. Migne, *Patrologia Latina*, xxii, col. 1080] and *Hieronymi Chronicon* [*Die Chronik des Hieronymus. Hieronymi Chronicon*, in *Eusebius Werke*, vii, ed. Rudolf Heim (3rd edn., Berlin, 1984), 88; see also the Latin reconstructed version of bk. 1 of the original *Chronicon* by Eusebius of Caesarea in Migne, *Patrologia Latina*, xxvii: *Eusebii Chronicorum liber I*, 46. 8, col. 193].

[44] Florus 1. 1. 8. **Translator's note:** References to Florus here follow the older four-book division familiar to Gentili rather than the two-book division common since the Teubner editions of Otto Jahn (1852) and Otto Rossbach (1896). This allows greater precision in pinpointing passages. Modern editions of Florus (e.g. Rossbach's Teubner and Forster's Loeb) do indicate the older book and chapter divisions marginally.

[45] *De spectaculis* 5.

[46] **Translator's note:** Cited without attribution from Lucan, *De bello civili* 1. 95, minus *primi*.

[47] **Translator's note:** Mommsen took the *tribunus equitum*, or *tribunus celerum*, to be a predecessor of the office of *magister equitum*, the dictator's subordinate in the time of the Republic. See Mommsen, *Staatsrecht*, ii. 169.

[48] Servius, *On Aeneid* 11. 603 [Here a certain Celer is made responsible for the murder on Romulus' behalf; Dionysius of Halicarnassus already gives Celer as the murderer at 1. 87. 4, as well as Ovid, *Fasti* 5. 469].

[49] **Translator's note:** This is probably a reference to *De civitate Dei* 3. 6, where Augustine records the exonerating accounts in which the blame was shifted to others—mentioned also by Plutarch at *Romulus* 10.

This was a wicked state of wicked men, in which the first crime was murder of kin, perpetrated by the founder, descendant of course of the kin-murderer Dardanus.[42] "Rome was consecrated by an act of kin-murder," says Jerome.[43] "Remus was the first sacrificial victim and consecrated the fortifications of the new city with his own blood," writes Florus.[44] Augustine, Cyprian, everyone in fact cast this act in the teeth of the fratricide, as Tertullian says.[45] "The walls became wet with a brother's blood."[46] And the man who actually killed Remus won from the kin-killer the office of tribune of the horse [*tribunus equitum*][47] as a reward for his deed.[48] And a certain one of the historians or poets reported—or invented—that Romulus neither killed his brother nor commited any crime (*flagitium*), as Augustine strongly brands the deed.[49] We, too, need to brand it strongly—and to derive from p. 11
this a powerful inference about how no base deed was ever done by the Romans, no matter how major and how publicly performed it may have been, which the writers did not turn upside down with their lies and twist about through every sort of contrivance. But the memory of this fratricide remains secure and endures, attested by enduring records.

What, then, son of Ilia, what was the reason for your fratricide? For you must defend yourself against a crime that you cannot deny that you were guilty of. But indeed first may you listen to the greatest of the jurists [Papinian], who replied to Bassianus Caesar [Caracalla], a parricide like yourself, that an act of parricide is easier to be perpetrated than excused.[50] "In the case of parricide, no sufficiently just cause can be offered for a defense against the crime."[51] "He mocked my walls," you say, "and crossed them in mockery." *Your* walls, Romulus? In the building of which your brother labored just as much as you did? And therefore he is called "partner": "The walls not to be inhabited by partner Remus."[52] He mocked them? He in fact by that leap warned and taught you that the rampart was not sufficient for the protection of the city—as is also found in the historical record.[53] No, no, in fact you killed a brother who was doing nothing wrong to you with no defense of justice but through desire for autocracy [*principatus*], which those same great theologians prove. Let the Romulus from Arpinum[54] himself deliver the verdict: "The walls were a specious show of rectitude, neither reasonable nor suitable in the least. You sinned, Quirinus."[55] You, before the time of the Younger Dionysius, that tyrant of Syracuse, denied partnership in life to the man to whom you owed partnership in rule.[56] What p. 12

But the word Augustine uses there for the parricide is *scelus*. At 15. 5, he uses the term *facinus*, just before quoting the line from Lucan Gentili cited a couple of sentences back.

[50] Aelius Spartianus (*Scriptores Historiae Augustae*), *Caracalla* 8. 5.

[51] Justin 16; Plato, *Leges* 9 (872 E).

[52] Tibullus, *Elegiae* 2. 5. 24.

[53] Paulus Diaconus, *Historia Romana* 1. 2 [in Sextus Aurelius Victor, *Historia de vita et moribus imperatorum Romanorum*, Paris, Simon de Colines, 1531].

[54] The phrase "Romulus Arpinas" for Cicero occurs in Pseudo-Sallust *In M. Tullium Ciceronem oratio* 4. 7.

[55] **Translator's note:** This supposed direct address of Cicero to Romulus is a garbled version of a third-person passage in *De officiis* 3. 41: "et tamen muri causam opposuit speciem honestatis, nec probabilem, nec sane idoneam."

[56] Justin 21.

reliquisti. Quæ item tua, Romule perfidia in augurio renunciando? Vidit augurium frater primus, an potius solus? an tibi ullum conspectum est, qui duplicatum avium numerum dupliciter ementiris? Illam tu tertio Regi Romano, et Cæsari tuo præivisti sententiam, regni caussa violare ius, pietatem in reliquis colere oportere? Recolamus auguria hic, aves rapto viventes.

Sed et horum puerorum altricem picum, furacissimam, audacissimam avem. Sed et altricem feram, cuius dentes famelicos, et profundum inexplebile nullæ unquam satiare rapinæ possint. [a] *Lacte quis infantes nescit crevisse ferino? Et picum expositis sæpe tulisse cibos*? Ostenta hæc, et portenta sunt civitatis futuræ, Romuli iam unius filiolæ: quæ quotidie aliena per infinitam rapinam sibi arripere, de aliis undique eripere habuisset. Hic Antiochus ille Hierax, qui annos quatuordecim natus, et fratri, partem regni donanti, latronis more totum eripere voluit: et in alienis eripiendis sectatus vitam accipitris, cognomen illud sibi peperit.

Age tu, M. Tulli, respice ad parentis virtutem vestri: qui novæ urbis agro fines non ponit, quo vicinis subinde præriperet: et bellandi libidine insanus (hoc ei nomen Plutarchus tribuit) occasionem bellandi primo statim die nascentis urbis nancisceretur. Quid? Cum nec fraude ista proficeret: essent-
p. 13 que | Itali almæ studiosiores pacis, quam ut cum barbaris turpissimis, et perditis parricidis digladiari vellent: tum sacris in spectaculis mediis, tum verus Martis pullus, hoc est, ut voluit Aristophanes, homo ad omnem audaciam proiectissimus, mulieres ad se invitatas rapit: et iura divina disturbat: iura gentium profligat: hospitalem gratiam, apud alias barbaras gentes omnes inviolabilem, violat: sanctissimum fidei pignus penitus tollit perfidus. Adde sacrilegium hominis: qui Consi Dei consilium sceleri huic obtendit scelerosissimo. [b] Et quæ improbarentur facta ab homine quovis, ea interposito divino nomine defenduntur? Etiam atrocissimum est, facere hoc prætextu, si quid non licet.

[a] *Ovid.* 3. *Fast. Plut. probl. Ro.* 21. [b] *Demost. Leptin.*

[57] **Translator's note:** This maxim from Euripides' *Phoenissae* 524–5 was a favorite of Caesar's, according to Cicero, *De officiis* 3. 82. As for the third Roman king, Tullus Hostilius, Livy at least records (1. 22. 2) that he was "ferocior etiam quam Romulus fuit," and that he eagerly sought excuses for spreading his rule through warfare.

[58] Ovid, *Fasti* 3. 53–4; cf. Plutarch, *Quaestiones Romanae* 21.

[59] [Aristophanes, *Birds* 835: Ἄρεως νεοττός.]

[60] Demosthenes, *In Leptinem* 126.

was your perfidy, Romulus, in the announcing of the portents? Did your brother see the portent first—or, rather, was he the only one to see it? Or did you see any portent at all, you who duplicitously lied about the doubled number of birds? Did you dictate in advance that famous maxim to the third Roman king and to your Caesar: "for the sake of rule one ought to violate justice, but cultivate piety in other matters."?[57] Let us consider the omens here: birds that live by preying.

Let us also consider the nurturer of those boys, a woodpecker, the most thievish, the most audacious of birds. And let us consider their wild nourisher as well, whose famished teeth and unfillable belly no snatched prey would ever have been able to satiate. "Who doesn't know that the babies grew through a wild beast's milk? And that a woodpecker often brought food to the exposed ones?"[58] These are prodigies and portents of the future city, the daughter now of Romulus alone, which has daily through endless rapine snatched other people's goods to its own bosom and ripped them everywhere from the hands of others. What we have here is that famous Antiochus Hierax ("Hawk"), who at the age of 14 when his brother offered him a part of the kingdom wanted to seize the whole of it like a brigand and in the seizing of others' possessions following the life of a hawk acquired that nickname for himself.

Come on, Marcus Tullius Cicero, look at the virtue of your own ancestor, who placed no boundaries for the fields of his new city, so that he might repeatedly plunder his neighbors and, insane (this term Plutarch applies to him) through lust for making war, might discover a pretext for warfare right from the first day of the growing city. What? When he failed to succeed even with that trick—and there were Italians too eager for kindly peace to want to p. 13
fight it out with the basest of barbarians and abandoned parridicdes—then in the midst of holy games, then the true chick of Mars—that is, as Aristophanes put it,[59] a man most inclined to any sort of impudent daring—seizes women who had been invited to visit him and throws into confusion divine laws, ruins the laws of nations, and violates the grace of hospitality, something inviolable among all other barbarian peoples. The perfidious man utterly destroys the most sacred assurance of trustworthiness. Add to that the sacrilege of the man who pleads the advice of the god Consus as a pretext for this most criminal crime. Are crimes that would be censured by any human being at all defended by the throwing in of a god's name?[60] Rather, if something is not permitted, it is especially dreadful to do it under this pretext.

[a] Invectus autem in facinus facinorosum sæpe Tertullianus, invectus Augustinus, invectus Minutius: qui, desponsatasque, destinatas, maritas raptas, scribit: contra quam persuadere alii de virginibus solis voluerunt. [b] Exclamat Virgiliusque, et *raptas sine more Sabinas*: sine exemplo, contra decus, malo more, et contra leges. Et de quo mores tamen fuere: quod damnat facinus magis: [c] *Tu criminis auctor, nutritus duro, Romule, lacte lupæ. Tu rapere intactas docuisti impune Sabinas.* Quod si nobiles illi populi connubia vobis denegarunt: an tu iure indignari potes Romule: [d] qui in tua illa
p. 14 sicariorum turba vix centum deprehendisti, qui patrem ciere potuerint: quos | et senatores fecisti? cum reliqui omnes, tui similes, sine lare, sine nomine, nothi, ignoti, terræ filii aut filii potius Erebi essent. Vos, patriciis cum populi vestri reliquis, cum aliis civibus vestris ius nuptiarum esse non voluistis. Alienos a vobis hic socios etiam Latinos fecistis. [e] Hos et per turpem fraudem afflixistis, connubia vestra petentes: per quæ exsolescens necessitudo vos inter, et illos instauraretur. Et vobis olim illustres illæ gentes connubia non denegassent? Et dominæ in manum fugitivorum convenissent? Ingenuæ nupsissent servis? Honestæ scelestis traditæ fuissent? Sed negaverint etiam iniuste, et non probe vobiscum detrectaverint affinitatem: num tu propterea iuste talem, ac tantum raptum confeceris? [f] Prædo est, qui sua auctoritate capit, quod sibi est debitum.

Necessitas (quod dicebas) vim excusabit? At non vis turpitudinem. [g] At necessitas non excusat, si exemplo, auctoritateve aut generali, aut speciali factum non adfirmatur. Ubi exemplum sine more facti? Ubi auctoritas vituperati ab omnibus auctoribus facti? Bello quæsiisses negatas nuptias non spectaculi fraude: ut sic Augustinus tibi respondet. [h] *Sed an etiam si necesse fuit facere, ignoscendum propterea est? Ad quœdam nulla debet necessitas compellere.* [i] Fœda, flagitiosa ne conservandæ quidem patriæ causa facienda sunt. Contra
p. 15 naturam est, et con | tra leges populorum, hominis incommodo suum

[a] *Tert. de spect. et adv. Val. Aug. 2. de civ. Minut. Oct.*
[b] *Virg.* 8. *Æn. Schop.* 4. *veris.* 4. *Serv. Æn.* 7. [c] *Prop.* 2. *eleg.* 6.
[d] *Plut. pr. Ro.* 58. *Manut.* 9. *fam.* 21. [e] *Macr. I. Sat.* 11. [f] *l.* 5. *de adq. pos.*
[g] *Cuch. Dec. l.* 122. *de reg. iu.* [h] *Sen.* 7. *contr.* 2. [i] *Cic. l.* 3. *de off.*

[61] Tertullian, *De spectaculis* 5 and *Adversus Valentinianos* 32; Augustine, *De civitate Dei* 2. 17; Minucius Felix, *Octavius* 25. **Translator's note:** Minucius' phrasing was "mox alienas virgines iam desponsatas, iam destinatas et nonnullas de matrimonio mulierculas sine more rapuit . . .".

[62] Vergil, *Aeneis* 8. 635; Caspar Schoppius, *Verisimilia* 4. 4 [*Verisimilium libri quatuor*, Amstelodami, Apud Judocum Pluymer, 1662, p. 138].

[63] Propertius 2. 6. 19–21.

[64] **Translator's note:** Erebus, in Greek mythology the personification of darkness.

[65] Plutarch, *Quaestiones Romanae* 58; Paulus Manutius [Paolo Manuzio], *M. Tullii Ciceronis epistolae ad familiares. Annotationes breves in margine adscriptae*, Coloniae Agrippinae, Apud Cholinum, 1604, 9. 21 [the reference is unclear].

[66] Macrobius, *Saturnalia* 1. 11. 37–40.

[67] *Digest* 41. 2. 5.

[68] Postilla of Hieronimus Chuchalon Hispanus to *Digest* 50. 17. 162, in Philippus Decius [Filippo Decio], *De regulis iuris*, Lugduni, Apud Nicolaum Parvum, 1539, fols. 156^{v}–157^{v}.

Moreover, often Tertullian, Augustine, and Minucius Felix attacked this most felonious felony—the last writes that "betrothed women, promised women, married women were seized," which contradicts those who have wished to persuade us that they were seized only from among the virgins.[61] And Vergil exclaims "the Sabine women seized in defiance of custom"—in an unparalleled way, dishonorably, through bad behavior, and against the laws.[62] And there did exist customary laws about this, a fact which condemns the crime all the more. "You, the author of the crime, Romulus, nourished by the harsh milk of the she-wolf, you taught how to seize untouched Sabine women with impunity."[63] But if those noble peoples refused intermarriage with you, can you rightly be insulted, Romulus, when in that your crowd of cutthroats you scarcely found a hundred who could name their fathers—men whom you in p. 14
fact made senators—and when all the others were men like yourself, without homes, without a name, bastards, nobodies, sons of the earth (or rather sons of Hell[64]])?[65] You Romans have not wished that patricians have the right of marriage with the rest of your people, with your other citizens. You have made foreigners even of the Latins, your allies. You have afflicted them through base deception when they seek marriages with you, through which a growing connection might be established between you and them.[66] And would not those distinguished peoples once have refused intermarriage with you? And would ladies have entered into marriages where they were fully under the authority of fugitives? Would freeborn women have married slaves? Would respectable women have been handed over to criminals? But even if they had refused unjustly and had improperly declined a marital connection with you, would you on that account have been justified in committing an abduction of that sort and on such a scale? That man is a robber who seizes upon his own authority even that which is owed to him.[67]

Will necessity (as you were saying) excuse violence? But violence won't excuse baseness. And necessity does not excuse a deed unless it is supported by a precedent or by a general or particular authority.[68] Where would there be a precedent for a lawless deed? Where would there be authority for a deed censured by all authors? By open warfare, not by the deceit of a public spectacle, you should have sought the marriages refused to you, as Augustine answers you.[69] "But even if there was a necessity to do the deed, is it to be pardoned on that account? There are some acts to which no necessity ought to compel one."[70] Repulsive and criminal acts ought not be done even for the sake of saving one's country.[71] It is contrary to nature and contrary to the laws p. 15

[69] [Presumably, Augustine, *De civitate Dei* 2. 17: "Iustius autem bellum cum ea gente geri potuit..."]

[70] Seneca the Elder, *Controversiae* 7. 2. 9.

[71] Cicero, *De officiis* 1. 159. **Translator's note:** In *De officiis*, it is the Stoic sage (*sapiens*), who would not engage in such acts even for the sake of the fatherland.

commodum augere. Etiam si omnia incommoda essent subeunda, vel externa, vel corporis, vel etiam ipsius animi, quæ iniustitia vacent: non tamen de commodis alienis licet detrahere. Ait Cicero. [a] Non hic excusat necessitas adversus hominem [b] Nullibi excusat necessitas, quæ non necessitas esse potest.

[c] Neque enim vere est necessitas, cum potest casui aliter provideri. An a patribus Albanis, an ab avo rege Albanorum, qui et manu tua restitutus in regnum erat, sicuti viros, ita etiam mulieres impetrare non potuisses, si non belli caussam quæsiisses cum aliis? Et non vobis, quemadmodum viri, pares et coniuges in asylo inventæ? *Ut matrimonium facias, rem concordiæ per discordiam auspicaris: rapis, ferocis, fallis: et nuptiæ tibi sunt rupta hospitii fœdera.* Quæ tibi Cyprianus. Ecce autem nobis virtutis illius Romanæ specimina prima. Ecce specimina militaris virtutis. Strenui isti, hospitum inermium, puellarumque victores, et muliercularum, dum armatos mox habent, etiam mœnibus, et parietibus suæ urbis inclusos, cum quibus conferant manus, fugantur in illa sua urbe trepidi, et conciduntur. Et qui regni consortem, regni confundatorem, et fratrem ferre geminum, atque [d] primogenitum nequiit, is hostem in regni partem habere coactus est. Habes, Romule,
p. 16 quod | meruisti. Non fratrem, hoc est, te alterum, [e] et eum geminum, quod plus est aliquid, ferebas: et, feras peregrinum, hostemque, necesse est. Immo vero necesse non est. Quem enim spoliare armis per Tarpeiæ virginis dolum non potuit: nec satis per allegatas fraudare Sabellas: insidiis illum obtruncari Lanuviorum, sibique de medio tolli curat.

[f] Legimus apud Dionysium, quam virgo illa vafram inierit rationem, ut hostes perderet. Pacta arcis deditionem, si acciperet gesta hostium in sinistris: ut ita scutis nudaret, et ita traderet cædendos suis. De scutis, non de armillis pepigit: et scutis obruta est. An vero puellæ commentum existimamus? An virorum verius, qui Tarpeiæ inferias constituere sollemnes, annuas, perpetuas? Quid etiam per Sabellas tentatum existimamus? Non eæ sponte sua inter tela

[a] *Ceph. cons.* 451. [b] *Tertu. exh. cast.* [c] *Alc.* 8. *cons.* 35.
[d] *Ior. de re. suec.* [e] *Sen.* 9. *contr.* 3. [f] *Dionys.* 2.

[72] Ioannes Cephalus [Giovanni Cefalo], *Consilia* 451, fols. 10ʳ f. [*Consiliorum sive responsorum libri quinque*, Francofurti ad Moenum, Apud Ioannem Feyerabendt, impensis Sigismundi Feyerabendts, 1579].
[73] Tertullian, *De exhortatione castitatis* 7. 5.
[74] Alciatus, *Consilia* 8. 35, col. 1147.
[75] [[Ps.-]Cyprian, *De idolorum vanitate*.]
[76] Jordanes, *Romana* 87–9. [Cf. Jordanes, *Getica* 35. 180 f.]
[77] Seneca the Elder, *Controversiae* 9. 3. 3.
[78] Dionysius of Halicarnassus 2. 39.

of peoples for one to increase his own advantage to the disadvantage of another man. Even if one had to undergo all sorts of disadvantages that did not involve one in wrongdoing—disadvantages for one's possessions, for one's body, even for one's own life—even then one is not allowed to detract from the advantages of others. So says Cicero. Necessity does not offer us an excuse here against a fellow human being.[72] Nowhere can a necessity provide an excuse where it is not a necessity in the first place.[73]

For there is no true necessity when it is possible to provide for the situation in some other way.[74] Would you not have been able to procure women, just as you had procured men, from the Alban fathers, or from your grandfather the king of the Albans, who had been restored to his kingdom by your hand—if, that is, you weren't looking for an excuse for warfare with others? And couldn't there have have been found for you in your refuge wives like yourselves, just as men were found? "In order to make a marriage, you find the auspices for a matter of concord through discord: you seize, you rage, you deceive—and for you marriages are the broken pacts of hospitality." That is what Cyprian tells you.[75] Behold the first indications of that celebrated Roman virtue! Behold the first indication of their military valor. Victors over powerless guests and girls and helpless women, when they soon had to deal with men in arms, even though those men were penned up within the walls of their city, these vigorous men were put to flight in fear and trembling and were cut down in that famous city of theirs. And the man who was unable to endure a twin brother (and the first-born, at that[76]) as partner in and cofounder of his kingdom—he was forced to let an enemy share his kingdom. You have what you have deserved, Romulus. You weren't able to p. 16
endure a brother—that is, a second self—and a twin brother at that, which is something more than just a brother[77]—and now you have to endure a stranger and an enemy. Or, rather, you *don't* have to. For the man whom Romulus could not plunder of his arms through the trickery of the maiden Tarpeia nor deceive sufficiently through the suborned Sabine women, he arranges to be killed by the wiles of the Lanuvians and thus to be gotten out of his way.

We read in Dionysius what a cunning plan that maiden [Tarpeia] entered into in order to destroy the enemy.[78] She agreed to betray the citadel if she could receive the things they carried on their left arms, in order that she might thus denude them of their shields and thus hand them over to her own people to be killed. For she made an agreement about shields, not armlets—and it was by shields that she was overwhelmed. Or are we to really imagine that this was the deception of a girl? Was it not more likely that of the men who established solemn, annual, and perpetual memorial observances for Tarpeia? And what are we to suppose was attempted by way of the Sabine

volantia se tulerunt: ut pulchra est Livii fabula: sed legatæ missæ ab iisdem sunt viris Romanis: ut Dionysius scribit, fidus ille, et cautus scriptor, et Livio inventus certior. [a] Quod scribunt critici doctissimi. Tentata proculdubio fuerunt alia omnia quam partitio, quæ secuta regni est. Tatii porro cædem nec sine [b] auctoribus adscribimus Romulo, nec sine ratione damus parricidæ sollemni: quæ et patrata a cognatis Laviniensibus, et bono eidem fuit. [c] Facti
p. 17 suspicio confirmatur, si adeptio commodi, vitatio incommodi osten|datur. Inquis Cicero. [d] Qui quid lucratur ex crimine, is consilium ad crimen dedisse, is tractasse de crimine creditur, ei gestum negotium intelligitur. Id Baldus, et reliqui iurisconsulti. De quibus illud iam vulgatum, *Semel malus*. Dico autem parricidam sollemnem: [e] qui non fratrem solum, sed et avum Numitorem, aut avum Amulium (quid moremur nominis varietatem?) interfecit avum. Avum, an patrem Amulium? semper parentem occidit parricida. [f] Parricida semper, etsi nec legitimum (qualis propatruus fuit Amulius) occidit: quia ius sanguinis in natura est, non in lege. Parricida etiam qui occidit patruum: adeoque et propatruum. Quod propter scelus inexpiabile hereditate Romulum Albani regni excidisse, unum sive Numitoris, sive Amulii hæredem, aut quam aliam ob caussam non regnasse Albæ existimemus? Verum non fuerit Romulus auctor cædis Tatii: cur tamen nec ultionem quærit socii regis? An desiit bellicosus esse? Aut pius, iustusque fuit numquam.

Et immo ex sequenti hoc facto apparet auctor. Sistentes se noxios ad ipsius tribunal absoluit: et iudicat, cædem iure factam, vi scilicet pro vi reddita. Et vim fecerit Tatius, qui Sabinos suos, a te victos, inimicisque deditos, eripuerit? Et neglexerit Tatius iustissimas Lanuviorum querelas: an propterea
p. 18 Romulus, nihil cunctatus (sic Dio|nysius) alterius sibi partes assumserit? Et quoniam, id in se fieri, non est passus Tatius, cæsus iure a Lanuvinis erit? Et quoniam istis illico non fit a Tatio satis, regem propterea, sacrum gentibus quibusque caput, etiam interque aras deorum: et in sollemni sacrificio tamquam victimam mactare, fas fuerit? Lanuvium ad sollemne sacrificium

[a] *Manut. Asco. pro Cor. Lips. de mag. c.* 16. [b] *Oros.* 2. *c.* 4. *P. Diac.* 1. [c] *Cic. part.*
[d] *Bal.* 5. *co.* 506. [e] *Oros. Cedr. Fris.* 2. *c.* 3. [f] *Inst. de nupt. l.* 1 *de par. l.* 6. *de in ius vo. l.* 50. *de V. S.*

---

79 Paulus Manutius [Paolo Manuzio], *Scholia ad Asconium*, fol. 100r [*Asconius Pedianus, Explanatio in Ciceronis orationes in C. Verrem, in orationem pro C. Cornelio, in orationem contra competitores, in orationem pro M. Scauro, in orationem contra L. Pisonem, in orationem pro Milone. Scholia Pauli Manutii*, Venetiis, 1563]; Justus Lipsius, *De magistratibus veteris populi Romani*, ch. 17 [in *Tractatus ad historiam Romanam cognoscendam apprime utiles*, Cantabrigiae, 1592; Gentili must have ch. 17 of *De magistratibus* rather than ch. 16 in mind, where Dionysius is contrasted favorably with Livy and described as *fidus* as well as *cautus scriptor*].

80 Orosius 2. 4. 6; Paulus Diaconus, *Historia Romana* 1. 2. [The passage in Paulus Diaconus does not confirm that Romulus murdered Tatius.]

81 Cicero, *De partitione oratoria* 32. 111.

82 Baldus de Ubaldis, *Consilia* 5. 506, fols. 135v f. [*Consiliorum, sive responsorum*, vols. 1–5, Venetiis, 1575]. [Cf. Gentili, *De iure belli* 3. 24.]

83 Orosius 2. 4. 3; George Cedrenus, *Historiarum compendium* 257 [J.-P. Migne, *Patrologia Graeca*, cxxi, col. 291/292]; Otto of Freising, *Chronicle* 2. 3 [*Chronica sive historia de duabus civitatibus*, rec. Adolfus Hofmeister, Hannoverae et Lipsiae, 1912, p. 71].

84 *Institutes* 1. 10; *Digest* 48. 9. 1; *Digest* 2. 4. 6; *Digest* 50. 16. 50.

women? They did not of their own accord venture forth amidst flying weapons, as the pretty tale of Livy has it. Rather, they were sent as ambassadors by their Roman husbands, as Dionysius writes, that trustworthy and cautious writer, and one who has been found more reliable than Livy. And this is what the most learned judges write.[79] No doubt everything was attempted, short of a partition of the kingdom—and in fact that followed as well. Moreover, it is not without authorities that we attribute the murder of Tatius to Romulus,[80] nor without reason do we ascribe it to the habitual kin-killer, an act which was at one and the same time performed by his relatives the Lanuvians and was a blessing to himself. Suspicion for a deed is strengthened if the attainment of an advantage and the avoidance of a disadvantage can be demonstrated. You say so, Cicero.[81] The person who p. 17
profits from a crime—that person is believed to have given advice to commit the crime, that person is believed to have been involved in the crime, and the business is understood to have been carried out for him. So say Baldus and the other jurisconsults—from whom comes that already trite phrase "Once a wicked man, [always a wicked man]."[82] Now, I call this man a habitual kin-killer, for he not only killed his brother, but also his grandfather Numitor—or his grandfather Amulius (why should we linger over the difference in names?)—either way, he killed his grandfather.[83] Was Amulius his grandfather—or his father? Either way, he killed a male ancestor. Either way, he is a kin-killer, even if he kills someone not his legitimate kin (such as his great-uncle Amulius), for the right of blood lies in nature, not in law. He is a kin-killer who kills his uncle, and even his great-uncle.[84] On account of this inexpiable crime we judge that Romulus forfeited his claim to the Alban kingdom, though he was the sole heir of Numitor (or Amulius)—or for what other cause are we to suppose that he did not reign over Alba? And let's suppose that it was true that Romulus was not the one who contrived the murder of Tatius. Why does he not then seek vengeance for his associate king? Has he left off being warlike? In fact, he was never either dutiful or just.

Furthermore, it is clear from the following fact that he was the one behind the deed. For he absolves those who appear in court as the guilty parties, and he delivers the verdict that the murder was done lawfully, violence naturally being returned for violence. Would Tatius have been guilty of violence when he would have rescued his Sabines when they were conquered by you and handed over to their enemies? Would Tatius have paid no attention to the perfectly just complaints of the Lanuvians? And would Romulus for that reason and without the slightest delay (so Dionysius) have taken the side of p. 18
the other party? And because Tatius did not put up with this being done against him, was he justly murdered by the Lanuvians? And because Tatius did not immediately make amends to those people, would it have been on that account perfectly proper to slaughter a king, a life held sacred among all nations, among the altars of the gods, no less, and in a solemn sacrifice—like a sacrificial victim? Old Tatius had come to Lanuvium to a solemn sacrifice.

venerat senex Tatius. Num credimus, in Lanuvinos, admissi ullius a se peccati fuisse conscium? [a] Periti docent, innocentiæ signum esse maximum, si veniat in carcerem sponte, qui accusatus criminis est: Censent adversum fugientes: censent pro manentibus: et magis igitur pro venientibus in periculi locum. Innocentia præstat securitatem. Et sic Tatius Lanuvium venit: et ibi hospes, rex, sacerdos, in conspectu deorum immortalium, interficitur iuste. Sed ecce dii illi, late immissa in noxios pestilentia, cædem vindicant, quam Romulus iustam pronunciavit. [b] Et Remique cædem paria vindicarunt mala: de quibus Plutarchus, et alii exposuerunt.

Hic vero fraudis, et perfidiæ a raptu mulierum finis: Verum ex finibus agro non positis fraus, quam ardentissime quæsiit, infinita. Romule, terminos cur agro non ponis tuo? [c] *Dimensiones terrarum, terminis positis, vagantibus, ac discordantibus populis pacis utilia præstiterunt.* At pacem Romulus non quæ-
p. 19 rebat. [d] Audiamus Plutar|chum, *Noluit Romulus mensura proprii agri prodere mensuram alieni: siquidem virium compedes terminos esse, si servarentur: et iniuriæ indicium, si non servarentur.* Aut quid testes advocamus? Re ipsa tu, hoc tuum fuisse consilium, ostendisti, Romule. Nam hinc arripis belli caussam in Fidenates: ac si isti de tuo agro Romano prædas abegerint. Et eripi vobis quidquam valuerit: quorum patrii soli ([e] ut Florus loquitur) gleba nulla esset, sed statim pomœrium, et omnibus portis in alienum exiretur. Ista autem (quod idem scribit) contagione per singulos itum est: et proximis quibusque correptis totam sub vos redegistis Italiam [f] *Assumtis semel armis nunquam quies*: (en testem alterum) *quippe quibus egestas turpis, atque obscœna fames domi timerentur, si paci unquam, aut fœderi adquievissent.* Vi igitur, atque iniuria sub Romulo occupatum imperium, scribit idem Florus verissime. Nam bella inferre finitimis, et inde in cetera procedere, ac populos sibi non molestos sola regni cupiditate conterere, et subdere, dic, age, responde Augustino, quid aliud, quam grande latrocinium nominandum est? Immane huius unius latrocinium regis: qui non supra tria hominum millia habuit primum, et non habuit pedem terræ: moriens ad mare usque tenebat, hominum vero millibus quinquaginta imperitabat.

[a] *Ceph. cons.* 721. *Alc.* 5. *cons.* 6. *Deci.* 3 *cons.* 96. 104. [b] *Cedr. Serv.* 1. *Æneid.*
[c] *Boeth. geometr.* [d] *Plut. Nu. et pr. R.* 15. [e] *Flor. lib.* 1. [f] *P. Diac.* 5.

---

85 Cephalus, *Consilia* 721.

86 George Cedrenus, *Historiarum compendium* 258 [J.-P. Migne, *Patrologia Graeca*, cxxi, cols. 291–4]; Servius, *On Aeneid* 1. 280 [cf. also *On Aeneid* 1. 296].

87 Ps.-Boethius, *De geometria.*

88 Plutarch, *Numa* [where the proper sense of the first sentence of Plutarch's work is: "He did not wish, by measuring his own territory, to acknowledge how much he had seized of other people's"]; *Quaestiones Romanae* 15.

89 Florus 1. 9. 7. **Translator's note:** Gentili has rendered Florus' somewhat obscure phrase "set statim hostile pomerium" quite unintelligible by omitting "hostile."

90 Paulus Diaconus, *Historia Romana* 5. **Translator's note:** It actually is a citation not of Diaconus, but of Orosius 2. 4. 8: "adsumptis semel armis numquam quies, quippe quibus egestas turpis atque obscena fames domi timerentur, si umquam paci adquieuissent."

91 [Citation from Augustine, *De civitate Dei* 4. 6.]

Are we to believe that he was aware of any wrongdoing he had perpetrated against the Lanuvians? The learned teach that it is the greatest indication of innocence if someone who is accused of a crime comes to prison of his own free will.[85] They pass judgment against those who take to flight; they pass judgment on behalf of those who stay put—and even more, accordingly, for those who venture into a place of danger. Innocence offers one a sense of security. And thus Tatius came to Lanuvium, and there as a guest, a king, a priest, in the sight of the immortal gods, he was killed "justly." But behold: those gods, by unleashing a pestilence upon the guilty parties, punish the murder which Romulus pronounced justified. And similar misfortunes, about which Plutarch and others have expounded, punished the murder of Remus.[86]

This, indeed, was the end result of the trickery and perfidy arising from the abduction of the women. But the deceit arising from the fact that boundary stones were not placed in the field, a deceit which he most eagerly sought out—this deceit has no boundaries to it. Romulus, why do you not place boundaries in your territory? "Measurements of land, when boundary stones have been placed, have offered to wandering and contentious peoples the benefits of peace."[87] But Romulus wasn't seeking peace. Let us listen to
Plutarch: "Romulus did not wish to reveal the extent of someone else's p. 19
territory by making a measurement of his own. For he knew that boundaries are restraints upon power if they are preserved—and evidence for injury if they are not."[88] But why should we summon witnesses? You have shown by the fact itself that this was your advice, Romulus. For it was from here that you seized upon an excuse for war against the inhabitants of Fidenae—as if those men drove off booty from your Roman territory. And as if you had anything worth the plundering—you men of whose ancestral soil (as Florus says) there was not a single clod, but it was hostile territory from the pomerium on, and from all the gates one went forth into foreign territory.[89] Through that contagion (as the same man writes) the process went on from one group of people to the next, and when whatever peoples were nearest had been seized you reduced all of Italy to your power. Another witness writes: "Once arms were taken up, there was never peace again for those men who feared base want and disgusting hunger at home if they ever consented to peace or a treaty."[90] That same Florus very truly writes that under Romulus power was seized by violence and wrongdoing. For to bring war upon one's closest neighbors and from there to move on to other crimes, and to wear down and subdue peoples who have done you no harm simply through lust for rule—come now, speak; answer Augustine: what else is this to be called but brigandage on the grand scale?[91] Monstrous was the brigandage of this one single king, who had no more than 3,000 men at first and possessed not a single foot of soil. But upon his death his rule extended all the way to the sea, and he ruled over 50,000.

p. 20 Sed an exorsi lon|gissimam orationem non sumus, si regum omnium, ducumque gesta expendimus? Utar deinceps compendio: nam et stat generale testimonium, [a] *Cum Romulo, regibus ceteris, postremisque ducibus disciplinam communem: prædamque audaciæ esse, quicquid Romani sub imperium retinerent.* [b] Sane vero et Cicero, et Livius, et alii faciunt reges omnes, excepto Superbo, pares: etsi probos. At de probitate nunc in Romulo ostensum contrarium est. Et id ergo sequitur nobis bellissime, quod si pares fuerunt omnes: et Romulus, divus ille unus in omnibus, fuit improbissimus: omnes improbissimi multo fuerunt. Et ego tamen excipio item unum, sed Numam. Vidit omnium improbitatem Orosius, et ostendit: quod si unus fuisset rex improbus, non sustulissent regnum Romani, sed illum regem.

Et itaque urbis exordium hoc, et Romuli virtus hæc est.

De Numa, et reliquis regibus.
CAP. III

Quis procul ille autem, ramis insignis olivæ Sacra ferens? nosco crines, incanaque menta Regis Romani: primus qui legibus urbem fundabit. Recte a sanguinario Romulo, et illege procul, qui sequitur Numa, ut alibi etiam longe a templis, domiciliis deorum, sunt inferi: *hinc procul addit tartareas etiam sedes.* Procul a
p. 21 Romulo iste: vir Italicus: et fidei | colentissimus, et pacis: et iustissimus unus. Sub cuius regno longissimo animi illi feri quievere Romulidarum: et aurea patris Iani secula Latio rursus, regnata per arua Saturno quondam, condita sunt. Neque enim finitimi populi, læsi licet vehementer a Romulo fuerint, licet et Numæ contemnere animum potuissent, pacem unquam sollicitarunt. Ut intelligamus, bella omnia fuisse Romanis volentibus, moventibus. Ecce hi pacem sollicitant mox a Numa: qui frenum effreni alioqui, et impotenti belluæ fuit.

[a] *Minut. Oct.* [b] *Cic.* 1. *Parad. Liv.* 2.

---

92 Minutius Felix, *Octavius* 25. 4–5 [considerably abridged by Gentili].
93 Cicero, *Paradoxa Stoicorum* 1; Livy 2. 1. 2.
94 [Orosius 2. 4. 13 ff.]
95 [Anchises to Aeneas in the Underworld, Vergil, *Aeneis* 6. 808–11.]
96 [Vulcan forging the shield of Aeneas: Vergil, *Aeneis* 8. 666–7.]
97 **Translator's note:** Gentili is applying to Numa a paraphrase of words Anchises applied to Augustus at *Aeneis* 6. 792–4. I am assuming that "Saturno quodam," "a certain Saturn," found in both the 1599 and 1770 editions, is Gentili's rather catty alteration of Vergil's "quondam." But it could well be a misprint.

But have we not stated merely the introduction here to a very long oration p. 20
if we are considering the deeds of all the kings and commanders? Henceforth, then, I shall make use of a shortcut, for it stands as a general proof: "With Romulus, the other kings and the most recent leaders this is the common practice—and whatever the Romans hold under their sway is the booty of shameless behavior."[92] True enough, Cicero and Livy and others made all the kings, with the exception of Tarquin, out to be all alike—though alike in virtuousness.[93] But now, in the case of Romulus, the opposite has been demonstrated in respect to virtue. And so this follows for us most elegantly: that if they were all alike, and Romulus, that sole apotheosized one among the lot of them was utterly wicked, then they were all utterly wicked. And yet even I nonetheless make an exception of one of them: Numa. Orosius saw the wickedness of all of them and pointed out that if there had been only one wicked king the Romans would not have done away with the monarchy; they would just have done away with that one king.[94]

And so this is the city's beginning—and this is the excellence of Romulus.

CHAPTER 3
On Numa and the Other Kings

"Who is this at a distance, distinguished by sprigs of olive, bearing sacred objects? I recognize the gray hairs and chin of a Roman king—the one who will first establish the city with laws."[95] Rightly does Numa who follows stand at a distance from bloody and lawless Romulus, just as in another passage those of the underworld are at a distance from the temples, the homes of the gods: "At a distance he adds as well the dwellings of Tartarus."[96] That Italian
man stands far from Romulus, for he is most devoted to trustworthiness and p. 21
peace and is a man of unparalleled justice. Under his very lengthy rule the savage spirits of the sons of Romulus grew peaceful, and the golden age of Father Janus, throughout the fields ruled over by a certain Saturn, were established again for Latium.[97] For while it may be that the neighboring peoples might have been grievously harmed by Romulus, and while it might be that they could have despised the unwarlike inclination of Numa, in fact they never disturbed the peace. Thus we can understand that all the wars came about because the Romans wanted them and set them in motion. Behold, *these* people soon disturbed the peace after the time of Numa, who acted as a bridle upon an otherwise savage and headstrong animal.

Cui deinde subibit, Ocia qui rumpet patriæ, residesque movebit Tullus in arma viros. [a] Tullus: cuius incunabula agreste tugurium cœpit: et adolescentia in pecore pascendo fuit occupata. [b] Quem in patres Albanos nihil aliud movit, Virgilio dicente, Augustino adnotante, nisi resides ut moveret in arma viros. Et hæc iusta Romanis bellandi caussa scilicet, arma ne rubiginem traherent, aut otiarentur. Non audis Suetonium narrantem, bellum ab Augusto nullum cuiquam sine iustis, et necessariis caussis fuisse illatum? [c] et Velleium, et Dionem, illatum ab Augusto bellum Pannoniis, quo arma Romana exercerentur? [d] Ecquis ille Fabius, qui Cretam invadit, ne haberet (ita Livius) provinciam ociolam? Sed de Tullo. *Ferocior Romulo, undique materiam exci-*
p. 22 *tandi belli quærebat*: quod itidem Livius. Apud | quem, et apud Dionysium, et apud alios legimus reliquas Albani belli rationes regis huius improbissimas, et crudelissimas: et una hora quadringentorum annorum opus, quibus Alba steterat, urbem regiam a primo ortu, urbem Latii principem, urbem parentem exscidio datam a suis colonis, qui filii parricidæ ipsi, et parricidarum parentes.

Iam audies. *Sequitur iactantior Ancus*: [e] id est, qui plurimum sibi arrogat: et *nimium gaudens popularibus auris*: favoribus populi, quos non quærunt sapientes. [f] Et is condemnavit superiores: quod vidisse dicitur, populum Romanum ardentem amore bellorum, inferentemque gentibus bella plerumque ratione nulla iustæ exstante: et itaque fecialia iura (remedium huic iniquitati) de Æquicolis accepisse: Hoc Servii Honorati testimonium. At remedium, an emplastrum, atque fucum dicimus potius? Fucum potius. [g] Ecce nobis Picenus noster Firmianus Lactantius: *Quantum a iustitia recedat utilitas, populus ipse Romanus docet: qui per feciales bella indicendo, et legitime iniurias inferendo, semperque aliena cupiendo, atque rapiendo, possessionem sibi totius orbis comparavit.*

De Prisco, Servio, Superbo, tribus invasoribus regni, hoc satis. Et Superbus, qui laudatur foris, (etiam istum laudant) num fraude mala non
p. 23 aggressus est Gabios? Num contra Rutulos bellum non | movit, quia divites erant? Num per scelus inauditum non sustulit Hordeonium Turnum? Sed de regibus reliquis, simul et de superioribus nunc notemus, quemadmodum senatorum manibus Romulus discerptus suit. Hic raptus in cælum. [h] *Rude illud, et ferox seculum conditoris sui cruore fœde maculatum ne summa quidem posteritatis dissimulare pietas potest.* Hoc aliorum, hoc Valerii Maximi. [i] Tullus

[a] *Val.* 3. *c.* 4. [b] *Aug.* 3. *de civ.* 14. [c] *Dio.* 49. [d] *Liv.* 37. [e] *Donatus.*
[f] *Serv.* 10. Æn. [g] *Lact.* 4. *Inst.* 9. [h] *Val.* 5. *c.* 3. [i] *Zonara.*

---

98 [Vergil, *Aeneis* 6. 812–14.] 99 Valerius Maximus 3. 4. 1. 100 Augustine, *De civitate Dei* 3. 14.
101 [Dio Cassius 49. 36; Velleius Paterculus alludes to Augustus' acquisition of Pannonia at 2. 39. 3, but he does not give a reason for it.]
102 Livy 37. 60. 2. 103 [Livy 1. 22. 2.] 104 [Vergil, *Aeneis* 6. 815–6.]
105 Donatus [Tiberius Claudius Donatus, *Interpretationes Vergilianae*?]. 106 Servius, *On Aeneid* 10. 14.
107 **Translator's note:** Picenus is misled by the name Firmianus into thinking that Lactantius hails from Fermo, the ancient Firmum Picenum. Lactantius was really a native of North Africa. Gentili knows this; see the response by the Roman in 2. 3, pp. 190–1 to this effect.
108 Lactantius, *Divinae institutiones* 6. 9. 3–4. **Translator's note:** This is a loose summary by Lactantius of part of Philus' anti-imperialist argument in Cicero's *De republica*.
109 Valerius Maximus 5. 3. 1.

"Next Tullus will succeed him, a man who will shatter his country's leisure and stir idle men to arms."[98] Tullus—who spent his childhood in a rustic hut and whose youth was spent in pasturing a herd.[99] Tullus—who had no other motive to attack the Alban fathers except a desire to stir idle men to arms, as Vergil notes and as Augustine also observes.[100] And this, I suppose, is a just cause of warfare for the Romans: to prevent their weapons from rusting or from sitting inactive. Do you not hear Suetonius relating that Augustus waged no war against anyone except for just and necessary causes? At the same time, though, don't you hear Velleius Paterculus and Dio Cassius saying that Augustus waged war against the Pannonians so that Roman arms might be put to use?[101] And what of that Fabius who invaded Crete lest he be in charge of a province that was more or less at leisure (so Livy says)?[102] But of Tullus himself we read: "Fiercer than Romulus, he used to seek an opportunity everywhere for stirring up war," as Livy also writes.[103] We read in Livy, Dionysius of Halicar- p. 22
nassus, and others of this king's utterly wicked and cruel reasons for the Alban war, and we read how in one hour the work of the 400 years in which Alba had stood, a royal city from its first beginnings, the chief city of Latium, a parent city, was given over to destruction by the colonists it had sent forth, who were themselves the sons of a parricide and the parents of parricides.

Now you shall hear: "Next comes the more boastful Ancus"—that is, he who lays claim to as much as possible—"and takes too much pleasure in the popular breezes"[104]—that is, in the favor of the people, which wise men do not seek.[105] And he censured his predecessors because he is said to have seen that the Roman people was passionate with love for wars and ready to inflict war upon peoples when there was often no just cause, and so he adopted the fetial laws from the Aequicolii as a remedy to this injustice.[106] This is what Servius testifies. But are we to call it a remedy—or rather a sticking plaster and rouge? Rouge would be the better term. Look what our fellow Picene[107] Firmianus Lactantius tells us: "Just how far utility stands from justice the Roman people itself teaches us, for by declaring wars through the fetial priests and imposing wrongs under cover of law and by always craving and plundering other peoples' things they acquired for themselves possession of the entire world."[108]

This will suffice also for Tarquinius Priscus, Servius Tullius, and Tarquinius Superbus, three usurpers of the throne. And Superbus, who is praised abroad (they praise even him!)—did he not attack the Gabii with a wicked trick? Did he not set a war in motion against the Rutulans because they were p. 23
wealthy? Did he not make away with Hordeonius Turnus through an unheard-of crime? But about these other kings, just as about the earlier ones, let us now simply observe how Romulus was torn apart by the senators. *This* was his rapture into heaven. "That rude and savage age, foully stained by the blood of its founder, not even the most extreme piety of posterity could hide."[109] What Valerius Maximus says here is true of the other kings as well. Tullus

cum tota domo exustus per insidias Anci. Et Ancus per insidias Prisci sublatus est: certe per insidias: [a] nam, excepto Numa, absumtus suo fato (sic Plutarchus) est nemo: sed insidiis occubuere: et Superbus actus in exsilium fuit: quæ civilis mors. Priscum scimus occisum procurantibus filiis Anci. Servium generi manu cæsum, et filiæ calcatum pedibus cernimus. Superbum a filio sororis Bruto, a cognato Tarquinio spoliatum regno, spoliatum domo non ignoramus. Et virtutis quidquam in ea civitate fuisse credamus; in qua aliud super aliud scelera tragica, et parricidia infanda tenemus? Num foris iusti cum aliis fuerint: qui domi ne tantillum quidem iustitiæ habuerunt? Quasi scilicet ut aliæ sunt domi vestes, aliæ foris, aliæ viatoriæ, ita isti in civitate per omnem viventes iniustitiam cum externis iustitiam colerent.

Atque hæc infantia populi Romani dicitur: cum in visceribus matris catulus p. 24 viperinus luctatus, | et grassatus est. [b] *Viperei coeunt abrupto corpore nodi.*

De Brutis duobus, et Scævola, et aliis similibus. CAP. IV

Secundus conditor civitatis ille est: [c] cui a brutis moribus nomen obtigit. Non eum magis decuisset, hominem ante mori, quam agere vitam brutorum, et bruti appellationem subire? Sane accepimus, Socratem nec orationem unam recitare sustinuisse paullo molliorem: atque, quod superesset, ex vita perire sibi, quam quod præterierat, maluisse. Vita brevis: vita hominis bulla: et ad mundi ævitatem collata, ferme nulla. Quo argumento a scientia rerum, et harum quidem obviarum, ducto docemur, nec magni facere rem parvam, nec oportere pro re parva retinenda peccare.

Brutus is, alter reipublicæ Romanæ pater, in regem perfidus, et avunculum suum censebitur nihilominus, quam progenies eius perfida in Cæsarem dictatorem exstiterit: [d] quæ damnata sententiis summorum virorum, et summorum theologorum est. [e] Mitto posterioris huius aliam brutitatem: qui, in

[a] *Plut. Nu.* [b] *Lucan. Ser. 3. Geor. Apul. Apol. 2.*
[c] *Macr. 3. Sat. ult.* [d] *Dio. 44. Marty. 3. Iud. Dant. inf. Melan. epit. ph. mo.*
[e] *Card. 3. de sap. Sen. 2. de benef.*

[110] Zonaras 7. 6. [111] Plutarch, *Numa* 22. 6–7.

[112] Lucan, *De bello civili* 6. 490; Servius, *On Georgics* 3. 426; Apuleius, *Apologia de magia* 85. **Translator's note:** The Lucan passage is about the powers of Thessalian witches to alter nature. Its application to the present context is not entirely clear.

[113] Macrobius, *Saturnalia* 3. 20. 5.

[114] Dio Cassius 44; Vermilius 3 [Peter Martyr Vermilius, *In librum iudicum commentarii*, Tiguri, Excudebat Christophorus Froschoverus, 1571]; Dante, *Inferno* 34. 64–6 [*Divina commedia*, Venetia, 1529]; Philipp Melanchthon [Philip Schwarzerd], *Philosophiae moralis epitomes libri duo*, Argentorati, Apud Cratonem Mylium, 1546.

was incinerated with his entire household by the plotting of Ancus.[110] And Ancus was done away with by the plotting of Priscus—of course by plotting, for with the exception of Numa not one of the kings lived out his natural life (according to Plutarch), but died through plots, and Superbus was driven into exile, which was a kind of civic death.[111] We know that Tarquinius Priscus was killed by the machinations of the sons of Ancus. We know that Servius was killed at the hand of his son-in-law and his body was trampled upon by his daughter. And we are aware that Tarquinius Superbus was deprived of his kingdom and his home by Brutus, his sister's son—that is, by a relative in the Tarquin family. And what virtue could we believe there was in that state, in which we have the record of a succession of crimes worthy of the tragic stage and unspeakable parricides? Could they have been just towards others abroad when at home they possessed not the smallest particle of justice? No doubt just as there are some clothes one wears at home, others abroad, and others again while traveling, so those men, I suppose, while living lives of utter injustice in their own state, practiced justice with foreign peoples.

And this is what is called the infancy of the Roman people, when an infant viper struggles and attacks while still in the innards of its mother. "Vipers' p. 24
knots come together again after the body is broken."[112]

CHAPTER 4

On the Two Brutuses, Scaevola, and Others of that Sort

The second founder of the state was that man whose lot it was to bear a name derived from his brutal character.[113] Would it not have been more proper for him to die as a human being before living the life of brute beasts and endure the name of a brute? Indeed we have learned that Socrates could not bring himself to utter just one speech that was a little more conciliatory and that he preferred to lose that bit of his life which might have been left him rather than see the life he had already lived be destroyed. Life is short; the life of man is a bubble—and, when compared with the age of the earth, almost nothing. By this argument drawn from the nature of things (and quite obvious things at that), we are taught not to make much of a small matter and that we ought not sin in order to hold onto something trivial.

This Brutus, the second father of the Roman state, will be judged no less faithless to his king and uncle than his descendant, who proved faithless to Caesar the dictator and was condemned by the judgments of the most distinguished men and most distinguished theologians.[114] I pass over here the other brutishness of this later man, who stupidly believed and hoped that

magna republica instaurari libertatem, ut in parva, potuisse, opinatus est stulte et speravit, ibi libertatem futuram, ubi tam magnum erat præmium imperandi, et tanta serviendi voluntas: et existimavit, civitatem in priorem p. 25 formam posse revocari, amissis | pristinis moribus: et credidit, futuram ibi æqualitatem iuris civilis, et staturas suo loco leges, ubi viderat, tot millia hominum pugnare, non si servirent, sed cui servirent domino. Quanta illum aut rerum naturæ, aut urbis suæ tenuit oblivio: qui, uno interemto, defuturum alium, censuit, qui idem vellet: cum Tarquinius esset inventus post tot reges ferro, ac flammis occisos? Hæc prudentiæ cum Bruto non exputo. Animum illi exprobro immanem: qui vitam adimere Cæsari potuit: a quo fuerat in vita conservatus: ornatus dignitatibus: quasi filius habitus. Iniustitiam illius vitupero: qui optimum reipublicæ statum, qui sub rege iusto est, et ad illud temporis necessarium subvertere conatus est. [a] Popularis status ad magnum evectus imperium recte se habere deinceps nequit. Et id ratio, et id experientia contestatur.

Quid mihi libertatem obtendis patriæ: et iustitiam propterea unam cordi tibi fuisse contendis? Obsistere potueris invadenti principatum: factum principem tollere non potuisti. Non hæ sunt partes subditorum: non tuæ, qui magno in Cæsaris principatum obstrinxisti te iuramento. [b] In principatum Cæsaris te obstrinxisti, maximo studio (sic historia) senatus exquisitum, atque delatum.

Sed ecce ulciscitur velox nemesis istum, et reliquos parricidas: ecce brevi p. 26 temporis spatio miserabi|liter exstinctos omnes. Vlta Nemesis facinus prioris Bruti: qui uno quasi momento cæcidit super occisos filios parricida. *Infelix, utcunque ferant ea fata minores*: de Bruto isto cecinisse Virgilium, scimus. Et iste quod auferre regnum cognatis Tarquiniis voluit, an etiam studio libertatis? Certe osculum terræ tulit, quo præriperet regnum sibi: et prærepti retinendi viam præivit. Quem hic a Tarquinio rege magistratum tenebat in Tarquinium exercuit perfidus.

[c] Perfidus et in collegam, bonum, atque innocentem virum, levicula, aut nulla potius nominis occasione: quod Augustinus adnotavit. [d] Et, tu, Cicero,

[a] *Dio.* 47. 54. [b] *Val.* 1. *c.* 6. [c] *Aug.* 2. *de civ.* 17. [d] *Cic.* 3. *de off.*

---

115 Hieronymus Cardanus [Girolamo Cardano], *De sapientia* 3 [*De sapientia libri quinque: quibus omnis humanae vitae cursus vivendique ratio explicatur; Eiusdem De consolatione libri tres. His propter similitudinem argumenti, & ipsius Cardani commendationem, adiecti sunt Petri Alcyonii De exilio libri duo*, Aureliopoli, Apud Petrum & Iacobum Chouët, 1624]; Seneca, *De beneficiis* 2. 20. 1–3. **Translator's note:** The whole passage from *speravit* onwards is in fact a more or less accurate citation from Seneca.

116 Dio Cassius 47. 39. 5.

117 Valerius Maximus 1. 6. 13. **Translator's note:** The passage reads: "te enim accepimus eo die, quo purpurea ueste uelatus aurea in sella consedisti, ne maximo studio senatus exquisitum et delatum honorem spreuisse uidereris ..." The person addressed here is C. Iulius Caesar.

118 [Vergil, *Aeneis* 6. 822.]

119 **Translator's note:** The reference here is to the story told by Livy 1. 56. While consulting the Delphic oracle, the sons of Tarquin, accompanied by Brutus, asked which of them should be king of Rome. The Pythia replied that it would be the one who first gave his mother a kiss. Brutus, grasping the real meaning of the oracle, purposely stumbled upon leaving the oracle and kissed the earth.

liberty could be restored in a large state as it could be in a small one, and who imagined that liberty could come about where there was such a great reward for ruling and such a willingness to obey; who believed that the state could be summoned back to its earlier form after the original mores had been lost, and p. 25
who thought that there could be equality before the civil law and that the laws were going to stand firm in their place when he saw so many thousands of men fighting not to determine if they *would* be slaves, but simply to determine which master they would be slaves to. What ignorance of either the nature of things or of his own city possessed the man who imagined that upon the death of one man there would not be another who would desire the same thing, when a Tarquin would be found after so many kings killed by fire and sword?[115] I do not share the view of Marcus Brutus that all this shows good sense. I reproach that man for his monstrous heart, for he could bring himself to deprive Caesar of his life—the man to whom he owed his livelihood, by whom he was adorned with offices, by whom he was considered virtually a son. I denounce the injustice of that man, who attempted to overturn the best government of a state, which is to be under a just king, a government necessary for that moment in time. A democratic government which has grown to a great empire is subsequently unable to maintain itself properly.[116] Both reason and experience bear this out.

Why do you offer me the liberty of your country as an excuse and claim that therefore justice alone was your concern? You could have opposed him when he was usurping the principate; but you couldn't make away with him when he had become ruler. This isn't the role of subjects; it wasn't your role, who bound yourself by a great oath to Caesar's principate. You bound yourself to Caesar's principate, that the Senate had created and bestowed upon him with the greatest enthusiasm (so history tells us).[117]

But behold: swift retribution takes vengeance on that man and on the other parricides. Behold: in a brief space of time they are all wretchedly p. 26
obliterated. Nemesis thus avenged the crime of the earlier Brutus, who in one moment, as it were, fell as a parricide upon the bodies of his sons. "Unhappy man, however your descendants may tell of that fate"—so sang Vergil about that Brutus, as we know.[118] And the fact that that man wished to take rule away from his relatives, the Tarquins—was it through eagerness for liberty? Indeed, that man gave the earth the kiss by which he would snatch away rule for himself—and then pioneered the path of retaining it once he had snatched it.[119] The magistracy that he held from King Tarquin he disloyally used against Tarquin.

He was also disloyal to his consular colleague, a good and innocent man, for the very trivial reason—or non-reason, rather—of his name, as Augustine

scribis, factum non admodum cum honestate coniunctum: etsi eo colore tentas defendere, quod patriæ exstiterit utilissimum: in quo discedis tu a te, et a documentis tuis. Nihil enim utile, quod non honestum: et quod non honestum est, id ne servandæ patriæ quidem disputas admittendum.

Ecce autem nobis in bello hoc regio iniustissimum illud Scævolæ facinus, quod Romano adprobante senatu sicarius ille aggressus est. Neque enim licet, non licet, latronis, et sicarii more hostibus insidiari. Latuit inter Etruscos Scævola: [a] edoctus iam a nutrice Etruscam linguam: [b] Non licet, non in bello uti desperatis his rationibus: ut cum aliena cæde, cui inhies uni, certam p. 27 semper cædem tuam coniunctam ve|lis. Hi mali sunt, qui mortem non timent, nec enim abstinent a delictis.

Sed audi etiam Sinonem Romanum: et quid regi optimo pro clementissimo in se affectu respondit: *Quandoquidem est apud te virtuti honos, ut beneficio tuleris a me, quod minis nequisti: trecenti coniuravimus iuventuti Romane, ut in te hac via grassaremur* et cetera, quæ sequuntur apud Livium plusquam Sinonica. Et hæc Romanæ virtutis sexcenta sunt.

[c] Ita idem senatus probavit dolos turpes Martii; callidatem Græcam, versutiam Punicam ait Livius; et patrias Romanas artes dixisset rectius. Audiamus et istum: *Favent pietati fideique dii: per quæ populus Romanus ad tantum fastigii venerit.* Sic Martius loquitur; qui et suis habitus turpis impostor. [d] Quid dicam Fabii præstigias (ut sic Valerius nominat) in secando naves Antiochi omnes? [e] Quid quod ille divum genus Scipio bellum, et perniciem extremam Siphaci parat intentissime: et de pace interim legatos ad regem mittit, qui specularentur apta insidiis, et pacis spe incautum, improvidum hostem facerent: cumque omnia parata sibi sensisset: tum nuntiat regi, placere quidem sibi tractata omnia, sed consilio suo improbari: itaque redeundum esse ad bellum. Itane magnanimus ille Scipio, a Punicis p. 28 abhorrens factis? Hic mihi de aliis dicendum esset. [f] De triumphatore Illyrii: |

[a] *Diony.* 5. [b] *Dio lib.* 46. [c] *Liv.* 42.
[d] *Val.* 7. *c.* 3. [e] *Polyb.* 14. *Liv.* 30. [f] *App. Illyr.*

[120] Augustine, *De civitate Dei* 2. 17. **Translator's note:** Brutus' colleague was Lucius Tarquinius Collatinus, and Brutus had him exiled because of his name and family connection to the Tarquins.

[121] Cicero, *De officiis* 3. 40.

[122] Dionysius of Halicarnassus 5.

[123] Dio Cassius 46.

[124] **Translator's note:** Livy 2. 12. 15. Gentili has garbled Livy's "trecenti coniuravimus principes inventutis Romanae" as "trecenti coniuravimus iuventuti Romanae." Sinon was the wily Greek who persuaded the Trojans to accept the Trojan Horse in *Aeneis* 2.

[125] Livy 42. 47. 7.

[126] Livy 44. 1. 11.

[127] Valerius Maximus 7. 3. 4b. **Translator's note:** Fabius had made a treaty with Antiochus in accord with which the king would yield half his ships. Fabius had all his ships sawn in half.

[128] Polybius 14. 1–2; Livy 30. 4.

noted.[120] And you, Cicero, write that that deed was not exactly in conformity with propriety, even though you attempt to defend it with the excuse that it was the most useful thing for the country—in which you yourself depart from yourself and from your writings.[121] For nothing is useful which is not honorable, and that which is not honorable you argue should not be allowed even to save one's country.

Moreover, behold: we have that most unjust crime of Scaevola in that war waged by the king, a crime which that assassin undertook with the approval of the Roman Senate. For it is not permitted—it is simply not permitted—to lie in wait for your enemies in the manner of a brigand and assassin. Scaevola lay in wait among the Etruscans, having earlier learned the Etruscan tongue from his nurse.[122] It is not allowed, simply not, to make use of such desperate measures in war that you would wish that your own certain slaughter be always attendant upon that slaughter of a foreigner you are so intent upon.[123] p. 27
For those men are wicked who have no fear of death and so do not refrain from crimes.

But just listen to this Roman Sinon and his answer to the excellent king in return for his most merciful feelings towards him: "Since among you honor is paid to courage, so that you might get by doing me a favor what you could not get through threats, I shall tell you: three hundred of us have sworn an oath to the youths of Rome to attack you in this manner"—and other things that follow in Livy, worse than Sinon's words.[124] And there are six hundred examples of this Roman valor.

Thus the same Senate approved of the base tricks of Quintus Marcius Philippus—Greek shrewdness and Punic cunning, Livy says, but he would more correctly have called it native Roman crafts.[125] And let us hear that man's words: "The gods favor the piety and faith through which the Roman people arrived at such heights."[126] So speaks Marcius, who even among his own people was viewed as a base deceiver. What shall I say of Fabius' sleight of hand (as Valerius Maximus terms it) in cutting in two all the ships of Antiochus?[127] What shall I say of that fact that Scipio, that descendant of the gods, most intently prepared war and destruction for Syphax and while he was doing so sent ambassadors to the king to scout out fit opportunities for ambushes and to make an enemy lacking in foresight incautious through hope for peace? And when he was aware that everything was ready for him, then he announced to the king that everything they had agreed upon was pleasing to him personally, but did not meet with the approval of his council; and so they would have to go back to war.[128] So is this how that famous Scipio was so great-souled, recoiling from Punic deeds? This would be the place for me to speak of other such men—for instance, about the man [L. Anicius Gallus] who celebrated a triumph over the Illyrians, who, when p. 28

qui Gentium regem, venientem publica sua ad se fide, supplicem retinet, in triumphum ducit. Qui urbibus Illyrii septuaginta pollicitus veniam, si omne argentum darent, eas depredatur, quæ omne argentum dederant. Sed, ut dico, sunt hæc plurima. Neque ego intelligo facta privatorum, aut non probatorum Romæ hominum, at publica; at eorum magistratuum, qui exempla aliis effulsere virtutis in civitate universa: et quorum si convellimus existimationem, salva civitatis existimatio esse non valet. [a] Neque enim aliud est civitas, quam cives, magistratusque: in quibus si indigni sint, qui digniores habiti sunt: reliqui minus digni quales erunt?

Romani bellis victi.

CAP. V

Porro autem facere non valeo hic, quin in mancipia Romana, in Romanorum rerum scriptores non commovear vehementer: quorum est illud, [b]*Populus Romanus victus vi, et superatus præliis sæpe est multis, bello vero nunquam, in quo sunt omnia*. Nunquam, Lucili, nunquam, Livi, victus bello populus Romanus?

At vicit Tatius: qui regemque se, et Sabinos, Curetes suos in urbem intulit: [c]quique nomen mutavit isti populo, et de Romanis Quirites fecit, non solum dedit nomen uni colli Aventino, uni trium tribuum Tatiensi. At bello hoc
p. 29 regio vicit Porsena: qui Romanos agro multavit: sub præsidiis posu|it: spoliavit armis, et omni ferro, præter quam in agriculturæ usum. Huic regi liberum iudicium, quod bello quærebatur, in caussa pulsi Tarquinii permissum est: huic dedita Roma est. [d] Quæ Dionysius, Tacitus, Plutarchus, Plinius commemorarunt. [e] Alii et tributa memorant: atque, quod audis ex his, probe: ut ut idem Plutarchus non hos auctores, non hoc probet.

[a] *l. 2. de re. du.* [b] *Non. diff. dict. Liv. 9.* [c] *Festus. Dionys. Serv. 5. 7.*
[d] *D. 2. T. 3. hist. Plut. de clar. mul. Pli. 34. c. 14.* [e] *Plut. pr. R. 18.*

---

[129] *Digest* 34. 5. 2. **Translator's note:** This seems also to be taken from Aristotle's discussion of citizenship in connection with his attempt at defining the *polis*; cf. Aristotle, *Politica* 3. 1 $1274^{b}32$–$1275^{a}33$, esp. $1274^{b}39$ ff. and $1275^{a}22$ ff.

[130] *Nonii Marcelli de compendiosa doctrina libros XX*, ed. Wallace M. Lindsay, Lipsiae, 1903, 437. 17–18; Livy 9. 18. 9. **Translator's note:** The quoted words are by Lucilius (F. Marx, *C. Lucili carminum reliquiae* I–II, Lipsiae, 1904–5, pp. 613–14).

[131] *Sexti Pompei Festi de verborum significatu quae supersunt cum Pauli Epitome*, ed. Wallace M. Lindsay, Lipsiae, 1913, s.v. Curis, p. 43 [cf. also s.v. Dici, p. 59]; Dionysius of Halicarnassus 2. 46. 2; Servius, *On Aeneid* 8. 635.

[132] Dionysius of Halicarnassus 2 [Gentili here probably meant to refer to 5. 35. 1, where the Senate is said to have voted to send Porsenna a throne and other regal insignia; or 5. 22. 3, where Porsenna is said to have taken the Janiculum; however, Rome does not surrender in Dionysius' account]; Tacitus, *Historiae* 3. 72; Plutarch, *Mulierum virtutes* 250 B; Pliny the Elder, *Historia naturalis* 34. 139.

king Gentius came to him under safe conduct, detained the suppliant and led him in his triumphal procession—who having promised mercy to seventy cities of Illyria if they would give him all their silver then sacked those who had given him all their silver. But, as I say, there are very many examples of this. Nor do I mean the actions of private men or of those who were not distinguished men of Rome, but public acts, acts of those magistrates who shone as examples to others in the whole human community—and once we have destroyed the reputation of these men, the reputation of the state itself cannot be saved. For a state is nothing more than its citizens and its magistrates.[129] And if those of them who have been considered more worthy than others were in fact unworthy, then what sort will the others who are less respectable prove to be?

CHAPTER 5
The Romans Defeated in Wars

Next, moreover, I cannot here keep myself from being deeply angry at those slaves of the Romans, the writers of Roman history, whose claim is: "The Roman people, though it was often defeated by superior force and overcome in many battles, was never defeated in an actual war—and that is all-important."[130] *Never*, Lucilius, *never*, Livy, was the Roman people defeated in a war?

And yet Tatius defeated them, he who forced upon the city both himself as king and his Sabines, his Curetes, and who changed the name for that people, and from Romans made the Quirites, and not only gave a name to one hill, the Aventine, but also to one of the three tribes, the Tatiensis.[131] And in that war over the king [the expelled Tarquin], Porsenna conquered, for he deprived the Romans of territory, placed them under garrisons, and deprived p. 29
them of arms and of all iron beyond that needed for agriculture. This king was allowed unfettered jurisdiction (which was the purpose of the war) in the case of the expelled king Tarquin; Rome was surrendered to him. Dionysius, Tacitus, Plutarch, Pliny all mention this.[132] Others mention tribute as well, and, according to what you hear from these authors, it was justly exacted—no matter if the same Plutarch does not bear out these authors or this action.[133]

[133] Plutarch, *Quaestiones Romanae* 18. **Translator's note:** Plutarch here refers to the story, which he regards as fabulous, that the Romans offered sacrifice to Herakles because he freed them from Etruscan tribute. There is no reference here to Porsenna.

At vicit Romanos Brennus, vicerunt Senones: scelere Romanorum provocati: sceleratis Romanorum armis petiti. Urbem illi tenuerunt: etiam rupem illam Tarpeiam, etiam [a]*Capitolium Senones occupaverunt*: sic Tertullianus: *Tarpeia sede perusta Gallorum facibus*: ita Lucanus. *Infelices vix mille hominum reliquiæ fame, peste, desperatione, formidine territæ subactæ, venditæ mille auri libris*: quod Orosius. Non bello victi? Non *Capitolia capta*? quod apud Silium: et non *capti Quirites*?

Nam cæsos, fugatosve a Camillo Gallos post fuisse, hoc demum impudentium mancipiorum est scribere. Quandoquidem exsulem inopem, republica accisa, et prostrata, id potuisse, tum credere homines potuissent, cum fortisque viri vim truncatus pedum, manuumque, et trunco reliquo affictus humi vincere visus fuisset. Aut num fatebimur Gallos victos ex Polyeni etiam testimonio? [b]*Capta urbe*, inquit ille *fædus est cum Gallis ictum, ut his Romani*
p. 30 *tributa pende | rent; et portam apertam omni tempore præberent; terram darent, et aquam*. Et hactenus Romani victi: et sub servitutem Gallorum ex conventu adacti. *Sed Romani mox tamquam ad amicos munera mittunt hospitalia, et in his vinum, quo Galli inebriati occidione deleti omnes ab eis sunt*. Sic Romani victores: sed proditores, perfidi fœdifragi. [c] Quæ victoriæ partæ contra æquum deteriores omnibus sunt cladibus.

[d] Verum de Polybii, et aliorum libris, pacem cum Gallis pro istorum arbitrio initam, naves ad Tyberim transeundum Gallis tributas, et alio exercitum invictum proficiscentem, de victoria, et urbe subacta, longumque possessa, litteras ad suos exaravisse, ad eosque tandem fortunis integris omnibus rediisse constat. [e] Sic Livius Drusus proprætore ex provincia Gallia retulisse traditur aurum, Senonibus olim in obsidione Capitolii datum, nec, ut fama, extortum a Camillo. Sic Suetonius. Quid tamen vetera ista conquiro, et me quasi in obscurum aliquod antiquitatis antrum concludo? Nos, nos Piceni, ducibus Asculanis meis, amantissimis illis patriæ meæ, amantissimis familiæ: nos in summo Romani imperii fastigio Romanos bello vicimus. [f] Et nostra iustissima caussa fuit. Petebamus enim eam civitatem: cuius imperium armis defendebamus: et per annos omnes, per omnia bella duplicem illi
p. 31 militum, equitumque numerum explebamus: necdum tamen in ius | eius

[a] *Tertu. apolog. c.* 40. *Luc.* 5. *Oros.* 2. *c. ult.* [b] *Polyen. lib.* 8. [c] *Isocr. pana.*
[d] *P.* I. 2. *Front.* 2. *c.* 6. *Bod.* 5. *de rep.* 5. [e] *Suet. Tyb.* [f] *Paterc.* 2.

---

134 Tertullian, *Apologeticus* 40; Lucan, *De bello civili* 5. 27–8; Orosius 2. 19. 8 f.
135 [Silius Italicus, *Punica* 4. 156 and 48.]
136 Polyaenus, *Strategemata* 8. 25. I.
137 Isocrates, *Panegyricus*.
138 Polybius I. 2; Frontinus, *Strategemata* 2. 6; Jean Bodin, *De republica* 5. 5 [*De republica libri sex*, Francofurti, Apud Ioan. Wecheli viduam, sumtib. Petri Fischeri, 1594].
139 Suetonius, *Tiberius* 3. 2.
140 Velleius Paterculus 2. 15.

And yet Brennus and his Senones defeated the Romans, provoked by the crime of the Romans and attacked by the criminal arms of the Romans. They held the city, and the Tarpeian Rock, and "the Senones occupied the Capitoline" too, says Tertullian. "The seat of Tarpeia was burned by the torches of the Gauls," says Lucan. "Scarcely a thousand survivors, terrified and overcome by hunger, disease, desperation, and fear, were ransomed with a thousand pounds of gold," says Orosius.[134] Were they not defeated in war? Was not "the Capitoline captured" (as Silius says), and were not the "Quirites captured?"[135]

As for the notion that the Gauls were subsequently slaughtered and put to flight by Camillus—this is simply something for shameless slaves to write. For people would have been able to believe that a destitute exile could accomplish this at a time when his country was cut down and lying prostrate only if it would have seemed possible that a man mutilated in feet, hands, and the rest of his body and tied to the ground could have overcome the strength of a mighty man. Or are we to admit that the Gauls were defeated on the basis of the testimony of Polyaenus, no less? "When the city was captured," he says, "a treaty was struck with the Gauls stipulating that the Romans were to pay them tribute and to keep their gate open at all times and to give them p. 30
earth and water."[136] Up to this point, then, the Romans were defeated and reduced to servitude under the Gauls by the agreement. "But the Romans soon sent them guest-gifts as though to friends, and among these was wine, by which the Gauls were made drunk—and then slaughtered to the last man by the Romans." Thus the Romans were victors, but also betrayers, perfidious treaty-breakers. Victories obtained contrary to justice are worse than any sort of military disaster.[137]

But from the books of Polybius and others it is clear that the peace with the Gauls was entered into at the will of the Gauls, that boats for crossing the Tiber were given them as tribute, that their army set forth for other parts undefeated, and that they sent off a letter to their own people telling of their victory and of the city which had been conquered and held for a long time, and that they returned to them at last with all their fortunes intact.[138] Thus Livius Drusus as propraetor is said to have brought back from the province of Gaul gold that had once been given to the Senones during the siege of the Capitol and so was not, as the story has it, recovered by Camillus. This is in Suetonius.[139] But why do I collect these ancient doings and shut myself up, as it were, in some dark cavern of remote antiquity? We ourselves, we Picenes, with my own Asculans as leaders, those men most devoted to my country and my family, defeated the Romans in war at the very height of the Roman empire. And our cause was most just.[140] For we were seeking citizenship in a state whose empire we used to defend with our arms, and throughout all the years and all the wars we used to supply for her a double number of infantry and cavalry, and yet we were not yet being accepted into her full rights, but we p. 31

recipiebamur: at, qui illam in id ipsum deduximus fastigium, homines eiusdem et gentis, et sanguinis ut externi alienique fastidiebamur. Quæ Velleius omnia. Et quæ virtutem, humanitatem, gratitudinem, et iustitiam Romanam satis ostendunt.

At quod Velleius addit, et concludunt alii, bellatum ab Italicis pro civitate Romana consequenda: eosque civitatem consecutos: sed bello tamen fuisse victos hoc quidem est, de quo dicimus: et in quo scriptores isti deridendi sunt maxime. Nam cur victos Italicos affirmant? Quia victi præliis multis sunt, et plures ipsorum urbes, et ipsum Asculum, captæ sunt? At non hoc est bello vinci, sed præliis. Bello vinci est, petitis: excidere, hostibus certata relinquere. Non id etiam est vinci pro tribunalibus? Non sumtus, non damna litis, non contrariæ interlocutiones victum efficiunt, sed sententia, quæ finem controversiis facit re iudicata, adiudicata. Et igitur Italici non victi, sed victores iustissime censeantur: qui potiti voto sunt, re petita. Etiam nec ridebat Roma, cum lugeret Italia. Sileant, si qui putant, victis voluisse Romanos dare hostibus, quod amicis, armatis noluissent. [a] Prætextas, ornamenta magistratuum posita, saga sumta Romæ scimus. Debilitatas manus, et murcios illic factos non ignoramus: in civitate nepotum Veneris timidissimos homines,
p. 32 qui | vitandæ militiæ præciderent pollices sibi, sæpe visos, invisos alibi gentium. Etiam ad auxilia Latini nominis, externarumque gentium abiit inclita Roma: et (quod nunquam antea) libertinos milites sumsit. Fugatus ab Asculo Pompeius: recepti populi complures: capti Romani magistratus: cæsi legati: cæsi consules: expugnatæ urbes: deleti exercitus. Et, cum isthæc ita se haberent, delata nobis civitas est. Nos victi sumus?

Quid nunc memorem Parthos, Romanorum victores semper? [b] Memorat Trogus. Vincendos ego dixerim Romanos semper: nisi unus, itidem noster Picenus, Ventidius ille Asculanus exstitisset: qui Parthos semper victores ipse unus victos effecisset Romanis. [c] Tribus præliis eos fudit: et de eis triumphavit solus, aut certe primus, aut etiam merito solus. [d] Nolo hic aut Antonii

[a] *Val.* 6. *c.* 3. *Front.* 3. *c.* 17. *App.* 1. *civ. Liv.* 72. *seq.* [b] *Iusti.* 46.
[c] *Gell.* 15. 6. 4. *App. Parth. Flor.* 4. [d] *Dio.* 49. *Cic.* 10. *fa.*

[141] [Velleius Paterculus 2. 15. 2: "Quorum ut fortuna atrox, ita causa fuit iustissima: petebant enim eam civitatem, cuius imperium armis tuebantur: per omnis annos atque omnia bella duplici numero se militum equitumque fungi neque in eius civitatis ius recipi, quae per eos in id ipsum pervenisset fastigium, per quod homines eiusdem et gentis et sanguinis ut externos alienosque fastidire posset."]

[142] Valerius Maximus 6. 3. 3; Frontinus, *Strategemata* 3. 17; Appian, *Bella civilia* 1; Livy 72 f. [?].

[143] **Translator's note:** The Pompey in question is Cn. Pompeius Strabo, father of Pompey the Great. Far from being driven off from Asculum, he conducted a successful siege of the city and celebrated a triumph over his victory.

[144] Justin 46.

who had brought her to that very summit of power, we men of the same race and blood, were disdained like strangers and foreigners. Velleius records all of this.[141] And this sufficiently demonstrates Roman virtue, humanity, gratitude, and justice.

But as for what Velleius adds and others as well conclude—that war was waged by the Italians to obtain Roman citizenship, that that they did in fact obtain it, but that they were nonetheless defeated in the war—this is indeed that very thing of which I have spoken, the thing that makes those authors most to be derided. For why do they claim that the Italians were defeated? Is it because they were defeated in many battles and many of their cities, including Asculum itself, were captured? But this is not to be defeated in war, but in battles. To be defeated in war is to withdraw from what one had sought and to relinquish what was fought over to the enemy. Is that not even what it means to be defeated in a court of law? It is not financial outlay, not a fine, not unfavorable sentences passed while the case is pending that cause someone to be defeated; it is the judge's decision, which makes an end for the disputants when the case is judged and adjudicated. And therefore the Italians should most justly be judged not the vanquished but the victors, for they obtained their request, the very thing they had sought. In addition, Rome did not rejoice when Italy was in mourning. If there are any who suppose that the Romans would have wished to bestow upon defeated enemies what they wouldn't have wished to give to friends under arms, let them be silent. We know that at Rome purple-bordered togas, the ornaments of magistrates, were removed and military cloaks puts on. We are not unaware that troops were maimed and men made self-mutilated, that there were often seen in the city of the grandchildren of Venus very timid men who cut off their p. 32
own thumbs to avoid military service—though such men were not seen among other peoples.[142] Glorious Rome even had recourse to Latin allies and foreign peoples and—something unheard of before—took on freedmen as soldiers. Pompey was driven off from Asculum,[143] very many peoples were received into citizenship, Roman magistrates were captured, legates slaughtered, consuls slaughtered, cities sacked, armies destroyed. And when things were in such a state, citizenship was granted to us. Were we, then, defeated?

Why should I now mention the Parthians, who were always the victors over the Romans? Pompeius Trogus mentions them.[144] I would have said that the Romans were always to be defeated, were it not for the existence of one man, once again a fellow Picene, that famous Ventidius Asculanus, a man who himself single-handedly rendered the ever-victorious Parthians defeated for the Romans. He overthrew them in three battles and was the only person to celebrate a triumph over them—or at least the first, or even the only one to do

invidiam vestri, non vestrum, non Planci tui, Cicero, contumelias indignas dicere, quibus virum fortissimum lacerare solebatis. Hæc ad cæteras virtutes vestras accedant per me tacita.

Ostendi, vos victos variis, pluribusque bellis. Ostendi mendacia historicorum. Mendacia; non quod facere consueverunt poetæ, qui res scribebant vestras, ut vestras præterirent calamitates: [a] ut apud te legimus: sed mendacia: quæ historicos dedecent.

p. 33

Fraus Romanorum in fœderibus.

CAP. VI

Mihi redire ad Gallos placet et ad tertium civitatis fundatorem Camillum. Gallos iste (cæsi Galli, aut fugati credantur) cur fugat, cur cædit? [b] Numquid senatus, populus, et quicquid erat Romæ sine isto magistro pacisci cum Gallis victoribus nequiit? [c] Cur ergo Caudinæ pactioni non statur: quam tot magistratus pepigerunt? Pallium scilicet ([d] ut est in proverbio) revolvitur hic: et, magistratus absque populi, et senatus auctoritate non convenire potuisse, contenditur. [e] Itaque Corsi, ita decepti Numantini. Et ita sive in urbe cum istis contraxeris, sive peregre, certum nihil, et nihil recte contractum censebant, quod libidini ipsorum non satisfaceret. Ita Mithridates, ita Iugurtha, ita alii circumventi.

Atque est illud utique importunissimum in argumento hoc fœderum, quod Romani ducum suorum pactionibus se obstringi non posse contendant, nisi easque ratas ipsi habuerint: alios populos tamen eorum ducum conventis obligare velint, nec si populi illi conventiones ducum adfirmassent. [f] Id in fœdere cum Asdrubale icto voluerunt: quo Carthaginenses se non teneri, ab se non sancito, iustissime respondebant. Et vana est Livii, Polybiique contra-
p. 34 ria disceptatio: qui Romanos tuentur, quia adiici ex Romano|rum ducum

[a] *Cic. pro le. Ma.* [b] *Liv.* 5. [c] *Liv.* 9. 56. [d] *Alc. lib.* 4. *de V. S.*
[e] *App. Hisp. Val.* 9. *c.* 3. [f] *Liv.* 21. *Polyb.* 3.

145 Aulus Gellius 15. 6; Appian, *Parthica* [**Translator's note:** Originally part of bk. 11 of Appian's *Roman History*, the account of the Parthian war is only partially preserved, perhaps having been left unfinished at Appian's death. What Gentili read was a Byzantine fake commonly printed to eke out the truncated 11th book]; Florus 4. 9. 5.

146 Dio Cassius 49; Cicero, *Epistulae ad familiares* 10.

147 *Pro lege Manilia* 25.

148 Livy 5. 48 f.

149 Livy 9. 5–6.

150 Alciatus, *De verborum significatione, liber quartus* [in *Opera Omnia in quatuor tomos*, Tomus IIII, Basileae, Apud Thomam Guarinum, 1582, cols. 999 ff.; the reference is unclear].

151 Appian, *Iberica* 79. 338–80. 350; Valerius Maximus 9. 3.

152 Livy 21. 19; Polybius 3. 21.

so deservedly.[145] I do not wish to mention here either the envy of your Antony or of all of you Romans or the unworthy slanders of your friend Plancius, Cicero, envy and slanders with which you Romans were in the habit of wounding a man of the utmost bravery.[146] Let these deeds of his be added to your other virtues with no further words from me.

I have shown that you were defeated in various and numerous wars. I have shown the lies of the historians. They were lies: not the sort of thing that the poets were accustomed to do, who wrote of your deeds in such a way as to pass over disasters, as we have read in your works, Cicero,[147] but lies which are unsuitable for historians.

CHAPTER 6 p. 33

The Deceptiveness of the Romans in Treaties

I want to return to the Gauls and to the third founder of the city, Camillus. Assuming that the Gauls were slaughtered or put to flight, *why* did your Camillus put them to flight or slaughter them? Was the Senate, the people, or anything else at Rome unable to make a pact with the victorious Gauls without that man as leader?[148] Well then, why did they not abide by the treaty at the Caudine Forks, which so many magistrates agreed upon?[149] Then the cloak is turned inside out (as the proverb has it[150]), and it is claimed that the magistrates could not make an agreement without the authority of the people and the Senate. Thus were the Corsicans deceived, and so too the Numantines.[151] And so either you would negotiate with those Romans in their own city, or if you were to do so outside the city they were in the habit of deeming that nothing was fixed, nothing was properly agreed to that didn't suit their pleasure. In this way Mithridates, in this way Jugurtha, in this way others as well were tricked.

And surely the most annoying thing in this business of treaties is the fact that the Romans would claim that they could not be bound by the pacts made by their generals unless they themselves formally confirmed them—and yet they would wish to bind other peoples by the agreements of *their* generals, and not just if those peoples affirmed the agreements of their generals. This is what they wanted in the treaty struck with Hasdrubal, by which the Carthaginians very justly said they were not bound, as it had not been ratified by them.[152] And empty is Livy's reasoning to the contrary, and so too that of Polybius, who defend the Romans on the ground that it used to be added in treaties on the part of the Roman generals "So it shall be valid, if the people should have p. 34

parte diserte soleret in fœdere, *Ita id ratum fore, si populus censuisset*: ex Asdrubalis autem latere exceptum quicquam tale non fuerit: et tot annorum silentio ita vivo eo comprobatum sit fœdus, ut ne mortuo quidem quicquam mutaretur.

Quid enim si disceptationis caput primum, quod huius est proprium loci, brevicula interrogatione disperdo? An igitur si sine illa exceptione dux Romanus ineat fœdus, hoc Romanos tenebit? Eccur igitur tenuerit Carthaginenses? Et tantos historicos vanitatis tantæ non pudet?

Alterum caput de silentio per iuris itidem imperitiam induxerunt: quando non ex silentio, re nihili, sed ex verbis, factisve obligari homines, ius ostendat. *Qui tacet, non consentit*: ut regula iuris est: et vulgi. [a]*Silentium nihil est: nec unquam invenies dictum, silendo aliquos concordasse.* Patientia non est verus hominis actus: quia silentium est quædam privatio, non actus. Cum id genus aliis: quæ maximi interpretes iuris docuere.

Quid præterea si Asdrubalis fœdus non sic observatum fuit tacite, ac si ratificatum, aut ictum expresse fuisset? id est, quid si non publico tacito fuit observatum, sed aliquorum privato? et privatum dico etiam ducum, et magistratuum, et ipsius Asdrubalis: quem servasse pactum suum, nec mirum sit.
p. 35 [b] Isto casu non obligari universitatem, certum est: | et si aliqui universitatis non observassent, vel pauci; hi iura universitatis omnibus conservassent. Ecce Annibal non observat. Sed quam illud difficile, ut ostendatur, publico observatum consensu quid exstitisse?

Ceterum si vos, Romani, pactiones ducum vestrorum non tenent: et illas vos pro libitu, et libidine vestra respuitis: num etiam non censebitis æquum, integra omnia adversariis conservari? [c]*Restitutio ita facienda est, ut unusquisque in integrum suum recipiat*: ait Paulus. *Restituere videtur, qui in pristinum statum reducit*: inquit Ulpianus. *Restituere est possessorem facere*: dicit Caius. *Est caussam reddere, et omnem conditionem*: ut Proculus loquitur. *Est id facere, quod fuerat*: ut scribit Tertullianus.

Quid ni igitur, Romane, si sponsionis ad furculas Caudinas factæ pœnitebat, legiones restitueris, unde per sponsionem eductæ sunt? Quid ni recipiat Samnis, quod integrumque illi fuit, pro arbitrio statuere de legionibus vestris? Recipiat saltus illos, et vos imis inclusos angustiis? Possessionem corporum

[a] *Bal.* 1. *cons.* 396. 437. 5. 321. *Rom.* 311. *Alex.* 1. 136. 6. 191. [b] *Alc.* 7. *cons.* 3.
[c] *l.* 2. *ne q. in lo. p. l.* 38. *de usur. l.* 22. 35. *ult. de V. S. Tert. apol.*

[153] Baldus, *Consilia* 1. 396, fol. 127^{v}; 1. 437, fol. 140^{v}; 5. 321, fol. 80^{r} [*Consilia vel responsa*, vols. 1–5, Venetiis, [Apud Hieronymum Polum,] 1575]; Ludovicus Pontanus Romanus [Lodovico Pontano Romano], *Consilia et allegationes* 311, Venetiis, Bonetus Locatellus, 1500, fol. 96^{v}; Alexander Tartagnus Imolensis [Alexander of Imola], *Consilia* 1.136, fol. 143^{v}; 6. 191 [*Consiliorum seu responsorum libri VII*, Venetiis, Ex Officina Iac. Antonij Somaschi, 1597].

[154] Alciatus, *Consilia* 7. 3, cols. 937 f. [The reference is unclear; he might rather have *Consilia* 5. 23, col. 510 in mind: "Constat enim non obligari universitatem, vel Castrum, nisi maior pars, communicato consilio, et re deliberata, deliquerint."]

[155] *Digest* 4. 4. 24. 4 [Paulus in this passage says in fact *ut unusquisque integrum ius suum recipiat*; Gentili quotes the passage also in chapter 2.6]; *Digest* 43. 8. 2. 43 [Ulpian]; *Digest* 50. 16. 22 [Gaius]; *Digest* 50. 16. 246.1 [Gentili alludes vaguely to a passage by Pomponius, not Proculus]; Tertullian, *Apologeticus* 48. 2.

decreed," but that a similar clause was not stipulated on the part of Hasdrubal—and also on the ground that the treaty was so strongly confirmed by the silence of so many years while he was still alive that nothing was changed even when he was dead.

What if I do away with the first issue of this dispute by means of a brief bit of questioning, as befits this section? Will it, then, be the case that if a Roman general should enter upon a treaty without that stipulation, then this treaty will be binding upon the Romans? Then why would it have bound the Carthaginians? And are not such great historians ashamed of such foolishness?

The other issue, the one about silence, they have likewise introduced through ignorance of the law; for the law shows that men are bound not by silence, which is a non-thing, but by words and deeds. "He who is silent does not give consent," as the rule of the law is—and the rule of common practice as well. "Silence is nothing; nor will you ever find it said that people agree to something by keeping silent."[153] Putting up with something is not a genuine act of a man, because silence is a kind of lack, not an act—along with other things of this sort, which the greatest interpreters of the law have taught.

Moreover, what if the treaty of Hasdrubal was not observed tacitly in quite the way it would have been had it been formally struck and ratified? That is, what if it was observed not by a public body that maintained silence but only by the private approval of certain men? And by "private" I mean even the approval of generals, magistrates, and Hasdrubal himself (and it would be no wonder if he abided by his own pact). It is clear that a whole state is not bound by that sort of circumstance, and if some members of the whole state p. 35 did not abide by the agreement, or if even just a few did not, they would have preserved the rights of the whole state for everyone.[154] Behold: Hannibal does not abide by the agreement. But how hard it is to show that there existed any agreement here at all that was ratified by public consent?

Furthermore, if the pacts made by your generals do not constrain you Romans, and you reject them arbitrarily and on your own whim, will you not even deem it fair that all things be maintained in their original condition for adversaries? "Restitution ought to be made in such a way that each person gets his own back in its original condition," says Paulus. "That man appears to make restitution who brings about a restoration to the original situation," says Ulpian. "To make restitution is to make someone a full possessor," says Gaius. "It is to give back the issue in dispute and the whole original state of affairs," as Proculus says. "It is to bring about that which had been," as Tertullian puts it.[155]

Therefore, Roman, if you regretted the agreement made at the Caudine Forks, why didn't you hand over the legions to the very spot from which they were marched out in accord with the agreement? Why shouldn't the Samnite get back that which was his original right: to make what determination he pleased with regard to your legions? Should he get back again those narrow passes—and you yourselves trapped in the bottom of the defiles? Should he get

vestrorum recipiat? Caussam vestram, et conditionem omnem deploratissimam ex integro habeat? [a] Hæc vobis et Samnites dixerunt: et dicunt postea Numantini: aut pro Numantinis Orosius. Nunquamne caussa deficiet, cur victi pacto non stetis? Obsides Porsenæ dedistis: furto (hoc credam, non
p. 36 tranasse Tyberim il|las puellas) subduxistis, auro civitatem a Gallis redimistis: inter accipiendum aurum cæsi sunt. Pacem cum Samnitibus pepigistis: eam irritam facitis: et semper aliquam fraudi speciem iuris imponitis.

Quid ludibria illa religionum referam: et pueris vix dignas ambages, quas senes vestri, ac consulares fallendæ fidei exquisiverunt? Iuste, Livi, hæc tu: et caute tamen ex persona hostis Romanorum dictas: ne cum Patavinitate, et studio partium etiam hostilitas tibi obiiceretur.

Dum Samnitibus deditur Postumius, qui sponsionem inierat, fæciali Romano femur perculit, et clara voce ait, se Samnitem civem esse: fæcialem a se contra ius gentium violatum: eo iustius bellum Romanos gesturos. An hæc ludibria non sunt, et lusus? Et his fides publica liberatur? *Forsitan*: ais, Livi. *Forsitan*: et rides ridicula. Hæccine restitutio? Civis Samnis Postumius, quem Samnites non receperunt? [b] Civis an Romanus manserit, disputent Manilius, Scævola, Brutus, Pomponius, Modestinus, alii iurisconsulti: sed factum civem Samnitem nullus dixerit. [c] Ut enim donatio, ita deditio intelligi sine acceptione non potest: quod etiam Cicero scribit. [d]*Etiam qui erant Romæ rerum capitalium condemnati, nec prius eam civitatem amittebant, quam erant in eam recepti, quo vertendi, hoc est, mutandi soli caussa venerant. Non universi*
p. 37 *populi Roma|ni potestas aliter potuit.* Certe et civis manserat Romanus Postumius. [e] Quod alteri non adquiritur, id non perditur. Quod non adquiritur recipienti, id remanet penes dantem, inquit Baldus. [f]*Si fidem fœderis, quam sibi Romani servari a subiectis volunt, ipsi subiecti Samnitibus servassent, hodie aut omnino non essent, aut Samnio dominante servirent.* Hic ita concludant verba historiæ.

[a] *Oros.* 5. *c. i.* [b] *Cic. Top. l. ult. de lega. Alc.* 8. *cons.* 14. [c] *l.* 19. *de don.* [d] *Cic. pro do. su.*
[e] *Bal. l.* 3. *de off. præt. l.* 21. *de sta. ho.* [f] *P. Diac.* 2.

---

156 [This is a reference to the speech of the Samnite Pontius in Livy 9. 11.]

157 Orosius 5. 1.

158 [Again, the reference is to Pontius in Livy 9. 11.]

159 [According to Quintilian 1. 5. 56, Pollio accused Livy's style of "Patavinity," i.e. traces of Paduan dialect.]

160 [See Livy 9. 10. 10.]

161 [Livy 9. 11. 13.]

162 Cicero, *Topica; Digest* 50. 7. 18; Alciatus, *Consilia* 8. 14. **Translator's note:** The Cicero reference seems to be to *Topica* 8. 37, where the subject is *postliminium*, whereby a Roman captive lost his civil rights in Rome, but regained them upon his release. But the general in question in that passage was not Postumius, but Mancinus. Cicero does allude to the situation of Postumius at *De inventione* 2. 30. 91.

163 *Digest* 39. 5. 19. 2.

164 Cicero, *De domo sua* 30. 78.

165 Baldus, *On Digest* 1. 14. 3, fols. 50^r ff.; 1. 5. 21, fol. 30^v [*In primam Digesti veteris partem commentaria*, [n.p.], 1535].

166 Paulus Diaconus, *Historia Romana* 2. 9.

back the possession of your bodies? Should he possess your original state and your whole utterly deplorable original condition? The Samnites themselves said this to you,[156] as did the Numantines later on—or Orosius speaking on behalf of the Numantines.[157] Will you never lack an excuse not to abide by a pact when you are defeated? You gave hostages to Porsenna—and you spirited them away by stealth (this is what I shall believe—not that those maidens swam across the Tiber). You ransomed the state from the Gauls with gold— p. 36 and they were cut down in the midst of their receiving the money. You agreed upon peace with the Samnites—and then you rendered this invalid and consistently bestowed upon deception some appearance of justice.

Why should I mention those mockeries of religious excuses and subterfuges scarcely worthy of children that your senators and men of consular rank have sought out for the sake of deceiving trust? You have mentioned these things justly, Livy; and yet you cunningly utter them from the mouth of an enemy of the Romans,[158] lest in addition to your Paduan style and your party zeal outright hostility to Rome be cast in your teeth.[159]

When Postumius, who had entered upon the agreement, was being handed over to the Samnites, he struck the thigh of a fetial priest and said in a loud voice that he was now a Samnite, and that a fetial priest had been violated by him against the law of nations, whereby the Romans were going to wage war with greater justice.[160] Was this not mockery and playacting? Was the people's pledge cancelled even by such things as these? "Perhaps," you say, Livy.[161] "Perhaps"—and you laugh at this foolish stuff. *This* is restitution? Was Postumius, whom the Samnites themselves did not accept, a Samnite citizen? Manilius, Scaevola, Brutus, Pomponius, Modestinus, and other jurisconsults may debate as to whether he remained a Roman citizen, but none will have said that he became a Samnite citizen.[162] For just like a donation, so also a surrender cannot be understood without an act of acceptance,[163] as also Cicero writes: "Those condemned on capital charges in Rome used not to lose their citizenship before they were received into that state to which they had gone in order to 'turn', i.e. change, their soil. The power of the whole Roman people could not do otherwise."[164] Surely Postumius p. 37 remained a Roman citizen. That which is not acquired by someone else is not lost; that which is not acquired by a recipient remains in the power of the giver, says Baldus.[165] "If the Romans, when they themselves were subjects to the Samnites, had maintained their good faith in the treaty—precisely that good faith which they wish their own subjects to maintain towards them—then today they would either not exist at all, or they would be serving a Samnite master."[166] This is how the words of a history conclude here.

Samnitici belli caussa iniusta.
CAP. VII

At vero caussam Samnitici belli etiam intelligamus. Decet enim, et cœpimus confutare historicos, [a] qui, arma nunquam nisi iustis de caussis sumta a Romanis, tradunt. Scilicet iusta caussa (ut audivimus) ad arma ipsa exercenda, et ad otium fugiendum. Iusta est caussa, bellis petere ignotos, et quietos: [b] ut hoc Romani fecerunt: [c] et itaque etiam belli iura, etsi (ridiculum) non bellum cum his esse, non esse hos hostes voluerunt. Iusta est caussa, occasiones quasvis cupide arripere ([d] et hoc Romani) augendi imperii.

[e] Negant Campanis auxilia contra veteres socios: in ditionem tamen venientibus largiter opitulantur. Quid tamen aut in ditionem accipiunt litigiosam rem? et sociis ferme adquisitam? [f] Feram vulneratam intercipi vulneranti ab alio non oportere, Trebatius iurisconsultus admonuit: cuius et opinio
p. 38 probata a | Friderico Cæsare: et moribus adfirmata, atque recepta est. [g] *Scilicet honestum non est, competentia compendia aliis, vel debita, vel parata avertere*: ait Ambrosius. [h] Non potest quis absque facto suo privari spe sua. Spes etiam ex conditione sic est. Actio etiam est pro spe: et id genus alia, quæ tradunt periti iuris. Spes pro veritate habetur. Neque tu mihi diversam plerorumque sententiam, et probatam a Iustiniano Cæsare renarres: ut non aliter intelligatur facta fera vulnerantis, quam si et capta eidem fuerit. Tractarunt enim posteriores imperatores, et iurisconsulti quædam diligentius, quam fecerunt priores: quod magnus Galliæ iurisconsultus scribit Cuiacius: inque certa hac ratione adfirmat.

Mirandum sane, fuisse desertam Trebatii sententiam de fera vulnerata. Sed evaluit consuetudine, quod erat naturaliter verum. *Opinionum commenta delet dies, naturæ iudicia confirmat.* Scilicet natura est, quod verum est. [i] Et id quidem sic factum alibi cum opinionibus Trebatii est, et aliorum: ut, quod

[a] *Diony.* 2. [b] *Oros.* 3. *c.* 20. [c] *l.* 5. *de capt.* [d] *App. Mitr.* [e] *Liv.* 7. [f] *l.* 5. *de ad. re. do. Cuia.* I. *feud.* 1. [g] *Ambr.* 3. *de off.* 9. [h] *Decian.* 2. *cons.* 17. [i] *l.* 39. *de statul.*

---

167 Dionysius of Halicarnassus 2. 72. 168 Orosius 3. 20.

169 *Digest* 49. 15. 5. **Translator's note:** The passage deals with the Roman law of *postliminium* and seems arbitrarily chosen as there is nothing on just causes of war in it.

170 Appian, *Mithridatica.* 171 Livy 7. 29–32.

172 *Digest* 41. 1. 5. 1; Iacobus Cuiacius [Jacques Cujas], *De feudis, libri quinque* 1. 1, col. 810 [in *Opera quae de iure fecit*, Tomus secundus, Lutetiae Parisiorum, 1617]. [Frederick, as rendered by Cujas, actually puts forward more differentiated a stance than Gentili's prosecutor admits here; if the animal had been hunted down by shepherd's dogs as opposed to hunting dogs, Frederick does not adjudicate in favor of the hunter. Cujas takes this from Radevicus, *De gestis Friderici* 1. 26.]

173 Ambrose, *De officiis* 3. 9. 58. **Translator's note:** I have used the translation of Ivor J. Davidson (Oxford: Oxford University Press, 2001), i. 389. Ambrose was referring to inheritances.

174 Tiberius Decianus, *Consilia* 2. 17, fol. 68[v] [*Responsa*, Venetiis, Apud Vassallinum, 1602].

175 [Cicero, *De natura deorum* 2. 2. 5.]

CHAPTER 7
The Unjust Cause of the Samnite War

But let us by all means also understand the cause of the Samnite War. For this is fitting, and we have already begun to refute the historians who propound that wars were never undertaken by the Romans except for just causes.[167] No doubt it was a just cause (as we have heard) to go to war for the sake of keeping weapons in use and dispelling leisure. It is a just cause to assault with wars peoples who were unknown to them and causing no trouble, for the Romans did precisely this[168]—thereby assaulting at the same time the laws of war,[169] even though those peoples did not absurdly want war with the Romans and did not want the Romans as enemies. It is a just cause to avidly seize upon any and all opportunities (and this, too, the Romans did[170]) of augmenting their empire.

They deny aid to the Campanians against their old allies; but they bountifully aid them when they come under their power.[171] But why do they accept into their rule a quarrelsome state and one nearly annexed by its allies? A wounded beast ought not to be robbed from the hunter who wounded it by some other party, the jurist Trebatius warned, and his judgment was seconded by Caesar Frederick [Frederick II],[172] and it has been affirmed p. 38
and accepted by custom. "For it is not honorable to divert hard earned savings which may be due to others or set aside for them," says Ambrose.[173] One cannot be deprived of his expectation unless as a result of something he has done himself.[174] An expectation is thus dependent on a condition. And a suit is made on behalf of an expectation—and other things of that sort which the experts in the law propound. An expectation is viewed as a truth. Nor should you parrot back a dissenting opinion of a number of people, one approved by the Emperor Justinian, to the effect that the animal is understood as being made to belong to the one who wounds it only if it has also been seized by him. For the later emperors and jurists handled certain matters rather more economically than did the earlier ones, as the great French jurist Cujas writes, and he declared against some of the later rulings on this ground.

It is indeed astonishing that the ruling of Trebatius on a wounded animal had ever been abandoned. But it has had power through custom, which is the truth by nature. "Time destroys the inventions of opinions, but confirms the judgments of nature."[175] Indeed, nature is that which is true. And it has been in other cases as well been carried out in accordance with the views of

naturalem habet rationem, in usu obtineat, etsi est in disputationibus reiectum.

Aut num rationem naturalem non habet, ut parata aliis compendia non avertantur? [a] *Iure naturæ æquum est, neminem cum alterius detrimento, et iniuria fieri locupletiorem.* Illud rationem naturalem non habet, *Omnia, quæ volumus*
p. 39 *alios nobis facere,* | *nos et aliis faciamus*? [b] quæ volumus, id est, quæ velle debemus. [c] Non habet rationem naturalem, quod ex sensu et affectu est communi? Sed me dies hic deficeret, si omnia velim dicere, quæ naturalem rationem ostendunt.

Etiam ego dico captum, quod aufugere non potest, pro actu enim est potentia proxima actui: condemnandus in proximo est pro condemnato: et id genus alia: quæ vel in subtili disceptatione pro Trebatio afferuntur. [d] Quid, quod reliquorum quoque iurisconsultorum mens hac stat? Ratio enim, cur non tribuant alii feram vulneranti, illa est, quoniam accidere possint multa, ut eam ille non capiat. Itaque si nihil multum possit accidere, cur non capiat, feram ei interverti non oporteat. [e] Examen, quod evolaverit ex alveo nostro, manet nostrum, donec in conspectu nostro est, nec difficilis eius persecutio est. Manet nostrum: hoc est, interverti nobis non oportet. [f] Nam feræ, pisces, aves desinunt nostra esse, cum effugerunt: etsi recuperari adhuc possunt. [g] Ut libertatis species est fugisse. Et nec igitur dico quæsitam vulneranti; sed non averti illi oportere spem tantam quærendi.

[h] Videndum et hoc ait Proculus, utrum in laqueo ita hæserit aper, ut expedire se non possit ipse; an diutius luctando expediturus se fuerit: ut si quis eum exemerit, teneatur mihi, qui laqueum venandi caussa posui.
p. 40 Vi|delicet ut non sit aper statim meus, atque incidit vel tenacissime in laqueum: hoc tamen casu, actionem esse mihi adversus eximentem, semper est verius: aut iurisconsultus videndum voluit, quod attinebat nihil.

Huc modo advertatur disputatio, si Campanos vulneratos a Samnitibus potenter, et iam iam capiendos, sic eripuerint Romani iuste? [i] Pro capto est reus, qui sub oculis est magistratus: itaque delinquat, qui illum offendit nunc, alias offensurus impune. Disserit ad quæstionem vulneratæ feræ plura in sententiam nostram Ioannes Cephalus, iurisconsultus primus in academia

[a] *l.* 206. *de reg. iur.* [b] *Decian.* 2. *cons.* 29. [c] *Decian.* 2. *cons.* 9.
[d] *Ceph. cons.* 136. [e] *l.* 5. *de ad. re. do.* [f] *l.* 44. *de ad. re. do.*
[g] *l.* 17. *de ad. ed.* [h] *l.* 55. *de ad. re. do.* [i] *Bal. l.* 4. *de sta. ho.*

---

[176] *Digest* 40. 7. 39. **Translator's note:** Gentili is presumably alluding to 40. 7. 39. 4, where it is said that an opinion of the jurists Labeo and Ofilius concerning the status of a statuliber was reasonable, yet not consonant with the law in force: "Labeonis et Ofilii sententia rationem quidem habet, sed hoc iure utimur, ut is servus ex testamento liber sit." However, this seems rather confused, as the rational opinion in this passage is portrayed as not being in use.

[177] *Digest* 50. 17. 206. [178] Decianus, *Consilia* 2. 29, fols. 94v ff.

[179] Decianus, *Consilia* 2. 9, fol. 46r. [Gentili here paraphrases Decianus, according to whom "naturalis ratio nil aliud est nisi sensus quidam communis, et ex affectu omnium communi procedens."]

[180] Cephalus, *Consilia* 136. [181] *Digest* 41. 1. 5. 4.

[182] *Digest* 41. 1. 44. [183] *Digest* 21. 1. 17. 10. [184] *Digest* 41. 1. 55.

[185] Baldus, *On Digest* 1. 5. 4, fol. 26v.

Trebatius and others, that that which has a natural justification may prevail in use, even if it has been rejected in legal disputations.[176]

Or is there no justification in nature for the principle that profits acquired by others not be taken away from them? "It is just according to the law of nature that nobody become wealthier at the cost of the loss or injury of another person."[177] Does this principle not have a justification in nature, "Everything we wish others to do for us, we should ourselves do for others"? p. 39
"What we wish"—that is, what we *ought* to wish.[178] "Does not that which arises from common sense and feeling have a grounding in nature?"[179] But time would fail me if I were to wish to mention everything that does show a natural grounding.

Also, I call something "captured" that wasn't able to flee; for a capacity that is very close to an act counts as an act; and someone who ought to be condemned is in effect someone who *is* condemned; and likewise many other cases of this sort, which are affirmed in a subtle disputation on behalf of Trebatius. What of the fact that the views of other jurists as well stand on this side?[180] For the reason why some others don't award the beast to the man who wounded it is that many things could occur to keep him from seizing it. Accordingly, if nothing of consequence might happen to prevent him from capturing it, the beast ought not to be filched from him. A swarm which will have flown off from our beehive remains ours for as long as it is in our sight, and pursuit of it is not difficult.[181] It remains ours—that is, it should not be intercepted. For beasts, fish, and birds cease to be ours when they have escaped; even though they might be up to that point capable of being retrieved.[182] For to have escaped is a kind of liberty.[183] And therefore I don't declare the beast which has been demanded to be the property of the one who wounded it, but at least the hope of obtaining it ought not to be taken away from him.

Also, Proculus says that we need to consider this: whether a boar might be caught in a trap in such a manner that it could not disentangle itself; or whether it would have disentangled itself by struggling longer; so that if someone should take it out, it might be held as mine, when I was the one who laid the trap for the purpose of hunting.[184] It is evident that the boar is not p. 40
immediately mine, even though he fell even more inextricably into the trap; and yet in this case it is always more reasonable that I have a suit against the person who freed the beast—either that, or the jurist wanted attention paid to something of no consequence.

Is the dispute as to whether the Romans justly snatched away the Campanians who had been strongly wounded by the Samnites to be turned in this direction? The defendant who is under the eyes of a magistrate is virtually a captive; therefore he who strikes him now would be at fault, even though on another occasion he will strike him with impunity.[185] Joannes Cephalus

prima Patavina concludit, quod qui hostes persequebatur, et iam assequebatur, is agere saltem possit pro suis damnis, et interesse omni adversus interceptorem: qui caussa fuerit, quominus ipse tanti laboris, atque discriminis mercedem meritam consequeretur. Hæc, Romani, effecistis Samnitibus sociis. Hæc illis debita retinetis.

Verum dicite nunc, quare etiam Sidicinos, itidem dedentes se vobis, non recepistis, et contra eosdem Samnites non defenditis? Seram deditionem, ultimaque tandem necessitate expressam aspernamini? An magis illicuere cupidinem vestram Campanæ maiores opes, uberrimus ille totius Italiæ ager, certamen ([a]ut dicunt) Liberi, Cererisque, et naturæ gaudentis opus? p. 41 Hoc verius in pari alioqui caussa Si | dicinorum, et Campanorum. Et sic puncto tempore, fidem esse utilitate antiquiorem, obliti estis. Fidem utilitate antiquiorem, paullo ante deditionem, Campanis respondebatis: et fœdus vobis cum Samnitibus servandum esse.

Quid iam alias memorem Italicas gentes, iniquis Romanorum armis oppressas? Aut quomodo memorem? [b] Nos, in ultimo temporum positi, mala Romanorum scire non possumus nisi per eos, qui laudavere Romanos. Sed intelligimus tamen, quam valde multa iniusta fuerint Romanorum facta, qui videmus, emanasse non pauca iniustissima in tanto studio laudandi. Deleta Ausonum gens vix certo defectionis crimine, perinde ac si internecino bello certatum esset: ut scribit Livius. [c] Calabriæ arma illata: quasi excepissent Pyrrhum Calabri: sed re vera ut Brundusio potirentur, portu in Græciam oportuno: ut alii adnotarunt: de quibus Zonara retulerit.

At placet, a patriis calamitatibus avertere alio animum, et in regiones alias convertere orationem. Hæc vero populi Romani adolescentia fuisse dicitur, cum Italiam subiugavit.

[a] *Ior. de re. succ. Pli.* 3. *c.* 5. [b] *Oros.* 4. *c.* 5. [c] *Zonara.*

---

186 [Cf. Livy 8. 2.]
187 Jordanes, *Romana*; Pliny 3. 5 [cf. Florus 1. 16. 3].
188 [Livy 7. 31. 1.]
189 Orosius 4. 5.
190 [Livy 9. 25. 9.]
191 Zonaras 8. 7.

argues many points with regard to the question of the wounded animal in accord with our opinion. A first-class jurist in the first-class university of Padua, he concludes that the person who was pursuing and overtaking enemies should at least have the power to lodge an action on behalf of his losses, and everyone has an interest against the interceptor who was the reason that prevented that man from being able to achieve his due reward for so much labor and risk. This, Romans, is what you did to your allies, the Samnites. You kept for yourself these things that were owed to them.

But tell us now why you did not also accept the Sidicini, who had surrendered to you in exactly the same way, and did not defend them against those same Samnites?[186] Did you reject a tardy surrender and one forced out finally only by the most extreme necessity? Or was it more that the greater Campanian resources enticed your greed? Campania was the most fertile region of all of Italy, a prize fought over by Bacchus and Ceres (as they say), and a product of rejoicing nature.[187] This is what is more likely in the otherwise identical case of the Sidicinians and the Campanians. And thus, p. 41
at a certain point in time, you forgot that loyalty is preferable to profit. A little while before their surrender you replied to the Campanians that loyalty is preferable to profit, and that your treaty with the Samnites had to be preserved.[188]

Why should I now mention other Italian peoples oppressed by the unjust arms of the Romans? Or *how* shall I mention them? Placed as we are at such a remote distance in time, we can only know the misdeeds of the Romans through those who have praised the Romans.[189] Nonetheless, we know how very deeply unjust were the deeds of the Romans, since we see that several extremely unjust acts emerge even in the course of such eagerness to praise. The Ausones were destroyed scarcely through any firm charge of defection but exactly as though they had struggled against the Romans in a murderous war, as Livy writes.[190] Arms were taken away from Calabria, as though the Calabrians had received Pyrrhus; but if truth be told, it was so that the Romans might gain control of Brundisium, a port conveniently placed for sailing to Greece, as noted by others, of whom Zonaras has informed us.[191]

But now it pleases us to turn our thoughts away from our ancestors' disasters and to direct our discourse into other regions. This, indeed, is said to have been the adolescence of the Roman people, when it subjugated Italy.

De bellis Punicis.
CAP. VIII

In Siciliam quæ caussa devexit arma Romana? [a] Cum viderent (ait Florus) opulentissimam in proximo prædam, cupiditate eius exarserunt. Et hac
p. 42 quidem præda sollicitan|te, sed specie Messanæ oppugnatæ, et fabulosæ originis, [b] qua se Mamertini imputavere Romanis, arma illa in Siciliam devecta sunt. [c] Et iudicatum Romæ tamen turpissimum fuit, iuvare Mamertinos, flagitiosissimos homines. Hinc autem primum cum Pœnis, veterrimis sociis. [d] Nam auxilia tandem cum decreta Mamertinis essent, nec mitterentur: Mamertinique ad Pœnos refugerent, atque accepissent e Pœnis: tum Romani Messanam, factam Carthaginensium, libertati reddere volunt. Vincuntur autem primo: et a Pœnis recipiunt amissas triremes: ut fœderis arguerentur clarius fracti. Sane enim violarunt Romani fœdus: qui in Siciliæ partes, quæ parebant Carthaginensibus, navigare ex fœdere non potuerunt: atque Carthaginensibus Messana parebat. Tantum abest, ut eo etiam oppugnatum socios valuerint proficisci. Et non apte in quæstione ista contrarium, et adversus Philenium in quæstione ista Polybius disputavit.

Pergo porro. Venit in colloquium dux Carthaginensis: capitur improbe, a Mamertinis, an a Romanis dominis? Excedit cum omni exercitu tota Sicilia. Petitur, ut Romanus excedat quoque. Sed huic surdæ sunt aures ad tantam, et tam evidentem æquitatem.

Sic bellum primum Punicum, violatis fœderibus, adiutis improbis, Et
p. 43 secuta iniquam istam illic prædam præda | iniquior Sardinia, per summam iniuriam, contra iura omnium fœderum ablata: ut omnium historicorum sententia convenit: et Polybius declarat luculentissime.

Sed secundi belli non melior caussa, quam primi fuit. Et de Sagunto illud prius notem, quæ caussa creditur huius belli: eam immo Annibali civitatem perfidam exstitisse: omni dignissimam fuisse malo: et habitam tamen ab Annibale clementissime. [e] Ita Plutarchus. [f] Et alii sic tradunt, obsessam a

[a] *Flor.* 2. [b] *Panegy. Fla.* [c] *Polyb.* 1. [d] *Zonara.*
[e] *Plut. de cla. mu.* [f] *Vet. com. Iuv. sat.* 15.

---

[192] [Florus 2. 2. 2.]

[193] Paneg. Flav. **Translator's note:** This is a reference to what is usually called "Panegyric V" of the *XII Panegyrici Latini*. It is a *gratiarum actio* to Constantine. The passage in question is sect. 3.1. In Gentili's day it was probably called the "Panegyricus Flaviae." "Flavia," mentioned in the first sentence of the panegyric, was the city of Flavia Aeduorum, i.e. modern Autun. The panegyric is constructed as a *prosopopoeia*, with Flavia Aeduorum imagined as addressing her thanks to Constantine.

[194] Polybius 1. 10.

[195] Zonaras 8. 8. **Translator's note:** Zonaras, a Byzantine epitomator of the early 12th c., was summarizing a passage from bk. 11 of *Dio Cassius*. Judging by Polybius 1. 15. 2, the account of an initial Roman defeat apprears to derive from the pro-Carthaginian historian Philinus of Acragas, though Polybius does not specifically attribute to Philinus Hanno's restoration of the triremes. Polybius' own account of the outbreak and first stages of the war seems to have followed that of Q. Fabius Pictor.

[196] Plutarch, *De mulierum virtutibus* 248 E–249 B. **Translator's note:** Plutarch is writing about Salamanca here, not Saguntum.

CHAPTER 8
On the Punic Wars

What excuse carried Roman arms to Sicily? Since they saw (says Florus) a very rich prize lying very nearby, they became inflamed with desire for it.[192] And though this prize was very tempting in itself, it was through the pretext of the p. 42 siege of Messana and the bogus ancestral origin by which the Mamertines imposed themselves on the Romans that Roman arms were carried into Sicily.[193] And yet it was judged at Rome that it was most disgraceful to come to the aid of the Mamertines, the most wicked of men.[194] From this source arose the first war with the Carthaginians, who had been their allies of old. For when aid had at last been decreed for the Mamertines but was not yet being sent, and the Mamertines took refuge with the Carthaginians and received aid from the Carthaginians, then the Romans wished to restore Messana, which had been made the property of the Carthaginians, to its liberty. But at first the Romans were defeated—and then received back from the Carthaginians their lost triremes, so that they [the Romans] might be more manifestly convicted of having broken the treaty.[195] For the Romans had indeed violated the treaty, since they were by the treaty forbidden to sail to those parts of Sicily that were subject to the Carthaginians, and Messana *was* subject to them. So far were they from having any right to hasten off there to attack allies! And Polybius did not properly take the opposite side to that of Philinus in this dispute.

But I proceed onwards. The Carthaginian commander comes to a conference; he is wickedly seized by the Mamertines—or is it by their Roman masters? He withdraws from all of Sicily with his entire army—and he asks that the Roman commander withdraw also. But the latter's ears were deaf to such and so evident fair dealing.

Thus began the First Punic War, with treaties broken and wicked men aided. And there followed upon this unjustly seized prize an even more unjustly seized prize: Sardinia, which was seized through the greatest p. 43 wrong, against the terms of all the treaties, as the opinion of all the historians agrees, and as Polybius makes abundantly clear.

But the cause of the second war was no better than the first. And I would first make this comment about Saguntum, which is believed to be the cause of this war: that state was in every way utterly disloyal to Hannibal; it was thoroughly worthy of every possible misfortune—and yet it was treated with the utmost mercy by Hannibal. So Plutarch.[196] And others record thus:

Romanis Saguntum, non ab Annibale. Et is ipse igitur Annibal non per vanitatem ait, Romanos Sagunti fecisse inique.

Attamen sic se habeat res, ut descripta a Livio est: quid nos in Pœno reprehendimus, si Saguntum, suorum hostium munimen, atque perfugium, armis aggreditur? Non sane pro iniustis viris Romani contra Carthaginenses sexto iam fœdere iunctos, et iustum ius prosequentes, capessere bellum debuerunt. Nihil hic dissero, si Saguntinis postumis sociis cautum fœdere erat. Qua tamen in re definienda præcipitem fuisse Livium, animadvertere est. [a] Etenim plures sunt iurisperitorum sententiæ, quæ significant, actum videri de præsenti, non de futuro: et itaque fœdere illo prospectum præsentibus solis, non etiam futuris sociis.

[b] Quid, quod Appianus tradit, Romæ ita decretum fuisse, ne auxilia
p. 44 Saguntinis mitterentur: quoniam | non fœdere comprehensi, sed liberi relicti essent? An ita? An, quod fecistis cum Mamertinis, exspectabatis, se Saguntum defendere, et debilitari Pœnum, sine vestro incommodo? An etiam, Saguntum perdi, quam vobisque intersepturam iter ad Hispaniarum imperium credebatis?

Non ingrediar imperii vestri arcana. Perfidi, si Saguntinis sociis auxilia denegastis. Perfidi, si pro non sociis Saguntinis contra socios Carthaginenses pugnastis. Perfidi semper, qui contra veteres pro novis stetistis sociis. [c] Num quæstio est subdifficilis, si amici novi sint veteribus anteponendi? Indignam homine dubitationem, et tu ais illico, M. Tulli, ac subdifficilem quæstionem aiebas.

Romanorum etiam socios, iniurios sibi, potuisse Annibalem bello persequi, quis neget? [d] Etiam hoc ad iniustitiam Saguntinorum acccedit: qui relicti per fœdus in libertate, et medii, tradiderunt se, et addixerunt Romanis totos. Nam hoc est contra fœdus, a partibus tributis longe abire. Male Saguntini a medio ad extremum iere. Et Romani in suum extremum recepere medium male. [e] Etiam cum dicitur, licere cuilibet non adscriptorum fœderi, ad utros velit, se conferre: non tamen pactum hoc est ita intelligendum, ut quid fieri inque perniciem partis alterius possit. Quod prudenter edisserunt Corinthii
p. 45 legati, ne se contra, fœdera|tos primos, susciperent Athenienses Corcyræos defendere.

[a] *Ceph. cons.* 693. 733. [b] *App. Hisp.* [c] *Cic. Læl.*
[d] *Plut. Ann.* [e] *Thucyd.* I.

---

[197] Scholia on Juvenal, *Satirae* 15. 93–4. **Translator's note:** Late antique scholiasts of Juvenal seem to have confused Juvenal's reference to the Vascones, besieged by the Romans in 72 BC, with the siege of Saguntum, which one scholiast attributed to Metellus rather than Hannibal.

[198] Cephalus, *Consilia* 593; 733. [199] Appian, *Iberica* 11. 43. [200] Cicero, *De amicitia* 19. 67.

[201] Plutarch, *Ann.* **Translator's note:** The accuser seems to have in mind a life of Hannibal here, but Plutarch wrote no biography of Hannibal. Cf. *De armis Romanis* 2. 8, pp. 260–1, where the defender of the Roman cause refers to this reference and emphatically declares that "some recent writer" is meant, adding that "that was *not* Plutarch."

[202] Thucydides 1. 52–3.

Saguntum was besieged by the Romans, not by Hannibal.[197] And therefore Hannibal himself says—and not through his own vanity—that the Romans behaved unjustly at Saguntum.

But let the matter rest as it has been described by Livy. What criticism can we offer of the Carthaginian if he attacked with arms Saguntum, the rampart and refuge of his enemies? Surely the Romans should not have entered upon a war on behalf of unjust men against the Carthaginians who had been joined to them by six treaties already and who were pursuing a justified right. I am not discussing here if later Saguntine allies were provided for by a treaty. It is to be noted that Livy in properly defining this matter was over-hasty. For truly there are many opinions of jurists which point out that an act is to be viewed from the perspective of the present, not the future, and so provisions were being made by this treaty only for present allies, not future allies.[198]

What of what Appian records? He says that it was decreed at Rome not to send aid to the Saguntines, since they weren't covered by the treaty but were p. 44
left free.[199] Was it thus? Did you do what you did with the Mamertines—that is, were you expecting that Saguntum would defend itself and that the Carthaginian would be weakened without any inconvenience on your part? Or did you go so far as to believe that Saguntum should be lost rather than deprive you of the path to rule over the Spains?

I shall not enter upon the secrets of your empire. You were faithless if you denied aid to the Saguntines. You were faithless if you fought against the Carthaginians, who were your allies, on behalf of the Saguntines, who were not your allies. You were always faithless, you who took a stand against old allies on behalf of new ones. Is it really a "somewhat difficult question" whether new friends are to be preferred to old ones?[200] Even you, Cicero, say in that very passage that this doubt is unworthy of a human being, and yet you did call it "a somewhat difficult question."

Who would deny that Hannibal was able to wage war even against allies of Rome if they had done him wrong? Even this very fact adds to the injustice of the Saguntines: that, left in freedom and in the middle by the treaty, they handed themselves over to and joined themselves utterly to the Romans.[201] For this is against the treaty, to depart a considerable distance from assigned roles. The Saguntines wickedly went over from the middle to the extreme. And the Romans wickedly received this middle to its own extreme. Even when it is said that it is permitted for any of those not covered by the treaty to betake themselves to either side, this pact is nonetheless not to be understood as making possible something that tends to disaster for either side. The Corinthian ambassadors prudently pointed this out, lest the Athenians p. 45
should undertake to defend the Corcyreans against them, their original allies.[202]

Sive igitur Annibalis partem consideramus, sive partem Romanorum, semper liquido iniustitiam horum deprehendimus. Porro belli huius secundi accessio est Hispania: in quam Sagunti prætextu malo excercitus transportarunt. Saguntum dicimus? [a] Ad fodinas auri petitam Hispaniam: ait testis magnus, Macchabeicus. *Auri sacra fames.* Numantiam in Hispania exsciderunt: [b] quam illic urbem iniustissimo bello petierunt: ut sic Florus: cui urbi conventiones abruperunt: ut sic dictum antea: a qua urbe nullis conditionibus, nisi mortibus omnium mortalium, et ruina omnium rerum moveri potuerunt: ut omnis clamat historia. Nam quid de indignitate dicam, quod non nisi vincere fame Numantinos voluerunt? [c]*Neque dignum videbatur, famem hostium operiri*: Tacitus de Tito, qui Hierosolyma oppugnabat: locum illum munitissimum, et abnuentem impetus belli, [d] cum sine mœnibus, undique pervia Numantia esset. Turpissimi homines, toties cæsi innumeri a pauculis, vivere tantam virtutem, et testem superesse ignominiarum Romani populi, non tulerunt.

Est belli secundi accessio et Sicilia universa: præda illa iam antea expetita, et per tot annos, perque tot discrimina deprædata. Age, fidelem socium te
p. 46 præsta, Hiero, et amicum certum Roma|nis: age: nunc puero nepoti tuo nec parcunt isti, nec civitati tuæ.

Sed in Corsos, residuam insulam, quæ caussa, aut occasio belli? [e] Incognitam sibi profitentur peritissimi antiquitatum. An fuit nulla? [f] In fœderibus Punicis fuit, ut Corsica media esset inter Romanos et Carthaginenses. Sed boni illi viri medium sic interpretari consueti, veluti suum. Non audivimus de Sagunto: In fœderibus deceptos Corsos, ante cognovimus. Et ita igitur Italiam habent, Hispaniam, insulas.

Agite: in ipsam Africam traiiciamus: bella concludamus Punica: Neque enim singula istorum bellorum exquirenda sunt per immensam orationem. [g]Quanta illa erat in primo iniustitia, quod, redire Regulum, nollent? etiam iuramentum redeundi nihili interpretantes, iuratum vi. Sic senatus populusque, non propinqui soli reditum morantes. Hos tu damnas, Cicero, omnes: qui Reguli reditum iustum dilaudasti. Regulus et ipse iniustus: qui contra susceptum legationis officium agit Romæ: et iuste igitur necatus a Pœnis: et iniuste igitur Romani tot nobiles Carthaginenses excarnificandos Reguli filiis

[a] 1. *Maccha.* 8. [b] *Flor.* 2. [c] *Tacit.* 5. *histor.* [d] *Lips. de mach.*
[e] *Sigo. de ant. iu. pro.* [f] *Serv.* 4. *Æneid.* [g] *Polyen.* 8. *Zon. Sui. Horat.* 3. *od.* 5.

---

203 1 Maccabees 8: 3–4. 204 [Vergil, *Aeneis* 3. 57.] 205 Florus 2. 18. 3.

206 Tacitus, *Historiae* 5. 11.

207 Justus Lipsius, *De machinis* [*Poliorceticon sive de machinis libri quinque*, Antverpiae, Ex officina Plantiniana, Apud Viduam et Ioannem Moretum, 1596].

208 **Translator's note:** In the First Punic War, Hieron II of Syracuse, after initially siding with the Carthaginians, soon became a firm ally of the Romans. He supported the Romans also in the Second Punic War, but upon his death in 215 his grandson and successor Hieronymus shifted allegiance to the Carthaginians. Though he was soon murdered at Lentinoi, Syracuse remained on the Carthaginian side, and this led to its siege and destruction by Claudius Marcellus in 211.

209 Sigonius [Carlo Sigonio], *De antiquo iure provinciarum libri tres* 1. 4, col. 487 [Sigonio, *Opera omnia*, Tomus V, Mediolani, In aedibus palatinis, 1736]. 210 Servius, *On Aeneid* 4. 628.

211 Polyaenus, *Strategemata* 8. 12; Zonaras 8. 15; *Suda*, ed. Adler, rho, 126; Horace, *Carmina* 3. 5.

Therefore, if we consider the role of Hannibal or that of the Romans, we always clearly grasp the iniquity of the latter. Moreover the thing gained in this second Punic war was Spain, to which they shipped armies over on the base pretext of Saguntum. Saguntum, do I say? Spain was attacked for its gold mines, says a great authority, the Book of Maccabees.[203] "Accursed hunger for gold!"[204] They razed Numantia in Spain, a city they attacked there in a most unjust war, as Florus records[205]—a city with which they broke compacts, as was mentioned earlier—a city by which they could be moved by no terms short of the death of all its mortals and the destruction of all of its things, as every history shouts out. For why shall I speak of the baseness of the fact that they did not wish to defeat the Numantines by any other means than hunger? "Nor did it seem a worthy thing to wait for the hunger of their enemies"—so Tacitus about Titus, who was besieging Jerusalem, a place that was highly fortified and one that repelled the assaults of war,[206] while Numantia, on the other hand, was without walls and was penetrable on all sides.[207] Basest of men, so often cut down in vast numbers by very small numbers—they could not endure that such valor should live and that a witness to the disgraces of the Roman people should survive.

The whole of Sicily was the acquisition of the Second Punic War—that prize they had long sought and had ravaged for so many years and through so many crises. Come now, Hieron, offer yourself to the Romans as a loyal ally
and firm friend: come, do those men now spare your young grandson or your p. 46
city?[208]

But what cause or occasion of war was there against the remaining island, Corsica? Those most learned in antiquities admit that the reason is unknown to them.[209] Was there none at all? In the treaty with the Carthaginians it was agreed that Corsica would be neutral between the Romans and the Carthaginians.[210] But those fine men were accustomed to interpret "neutral" to mean "their own." Haven't we heard about Saguntum? We learned earlier that the Corsicans were deceived in treaties. And therefore in this way the Romans possess Italy, Spain, and the islands.

Come now: let's cross over to Africa; let's finish the Punic Wars. There is no need to seek out the details of those wars in an immense oration. How great was their injustice in the first war, when they did not want Regulus to return—and even, in fact, judged his oath to return as of no value, as sworn under duress?[211] Thus the Senate and the people, not just his relatives, attempted to hinder his return. You condemn them all, Cicero, for you praised Regulus's return as just. But Regulus was himself unjust, for while in Rome he acted against the duty of the embassy he had undertaken; and thus he was justly killed by the Carthaginians, and the Romans thus acted unjustly in handing over so many Carthaginian nobles to the sons of Regulus

in vindictam tradunt. En sævos: en iniustos. Sævi in secundo bello cum homine mortuo: ut post dico: iniusti in captivis periuris ad Annibalem non remittendis aut si remissos dicentibus credimus magis; etiam hoc faciamus,
p. 47 ut, quia re|mittere nolebant Regulum, de ipsis sit, [a]*Servandam in parvis iustitiam, ut iniustus esse in maioribus possis.* In vilibus capitibus colere iustitiam voluere, qui colere in magno recusabant.

Ceterum dico bellum tertium. Urbem Carthaginem, et Punicum imperium quo tandem iure, quibus artibus exstinxerunt! Ius dictum omnibus, quod æmulam in propinquo potentiam rebus tutam suis non censuerunt. Audiamus, quid tamen scribat historicus, [b]*Mihi, studiose quærenti, nusquam omnino caussa belli Punici tertii eluxit: alii volebant propter securitatem dirui: alii manere ad virtutem acuendam: igitur caussa non ex iniuria lacessentium.* Audiamus alium, qui et de Scipione hic tradit, [c]*Eam urbem magis invidia imperii, quam ullius eius temporis noxiæ invisam Romano nomini funditus sustulit.* Adde cum eodem auctore, *Magis, quia volebant Romani, quicquid de Carthaginensibus diceretur, credere, quam quia credenda afferebantur, statuit senatus Carthaginem exscindere.* [d] Catonis ficum meminimus, et cavillationes.

Artes nihilo iustiores in bello, consilia vaferrima, doli pessimi. Masinissam vicinum apponunt infestissimum: ad cuius iniurias manifestas connivent: cum et possent, et deberent eas prohibere: et simularent, etiam legationibus
p. 48 missis, prohibituros. Quid enim, quid Livius? [e]*Masinissa, postquam infames | Carthaginenses sensit, et discordes inter se, locum iniuriæ esse ratus, agrum depopulatur*, &c. Quid enim, quid Numida ille obtendit, ut iure rapere Carthaginensium bona videretur? Scilicet Carthaginensibus in Africa nec terræ pedem extra Byrsam esse oportere: [f] tantum enim, et hoc tantum callidis Tyriæ commentis acceptum. Sed ita ne spernimus septingentorum annorum possessionem? et iura sic convellimus vetustissima?

[a] *Plut. de tu. bo. va.* [b] *Oros.* 4. *c.* 23. [c] *Paterc.* 1. [d] *Plin.* 15. *c.* 18.
[e] *Liv.* 34. [f] *Iust.* 18.

---

212 [Diodorus Siculus 24. 12; Zonaras 8. 15.]

213 **Translator's note:** Gentili is referring here to a delegation of ten prominent Romans, captured at Cannae, whom Hannibal sent to Rome to negotiate the ransoming of the other Roman prisoners. According to Polybius 6. 58 (followed and expanded by Livy, 22. 58–61), the Senate rejected the ransom and duly returned the ten envoys (one of them unwilling and in chains) to Hannibal. But at 22. 61 Livy also records another account, in which the Senate narrowly agreed to let the envoys break their oath to Hannibal and remain in Rome.

214 Plutarch, *Moralia, De tuenda sanitate* 135 F. **Translator's note:** In this passage the tyrant Jason of Pherae is quoted as saying that we need to do wrong in little ways in order to do good in big ways. Obviously Gentili was turning these words inside out.

215 Orosius 4. 23.

216 Velleius Paterculus 1. 12. 5.

217 Velleius Paterculus 1. 12. 2.

218 Pliny the Elder 15. 18. **Translator's note:** Cato the Censor displayed an early ripe fig in the Senate house, announcing that it had been plucked just two days earlier in Carthage—"so near is the enemy to our walls!"

219 Livy 34. 62. 1–2.

to be slaughtered.[212] Behold savage men! Behold unjust men! In the second war they were savage along with the dead man [Regulus]: and, as I say next, they were unjust in not handing over to Hannibal captives who were perjured, or if we put more faith in those who claim that they *had* been handed over,[213] let us do so in order that, because they were unwilling to hand over Regulus, p. 47
it might hold true about these same people that "justice is to be observed in small things so that you might be unjust in important things."[214] They wished, then, to observe justice in the case of lesser persons, for they refused to observe it in the case of a great man.

But I now mention that Third Punic War. By what right, finally, by what arts did they extinguish the city of Carthage and the Carthaginian empire? Their "right" was made manifest to all: that they did not judge that a rival power nearby was safe for their own state. Let us hear, however, what a historian writes. "Though I search diligently, nowhere at all has the excuse for the Third Punic War shone forth. Some wished for Carthage to be destroyed for their own security; others wished it to survive as a stimulus to courage. Therefore the pretext does not arise from any injury suffered by those who provoked the war."[215] Let us listen to another historian, who records of Scipio here: "He destroyed from its very foundations that city which was hateful to the Roman name more from envy of its power than from any harm it was doing at that time."[216] Add this, from the same author: "It was more because the Romans wished to believe anything that might be said about the Carthaginians than because they maintained that these things were worthy of belief that the Senate decided to destroy Carthage."[217] We call to mind the fig and the sophistries of Cato.[218]

Their crafts in war-making were in no way more just than that; their plans were most cunning; their tricks the very worst imaginable. They established Masinissa as a most hostile neighbor to Carthage, and then connived at his open wrongdoings when they could and should have prohibited them, and they pretended that they were going to prohibit them by sending ambassadors. What, now, does Livy say? "Masinissa, after he became aware that the p. 48
Carthaginians were disgraced and were quarreling among themselves, and judging that he had an opportunity for doing wrong, ravaged their countryside."[219] What on earth did that Numidian offer as a pretext so that he might seem to be plundering the goods of the Carthaginians justly? No doubt it was that there ought not to be a foot of ground in Africa for the Carthaginians beyond the Byrsa—for this much and only this much was owed to the clever tricks of the Tyrian woman.[220] But did we thus spurn a right of possession that had lasted 700 years, and did we thus uproot rights of great antiquity?

---

220 Justin 18. 5. **Translator's note:** The Tyrian woman is Elissa/Dido. Justin writes: "Having then bargained for a piece of ground, as much as could be covered with an ox-hide, . . . she directed the hide to be cut into the thinnest possible strips, and thus acquired a greater portion of ground than she had apparently demanded; whence the place had afterwards the name of Byrsa." John Selby Watson, trans., Bohn's Library, London, 1853.

Et vobis igitur, Romani, probe Carneades, quod si iusti esse velletis, ad casas redire vos, unde prodiistis primum, et imperium isthoc orbis terrarum relinquere vos oportuisset. Non ita a casis? [a]*Roma, nisi immensum vires promosset in orbem, Stramineis esset nunc quoque densa casis.* [b] Etiam Romuli regis casa, *Romuleoque recens horrebat regia culmo.* [c] Etiam reliqua urbis sic erant: quod et alii canunt poetæ: [d] et ille sanctus, *Ipsa casas fragili texat gens Romula culmo: sic tradunt habitasse Remum.* Barbaram rationem barbari Numidæ. Age tamen, age rex Masinissa: obliviscere Hieronis liberos: inservi Romanorum cupiditati: [e] ne audi, quod in suis curiis, templisve disserebant, abutendum te contra Carthaginenses ad suæ utilitatem reipublicæ. Et tu mox audies tui exscidium regni connivente tuo hoc populo Romano ad mortes
p. 49 lamentabiles liberorum tuorum: et eas ulciscente mox ad prædam acci-|
piendam adeo turpiter: ut verissime exclamasse sciamus nepotem tuum. [f] *Urbem venalem.* Sic regibus abusa omnibus Roma est. Sic sustulit omnes, cum opus servitio illorum postea non haberet. [g] Inservientes hi reges nominati, et habiti.

[h] Sed ecce Pœni adusque Romanorum pedes devoluti, intolerandam Masinissæ avaritiam, et superbiam conqueruntur: si trium rerum unam sinerent impetrari, rogant cum lacrymis: ut vel ex æquo apud socium populum, quod cuique esset, disceptarent: vel permissum sibi esset, ut adversus iniusta arma pio, iustoque se tutarentur bello: vel ad extremum, si gratia plus quam veritas apud eos valeret, semel statuerent, quid donatum ex alieno Masinissæ vellent.

Et cetera, quæ exsecutus est ipse Livius. [i] Missi in Africam conciliatores: sed cum mandatis, ut faverent regi, quantum possent: et iterum alii cum iisdem mandatis clam, ut regis utilitatem promoverent. Et quidem sic negotium utrique conficiunt pro Masinissa. Neque dum quiescit is tamen. Et arbitros ergo Pœni rursus implorant. Et promissi arbitri, nec missi prius, quam speratum Romæ esset, victos Pœnos, victorem Masinissam exstitisse. Etiam probus ille Africanus missus: qui passus vigere inimicitias, qui pastus dulcissimo (sic et fari ausus) spectaculo, e colle prospectans prælia Africæ,
p. 50 sanguinem, et cladem | Lybiæ, Numidiæque. [j] *Suave etiam belli certamina*
magna tueri per campos instructa tua sine parte pericli?

[a] *Ovid. 2. eleg. 9.* [b] *Virg. 8. Æn.* [c] *Prop. 4. eleg. 1.* [d] *Prud. 2. co. Sym.*
[e] *App. Puni.* [f] *Liv. 64. Flor. 3.* [g] *Tac. 2. hist.* [h] *Liv. 42.*
[i] *App. Pun.* [j] *Lucr. 2.*

---

[221] **Translator's note:** From Cicero, *De republica* 3. 21, which Gentili can only have known from a passage in Lactantius, *Divinae institutiones* 5. 16. 2–5, the end of which is: "omnibus populis qui florerent imperio, et Romanis quoque ipsis qui totius orbis potirentur, si iusti velint esse, hoc est si aliena restituant, ad casas esse redeundum et in egestate ac miseriis iacendum." The point is made in the context of Carneades' argument that justice consists in stupidity.
[222] Ovid, *Amores* 2. 9. 17–18. [223] Vergil, *Aeneis* 8. 654. [224] Propertius 4. 1.
[225] Prudentius, *Contra Symmachum* 2. 298 f. [226] Appian, *Punica* 3. 13–14.
[227] Livy, *Periochae* 64; Florus 3. 1. 18. **Translator's note:** The grandson of Masinissa was Jugurtha.
[228] Tacitus, *Historiae* 2. 81. 1. [229] Livy 42. 23. [230] Appian, *Punica* 10. 67.
[231] Lucretius 2. 5–6. **Translator's note:** In Lucretius' text, this is not a question.

And thus Carneades quite properly told you, Romans, that if you wished to be just, you ought to return to those huts from which you first set forth, and you ought to surrender this empire of the world.[221] Was it not from huts you set forth? "Had Rome not moved forth its power into the vast world, she would even now be filled with straw huts."[222] Even King Romulus had a hut: "The newly built palace was rough with Romulus' straw."[223] Even the other parts of the city were like this, as other poets sing,[224] among them that holy poet [Prudentius]: "Let the people of Romulus weave together huts with fragile straw: thus they say Remus lived."[225] The barbarian Numidians had a barbarous pretext. Go on, king Masinissa, go on: forget about what happened to the children of Hieron; be of use to the greed of the Romans; don't listen to what they say in their Senate halls and temples: that you are to be used against the Carthaginians for the profit of their own state.[226] And you will soon hear of the destruction of your own kingdom, with that Roman people of yours turning a blind eye to the lamentable deaths of your children—and then soon avenging those deaths for the sake of getting booty so basely that we know p. 49
that your grandson very truly exclaimed, "What a corrupt city!"[227] Thus the Romans made away with all those for whose servitude they no longer had any use. "Submissive kings" they were named—and considered.[228]

But behold: the Carthaginians, having almost fallen at the feet of the Romans, complain of the unbearable avarice and pride of Masinissa. They ask in tears if the Romans will allow them at least one of three things: that they might decide on an equal footing in front of an allied people what should belong to each party; or that it might be granted them to defend themselves in a pious and just war against unjust arms; or, at worst, if favor was going to carry more weight among them than truth, that they should once and for all decide what they wished should be granted Masinissa from the property of others.[229]

And there are other things which Livy himself proceeded to relate. Peacemakers were sent to Africa, but with orders to side with the king as much as they could, and others again were sent in secret with the same orders to promote the profit of the king.[230] And indeed both groups settled the business in Masinissa's favor. And yet he wasn't keeping still even then. And therefore the Carthaginians begged for arbitrators again. And arbitrators were promised, but not sent before it was expected at Rome that the Carthaginians would emerge defeated and Masinissa would be the victor. It was even the upright Scipio Africanus who was sent, who allowed the hatreds on both side to flourish and feasted upon the very sweet (so even he dared to call it) spectacle, viewing from a hill the battles of Africa and the blood and slaughter of Libya and Numidia. "Is it sweet to view even great contests of p. 50
war marshaled across the plains without any danger to you?"[231]

Atque ita tandem cum prospicere ipsi sibi Carthaginenses cogerentur, violati fœderis rei facti, et hostes declarati. [a] Quasi scilicet aut lex, aut pactio valeat, ne quis se defendat. Bellum in eos simul indicitur, et infertur. Nam sollemnia illa, et iusta, res repetendi, tum desierant. Excusationes eorum æquissimæ non audiuntur: iubentur satisfacere aliter: rogantibus, quid esset hoc *aliter*, non exponitur, nisi scire eos et hoc *aliter*. At Pœni damnaverant iam omnes, quos fecisse contra fœdus, et voluntatem Romanorum credebant. Obsides nunc, et alia iussi dedunt. Ceterum, quod mandatum a principio fuit, consulibus idem nunc iteratur clam, non absisterent bello prius, quam diruta Carthago foret: quam tamen mansuram liberam, semper promittebatur. Rursum igitur iubent consules, arma tradi, et naves: et naves, et arma traduntur.

Atque ecce profertur tandem arcanum: ad quod per tot frustrationes, et fraudes ventum est: et quod Pœnis probe antea fuit cognitum, nec arcanum. Subruenda Carthago est: urbs alia longe illinc ædificanda. Equidem exclamem, O monstra! Sed de civitate, quæ civibus, et hominibus constat, non de urbe, quæ in tectis, et parietibus est, Pœnis relinquenda libera promissum est.
p. 51 Sed | iterum, O monstra, et portenta terrarum! An potuit de civitatis libertate intelligi pollicitatio, cum esset iam a bello primo Carthago civitas vobis stipendiaria, et serva? Sic vos appellabatis Annibalem ipsum stipendiarium vestrum, et servum. Turpem vero captiunculam, vocularum nec certam distinctiunculam: quam nec admittere queant sine stomacho, qui a syllabis toti pendent, causidici.

Quid recitem consulis orationem, huius sceleris administri? qua deceptis Pœnis ruinam patriæ adprobare nititur, et novæ ædificationem urbis. Non est in parietibus respublica: est tamen in aris, et focis: [b] ut tu contra Pompeium dicebas Cicero: qui reliquerat urbem. [c] Ite Quirites, ite ad Camilli orationem: quæ vos in ruinis urbis vestræ, in ruderibus, in cineribus olim retinuit: et capedunculam istam vestram urbis, et civitatis turpem, nefariamque vobis ostendet. [d] *Si transferre sedes cogerentur, maior vitæ metus, quam mortis*: ait de Iudæis Tacitus. Adeo nihil est solum patriæ? nihil ea terra, quam appellamus matrem? et assueta oculis regio? et cælum, sub quo sumus nati, et educati? Quid locus ille Carthaginis, ager, mare, loci genium? ubi parva exsulum

[a] *Bal.* 4. *cons.* III. [b] *Cic.* 7. *Att.* II. [c] *Liv.* 5. [d] *Tacit.* 5. *histor.*

---

232 Baldus, *Consilia* 4. 111, fols. 28r f.
233 [Appian, *Punica* 11. 74.]
234 Cicero, *Epistulae ad Atticum* 7. 11. 3.
235 Livy 5. 51–4. **Translator's note:** I have rendered Gentili's word *capeduncula* as "sophistical distinction" on the assumption that he is using it similarly to his other diminutives in this section, *captiuncula* and *distinctiuncula* . In fact, a *capeduncula* should mean a small dish used in sacrifices; cf. Cic. *De natura deorum* 3. 17. 43.
236 Tacitus, *Historiae* 5. 13.

And so, at last, when the Carthaginians were forced to look to their own interests, they were made guilty of the violated treaty and proclaimed as enemies. As though, indeed, either a law or a pact could have any power if one were not permitted to defend oneself.[232] War was at one and the same moment declared and inflicted on them. For that famous and fair ritual of seeking restitution ceased to be in effect. The Carthaginians' very fair excuses were not heard. They were ordered to make satisfaction "in another way." When they asked what this "other way" might be, nothing more was laid out to them beyond the fact that they *knew* what this "other way" was.[233] But the Carthaginians had already condemned all those who they believed had acted against the treaty and the will of the Romans. Now they handed over hostages and other things when so ordered. Furthermore, that which was ordered from the first is now secretly repeated to the consuls: that they will not leave off the war until Carthage should be destroyed—a state which nevertheless was always promised it would remain free. Thus the consuls again order that arms and ships be handed over; ships and arms *are* handed over.

And behold at long last the secret is brought to light: the goal to which they had been tending through so many deceptions and frauds, and which was previously quite thoroughly known and not a secret at all to the Carthaginians. Carthage had to be razed; another city was to be built at a considerable distance from it. Indeed I would exclaim, "O monsters!" But as to the state, which consists of citizens and people, and not the city, which consists of houses and walls, the Carthaginians were promised that it was to be left free. But again, "O monsters and portents of the earth!" Could the promise be p. 51
understood to be about the liberty of the state, when from the time of the First Punic War the state of Carthage was tributary to you and your slave? Thus you used to call Hannibal himself your tributary and your slave. Indeed a base sophism, not even a fixed subtle distinction of sounds, one that lawyers, who entirely depend upon syllables, could not allow without disgust.

Why should I repeat the speech of the consul, the minister of this crime? With this speech he strove to render acceptable to the deceived Carthaginians the overthrow of their country and the building of a new city. A state is not in its walls, but even so it *is* in its altars and hearths, as you, Cicero, used to say against Pompey, who had forsaken his city.[234] Go, Romans, go to the speech of Camillus, the speech that once upon a time kept you in the ruins of your city, in the rubble and the ashes, and which will show you how base and nefarious is that sophistical distinction of yours between a city and a state.[235] "If they were forced to relocate, they feared life more than death," said Tacitus of the Jews.[236] Indeed, is the soil of one's fatherland nothing? Is that land which we call our mother nothing? And the region to which our eyes have become accustomed, and the sky under which we were born and brought up? What of Carthage's location, its farmland, its sea, the tutelary

manus duce fæmina, inter tot vetustos principatus, inter tot gentes validissi-
p. 52 mas ita crevit, ut iam columen omnium facile esset, et censeretur. Ergo æmu-|la illa imperii vestri: quæ et vos bonos esse cogebat, aut simulare: illa deleta Carthago est. Hæc in meridie, Numantia ad occidentem Solem Romanæ improbitatis, et feritatis insignia monumenta. [a] Quid loca, quid urbes peccavere? Quod tu dicis crimen in illis?

De Græcia et Syria.
CAP. IX

Sed quid factum in Oriente? Corinthus, totius Græciæ lumen eversa. [b] Et tu censes, M. Tulli, specie utilitatis in ea disturbanda, et evertenda peccatum. Nam historia clamitat, facinus indignum: quæ oppressa fuerit ante, quam in numerum certorum hostium referretur. [c] Illa commemorare non attinet, quæ Trogus, Pausanias, Polybius, et nemo non litteris tradidit, gesta a Romanis turpiter ad concilium dissolvendum Achaiæ: unde Corinthus, et reliqua Græcia conflagravit. [d] Ita voluerunt et coniunctionem dissolvi Agrippæ, et aliorum in Syria regum: quod Iosephus explanavit. Sane hoc vulgare, *Divide, et impera*, magistri omnis arcani imperii non ignorarunt.

Ceterum ad initia ire oportet, et caussas decet intellexisse, cur Græciam Romani adeundam, armis Orientem aggrediendum existimarint.[e] Græcia petita a Philippo in servitutem, et Annibal ab eodem adiutus pecuniis, auxiliisque, fecerunt eum regem hostem, et arma Romana in Græciam devocarunt. Ita apud Livium.

p. 53 [f] Sed ab | aliis audio, cultumque Philippum a Romanis postea quoque, quam illa Annibali præstita essent, et essent intellecta. [g] Ut, si dissimulatione, et tacito temporis aboletur iniuria, cultu magis aboleatur. [h] *Si tu cum illo postea in gratiam redisti: si domi illius aliquoties fuisti: si ille apud te post cœnavit: utrum te perfidio-*

[a] *Ovid. Met.* 10. [b] *Cic.* 3. *de off. Flor.* 2. [c] *Iust.* 34. *Paus.* 7.
[d] *Iose.* 19. *antiq.* [e] *Liv.* 45. [f] *Zonara.* [g] *l.* 11. *de iniu. l.* 5. *C. eo. Bal. l.* 5. *C. fa. erc.*
[h] *Cic. divin.*

237 Ovid, *Metamorphoses* 10. 230.
238 Cicero, *De officiis* 3. 46; Florus 2. 16. 1.
239 Justin 34. 2; Pausanias 7. 16.
240 Josephus, *Antiquitates Judaicae* 19. 338–42. **Translator's note:** By "Agrippa" is meant Marcus Julius Agrippa II, the last of the Herodians.
241 **Translator's note:** Perhaps *omnes* should be read: "all teachers of the secret of empire are familiar . . ."
242 Livy 45. 22. 6. 243 Zonaras 9. 4; 9. 15.
244 *Digest* 47. 10. 11. 1; *Code* 9. 35. 5; Baldus, *On Code* 3. 36. 5 [*Super primo, secundo, tertio Codicis commentaria*, Lugduni, 1539, fol. 222r].

deity of its place? This is where a small band of exiles, with a woman as leader, amidst so many ancient principalities, amidst so many very powerful peoples, grew so great that it could now easily be the summit of them all—and be deemed as such. Therefore that rival of your empire, which used to p. 52 force you either to be or to pretend to be good, that Carthage was destroyed. Carthage and Numantia were signal monuments of Roman wickedness and savagery, one to Rome's south, the other to her west. How did these places, these cities sin against you? What crime can you name among them?[237]

CHAPTER 9
On Greece and Syria

But what was done in the East? Corinth, the shining ornament of the whole of Greece, was overthrown. Even you, Cicero, decide that a wrong was done, on the pretext of profit, in uprooting and overturning that city.[238] For the historical record cries out against the unworthy crime—that the city was crushed even before it was placed on the official register of open enemies. This is not the place to mention those things which Pompeius Trogus, Pausanias, Polybius, and all the others recorded that the Romans did in order to break up the Achaean League—whence Corinth and the rest of Greece went up in flames.[239] In the same way, they wished to dissolve also the alliance of Agrippa and other kings in Syria—all of which Josephus sets forth.[240] Indeed, the teachers of every sort of secret of empire are familiar with that famous saying, "Divide and rule."[241]

But we need to go back to the beginnings and understand the reasons why the Romans decided that Greece had to be attacked and the East had to be invaded. The attempted enslavement of Greece by Philip V and the aid he gave Hannibal in money and reinforcements made that king Rome's enemy and summoned Roman arms into Greece. So we read in Livy.[242]

But from others I hear that Philip was actually cultivated by the Romans p. 53 even after that aid had been furnished to Hannibal and after it had come to be known.[243] So if an injury is done away with through dissimulation or through the silent passage of time, it may be even more done away when one cultivates the wrongdoer.[244] "If you have been subsequently reconciled to him, if you have on several occasions been at his house, if he has afterwards dined with

sum, an prævaricatorem existimari mavis? ait Cicero contra illum, qui inimicitias sibi dicebat cum Verre: et hæc tamen amici cum Verre animi signa dederat. [a]Etiam dominus servitium recipiens a vasallo inimico, feloniam videtur remittere, et iniuriam: ut sic loquuntur, et censent feudistæ. [b] Etiam qui omittit agere, ut sit gratior, non recte postea petet: ut divus Pius rescripsit. Perfidiosi igitur Romani.

Attamen veteratores nobilissimi nunc non veteres obtendunt iniurias, sed Græciæ libertatem unam. Ad quam videlicet defendendam rogatu accesserint Ætolorum. Quales socii! communes qui essent hostes omnium: rapacem semper, et ferinam ducerent vitam: nihil proprium cuiusque, sed prædæ cuncta exposita deputarent: non pacis, non belli ullum observarent modum: sacrilegi: Græcis omnibus detestabiles: ut hæc, aliaque scribit Polybius plura.

Ad prædandam igitur, non ad servandam Græciam profecti sunt: deducti a p. 54 latronibus publicis: latrones ipsi, et latronum fautores certissimi. Num|quid a sociis coniectura potentissima non fuit semper? Et ipsos non audivimus, vidimus latronum filios? Et ipsos (Romanos dico) non latronum intelligimus tuitores? [c] At superest vestigium legis duodecim tabularum, quæ piraticas societates adprobabat. [d] Exstat Alexandri, et Demetrii regum exprobatio Romanorum latrociniorum, et Romanæ piraticæ. Hæc piratarum latrocinia: quæ grassata maxime in Italia: [e] ut ait Plato. [f] Hæc tum Italia erat, Oenotria illa, Saturni latibulum, Evandri regnum. Caverunt sibi Carthaginenses adversus ea: in legibus primi fœderis adscribentes: ne Romani ultra promontorium Pulcri navigarent aut mercaturæ gratia, aut prædæ. [g] Quid senatusconsultum, quo data senatoribus impunitas tanti criminis est?

[h] Et Balearibus tamen propter huiusmodi improbos paucos bellum inferunt. Propterea inferunt bellum Illyriis: cum horum tamen regina promitteret, effecturam se, ne qua a suis iniuria publice Romanis inferretur. Nam de privatis spondere, aut præstare quis potest? *Singuli nec nocent universitati.* Hoc sub prætextu bellatum cum Histris, cum Dalmatis, cum Liguribus, cum

[a] *Iser. c.* 1. *de fe. si. cu. non am.* [b] *l.* 17. *de usur.*
[c] *l. ult. de colleg. Bod.* 3. *de rep.* 6. [d] *Stra.* 5. [e] *Pla.* 6. *de legi.*
[f] *Virg.* 3. 8. *Æn. et Stra. lib.* 6. [g] *Dion.* 49. [h] *Stra.* 3.

245 Cicero, *Divinatio in Caecilium* 18. 58.

246 Andreas Isernas [Andrea d'Isernia], *De feudo sine culpa non amittendo*, fol. 58v [*In usus feudorum commentaria*, Neapoli, 1571].

247 *Digest* 22. 1. 17. 1.

248 *Digest* 47. 22. 4; Bodin, *De republica* 3. 6. **Translator's note:** The passage in the *Digest* does not say anything concerning pirates—quite to the contrary, nothing agreed upon among the members of an association (*collegium*) may contravene public statutes.

249 Strabo 5. 3. 5.

250 Plato, *Leges* 6, 777 c.

251 Vergil, *Aeneis* 3. 165; 8. 319–23; Strabo 6. 1. 4.

252 Dion. 49. **Translator's note:** There is no 49th book of Dionysius of Halicarnassus. Dio Cassius, whom Gentili usually calls "Dio," has a Book 49, but I cannot find this passage there.

253 Strabo 3. 5. 1.

you, which do you want to be considered: perfidious or crooked?"[245] So says Cicero against that man who had assured him of his hatred for Verres and then nonetheless had given these indications of a disposition friendly to Verres. Even a lord who is receiving the servitude of a vassal who has been hostile to him seems to forgive his breach of feudal vows and the injury he has done, as the experts of feudal laws say and judge.[246] Even he who chooses not to act in order that he might be more ingratiating will not have the right to make a demand later, as the divine Antoninus Pius declared in a rescript.[247] Therefore the Romans were perfidious.

And yet these most noble knaves do not now offer old injuries as a pretext, but solely the liberty of Greece. Supposedly it was to defend this that they came at the request of the Aetolians. What allies were these, the common enemies of all, who lived a rapacious and bestial life always, who considered no one's possessions his own but regarded everything as available for plundering, men who observed no moderation in either peace or war, sacrilegious men, hateful to all the Greeks—as Polybius records all this, and much more.

Thus they set out not to save Greece, but to plunder her—led in by public brigands, brigands themselves, and the most manifest supporters of brigands. Has not the best conjecture about people always been from the company they p. 54
keep? Have we not heard and seen that the Romans were themselves the sons of brigands? Don't we know that they themselves—the Romans, I mean—are the protectors of brigands? And there survives a part of a law of the Twelve Tables that approves of associations of pirates.[248] There exist denunciations by kings Alexander and Demetrius of Roman acts of brigandage and Roman piracy.[249] This was the depredation of pirates that prowled about most extensively in Italy, as Plato says.[250] This is what Italy was then, that famous Oenotria, the hiding place of Saturn, the kingdom of Evander.[251] The Carthaginians protected themselves against this when, in the terms of the first treaty, they adjoined a clause forbidding the Romans to sail past Cap Bon either for the sake of trade or booty. What of the senatorial decree granting senators immunity from such a charge?[252]

And yet they waged war against the Balearic Islanders because of just a few men of this sort.[253] For this reason they waged war against the Illyrians, even though their queen promised them that she would see to it that no injury might be inflicted on the Romans by her people in an official capacity—for who can give an assurance or answer for what is done by private men? "Private individuals do no harm to the whole group." Under this pretext war was waged with the Istrians, the Dalmatians, the Ligurians, and with others from

aliis ab urbe condita: a prædonibus istis ab urbe condita: nec odio latrociniorum, sed quod soli esse latrones cuperent latrones in bello, latrones in pace:

p. 55 [a] Iudicium in Ardeatium, et Aricinorum | caussa an obscurum? quo rem litigiosam neutri partium, sed sibi boni arbitri addixerunt. Iudicium turpi in caussa Neapolitanorum, et Nolanorum ignoramus? [b] An mentitum te, Cicero, existimemus: qui, piratarum fidem meliorem, quam senatus, aliquando facis? An illic, ubi piratas immunes, socios vectigales vobis narras? Audin', piratas immunes? Adiunge aliis testimonium. Audin', socios vectigales? Adde (quod nunc dicimus) spoliatos, nudatos. Quid mihi paucorum paupertatem, aut etiam integritatem obiicies: si opes aliorum immensas, et privatorum, et publici cernimus? Non ego Verrem accuso, sed populum everriculum orbis.

Ceterum a bellis, et ab Ætolis non discedamus. [c] His auxilia nec submissa, at speculatores rerum Macedonicarum immissos, Pausanias notat. [d] Et itaque Ætolos desertos (Livii utor verbis) quibus voluit conditionibus ad petendam, et paciscendam secum pacem Philippus subegit. Atque hoc tamen in partem pessimam Romani capiunt: et Ætolis sic irascuntur vehementissime. Quid autem? Exscindi se, spectantes auxilia vestra, veluti Saguntini, exspectassent.

Sic Saguntinis, sic Mamertinis, sic Ætolis; sic aliis post collisas omnium vires vos integri supervenire malebatis versuti. [e]*Non defendi homines sine*
p. 56 *vituperatione fortasse possunt, sed defendi negligenter sine scelere non | possunt*: Cicero dixit. Quid igitur vobis hic est, qui Ætolos defendebatis et negligenter, et fraudolenter? Verum elegans est commentum alterum, quo in Ætolos ipsos moventur pro Acarnensibus. [f] Nempe soli Acarnanes Ilium non profecti olim: et matrem illam Æneadum cum reliquis Græcis, et cum his ipsis Ætolis non oppugnarunt. Putabamus, Romanis ingeniis usquam defuisse acumen? [g] Sic sane Turca mirabatur, Italos pro Græcis stare, non potius secum ire [h] *ultum avos Troiæ, templa et temerata Minervæ.*

[a] *Diony. ult. Liv.* 3. *Val.* 7. *c.* 5. [b] *Cic.* 3. *de. off.*
[c] *Paus.* 7. [d] *Liv.* 29. [e] *Ammian.* 30. [f] *Iusti.* 28.
[g] *Mont.* 2. *ess.* 36. [h] *Virg.* 6.

254 Dionysius of Halicarnassus 5. 61–2; Livy 3. 71–2; Valerius Maximus 7. 5.

255 **Translator's note:** Both editions print *turpis*, which makes no sense. I assume that *turpi* was meant. Cf. the phrase *turpis causa* in Caesar, *Bellum civile* 3. 20.

256 Cicero, *De officiis* 3. 87.

257 [Cicero, *De officiis* 3. 49.]

258 [Cicero labeled Verres an *everriculum* in the second speech *In Verrem*, 2. 4. 53.]

259 Pausanias 7. 7. 7.

260 Livy 29. 12. 1.

261 Cicero, quoted in Ammianus Marcellinus 30. 4. 7.

262 Justin 28. 1.

263 Montaigne, *Essays* 2. 36.

264 Vergil, *Aeneis* 6. 840.

the time of the founding of the city—and waged by those who were freebooters from the time of the founding of the city—not through hatred of acts of brigandage, but because they wanted to be the only brigands around: brigands in wartime, brigands in peacetime.

Was the judgment in the dispute between the people of Ardea and Aricia at p. 55
all obscure, by which those fine judges settled the matter in dispute to the satisfaction of neither party but to their own?[254] Do we not know of the judgment in the base dispute between the people of Naples and those of Nola?[255] Or should we judge that you were lying, Cicero, when you made the trustworthiness of pirates out to be sometimes better than that of the Senate?[256] Or were you lying when you said that pirates were immune, but allies were subject to taxation?[257] Do you hear? Pirates are immune. Add that testimony to the others. Do you hear? Allies are subject to taxation. Add (which we have just said) that they are despoiled, left naked. Why do you hold up to me the poverty or even the integrity of a few men, when we see the vast wealth of other private men—and of the public? I, for one, do not accuse Verres of being a dragnet of plunder, but rather I accuse the whole Roman people of being the dragnet of the plunder of the whole world.[258]

But let us not get distracted from wars and from the Aetolians. Pausanias notes that what were sent to the Aetolians were not reinforcements but spies on the affairs of the Macedonians.[259] And so Philip reduced the Aetolians who had been abandoned by the Romans (I am using the words of Livy here) to seek and conclude peace with him on whatever terms he wished.[260] And yet the Romans took this in the worst possible sense and so were extremely angry with the Aetolians. But why? Was it as though they were expecting them to destroy themselves while awaiting your aid, like the Saguntines?

Thus you shrewd people preferred to come upon the Saguntines, the Mamertines, the Aetolians, and others with your own forces intact after the powers of all the other parties had been shattered. "Perhaps men cannot be defended without the defenders incurring censure, but they cannot be defended negligently without the imputation of wickedness"—so said p. 56
Cicero.[261] What, then, have you to say for yourselves, you who defended the Aetolians both negligently and fraudulently? Indeed it was another clever trick by which the Romans were moved against the Aetolians themselves on behalf of the Acarnanians. Supposedly, the Acarnanians were the only ones who did not set forth once upon a time for Troy, and so they did not besiege that mother of the sons of Aeneas along with the rest of the Greeks—among them these same Aetolians.[262] What?—did we suppose that Roman wits ever lacked subtlety? This is very much like how a Turk used to wonder that Italians stood up for Greeks[263] and did not join him in going "to avenge the ancestors of Troy and the violated temple of Minerva."[264]

[a] Atque tandem hos ipsos socios Ætolos: quorum inductu, opibusque vicerunt Macedoniam, suum sub imperium cur redegerint, si quis de Romanis petat; responsum non accipiet magis, quam hoc ipsum interroganti alicubi Alexandro responderit Iulius Cæsar. Ætolorum casu oppressus Antiochus, et in regna Orientis penetratum est. Quæ quidem regna attrectarunt certe impudenter: si ([b]quod est in historiis) Iudæis a rege suo deficientibus libertatem tribuerunt, fœderatos se adiunxerunt: libertatem (ait Trogus) facile largiti sunt de alieno. [c] Videlicet hæc quoque species lucri est, utcumque inodori (nam furtum est) de alieno largiri. At his furibus omnibus, non uni eorum sordido, bonus odor lucri ex re qualibet.

p. 57 Sic tenent Græciam. Quomodo insula Græciæ? [d] Creta est Metelli | præda perfidiæ, et ambitionis: et Cretici tamen cognomento insigniti ad laudem posteritatis: ad æmulationem Macedonici, Numidici, Dalmatici, Balearici, itidem Metellorum. *Fato Metelli Romæ fiunt consules.* Sed Macedonicus factus: nec tamen cum iusto hoste rem habuit in Macedonia. Factus Numidicus: cum eius succcessor provinciam illam vicerit, et Iugurtham regem. Factus Dalmaticus: de amicis, et hospitibus agens triumphum, et nomen referens quod Appianus ait. Factus Balearicus, factus Creticus: quemadmodum modo dicebamus.

O vanos, o iniquos! [e] Tenent Cyprum, Clodii quæstum turpissimum, ab omnibus scriptoribus vituperatum: a Catone tamen illo sanctissimo, an perinvito? itaque factum civitatis condemnante: sed certe non sine grandi nota avaritiæ intolerandæ confectum: ut qui etiam venena vendiderit: [f] quæ perdi, volunt leges, et corrumpi protinus.

Nunc de Antiocho absolvamus. [g] Blanditi et huic sunt muneribus, legationibus, dum simul timent a Philippo: insultarunt mox: et nullam pacis, aut honestæ, aut tolerabilis, spem reliquerunt. Ita et cum Perseo post: ita cum aliis egerunt omnibus. Ut, si quid secum non probe actum caussati semel potuerint, id alia ratione emendari passi sint nunquam, quam adversæ partis p. 58 exscidio supremo. Nam quod illud a Per|seo actum est, quod expiari non

[a] *Iulia. Cæss.* [b] 1. *Macc.* 14. *Iust.* 36. [c] *l.* 54. *de fur.*
[d] *Dio.* 36. *Flor.* 3. [e] *Amm.* 14. *Dio.* 38. *Cic. pro Sex. et Sex. Ruf. Flor.* 3.
[f] *l.* 4. *fam. erc.* [g] *Zon. Liv.* 33.

265 [Julian, *Caesares* 324 AB. This is a dialogue of the dead featuring Alexander, Julius Caesar, and various Roman emperors.]

266 1 Maccabees 8 [14?]; Justin 36. 3.

267 *Digest* 47. 2. 55. 1.

268 [Naevius, quoted by Ps.-Asconius on Cicero, *In Verrem* 1. 29.]

269 Ammianus Marcellinus 14. 8. 15; Dio Cassius 38. 30. 5; Cicero, *Pro Sestio* 26. 56. 7; Festus, *Breviarium rerum gestarum populi Romani* 13. 1; Florus 3. 9. 1–5.

270 *Digest* 10. 2. 4. 1–2.

271 Zonaras 9. 20; Livy 33. 30–1. **Translator's note:** Livy describes the terms of the peace reached.

And if anyone should ask why they finally reduced those very Aetolian allies of theirs, at whose invitation and with whose help they defeated Macedonia, one would get no more of an answer than Julius Caesar gave Alexander somewhere when he asked the same question.[265] Antiochus was reduced to dire straits by the disaster of the Aetolians, and the Romans made inroads into the kingdoms of the East. Assuredly, they meddled with these kingdoms imprudently if (as is recorded in the histories[266]) they bestowed freedom upon the Jews who were revolting from their own king and joined themselves to them as allies. It was easy for them to bestow liberty upon them when it was not theirs to give (as Pompeius Trogus says). Clearly, this also is a kind of gain, though it lacks the good odor of one (for it is, after all, a theft): to bestow something from someone else's property.[267] But for all these thieves, not just for one sleazy specimen among them, a good odor of profit emanated from whatever opportunity came their way.

This is how they came into possession of Greece. And how did they get the Greek island of Crete? Crete was the booty of the perfidy and the p. 57
ambition of Metellus, distinguished by the cognomen Creticus to the glory of his descendants, in emulation of the cognomina Macedonicus, Numidicus, Dalmaticus, and Balearicus—likewise acquired by members of the Metellus family. "It's our fate that the Metelli become consuls at Rome."[268] But the Metellus who became Macedonicus had no dealings with a legitimate enemy in Macedonia. And another became Numidicus even though it was his successor who conquered that province and King Jugurtha. And the one who became Dalmaticus got the name by celebrating a triumph over friends and hosts, as Appian says. And a Metellus became Balearicus and Creticus in the manner we have just been mentioning.

O vain men! O unjust men! They possess Cyprus, the most disgraceful acquisition of Clodius, criticized by all the writers, subdued by that most holy man, Cato the Younger. Did he do so unwillingly and thereby condemn the action of his state? But he certainly did not do so without abundant indication of intolerable ambition.[269] He acted like one who sells poisons that the laws wish to be straightway thrown away and destroyed.[270]

Now let us deal quickly with Antiochus. They flattered him, too, with gifts and embassies while they had something to fear from Philip; but soon they abused him and left him no hope of a peace that was either respectable or bearable.[271] They dealt in similarly fashion with Perseus later on—and likewise with all the others. They dealt with them in such a way that, if once they could allege that they had been improperly treated in some respect, they would never allow restitution by any other method than by the most extreme destruction of the other party. For what was it that Perseus did that p. 58

potuerit aliter, quam si se, regnumque suum, et sua omnia dedidisset? Vestris amicis iniurius fuit? Immo his restitit, iniuriam, et arma inferentibus. Qui vestræ controversiæ cardo est. Si enim vera Persei est isthæc defensio, quam [a] Livius recitat: nihil attinet, de iure fœderis disputare. Sed et fœdus amplexurum se Perseus, quod contraxerat pater, iam ait: et iam sic potest: [b] et in contractibus bonæ fidei (quales omnes sunt principum) semper admitti debet purgatio moræ, quod omnes tradunt interpretes iuris. Purgatio moræ fundata in æquitate est: et itaque Canonico iure, quod æquitatem respicit, semper admittitur: coram principe, qui æquitatem respicere habet vel maxime, admitti debet vel maxime.

Sed ecce, etiam Perseus, satisfacturum Romanis per omnia, etiam cum vicisset nobili prælio, spondet ultro: nec auditur, nisi se dedat, et de summa rerum senatui liberum permittat de se, deque universa Macedonia statuendi ius. [c] Sed hoc ius non est, sumere bellum quasi in iniurium, qui iure agere, et satisfacere paratus est. Fœdus abrupit? Pœnituit. Vos igitur abrumpitis: qui pœnitentiam non admittitis. [d] Si pœnituit eum, qui libellum divortii dedit: at is, qui accepit, matrimonium solvere voluit: et per istum solvi matrimonium dicitur.

p. 59 Ecce pœnamque spondet Perseus, non | affert vobis pœnitentiam solam, [e] *Est autem ulciscendi, et puniendi modus*. Haud autem scis, Cicero, an satis sit, eum, qui lacessierit, iniuriæ suæ pœnitere? [f] Aristoteles ait, et cum Aristotele interpretes iuris, nihil errare iudices, qui liberent reum usque adeo emendatum, ut nihil præterea delinquere velit. An tu nescis, M. Tulli? At scis tamen, et dicis satis. At etiam scribis rotunde, *Ulciscamur eos, qui nocere nobis conati sunt: tantaque pœna afficiamus, quantam æquitas, humanitasque patiatur*. An ergo Persei facinus tantum, quod dictam a vobis mereretur pœnam? [g] Iustum est bellum pro rebus repetendis, sed quoadusque sit satisfactum. Vere hic, vere, quod ait Pindarus, [h] *Contentionem, susceptam adversus potentiores, deponere, difficile*. Etiam quid Antiochus tantum meruit mali, ut nisi maxima

[a] *Liv.* 42. [b] *Dec.* 2. *cons.* 32. [c] *Thucyd.* 1. [d] *l.* 7. *de divor.*
[e] *Cic.* 1. 2. *de off.* [f] *Decian.* 2. *cons.* 5.
[g] *Cur. Castr. l.* 4. *de iu.* et *iu.* [h] *Pind. Olymp.* 10.

---

[272] Livy 42. 25. 8–12.

[273] Decio, *Consilia* 2. 32 [the reference is unclear; neither Consilium 32 nor Consilium 232 fits here, the only Consilium where Decio deals with *purgatio morae* being Consilium 452, where *purgatio* is admitted only in the context of equity in canon law: *Consiliorum pars quarta*, Lugduni, Apud Iacobum Giuntam, 1546, fol. 12r (for circumstances that do not admit of *purgatio* see fol. 12v)]. **Translator's note:** *Purgatio morae* is the purging of a failure to discharge a legal duty in Roman law.

[274] Thucydides 1. 85. 2. [275] *Digest* 24. 2. 7.

[276] Cicero, *De officiis* 1. 33.

[277] Decianus, *Consilia* 2. 5, fol. 37v.

[278] [Cicero, *De officiis* 2. 18.]

[279] *Cur.* [probably Franciscus Curtius Junior (Francesco Corti)]; Paulus Castrensis [Paolo de Castro], *On Digest* 1. 1. 5, fol. 4v [*Prima super Digesto veteri, commentariorum in Digestum vetus pars prima*, (Lugduni, Apud S. Gryphium,) 1531.] **Translator's note:** Cf. Cicero, *De officiis* 1. 36: "Ex quo intellegi potest nullum bellum esse iustum, nisi quod aut rebus repetitis geratur aut denuntiatum ante sit et indictum."

[280] Pindar, *Olympian Odes* 10. 39–40.

could not be expiated in any other way than if he surrendered himself, his kingdom, and all he possessed? Was he harmful to your allies? Indeed he did resist them when they were bringing injury and arms upon him. Hence arose the key point of your dispute. For if that defense of Perseus related by Livy is true, it is irrelevant to dispute over the terms of the alliance.[272] But Perseus now said that he was going to embrace the treaty that his father had contracted, and now he was able to do so; and in contracts in good faith (as are all of those of princes) a *purgatio morae* always ought to be admitted, as all the interpreters of the law hand down.[273] *Purgatio morae* is founded in fairness, and thus it is always admitted in canon law, which has a regard for fairness. In the presence of a prince, who is required to have a regard for fairness to the highest degree, it ought to the highest degree be admitted.

But behold: Perseus went so far as to promise of his own accord to make amends to the Romans, even when he had emerged victorious from a noble battle; but he was not heard, unless he were to yield himself up and grant the Senate the free right of making decisions about the general welfare of himself and of all of Macedonia. But this is not just: to undertake a war as though against a wrongdoer when it is in fact someone who is ready to act justly and to offer satisfaction.[274] Did he break the treaty? He was sorry for it. You, therefore, broke the treaty in that you did not accept his penitence. Thus, if the person who files a petition for divorce changes his mind, but he who accepted the petition wishes to dissolve the marriage, then the marriage is said to be dissolved through the action of that man.[275]

Behold: Perseus promises to pay a penalty; he doesn't just offer you his p. 59
penitence. "But there is some limit to taking vengeance and punishing."[276] But do you go on to say, Cicero, that you scarcely know if it is enough that he who has done harm repents of his injury? Aristotle says—and with Aristotle the interpreters of the law—that those judges do no wrong who free a defendant who has reformed to the point where he wishes no longer to do wrong.[277] Are you unaware of that, Cicero? But at least you know and say enough: "Let us punish those who have attempted to harm us; let us visit them with just so much punishment as fairness and humanity would allow."[278] Was the crime of Perseus so great as to deserve the punishment decreed by you? A war made for reparations is just, but only up to the point where satisfaction is achieved.[279] Very true in this instance is what Pindar said: "It is hard to set aside a dispute undertaken against those who are more powerful."[280] Further, what did Antiochus do to deserve so much evil that he

imperii parte spoliatus, ingenti stipendio oppressus, immani pecuniarum summa multatus, classe exsutus, elephantis privatus, pacem a vobis nequierit obtinere? O profundam imperii cupidinem, et divitiarum! Hæc una bellandi caussa dicta Sallustio vestro, an non de vobis? Annibal certe, cum rex iste splendidum belli in vos apparatum suum ostentaret, satis, inquit, Romanis, etsi illi avari valde sunt.

p. 60

De Mithridate, et Annibale.
CAP. X

Superest Mithridates. Hunc artibus consuetis circumventum a Romanis, liquet. [a] Nam scimus, instigatum Nicomedem, qui fines Mithridatis infestaret: et vinceretur: itaque pro victo socio bellum ipsi susciperent, et vincerent victorem regem. Hoc istorum institutum perpetuum, tentare per alios prius, quem ipsi aggredi constituerent: eius vires imminuere, certe intelligere, et artes cognoscere in re præsenti, et in ipso experimento, non per coniecturas, et ambages, quæ fallerent.

[b] At iustitiæ colorandæ et illud Iasonis Thessali didicere, *Opus esse, ut iure facere iniuriam possis, alium tibi fuisse iniurium prius.* Atque hoc aliud Romanæ dominationis arcanum fuit: ut tenderent amicitias late, et acciperent in societatem plurimos: non ideo ut amicos, sociosque defenderent, et ornarent: sed ut illorum occasione alios opprimere possent, qui sociis suis, et amicis molesti esse viderentur. *Noster populus sociis defendendis, terrarum iam omnium potitus est*: ut erat Ciceronis testimonium. Atque ut hoc est defendere, si evertas omnes, et cuncta rapias ad te unum. Hoc est patrocinium, [c] quod itidem Cicero iactat, orbis terræ, si orbem terræ exsuas libertate, dominationi tuæ subiicias.

p. 61 Sic sane, sic fuit illa sociorum defensio, quemad|modum et Cæsar contestatur, [d]*Maiores nostri tantam urbem nostram fecerunt, cum suas fortunas, tamquam, alienam possessionem semper periculis obiecerunt: aliorum autem ditionem, tamquam pertinentem ad se haud cunctanter suam facerent.* Itaque vicerint Mithridatem: et regna illius sua fecerint. [e] Vicerint Mithridatem? *Pompeius*

[a] *App. Mithrid.* [b] *Arist.* 1. *rhet.* [c] *Cic.* 2. *de off.* [d] *Dio.* 38. [e] *Pater.* 2.

---

281 Appian, *Mithridatica* 11.

282 Aristotle, *Rhetorica* 1373 A. **Translator's note:** This seems confused. Jason of Pherai is cited there as saying that one should commit a few crimes so as to be able then to do a number of acts of justice.

283 [Cicero, *De republica* 3. 35. Gentili must have known this passage from Nonius 498. 18.]

284 Cicero, *De officiis* 2. 27.

285 Dio Cassius 38. 37. 4. **Translator's note:** The concluding phrases in Dio can more simply be rendered: "always putting their own things at risk as though they belonged to others, and readily taking possession of other's things as though they were their own."

was stripped of the greatest part of his empire, oppressed with a huge levy, fined a huge sum of money, deprived of his fleet and elephants, and yet was unable to obtain peace from us? O the profound lusts for rule and riches! This was the sole cause of going to war mentioned by your Sallust—and was he not talking about you? Hannibal indeed, when that king was displaying his magnificent preparations for war against you, said: "This is enough for the Romans, no matter how exceedingly grasping they are."

CHAPTER 10 p. 60

On Mithridates and Hannibal

There remains Mithridates. It is clear that this man was deceived by the Romans through their customary tricks. For we know that Nicomedes was urged on to harass the borders of Mithridates and to be defeated, so that the Romans themselves could undertake a war on behalf of their defeated ally and defeat the victorious king.[281] This was the standard procedure of those people: to make an attempt through others upon someone they themselves decided to move against; to diminish his forces, gather clear intelligence, and learn his procedures on the spot in an actual test, not through guesses and roundabout methods, which tend to let one down.

But for giving the appearance of justice they have also learned that saying of Jason of Pherae: "In order that you might be able to commit an injustice justly, it is necessary that there first be some other injury against you."[282] And this was another secret of Roman domination: that they would offer friendships far and wide and accept very many people into an alliance, not so that they might defend and honor their friends, but so that they might use them as an excuse to be able to oppress others who might seem to be troublesome to their allies and friends. "By defending its allies our people have now gotten control over all the lands," as was Cicero's testimony.[283] As if *this* were defending: if one overthrew everyone and carried off everything for yourself alone. This is that protection of the whole world that Cicero likewise discusses—if you deprive the world of its liberty and subject it to your own domination.[284]

Thus, indeed, thus was that defense of allies to which Caesar also bore p. 61
witness: "Our ancestors made our city so great since they always exposed their own resources to dangers as though they were the property of others—and without hesitation appropriated other people's political authority as though it naturally belonged to them."[285] And so they would have defeated Mithridates and made his kingdoms their own. They would have *defeated* Mithridates?

per ambages, et moras fregerit invictum: ut sic Ammianus. Vicerint Mithridatem, *omnium sui iuris regum ultimum: bello acerrimum, virtute eximium aliquando fortuna, semper animo maximum*: ut sic est Paterculi testimonium.

Ego tamen quid dico victum? Etiam hic parricidas Romanos defero. [a] Aut si filio Pharnaci auctores parricidii non fuere: ei cur in parricidii præmium tribuere regnum paternum? cur sociis, et amicis parricidam adscribunt? [b] *Cæsaris iniussu cæcidit Farnesius heros, at data sunt iussu præmia sicariis*: cecinit ille in Carolum V. qui suo cæsum iussu negabat Farnesium, Parmæ ducem: sed, præmia sicariis a se data, negare non poterat. O mendax carmen, [c]*Romani scelerum semper sprevere ministros.* [d] Proditori arcis Artenæ, præter libertatem, an non etiam duarum familiarum bona in præmium data? [e] Demetrio proditori Illyriorum non præmia contributa? [f] Papirius Cursor (laudatos laudo) non
p. 62 corrupit Tarentinum legatum: qui arcem sibi proderet? [g] Quid dicam Me|telli, illius Numidici, plura eiuscemodi tentamenta? [h] Ipse Bocchus non socius populi Romani dictus, ac multa Numidiæ parte donatus: quia Iugurtham prodidit socerum parricida? O solentissimum usque a patre Romulo Romanorum crimen.

At pergo, Magni Pompeii os illud accusare probum, cetera non probum. [i] Albanos, et cognatos, et pactis securos, opprimit. [j]*Albani, memores Italicæ originis, exercitum Cn. Pompeii fratres salutavere*, Perfidus Phraati est. Antiochum spoliat regno Syriæ, inermem, et nunquam de populo Romano meritum male, prætextu inepto. Huius est probi oris vox illa improbissima, *Armatus ut leges cogitem*? Et propter hæc, quæ ad animum suorum pertinebant, dictus iste Magnus? Aut adulati sic sunt homini: qui longe inferior prioribus ducibus? [k] sic aiunt. Sed et Pompeium mitto.

Et quemadmodum rapior huc, illuc Romanorum sceleribus plurimis, ita et feror oratione, nec satis cum certo ordine. Ecce vobis Mithridates, eximius ille, et acerrimus, et maximus, parricidio Romanorum in Septentrione extinctus: et ad eam partem terrarum, quæ superesse videbatur incontaminata, scelerum Romanorum monumentum iacet.

[a] *Dio.* 37. *App. Mithr.* [b] *Nat. Co.* 3. [c] *Claud.* [d] *Liv.* 4. [e] *App. Illyr.*
[f] *Front.* 3. [g] *Sallust. Iugur.* [h] *Sigo.* 1. *De an. iu. pr.* 17. [i] *Dio.* 37. *App. Syr.*
[j] *Iustin.* 42. [k] *Iulia. Cæss.*

---

[286] Ammianus Marcellinus 29. 5. 33. **Translator's note:** What Ammianus actually wrote was that Theodosius "intended to overcome through roundablout methods and delays an enemy who was shattering his own attacks, as once Pompey did to Mithridates": "per ambages et moras hostem frangentem suos impetus oppressurus, ut quondam Pompeius Mithridatem."

[287] **Translator's note:** Velleius Paterculus; a composite of 2. 40. 1 and 2. 18. 1.

[288] Dio Cassius 37. 14; Appian, *Mithridatica* 16. 113.

[289] Natalis Comes [Natale Conti], *Universae historiae sui temporis libri triginta*, bk. 3, Venetiis, Apud Zenarum, 1581.

[290] Claudian, *De bello Gildonico* 1. 270. [291] Livy 4. 61. 10. [292] Appian, *Illyrica* 8.

[293] Frontinus, *Strategemata* 3. 3. 1. [294] Sallust, *Bellum Jugurthinum* 61 (Bomilcar); 83 (Bocchus).

[295] Sigonius, *De antiquo iure provinciarum* 1. 17, col. 533 [Sigonio, *Opera Omnia*, Tomus V, Mediolani, 1736].

[296] **Translator's note:** The phrase *illud os probrum* derives from Pliny the Elder, *Naturalis Historia* 7. 53, on the two "body doubles" of Pompey the Great.

[297] Dio Cassius 37. 3–5; Appian, *Mithridatica* 114. [Cf. also Livy, *Periochae* 101.]

"Through roundabout methods and delays, Pompey broke down the undefeated man," as Ammianus says.[286] They would have defeated Mithridates, "the last of the independent kings, most brave in war, preeminent in valor, always the greatest in spirit—and sometimes in success," as is the testimony of Vellcius Patcrculus.[287]

And yet why do I call him "defeated"? Precisely here I indict the Romans as parricides. Or if they were not the instigators of parricide for his son Pharnaces, why did they grant him his father's kingdom as a price for his parricide? Why did they enroll a parricide among their allies and friends?[288] "Not under Caesar's orders did the Farnesian hero fall, but at his orders rewards were sent to the assassins," as a certain author [Natalis Comes] wrote against Charles V, who denied that [Pier Luigi] Farnese, duke of Parma, had been killed under his orders.[289] Oh what a lying poem has this: "The Romans always spurned the ministers of crimes."[290] To the betrayer of the citadel of Artena did they not grant, in addition to liberty, even the possessions of two families as a reward?[291] Were not rewards bestowed upon Demetrius, the betrayer of the Illyrians?[292] Did not Papirius Cursor (I am simply praising those who have been praised) corrupt the Tarentine ambassador to hand over the citadel to him?[293] Why should I mention the attempts of this sort by that famous Metellus Numidicus?[294] Was not Bocchus himself declared an ally of the Roman people and granted a large portion of Numidia, because as a parricide he betrayed his son-in-law Jugurtha?[295] Oh, the most customary crime of the Romans from the time of father Romulus himself! p. 62

But I proceed now to accuse that "noble countenance" of Pompey the Great—but really not at all honorable.[296] He overwhelmed the Albani who were both relatives and protected by pacts.[297] "The Albani, remembering their Italian origin, greeted the army of Gnaeus Pompey as brothers."[298] He is faithless to Phraates. He plunders Antiochus of his kingdom of Syria, a man harmless and never deserving ill of the Romans, on a flimsy pretext. This very base utterance came from the honorable mouth of this man: "When in arms, am I to think of laws?"[299] And was it for these things, things that had a real bearing on the character of his people, that he was called "the Great"? Did they flatter the man thus, who was far inferior to earlier leaders? So they say, anyway.[300] But I'm giving up Pompey as well here.

And just as I am hurried along in this direction and in that by the very many crimes of the Romans, so am I carried along in my discourse, and not with a sufficiently fixed order. Behold, there you have Mithridates—that famous preeminent man, the most brave, the greatest—killed up in the north by an act of parricide engineered by the Romans—to be a monument to Roman crimes for that part of the world which seemed to remain as yet uncontaminated by them.

[298] Justin 42. 3. 4. [299] [Cf. Plutarch, *Pompeius* 623 D.] [300] Julian, *Caesares* 322 C–23 B.

[a] Nescis, Viriatum in Hispania? Non diximus; Iugurtham in Africa?
p. 63 Annibalem apud suos in Africa, apud alios in Asia, et Europa turpibus | petitum dolis Romanorum, ignorat nemo. Equidem audio nunquam Annibalis vocem illam supremam, [b]*Liberemus diuturna cura populum Romanum: quando mortem senis exspectare longum censent: et legatum consularem, qui auctor esset Prusiæ per scelus occidendi hospitis, miserunt*: hanc ego Annibalis orationem nunquam memini, quin ad immanitatem, et turpitudinem Romanam non cohorrescam.

[c] Nobilissimum illum ducem: cuius parem sol hactenus non aspexit: qui magis noluit, quam nequiit, Romanos vincere; aut potuerit vincere, nisi domi civium suorum invidia debilitatus fuisset: qui Romanos in Italia vicit semper: et post Cannensem pugnam castra in campo contraria non invenit: callidissimo etiam verba dedit Fabio: et invictus defensum patriam revocatus est. Ut hæc Cornelius Nepos.

Hunc ducem dum crudelitatis, impietatis, perfidiæ video accusari a Romanis testibus, non commovear vehementer? Ecquæ tu crudelia, Livi, impia, perfida Annibalis recensere potes? [d]*Iussit, puberes Sagunti omnes occidi: crudele, ceterum et necessarium*, ais tu: et iustum ego ex iure belli defendo: adeoque nec fuisse crudele. Quid Romani tui? [e]*Aennam aut malo, aut necessario facinore retentam*, scribis a tuis, et exsecrabile facinus nec a Marcello improbatum.
p. 64 [f] Quid in eadem Hispania cum Numantinis | egit Africanus? Fame eos confecit, morte longe sævissima: dum conditionibus nullis eos excipit, vere crudelis: nec armis sperat urbe potiri, pro timido sapiens nuncupatus. An conditiones Annibal nullas Saguntinis tulit? Ubi crudelitas? An non capit vi Saguntinos, et per virtutem? Quid in bello isto cum Annibale Maximus ille, unus qui cunctando vobis restituit rem? Proditione Brutiorum Tarentum recepit: sed, ad hanc proditionis famam exstinguendam, ante omnes trucidari Brutios imperavit. Cæsi et Tarentini plurimi, et venditi reliqui sub hasta sunt. Is perfidus: is crudelis. [g] Et vero sic traditur perfidiæ, et crudelitatis aspersus nota.

[a] *Iusti.* 31. [b] *Liv.* 39. [c] *Cor. Ne. Ann. Plut. de for. Ro. App. Ann. Iusti.* 38.
[d] *Liv.* 21. [e] *Liv.* 34. [f] *App.* 4. *civili.* [g] *Plut. Fab.*

---

301 Livy 39. 51. 9–11.
302 Cornelius Nepos, *Hannibal*; Plutarch, *De fortuna Romanorum*; Appian, *Hannibalica*; Justin 38.
303 Livy 21. 14. 3.
304 Livy 24. 39. 7.
305 Appian, *Iberica* 84–98. [Scipio Africanus the Younger is meant.]
306 Plutarch, *Fabius Maximus* 21–2.

Are you unaware of the fate of Viriathus in Spain? Have we not mentioned that of Jugurtha in Africa? And no one is unaware that Hannibal was attacked by the base tricks of the Romans among his own people in Africa p. 63
and among others in both Asia and Europe. Indeed, whenever I hear those famous last words of Hannibal—"Let us free the Roman people from their longstanding worry, since they consider it too long to wait for an old man's death; and they have sent an ambassador of consular rank to serve as Prusias's agent for the crime of killing of a guest"[301]—I say, I never call to mind that speech of Hannibal without shuddering at the cruelty and baseness of the Romans.

Most noble was that leader, whose equal the sun has not yet looked upon, who was more unwilling than unable to defeat the Romans, or he could well have defeated them had he not been weakened at home by the ill will of his own citizens; a man who always defeated the Romans in Italy and after the battle of Cannae found no enemy camp left in the field, who even tricked the very crafty Fabius, and was finally called away, still undefeated, to defend his homeland.[302] This is how Cornelius Nepos tells it.

When I see this leader accused of cruelty, impiety, treachery by Roman witnesses, am I not passionately upset? What cruel, impious, perfidious acts of Hannibal can you record, Livy? "He ordered all the adult males of Saguntum to be killed—a cruel act, but necessary."[303] So you say; and for my part, I defend it on the basis of the law of war, and in addition I say that it was not cruel. And what about your Romans? You write that Henna was held onto by your people "either through a wicked or a necessary crime"—and it was a detestable crime which Marcellus did not find fault with.[304] How did Scipio Africanus deal with the Numantines in that same Spain?[305] He did p. 64
them in by starving them out, a death by far the most savage, while he accepted no conditions from them, truly cruel man that he was; nor did he hope to gain possession of the city by force of arms, a man dubbed wise instead of what he was: timid. Did Hannibal offer no terms to the Saguntines? Where is the cruelty in that? Did he not capture the Saguntines through violence and valor? What comparison can there be in that war between Hannibal and that famous Fabius Maximus, the one man who by delaying saved the situation for you? He recovered Tarentum through the betrayal of the Bruttians, but in order to snuff out the report of this betrayal he ordered all the Bruttians to be slaughtered first. Very many of the Tarentines were cut down as well, and the rest were sold under the auctioneer's spear. It was he who was treacherous, he who was cruel. And indeed he is recorded as having been branded by the stain of this perfidy and cruelty.[306]

Numquid tamen singula memorem singulorum? [a] Romani non modo homines quosvis in captis civitatibus obvios cædere, sed et canes dissecare, et alia animalia membratim truncare soliti. Adde alia Annibalis, Livi. *Vicuvias, tamquam vi captas, non deditas, diripiendas tradidit.* Sed non me dies deficeret, si talia laudatissimorum Romanorum exponere velim? [b] Quid enim de Pomœtia scribis tu actum a tuis? *Nihilominus fœde actum cum ea dedita, quam si capta foret: principes securi percussi, alii venditi, urbs diruta.*

[c] Quid unus ille in optimis optimatum Æmilius, immo quid senatus cum urbibus Epiri egit septuaginta? Sub amicitiæ specie eas ingressus, dolo malo,
p. 65 peiori | perfidia, mendaciis turpissimis, diripit, et subvertit, et millia capitum centum quinquaginta rapit in servitutem. Non recito, quæ sunt innumera. Sed an Vicuvias tu non vi captas existimas? ad quas in eruptionibus pugnatum: ductus exercitus victor duorum consulum est. Num censes, agi tamquam cum deditis oportere semper, ubi se dedant aliqui, etsi isti iam, iam capti forent? Quid igitur prohibet, quominus vi capiatur nemo?

Sed Livi, perge. [d] *Maharbal fidem dat dedentibus se, abituros incolumes Annibal* (*quæ Punica fides*) *in vincula omnes coniecit.* Et iudicas igitur, iniussu maioris ducis posse minores pacisci pacta isthæc cum hostibus? [e] Eccur igitur Masinissæ pacta cum Sophonisba sibi Scipio servanda non ducit? Quanti res muliercula una, ut de ea rex Masinissa pacisci nequierit? nihili vero tot illi milites, de quibus pacisci Maharbal quierit? Aberras, Livi, a iure. [f] Hoc dicebat Annibal, quod est iuris, Maharbalem suo iniussu pactum facere non potuisse. Et illos captivos tamen dimittit Annibal mox, pusillo nescio quo adiecto ad conditiones liberationis. Sapienter: ne videri posset, crudelitate, avaritiaque magis, quam tuendi caussa iuris imperatorii, irritam fecisse Maharbalis pactionem.

Nunc loquatur Livius: si plura habet. [g] *Annibal, quas tueri urbes nequit,*
p. 66 *spoliat, ut vastata hosti relinqueret: præceps in ava|ritiam et crudelitatem*

[a] *Vopis. Aurelia. Polyb.* 10. [b] *Liv.* 2.
[c] *Plut. Æmi.* [d] *Liv.* 22. [e] *Liv.* 30.
[f] *App. Ann.* [g] *Liv.* 26.

[307] Vopiscus (*Scriptores Historiae Augustae*), *Aurelian* 22. 6; Polybius 10. 15. 5.
[308] [Livy, 21. 57. 9–13 (paraphrased).]
[309] Livy 2. 17. 6.
[310] Plutarch, *Aemilius Paulus* 29.
[311] **Translator's note:** Gentili seems to be envisioning a case where, in the process of a city being taken by storm, some individual defenders surrender. This would not constitute the formal surrender—*deditio*—of the city itself, and so the individuals who surrender would be considered in the same category as those captured by force.
[312] Livy 22. 6. 11–12.
[313] Livy 30.
[314] Livy 26. 38 ad init. [paraphrased].

But am I to record the individual acts of individuals? The Romans were in the habit not only of cutting down any men who fell into their path in the cities they captured, but even to tear apart the dogs and dismember other animals.[307] Go ahead, Livy, and add other deeds of Hannibal. "He handed over Vicuviae [Victumulae] to be torn apart, as though it had been captured by force, not surrendered."[308] But wouldn't the daylight hours fail me if I should wish to lay out similar deeds of your most praiseworthy Romans? For what do you record was done by your people concerning Pometia? "Nonetheless, when it surrendered it was foully dealt with as though it had been captured: the leaders were struck down with the axe, the others were sold off, and the city was uprooted."[309]

What did that unique man among the very best of the nobility, Aemilius Paulus—nay, rather, what did the Senate do with the seventy cities of Epirus?[310]
Entering them under a show of friendship, through an evil deception, even p. 65
worse treachery, with the most shameful lies, he tore them apart and overturned them and carried off 150,000 souls into servitude. I am not going through all the innumerable examples of this. But do you yourself not believe that Vicuviae [Victumulae] was captured by force, when an army that had defeated two consuls was led against it to fight a force that had sallied forth from it? Surely you don't believe that, when some individuals surrender, one must always treat them as people who have made a formal surrender, even though they have in fact already been captured?[311] If so, then what would prevent one from denying that anyone at all can ever be captured by force?

But proceed, Livy. "Maharbal made an agreement with those who surrendered, but as they were going away Hannibal (such is Punic faith) cast them all into chains when they were departing."[312] And do you judge that without orders from the superior commander the lesser leaders can make these kinds of agreements with the enemy? Then why did Scipio not believe that Masinissa's agreement with Sophonisba needed to be observed by him?[313] Was that insignificant woman of such importance that Masinissa, a king, would not be able to make an agreement with her? Or, conversely, were those very many soldiers about whom Maharbal wished to make a pact people of no significance at all? You are wandering off from the question of law, Livy. This is what Hannibal was trying to say: that it was a question of law that Maharbal not be able to make a pact without his express orders. And yet Hannibal soon afterwards released those captives, after an insignificant addition had been made to the conditions for their freedom. He did this prudently, lest he might seem to have rendered the pact of Maharbal invalid more from cruelty and greed than for the reason of protecting his right of command.

Now let Livy talk on, if he has more to say. "Hannibal despoiled the cities he was unable to put a guard over, so that he might leave the enemy only
devastated territory; he had a spirit prone to greed and cruelty."[314] This p. 66

animus. Hoc videlicet eius historici magni imperitiæ iuris bellici testimonium magnum est. Num est iniustum perdere hostilia, et hostibus incommodare? [a] Fruges, loca, alia, quæ defendi nequeunt nostra, perdi licite possunt, et quotidie solent. [b] Politorium tui diruunt Romani, ut tu scribis, ne hostibus foret receptaculum. Et hæc sunt omnia, quæ narrare contra Annibalem potuisti? [c] Eius singularem humanitatem, et benignitatem cum captis ad Trebiam, ad Thrasymenum, ad Cannas notasti tamen. Fidem erga præsidium Casilini asseruisti. Pietatem in Gracchi, Æmilii, Marcelli exsequiis suspexisti. [d] De qua alii, et poetæ exposuere magnifica: *credas, Sidonium cecidisse ducem*. [e] Etiam Flaminii corpus, ut funeraret, decoraretque virtutis caussa, quæsivit magna cum cura. [f] Aut quæ illa huius invisi ducis vox ad Cannas, *Parce ferro*, suos a cædibus revocantis?

Quid iam post hæc omnia Romani? [g] Sæviunt in cadaver Asdrubalis: cuius præcisum caput ante Punica castra, et ante Annibalis fratris oculos abiecerunt: itaque humanitati, et pietati Annibalis gratias retulerunt. Itane barbari? Ista aut belli iura sunt in hostes cæsos? Aut hostes iam sunt, qui cæsi sunt? *Neque enim finito Marte vocandus hostis est*. Itane belli iura cum captivis p. 67 Pœnis? [h]*ne minus decem pondo compedibus vincti in carceris publici | custodia essent*. Sic, sic Romani: [i]*civitas minime in captivos iam inde antiquitus indulgens*.

Quo me tamen iusta illa indignatio, et iusta hæc Annibalis defensio traxit? De Mithridate erat oratio? Qui per dolos, et iniustitiam Romanorum tractus in bellum: et eodem modo dolose, iniuste extinctus est.

Primum, et postremum dixi: de quibus medium, tempus annorum eius belli sex et quadraginta, tacite censeamus. Quis Murenæ improbitatem abominetur satis? [j] Bellum a Sylla compositum suscitat per suam triumphi nescis cuius cupidinem. Et fœdera ei cum obiectarentur, hæc negat impudens: videlicet quia non perscripserat ea, contentus exsecutione pactorum, Sylla.

Rex legatos usque mittit Romam: ubi Syllaque censet indignum, infestari fœderatum Mithridatem bello. Et egregius quidem senatus palam iubet, desistere a bello Murenam: clam autem contrarium monet. [k]*Nullus clam facit, nisi sciat illicitum. Qui male agit, odit lucem*. Specta regis fortissimi

[a] *Bal. l.* 3. *de di. re.* [b] *Liv.* 1. [c] *Liv.* 22. 23. [d] *Val.* 5. *c.* 1. *Sil.* 10. 15.
[e] *Plut. Fab. Liv.* 2. [f] *Ior. de re. succ.* [g] *Liv.* 27. [h] *Liv.* 32.
[i] *Liv.* 23. [j] *App. Mith.* [k] *Serv.* 1. *Æneid.*

---

[315] Baldus, *On Digest* 1. 8. 3, fol. 44v.
[316] Livy 1. 33. 3.
[317] Livy 22; 23.
[318] [Livy 23. 19. 16.]
[319] Valerius Maximus 5. 1. ext. 6; Silius Italicus 15. 389–90.
[320] Plutarch, *Fabius Maximus* 3. 3; Livy 22. 7. 5.
[321] Jordanes, *Romana* 189. [322] Livy 27. [323] [Ovid, *Metamorphoses* 14. 246–7.]
[324] Livy 32. 26. 18. [325] Livy 22. 61. 1. [326] Appian, *Mithridatica* 9. 64.
[327] Servius, *On Aeneid* 1. [Servius does not write this; the second clause is a citation from *John* 3: 20; cf. also *Liber Extra* 5. 7. 12.]

passage is obviously great testimony to this great historian's ignorance of the law and rights of war. Is it unjust to destroy the enemy's things and to injure him? Crops, places, and other things of ours that we cannot defend can be destroyed licitly—and this happens daily.[315] Your Romans destroyed Politorium (as you write) lest it become a refuge for your enemies.[316] And are these all the things that you have been able to relate against Hannibal? You have noted his remarkable humanity and kindness with those captured at the Trebia, Lake Trasimene, and Cannae.[317] You have declared the way he kept his word with the garrison of Casilinum.[318] You have admired the piety he showed in the funeral rites for Gracchus, Aemilius, and Marcellus, concerning which others, even poets, have laid out fine words: "You would believe that it was a Sidonian leader who had fallen."[319] He even made a very careful search for the body of Flaminius so that he might give it proper funerary honors on account of his valor.[320] And what were the words of this hated leader at Cannae, when he was recalling his men from slaughter? "Spare the sword."[321]

And what did the Romans do after all these things? They outraged the body of Hasdrubal, whose severed head they cast before the Carthaginian camp and before the eyes of his brother Hannibal; and so they offered thanks to the humanity and piety of Hannibal.[322] Were they such barbarians? Were those the laws of war against enemies who had been killed? Or are those who have been killed still enemies? "For one ought not be called an enemy when the fighting is over."[323] Were the rights of war thus observed with the Carthaginian captives? "Bound with shackles of no less than ten pounds' weight, they were kept in the custody of a public prison."[324] Thus, thus did p. 67
the Romans behave: "From the earliest times the state showed very little mercy to prisoners of war."[325]

But where has that just indignation and this just defense of Hannibal carried me off? Were we talking about Mithridates? He was drawn into a war through the deceptions and the injustice of the Romans, and in the same manner he was deceitfully, unjustly killed.

I have spoken about the beginning and the end; let us pass judgment in silence over the intervening forty-six years. For who could sufficiently express detestation for the wickedness of Murena? Through his lust for any sort of triumph, he stirred up again a war that Sulla had brought to an end.[326] And when the treaty was held up to him he impudently rejected it, supposedly on the grounds that Sulla had not written it out in full, content as he had been with the actual carrying out of the treaty's terms.

The king went so far as to send ambassadors to Rome, when even Sulla judged it unworthy that Mithridates, now treaty-ally, be harassed with war. And indeed the noble Senate openly ordered Murena to desist from the war—but it secretly advised him the opposite. "No one acts in secret unless he knows his act is illicit. He who acts badly hates the light."[327] Behold the

patientiam, et æquanimitatem: qui interim dum agit rem per legatos Romæ: non Murenæ deprædanti omnia, etiam sacra, occurrit: at reditum legatorum quietus exspectat. Eadem et usus patientia primum, ante quam contra Nicomedem, et Ariobarzanem, illos emissitios, commoveretur.

p. 68 Neque tamen adnotabo singula: et quod feci in tota hac mea | defensione orbis, id hic quoque teneo: ut pauca de plurimis aperiam Romanorum facinora. [a] Ergo tentatus Mithridates insidiis per hospitem Attilium: tentatus per Archelaum ducem: quem Sylla, gnarus bene gestæ rei contra Iugurtam, ad proditionem sollicitavit. [b] Etiam Africanus ducem Carthaginensium sollicitarat. Sed Mithridates parricida tandem confectus, ut dixi, manu. [c] Magnus ille etiam Hiempsalem armavit contra patrem: etiam et ornavit eum regno paterno parricidam. Idem nunc agit cum Mithridate. [d] Atque Mithridates rex exstinctus totum Septentrionem ruina sua involuit.

Hæc autem iuventus dicitur eius populi: cum prolata arma sunt extra Italiam, perque omnes partes orbis circumlata terrarum.

De Cæsaribus.
CAP. XI

Vidimus Romulos in infantia, et reges reliquos. Vidimus in adolescentia Brutos, Scævolas, Camillos, Postumios. Vidimus in iuventute Fabios, Africanos, Catones, Martios, Metellos, Claudios, Magnos. Vidimus hæc urbis lumina, et urbem totam. Et pervenimus iam ad Cæsares: quibus quasi filiis tradidit se Roma in senectute, [e] ut loquitur Ammianus.

De Cæsaribus autem quid dicemus? An filii meliores, quam parentes fuerunt, aut quam ipsa exstitit mater? Progenies patribus vitiosior. [f] An expedierit, nec ne
p. 69 nasci Iuli | um, quæstio est. [g] Hic vir, hic est, qui prætor turbavit quiescentem Hispaniam, et a bello in bellum rapuit: qui Galliam quietissimam proconsul commovit, et afflixit totam: qui adiit Britanniam istam sepositam: et magnam Germaniam attentavit. Et profunda illa imperii cupido motuum

[a] *App. Mith.* [b] *Liv.* 50. [c] *Manut. agr.* 2. [d] *Flor.* 3. [e] *Amm. lib.* 14.
[f] Sen. 5 *nat. q.* [g] *Dio.* 37. 38. 40. *Suet.* 7. *Plui. apoph. reg. et du.*

---

[328] Appian, *Mithridatica.*
[329] Livy 50 [summary].
[330] Manut. *agr.* 2. [Paulus Manutius' commentary on Cicero's *De lege agraria* is meant; the reference is unclear, however. Pompey's help for Hiempsal—not his being armed against his father, however—is mentioned by Manutius in his comment on Cicero's first speech *De lege agraria*; see *M. Tullii Ciceronis Orationes*, Tomus II, Pars I, Amstelodami, Ex Typographia P. & I. Blaeu, 1699, p. 276.]
[331] Florus 3. 5. 21. [332] Ammianus Marcellinus 14. 6. 5.
[333] Seneca, *Naturales quaestiones* 5. 18. 4. [Seneca attributes this sentiment to Livy.]
[334] Dio Cassius 37. 52; 38. 31; 40. 32.

patience and even-temperedness of the king, who in the interval when he was negotiating at Rome through his ambassadors did not oppose Murena who was pillaging everything, even sacred objects; rather, he peacefully awaited the ambassadors. He had also used this same patience before moving against those spies Nicomedes and Ariobarzanes.

And yet I shall not record all the particular events; and what I have done in this entire defense of the world [i.e. against the Roman predators] I have been p. 68
engaged in, that shall I keep to here as well: so that I may unfold just a few of the very many crimes of the Romans. Thus, an attempt was made on Mithridates's life through a plot with his host Attilius; and an attempt was made on his life through his general Archelaus, whom Sulla, once he knew that things were going well against Jugurtha, tempted to betray him.[328] Scipio Africanus, also, had tempted a Carthaginian general.[329] But Mithridates was finally done in by the hand of a parricide, as I have said. That famous Pompey the Great armed Hiempsal against his own father, and he even honored that parricide with his father's kingdom.[330] He now does the same with Mithridates. And in his death Mithridates involved the whole of the north in his own ruin.[331]

And this is called the youth of this people, when their arms were brought forth beyond Italy and carried about through all parts of the world.

CHAPTER 11

On the Caesars

In Rome's infancy we have seen Romulus and the other kings. In her adolescence we have seen men like Brutus, Scaevola, Camillus, and Postumius. In her vigorous youth we have seen people like Fabius, Scipio Africanus, Cato, Marcius, Metellus, Claudius, and Pompey the Great. We have seen these glories of the city—and we have seen the city as a whole as well. And now we have arrived at the Caesars, to whom in her old age Rome bequeathed herself as to her children, as Ammianus puts it.[332]

But what are we to say about the Caesars? Were the sons better than the parents had been—or than their mother herself was? The offspring was worse than the parents. It is a question whether it would not have been better had Julius not been born.[333] This man, this it was, who as a praetor stirred up p. 69
peaceful Spain and harried it on from war to war; who as proconsul threw utterly quiet Gaul into turmoil and harassed the whole of it; who went to distant Britain and made an attempt on great Germany.[334] And it was a

caussa tantorum: quæ et ad lacrymas adegit hominem: cum Gadibus statuam Alexandri vidisset: simul et meminisset, se nihil ea ætate magnum egisse, in qua Asiam Alexander domuerit universam. [a]*Sic belli occasione, ne iniusti quidem abstinuit, tam fœderatis, quam infestis gentibus ultro lacessitis.*

Sic M. Cato, dedendum his gentibus auctorem hunc Cæsarum, censuit, iniqua inferentem bella. Sed te, Cato, non audivit pulchra Roma: non purpurea secuta est curia, *prospere decedentibus rebus*: ut ait historia. Quamquam et solens Roma, agi cum Gallis improbe. [b] Meministis, nec deditum Fabium Gallis, violatorem iuris gentium sanctioris. Meministis perfidum Domitii factum cum Arvernorum rege: quod nec rescidit, sed adfirmavit senatus. Meministis alia. Non gessit alia Iulius occupata republica: et illico periit.

Filius Augustus movit Cantabris bellum. [c] Nam angebatur, non esse suum in Hispania illud Cantabriæ terræ perpusillum. Movit bellum Pannoniis: p. 70 ut arma exerceret Romana: quod antea dictum est. Cicero, quid ille | Brutus tuus in bellorum caussis dedit symbolæ? [d]*Progressus sum ad inalpinos cum exercitu, non tam nomen captans imperatorium, quam cupiens militibus satisfacere.*

Ceterum quæ privatæ horum, et Cæsarum filiorum cupiditates nunc dici valent, eæ matri venerandæ non adscribantur. Et ipsos quoque quid insecter oratione Cæsares? Quid Iulium, ceterosque vincam tyrannos? In quo nomine uno scelera omnia concluduntur. Ille Iulius Nicomedis sponda. Patrui Augustus sponda. Nequam Tyberius. Furiosus Caius. Stolidus Claudius. Parricida Nero. Spurcus Galba. Luxuriosus Otho. Lurco Vitellius. Sordidus Vespasianus. Hypocrita Titus. Sanguinarius Domitianus. [e] Corruptor adolescentis principis Nerva: ipse nullus. Vinolentus Traianus: herba parietaria: infamis flagitii compertissimus. Adi mihi unum Suetonium: qui licentia pari Cæsarum scripsit vitas, atque illi egerunt.

[a] *Suet.* 24. *Plut. Cras.* [b] *Val.* 9. c. 6.
[c] *Oros.* 6. *c.* 21. [d] *Cic.* 11. *fam.* [e] *Suet. Dom.* 1. *P. Dia. Eu.* 12. *Amm.* 27.

---

[335] Plutarch, *Regum et imperatorum apophthegmata* 206 B; Suetonius, *Divus Iulius* 7.1.
[336] Suetonius, *Divus Iulius* 24. 3; Plutarch, *Crassus.*
[337] [The quoted words are from Suetonius, *Divus Iulius* 24. 3.]
[338] Valerius Maximus 9. 6. 3.
[339] Orosius 6. 21.
[340] Cicero, *Epistulae ad familiares* 11. 4. 1.
[341] Suetonius, *Domitianus* 1. 1 [for the story that Neva corrupted the young Domitian]; Paulus Diaconus, *Historia Romana* 7. 22 [on Domitian's vices]; Eutropius 8. 4 [on Trajan's fondness for partying with friends—Paulus Diaconus, whose *Historia Romana* is an enlarged version of Eutropius' work, copies Eutropius word for word in this book]; Ammianus Marcellinus 27. 3. 7 [according to Ammianus, Constantine the Great called Trajan "wall-wort," *herba parietaria* or *parietina*, because of the multitude of inscriptions bearing his name].

profound passion for rule that was the cause of such great disturbances—a passion that drove the man even to tears when he saw a statue of Alexander at Cadiz, and he recalled that he himself had done nothing in that same time of life in which Alexander had conquered all of Asia.[335] "Thus he never refrained from an opportunity of making war, not even an unjust war—with not just enemies wantonly provoked, but allies as well."[336]

Thus Marcus Cato believed that this Caesar ought to be handed over to those peoples as the instigator, bringing unjust wars upon them as he did. But lovely Rome did not listen to you, Cato; the purple-clad Senate did not follow you, "since things were proceeding prosperously," as the history records.[337] Even though Rome herself was in the habit of behaving basely with the Gauls. You all have remembered, surely, that Fabius was not surrendered to the Gauls, even though he violated the quite holy law of nations. You all remember the treacherous act of Domitius with the king of the Arverni—an act which the Senate not only did not rescind, but in fact affirmed.[338] You all remember other such deeds. Julius did not act otherwise when he had seized the Roman state—and he perished on the spot.

His son Augustus set in motion a war against the Cantabrians. For he was tormented by the fact that that tiny bit of Cantabrian territory in Spain was not his.[339] He instigated a war against the Pannonians in order to keep Roman arms in practice, as we have mentioned earlier. What kind of contribution, Cicero, did your friend Decimus Brutus make in the business p. 70
of coming up with reasons for wars? "I advanced with my army against the inhabitants of the Alps, not so much because I was trying to claim the title of a commander-in-chief as because I wished to make my soldiers happy."[340]

But let not what private lusts may be mentioned of these Caesar "sons" be ascribed to that venerable "mother" Rome. And why should I inveigh against the Caesars themselves in my speech? Why should I trounce Julius and the other tyrants, in which single term all crimes are enfolded? That famous Julius was called "the bed of Nicomedes." And Augustus was his uncle's "bed." Worthless Tiberius. Mad Gaius. Stupid Claudius. Parricide Nero. Foul Galba. Extravagant Otho. Gluttonous Vitellius. Stingy Vespasian. Hypocritical Titus. Bloody Domitian. Nerva, a nonentity who corrupted a young prince. Alcoholic Trajan, the "wall-wort," a man with the most consummate knowledge of shameful crime.[341] Just visit for me one single author, Suetonius, who wrote up the lives of the Caesars with a license equal to that with which they lived those lives of theirs.

Et sub istis principibus regna titulo (ut volunt) iustissimo quæsita plurima per testamenta. De quibus scilicet abiecti heredes fuere naturales: quorum ius non a voluntate regis, sive morientis, sive desipientis, sed ab immutabili successione, aut a certo pendet consensu populorum. Quis Asiam vobis reliquit. [a] Ille parricida scelestæ rabiei: qui, mox pœnas pendens manibus
p. 71 interfectorum, non aliquod signum sani hominis habuit. Adi Trogum. |

Sed neque sapientissimi hæc est facultas. Quod, quod enim in regnum est ius, id cum regis vita protinus finit. [b] Amplissima papæ Romani potestas limitibus vitæ continetur. [c] Feudum, quæsitum descendentibus ex investitura, nequit post mutari pacto ascendentium, etiam si ipseque velit feudi dominus. [d] *Habeat*, inquiebat rex Gallus, *regnum Carolus, Balbi filius: a quo amovere orbis terrarum nequit universus.* [e] Inquit Baldus, *Regnum quis, velit, nolit, transmittit ex maiestate radicis: quæ semper radicat.* Non est, sane non est lex ulla, aut ratio, quæ principi de imperio faciat potestatem testandi: ut privato de rebus privatis facit. Quod si etiam dari testamento regnum potest, cur non etiam contractu? Cur non donari? vendi? et veluti venalia pecora haberi homines? [f] Subditi non eiusmodi sunt liberæ voluntati, sed ut regantur commodius.

Absolvo Cæsares. [g] Occiditur Iulius. Veneficio uxoris perit Augustus. Strangulatur Tyberius. Interficitur Caius. Veneno Claudius tollitur ab uxore. Nero sui carnifex. Trucidatur Galba. Otho iugulum aperit sibi. Vitellium et cum ludibriis tollunt. Vespasiano mors a Tito filio. Tito mors est a fratre. Domitianus gladio occumbit. Traianus ab uxore conficitur, et a filio. Nullus Nerva nullus obiit. Hi sancti principes: ille populus sanctus: atque ista
p. 72 Palatinæ urbis virtus: cui pa|rere orbis terrarum debuerit universus.

[a] *Iustin.* 36. [b] *Alc.* 4. *cons.* 2. [c] *Alc.* 9. *cons.* 17. [d] *P. Æmil.* 9.
[e] *Bal.* 2. *cons.* 275. [f] *Alc.* 5. *cons.* 23. [g] *Xiph. Cedr. Philostr.* 6. *vi. Ap.*

[342] Justin 36. 4. **Translator's note:** The supposedly mad king in question was, of course, Attalos III of Pergamum. It is not entirely clear why Gentili sets forth an event that occurred in 133 BC in his chapter on the Caesars.

[343] Alciatus, *Consilia* 4. 2, col. 369.

[344] Alciatus, *Consilia* 9. 17.

[345] Paulus Aemilius [Paolo Emili], *De rebus gestis Francorum Libri X*, Lutetiae Parisiorum, Ex officina Vascosani, 1566, bk. 9. **Translator's note:** This appears to refer to the Carolingian king Charles the Simple, posthumous son of Louis the Stammerer.

[346] Baldus, *Consilia* 2. 275, fol. 76^{v}. **Translator's note:** The sentence in Baldus reads: "sed regnum, et dominium transmittit, quis velit, nolit ex maiestate radicis, quae semper radicat."

[347] Alciatus, *Consilia* 5. 23, col. 510.

[348] Johannes Xiphilinus, *Epitome Dionis Cassii*, Lutetiae, 1551; George Cedrenus, *Historiarum compendium* 300; 346 [J.-P. Migne, *Patrologia Graeca*, cxxi, cols. 335–8; 383]; Philostratus, *Life of Apollonius* 6. 32. **Translator's note:** The passage from Philostratus is offered in support of the notion that Domitian killed Titus.

And under these princes very many kingdoms were acquired through a utterly just title (so they claimed) by being left them in wills. That is to say, the rightful heirs were expelled from these kingdoms, for their right did not depend upon the will of a dying or mad king, but the unalterable laws of succession or the fixed consensus of their peoples. Who left Asia to you in his will? It was that parricide afflicted with wicked madness, who, soon paying the penalty for his crimes to the shades of those he had killed, displayed not a single indication of a sane man. Go to Pompeius Trogus and find out.[342]

But this capability of bequeathing a kingdom does not belong even to a p. 71
very wise king. Whatever right one has to a kingdom comes to an end immediately with the life of the king. The very wide-ranging power of the Roman Pope is confined within the limits of his lifetime.[343] A fiefdom that has been acquired for descendants through investiture cannot later be altered through an agreement of the parents, even if the lord of the fiefdom himself should be willing.[344] A French king used to say, "Let Charles, son of the Stammerer, have the kingdom, from which the entire world has not the power to remove him."[345] Baldus declares: "Who either intentionally or unintentionally hands over a kingdom does so on account of the sovereignty of its origin; which is always what provides the basis."[346] There is not, indeed there surely is not any law or rational principle which creates for a prince the power of making a will concerning his rule, as it is permitted for a private man to do concerning private possessions. But if a kingdom can be given in a will, why could it not just be given away? Or sold—as though men were considered cattle for sale? They are not subject to a king's free will in this way, but only in order that they may be ruled more effectively.[347]

I am bringing this account of the Caesars to an end. Julius was murdered. Augustus perished through his wife's poison. Tiberius was strangled, Gaius was killed. Claudius was carried off by poison administered by his wife. Nero was his own butcher. Galba was cut to pieces. Otho cut his own throat. They made away with Vitellius with derision. Vespasian died at the hands of his son Titus. Titus died at the hands of his brother. Domitian fell on his sword. Trajan was killed by his wife and his son. The nonentity Nerva died the death of a nonentity.[348] These were the august princes; this was the august people; and this was that excellence of the Palatine city which the whole world was p. 72
supposed to obey.

De Romanis et Alexandro.
CAP. XII

At fortuna factum Romanum imperium, Plutarchus disseruit. Fortuna muliebris servavit a Volscis urbem: et illi muliebri positum templum fuit. Anser a Gallis servavit urbem. *Romulidarum arcis servator candidus anser*: Lucretius. *Mira fortuna, viros, qui universum orbem erant missuri sub iugum, avis una servavit*: Vegetius. [a] Et itaque prima censoris cura, locare illis avibus victum in Capitolio: quod Plinius narrat: et quis non? Quid, quod refert urbis augmentum Augustinus in sacram quamdam occasionem? Putat, Babylonem in Occidente quoque esse oportuisse. Quæ hæc fuerit urbs amplissima, plena confusionum, atque blasphemiarum, Audistin' qui in Babyloniæ campis minitatus cælo est? [b] Audi Cæsarem ferocientem, *Decem habere legiones populum Romanum, quæ etiam cœlum diruere possent.* [c] Audi Prosperum, *Quis non intelligat, quam dicat apocalypsis ferentem poculum plenum exsecrationibus immundiciæ, et fornicationis terræ? æterna cum dicitur, quæ temporalis est, utique nomen est blasphemiæ.* Urbs æterna sic audiit Roma apud Ammianum, et alios.

In hæc tamen mysta non penetro: at de virtute exputo: Disserit idem
p. 73 gravissimus auctor Plutarchus de Alexandri vir|tute. [d] Cui Livius dictam virtutem Romanam, late secedens a suo opere, præponere non veretur. Ita cæcus ubique ab amore suorum est. Et suis illis Corvinis, Torquatis, Deciis, Papiriis non fuisse in Alexandri exercitu, qui obiicerentur, dememinit, Ptolomæos, Lysimachos, Seleucos, Antigonos, Antiochos, Eumenes, alios plures, viros regales, et quos regno Alexandri non indignos, qui nec Alexandri virtutibus inferiores fuissent, veterum sententiæ singulos censuerunt.

Sed et qui illi Corvini? Quibus item avis et victorias dedit, et nomina. Qui Torquati? stolidi viri: feræ immanes. Qui Decii? Præstigiatores, et necromantici. [e]*Incurrite mecum, et prosternite humo iuvenem magica arma moventem.* Nos contra Decium utrumque, quam ille dixerit contra Perseum, dicimus iustius. Qui Papirii? Respondeo, supra responsum esse. Hæ sunt illorum

[a] *Cic. pro Ro. Amm. Plut. pr. R.* 98. [b] *Hirt. Hisp.* [c] *Prosp. di. te. c.* 7.
[d] *Liv.* 9. [e] *Ovid.* 5. *Metam.*

349 [Plutarch, *De fortuna Romanorum* 318 F.] 350 [Lucretius 4. 683.]
351 [Vegetius 4. 26.]
352 Cicero, *Pro Roscio Amerino* 20. 56; Plutarch, *Quaestiones Romanae* 98; Pliny the Elder, *Historia naturalis* 10. 22. 51.
353 [Augustine, *De civitate Dei* 16. 17.] 354 Ps.-Hirtius, *De bello Hispaniensi* 42. 7.
355 Ps.-Prosper, *Liber de promissionibus et praedictionibus Dei* 4. 7. 14 [J.-P. Migne, *Patrologia Latina*, li, cols. 843–4].
356 [e.g. Ammianus 23. 1. 4.] 357 Livy 9. 17–19.
358 **Translator's note:** See Florus 1. 13. 20. In a battle with the Gauls, a sacred crow landed upon the helmet of a Valerius, who became victorious in the battle. Subsequently he took the name Corvinus, from *corvus*.
359 Ovid, *Metamorphoses* 5. 196–7.

CHAPTER 12
On the Romans and Alexander

But Plutarch argues that the Roman Empire was created by luck. Fortuna Muliebris saved the city from the Volscians, and a temple was established for this Female Fortune.[349] A goose saved the city from the Gauls. "The savior of the citadel of the sons of Romulus was a white goose," wrote Lucretius.[350] "Through a remarkable stroke of Fortune, a single bird saved the men who were going to send the entire world under the yoke," wrote Vegetius.[351] And so the first job of the censor was to put out a contract for the feeding of those birds on the Capitol, as Pliny records—and who does not?[352] What of the fact that Augustine refers the expansion of the city to a certain divine explanation? He also believes that Rome ought to be considered "the Babylon of the West."[353] For this city of Rome was huge, full of confusions and blasphemies. Have you heard who in the plains of this Babylon threatened Heaven? Listen to raging Caesar: "The Roman people have ten legions which are even able to tear down the heavens."[354] Listen to Prosper: "Who would be unaware whom the Apocalypse says is bearing a cup full of the curses of the uncleanness and fornication of the earth? When she who is temporal is called "eternal," that is indeed a name of blasphemy."[355] The city of Rome is thus termed "eternal" in Ammianus and other writers.[356]

But I am not entering into these secret rites; rather, I am making an examination about valor. That same very weighty authority Plurarch discourses on the valor of Alexander. Livy, digressing wide from his subject, is p. 73
not afraid to set the so-called valor of the Roman people over that of Alexander.[357] He is blind in this way everywhere in his work through love for his own people. And when he claims that there were none in Alexander's army who could have been a match for his own Corvini, Torquati, Decii, and Papirii, he forgets the people like Ptolemy, Lysimachus, Seleucus, Antigonus, Antiochus, Eumenes, and many others, men of regal stature, whom the opinions of the ancients judged as in their own right not unworthy of the kingdom of Alexander, since they had been not inferior to the excellences of Alexander.

But who were these Corvini, anyway? People to whom a bird gave both a victory and a name.[358] Who were the Torquati? Dull-witted men, savage beasts. Who were the Decii? Impostors and necromancers. "Attack with me and lay on the ground the young man who is wielding magical arms"—we say this more justly against either of the Decii than Eryx said it against Perseus.[359] Who were the Papirii? My answer is that I have answered this

virtutes, qui senes, pueri occurrere Alexandro, et florentibus Macedoniæ viris habuerunt. Hic ille senatus Romanus, qui sedens intra pomœrium urbis gerere bellum habuit cum Alexandro, et senatu eius regis, in castris, in aciebus agente.

Ego tamen quid abeo in disputationem novam, qui propositam actionem ferme absolui? Paresne Alexandro fuissent isti, [a] qui Alexandrum, in alio
p. 74 propemodum orbe versantem, venerati legationibus sunt? Et illic veriti sunt | Alexandrum. [b] Tu enim ais, M. Tulli, nomen ipsum legationis ultro missæ signum esse timoris videri. Aut quid vobis erat et Alexandro? Ubi factum non habet nisi caussam unam, factum ex ea caussa credere necesse est. Vel timuistis postea Philippum, et Antiochum, regulos, si conferas Alexandro, at Alexandrum non timuistis? Vos pares Alexandro? qui Pyrrho (quantulus et iste rex, Alexandro admotus, et regnis, et exercitibus Macedoniæ?) Pyrrho ita concesseratis: [c] ut vester cæcus optaret se surdumque, ut quemadmodum ora intueri vestra pallentia, frigidaque non poterat, et reliqua timoris signa certa, ita nec audire consilia abiecta, et complorata valeret. Isthæc sollemnia vobis, pavere, et desperare.

[d] Et sic vestra illa erant tacita senatusconsulta: cum vis ab hoste immineret, quæ vos cogeret vilia (ut dico) captare consilia. Annibal unus, civium suorum odiis iactatus, fortuna civitatis suæ destitutus, barbaro Hispanorum exercitu stipatus malefido, victor per magna prælia insultavit portis urbis, et Italiam annos sexdecim insedit: de qua nec ductus, nisi iuvenis unius fortuna: [e] ut sic Scipionem acres iudicio viri fortunatum utrumque, magis quam fortem, viri in populo vestro principes censuerunt.

An vero defuisset fortuna Alexandro: quem dicitis fortunatum omnes?
p. 75 cuius virtuti comitem fortunam di|xissetis æquius: aut etiam ancillantem, cum Plutarcho verius. Non Macedonum odia potuistis sperare, non infidelitatem. Aspicite, si quando versatur in periculo Alexander, quemadmodum pro salute illius commoveantur; ruant in ferrum, penetrent arces, et limina pervadant inaccessa. Aspicite, si quando illis subiratus fuit, quemadmodum iacent in luctu, vivere nolunt; et vitam tum demum, ac Solem putant redditum sibi, cum sibi propitius redditus est Alexander. Nam quid attinet hic

[a] *Pli.* 3. *c.* 5. [b] *Cic. phi.* 5. [c] *Plu. nu. sc. ge. re. Val.* 8. *c.* 3. *l.* 2. *de orig. iu. l.* 1. *de postu.*
[d] *Capitol. Gord.* [e] *Spar. Nigr.*

---

360 [Reference to Papirius Cursor, *De armis Romanis* 1. 10, pp. 84–5.]

361 Pliny, *Historia naturalis* 3. 57. 362 Cicero, *Orationes Philippicae* 5. 26.

363 Plutarch, *An seni respublica gerenda sit* 794 E; Valerius Maximus 8. 13. 5; *Digest* 1. 2. 2. 36 [**Translator's note:** This passage does not seem to provide support for Picenus' claims, as Appius Claudius here is only said to have opined that Pyrrhus should not be received into the city]; *Digest* 3. 1. 1. 5 [**Translator's note:** Here the subject matter is whether a blind man such as Appius Claudius can hold the office of a magistrate].

364 Aelius Capitolinus (*Scriptores Historiae Augustae*), *Gordiani tres* 12. **Translator's note:** This late antique fabricator claims that the Senate occasionally met in closed session, with senators taking on the role of scribes, and passed "secret decrees" when they had a need to keep their deliberations secret. No reputable ancient source confirms this.

365 Aelius Spartianus (*Scriptores Historiae Augustae*), *Pescennius Niger* 12. 2.

above.[360] These are the virtues of these men who as boys and old men would have had to meet Alexander and the men of Macedonia in their prime. This is that famous Roman Senate which, sitting within the Pomerium of the city, would have had to wage war with Alexander and his royal council which was active in the camps and the ranks of battle.

But why should I go off into a new disputation when I am almost through with the case I proposed to lay out? Would those men have been the equals of Alexander who honored Alexander with embassies when he was operating in what one might almost call another world?[361] And in this they showed that they feared Alexander. For you, Cicero, say that the very name of "embassy" p. 74
sent on one's own initiative would seem to be an indication of fear.[362] Otherwise, what business would you have had with Alexander? Where an action has but one cause, it is necessary to believe that the action arises from that cause. Or did you afterwards fear Philip and Antiochus, kinglets when you compare them with Alexander, but did not fear Alexander himself? Were you the equals of Alexander, you who made such concessions to Pyrrhus (and what a paltry king he was, when set beside Alexander and the kingdoms and armies of Macedonia) that your blind old man [Appius Claudius] wished himself deaf as well, so that just as he wasn't able to look upon your pale and cold faces and other sure signs of terror, so too he might not be able to hear your abject and lamenting deliberations?[363]

Those were customary practices for you: to fear and despair. And such were those silent senatorial decrees of yours, when violence from an enemy threatened, which would force you to snatch at base (as I call them) plans.[364] Hannibal, a single man, buffeted about by the hatreds of his own citizens, bereft of the prosperity of his state, surrounded by an untrustworthy barbaric army of Spaniards, nonetheless victorious in many battles, mocked at the gates of the city and for sixteen years occupied Italy, from which the only thing that drew him away was the good luck of a young man, for thus men shrewd in judgment—leading men among your own people—judge both Scipios to be more lucky than brave.[365]

Or would luck have been lacking to Alexander as well—he whom you all call the man favored by fortune? You would more justly have said that fortune was his companion—or even his handmaiden, as Plutarch more accurately p. 75
put it. You would not have been able to hope that the Macedonians might show hatred or lack of loyalty to him. See how, whenever Alexander was in a tight spot, the Macedonians were roused to save him—and how they would rush into battle, break into citadels, and rush across inaccessible boundaries. See how, if he were on occasion somewhat angry with them, they would lie grief-stricken and would wish they were dead, but would think that life and the light of the sun had at long last returned to them when Alexander was

enarrare, quomodo fracti, laceri, confecti senio secuti eum sint per tot annos continuos, per tot ferocissimas nationes, per loca fera, per discrimina rerum omnium, per infinitam viam? Quid mœrorem, squalorem, prope mortem omnium in ipsius unius morte? Aut quid est, cur caussa tanti amoris, tantæ fidei indagetur, si fides cernitur, et amor? Etiam ille exercitus veteranorum erat (et hoc nota) Philippi patris, regis sapientissimi, exercitatissimi, [a] discipuli Pelopidæ, et Epaminondæ. Sic Alexandrum colebant natum sibi regem, diligebant veluti filium, amplexabantur alumnum.

Non sperare cum Alexandro licebat, non illa, quæ vos Annibali subduxerunt. [b] Etiam scriptum est a Polybio, quod si Annibal, omissis Romanis, intulisset primum bella aliis gentibus, utique vincere potuisset omnes: et, p. 76 victis reliquis, vincere | etiam Romanos potuisset. Et hoc igitur Alexander, subacta plurima Africa, universa Asia, cum tantis Europæ opibus, Macedoniæ, Græciæ, Thraciæ, Illyrii, non effecisset? [c] Quem unum iuvenem regem Annibal sibi, et Pyrrho, et omnibus in re militari, et in arte imperatoria præferebat. Merito.

[d] Audi de Alexandro virum sapientem: hoc est, loquentem decenter, non indulgentem affectibus: *Solus a condito ævo fortuna sua maior: successus amplissimos et provocavit ut strenuus, et æquiparavit ut meritus, et superavit ut melior: solus sine æmulo clarus: adeo ut nemo eius audeat vel sperare virtutem, vel optare fortunam. Alexandri facinora fatigaberis admirando*: et cetera: quæ Apuleius habet.

Sed illic ridendum utique fuit: ubi Livius terrere vanis etiam imaginibus pectus cogitat Alexandri. Saltus Apuliæ, Lucanos montes, vestigia recentia domesticæ cladis ostendit. Et suavis sane sonus illorum verborum est Livii: et de quo dulcis nescio quis error accidere ad aures potest, sed qui tamen non pertingat, pertentetve pectora, non pectus illud Alexandri ullo motu. Nam quid aliud ostendit Livius tandem, aut quid insinuat Alexandro, nisi ut caveret insidias Lucanorum: [e] quibus et Romanus proconsul absumptus est? Caveret sicariorum perfidiam: [f] qua ille avunculus Alexandri occubuit: postp. 77 quam Brutias | sæpe, Lucanasque legiones fudisset: Heracleam Tarentinis,

[a] *Diod. Sic.* 17. *Iusti.* 6. 7. [b] *Polyb.* 11. [c] *Liv.* 35. [d] *Apul.* 1. *flor.*
[e] *Sil.* 12. *Val.* 1. *c.* 6. [f] *Liv.* 8.

366 Diodorus Siculus 16. 2. 2–3; Justin 6. 9.
367 Polybius 11. 19. 6.
368 Livy 35. 14. 7.
369 Apuleius, *Florida* 1. 7. 2–4.
370 **Translator's note:** Gentili is quoting Livy 9. 17. 17. The "domestica clades" refers to the death of Alexander's uncle, Alexander of Epirus, in a battle against the Lucanians in 326. See below.
371 Silius Italicus 12. 475–8; Valerius Maximus 1. 6. 8.

restored to them in a kinder mood. For what point is there here in recounting how, shattered, mutilated, worn out by age, they followed him through so many years without a break, through so many utterly fierce peoples, through wild regions, through situations of utter crisis, through a journey without end? Why should I relate the mourning, the dirty garments, the virtual death of all of them upon that one man's death? Or what is the reason why we need to seek out the cause of such love, such loyalty, when the love and the loyalty are there to be seen? Moreover, that was an army of veterans (and take note of this) of his father Philip, a very wise king and one thoroughly trained in warfare, the student of Pelopidas and Epaminondas.[366] Thus they served Alexander as one born to be their king, they loved him as a son, and they embraced him as pupil.

You wouldn't have been allowed if facing Alexander to hope for those circumstances that rescued you from Hannibal. It was even written by Polybius that if Hannibal, leaving the Romans aside, had first attacked other peoples he would certainly have been able to defeat them all and, when all the rest had been defeated, he would have been able to subdue the p. 76 Romans as well.[367] And therefore would not Alexander have accomplished this as well, with most of Africa and all of Asia subdued, with such resources of Europe, Macedonia, Greece, Thrace, and Illyria? Hannibal himself used to place this one young king above himself, above Pyrrhus, and everyone else in military skill and in the art of commanding.[368] And quite rightly, too.

Listen to a wise man about Alexander—that is, a man who speaks properly, not giving way to his feelings: "From the beginning of time, he alone proved greater than his own fortune. As he was vigorous, he offered a challenge to the greatest successes of the past; as he was worthy, he equaled them; as he was greater, he surpassed them. He stands alone in his fame, without a rival—to such an extent that no one could dare either to hope for his valor or to wish for his good fortune. You will wear yourself out admiring the deeds of Alexander,"—and other things which Apuleius writes.[369]

But it is certainly laughable when Livy thinks he can terrify the breast of Alexander with empty phantoms. He shows him "the passes of Apulia, the mountains of Lucania, and the fresh traces of a slaughter of his kin."[370] No doubt the sound of those words of Livy is pleasing, and from them some pleasing error can reach people's ears, but it couldn't, however, reach or seize people's hearts—and certainly not that stout heart of Alexander—with any true emotion. For what does Livy show or insinuate to Alexander, finally, beyond the fact that he should be on his guard against the ambushes of the Lucanians, by which a Roman proconsul as well was killed?[371] And he should be on his guard against the treachery of assassins, by which that uncle of Alexander died—after he had often routed the Bruttian and Lucanian p. 77

Brutiis Acerras, plures Lucanis, alias Messapiis cepisset validas urbes nobilissimas: postquam et trecentas illustres familias, quas obsidum numero haberet, in Epyrum misisset.

Quid facies Romanis scriptoribus? Terreri illis inanibus Alexandrum potuisse volunt. Sed et coniuratione nescio qua populorum terreri potuisse volunt. Et putant coniurare etiam potuisse Samnites? Hi autem si Alexandro se coniunxissent, servare salus Romanos valuit? Coniurassent certe contra Romanos: contra quos concitarunt genus omne virorum, et barbarorum genus omne: a quibus spoliatos se perfide Italiæ principatu, traductos in servitutem iniustissimam fremuerunt ad ultimum vitæ semper.

Obiectat socios Pœnos contra communem hunc hostem: et Pœnis fidit, contra quam solet: et Pœnis fidit: [a] qui Tyriis parentibus auxilium contra istum Alexandrum non attulere. Et Pœno fidit militi mercenario adversus proprium, veteranum Macedonem. Levia hæc in coniurationibus istis. Levissimum illud, Alexandrum ne fama quidem fuisse Romanis notum: quem a fronte, a tergo, supra, infra, longe, prope ipsis omnes obstupescebant, et magno cultu prosequebantur.

Illud falsissimum, Romanos nunquam ab equite hoste, nunquam a pedite,
p. 78 nunquam | aperta acie, nunquam æquis, nunquam iniquis locis adversus Macedones laborasse. [b] Etiam Livius scribit, victos Romanos a Perseo aperta acie: et ita quidem, ut pavorque occuparit eos, ne extemplo castra hostis aggrederetur: et (quod addit) si rex parvo momento adiuvisset vincentes suos, debellatum fuisset. Hic autem sibi defuisset vis illa Alexandri propria: quam aut stimulabat sibi Perseus frustra, aut simulabat inepte. Hic exercitui dux defuisset? [c] Tu idem hoc notas, Livi, ducibus validiorem, quam milite rem Romanam fuisse. Vere. Nam unus vos vester afflixit Coriolanus: unus vobis rem perdidit absens, et reddidit præsens Camillus: unus homo vobis cunctando restituit rem perditam Fabius.

[a] *Iust.* 11. [b] *Liv.* 42. *Plut. apop. reg. et duc.* [c] *Liv.* 2.

---

372 Livy 8. 24.
373 [Livy 9. 19. 4–5.]
374 **Translator's note:** Gentili's words "servare salus Romanos valuit?" derive from a word-play common in Roman comedy: e.g. "neque iam Salus servare, si volt, me potest," Plautus, *Captivi* 529.
375 [Livy 9. 19. 13–14.]
376 Justin 11. 10.
377 Livy 42. 60; Plutarch, *Regum et imperatorum apophthegmata* 197 EF.
378 Livy 2. 39. 2.

legions, after he had captured Heraclea from the Tarentines, Acerrae from the Bruttians, many cities from the Lucanians, and other strong and very noble cities from the Messapians, and after he had also sent back to Epirus three hundred noble families whom he was keeping among his hostages.[372]

What can you do with these Roman writers? They would have it that Alexander could be frightened by those empty fears. But they also want him to have been able to be terrified by some sort of sworn league of Italian peoples.[373] Do they even think that the Samnites, too, could have joined the league? If, on the other hand, the Samnites would have conspired with Alexander, would even [the goddess] Safety herself have had the power to save the Romans?[374] They would indeed have conspired against the Romans, against whom they had stirred up every sort of men and every sort of barbarians, and by whom they always grouse to the end of their lives they were treacherously robbed of the leadership of Italy and reduced to a servitude most unjust.

Livy sets up the Carthaginians as our allies against this common enemy, and he trusts the Carthaginians, contrary to his usual practice.[375] Yes, he even trusts the Carthaginians, who did not bring any help to their mother-city of Tyre against Alexander.[376] He even trusts a Carthaginian mercenary solider against a native, battle-hardened Macedonian. There are all of these silly things in the part about the sworn leagues, but the silliest thing of all is the notion that not even by rumor was Alexander known to the Romans—Alexander, whom all peoples in front of him, behind him, above him, below him, far-off, close at hand marveled at and honored with great veneration.

And the falsest thing of all is Livy's claim that the Romans never strove p. 78
against the Macedonians in a cavalry engagement or an infantry engagement or on an open field or on favorable ground or even on rough ground. Even Livy writes that the Romans were defeated by Perseus in the open field—and in such a way, indeed, that they were seized by the fear that the enemy might immediately attack their camp; and (as he adds) if the king had even just briefly reinforced his victorious troops the war would have been brought to an end right then and there.[377] Here in Italy would Alexander's characteristic energy have failed him—an energy which Perseus either whipped up in himself fruitlessly or feigned incompetently? Here in Italy would the commander have let the army down [as Perseus did in Macedonia]? You yourself make this same observation, Livy: that the Roman state was stronger through its commanders than its army.[378] Indeed. For a single man of yours, Coriolanus, shattered you all; and a single man, Camillus, by his absence ruined your state, and by his presence brought it back; and a single man, Fabius, restored your state for you by his strategy of delay.

Etiam Alexandri successores spernis, Livi? etiam Pyrrhum? [a] etiam illa Ciceronis non legisti? *ex veterum rerum monumentis, vel maximum bellum populum Romanum cum Antiocho gessisse, video.* [b] Quanta Romanis negotia exhibuerint gentes istæ, tibi (Livi) contemtæ, etiam Cappadoces, priusquam in illorum ditionem redigerentur, non ignorant veteris eruditionis studiosi. Quod tibi magnus dicit Iustinianus. Nec tu ignorabas ineruditus, sed obscurabas malevolus.

Arma, artem militarem, disciplinam eorum temporum etiam iactitas, Livi, p. 79 Romanorum? Nescio, si feceris merito in comparatione Volsco | rum, Hernicorum, Æquorum, Samnitium: quibuscum Romani per illa tempora præliabantur. [c] Nam verutum a Volscis, scutum a Samnitibus, alia ab aliis arma, et a Græcis, Gallis, Hispanis, Afris, instrumenta bellica, machinas post didicerunt. Neque Romana militia simul nata, simul perfecta est. A Pyrrho alia, et rationem castrorum, rem Romanam firmissimam, acceperunt.

Cedite Romani scriptores, cedite. Non sunt Romani Alexandro pares. [d] Etiamne audetis conferre Germanicum? [e] Quem, ut laudetis certatim omnes, ignaviæ tamen nota non exemistis. At Alexandri ebrietatem, crudelitatem accusatis, alia, quæ in ducibus vestris vidistis: [f] et a quibus alii item vestri scriptores liberant Alexandrum. Etiam amatorias voluptates obiicitis? [g] Sed, his alienum Alexandrum fuisse, magis convenit: et ratio quoque dicitur, si vino deditus fuit, ut in rebus esse Veneris non valuerit. Consule magistros naturæ.

Amat captivam Alexander. Quidni, iuvenis? Sed et matrimonii contrahendi sustinet moram probus, et contumeliam non infert iustus captivæ. Securus ab hac parte Alexander. Discipulus ille Aristotelis pulchras mulieres Persicas, reginam pulcherrimam intueri coram non timet. Tuus ille maior Africanus, Tite, contueri Hispanam veretur: vitæ suæ anteactæ conscius, et libidinis: de p. 80 qua nec | tacuit fama, nec poesis. [h] Quid, quod Antias Valerius, eorum temporum scriptor, non redditam patri Hispanam, sed retentam, atque in deliciis, et amoribus a Scipione usurpatam, scribit? Tu Livio credes? [i] Tu credes Maximo Valerio: qui assentitur de vita Scipionis solutiori in

[a] *Cic. pro Mure.* [b] *Nov.* 30. [c] *Virg.* 2. *Geor. Athe.* 4. 9. *Sym.* 3. *ep.* 11. *Val.* 2. *c.* 3. *Fro.* 4. *c.* 1.
[d] *Tac.* 2. *ann.* [e] *Paterc.* 2. [f] *Lampr. Alex.*
[g] *Plut.* 1. *Symp.* 6. *Ath.* 10. *Arist.* 3. *Probl.* 11. et 32. [h] *Gell.* 6. *c.* 8. [i] *Val.* 6. *c.* 7. 9.

---

379 Cicero, *Pro Murena* 14. 31. 380 *Novellae* 30 (*De proconsule Cappadociae*).

381 Vergil, *Georgica* 2. 165–72; Athenaeus 4. 9; Symmachus, *Epistulae* 3. 11; Valerius Maximus 2. 3; Frontinus, *Strategemata* 4. 1. 4.

382 Tacitus, *Annales* 2. 73.

383 Velleius Paterculus 2.97.2. **Translator's note:** Gentili appears to take Velleius's comment that it was hard to tell whether Germanicus was suited more to military or civil life as a veiled accusation of laziness.

384 Lampridius (*Scriptores Historiae Augustae*), *Alexander Severus* 30. 3.

385 Plutarch, *Table Talk* 1. 6. 1; Athenaeus, *Deipnosophistai* 10, 434 F–435 A; Aristotle, [*Problemata*] 3. 11; 3. 31.

386 Aulus Gellius 6. 8. 387 [Livy's account of this incident is at 26. 50.]

Do you even hold the successors of Alexander in contempt, Livy? Even Pyrrhus? Have you not even read those words of Cicero: "On the basis of the records of ancient history, I see that the Roman people fought its greatest war with Antiochus"?[379] Those who are diligent in ancient learning know just how much trouble those peoples whom you despise, Livy, gave the Romans—even the Cappadocians—before they could be brought back under their sway. The great Justinian tells you this.[380] And yet you are not unaware of the truth through ignorance; you are hiding the truth through malice.

Do you even boast, Livy, of the arms, the military skill, the discipline of the Romans of those days? I'm not sure that you did so deservedly when the Romans are compared with the Volscians, the Hernici, the Aequi, and the p. 79
Samnites, with whom the Romans battled through those ages. For the Romans learned of the javelin from the Volscians, the shield from the Samnites, other arms from other peoples, and later on instruments and machines of war from the Greeks, the Gauls, the Spaniards, and the Africans.[381] For Roman warfare was not born and perfected all at once. They received from Pyrrhus, among other things, the manner of making a camp, a thing regarded as thoroughly Roman.

Yield, Roman writers, yield. The Romans are not the equals of Alexander. Do you even dare to compare Germanicus to him?[382] Even when you are all outdoing one another in praising Germanicus, you have nonetheless not removed all indications of his laziness.[383] But you arraign the drunkenness and cruelty of Alexander—which are other things you have seen in your own leaders, and charges from which other writers of yours exonerate Alexander.[384] Do you accuse him of lustful pleasures? But there is greater agreement that Alexander was foreign to these; and if it is true that he was given to wine, then it stands to reason that he would not have had potency in the business of Venus: just consult the natural philosophers.[385]

Alexander loved a captive woman? How could he not? He was a young man. But he also worthily endured a delay before the undertaking of the marriage, and he justly refrained from reproaching the captive. Alexander is safe from attack in this direction. That pupil of Aristotle was not afraid to look beautiful Persian women, including the most beautiful queen, full in the face. But your Scipio Africanus the elder, Livy, was afraid to look upon a Spanish captive maiden, conscious as he was of his earlier life and his lust, about which neither rumor nor poetry is silent. What do you make of the fact p. 80
that Antias Valerius, a writer of that period, writes that Scipio did not return the Spanish girl to her father, but kept her and enjoyed her among his girlfriends and lovers?[386] Are you going to trust Livy?[387] Or are you going to trust Valerius Maximus, who acknowledges Scipio's rather loose way of life

adolescentia: et addit, citra luxuriæ crimen stetisse? Itane Maxime? Ais tamen de seniori, quemadmodum ancilla ipsi uxoris, et in uxoris oculis, placuit. Credes istis scriptoribus? Credes hoc postremum Maximo, laudatori Scipionis perpetuo. [a] Quid enim cuiquam credemus, si fidem laudantibus non habemus? hic Lactantius diceret. Quod valet dictum firmissimum et cum aliis omnibus, qui professi laudatores sunt Romanorum: de quibus tamen et vitia Romanorum collegimus, atque notavimus.

Nunc Romani cedite Alexandro, et virtuti eius. [b] Quod vos plusquam decies centenis millibus hominum ex urbe vestra cæsis, post annos mille vix quæsiistis: id unus Alexander, nec quadraginta millibus militum, annis decem paravit.

Tyrannis Romanorum.
CAP. XIII

Iam satis, iam vidimus, audivimus, cœpimus de Romana virtute. Vim vidimus, per quam, [c] ut in veteri proverbio est, *Romanus sedendo vincit*: id est, ut
p. 81 audivimus, dolis, ac fraudibus magis, quam viribus vincit. [d] Ro|mani ipsi inquiunt, *Moribus plura, quam viribus vicimus*. Quod rectius dictum evolvitur in idem tamen: si perfidiam Romuli, fallaciam Tulli, astum Anci, proditionem Bruti, sicam Scævolæ, versutiam Martii, præstigias Labeonis, mentitiones Scipionis, iniurias Anicii, cavillationes Catonis, et id genus alios mores aliorum cepimus, qui sunt expositi. Facit Plutarchus alicubi, animal Ulyssi dicere captos ab hoc homines fraudibus: qui, nescii fallendi, secuti essent ingenuum belli morem, et generosum. Hic autem (cernis) populus Romanus Ulysses est.

Habes dissimulantem iniuriarum, adulantem inimicis, desertorem amicorum, contemtorem fœderum, itaque prædatorem omnium, et omnibus immitem. Vides veros istos Suevos: et agros circa se undique vacantes latissime? et quibus in locis (ut historia observat) nobilissimæ olim urbes cernebantur, illic tuguria Romanorum servitiorum manere. Iure aquilam sibi

[a] *Lact.*1. *Inst.* 9. [b] *Card.* 3. *de sap.* [c] *Var. pr. de r. r.* [d] *Quinct. decl.* 3. *Pli.* 6. *ep.*

---

[388] Valerius Maximus 6. 7. 1; 6. 9. 2.

[389] [Valerius Maximus 6. 7. 1.]

[390] Lactantius, *Divinae institutiones* 1. 9.

[391] Varro, *De re rustica* 1. 2. 2.

[392] Quintilian, *Declamationes* 3; Pliny, *Epistulae* 6.

[393] **Translator's note:** The reference is to the *Gryllus, or the Rationality of Animals, Moralia* 987 C. In this dialogue Gryllus is a man turned into a pig by Circe. He explains to Odysseus that he is happier as a pig than he was as a human being. Gentili also alluded to this passage in bk. 2, ch. 3 of *De iure belli.*

in his younger years—and adds that he stayed just this side of the charge of dissipation.[388] Was it so, Valerius? But you nevertheless tell how even as an old man he fancied a slave girl—while his wife was looking on, yet.[389] Will you trust those other writers? Well, you will at least trust Valerius Maximus, an unstinting encomiast of Scipio. For why will we trust anyone about anything if we don't trust those who write in someone's praise [when they mention something discreditable about him]? This is what Lactantius would say here.[390] This principle is especially secure with regard to all those other writers who are professed encomiasts of the Romans, from whose writings nonetheless we have gathered and recorded the sins of the Romans.

Now, Romans, yield to Alexander and to his excellence. What you scarcely acquired after more than tens of hundreds of thousands of men from your city were slaughtered and after a thousand years had passed, one man, Alexander, acquired with no more than 40,000 men in ten years.

CHAPTER 13
The Tyranny of the Romans

We have already seen, heard, and begun to speak enough about Roman virtue. We have seen the might by means of which, as the old proverb has it, "the Roman conquers by sitting still."[391] That is to say, as we have heard, he conquers more by stratagems and deceits than by force. The Romans p. 81
themselves say: "We have conquered more things by our character than by force."[392] This, when said in a straighter way, comes round to the same point, if we have grasped the treachery of Romulus, the deceitfulness of Servius Tullius, the cunning of Ancus, the treason of Brutus, the dagger of Scaevola, the craftiness of Martius, the tricks of Labeo, the lies of Scipio, the misdeeds of Anicius, the scoffings of Cato, and others' habits of this sort, which have been related. Somewhere Plutarch has an animal tell Ulysses that he had seized with his wiles men who, innocent of guile themselves, would have followed an open and noble way of waging war.[393] Now this Roman people, you notice, is Ulysses.

You have a people who hide their wrongdoings, fawning upon enemies, abandoning friends, despising treaties—and accordingly plunderers of all and savage to all. Do you see those veritable Suevi and the fields lying empty far and wide all around them? And do you see that in those places where, as history tells, the noblest cities were once to be seen only the huts of the Romans' slaves remain? Quite properly did they take for themselves the eagle

sumpserunt avem insigne, [a] ut enim illa longum, latumque tractum tenet, et vicinam aliam non patitur: ita Romani circum se omnia unis patere sibi voluerunt, et per omne nefas effecerunt. [b] Iure sumserunt insigne lupos, luparum alumni: [c] Italicæ raptores libertatis, lupi dicti a fortissimo illo Pontio
p. 82 Telesino. Etiam vide remotiora. Capuam aspice: in qua lenitatis specimen | ostentare voluerunt. [d] Plebs dissipata, venundata: nobiles crudeliter cæsi: urbis tecta relicta, ut esset aliqua aratorum sedes: sepulcrum, et monumentum Campani populi: relicta crudelius habitanda, quam si deleta foret. Quæ non mea sunt verba. At de propioribus illis num cantiunculas etiam concinnarunt? [e]*Et Veii veteres, et Volscum regna fuistis: et vestro posita est aurea sella foro. Nunc intra muros pastoris buccina lenti cantat: et in vestris ossibus arva metunt.*

Nunc longe, nunc longius adverte oculos ultra mare, quod supra, quodque alluit infra. [f] Regna vides Illyrii, et Macedoniæ secta in partes: commercia omnia partibus interdicta per humani desertionem iuris: distracta tamquam animalia in artus, alterum alterius indigentes. Hæc huius tyranni populi sollemnis æquitas: [g] ut sic quoque Latinis populis connubia, commercia, concilia multo ante ademerat.

Sed ecce ad Perseum regem specta, et ad regem Illyriorum, et ad Siphacem: reges quasi belluæ, catenis vincti ante currum superbi civis Romani aguntur. [h] Abite nunc mei iurisconsulti, qui docetis; oportere parci nobilibus: etiam cum lex diceret, misericordiam nullam deberi delinquenti: docetis, subtrahi nobiles oportere publicis istis spectaculis. Sed specta. Filii regum, omnis nobilitas in eamdem captivitatem abducuntur: carceribus sempiternis
p. 83 manci|pantur contra omnem belli rationem, et legem. [i] Sed et morte Perseum miserrima confecere, vigiliis. Aut verius est, quod legebamus apud Sallustium. *Apud Samothracas deos Perseum acceptum in fidem, callidi, et repertores perfidiæ, quia pacto vitam dederant, in somnis occidere.* Sic ius Turcicum hodie, dormientem inter vivos non censeri. Et sic magnus quidam ab imperatore Turcarum necatus: cui vita fuit ex promisso, et iureiurando

[a] *Arist.* 9. *hist.* 32. [b] *Pl.* 10. *c.* 4. [c] *Paterc.* 2. [d] *Liv.* 26. [e] *Prop.* 4. *eleg.* 11.
[f] *Liv.* 45. [g] *Liv.* 8. [h] *Decian.* 2. *cons.* 5. [i] *Iov.* 33.

---

394 Aristotle, *Historia animalium* 9. 32.

395 Pliny the Elder, *Naturalis historia* 10. 4.

396 Velleius Paterculus 2. 27. **Translator's note:** Pontius Telesinus was the leader of the Samnites in the Social War. Leading an assault on the forces of Sulla near the Colline Gate, he declared that "the wolves, plunderers of the liberty of Italy, will never leave off unless the forest in which they were accustomed to take refuge has been cut down."

397 Livy 26. 16.

398 Propertius 4. 10. 27–30. **Translator's note:** This is identified as 4. 11 in the marginal note. For the first words "et Veii," offered by some manuscripts, most modern editors adopt Luetjohann's "eh Veii." Also, Gentili's text offers "Volscum" for the manuscripts' "vos tum" in line 27. The line should probably read: "Alas, ancient Veii: you too were once a kingdom!"

399 Livy 45. 400 Livy 8.

401 Decianus, *Consilia* 2. 5, fol. 37v.

402 Giovius [Paolo Giovio] 33 [the reference is unclear; probably *Historiae sui temporis* 27, Tomus secundus, Lugduni, Apud Haered. Seb. Gryphii, 1561, pp. 669 ff.]. [Cf. Plutarch, *Aemilius Paullus* 37. 3.]

as a military standard. Just as the eagle holds a long and wide territory and does not endure another neighbor,[394] so the Romans wanted everything around them to lie open to themselves alone, and they brought this about by means of every possible crime. Rightly did they adopt as a symbol wolves, these nurslings of wolves[395]—these men called "the plunderers of Italian liberty, wolves," by that very brave man Pontius Telesinus.[396] Also, look at things further in the past. Look at Capua, in which they wished to display an p. 82 example of gentle behavior. The common people dispersed, put up for sale; the nobles cruelly slaughtered; the city's buildings left to stand, so that the tomb and monument of the Campanian people might serve as a habitation for ploughmen, derelict buildings that were to be to be inhabited more cruelly than if they had been destroyed.[397] These are not my own words. But have they composed alluring songs yet about these more recent events? "And ancient Veii: you, too, were once the kingdom of the Volscians, and a golden throne was placed in your forum. Now within your walls the horn of the sluggish shepherd sounds, and they reap fields amidst your bones."[398]

Now turn your eyes far off—and even farther off—beyond the sea which washes above [the Adriatic] and that which washes below [the Tyrrhenian Sea]. You behold the kingdoms of Illyrium and Macedonia divided into segments; all trade prohibited to certain parts through the abandonment of human law; regions torn apart like animals torn limb from limb; each region in need of some necessity.[399] This is the customary justice of this tyrant people—just as it had in the same way taken away much earlier also from the Latin peoples the right of intermarriage, the right of free trade, and their assemblies.[400]

But behold, look at king Perseus, at the king of the Illyrians, and at Syphax. Bound in chains, kings are driven like beasts before the chariot of a proud Roman citizen. Go away now, my jurists, who teach that men of noble birth ought to be spared—even though the letter of the law would say that no mercy is owed to the wrongdoer.[401] You teach that nobles ought to be spared those public spectacles. But behold. The sons of kings, all of the nobility are led off into the same captivity and handed over to everlasting imprisonment against every policy and law of war. But they killed Perseus p. 83 with the most wretched kind of death: by keeping him awake.[402] Or perhaps more reliable is that which we were reading in Sallust: "When he had surrendered at the sanctuary of the Gods of Samothrace, clever inventors of perfidy killed him while he was asleep, for they had granted him his life through the agreed-upon terms."[403] Thus Turkish law today holds that someone asleep is not counted among the living. And a certain great man was killed by the emperor of the Turks in this manner, a man whose life was

[403] Sallust, *Historiae* 4, frag. 69.7. **Translator's note:** This is a letter from Mithridates, included in Sallust's now-lost *Historiae*. Gentili transcribed "in somnis occidere," where modern editions of Salllust print "insomniis occidere," which would be in accord with the version of Perseus' death offered by Plutarch and Giovio.

tyranni tuta. [a] Sic ius antea Persicum, cinere suffocare, quos non vi, non veneno per pactum posses. At unde etiam ius hoc sævissimum belli, unde est; ut reges hostes captivos necaretis? Et istam quoque immanitatem celebratis carminibus? [b]*Haurire venena compulimus dirum Siphacem.*

Et, reges sic meritos, vincetis unquam? Et, Siphacem dirum, vincetis? Qui naturæ secutus iudicium, latissimo distinguentis mari Libyca, et Italica regna: secutus tot icta vobis cum Carthaginensibus fœdera, iubentia, populum utrumque illis naturæ finibus contentum esse: secutus iura regnorum certissima, ne quod permittatur tantum inter alia caput efferre, ut timendum reliquis omnibus ab eo sit: secutus æquissimam regni sui conditionem, quæ in discrimen præsentissimum ducebatur, Masanissam vobis in Africam redu-
p. 84 centibus: secutus cum Pœnis iura consanguinitatis, et communis pa|triæ, et deorum communium Africæ: vos voluit, vos monuit, Africam Afris relinquere, quibus natura dedit, adstipulati vos essetis, vindicabat ius commune regnandi, regni sui flagitabat securitas, et, quicquid esset in terris sanctum, et videretur in cælis, adiudicabat. Hæc ictum cum Scipione vestro fœdus tollebant: aut etiam pro Siphace ita interpretabantur. Illud fœdus vos abrupistis primi: abrupit Scipio primus, Masinissa sumto socio armorum, et belli. Nescitis, violari fœdus, si cum hoste fœderati fœdus percutitur, et iam arma adsumuntur? Et itaque Siphacem vincitis dirum.

Exeo autem Africam: unde non tam est novi aliquid semper, et monstri, quam est illic novum semper aliquod, et monstrosum factum Romanorum. [c] Ecce, Iubam Mauritaniæ regem vivere propter eius eruditionem, voluerunt: at duxerunt in triumphum, et ceciderunt flagris. Exeo, exeo Africam. In Græciam redeo: unde divertimus. [d] Ecce, alter regis Persei filius Albano magistratui scriba factus: alter artem faciens ferrariam: uterque ut victum quæritent, et vitam tolerent. Quæ iactata populi Romani, et laudationibus concelebrata clementia, et liberalitas: ut filios regum, et ipsos crudeliter tractarit reges. Nos vero, ab hominibus huius cæli hæc potuisse fieri, cogitare potuissemus?

[a] *Val.* 9. *c.* 2. [b] *Clau. be. Gild.* [c] *Suida.* [d] *Amm.* 14. *Zona. Oros.* 4. *c.* 20.

---

[404] Valerius Maximus 9. 2. ext. 6. **Translator's note:** Gentili here elevates into "ius Persicum" an anecdote about Darius II, who evaded an oath not to kill those who had conspired against him by perching them on beams above beds of hot ashes, into which, when overcome with sleep, they would fall to their deaths. This is also alluded to by Ovid in the *Ibis*, lines 315 f.

[405] Claudian, *De bello Gildonico* 91.

[406] *Suda*, ed. Adler, iota, 399.

[407] Ammianus Marcellinus 14. 11. 31; Zonaras 9. 24; Orosius 4. 20.

supposedly secure on the basis of a promise and oath of the tyrant. And thus it was formerly Persian law to suffocate with ashes those whom you weren't able to kill with violence or poison on account of a treaty.[404] But whence, whence came this most savage law of war, that you would kill captive enemy kings? And do you celebrate this cruelty even in poems? "We forced dreadful Syphax to drink poison."[405]

And will you ever truly conquer kings who are so meritorious? And will you ever truly conquer "dreadful Syphax"? This king gave heed to the decision of nature which separates the Libyan and Italian kingdoms by a very wide sea; he gave heed to so many treaties that you made with the Carthaginians requiring both peoples to rest content with those natural boundaries; he gave heed to the most settled laws of kingdoms that forbid one of them to raise its head so high among the others that it becomes a source of fear to all the rest; he gave heed to the most equitable situation of his own kingdom, which was brought into the most immediate danger when you brought Masinissa back to Africa; and he gave heed to the laws of kinship and common fatherland with the Carthaginians, as well as the shared gods of p. 84
Africa. He wanted you and advised you to leave Africa to the Africans, to whom nature gave it, to whom you yourselves had granted it, for whom the common law of governance protected it, for whom the security of his own kingdom demanded it, and to whom whatever is holy on earth or seems so in heaven awarded it. These facts were making void the treaty he had struck with your Scipio; or at least they were offering an explanation on Syphax's behalf. You yourselves first broke off that treaty, Scipio first broke it off, when Masinissa was taken up as an ally of your arms and war. Are you unaware that one treaty is violated if another treaty is struck with an enemy of the party with whom you made the first treaty and weapons are already being taken up? And thus you conquer dreadful Syphax.

But I am leaving Africa behind, a land from which nothing ever comes so strange and monstrous as some strange and monstrous deed of the Romans performed there. Behold, it was their will that Juba, king of Mauritania, live on account of his erudition; but they conducted him as prisoner in triumph and killed him with whips.[406] I am leaving, *leaving* Africa. I return to Greece, from which we got turned away. Behold, one son of king Perseus was made scribe to a magistrate of Alba; the other was plying the trade of a blacksmith—each one in order to seek sustenance and endure their lives.[407] That is the boasted clemency and kindness of the Roman people, celebrated in speeches of praise: that it has cruelly treated the sons of kings and the kings themselves! But would we have been able to imagine that these things could be done by men of such exalted honor?

p. 85 Sed principibus summotis, populos in liber|tatem duxit, terris universis pacem adduxit, atque constituit Roma. Dicant historiæ. Quibus retentum imperium artibus? [a] Voluptatibus: ut Tacitus ait. [b]*Orbem, quem subegimus, lascivitas nostra defendit*: scribit Seneca. Arcanum hoc imperii, per quod suavis creditur principatus, quæ sæva dominatio est. Aut num quid sævius esse potest, quam si evirentur homines, et effeminentur? si per voluptates, et lascivitates etiam infra omnem hominis conditionem deiiciantur? Quid libido dominatoris aut non audebit, aut non poterit cum pecoribus his, quæ prona humi, et cæno obvoluta os sublime tollere nesciunt, cælumque tueri? Sic est arcanum imperii, quod dum firmat maxime dominationem, id tegit maxime, et vultum huius contrarium præfert. [c] Vanam itaque speciem, et inane nomen libertatis dicebant Ætoli: quorum nec vanam criminationem Livius cogitur confiteri. [d] Hæc illa libertas est, quam Philippus Græcis, a se deficientibus ad Romanos, prædixlt, dominationi diuturniori eos submisisse colla. Etiam crudeliori, etiam. Aspice fasces, secures: vide rapinas, rapacitatem, sectionem publicanorum, calumnias litium, iussa magistratuum, et vexationes. [e] Respice ad tot vectigalium genera, et tributorum: et saxa, et rupes
p. 86 sub tributo habuerunt: et a viris, feminis, pueris, servis, mendicis, sive in | oppidis, sive in agris, etiam pro quolibet animali, etiam pro cane aliquid exigebant, illoque nomine immundo stercoris, et urinæ. Miseram Siciliam: haud quadragesimam partem eius imperii, solvisse ex decumis, portoriis, pastionibus supra quadringenties, hoc est millionem. Infelicem Ægyptum: quæ, cum daret regibus suis (immane) septem milliones, et semissem, dare his amplius duodecim habuit. Perditam Galliam: quæ referta olim et sacris opibus, et profanis, mox direpta, expilata a Cæsare, sæpius (ut inquit Suetonius) ob prædam, quam ob delictum, illico milliones decem annuos, illico viginti debet. Avarissimi hominum, et crudelissimi. Supra centum et quinquaginta milliones ex solis illis tributis conficiebant annuos: quantum non universus nunc orbis, et vetus, et novus principibus omnibus dependet in omnibus. Si enim vigesimas, centesimas, et id genus alia numero: si metalla excutio, quæ sua ubique esse voluerunt: si aurum metior coronarium: si cetera

[a] *Tac. 4. hist.* [b] *Sen. de cons. ad ma.*
[c] *Liv. 53. 34.* [d] *Plut. de Herc. ma.* [e] *Lips. 2. de ma. Ro.*

---

408 Tacitus, *Historiae* 4. 64. **Translator's note:** Ambassadors from the German Tencteri appealed to their fellow Germans of the Colonia Agrippinensis: "Take up again the customs and ways of your ancestors, having left off the pleasures by which more than by arms the Romans hold sway over their subject peoples."

409 Seneca, *De consolatione ad Marciam*. **Translator's note:** It is unclear whether this reference is correct. Note the misidentification in *De armis Romanis* 2. 13, pp. 376 f., n. 752.

410 **Translator's note:** The language here (*os sublime nesciunt caelumque tueri*) recalls Ovid's account of the creation of man: "os homini sublime dedit caelumque videre / iussit," *Metamorphoses* 1. 85 f.

411 Livy 33. 31. **Translator's note:** The marginal note reads "33. 34."

412 Plutarch, *De Herodoti malignitate* 855 A.

413 Justus Lipsius, *Admiranda, sive De magnitudine Romana libri quattuor* 2. 4, Antverpiae, Ex Officina Plantiniana, Apud Ioannem Moretum, 1598, p. 54.

But when the chiefs had been removed, Rome led the subject peoples into liberty, and she introduced and established peace in all the lands. Well, let p. 85 the histories speak. By what arts was rule maintained? By pleasures, as Tacitus says.[408] Seneca writes: "Our wantonness protects for us the world which we have subdued."[409] This is the secret of empire: by which a dominion is believed to be agreeable which is in fact savage despotism. Or can there be anything more savage than that men be emasculated and feminized, that by means of pleasures and wanton behavior they be cast down even below any truly human condition? What will the whim of the despot not dare or not be able to do with herds like these, which, hugging the ground and covered with mud, do not know how to raise their faces up and look upon the sky?[410] Thus is the secret of empire: which while it most fully strengthens domination it most fully conceals it and presents the face of its opposite. Thus the Aetolians spoke of the empty pretense and void name of "liberty," whose accusation—which is *not* false—Livy is forced to acknowledge.[411] This is that "liberty" which Philip meant when he warned the Greeks, who were defecting from him to the Romans, that they had sent their necks under a domination that would be even more long-lasting than his.[412] And even crueler, also! Behold the fasces, the axes. Witness the plunderings, the greed, the confiscations of the tax-collectors, the malicious charges in lawsuits, the orders and harassments of magistrates. Consider so many kinds of taxes and tributes. Even rocks and cliffs they held under tribute. They collected something from men, women, boys, slaves, beggars, either in the towns or in the countryside, even for any sort of animal, even for a dog—on that filthy p. 86 pretext of manure and urine.[413] Wretched Sicily, scarcely a fortieth of that empire, to have paid from produce tithes, port duties, and pasturage fees over forty million. Unlucky Egypt, though it used to give its own kings (monstrous!) seven and a half millions, it had to give the Romans twelve times this. Ruined Gaul, which was once replete with sacred and secular riches, but was pillaged and plundered by Caesar, more often (as Suetonius says) for the sake of booty than for any fault of her own, there she owes ten millions a year, there twenty. Greediest and cruelest of men! Annually they made upward of 150 million solely from those tributes—a figure which the entire modern world, both the old and the new, will not pay to all the princes in all the years. For if I count up twentieth-part taxes and hundredth-part taxes, and others of that sort, if I investigate the metals, which they everywhere wanted as their own; if I estimate the *aurum coronarium*,[414] if I do an inventory of all the

[414] **Translator's note:** This was gold collected in provinces for wreaths for victorious generals.

percenseo, audies tu, positos istos homines in orbe, vel orbi impositos, qui ferro sanguinem orbi, et rapto opes orbi exsugerent. Etiam soliti, se vendere homines, ut his canibus tributa penderent.

Sævissimi hominum. Audi sævitiæ, [a] audi vocem: *Remi salvi sint: nam*
p. 87 *remiges non deerunt, dum in Græcia homines erunt.* Hæc libertas. *Liberos cuique* | *suos natura carissimos esse voluit: hi per dilectus alibi servituri auferuntur. Bona aguntur in tributum.* Quæ sunt iura populi Romani, non privati alicuius iniuriæ. Abi, et Turcicam hic mihi barbariem memora. Audis, et provinciarum sanguine provincias victas. [b] Ubi autem solitudinem fecerunt, ibi pacem se constituisse defendebant: quod Britannus clamabat. Prædones orbis terrarum: quos neque Oriens, neque Occidens satis expleverit: quique cum in urbe illa integrum orbem concluserint, etiam tuguriola Britannorum concupierunt: ut itidem Britannus exclamat, [c]*Quasi inexplebilis venter Roma, cuncta consumens, et semper esuriens: cum in sinus ipsius eversarum omnium urbium, nudatarumque terrarum abrasæ undique opes cogerentur*: et cetera, quæ pius, ac religiosus testis habet Orosius. [d] *Civitatem unam in humani generis perniciem natam*, Arnobius, vir sanctus ait.

[e]*Quam vincit illa feliciter, tam infeliciter, quicquid extra est, vincitur Felicitas urbis, infelicitas orbis. Infelicem sub isto victore orbem, arguto insidiatore, hoste infesto, domino immiti*: ut idem pro testimonio dicit Orosius religiose. Nisi illud forte verum non sit, quod de felicitate censuit urbis.[f] Et immo ipsa tanto miserior, quanto est detestabilius, et calamitosius, facere, quam pati iniuriam.
p. 88 [g] Non est felix civitas: quia exercuerit cives aliis imperare. Non est | in hoc exercitatio rerum bellicarum felix, ut alii servi fiant: qui neque nati sunt ad serviendum, neque meriti per culpam aliquam sunt istam adversitatem. Ad servitutem, et iniuriam propulsandam, ad utilitatem subiectorum vis est armorum iusta, et iustum imperium. De qua iustitia est felicitas vera. Quam iustitiam (et itidem de vera, non de simulata dico) Romana civitas

[a] *Oros.* 6. *c.* 19. [b] *Tac. Agri.* [c] *Oros.* 5. *c.* 18. [d] *Arnob. ad. ge.*
[e] *Oros.* 5. c. 1. *lib.* 6. *c.* 12. [f] *Pla. Gorg.* [g] *Arist.* 7. *polit.*

---

415 Orosius 6. 19. **Translator's note:** The words are those of Antony, who learned before the battle of Actium that almost a third of his rowers had died of hunger.

416 **Translator's note:** Though Gentili offers no marginal note here, this passage is derived from the speech of the British chief Calgacus in Tacitus' *Agricola* (31. 1–2), which Gentili proceeds to cite again shortly.

417 Tacitus, *Agricola* 30. 6 **Translator's note:** Gentili offers a rather cumbersome version of Calgacus's terse "atque ubi solitudinem faciunt, pacem appellant."

418 **Translator's note:** A free paraphrase of Tacitus, *Agricola* 30. 4–5. Gentili is using here the word *praedones* ("robbers"), a term designating a inferior legal status than that of "enemy" (*hostis*); see Cicero, *De officiis* 3. 107; see also the explanation of *praedones* in *Digest* 50. 16. 118: " 'Enemies' [*hostes*] are those who have publicly declared war on us or on whom we have publicly declared war, others are 'bandits [*latrones*] or 'brigands' [*praedones*]."

419 Orosius 5. 18.

420 Arnobius, *Disputationes adversus gentes.*

421 Orosius, 5. 1; 6. 12. **Translator's note:** Gentili has very freely adapted these passages.

other imposts, you will hear that those men were placed on the earth—or, rather, imposed upon the earth—to drain blood from the earth by the sword and wealth from the earth once they had seized it. Men were even accustomed to sell themselves in order to pay tribute to these dogs.

Most savage of men! Hear the voice of savagery: "Let the oars be saved. For there won't be oarsmen lacking while there are men in Greece."[415] This is "liberty." "Nature has willed that for everyone his own children are most dear. p. 87
These children of ours are carried off through conscription to be slaves elsewhere. Our goods are gathered for tribute."[416] These are the laws of the Roman people, not the offences of some private person. Go off and tell me about Turkish barbarity! You hear of provinces conquered with the blood of provinces. Where they have made a solitude, there they used to allege that they had established peace, as the Briton complained.[417] Robbers of the whole world, whom neither the East nor the West will have satisfied, and who, although they have shut up the whole world in that city of theirs, nonetheless coveted the little huts of the Britons—as the Briton cries out in the same place.[418] "Like a stomach that can't be filled is Rome, consuming everything and always hungry still, since into its lap are gathered the riches scraped away from all the overthrown cities and the denuded lands"—and so on. (The pious and religious witness Orosius writes these things.[419]) "The one and only state born for the destruction of the human race," says Arnobius, a holy man.[420]

"That city conquers through its own good luck, just as it is bad luck for whatever outside the empire is conquered. The city's good luck is the world's bad luck. The world is unlucky under that victor, a shrewd plotter, a dangerous enemy, a cruel master," as the same Orosius piously says by way of testimony.[421] But perhaps what he said about the good luck of the city was not true. For indeed she herself is all the more wretched, insofar as it is more detestable and disastrous to perform an injury than to endure one.[422] The state is not fortunate, for it has trained its citizens to rule over others.[423] That training in military affairs is unfortunate that has as its aim p. 88
that others shall become slaves, people who were neither born to be slaves[424] nor have merited adversity through any fault of their own. The just might of arms and just rule are for warding off slavery and injury and for the advantage of subjects. From this justice derives true good fortune. This justice (I am still speaking here of true, not simulated justice) the Roman state

---

[422] Plato, *Gorgias* 489 A.
[423] Aristotle, *Politica* 7.
[424] **Translator's note:** Cf. *Institutes* 1. 3.

nunquam, ne de facie, novit. Civilem, hoc est, versutam iustitiam, in republica tua, Cicero, dices, fuisse, contendesque: sed veram, sed germanam fuisse, non vinces: ut docte disputat contra te Lactantius, et admonet Augustinus.

[a]*Augeri rempublicam sine iniustitia non posse*, apud vos, et vobis, natum est verbum. Atque hæc virtus vestra est: quæ virtutes omnes in se complectitur, avaritiam, abiectionem, perfidiam, ceteras virtutes vestras Fortuna, fortuna, non virtute factum vestrum imperium: fortuna, quæ ad deterrimos semper aberrat. Fortunæ vos templa multa, ab urbe statim condita, et publice posuistis fortunæ filii furiosæ. Virtuti vix unum, et sero, et privatus collocavit in isthoc virtutis hostico. [b] Sed et cum innumeros, atque propudiosos in oppido deos habueritis. Quietis templum, quasi hostis, extra mœnia esse, voluistis. [c] Ecquando vobis fuit aut Pacis templum? Ecquando belli signum clausum Ianum? [d] Inhiasti tu
p. 89 quidem Italia | per annos quadringentos exscidio huius sanguinariæ lupæ. Sed importune humana eras, cum reliquias Danaum, et mitis Achilli suscepisti in sinum: et ad tuam, et ad reliqui perniciem orbis confovisti: progeniem periuri Laomedontis, Laomedonteæ Troiæ perfugas, perfidi Paridis cognationem, [e] Æneæ proditoris manum, [f] Æneæ necromantis sanguinem, Æneæ Laomedontii: [g] ut sic Virgiliusque coactus aliquando est suum Æneam nominare perque infamatum sibi nomen. [h] Ænea, inculpatum deprædicas Laomedontem? Quin tu igitur sis Laomedontiades? [i] Quin tu omnino sis Dardanius Æneas, a fratricida ortus, et exsule Dardano? Ades et tu exsul. [j] Te dominum peregrinum (fatale malum Italiæ) civi pertulimus.

Sed Italia gaude. Omne tibi visum considere in ignes Ilium, et ex imo verti Romulia Troia. Qui sine virtutis cultu ullo per annos sexcentos, sine ipsa virtute semper, semper et sine quiete: in parricidiis, sacrilegiis, perfidiis, proditionibus, cædibus, rapinis, cupidinibus insatiabilibus nati, educati ab ortu primo per ætates omnes, et in tantum imperium a fortuna insaniente ducti, diuque per artes pessimas dominantes: ecce hic tandem conciderunt. Imperium male partum, administratum peius, dispersum penitissime, et dissipatum funditus, iam diu universus orbis, servituti subtractus lamentabili, intuetur, et ridet.

[a] *Aug.* 2. *de civ.* 21. [b] *Aug.* 4. *de civ.* 16. [c] *Baron.* 1. vol. *an. ec.* [d] *Oros.* 6. *c.* 1.
[e] *Dar. Phryg.* 6. [f] *Oth. Phris.* 1. *c.* 2. *Serv.* 1. 6. *Æn.* [g] *Virg.* 7. 8. *ubi Donat.*
[h] *Hom. Iliad.* 20. [i] *Servius* 3. *Æneid.* [j] *Scal.* 3. *Poet.* 28.

---

425 **Translator's note:** The differentiation between "civil," wise justice on the one hand and "natural," stupid justice on the other stems from the speech made by L. Furius Philus in Cicero's *De republica* (3. 31) and was known to Gentili through a passage in Lactantius' *Divinae institutiones* (5. 16. 5–13).

426 Augustine, *De civitate Dei* 2. 21. 427 Augustine, *De civitate Dei* 4. 16.

428 Caesar Baronius [Cesare Baronio], *Annales ecclesiasticae*, Moguntiæ, Impensis I. T. Schönwetteri, 1614, vol. 1.

429 Orosius 6. 1.

430 **Translator's note:** This is a sarcastic reworking of the words "reliquias Danaum atque immitis Achilli" at *Aeneis* 1. 30: "the remnants of the Danaans and survivors of *savage* Achilles."

431 Dares Phrygius 6.

has never come to know—has not even had a nodding acquaintance with it. Cicero, you will say and contend that civil—that is, cunning—justice existed in your state, but you will not persuade us that it was true, genuine justice, as Lactantius learnedly argues against you and as Augustine points out.[425]

"A state cannot be enlarged without injustice"—among you Romans and for your benefit was that saying born.[426] And this virtue is yours: one which embraces all the virtues: avarice, the humbling of rulers, oath-breaking, and all your other virtues. It was by luck, luck, not virtue that your empire was created: luck that always gravitates towards the basest men. Sons of mad luck, you publicly founded many temples to Fortune, from the very foundation of the city. It was only late that a private citizen founded but a single temple to Virtue in that territory hostile to her. And although you had countless very shameful divinities inside your city, you wished for the temple of Quiet to be outside your walls, like an enemy.[427] Did you at any time have a temple of Peace?[428] Was the symbol of war, Janus' temple, ever closed? Italy, for four hundred years you longed for the destruction of this bloody wolf.[429] But you p. 89
were inopportunely humane when you gathered to your bosom the remnants of the Danaans and survivors of gentle Achilles[430] and fostered for your own destruction and that of the rest of the world the offspring of perjured Laomedon, the refugees of Laomedon's Troy, the kindred of perfidious Paris, the band of the traitor Aeneas,[431] the blood of Aeneas the necromancer,[432] of Laomedontian Aeneas, as Vergil was at times forced to call his dear Aeneas by a name that was disgraceful to himself.[433] Aeneas, do you proclaim Laomedon guiltless?[434] Then why wouldn't you be Laomedontiades? Why wouldn't you indeed be "Dardanian Aeneas," since you are sprung from the fratricide and exile Dardanus?[435] You show up here as an exile yourself. We have preferred you as a foreign master to a citizen (a fatal evil for Italy).[436]

But rejoice, Italy. You have seen all of Ilium sink into the flames, and Roman Troy has been overturned from its foundations. Those who, without any cultivation of virtue over the course of six hundred years, always without virtue itself and always without rest, have been born and brought up in acts of parricide, sacrilege, perfidy, betrayal, slaughter, rapine, insatiable desires, and have been led to so great an empire by mad fortune, ruling for a long time through the basest arts—behold, here they have at last collapsed. Now at long last the whole world, freed from lamentable servitude, beholds and mocks an empire badly acquired, worse governed, now scattered far and wide and utterly broken.

---

[432] Otto of Freising, *Chronicle* 1. 25 [*Chronica sive historia de duabus civitatibus*, rec. Adolfus Hofmeister, Hannoverae et Lipsiae, 1912, p. 56]; Servius, *On Aeneid* 1. 31 f.; 6 [the reference to bk. 6 is unclear].

[433] Vergil, *Aeneis* 7. 105; 8. 18; see Donatus. **Translator's note:** In fact, only 8. 18 refers to Aeneas.

[434] *Iliad* 20. 236.

[435] Servius, *On Aeneid* 4. 365.

[436] Scaliger, *Poetices libri septem*, [Genevae] Apud Petrum Santandreanum, 1594, 3. 28.

p. 90

ALBERICI GENTILIS
DE ARMIS ROMANIS

LIBER II
VEL
De iustitia bellica Romanorum
DEFENSIO.

Testimonia certa Romanæ iustitiæ.
CAP. I

Facilem defensionis caussam, quam suscipio Romanorum meorum, facit Picenus, accusator noster: qui, a principio usque accusationis suæ, pugnare se, et disceptare contra receptam temporum omnium, et omnium hominum opinionem, professus est. Ego enim, probari omnibus sententiam illam existimo. [a]*Ut, de quo omnium definitio consentit, id verum esse, necesse sit.* Itaque si iustum Romanorum imperium, et iusta Romanorum bella cuncti
p. 91 mortales, decursu ist|hoc duorum annorum millium, una voce, tenore perpetuo censuerunt: quod testimonium accusatoris est: vicimus. Quid enim, quid, quibus universa assultat adversaria disceptatio, vel testimonia obscurissima, vel indicia tenuissima, vel leves prorsus argutationes contra clarissimorum virorum auctoritatem, contra iudicia gravissima, et contra robur invictarum rationum efficerent? P. Diaconus, Zonara, Orosius, Cedrenus, alii, et quorum nec dicere nomen frons fuerit accusatori, testes eius, qui Dionysio opponantur, Polybio, Plutarcho, Livio, suspectis historicis, mendacibus Romanorum laudatoribus.

Exploremus, accusator, exploremus testes. Quis Polybio sapientior, Dionysio diligentior, Livio simplicior, Plutarcho doctior? Et potuerit doctrina decipi, voluerit decipere simplicitas, potuerit errare diligentia, voluerit errores sapientia? Contumeliosa illa levitatis Græcorum, et infidelitatis non ad hos viros attingunt, utcumque Græcos. Ad illos pertinent accusatoris, Zonaras, Cedrenos, alios de plebe homulos, monachos Græculos esurientes. Nam et Græcia habet suos Aristides, Phociones, Epaminondas, alios innumerabiles:

[a] *Cic.* I. *de na. deo. Xenoph. apol.*

---

[1] **Translator's note:** Gentili was born in the Marche of Ancona, the territory of the ancient Piceni.

[2] Cicero, *De natura deorum* I. 44; Xenophon, *Apologia* I. I.

ALBERICO GENTILI p. 90

ON THE WARS OF THE ROMANS

BOOK 2

OR

Defense of the Justice of the Romans in Warfare

CHAPTER 1

Firm Testimonies to Roman Justice

Picenus,[1] our prosecutor, renders easy the case I have undertaken in defense of my Romans, for he has admitted from the very beginning of his indictment that he is fighting and disputing against the received opinion of all times and all men. For I think that this well-known pronouncement meets the approval of everyone: "That must be true, concerning which everyone's explanation agrees."[2] Therefore, if all men over this course of two thousand years have p. 91
judged uninterruptedly with one voice that the empire of the Romans was just and that the Romans' wars were just—a fact borne out by the prosecutor's own testimony—then we have triumphed. For when opposed to the authority of the most famous men, the weightiest judgments, and the force of undefeated arguments, what service might the most obscure testimonies, the shoddiest pieces of hostile evidence, or utterly worthless carpings perform for those who are assailed by a unanimous judgment? Paulus Diaconus, Zonaras, Orosius, Cedrenus, and others whose names the prosecutor wouldn't have the audacity to mention—these are his witnesses who are to be opposed to Dionysius, Polybius, Plutarch, Livy, whom he regards as suspect historians and lying encomiasts of the Romans.

Let us test, prosecutor, let us test the witnesses. Who is wiser than Polybius, more diligent than Dionysius, more honest than Livy, more learned than Plutarch? And could learning be deceived? Would honesty want to deceive? Could diligence err? Would wisdom tolerate errors? Those reproaches against the fickleness and untrustworthiness of the Greeks do not touch those men, Greeks though they may have been. They *do* suit those authorities of the prosecutor—Zonaras, Cedrenos, and other little men of base birth, hungry Greekling monks. For even Greece has its men like Aristides, Phocion, Epaminondas, and countless others, who were so eager

[a] qui sic studiosi exstitere veritatis, ut ne ioco quidem, ne propter maximam quidem utilitatem dicere mendacium velint, viri iustissimi.

p. 92 Ad Gallos accusatoris, et ad Hispanos illa | pertinent, quæ idem accusatoris auctor M. Tullius detonat adversum Gallos vehementius: [b]*An vero istas nationes religione iurisiurandi, ac metu deorum immortalium in testimoniis dicendis commoveri arbitramini? quæ tantum a ceterarum gentium more, ac natura dissentiunt*, &c. et quæ sunt nunc aptissima: *An vero dubitatis, iudices, quin insitas inimicitias istæ gentes omnes et habeant, et gerant cum populi Romani nomine?*

Græci si male audiunt (neque isti tamen) in historiis, illic id est, ubi de ipsorum agitur Græciæ rebus, et ubi effusi in laudes suas illi scriptores sunt. Sed ista vacat ratio hic. De rebus aliorum hic agitur; ubi etiam avari scriptores Græci esse consueverunt. Ridiculum illud est de exteris: nisi scribere historiam melius possunt obscuri illi monachi, id est tenebriones, nec modo exteri reipublicæ, sed hominibus omnibus, quam viri civiles, et eruditi, et diligentes, ut nati in terris aliis. Neque affectus locum apud istos invenerint: qui nec Romani fuerunt: nec habuere caussam mentiendi. Recipe tuum, Picene, illud, *Cui bono*? Desine viros gravissimos insimulare mendacii, quibus nulli bono mendacium fuit. [c]*Cum sint præmia falsi nulla, ratam debet testis habere fidem.* [d] Quod et Hieronymus. *Ex quo colligitur, fidele esse testimonium, quod caussas*
p. 93 *non habet mentiendi.* [e] Vani, leves, ignominia, spe, metu, iracundia, mi-| sericordia impulsi, præmio, gratia adducti, hi illi sunt testes, quos fide indignos censent leges, et auctores. At vanos, leves non appellaveris, nisi tu levis, et vanus sis, qui editis operibus, et monumentis ingenii nobilissimis viros se gravissimos cuncto orbi, et longæ vetustati temporum adprobarunt.

Hoc experimentum hominis, opus eius. Hinc de homine iudicium certum. *Loquere, ut te videam.* Nulla hic spes, nullus metus: [f]*dum res populi Romani memorabantur pari eloquentia, ac libertate: neque referebat cuiusquam, Punicas, Romanasve acies laetius extulisses.* Vacat hic iracundia adversum victos: contra quos testimonia scriptorum sint. Vacat misericordia erga victores: pro quibus dicta testimonia fuerint. Neque enim isti misericordia sunt prosequendi: neque est quisquam hominum adeo barbarus, et immanis, ut afflictis, mis-

[a] *Cor. Ne. Epam. Plut. Aristi. Thom.* [b] *Cic. pro Font.* [c] *Ovid.* 3. *Trist.* 10.
[d] *Hier. ep.* 9. et *Cic.* 2. *de fin. et Deci.* 2. *cons.* 25. [e] *Cic. part.* [f] *Tac.* 1. *hist.* 4. *ann.*

---

[3] Cornelius Nepos, *Epaminondas* 3. 1; Plutarch, *Aristides* 2. 2; 6; *Themistocles* 29. 2–3.
[4] Cicero, *Pro Fonteio* 30; 33.
[5] Ovid, *Tristia* 3. 10. 35–6.
[6] Jerome, *Epistulae* 9; Cicero *De finibus* 2; Decianus, *Consilia* 2. 25, fols. 82^{v} f.
[7] Cicero, *Partitiones oratoriae* 14/49.
[8] **Translator's note:** The earliest attestation of this proverb appears to be Apuleius, *Florida* 2, where it is attributed to Socrates.
[9] **Translator's note:** This is a conflation of Tacitus, *Historiae* 1. 1 and *Annales* 4. 33. 4.

for the truth that they were not willing to tell a lie even in a joke, not even for the greatest possible benefit—men of consummate justice.[3]

To the accuser's Gauls, to his Spaniards belong those things that none p. 92
other than Cicero, the prosecutor's authority, thunders vehemently against the Gauls: "Or do you think that those nations are moved by the sanctity of oath-swearing or by the fear of the immortal gods in the giving of evidence? These nations differ from the custom and nature of other peoples . . . etc." And he adds these words most suitable in this context: "Or do you really doubt, judges, that all those peoples possess and act upon deep-seated hatreds against the name of the Romans?"[4]

If the Greeks have a bad reputation (and yet the above-mentioned authors do not) in the writing of histories, it is with regard to the affairs of Greece—and in cases where those authors are lavish in their own praise. But that motive is lacking here. Here the subject is the deeds of others, where Greek writers have tended to be even stingy. That matter of their foreign birth is a ridiculous charge. Or were those obscure monks, i.e. light-shunning swindlers, men foreign not only to the state but to all mankind, able to write history better than men who were civic-minded, learned, and diligent, no matter if they may have been born in foreign lands? Nor would those monks find any room for partiality among those authorities [i.e. the Greek writers], men who were neither Romans nor had a reason for lying. Picenus, here is your own phrase back at you: "Cui bono?" Stop making accusations of mendacity against the most serious of men, men to whom no advantage would accrue from lying. "When there are no rewards for falsehood, the witness ought to have firm trust."[5] Ditto Jerome: "From which it is to be understood that that testimony is trustworthy which has no motives for lying."[6] Those who are
deceptive and erratic, who are driven by disgrace, hope, fear, anger, compas- p. 93
sion, who are attracted by reward and favor—these are the witnesses whom the laws and authorities judge untrustworthy.[7] But unless you were lying and erratic yourself, you would not call lying and erratic those men who through the production of the noblest works and monuments to their genius have shown themselves to the whole world and to the vast stretches of time to be the most respectable of men.

This is the true test of a man: his work. Hence comes sound judgment about a man. "Speak, so that I may see you."[8] There is no expectation, no fear evident in this: "When the affairs of the Roman people were recorded with equal eloquence and freedom, it didn't matter to anyone if you more gladly extolled the armies of the Carthaginians or the Romans."[9] Here there is no place for anger against the defeated, against whom the testimonies of the writers might be directed. Here there is no place for compassion towards the victors, on behalf of whom testimonies might be delivered. For just as the victor ought not to be attended with compassion, neither is there anyone so barbaric and cruel as to wish to be angry at the afflicted and wretched and

erisque irasci, perque iracundiam maledicere velit. Potuit Livius esse Pompeianus plurimum: si hosti Pompeianorum, qui hic citatur, credendum est Augusto: vixit enim Livius, cum aut partes illæ vigerent, aut partium studia superessent.

[a] Hoc Plutarchus notat difficillimum in scribenda historia, quod qui fuere præsentes, et de quibus est accipiendum, illi odio, gratia, aliter veritatem corrumpunt. Si Polybio teste uteremur pro Africano: etiam posset Polybio p. 94 reiici de affectu: | quo erga eum teneretur, cui comes, atque familiaris convixit. Ceterum non hoc pertinet studium ad ætates superiores. Et est ridiculum Castelvetrii (huius illud est) argumentum in Livium, qui hostes nominet, contra quos gererent Romani bellum. [b] Ut namque bella a parte victa nominari solent, Punicum, Italicum, Annibalicum, Mithridaticum: ita et hostes dicuntur, qui victi sunt. Etiam desierant tum hostes esse, et amici erant omnes, cum scriberet Livius. [c] Itaque vel Livio hosti crederetur testi, postquam reconciliata omnium amicitia, et quidem longo post tempore in summa animorum, et voluntatum consensione dicit testimonium.

Esset aliquid, quod aliud addit Picenus, quod si in uno falsus, ac mendax ostenditur Livius, iam in nullo fidus, ac verax deberet existimari. Ceterum quod illud est unum mendacium Livii? Unum in Pompeianorum notatur caussa: sed, ut dico, teste hoste illarum partium longe sævissimo, et contra quem antiquitas omnis, et quæ secuta in hunc diem omnis est ætas, [d] summi iudicii vir Lucanus, respondet: quæ pro Pompeianis semper iudicavit.

Non etiam verum est, non, ut testis aliquando mendax in caussa aliqua, ille idem in caussis omnibus semper veluti mendax reiiciatur. Non est verum, non, ut, si instrumentum quoddam sit tabellionis falsum, falsa omnia eiusp. 95 dem in | strumenta debeant reputari. Et ratio illa fidei individuæ sic est: quæ individua caussæ est individuæ, non caussis pluribus, variis, late dissitis: in quibus nec possit criminis eiusdem admittendi occasio esse.

Aut quid si non mendacium, ac dolus est testis, sed error? Id potius credendum est: ut criminis vitetur ([e] quod leges iubent) interpretatio: et iam nihil de fide, de auctoritate forte detrahi non nihil potest: quasi hominis eius, qui notitiam non teneat rei plenam, et abundantem. At sunt hic quoque replicationes illæ firmiores: quod in diversis caussis error non ostenditur per errorem, qui admissus in una est. Multa sunt vetustiora, et multis modis

[a] *Plutarch. Pericle.* [b] *Paus.* 4. [c] *Nell. de testi. ver.* inimicus. *Decian.* 3. *cons.* 34.
[d] *Mont.* 2. *ess.* 10. [e] *l.* 51. *pro soc.*

---

[10] **Translator's note:** For Augustus on Livy as Pompeian, see Tacitus, *Annales* 4. 34. 3.

[11] Plutarch, *Pericles* 13. 16.

[12] [Lodovico Castelvetro, *Poetica d'Aristotele vulgarizzata et sposta*, Basilea, Stampata ad instanza di Pietro de Sedabonis, 1576.]

[13] Pausanias 4. 6. 1.

[14] Nellus de Sancto Geminiano, *Tractatus de testibus*, in *Tractatus universi iuris*, Venetiis [Franciscus Zilettus], 1584–6, vol. 4, fol. 80^r, s.v. inimicus; Decianus, *Consilia* 3. 34.

[15] Montaigne, *Essays* 2. 10. [16] *Digest* 17. 2. 51.

to speak ill of them through anger. Livy was able to be predominantly a Pompeian, if we must believe Augustus, the enemy of the Pompeians, who is here cited. For Livy lived either when those factions were strong or when their passions were still surviving.[10]

Plutarch notes that the most difficult thing in writing history is that those who were present and whose testimony we must accept perverted the truth through hatred, partiality, or in other ways.[11] If we are to use Polybius as a witness on behalf of Scipio Africanus, it would even be possible for Polybius to be rejected because of the fondness that he felt towards the man with p. 94
whom he lived as companion and close friend. But this zeal does not extend to earlier ages. And it is a laughable charge of Castelvetro[12] (for it is in fact his) against Livy that he termed "enemies" those against whom the Romans waged war. For just as wars tend to be named after the losing side (e.g. the Punic, the Italian, the Hannibalic, the Mithridatic), so are those who have been defeated termed "enemies."[13] But at the time Livy was writing, they had in fact ceased to be enemies and were friends. Therefore even Livy, an enemy, could be trusted as a witness, after the friendship of all of them had been reestablished, and he offers testimony after a very long time had passed, during a period of the greatest accord of minds and wills.[14]

There might be something in what Picenus adds, that if Livy is shown to be false and a liar in one thing, then he ought to be judged trustworthy and reliable in nothing. But what is that one supposed lie of Livy? It is just one: that he is branded as being on the side of the Pompeians. But, as I say, that is on the testimony of far and away the most savage enemy of that party, a man contradicted by all of antiquity and every age that has followed to the present day, as well as by Lucan, a man of the highest judgment.[15] Every age has always judged in the favor of the Pompeians.

Nor is it even true—not at all—that a witness who is on occasion lying in a certain case is always to be rejected as lying in all cases. It is not true—not at all—that if a certain document of a notary is false then all the documents of that same person ought to be considered false. And that well-known p. 95
principle of indivisible trustworthiness works thus: that it is indivisible for a particular case, not for many differing and widely scattered cases in which there would not even be a likely pretext for admitting the same charge.

Or what if there is no lying involved, and the witness is not deceptive, but there is simply an error? That is what is preferable to believe, in order that the suggestion of a charge might be avoided (as the laws ordain).[16] And in this case, while something might perhaps be subtracted from a witness's authority, nothing is lost of his general trustworthiness, for it is that of a man who does not have full and abundant information on the matter. But in this instance there are also these firmer replies: that in very different cases one error is not exposed through another error that is admitted in a single instance. There are many matters which are rather remote in time and in

obscuriora: in quibus errare etiam prudentissimi, et diligentissimi possunt, qui in aliis non erraverint. [a] Ipse sic Livius, certiora esse omnia post urbem a Gallis receptam, fatetur: cum, quæ antea gesta essent, ea aut scriptorem non invenerint, aut per Gallicum illud incendium amiserint memorias suas.

Væ tibi, Picene: væ testibus tuis, illis historicorum dehonestamentis, si argutationes hæ tuæ fidei, et auctoritati testium imminuendæ valent: civis Romanus est; itaque Romanis adblanditur: mendax in uno est; ergo abiiciendus in omnibus est: errat aliquando; nullibi igitur ulla est hominis auctoritas. p. 96 Quid enim, ut tibi tuum potiorem appellem, quid Orosius? Hispanus | est; itaque Numantinis ablanditur: hostis Romanorum est; itaque Romanis iniquus est. In Orosio hoc amplius mihi consideres, non tam illum esse historicum, quam apologistam, et quidem contra quietem, ac tranquillitatem Romani imperii: itaque credendum minus sit homini, utcumque integro; qui non fidem historicam prositetur, sed sedulam defensionem. Rapit enim iste, quicquid facit ad institutum operis: rapiturque in ea vicissim omnia, quæ suscepta poscit scriptio, et allatus scribendo cupit affectus. In Orosio, et reliquis Piceni hoc amplius, rhapsodos quosdam fuisse: quorum fides non constet absque auctoribus primis: certe, si auctoribus primis contradicunt: qui nostri illi Polybius, Dionysius, Livius, Plutarchus: et quibus si fides non constat historica, hominum quanta fides esse potest (ut de eo non disputem contentiose) periit ecce omnis historia, et magnum vitæ humanæ lumen perfusum est. Sed immo manet hoc lumen: manet historia: et optimorum illorum laudatur, placet, viget, relegitur, amatur.

[b] Optimis illis, et excellentibus historicis dandum et illud fuit, ut iudicarent facta, dicta, de quibus exposuerunt: et iure sibi sumerent, regere fidem lectorum ex sua. Namque in narrationibus pluribus, variisque eligere ipsi, qua erant vi præditi perspicacis iudicii, poterant veriores: et in contrariis p. 97 disce | ptationibus, qua instructi erant doctrina, poterant constituere iustiorem. Testium eadem ratio non est, plurimum idiotarum, atque imperitorum: et semper temerariorum, dum iudicando traiiciunt se in munus alius personæ, iudicis. Dicerem, esse testes, qui iudicantes audiantur:

[a] *Liv.* 6. [b] *Bru. de consecr. hist. Mont. d.* 10.

---

17 Livy 6. 1. 3.

18 Giovanni Michele Bruto [Ioannes Michael Brutus], *De historiae laudibus*, Cracoviae, Typis A. Petricovii, 1583; Montaigne, *Essays* 2.10. **Translator's note:** The first part of this reference is obscure. We take "Bru." to refer to Bruto, and we are assuming that "*De consecr. hist.*" is a misprint for "*De conscr. hist.*"—i.e. "*De conscribenda historia*," which we take to be Gentili's misremembering of the title of Bruto's short treatise, a work which shares Gentili's Roman defender's delight in early Roman history as a source for exemplary models. We do not believe that Lucian of Samosata's brief treatise *De conscribenda historia* is meant here.

various ways somewhat obscure in which even the most intelligent and diligent men can go astray, men who will not have gone astray in other matters. Thus Livy himself admits that everything became more certain after the city was recovered from the Gauls, since the things which were done earlier either did not meet with a chronicler or else lost their written records when the Gauls burned the city.[17]

Woe to you, Picenus. Woe to your witnesses, those disgraces among historians, if the trustworthiness and authority of actual witnesses can be diminished by carpings like these of yours: "He's a Roman citizen; therefore he's flattering the Romans. He's mendacious in one thing; therefore he's to be rejected in everything. He makes a mistake sometimes; therefore the man has no authority anywhere at all." What about Orosius (to summon for you a better man than you)? He's a Spaniard; therefore he's flattering the Numan- p. 96
tines. He's an enemy of the Romans; therefore he's unfair to the Romans. In the case of Orosius you might do me the favor of reflecting more fully that he was not so much a historian as he was a Christian apologist—and even an enemy of the peace and tranquility of the Roman Empire. Therefore one should put less trust in a man, even a worthy one, who does not profess historical trustworthiness but zealous justification. For that fellow seizes upon whatever contributes to the purpose of his book, and he is by turns carried away into all the things required by the composition he has undertaken, and driven by the very act of writing he seeks out strong passions. In the case of Orosius and the other authorities of Picenus, there is this further fact: some were compilers whose trustworthiness would not be secure in the absence of leading authorities, and it is certainly lacking when they contradict those leading authorities—by whom I mean Plutarch, Dionysius, Livy, Polybius, and all those who, if *their* historical reliability is called into question (insofar as there can be any reliability among humans—I wouldn't want to get into a heated dispute about that point), then, behold, all of written history has perished, and a great beacon of human life has been doused. But this light really does survive, and the historical work of those most eminent men survives, is praised, pleases, has power, is reread, and is loved.

And this is something that must be allowed to those greatest and most excellent historians: that they may judge the deeds and words they set forth and may lay a just claim to guide the beliefs of their readers in accord with their own.[18] For those very men were the ones able to select from among multiple and differing accounts the truest ones by means of that power of discernment with which they were endowed, and they were able to determine among conflicting contentions the ones that were more just by means of the p. 97
learning in which they were versed. This same procedure does not belong to witnesses, who are for the most part uneducated and inexperienced and always intemperate while by making judgments they thrust themselves into the task of another role, namely that of a judge. I would grant that there are

et quibus historici similiores sint, quam aliis. Sed omnino eadem ratio non est testium, et historicorum.

Porro de meliori nostra conditione in iudicio de Romanorum rebus gestis post tot secula non sic censuit Isocrates. [a]*Quæ nostra sunt ætate facta, de his nostrum iudicium non iniuria interponimus: in rebus vero a nostra memoria longe remotis, par est, nos illorum temporum assentiri peritis.* Sane quidem ut caligat corporis oculus ad ea, quæ nimium prope posita sunt: ad alia autem cæcutit, quæ per infinitam distantiam absunt: ita mentis oculus præsentium rerum affectibus obnubilatur, sed longissime remotarum ignoratione obtenebratur. Et igitur non Livio (age, indulgeamus accusatori) in civilibus bellis fides sit: non Tacito, non Suetonio contra Neronem. Valeat Cardani etiam verbum hoc pro ostento illo, ac monstro, nec in philosophia disputatione prolatum, sed in exercitatione ingenii. Sed itaque fides sit multo minor scriptoribus priscarum rerum recentissimis: cum veritas pluribus infracta modis, et multa
p. 98 rerum inscitia debi|litata iaceret. Istæ sunt testium, et testimoniorum veræ leges.

Nos autem, ut prooemio accusatoris illic respondimus, ubi disputare visus est: ita declamatiunculam reliquam manere patimur, et homini esse oblectamento. Agat, advocet in auxilium gentes. Aderunt Lybes: apud quos non enecta tantum a meis monstra, exscisa venena sunt; at reges, regulique, qui caussæ illic intestinorum bellorum, deleti, et publica tranquillitas, et tamquam unius bene coagmentati corporis sanitas constituta est. Favebunt votis omnibus Asiaticæ gentes: quæ mille Sardanapalis ereptæ, et portentis tyrannorum: raptæ in fidem, et clientelam populi Romani, in omnia tutæ, et in omnibus, pacem optatissimam tenuerunt. Plaudent Europei: quibus per virtutem Romanam de orbe reliquo partum imperium est. Nam quid Italos ciet in arma viros, lentos illos nunc, et longo otio marcidos? qui barbari ante Romanum imperium habiti non Græcis tantum, [b] verum etiam barbaris ipsis, mox et cultissimi, et principes omnium evaserunt. Quid Germanos? ad quos delatas a civitate mea artes omnes humanitatis: et itaque de rudibus, et agrestibus politissimos factos videmus. Quid Gallos? quorum de cervicibus

[a] *Isocr. enc. Hel.* [b] *Dru. 3. Obs. 3.*

[19] Isocrates, *Encomium Helenae* 22.
[20] [Cardanus, *Encomium Neronis* 1. 3.]
[21] Iohannes Drusius [Jan van den Driesche], *Observationes sacrae* 3. 3 [Antverpiae, Excudebat Aegidius Radaeus, 1584].

witnesses who would be listened to when passing judgment and to whom historians bear more resemblance than they do to others. But the method of witnesses and of historians is in general not the same at all.

Moreover, as to our supposedly superior vantage-point in passing judgment upon the deeds of the Romans after so many centuries, Isocrates does not agree: "Not without cause do we put forward our judgment about the things that were done in our own time. But in matters far removed from our memory it is proper that we assent to the learned men of those times."[19] Of course it is true that our bodily eye grows dizzy at things that are placed too close. On the other hand, it is blind to things that are distant at an immeasurable distance. Similarly, the mind's eye is beclouded by the sensations of present things, but is made dark by ignorance of things that have been moved a long distance away. And therefore let there be no trust in Livy (come, let's grant this much to the prosecutor) with regard to the civil wars—and no reliability in Tacitus or Suetonius against Nero. Let even Cardanus' declaration on behalf of that prodigy and monster be regarded as valid, even though it was not offered in a disputation in philosophy but in an exercise of cleverness.[20] But at the same time let there be much less faith placed in the most recent writers about ancient history, since the truth is injured in various ways and lies weakened through great ignorance of the facts. These, forsooth, p. 98 are the true laws of witnesses and testimonies.

Now, then, that we have made a response to the preface of the prosecutor in that place where he seems to be engaged in a disputation, so we are content to allow the rest of the little declamation to stand and to serve as an amusement for the fellow. Let him go then and summon the various peoples to his aid. The Libyans shall be present—among whom not only have monsters been killed off by my people and their poison eliminated, but also kings and chieftans, who were the sources of internal wars there, have been eliminated and public tranquility and, so to speak, the health of a single well-joined body have been established. The peoples of Asia shall no doubt heed all his prayers—men who, having been liberated from a thousand Sardanapuluses and monster tyrants and carried off into the security and patronage of the Roman people, safe for all things and in all things, have obtained the most desirable peace. The peoples of Europe will applaud—peoples who have through Roman valor obtained rule over the rest of the world. And yet—what rouses the men of Italy to take up arms for him, those men now sluggish and enfeebled by long leisure? Before the time of the Roman Empire those men were considered barbarians not only by the Greeks but even by the barbarians themselves, but soon emerged as the most cultivated people and rulers of everything.[21] What rouses the Germans to arms, men to whom we see that all the arts of civilization have been conveyed by my nation, and whom we see having been turned from rude and rustic men into the most polished? What rouses the Gauls to arms, from whose necks the excessively proud rule of

superbissimus Ariovisti dominatus, et immanis, ac perpetuus Germanorum p. 99 terror sublatus est. Quid Hispanos? qui Afro|rum olim, et latronum, atque piratarum præda, post sub Romano imperio frui fluminibus suis aureis, metallisque valuerunt, et esse beatissimi. Quid etiam Britannos concitat invictos? Invictos autem? quos victos qui negat, is ille est certe, qui negare omnem historiam potest? [a] Etiam nec desiderarunt, nec oblatam acceperunt pauperem tum, et negotiosam istam provinciam. Sed Britannos advocat: quibus si aliud nihil præstitissent Romani, quam quod divisos orbe toto in partem orbis, et hominum compegerunt: hoc illi beneficio uno immortali Romanum nomen perpetuo venerabuntur. Græcia in libertatem asserta, Macedonia de servitute vindicata deferent certe suis vindicibus, atque liberatoribus hanc coronam, et palmam virtutis. Nec denegabit lauream Carrhago magna: quæ terra, marique per annos quinquaginta in isto certamine gloriæ egit, et tribus bellis victa concessit. Et hæc summa Carthaginis laus est, quod cum populo victore omnium gentium bellavit fortissime omnium. [b] Nam, fuisse Carthaginem tributariam Syracusanorum, non ignoramus. Persæ, Medi, Assyrii a Romanis spoliati possessione plurimarum provinciarum: pulsi ultra Euphratem, et Tigrim: coacti in angustissimis finibus: et in his nec tuti nisi per solitudines, vastitudines immensas, et maria arenarum p. 100 interiecta: | non sunt de latibulis illis educendi, per loca sola ducendi, in contentionem producendi victi, qui florentes esse pares Romanis non valuerunt.

Eatur iam, eatur in rem præsentem: et singularia accusatoris discutiantur.

[a] *Str.* 2. 4. *App. proœ. Tac. Agri. Suet. Cla. Liv.* 105. *Serv.* 3. *Georg.*
[b] *Demosth. Lept.*

---

[22] Strabo 3. 4; Appian, *Prooemium*; Tacitus, *Agricola* 13; Suetonius, *Claudius* 17. 1; Livy 105; Servius, *On Georgics* 3. 25 [but *Eclogae* 1. 67 is what Gentili alludes to primarily].
[23] Demosthenes, *In Leptinem* 162.

Ariovistus and the terrible and unremitting fear of the Germans have been lifted? What rouses the Spaniards to arms, who, formerly the prey of Africans, brigands and pirates, were later able under the Roman Empire to p. 99
enjoy their own golden rivers and precious metals and be the most prosperous of men? What stirs up even the unconquered Britons? Or *were* they unconquered? He who denies that they were conquered is indeed he who is able to deny all of history. Nay, rather, the Romans did not crave that then poor and troublesome province and did not accept it when it was first offered. Nonetheless, he calls in the Britons to help him, men who, if the Romans offered them no service beyond the fact that they attached to a part of the world those who had been divided from the entire world, for this one immortal good deed will venerate the Roman name forever.[22] Greece having been declared free and Macedonia redeemed from servitude will certainly bring the crown and palm of valor to their avengers and liberators. Nor will great Carthage deny Rome the laurel, Carthage which for fifty years engaged in that contest for glory by land and sea and yielded after having been defeated in three wars. And this is the greatest praise of Carthage: that she waged war most bravely of all peoples with the victor of all peoples. After all, we are not unaware that Carthage once paid tribute to the Syracusans.[23] The Persians, the Medes, the Assyrians, deprived of possession of many provinces, were driven beyond the Tigris and Euphrates and constricted within the narrowest of boundaries and even in these were not safe unless made so through wastelands, vast empty reaches, and interposed seas of sands. They cannot be lured forth from those p. 100
lurking places, lured through empty territories, led forth into battle now that they have been defeated—these peoples who in their heyday were not strong enough to be equals to the Romans.

Now let us go forward, on into the business at hand—and let the particular points of the prosecutor be discussed.

Romulus.
CAP. II

Accusat Picenus in principio, mentitum a conditoribus urbis divinum genus. Attamen laudatissimus accusatori Piceno secundus rex per annos amplius quadraginta divinos congressus mentitus est. [a] Et celebratissimi quique latores legum, et civitatum conditores nobilissimi nunquam non aut genus deorum se deprædicarunt, aut non iubente Deo rem gerere publicam professi sunt. Ita videlicet voluere viri sapientissimi feros mortalium animos reverentia numinis molliores, et in obsequium reddere faciliores: qui alias intractabiles, alieni a communione omni, et omnis humanitatis expertes ævum duxissent. [b]*Nulla autem res efficacior multitudinem regit, quam superstitio: alioquin impotens, sæva, mutabilis.* [c] Sic auctores gravissimi, viris civilibus, et quibus necesse est, vitam suam adversus contumacem, et dissolutam turbam instituere, id tradunt, ut superstitionis quasi freno multitudinem compescant, et ad utilia torqueant. [d] Et id in Romana republica sic defendit Polybius diserte: ut
p. 101 propter ferocem illum populum necesse fuerit, | induxisse ea, et fovisse, quæ magnas superstitiones haberent, et probrosas apud alios omnes. Sic Lycurgus, Alexander, Africanus, [e] Augustus, alii congressus divinos, divinos ortus, divinos cultus probarunt animandæ plebi, extorquendæ obedientiæ, inducendæ reverentiæ. Quæ idem Polybius, idem Plutarchus, et Philo latiori folio prosequuntur. Non ergo Romulus accusetur, si vel ipse auctor superstitionis eius fuit. Sed declamitetur mecum in illam religionem: qua imbutus orbis propemodum universus, pulchrum existimavit, omnia de diis ad salutem publicam fingere: et sibi in animum quisque certissimo quodam induxerat præiudicio, cœtus hominum ita cogi, ita adfirmari, regi ita oportuisse.

Nec vero magnorum principum ortus quærere curiosius, at quales fuerint in republica, id demum evoluere sedulo, et explicare diligenter decet. [f] Non quærit venator, quod natum ex cane, sed qui canis: ut ita Plutarchus de politico viro. [g] Iactitabat probrosos natales suos Bion, et se ex se censendum ferebat. Sunt natales Romulo communes et viris aliis spectatissimis. Illuc mihi, illuc specta ad gesta Romuli: in quibus Romulum habes. Alienum

[a] *Val.* 1. *c.* 2. *Card.* 3. *de sap.* [b] *Cur.* 4. [c] *Plut. de ge. Socr.*
[d] *Polyb.* 6. 10. [e] *Phi. de legatio.* [f] *Plut. con. Ly. et Sy.* [g] *Laert.*

---

24 Valerius Maximus 1. 2. 1; Cardanus, *De sapientia* 2, p. 120.

25 Franciscus Curtius Junior [Francesco Corti], *Consilia* 4 [Venetiis, Ex officina Ioannis Baptistae Somaschi, 1575].

26 Plutarch, *De genio Socratis* 9 (580 A).

27 Polybius 6. 10. 28 Philo Judaeus, *Legatio ad Gaium* [see 36. 291; 40. 317].

29 Plutarch, *Comparatio Lysandri et Sullae* 2. 2. 30 Diogenes Laertius 2. 7. 46–7.

CHAPTER 2
Romulus

Right at the beginning, Picenus makes the accusation that the divine origin of Romulus was fabricated by the founders of the city. And yet the second king, who was most worthy to be praised in the view of the prosecutor Picenus, lied about meetings with a goddess [the nymph Egeria] for more than forty years. And all the most famous givers of laws and founders of states, too, have never failed to announce for themselves kinship with the gods or to claim that they govern through the will of God.[24] In this way, it is easy to see, the wisest men have wished to render the savage hearts of mortals gentler and more ready for obedience through respect for divine power. "Nothing more effectively rules the multitude than superstition. Without that, it is lacking in self-control, savage, and fickle."[25] Thus the most serious authors advise men in public life and those who must undertake a life in the face of the obstinate and dissolute crowd to restrain the multitude by the bridle, so to speak, of superstition and turn them aside to useful things.[26] And Polybius eloquently defended this in the case of the Roman republic thus: that on account of that wild people it was necessary [for the leaders] to p. 101
introduce and foster things which among all other peoples they considered massive and disgraceful superstitions.[27] Thus Lycurgus, Alexander, Scipio Africanus, Augustus,[28] and others approved of meetings with gods, divine origins, and divine worship for themselves for the purpose of inspiring the common people, extorting obedience, and inducing reverence. All this the aforesaid Polybius and Plutarch, as well as Philo in an even more extensive treatment, go over at length. Let not Romulus be accused then, even if he was himself the originator of this superstition. Rather, let others join with me in lauding that religious custom with which nearly the whole world was imbued when it judged it a fine thing to invent everything about the gods with a view to the public welfare—when everyone had come to believe by the most persuasive precedent that the gatherings of men ought to be convened thus, sanctioned thus, and governed thus.

But it is not proper to inquire into the origins of great princes too minutely; but their qualities in public life—that, certainly, we ought to diligently unfold and set forth. A hunter does not ask what bitch a dog is born from, but what sort of dog it is, as Plutarch says about a man in public life.[29] Bion used to make public mention of his base lineage and declare that he ought to be judged on his own merits.[30] The origins of Romulus were those he shared with many other highly distinguished men. Look instead over there for me—over there to the deeds of Romulus, for in them you have the true Romulus. The accuser complains that foreign territory has been seized for the city; and

agrum urbi occupatum clamat: et apertum in urbe asylum alienis hominibus
p. 102 rapiendis, et perditis omnibus attrahendis vociferatur. Quo in u | troque capite
reprehendendus acriter est accusator. Quid enim pro explorato ponit, Romam
in solo conditam alieno? Cur non in solo avi Numitoris? [a] in quod deducta avi
permissu colonia: in quo antea educati pueri a pastoribus avi: et quod præsidiis
regum Albanorum multo antea tenebatur. Etiamne fortuna, et felicitas Romæ
hæc, ut vicini eam in solo suo poni taciti paterentur? Etiamne fortitudo parvulæ
manus tanta fuit, ut vicini urbem in suo solo poni inviti paterentur? Asylum
autem tuetur Græcia: quam adversarius noster non vituperet. [b] Omnino certe
ius asylorum apud Græcos augustissimum fuit: adeo ut victis etiam hostibus
inviolatum conservaretur. [c] Hoc ius canonicum, imperiale, naturale, divinum
est: quod tibi Decianus clarissimus ostendit late: alii quidquid disputent.

Etiam tibi defendit Græcia, immo orbis totius invitamentum istud Romuli
in suam civitatem. Audin' Thesei edictum, *Huc pergite omnes populi*: quo ille
frequentare Athenas adproperabat. [d]*Romulus acer asylum Rettulit*, fecit ad
imitationem. Immo vero ingentes debent nostro Romulo gratias, quæ malis
hominibus exoneratæ civitates in asylum sunt Romuli. Et is simul existimari
divinus potuit vir: qui, supra quam divinus credebat Plato, illeges eos
p. 103 homines: et errones redigere in leges valuit, et aptos civitati, non esse bar-|
baros passus est. Moribus enim mox, sermoneque coaluerunt in civitatem
unam, qui ex civitatibus variis, linguis diversi, institutis discordes a principio
confluxerunt. Hæc Romuli, hæc illa est virtus, qua vecti in cælum sunt; qui
primos palantium hominum cœtus coegerunt, et orationis communitate,
atque æquitate imperii continuerunt.

[e] At etiam quid non Tarquinios plures, Claudios, Octavios dicimus Romam venisse, non transfugas, ac perditos alios? Familiæ illæ non ad asylum fugerunt. [f] Et Latinis legionibus avi Romulus cinctus venit. Ubi Ceninenses, Crustumini, Sabini, Camerini, Fidenates, Antemnates, Albani, reliqui populi, et victi, et in urbem, ac civitatem recepti? Fabii, Antonii, Æmilii, Cæcilii, alii plures Aborigines, et Troiani memorantur. [g] O utinam superesset Igini liber de Troianis his familiis: o utinam Varro. Iulii, Servilii, alii Albani, Curii, Fabritii, Porcii, Pompeii, Marii, alii ex aliis vicinis oppidis: non ab

[a] *Val.* 2. *c.* 2. *P. Diac.* 1. [b] *P. Ærod.* 1. *Decr.* 7. [c] *Decian.* 3. *cons.* 80. *Alc.* 7. *Parerg.* 6.
[d] *Virg.* 8. *ubi Serv.* [e] *Dionys.* 1. *Suet. Tyb. Serv.* 7. *Æn.* [f] *Paterc. ubi Lips.* [g] *Serv. Æn.* 6.

[31] Valerius Maximus 2. 2. 9; Paulus Diaconus, *Historia Romana* 1. 1a.

[32] Petrus Aerodius [Pierre Ayrault], *Decreta* 1. 7 [*Decretorum, rerumve apud diversos populos ab omni antiquitate iudicatarum, libri duo*, Parisiis, Apud Martinum Iuvenem, 1567].

[33] Decianus, *Consilia* 3. 80, fols. 192^{v} f.; Alciatus, *Parergon, seu Obiter dictorum iuris libri XII* 7. 6 [in *Opera omnia in quatuor tomos*, Tomus IIII, Basileae, Apud Thomam Guarinum, 1582, cols. 467 f.].

[34] Vergil, *Aeneis* 8. 342–3; Servius *ad loc.* **Translator's note:** Gentili follows Servius in taking Vergil's words "quem Romulus acer asylum / rettulit" as meaning that Romulus was founding Rome as an asylum in imitation of the Athenian Altar of Mercy, supposedly founded by Herakles.

[35] Dionysius of Halicarnassus 1. 85. 3; Suetonius, *Tiberius* 1. 1; Servius, *On Aeneid* 7 [the reference is unclear].

[36] Velleius Paterculus 1. 8. 5; Lipsius *ad loc.* [*C. Velleius Paterculus cum animadversionibus I. Lipsi*, Lugduni Batavorum, Ex officina Plantiniana, Apud Franciscum Raphelengium, 1591, p. 9.]

he exclaims that there was an open asylum in the city in order to snatch away foreign men and attract all sorts of desperate people. But in both these points p. 102
the accuser is to be sharply censured. For why does he take it as established that Rome was founded on foreign soil? Why not in the territory of his grandfather Numitor, into which the colony was led out at the grandfather's express permission, in which the boys were earlier brought up by the grandfather's herdsmen, and which much earlier used to be held by the garrisons of the Alban kings?[31] Was the good luck and prosperity of Rome already such that the neighboring peoples would have allowed it to be placed in their territory without protest? Was the value of the tiny band already so great that the neighboring peoples would have allowed the city to be located in their land against their will? Moreover, Greece, which our adversary does not pour scorn upon, observes the right of asylum. Beyond any doubt, the right of asylum was a most holy thing among the Greeks—to such an extent that it was observed inviolate even for defeated enemies.[32] This is true also of canon law, imperial law, natural law, divine law, which the most distinguished Decianus shows you at length, though others would offer some discussion as well.[33]

Greece also defends for you Romulus' invitation of the whole world into his state. Listen to the proclamation of Theseus: "Hasten here, all peoples"—by which he hastened to stock Athens. "Bold Romulus brought back asylum"—i.e. instituted it in imitation.[34] Why, in fact the cities that were relieved of bad men who went into Romulus' asylum owe a tremendous burden of thanks to our Romulus. And at the same time that man can be judged a divine man who, as more than divine Plato believed, had the power to bring under the power of laws men without laws and vagabonds and did not allow men fit for civilized life to be barbarians. For before long, men who p. 103
had at first streamed together from various polities, diverse in languages, discordant in their manners, coalesced into one state through shared practices and language. This, yes *this* was that remarkable excellence of Romulus, through which those who assembled the first gatherings of footloose men and sustained them through fellowship of language and justness of rule were conveyed to the very heavens.

But why don't we mention that various Tarquins, Claudii, and Octavii came to Rome—rather than those other runaways and desperate men?[35] Those families did not flee to an asylum. And Romulus himself came surrounded by the Latin legions of his grandfather.[36] Where else were the Ceninenses, the Crustumini, the Sabines, the Camerini, the Fidenates, the Antemnates, the Albans, and the other defeated peoples received into a city and a state? The Fabii, the Antonii, the Aemilii, the Caecilii, and many other native Italian and Trojan families are recorded. Would that the book of Hyginus on these Trojan

asylo, aut per asylum. Et de istis quasi sceleratis, et nocentibus populus facinorosorum congregatur?

Non hic igitur audimus magnos theologos: ubi historici minimi sunt. Non possunt magnæ esse auctoritatis, iure nobis per adversarium statuto, contra Romanos viri Afri, Carthaginenses. *Namque memor generis Carthaginis hæc*
p. 104 *pia proles Imminet Hesperiæ.* Etiam Mi|thridati credemus? Etiam Satyræ? At omnes historiæ de familiis, gentibus, et populis supradictis tradunt: quæ his theologorum, hostium, satyricorum adversantur. Non servum domino, non creditoribus nexum, non magistratibus criminosum reddebat Romulus? At neque omnes reddendi sunt scilicet. Qui fortunæ aliqua calamitate prolapsi in crimina sunt, et fugitivi facti sunt, non redduntur. Hæc est lex naturæ: [a]*Ne tradito servum domino suo, qui ad te eripuerit se.* [b] Pium hoc, et honestum, non modo utile: et cum libero quidem, quam cum servo, magis: qui honorare etiam videtur nos, dum supplicat nobis, et in nobis spem collocat suam. Quæ sapientes Hebræi ad sanctam illam legem explanant. Sic post asylum statuæ principum stetere calamitosis auxilium, hodie stant ædes sacræ. Tantum in natura est, ut recurrat semper, et se insinuet varie, quantumcunque trudatur, et furcillis quasi de medio expellatur. [c] Atque ut dolosis, et violentis ea lex Dei non staret, nec statua principis: qui et ab ipso altari Iehovæ ad supplicium trahebantur, etiam et ad altare occidebantur: tamen in territorio alieno et isti sunt tuti. Et hoc utimur iure: quicquid interpretes iuris contradicere videantur. Evalet consuetudine, quod est naturaliter verum: ut tu ais, Picene. Sic iniustitia negatur asyli.

p. 105 Etiam solum urbis, famam civi|tatis defendimus. Etiam famam defendimus senatus Romuli. [d] Invidiose scriptum est, dictos Romæ patres, quod soli possent tres ostendere: ceteram autem exstitisse turbam fugitivorum, quibus aut non noti, aut non ingenui patres essent. Patres ab ætate dicti: et quod

[a] *Deut.* 23. [b] *R. Moy. Ægypt.* 3. *duc. dub.* 40.
[c] 1. *Reg.* 2. [d] *Dionys.* 2.

[37] Servius, *On Aeneid* 6. 36 [*On Aeneid* 5. 704 contains a reference to the *libri* "quos de Familiis Trojanis scripsit"].

[38] **Translator's note:** Gentili seems to be referring to Augustine, Cyprian, and Tertullian.

[39] **Translator's note:** Though not glossed by Gentili, this is Lucan, *De bello civili* 8. 284–5: "namque memor generis Carthaginis impia proles / imminet Hesperiae," from a speech by Pompey expressing his distrust of the reception he will receive if he flees to Libya. But Gentili has misquoted, offering "hæc pia proles," which can be made to fit the sense, but spoils the meter.

[40] **Translator's note:** Picenus adduces Juvenal's *Satirae* in *De armis Romanis* 1. 2, pp. 20–1.

[41] **Translator's note:** A sort of debtor reduced to debt bondage, a sort of slavery, in the early Republic; see Cicero, *De republica* 2. 59 for a discussion of the abolition of debt bondage (*nexum*) by the Poetelian law; cf. Livy 8. 28 on the occasion for the law. The historicity of *nexi* and *nexum* is contested.

[42] Deuteronomy 23: 15.

families had survived! Would that Varro had![37] The Julii, the Servilii, the various Albani, the Curii, the Fabritii, the Porcii, the Pompeii, the Marii, and others from other neighboring towns—they didn't come from a place of refuge—or *for* a place of refuge. And does a nation of criminals come together from *those* kinds of supposedly villainous and dangerous types?

Accordingly, we aren't listening here to the major theologians, in a case where they are highly insignificant historians. In accord with a principle established for us by our adversary himself, men from Africa, Carthaginians,[38] cannot be men of great authority against Romans. "For this dutiful offspring of the race of Carthage, never forgetting, threatens Italy."[39] Are we going to p. 104
trust even Mithridates? Even satire?[40] But all the histories about the families, races, and peoples mentioned above hand down to us things that contradict those words of the theologians, enemies, and satirists. Is it true that Romulus did not hand over the slave to the master, the debtor [*nexus*[41]] to the creditor, the guilty man to the magistrates? But in fact not all of them ought to have been handed over. People who have fallen into criminal charges and have been made fugitives through some disastrous misfortune are not handed over. This is a law of nature: "See that you do not hand over to the master the servant who takes refuge with you."[42] This is a pious and worthy principle, not just a useful one—and even more so with a free man than with a slave, a free man who even seems to grant us honor as he supplicates us and places all his hopes in us. This is what the wise Hebrews are making clear with regard to that holy law. Thus, after the days of asylum the statues of princes stood as a recourse to those struck with disaster, and so today stand the holy churches. This is so deeply ingrained in nature that it always runs back in and will in various ways creep in as often as it may be thrust out and, as it were, driven out with pitchforks.[43] But although that law of God did not stay in effect for the deceptive and the violent—any more than a statue of a prince did—and such men were dragged off to punishment even from the very altar of Jehovah, or were even slaughtered at the altar itself—nonetheless even such men as these were safe in foreign territory.[44] And this is the right we make use of, whatever objections the interpreters of the law may seem to make to it. That which is true by nature acquires force also through custom—as you yourself say, Picenus. So thus the supposed injustice of the asylum is refuted.

So we have defended the territory of the city and the reputation of the p. 105
state. We have also defended the reputation of the senate of Romulus. It has been maliciously written that at Rome the senators were called "fathers" because they were the only ones who could reveal their own fathers, whereas the rest of the community was a crowd of fugitives whose fathers were either unknown or ignoble.[45] The "fathers" were so called from their age, and

---

[43] **Translator's note:** Ultimately a reference to Horace, *Epistulae* 1. 10. 24, "naturam expelles furca, tamen usque recurret," though this had become virtually proverbial.

[44] 1 Kings 2: [33] [1 Samuel 2: 33 AV].

[45] [A view cited by] Dionysius of Halicarnassus 2. 8. 3. [Cf. Livy 10. 8. 10.]

liberos iam haberent: et *cieri* (sic, sic, non *ciere*) poterant patres. Unde enim tanta spuriorum examina advolassent, et collecta essent, ut in tribus hominum millibus, quos primum habuit Romulus, centum soli essent non spurii? Iuvenes reliqui, nec mariti: qui iuvenem pariter regem secuti essent: quibus integer ævi sanguis, solidæque suo starent robore vires: et ut mos fuit semper, mittere in colonias iuventutem, illas maxime, quæ a vicinis non quietæ futuræ satis videbantur. [a] Plutarchus rationem eius nominis variam recitat: item et Sallustius: sed neuter istam sequitur, quam Dionysius dixerat invidiosam, et nos cernimus falsi compertam.

Etiam defendimus nunc de finibus agri Romuli. Si enim Albanorum colonia erat Roma, iam fines habere nequiit non finitos: si finitos habuit Alba. Quod si Numa terminos agro, et publico, et privato cuiusque posuit: hoc est tamen nihil, nisi quod privatum distinxit a publico: aut in agro sic fecit publico quem Romulus supra veterem illum, Albani partem, quæsierat. Et cui
p. 106 non fixit terminos: qui com|pedes (assentiamur Plutarcho coniectanti: audin', Picene, quod tu nolis tamen, coniectanti) compedes nascenti exsisterent civitati. Neque tamen iniuria statim est, ac terminos transilieris: et certum, et constitutum est, bello victos agro spoliare licere. Quid dixisses, si rex Romanus civitatis suæ fines, [b] quemadmodum Spartanus rex, hasta, et gladio finiisset? id est, qua armorum vis eos extendere valuisset.

Addat his noster iurisconsultus, finium regundorum iudicium non simplex, sed mixtum esse. Et non accuset Romulum solum, sed et vicinos. Cur enim non illi posuerunt agro suo? Hoc si fecissent, finitus et Romanus erat. Aut vicini non posuerunt prisco mortalium more, cum [c] *ne signare quidem, aut partiri limite campum, Fas erat. Non fixus in agris, qui regeret certis finibus arua lapis. Nullus in campo sacer divisit agros arbiter populis lapis.* Et quæ sexcenta sic sunt scriptorum omnium vulgata testimonia. Et itaque tanto iustior Romulus, quanto nec recessit a veteri, et sui temporis consuetudine vicinorum. Quod si etiam patrii soli gleba nulla fuit, sed statim pomœrium, et omnibus portis in alienum exibatur: ut ais, Picene: qui tum fines, et termini poni a Romulo debuerunt? Cui agro, si is nullus, potuerunt poni? Nihil igitur

[a] *Plut. Rom. Sallu. Catil.* [b] *Plut. apop.*
[c] *Cic. Ara. Virg.* 1. *Geo. Tib.* 1. *eleg.* 3. *Sene. Hipp.* 2. *Iusti.* 43.

---

46 **Translator's note:** Gentili is referring to Livy 10. 8. 10, where, however, the active is to be read, despite his attempt to read the passive: "en umquam fando audistis patricios primo esse factos non de caelo demissos, sed qui patrem ciere possent, id est nihil ultra quam ingenuos."

47 **Translator's note:** Though not glossed by Gentili or noted as a quotation, this is from Vergil *Aeneis* 2. 639 f.: " 'vos o, quibus integer aevi / sanguis,' ait, 'solidaeque suo stand robore vires'."

48 Plutarch, *Romulus* 13. 2. 5; Sallust, *Bellum Catilinae* 6. 6.

49 Plutarch, *Apophthegmata laconica* 210 E. [The king was Agesilaos.]

50 Cicero, *Ara.* [Neither Cicero's Aratea, his translation of Aratus' *Phaenomena*, nor his *Academica* seem to be meant here]; Vergil *Georgica* 1. 126–7; Tibullus 1. 3. 43–4; Seneca, *Phaedra* 528–9; Justin 2. 43 [2. 2, on the Scythians, is probably meant.].

because they already had children and were able to *be called* fathers—thus, thus, *not* call upon their fathers by name.[46] For whence might so great a troop of illegitimate men have flown and assembled so that among 3,000 men whom Romulus had at first only one hundred would not be illegitimate? The rest were youths, not husbands, who followed an equally youthful king, "who had the unimpaired vigor of their time of life and whose firm strength stood by their own power."[47] And as the custom always has been, they sent the young men off into colonies—especially those colonies that did not seem likely to be left undisturbed by their neighbors. Plutarch repeats a different account of this title ["fathers"]; likewise Sallust.[48] But neither follows the account that Dionysius called malicious and which we ourselves realize is guilty of falsehood.

Also, we now defend the boundaries of the territory of Romulus. For if Rome was a colony of the Albans, it could not have failed to have fixed boundaries, if Alba itself had fixed boundaries. But if Numa placed boundary stones upon both public and private land, this means nothing if not that he marked off private land from public, or that he set the stones in the public territory which Romulus had obtained beyond that old original land, the portion of Alban territory, and to which he did not fix boundary markers which would have existed as shackles for the nascent state (let us assent to p. 106
Plutarch's guesswork here—do you hear, Picenus? something you nevertheless won't allow: that he was guessing). And yet an injury is not perpetrated the minute you will have crossed borders—and it is a fixed and standard practice that it is permitted to deprive of their land those defeated in war. What would you have said if the Roman king had demarcated his state's boundaries the way the Spartan king did—with spear and sword—that is, as far as the power of arms had the power to extend them?[49]

Let our lawyer add to these considerations the fact that the decision as to how to set the boundaries is not simple but complicated. And let him not accuse Romulus alone, but his neighbors as well. For why did they not place boundaries stones to their own territory? If they had done this, the Roman territory would have been fixed as well. Or else the neighbors did not place boundary stones because they followed the ancient custom of mortal men, back when "it was not permitted even to mark or to divide the field with a boundary. No stone was fixed in the field which could rule the fields with definite boundaries. No sacred stone in the field divided the fields as a judge for the peoples."[50] And there are six hundred commonly cited testimonies of writers to this effect. And therefore Romulus was all the more just in that he did not depart from ancient custom and that of the neighbor peoples of his time. But if there was not even a clod of earth of his native soil, but it was immediately pomerium and from all the gates one went forth into foreign territory, as you say, Picenus, then what boundaries and limits ought to have been placed by Romulus? In what farmland could they be placed, if there was

p. 107 quicquam id de finibus est. Et nullo igitur modo damnabuntur, veluti ex | iniusto principio, quæ consecuta sunt postea bella propter res raptas, nec redditas. Non damnabitur partum per bella iusta imperium, quod terris æquatum: et quod [a]*gentibus est aliis tellus data limite certo: Romanæ spatium est urbis, et orbis idem.*

Huc adfert accusator etiam figmenta, lupam, picum: et portenta nobis de tripode post tot secula ab oraculis desitis interpretatur. Etiam avem, [b] a qua nomen suæ Picenæ gentis est, proscindere maledictis, non erubescit. Sed et vultures affligit: naturæ rerum, et iuris auguralis sane ignarus. [c] Vultures animalia innocentissima: quæ victu vivunt innocuo: et his vesci solis consueverunt, quorum esus, aut usus aliis non supersit. Hæc natura. Romuli civitas portendebatur: in quam perditi, et proiecti undique colligerentur innocenter. Hoc augurium. [d] Vultur accipitrem persequitur, avium persecutorem exsecrabilem. Hæc natura. Romuli civitas designabatur: quæ patrocinium calamitosorum susciperet. Hoc augurium.

Et ita posita Roma est. Ea parricidio dedicata non est. Remus occisus non fuit. Romulo supervixit: urbem Ravennam condidit. [e] Ita non unus est, qui tradit historicus. [f] Occisus fuit? In rixa, et turba: quam ipse cum aliis concitavit. [g] Scilicet fabulosum dicitur, quod de mœnibus dicitur. Sed cum
p. 108 Remus tempore augurii, Romulus numero avium certarent, | ille sic in pugna cæsus sit. [h] Invito Romulo occisus a Celere illo: qui itaque abiit in exsilium. Nec igitur finxisse isthæc dicetur, qui isthæc cum historiis dixit poeta, aut nec poeta, sed et ipse historicus in Fastis Ovidius, cum de fratre, interfecto a Celere, audisset Romulus: [i]*Lacrimis introrsus obortis Devorat, et clausum pectore vulnus habet. Flere palam non vult, exemplaque fortia servat: Sicque meos muros transeat, hostis, ait. Dat tamen exsequias: nec iam suspendere fletum, Sustinet: et pietas dissimulata patet. Osculaque applicuit posito suprema feretro: Atque, ait, Invito frater ademte vale.* Ipse Remus. *Noluit hoc frater: pietas æqualis in illo est.* [j] Dubium, an iussu fratris occisus sit? Et pro certo igitur

[a] *Ovid. 2. Fast.* [b] *Paul. Fest.* [c] *Plut. probl.* R. 93. [d] *Cass. 2. var.* 9. *Serv.* 11. *Æn.*
[e] *Egn. or. ge. Ro. Zos.* 5. [f] *Liv.* 1. [g] *Servius* 1. *Æneid.* [h] *Plut. Rom.*
[i] *Ovid. Fast.* 4. 5. [j] *Ior. de re. suec. Flor.* 1.

---

[51] Ovid, *Fasti* 1. 683–4. **Translator's note:** Just before this, Gentili's phrase "imperium, quod terris aequatum" alluded to Vergil, *Aeneis* 6. 782: "imperium terris, animos aequabit Olympo."

[52] Paulus Diaconus, *Epitoma Festi* [in *Sexti Pompei Festi de verborum significatu quae supersunt cum Pauli Epitome*, ed. Wallace M. Lindsay, Lipsiae, 1913, s.v. Picena, p. 235].

[53] Plutarch, *Quaestiones Romanae* 93.

[54] **Translator's note:** Both 1599 and 1770 editions read: "Haec natura Romuli civitas portendebatur; . . ." There needs to be a period after "natura" in order to maintain the symmetry between the two instances of "Haec natura." They are completely parallel—as are the two corresponding instances of "Hoc augurium."

[55] Cassiodorus, *Variae* 2. 9; Servius, *On Aeneid* 11.

[56] *Egn. or. ge. Ro.* [This is a reference to the late antique pastiche *De origine gentis Romanae*, 23. 6, where a writer by the name of Egnatius is cited as saying: "Contra Egnatius libro primo in ea contentione non modo Remum non esse occisum sed etiam uterius a Romulo vixisse tradit." The citation is probably spurious (cf. RE), although more recently some scholars, Arnaldo Momigliano among them, have regarded the citations in the *Origo* as fundamentally genuine; see Appendix 5, "Source Citations in the *Origo Gentis Romanae*" of A. Cameron's *Greek Mythography in the Roman World* (Oxford, 2004), 328–34]; Zosimus 5.

no farmland at all? Therefore this matter of boundaries is really nothing at all. And the wars which were subsequently undertaken on account of things seized and not handed back will not come under condemnation as arising from an unjust starting point. There will be no condemnation of an empire p. 107
gained through just wars, an empire extended through the lands and of which it may be said: "For other peoples the land has been given with a fixed limit; the space of the Roman city is at the same time the world."[51]

Here our accuser brings forward downright bogus things—the wolf, the woodpecker, and he even expounds to us portents from the oracular tripod after so many ages have past, from defunct oracles. Why, he didn't even blush to heap scorn upon the bird [woodpecker, *picus*] from which the name of his Picene people comes.[52] But he even lashes out against vultures, utterly ignorant of both the natural world and of augural procedure. Vultures are the most harmless of animals: they live upon a harmless diet; and they have been accustomed to feed only upon those things whose consumption or use is not left to others.[53] This is the natural world.[54] What was being portended was the city-state of Romulus, to which men who were desperate and cast out from everywhere could be gathered together in a way that caused no harm. This is augury. A vulture pursues a hawk, a loathsome pursuer of birds.[55] This is the natural world. What was being represented was the city-state of Romulus, which was to undertake the protection of those who had suffered disasters. This is augury.

And thus was Rome founded. It was not dedicated to parricide. Remus wasn't slaughtered. He survived Romulus—and founded the city of Ravenna. There is not just one historian who records it thus.[56] Or was he in fact killed?[57] If so, it was in a quarrel and a mob that he himself stirred up along with others. Indeed, that which is related about the walls is said to be legendary. Rather, when Remus at the time of the augury quarreled with Romulus over the number of the birds, he was thus killed in the fight.[58] p. 108
Against Romulus's will, he was killed by that man Celer, who therefore went off into exile.[59] And let not the poet who declared these things in accordance with the histories be said to have fabricated them—nor was he just a poet, for Ovid was a historian in his *Fasti*, where he wrote that when Romulus heard that his brother had been killed by Celer, he "swallows his rising tears and keeps his wound locked in his heart. He doesn't want to weep openly and keeps up a model of bravery, and says, 'Thus may an enemy pass over my walls.' Yet he grants funeral honors and no longer bears to check his tears, and the family feeling he'd hidden becomes clear. He placed final kisses on the bier when it had been set down, and he said, 'Brother taken from me against my will, farewell!' "[60] And Remus himself said, "My brother didn't want this; his love is a match for mine."[61] Is it uncertain that he was killed on

---

[57] Livy 1. 7. 2. [58] Servius, *On Aeneid* 6. 780. [59] Plutarch, *Romulus* 10.
[60] Ovid, *Fasti* 4. 845–52. [61] Ovid, *Fasti* 5. 471.

factum non adsumatur. Fama ea est vulgatior? At hæc non semper verior: et quæ hic in iudicio nostro pro explorata obtineat.

Sequamur illam et nos tamen. Et dicat peritus iuris, si in legibus non legit, [a] ut qui violaverit muros capite puniretur: et Remus ita occisus traderetur, quod transcendere murum voluerit. Hæc caussa cædis: et proculdubio iusta, quæ probata legibus est iusta cædes: per quam vim propulsata vis est. Ut hoc negare nequis accusator: quod et fama illa vulgatior habet: aut sequenda tibi per omnia, aut per omnia deserenda. Et sua Romulus mœnia probe aut adversus petulan-
p. 109 tem increpationem ([b] ea fuit moni | tio) vindicavit, firmavitque: *cæso mœnia firma Remo*. Sua mœnia per æqui conventionem iuris facta sunt Romuli. Quod enim de mentito obiicitur augurio: vanum est, vacuum auctoritate, cassum ratione. Adeantur historiarum verba pensiculate. Cogitet adversarius meus, si sine arbitris discessum sit ad auguria captanda: si sine arbitris ostendi mendacium possit. Hæc Remi cædes ad vindictam iusta. Nam de cupidine principatus scrutentur sibi, qui aiunt, theologi. Et de sua honestate neget Cicero: dum et necessitatem novi firmandi imperii, magnamque adeo utilitatem non inficietur: quod certe non faciet: ut in caussa mox Collatini audiemus.

Tatii autem et cædes Romulo cur adscribetur? Sunt, qui ita memorent rerum scriptores? Qui vero illi? Nominare non audes Orosios, et Diaconos tuos, aliosve, heri natos, mortuos heri. Qui, avumque, tradunt, a Romulo interfectum. Unde tertiumque obiectas Romulo parricidium. Sed levissimorum hominum testimonium levissimum est. Et levissima argutatio est accusatoris, ab hereditate amissa Albani regni. [c] Nam scribit Plutarchus, et idem Zonara accusatoris, quod etsi Albæ regnum pertineret ad Romulum, is tamen in populi gratiam iusserit, esse liberam civitatem: et ubi tamen
p. 110 crearet ipse per annos singulos magistratum. Ita nec exscidit illo re|gno. Ista vero Romuli avaritia, et dominandi libido: per quam potuit regno carere avito, et urbe principe Latii: etiam Fidenas, vi captas, libertati relinquere.

Sic sunt coniecturæ de cæde Tatii: cuius, cum novimus auctores, auctorem facere Romulum, est periniquum: cuius, cum scimus caussam, caussam coniectare aliam, est perabsurdum: etiam intolerabile, si id fiat ipsum ad aliorum

[a] *l. ult. de diu. re. Plut. probl.* R. 27. *Herodia.* 4. [b] *Flor. lib.* 1. *Prop.* 3. *eleg.* 8. [c] *Plut. Rom.*

---

62 Jordanes, *Romana* 89; Florus 1. 1. 8. **Translator's note:** Gentili takes Florus' words "dubium an iussu fratris," "it is uncertain whether (he was killed) by his brother's orders," and turns them into a rhetorical question.

63 *Digest* 1. 8. 11; Plutarch, *Quaestiones Romanae* 27, 271 A; Herodian 4. 5. 5.

64 **Translator's note:** The text here should probably read "per quam [sc. caedem] vi propulsata vis est." Cf. Cicero, *Pro Milone* 9: "atqui, si tempus est ullum iure hominis necandi, quae multa sunt, certe illud est non modo iustum verum etiam necessarium, cum vi vis inlata defenditur."

65 **Translator's note:** The parenthetical comment is a reference to Picenus' claim that in leaping over his brother's walls Remus was simply trying to warn Romulus that they were too low.

66 Propertius 3. 8. 50; Florus 1. 1. 8 ["prima certe victima fuit munitionemque urbis novae sanguine suo consecravit"].

67 **Translator's note:** In fact, Dionysius of Halicarnassus declares that both Romulus and Remus took men with them to confirm any auguries they saw: 1. 86. 2.

68 [See Cicero, *De officiis* 3. 40–1.]

69 Plutarch, *Romulus* 27. 1.

70 **Translator's note:** Gentili might have in mind that according to both Plutarch (*Romulus* 23. 6) and Dionysius of Halicarnassus (2. 53. 4.), part of the territory of Fidenae was seized and the town itself became a Roman colony, but at least it was not razed.

his brother's orders?[62] Therefore let not the deed be assumed as certain. Is the report of this more widely spread? But the more widely spread report is not always truer and able to pass for affirmed in our judgment.

But let us nonetheless ourselves follow this version. And let our legal expert tell us if he has not read in the laws that the man who has violated walls is punished by death—and that Remus was recorded as having been killed in this way, because he wished to overstep the walls.[63] This was the reason for his death—and it was without a doubt a just reason, one which has been approved by the laws as a justifiable homicide, through which act of violence another act of violence has been warded off.[64] Since you, the accuser, cannot deny this fact which even that more widespread account contains, you have to accept the account in all its details—or reject it in all its details. And Romulus defended his own walls properly and against an impudent rebuke (this was p. 109 that supposed warning Remus made).[65] And he made the walls stronger: "Through the death of Remus the walls were made secure."[66] Romulus's own walls were built through the compact of a just law. As for what is charged about the fabricated augury, it is empty, devoid of evidence, utterly lacking in reason. Let the words of the histories be attacked only with great caution. Let my adversary consider if one would have gone off to consult auguries without judges—or if without judges a lie could be detected.[67] This killing of Remus was justifiable as an act of punishment. For let the theologians who make the charge of lust for power themselves be carefully examined on this head. And let Cicero deny his own moral rectitude, provided that he not deny the necessity and even the great expediency of firming up a new order—something he indeed will *not* do, as we shall soon hear in the case of Collatinus.[68]

Moreover, why will the murder of Tatius be ascribed to Romulus? Are there writers who would thus record it? But who, in fact, are these men? You don't dare to mention your favorite writers, men like Orosius and Paul the Deacon, or others—born yesterday, dead yesterday. They even record that Romulus killed his grandfather. Hence you charge a third act of parricide against Romulus. But the testimony of the most inconsequential people is itself most inconsequential. And most inconsequential is the accuser's charge about the lost inheritance of the kingdom of Alba. For Plutarch writes—and likewise the accuser's Zonaras—that although the kingdom of Alba belonged to Romulus, he nevertheless ordered it to be a free city as a favor to the people, and he appointed a magistrate there annually.[69] Accordingly, he isn't deprived of kingship there. Such, in fact, was Romulus' alleged avarice and p. 110 lust for rule, thanks to which he could forego his ancestral kingdom and the principal city of Latium, and even left Fidenae, when captured by force, to its own freedom.[70]

The speculations on the death of Tatius are similarly insubstantial. It is highly unjust to make Romulus the initiator of it when we in fact know the instigators. It is utterly absurd, when we know the actual cause, to guess at

incommodum, atque perniciem. Lavinienses auctores: qui (hæc caussa) læsi a Tatio. Huic, propriæ caussæ, etiam propiori, adscribi factum, iubet natura, et omnis prudentia iuris. Coniecturæ accusatoris diversæ in re magis dubia diversantur: et isti concedunt interpretationi planissimæ.[a] Et itaque si est verum alicubi, hic est verissimum, quod scribitur generaliter, *iniquum esse, omnes, ad quos aliquid emolumenti ex aliqua re pervenerit, in suspicionem maleficii devocari.*

Romulus dein accusabitur iniustitiæ: qui Sabinos, violatores iuris gentium sanctissimi, dedendos violatis Lanuvinis censuerat? Et iniustus est, quia in partes alterius venerit? Sed unum Romæ regnum erat; quod duo illi reges communiter administrabant: non duo erant regna, Sabinorum unum, alterum Romanorum, unum Tatii, alterum Romuli. [b] Etiam privatus implet iudicis
p. 111 partes, quas is negligat: etiam iudex alienus. Sed et ius iustissimum, et rece| ptissimum dixit Romulus, dum temeratores legationum dedendos pronunciavit, et læsis addixit. Et Tatius, qui tantam contemsit iustitiam, facinorosos illos nec puniit, nec puniri passus est, *illorum pœnam in se vertit.* An ne hoc quidem nisi per iuris inscitiam Livius? Quid ad hæc rursum manifestissima respondere per coniecturas? Tatium non potuisse videri sceleris ullius conscium, qui Lavinium proficisci ausus sit. Quasi vero et manifestus coniurationis nec venerit in senatum Catilina. Quasi vero nec quidquam sperarit in religione Tatius: quam tu, Picene, obtendis saluti illius, clypei non enerrabile textum: *Hospes, rex, sacerdos, in conspectu deorum immortalium, ad ipsas aras.* Crimine tamen uno violatarum legationum perfringuntur iura isthæc, et, quicquid est iuris, omne consumitur. Criminosos, violentos ne quidem veri Dei tuetur altare: quos neque intuetur Deus, nisi iratus. Apage istas declamatiunculas in re seria gravissima. Apage divinationes. Abstrusa in cælis intimis non condemnabunt, quantum homini fas est proloqui, quod per omnem apertam rationem iustificatur. Aut si homines referebant seditiones, et pestes in cædes Remi, et Tatii: nos etiam scimus, hominum mentes superstitione perculsas, et similia, et longe vaniora edidisse iudicia.

[a] *Rh. ad Her.* 2. [b] *c.* 6. 7. *de off. ord.*

---

[71] *Rhetorica ad Herennium* 2. 3. 4.

[72] **Translator's note:** Gentili here makes a common confusion between the Laurentians and the Lanuvians. For the story of the maltreatment of the Laurentian envoys and the subsequent death of the Sabine Tatius in atonement, see Livy 1. 14. 1–3.

[73] *Liber Extra* [Decretals of Gregory IX] 1. 31. 6–7 [the passage discusses a judge supplying for the defects of the litigants].

[74] **Translator's note:** The quoted phrase is from Livy 1. 14. 2.

[75] **Translator's note:** Not identified by marginal gloss or italicization, this phrase, "clipei non enarrabile textum," is from Vergil *Aeneis* 8. 625, on the shield of Aeneas.

some other cause—nay, it is not to be borne when this happens to the detriment and harm of other people. The Lavinians were the instigators, men who were harmed by Tatius (that was their motivation). Human nature and a full knowledge of the law demand that the deed be ascribed to its proper cause, which is also more probable. An accuser's various guesses naturally vary in a matter that is rather doubtful, and they yield to an interpretation that is extremely obvious. And accordingly that which is written more generally, if it is ever true, is most true in this case: "It is unfair that everyone who has received some profit from any action be brought into suspicion of wrongdoing."[71]

Is Romulus next going to be accused of injustice because he deemed that the Sabines, the violators of the most holy law of the nations, were to be handed over to the Lanuvians who had been injured?[72] And is he unjust because he came down on the side of one rather than the other? But there was one kingdom at Rome, which those two kings governed jointly; there were not two kingdoms, one of the Sabines, the other of the Romans; the one of Tatius, the other of Romulus. Even a private citizen can take on the role of a judge when the judge himself is negligent—and so can even a foreign judge.[73] Romulus pronounced a very just and highly orthodox law when he p. 111
declared that those who had maltreated ambassadors ought to be rendered up and when he delivered them over to the ones who had been wronged. And Tatius, who had shown such contempt for justice and did not punish those who had committed the crime and did not allow them to be punished, "turned their punishment upon himself."[74] Does Livy say this only through ignorance of the law? Why, in the face of these facts that are so manifest, should we turn back to guesses? Why assume that Tatius could not have seemed party to any crime since he dared to head off to Lavinium? As though Catiline, manifestly guilty of conspiracy, did not go into the Senate! As though Tatius could put no faith in religious sanctions, which even you, Picenus, spread before him for his safety, "a shield's indescribable texture":[75] "guest, king, priest, in the sight of the immortal gods, at the very altars." Nevertheless by the single crime of the abused embassy those other rights are shattered, and whatever justice they had is utterly used up. Not even the altar of the true God protects the criminal and violent, whom God does not look upon except in anger. Away with those debating points in a serious matter of the gravest import! Away with divinations! Things hidden way off in the depths of the heavens will not condemn—even to the extent that it is permitted for a human being to declare them—something that is justified through every clear line of reasoning. Or if men used to attribute civil strifes and plagues to the deaths of Remus and Tatius, we are also aware that the minds of men have been ruined by superstition and have put forth judgments that are similar to this—or even much more foolish.

p. 112 Apage cædem Amulii quartam, et parricidium | parricidiis cumulatum. Apage tuos istos iam nunc Cedrenos, et Frisingenses: nomina ignobilia, et millesimo nostrum vix audita. Propatruum sustulit Romulus, tyrannum, ultus exsilium avi, matris necem, et fratris, et suam, et suum repetens regnum. Abest parricidium hinc, quod culpes. [a] Si filius patrem eiusmodi occidisset, sine scelere esset, etiam præmio adficiendus: ut omnes constituunt, et constituerunt. Nos disceptationi levissimæ dedimus nimis multa.

At de raptu Sabinarum, veluti in aperta caussa, acerbissime clamat: et magna secum nomina trahit magnorum patrum. Qui tamen nec magni extra suas quæstiones religionis, in his politicis humani iuris. Verum enimvero vidit etiam Augustinus in raptu isto principium Romanæ iustitiæ. Sed quia progressum reliquum impeditum, aut etiam præcisum multis quasi obicibus insuperabilibus existimavit, digressus in alteram partem est: et Romanos iniustitiæ condemnavit. Vidit Augustinus, connubia Romanis negata inique: et, ius propterea belli contra Sabinos, confessus est. At, quod fraude spectaculi usi Romani sint, hinc pronunciat iniustum bellum. [b] At vero *iudice me, fraus est concessa repellere fraudem. Armaque in armatos sumere iura sinunt. Fallere fallentem, fraudemque repellere fraude, Exemploque licet ludere*
p. 113 *quemque suo.* [c] Quod et | interpretes iuris afferunt. Et illud, malitiæ per malitiam occurri iuste: et non, eum dici calumnia uti, sed prudentia, qui alium fallit, ne fallatur: et, id genus alia. Ecquid autem vicinæ illæ civitates fraude immani, et vere sine exemplo, tot capitum millia circumvenissent: et pereuntium mortes per ludibrium domi desides prospectassent? Sacrilegium voluerint sacrilegiorum maximum: quo scilicet generationem, maximum sacrorum, et prima commendatum nobis voce Dei, ac naturæ, pessum dediderint? Primum iuris gentium caput everterint: quod humanæ est societatis, et coniunctionis? Naturam delerint humanam: non aliter atque ille, qui est aut in fabulis, aut in veris narrationibus, Timon? Nam quid interest, an fugiat vir unus societatem reliquorum, an civitas una reliquarum civitatum aspernetur? Et si Romani fugissent communionem aliorum, iam sociales esse, et homines desiissent? Alii, qui Romanos abominarentur, homines fuerint?

[a] *l.* 35. *de relig.* [b] *Ovid.* 3. *de ar.* [c] *l.* cum proponas. C. *de trans. Alc. ibi. Bal.* 1. *cons.* 142.

---

[76] *Digest*, 11. 7. 35. [77] [Augustine, *De civitate Dei* 2. 17.]

[78] **Translator's note:** The first couplet is Ovid, *Ars amatoria* 3. 491–2; for the second, see Ayala (*De iure et officiis bellicis et disciplina militari libri tres*, Duaci, Ex officina Ioannis Bogardi, 1582, fol. 68v), but he does not identify it—Alciati was Gentili's source (see next note).

[79] *Code*, 2. 3. 21; Alciatus, *On Code* 2. 3. 21 [*Commentariorum in Codicem* in *Opera Omnia in quatuor tomos*, Tomus III, Basileae, Apud Thomam Guarinum, 1582, col. 205, where Alciati cites the maxim from Ovid]; Baldus, *Consilia* 1. 142, fol. 43r.

[80] **Translator's note:** This resembles a Stoic explanation for the binding force of the law of nature and of its source; see e.g. Cicero, *De officiis* 1. 50, where Cicero deduces "natural principles" from the "human community and society (*communitas et societas humana*)" which is taken to be a "natural society"; Grotius was later to use this idea, ultimately based on the Stoic doctrine of *oikeiosis*, in the Prolegomena to his *De iure belli ac pacis*; see *Prolegomena* 8: "This maintenance of the social order (*societatis custodia*), which we have roughly sketched, and which is consonant with human reason, is the source of law (*fons iuris*) properly so called."

Away with that fourth murder, that of Amulius, a parricide heaped upon p. 112
parricides. Away now with those Cedreni and Frisingenses, base names, names never heard by one in a thousand of us. Romulus made away with his great-uncle, a tyrant, in vengeance for the exile of his grandfather, the death of his mother and her brother, seeking to regain the kingdom that was theirs. The parricide that you charge is absent here. If even a son had killed his father in this way, he would be without guilt—why, he ought to be given a reward, as everyone agrees and has agreed.[76] We have given far too much attention to a most insignificant controversy.

But he exclaims most bitterly about the abduction of the Sabine women, as though in an unambiguous court case, and he hauls in with him the great names of the great Church Fathers. But they were not, in fact, great at all in matters outside their own religious investigations—in these political issues concerning human law. And yet the fact is that even Augustine saw that the first stage in that abduction had the Romans in the right.[77] But because he judged that the rest of the story was entangled or even cut off by many insuperable obstacles, as it were, he went off in another direction and found the Romans guilty of injustice after all. Augustine did see that marriages were denied to the Romans unjustly, and that therefore the right of war against the Sabines was granted to the Romans. But because the Romans made use of the deception of the spectacle, he pronounces this an unjust war. But indeed "in my judgment, deception is allowed in order to fight back against deception. The laws allow one to take up arms against those who are in arms. It is allowable to deceive the deceiver and to repel deception with deception, and
to deceive anyone using the example he himself has established."[78] The p. 113
interpreters of the law make this same claim.[79] There is the principle that a malicious act is justly countered by a malicious act, and that he who uses deception so as not to be deceived himself is not said to be employing subterfuge but prudence—and all that sort of thing. Would those neighboring cities have cheated with a vast and indeed unparalleled trick so many thousands of lives and have viewed in scorn the deaths of those who were perishing while they themselves were sitting idly at home? Would they have wished for the greatest sacrilege of all sacrileges—that by which they would have destroyed nothing less than the begetting of offspring, the greatest of holy things and that which was commanded to us by the first commandment of God—and of nature? Would they have overturned the original source of the law of nations, which is that of human fellowship?[80] Would they have destroyed human nature itself—no less than that famous Timon, whether he is a figure of stories or in true historical accounts? For what difference does it make whether one man flees the fellowship of other men, or one state rejects that of other states? If the Romans had avoided the fellowship of others, would they have ceased to be social creatures and true human beings? Then would those others who loathed the Romans have been human beings?

Hic ignobilitatem, vilitatem, infamiam gentis Romanæ rursum accusat. At a me antea satisfactum huic est parti. Et igitur isthæc, quæ referebatur negati connubii, caussa iniusta fuit: quæ fuit falsa. Adeon' ignobilesque, vilesque: quibus nullæ possent mulieres copulari? Neque enim illustres, ac potentes,
p. 114 sed feminæ, petebantur. [a]*Cum pare quæque suo coeunt volu|cresque feræque: Atque aliquam, de qua procreat, agnus habet. Externis dantur connubia gentibus: et, quæ Romano vellet nubere, nulla fuit.* Etiam nulla abiecta in illis populis, quæ nubere abiecto posset? Etiam nullus Romæ honestus, et generosus, cui par esse uxor valuerit? Plebeis cum plebeis, patriciis cum patriciis, paribus cum paribus verum ius nuptiarum fuit Romæ. Quid obloqueris accusator? Cum Latinis, cum aliis nuptiæ Romanis non negabantur. Erant et cum externis aliis. Tantum ius civitatis nuptiis istis non tribuebatur. At nihil iuris civitatum cum Sabinis petiere Romani: ius gentium solum poscebant. Et poscebant quidem per honestissimas obtestationes pacifice. Ne tu mihi regeras accusator, quod et fabula est iisdem, [b] qui tibi narrarunt, auctoribus, connubia nostra petentes postea Latinos non auditos. Nam, si fabula hæc est vera, petierunt Latini connubia temporibus nostris iniquissimis, armati, positis castris ante urbem, nec ulla seria necessitate. Superbissimis imperatis concedere nihil oportuit. Honestissimis rogatis concedendum fuit.

[c]Turpissimis, et internecinis hostibus Beniaminitis ius hoc raptus tributum est: qui damnati suo pessimo erant merito, ne uxores nancisci possent. Et id decreti sancitum iurisiurandi religione fuit: vinculo Iudæis supra ius sancto:
p. 115 fraus tamen visa neces|saria est, et digna indulgentia, ne familia illa exstingueretur, ut, verbis decreti adservatis, sententia prorsus circumveniretur: datumque illis fuit, ut rapto acciperent, qui accipere de parentum manu non valuerunt.

Et Romanis, immeritis immanitatem coniurationis, obiicietur hospitalis gratia, et fides adversum fraudem? *Quicquid erat*, responderit Seneca, *quo mihi cohæreret, intercisa iuris humani societas abscidit.* Iterum dico, [d]*Qui per dolum resistit dolo, is dolosus non est. Sic ars deluditur arte.* [e] Licet per dolum, per vim,

[a] *Ovid. 3. Fast.* [b] *Plut. Cam.* [c] *Iud. ult.* [d] *Bal. 2. cons.* 165. 188. 3. 73.
[e] *Alex.* 1. *cons.* 135. *Alc.* 7. *cons.* 5. 6. *l.* 31. *depo. Cott. me.* dolum. *Cov.* 1. *reso.* 2. *Bal. l.* 5. *de iust.*

[81] Ovid, *Fasti* 3. 193–6 [but Gentili has substituted "agnus" (lamb) for the text's "anguis" (snake)].

[82] Plutarch, *Camillus* 3. 3. 2. **Translator's note:** Note that Plutarch, who indeed does call this the "mythodes" of the two accounts he offers, does not say that Rome was being besieged. The Latins supposedly made their demand of a Roman camp besieged on Mount Marcius.

[83] Judges 21: 15–24.

[84] **Translator's note:** Source not cited. It is Seneca, *De beneficiis* 7. 19. 8.

[85] Baldus, *Consilia* 2. 165, fol. 44r; 2. 188, fol. 71r [the sentence "sic ars deluditur arte" is quoted from here]; 3. 73, fols. 19r f.

Here he once again blames the baseness, the worthlessness, the bad reputation of the Roman people. But I have already sufficiently dealt with this point. And therefore this excuse for the denial of intermarriage that he brings back again was unjust, for it was false. Were these men so very ignoble and base that no women could be united with them? Nor was it distinguished and powerful women they were asking for—just women. "All birds and beasts come together with their own kind, and a lamb [*sic*] has a female p. 114
counterpart from whom he may procreate. Marriages are granted to foreign peoples, but there was no people who wished to wed with a Roman."[81] Was there not even a degraded woman among those peoples who could marry a degraded man? Was there furthermore no man at Rome who was respectable and well-born for whom a wife would not have been a fit match? There was a law at Rome, it is true, restricting marriages of plebeians to plebeians, patricians to patricians, equals to equals. What are you railing at, accuser? Romans were not forbidden marriages with Latins, with other peoples. There were in fact marriages with other foreign peoples as well. It was only the right of citizenship that they did not grant to these marriages. But the Romans sought nothing of the right of citizenship from the Sabines. All they called for was the law of nations. And in fact they asked for this through the most respectable entreaties, in a peaceful manner. Now, don't retort to me, accuser, something that is a mere story, even in the eyes of those very authors who have told it to you: that later on the Latins sought intermarriage with us—and were refused.[82] For if the story is true, the Latins sought marriage at a period most unfair to us—when they were under arms, with their camp pitched before our city, and not as a result of any pressing need of their own. One should not make any concessions to highly insolent orders. They should only have agreed to the most respectable requests.

This right of abduction was granted to the basest and most murderous of enemies, the tribe of Benjamin, who had been condemned through their own very abysmal offense to be unable to obtain wives.[83] And that decree [sc. forbidding the giving of wives to the Benjaminites] was sanctioned by the religious authority of an oath—for the Jews a holy bond above the law even. The oath notwithstanding, a subterfuge seemed to be a necessary and p. 115
respectable concession, lest that tribe be extinguished—so that, while the precise words of the decree were adhered to, its decision might be utterly circumvented. And so those who were forbidden to receive brides from the hands of their fathers were allowed to receive them by means of abduction.

And will their hospitable graciousness and honor in the face of deception be held against the Romans, who did not deserve the outrage of a conspiracy against them? Seneca will have answered, "Whatever it was that was binding me to him [sc. a bloodthirsty tyrant], his breaking off of the bond of human law has torn away."[84] I say again: "He who resists deceit with deceit is not himself deceitful. Thus craftiness is deceived by craftiness."[85] One is allowed

per furtum persequi ius suum: etiam cum non sua, sed debitoris res capitur: ut sic te docent, Picene, tui iuris magistri: in quibus et sunt, qui sic tenent, etiam cum magistratus copia est. Qua tamen de parte non contenderim: [a] nam ait lex, *non esse singulis concedendum, quod per magistratum publice possit fieri: ne occasio sit maioris tumultus faciendi.* Sed cum externis, cum his, qui iudiciis non tenentur, et bella esse necessaria, et fraudem istiusmodi licitam, nemo negat. Atque si quæsitam, in urbe conditam defendere Romani rem Marte aperto vix valuerunt: an Marte ire quæsitum aperto conditam apud hostes debuerint? Et fuit igitur hoc quoque necesse, ut fraude, et furto quærerent. Et hæc itaque obtenta merito necessitas est. [b]*Necessitas magnum humanæ imbe-*
p. 116 *cillitatis patrocinium.* [c] Quod non est licitum | lege, necessitas facit licitum. Non habet legem necessitas, sed ipsa legem facit. Necessitas facit probabile, quod erat alias improbabile. Et propter necessitatem receditur a solitis iuste. Et id genus alia plurima. Necessaria raptio, et defensio ista fraudolenta adversus fuit scelestissimam coniurationem, et capitalem offensionem. Et necessariæ defensioni nihil non condonatur. Et contra scelestissimum bellum nihil est, quod non iure rependi possit. Nihil non licet adversus internecinum.

Quid argutaris, actor? Ad quædam non debere nos per ullam compelli necessitatem? Probe. Sed an hoc tale est Romanorum factum? Hoc docendum. Doctum contrarium est. Etiam, nec necessitatem meis fuisse, tentas? Et in asylo fingis copiam feminarum, et ab Alba accersis? Scilicet ea est huius sexus audacia, ut suas et feminæ fugerint civitates. Scilicet ea est huius sexus occasio, ut multæ vertere solum cogantur. Ridicule creditur, magnam aliquam ad asylum fugam factam fuisse, sive feminarum, sive hominum.

Feminarum copiam a patribus Albanis, ab avo rege arcessis? Et nescis, dissidia esse adversum colonias solere parentibus? Nescis, Albam imperii æmulam Romani exstitisse? At ista mox tibi aperientur. Tu, mihi Tyrios relictos crudelitati Alexandri a Pœnis colonis, narrasti. Magnum Romuli
p. 117 animum vereri | senex Numitor potuit: qui antea et per insidias fratris de

[a] *l.* 176. *de reg. iu.* [b] *Sene.* 4. *decl.* 4.
[c] *l.* 27. *de ma. te. c.* 4. *de reg. iu. c.* 39. 1. *q.* 1. *Bal. l.* 5. *de iust. l.* 10. *C. de testa. et* 5. *cons.* 435.

[86] Alexander Tartagnus [Alexander of Imola], *Consilia* 1. 135; Alciatus, *Consilia* 7. 5, col. 945; 7. 6, col. 946; *On Digest* 16. 3. 31; Catellanus Cotta, *Memoralia, s.v. dolum* [Lugduni, Apud Antonium Vincentium, 1556]; Diego Covarruvias, *Variae resolutiones ex Pontificio, Regio et Caesareo iure* 1. 2 [in *Opera omnia*, Venetiis, Apud Gasparem Bindonum sumptibus sociorum, 1588]; Baldus, *On Digest* 1. 1. 5.
[87] *Digest* 50. 17. 176.
[88] Seneca the Elder, *Declamationes* 4. 4.
[89] [This is a quotation from the *Liber Extra*; see the reference below.]
[90] [This is a quotation of Gratian; see the reference below.]
[91] *Digest* 40. 4. 27; *Liber Extra* [Decretals of Gregory IX] 5. 41. 4; *Decretum Gratiani* C.1 q.1 d.p.c.39; Baldus, *On Digest* 1. 1. 5; *On Code* [possibly 6. 23. 10]; *Consilia* 5. 435, fol. 115^{v}.

to pursue what is one's right through deception, through violence, through theft—even when the thing seized is not one's own but one's debtor's.[86] This is what the teachers of your law teach you, Picenus—and among them are those who maintain that this is the case even when there is a supply of magistrates on hand. But I wouldn't care to argue from that position, for the law states that "something is not to be allowed to private individuals which could happen publicly through a magistrate, lest there be occasion for causing a greater civil disturbance."[87] But no one denies that wars are necessary—and deception of this sort is allowable—with foreigners, with those who are not constrained by legal proceedings. But if the Romans scarcely had the power to defend with open warfare something they had acquired and laid up in their own city, ought they have gone off to acquire through open warfare something laid up in their enemies' midst? And so this too was necessary: that they seek it through deception and theft. And so these excuses offered justly constitute necessity. "Necessity is the great defense of human weakness."[88] That which is not allowable according to the law necessity makes allowable.[89] p. 116
Necessity has no law, but it itself makes a law.[90] Necessity makes that acceptable which would otherwise be unacceptable. And because of necessity one justly departs from customary measures.[91] And there are many other maxims of that sort. The abduction was a necessary act, and it was a deceptive measure taken against a most criminal conspiracy and deadly hatred. And there is nothing that is not conceded to a defense that is forced upon one. And there is nothing that could not be justly paid back in kind against a highly criminal war. Nothing is not permitted against a war of extermination.

What are you prattling on about, plaintiff? Are you claiming that there are certain acts to which we should not be driven by any necessity? True enough. But was the act of the Romans of this sort? This needs to be demonstrated. In fact, the opposite has been demonstrated. Will you attempt to claim that my people were not forced by necessity? Do you imagine that there was an abundance of women even in the place of refuge—and do you summon women from Alba Longa? No doubt the boldness of their sex is such that women would have fled their own cities. No doubt the opportunism of this sex is such that many of them would think of changing their condition. It is foolish to believe that any large-scale flight would have been made to the asylum—be it by women or men.

Are you summoning an abundance of women from the Alban fathers or from Romulus' royal grandfather? Are you unaware that there tend to be matters of discord for mother cities against their colonies? Are you unaware that Alba was envious of Roman rule? Well, these things will soon be revealed to you. You yourself have recounted to me that the Tyrians were handed over to the cruelty of Alexander by their Carthaginian colonists. The old man Numitor could well fear the high spirit of Romulus, since he had p. 117

regno fuerat pulsus: et videbat, repeti iustius per Romulum posse a se regnum, quod et per Romulum restitutum sibi, et donatum fuisset.

Metiris tu tenuiter regum pectora, atque consilia ex nostris privatorum. Nobiscum ius valet gratitudinis: [a] principes odio habent, quibus se debere intelligunt. Nobis cara illa nomina, et arcta vincula cognationum: quibus nihil est in terris maius: sed principibus maius quid est, et habetur: cui ista omnia postponantur: principatus. Romulum non veritus esset Numitor: qui iuvenem vidit imperii cupiditate ita flagrantem, ut mortem exspectare senis longum censeret, et nova subito regna quæreret? Et quem vereretur, misissetque a se libens, iuvasset nunc; et crescenti eius, et iam vicinis verendæ potentiæ manum non subtraxisset, at tulisset opem? Istæ sunt potentissimæ coniecturæ, quæ a propria rerum natura, et ab experientia desumuntur quotidiana.

Nihil dico, si potuit avus dare feminas: quæ patriam nollent deserere, animal intra tecta suetum, domique naturali verecundia veluti affixum. Nihil, si potuit rex Albæ civibus non volentibus, auxilio nepoti esse: quod a conditione regum prisci illius ævi facile fuerit denegare: cives autem Albanos p. 118 noluisse, feminas dari, factum vicinorum plus satis ostendit: quorum | nec alia erga Romanum crescens imperium affectio esse, et caussa valuit. Nolebant, eum crescere regem, qui ipsis ferret se aliquando regem: et quem ipsi regem nollent, aut per feminam insertum stirpi regiæ; aut spurium ortum; aut transferentem alio decus regni, et sedem.

Ecce iterum, et meliores caussas tibi, propter quas, absque culpa sua omni, Romulus Albæ non regnarit: propter quas et quæsierit alias sedes: in quas missusque ab avo fuerit: qui sceptra Romulo sua relinquere non potuerit. Ecce autem, quod modo quærimus, necessitatem habes Romanorum, quærendi a vicinis connubia. Aut habes Romanorum probam, humanamque voluntatem: qui necessitudinem, et amicitiam cum vicinis quæsierunt maxime petitione ista, et isto facto connubiorum vel raptorum.

[a] *Commin.* 5.

---

[92] Cominaeus [Philippe de Comines], *Mémoires* 5 [ed. J. Blanchard, Paris, 2001].

earlier been driven from his kingdom through the plots of his brother, and he realized that the kingdom that had been restored and given to him by Romulus could more justly be demanded back by Romulus.

You trivially measure the hearts and plans of kings on the basis of those of us private citizens. With us, the law of gratitude is in force; but princes hate those to whom they know they are indebted.[92] For us, dear are the names and tight the bonds of kinship relations—there is nothing on earth of greater force. But for princes there is something which is considered greater—and actually is greater—something to which all other things are subordinated: rule. Wouldn't Numitor have feared Romulus when he saw the young man so aflame with the lust for rule that he thought it too long to wait for the death of the old man and instead immediately sought out new kingdoms? And if he was afraid of someone and gladly sent him away from him, would he then have given him help and, instead of withdrawing his support from his growing power which was already source of fear to its neighbors, would he have been apt to have brought him aid? Those conjectures are the most powerful which are derived from the particular nature of things and from daily experience.

I am quite mistaken if his grandfather actually had the power to give him women who were unwilling to forsake their country—for women are beings accustomed to living indoors and attached, as it were, to their houses by an inborn bashfulness. I am also mistaken if the king had the power to be of assistance to his grandson against the will of the citizens of Alba, assistance which it would have been easy to refuse on the basis of the situation of kings in that ancient period. But that the people of Alba did not wish for their womenfolk to be given away—this is something that the action of Rome's neighbors more than sufficiently demonstrates, for they were men whose p. 118
attitude towards and motives against the growing Roman empire could not have been otherwise than they were. They had no wish that a man would arise as king who might someday impose himself upon themselves as king—and whom they themselves didn't want as king, either insinuated into the royal line through a wife or of bastard birth or transferring elsewhere the glory and seat of rule.

Behold again, you have here even better reasons why Romulus, through no fault of his own, did not rule at Alba Longa and why he sought out other places to settle, into which he was sent by his grandfather, who could not hand over his scepter to Romulus. Behold also—the very thing we were seeking just now—you have here the necessity of the Romans to seek marriages from neighboring peoples. Or, rather, you have here the Romans' worthy and humane desire, as men who sought a family connection and friendship with their neighbors especially through that suit—and then through that act of marriages or abductions.

Nam est a verisimili alienum aliud, ut hinc quæsita fuerit belli occasio: quasi aliæ multo iustiores, et iustitiæ evidentioris ad bellum deesse caussæ potuissent: et quasi alia sit aut fertilior, aut paratior seges, quam occasionum est belli. Bellum inferre propter negatas nuptias potuerunt, et insuper aggesta probra. Bellum si provocare, non extorquere potius necessitudinem, voluissent: cur ille raptarum dilectus virginum: ut tanto videri minor læsio posset?

p. 119 An vero unum Minutium, auctorem non adeo aut re, aut nomine magnum | isthic sequemur? [a] Nam alii de una vix Hersilia scribunt nupta: de qua una et capi Minutii illa possunt, et *nonnullas de matrimonio raptas*: alioqui solas rapi virgines, et a viris lædendis, et a mulieribus abstineri (quæsita belli occasione scilicet) iussum. Quamquam nec fraus magna, raptis mulieribus, in illa matrimoniorum infirmitate: et in illa confusione rapiendi, ubi professas mulieritatem vix discrevisses.

Illa confusio est raptio sine more, quam Virgilius dicit. An et Virgilius, Romanæ gentis professus laudator, hic Romanos vituperet? [b] Sed sine more, id est, præter quotidianam consuetudinem, et usitatam rationem. [c]*Tempestas sine more furit*, &c. quæ ait alibi: quicquid ibi scribant Grammatici. Est sine ordine, et legitimis sollemnibus, et sine ceremoniis post inductis: [d]*Queis neque mos, neque cultus erat*: ut ait alibi. [e] Et ut Ovidius eodem sensu, *sine lege*, dixit. *In quem quæque inciderant raptæ*: inquit Livius. Hic est mos: exemplum non est: ut *sine more* Servius interpretatur, *sine ullo exemplo*. Immo enim nec sine exemplo fuit raptus: ut hoc ipsum explicat Dionysius. Quamquam et hoc ipsum quid esset, si sine exemplo esset? [f]*Delectabatur Duillius cereo funali, et tibicine: quæ sibi nullo exemplo privatus sumserat: tantum licentiæ dabat gloria*: inquit Cato. Cogebatur Romulus ad vim confugere, et ad dolum: ut sibi p. 120 nullo | exemplo raperet mulieres alienas: tantum licentiæ dabat necessitas: inquam ego.

[a] *Sext. Vict. Polyen.* 8. *Serv.* 8. *Æn.* [b] *Cic. pro Mur. Serv. Æn.* 7. *l.* 32. *de legi.* [c] *Virg. Æn.* 5. [d] *Virg.* 8. *Æn.* [e] *Ovid.* 1. *de ar.* [f] *Cic. Cat.*

---

93 **Translator's note:** Dionysius of Halicarnassus (2. 31. 1) alludes to the view of some unstated writers that the abduction was carried out in order to generate a pretext for war.

94 [Minucius Felix, *Octavius* 2. 5. 3.]

95 Ps.-Aurelius Victor, *De viris illustribus urbis Romae* 2. 2; Polyaenus, *Strategemata* 8. 3. 1; Servius, *On Aeneid* 8.

96 Cicero, *Pro Murena* 1. 1 [*more institutoque maiorum*]; Servius, *On Aeneid* 7; *Digest* 1. 3. 32.

97 Vergil, *Aeneis* 5. 694.

98 Vergil, *Aeneis* 8. 316.

99 Ovid, *Ars amatoria* 1. 119.

100 [Livy 1. 9. 11.]

101 Dionysius of Halicarnassus 2. 30. 5. [Dionysius has Romulus consoling the abducted women by observing that "this was an ancient Greek custom."]

102 Cicero, *De senectute* 13. 44. **Translator's note:** The 1599 edition prints *crebro funali*, "with many a torch," which is the reading of the manuscripts. I have supplied "returning from dinner" from Cicero's *redeuntem a cena*, omitted by Gentili but helpful for the sense.

For that other contention is highly improbable—that they were looking for an excuse for war on this pretext—as though many more legitimate causes of more evident justice were lacking for a war, and as though there were any crop that was more fertile or readier to hand than the crop of excuses for a war.[93] They were able to begin hostilities on account of the marriages denied them and the insults heaped upon them over and above that. If they had wished to provoke a war rather than to obtain a family connection by force, why then that well-known business of making a selection of the abducted women? Was it so that the harm might appear that much less serious?

But are we truly to follow in this matter a certain Minucius, an author important neither in terms of the subject matter nor of his name? For others p. 119
write about one woman, Hersilia, who had just recently been married. It was with regard to this one woman that those words of Minucius can be derived: "and some were snatched from marriage."[94] In other accounts the order was given that only maidens be seized and that they refrain from doing harm to the husbands and keep their hands off their wives—oh yes, they were obviously looking for an excuse for a war![95] And yet there was no great deception in the case of wives abducted, in those days when marriages were weak, and in that confusion of abduction, when you could scarcely distinguish those who claimed the status of wives.

This confusion is what Vergil alludes to by calling the abduction "without due order" [*sine more*]. Or would Vergil, the professed encomiast of the Roman people, have reproached the Romans here? Rather, "without due order" means contrary to daily custom and normal procedure.[96] "The storm rages without restraint [*sine more*], etc.,"[97] as he writes elsewhere—whatever the grammarians write on that passage. In the case of the Sabine women, it means without due order and the legitimate rights and without the ceremonies that were instituted later on. "For whom there was neither custom [*mos*] nor civilization," as Vergil writes elsewhere.[98] And as Ovid wrote "without due order" [*sine lege*] in the same sense.[99] "They were seized by whichever man they fell into the path of," says Livy.[100] Here *mos* is "due order," not "precedent," as Servius claims in glossing *sine more* as "without precedent." No, the abduction was not without precedent, for Dionysius shows precisely this.[101] And yet what difference would it make if this *were* without precedent? Cato says, "Duillius [returning from dinner] used to take delight in many a torch and flute, an extravagance in which, though a private citizen, he had indulged, though without precedent [*nullo exemplo*]; his fame granted him p. 120
that much license."[102] In similar fashion, I say: Romulus was being forced to resort to violence and trickery so that he might seize for himself foreign women, though without precedent; necessity granted him that much license.

At Picenus, nec excusare necessitatem, quæ exemplo, auctoritateve aut generali, aut speciali non adfirmatur: et factum hoc sine ullo exemplo, et vituperatum ab omnibus. Quæ ego nego omnia. Propter necessitatem receditur a solitis. Factum hoc neque sine exemplo, aut auctoritate est, certe generali. Nam quid Dionysius scribit? Quod illud cum Beniaminitis factum est? Quæ iurisconsultorum auctoritates, licere per dolum, ac furtum consequi ius suum? [a] Etiam nec esse raptum, nec damnari oportere, si quod est aut iusta, aut etiam iniusta raptum caussa. Sed hic iusta fuit: etiam iusta, vel si amor mulierum fuit: [b]*si modo nomina rebus Addere vera placet, non hoc iniuria factum, Verum amor est: neque erit nobis gener ille pudori*: ait Iupiter de raptu Proserpinæ. [c] Et Pisistratus filiis, qui gravissima malorum meditabantur in raptorem sororis. Quid, inquit, hostibus faciemus, si hæc amatoribus nostris fecerimus?

Tu rides, Picene, deos illos. Et bene rides, sed mihi, qui tecum rideo: sed non illi tempori, quod illos venerabatur deos: et ad quod dirigi præsens iudicium debet. Immo nec rides, sed excandescis: et sacrilegium accusas: quod Consi Dei consilium sceleri huic obtentum sit scelerosissimo. Animum p. 121 rege tamen: cogita, stratagema hoc | fuisse Romuli ad animandos suos: et commentum illis religionibus sacrilegum non exstitisse. Ita responsum et hic do sacrilegio sit. Sed et responsum de omnibus est per omnia. Neque enim exspectas, (scio) ut dicam etiam de Propertio: qui suum casum conqueritur, raptæ sibi amasiæ: itaque deos, itaque astra crudelia vocat.

Et ergo concludam cum Plutarcho. [d] Raptus admissi a Theseo (inquit) honesto carent velamento: nam sæpius, et nec nubilium, et citra necessitatem admissi: at Romulus semel, unamque sibi assumsit: et necessarie coactus ad raptum est. Magnæ et meminit charitatis, qua habitæ raptæ. Addit, sic factum, quod quærebatur, ut coniunctio cum vicinis esset. [e]*Hersiliam cerne, hirsutos cum sperneret olim Gens vicina procos, pastori rapta marito, Pressit leta thorum, et soceros revocavit ab armis*: et per eam coniunctionem mox potentia

[a] *Bald.* 4. *con.* 345. [b] *Ovid.* 5. *Metam.* [c] *Polyb.* 5. *Val.* 5. *c.* 1. *Plut. apopht.*
[d] *Plut. co. Th. et Ro.* [e] *Sil.* 13.

---

103 Baldus, *Consilia* 4. 345, fol. 77v.

104 Ovid, *Metamorphoses* 5. 524–6.

105 Polybius 5 [maybe 18. 43. 5, but the passage is really taken from Diodorus 9. 37. 1]; Valerius Maximus 5. 1. ext. 2; Plutarch, *Regum et imperatorum apophthegmata* 189 c [where Pisistratus is speaking to his wife after Thrasybulus kissed their daughter].

106 **Translator's note:** This sounds more like Vergil, *Eclogae* 5. 23, where the mother of the dead Daphnis "deos atque astra vocat crudelia."

107 Plutarch, *Comparatio Thesei et Romuli* 6. 2.

108 Silius Italicus, *Punica* 13. 812–15.

But Picenus says that not even necessity excuses things which are not supported by either a general or a specific precedent or authority—and he says that this deed was done without any precedent and was generally excoriated. All of this I deny. One departs from customary measures on account of necessity. This deed was done neither without precedent nor without authority—at least a general one. For what does Dionysius write? What of that which was done with the Benjaminites? What of the jurists' authorities, who say that it is allowable to pursue one's right through deceit or seizure? They go so far as to declare that if something has been seized for a just cause—or even for an unjust cause—it is not actually stolen or to be condemned.[103] But in this case the cause was a just one—at least, if love for women was just. As Jupiter says about the abduction of Proserpina: "If only you were willing to apply true names to what happens, this deed was no wrongdoing, but love; nor will that son-in-law be a source of disgrace to us."[104] And Pisistratus said to his sons, who were planning the gravest evils against the abductor of their sister, "What should we do to our enemies, if we shall have done this to those who are in love with us?"[105]

You laugh at those gods, Picenus. And you laugh properly—in my view, at least, for I share your laughter—but not so properly in the view of that period which used to venerate those gods, and it is to that period that the present judgment ought to be directed. But you don't really laugh; you grow hot with anger and lodge an accusation of sacrilege because the advice of Deus Consus was offered as a pretext for this most wicked crime. But control your anger. Consider: this stratagem of Romulus was for the encouragement of his p. 121 people and a fabrication was not a sacrilege in the eyes of those religions. Let our response about sacrilege be thus here as well. But a response about all cases will be valid for all cases. For I know you don't expect me to go so far as to talk about Propertius, who laments his misfortune when his girlfriend is stolen from him—and so calls the gods and the stars cruel.[106]

Therefore I shall end with Plutarch. The abductions perpetrated by Theseus, he says, lack the veil of respectability. For they were perpetrated too often, and not for marriage, and beyond necessity. But Romulus undertook only one abduction, took only one woman for himself, and was forced to abduction through necessity.[107] And Plutarch refers to the great kindness with which the abducted women were treated. He adds that it was carried out in such as way that (and this was its aim) there might be a rapprochement with their neighbors. "Behold Hersilia, though earlier the neighboring people spurned hairy suitors, once she had been abducted by a herdsman husband, gladly lay on his bed and called back his fathers-in-law from the fighting."[108] And through this joining of peoples the power of all of them soon will have

exsurrexerit omnium maxima. Sic eximium factum, et prudentissimum ad societatem hanc laudat.

Nunc in ipso isto bello Sabino proditionem Tarpeiæ virginis facit strata-gema Romanorum Picenus. Romanos, veluti columbas veniente aquila, Sabino ingruente fingit exanimari. Ego vero vanissimam hanc partem accu-sationis audenter affirmem. Quid enim ut Romani, quos vafros censet, et
p. 122 callidos, humeris puellæ rem tantam apposuissent? Et | in manu fecerint hostium, ut tenere arcem, neque adservatis cum puella conventis, valerent? Ecquis hominum ineptissimus ita unquam confidit hosti? Et non, quod factum est sæpius, Romani in arce insidias collocassent? Potuit commentum ineptum inire muliercula, sed viri nunquam inierint. Et hoc igitur dixerit de ipsa Tarpeia Dionysius. Et Tarpeiæ bono animo sollemnia debita sic sint. Et sic Romani constituerint sollemnes inferias. Aut quid etiam si Sabini: qui puellam contra pacta ceciderint: itaque placare illius manes voluerint?

Videamus tamen de iustitia. Licebat certe Romanis illa, quali, quali fraude uti. Sed non usi. Itaque condemnatur Tarpeia iam non ab uno: [a]*illa autem, quæ tondetur præcordia rostro alitis, En quantum resonat plangentibus alis Armiger ad pastus rediens Iovis, hostibus arcem Virgo, immane nefas, adamato prodidit auro Tarpeia, et pactis reseravit claustra Sabinis.*

[b] Et non aurum tamen adamatum, sed Tatium regem, alii latius canunt. Quamobrem Sabinos accuses tu, qui per turpe lenocinium exercent bella. [c] Iustus ille Minos, arbiter constitutus mortalium (ut finxerunt) æternus, abominatus aliam est, quæ per sui amorem itidem aperire sibi arcem volebat.

Cum Sabinis mox quid tentatum sit aliud, præter pacem, a mulieribus, sive
p. 123 sponte inferentibus se inter volantia tela, sive le|gatis, noster divinaculus explicet. Nobis nihil constat aliud, quam quod traditum ab auctoribus est. Sed Romanis hic Picenus timiditatem exprobrat: rectius Sabinis præter lenocinium, de quo diximus; et præter mercaturam, quæ aliena bellis eorum temporum; etiam impietatem, et inreverentiam religionum exprobraturus: [d] qui, nihil deos reveriti, quibus Romani operabantur, urbem solutiorem oppresserunt. Hostes crudelissimi, et impiissimi ferias religioni hostium vel invisissimæ tribuunt.

[a] *Sil.* 13. [b] *Prop.* 4. *eleg.* 4. [c] *Virg. Cei. et Ovid. Metam.* 8. [d] *Prop.* 4. *eleg.* 5.

[109] Silius Italicus, *Punica* 13. 839–43. **Translator's note:** The speaker is the Sibyl, giving a guided tour of Hades to the newly arrived father and uncle of Scipio Africanus.

[110] Propertius 4. 4.

[111] Vergil, *Ciris*; Ovid, *Metamorphoses* 8. 1–151. **Translator's note:** During the Cretan siege of Megara, the Megarean princess Scylla falls in love at first sight with the besieging Minos and cuts for him a lock of the magical hair of her father Nisus. Horrified by her betrayal of her father and her country, Minos spurns her.

[112] Propertius 4. 5.

risen forth as very great indeed. Thus Plutarch praises the remarkable deed—and one most shrewdly designed for the union of peoples.

Next Picenus makes the treason of the maiden Tarpeia in that very same war against the Sabines into a shrewd maneuver of the Romans. He pretends that upon the Sabines' attack the Romans were terrified, like doves when an eagle is coming on. But I would boldly mention that this part of the accuser's case is utterly frivolous. For does it make sense that the Romans, whom he deems shrewd and clever, would have placed so great a matter on the shoulders of a mere girl? And would they have put it in the power of the enemy to be able to p. 122 control the citadel, after having ignored their agreement with the girl? Has there ever been a man so foolish as to put his faith in the enemy like this? And would not the Romans in that case have laid ambushes in the citadel—something quite frequently done? A little woman might have entered upon an inept stratagem, but men would never have done so. And that is why Dionysius would have said this about Tarpeia herself. And thus solemn rites would have been owed to Tarpeia with right good will. And so the Romans would have instituted proper funeral rites for her. And yet, what if the Sabines, who killed the girl contrary to their agreement, wished to placate her spirit in this way?

But let us consider this from the standpoint of justice. It was certainly allowable for the Romans to make use of a deception of that sort. But they did *not* make use of it. Accordingly, Tarpeia stands condemned now not by just one authority. "Next there is that woman whose innards are plucked out by the beak of a bird—hear what a sound Jupiter's arms-bearer makes with his flapping wings as he returns to his feeding! The maiden Tarpeia handed over the citadel to the enemy (monstrous crime!) for beloved money and opened the gates to the Sabines with whom she had made an agreement."[109]

And others more fully sing that it was not just gold she loved, but also King Tatius.[110] Therefore you ought to indict the Sabines, who wage war through base pimping. That famously just Minos, who was (they fancied) set up as eternal judge of mortal men, loathed another woman who through love of him likewise wanted to open the citadel to him.[111]

As for what else the women soon attempted to gain with the Sabines beyond peace, either by throwing themselves amidst the flying weapons or by proxies, let our diviner set forth for us. For us, nothing stands firm beyond p. 123 what has been passed down by the authorities. But Picenus finds fault with the Romans here for their cowardice. He should rather find fault with the Sabines—not only for their pimping, about which we have spoken, and for their business deal, which was alien to the wars of those times, but also for their impiety and irreverence towards religious rites, for, showing no respect for the gods to whom the Romans were at that moment sacrificing, they attacked a city that had its guard down. Even the cruelest and most impious enemies concede festal days to even the most hated religion of their enemies.[112]

Nos tamen cum longa accusatoris oratione longiores iam sumus in Romulo. Quid fieret? Sic reis duplum temporis eius ad orandam caussam suam tribuitur, quod accusationi datum sit. Sic decet in seminibus ponendis Romanæ civitatis elaborare plenius, ut surgat facilius, tamquam a robustis radicibus arbor eniteat felicius, consistat firmius. Sic sequentur deinceps omnia breviora multo, et expeditiora. Atque de plurimis quidem Romanorum bellis stat in partem nostram tacita accusatoris confessio: qui in bellorum numero innumero de pauculis tantum dissertare ausus est.

Sed ubi tamen homini mens, cum a Fidenatibus exorditur? Non ipsi igitur Fidenates bellum concitarunt per rapinas, et populationes? [a] At scribit fidus
p. 124 ille, et cautus scriptor, Livio prælatus, Floro incom|parabiliter præferendus. Quis hic Florus, ut ei contra Livium, et Dionysium fides detur? Immo ager aliquis Romanus fuit: si nunquam colonia educitur sine agro: quod antea dictum est. [b] Et Strabo agrum aliquem Romulo tribuit: tantum abest, ut neget cum Floro glebam. Aut num iste loquitur hyperbolice, et de minutulo modo intelligit? Et tamen post Ceninenses, Antemnates, Crustuminos victos, et colonos ubique factos, etiam et post Sabinos in civitatem receptos, latusque fuerit agri Romani modus, necesse est: de quo itaque rapere, prædas abigere Fidenates potuerint. Ista sic itum contagione per alios proximos: qui, crescentis civitatis invidi, vexare Romana arma non destiterunt: donec victi, et sub imperium facti sunt omnes: Sic itum in Veientes: qui bellum Romulo movent, calamitate cognatorum commoti Fidenatium: timore colonorum Romanorum perculsi, positorum Fidenis. Neque ego Veientum noto aut timorem periculi sui a præsidio tam propinquo; aut commiserationem, et studium erga cognatos. Sed et Romani iuste cum Fidenatibus victis egerunt, et mox Veientibus arma inferentibus restiterunt. Ut sic iustum esse bellum utrinque potest.

Camerinis quis neget bellum factum iustissime? Colonos Romanos, secum
p. 125 habitantes, sustulerunt insidiose. Atque hæc bella sunt Romuli per | annos propemodum quadraginta: confecta (opinor) diebus non amplius quadraginta. O bellicosum regem, et bellandi libidine *insanum*! Etiam non vituperaveris cum isto Romulum verbo, non.[c] Insanum est magnum, adi ad Grammaticos.[d] Audies enim, Regulum sic laudari, *insano pugnæ tendebat*

[a] *Dionys.* 2. *Liv.* 1. [b] *Str.* 5. [c] *Serv. Ecl.* 9. *Georg.* 1. [d] *Sil.* 6. 11.

[113] Livy 1. 14. 4; Dionysius 2. 53. 2.

[114] **Translator's note:** Though Gentili cites Strabo, bk. 5, here, in fact Strabo seems to agree with Florus. At 5. 3. 2 he notes that the first Romans "did not have surrounding countryside of their own sufficient for a city," and at 5. 3 he observes that "in the beginning the good and abundant land roundabout belonged to others."

[115] **Translator's note:** Both 1599 and 1770 editions print "vexare Romana arma" here, but I suspect that Gentili actually wrote "vexare Romana arva" ("lay waste Roman fields"). Not only would *arva* fit the emphasis here upon the question of Roman farmland, but it also makes a more plausible direct object for *vexare*.

[116] **Translator's note:** I have added the phrase "despite Livy's account" to clarify Gentili's point here. After following Livy's account of a *contagio* of hostility to the Romans spreading among their neighbors, he qualifies Livy's account somewhat by offering his own opinion—*neque ego . . . noto*—that the Veiians lacked the justifying motives Livy ascribed to them. Note that the editors of the 1770 edition attempted to deal with Gentili's obscurity here by turning the sentence beginning "Sic itum in Vejentes" into a question, unlike the 1599 edition. But Gentili seems to have presented Livy's account "straight," then disputed part of it.

[117] Servius on Vergil, *Eclogae* 9 [line 43: "insani feriant sine litora fluctus"]; *Georgica* 1.

Though we were dealing with a long speech of our accuser, we are now taking even longer ourselves with Romulus. Why should that be? Defendants are allowed for pleading their own case twice the time that was allowed to the accuser. Thus it is fitting that we expand more fully in planting the seeds of the Roman state, so that it might rise more readily, like a tree from strong roots, be more splendid in its fruit, stand more firmly. Thus everything else may follow thereafter much more briefly and efficiently. But as for the very many wars of the Romans, the accuser's silent admission stands to my account, for despite the vast number of the wars he dared to discuss only a very few.

But what is the man thinking when he begins with the Fidenates? For did not the Fidenates themselves stir up the war through their depredations and ravaging? But that reliable and careful writer, the esteemed Livy, writes about this—a writer incomparably preferable to Florus.[113] Who is Florus here, that p. 124
he be trusted against Livy and Dionysius? Yes, there was indeed some Roman territory, for a colony is never led forth without territory for it, as was mentioned earlier. Even Strabo grants some territory to Romulus—so far is he from agreeing with Florus in denying farmland to Romulus.[114] Or is Florus just speaking hyperbolically and actually means just a very small amount of territory? At any rate, after the Ceninenses, Antemnates, and Crustumians had been defeated and everywhere made into colonists of the Romans—and even just after the Sabines had been brought into the state—it was necessary that there be a broad extent of Roman territory, from which the Fidenates would be able to plunder and drive off booty. That contagion of war-making thus spread through the other neighboring peoples, who, jealous of the growing state, did not leave off harassing Roman arms until they were all defeated and reduced under Rome's empire.[115] In this same way, the contagion spread to the people of Veii, who initiated a war against Romulus because they were troubled by the disaster of their kin, the Fidenates, and struck by fear of the Roman colonists who had been settled in Fidenae. And yet despite Livy's account I myself do not observe in the people of Veii either fear of danger from so near a garrison nor compassion and favor directed towards their kindred.[116] But the Romans acted justly with the defeated Fidenates and soon restored arms to the meddling Veiians. Thus it is that the war could be just on either side.

Who would deny that war was waged most justly against the people of Cameria? They made away with Roman colonists who were living with them. And these wars of Romulus over the course of almost forty years were p. 125
brought to conclusion, I believe, in no more than forty days each. "O warlike king, mad with lust for fighting!" And yet you did not really disparage Romulus with that word "mad"—not at all. "Mad" is "great"—consult the grammarians.[117] For you will hear Regulus praised thus: "he attacked with

amore: et Annibalem, *germanum furor acer agebat optatæ pugnæ*. Scilicet heroum virtus, quæ multo excedit communem hominum, non nisi his verborum excessibus notari potest.

Et hoc urbis exordium: et Romuli regnum hoc est: ita cœptum, ita ductum, ita auctum iuste: occupatum vi, et armis; sed abque iniuria; ut vis, et bellum absque iniuria quoque est. [a] Sic iustum aiunt et interpretes iuris Romanum imperium, quod consensu partim, et partim ense quæsitum fuerit, sic theologi, et Augustinus. [b]*Pro tantis bellis susceptis, et gestis, iusta defensio Romanorum est: quod irruentibus sibi importune inimicis resistere cogebat non aviditas adipiscendæ laudis humanæ, sed necessitas tuendæ salutis, et libertatis.* Audis aliam necessitatem, quam quæ a te dicta est, accusator, Romanorum bellorum, et Romanæ nunquam quiescentis civitatis. En, inquis, alterum testem: nec nominas: et iniuste facis: [c] nam est inauditum, testium, et accusatorum nomina non audiri, et legibus aversum bonis omnibus. Iniquitas aliorum (ait
p. 126 Augu|stinus) faciebat, ut bella iuste Romani gererent: et ut, iuste sic gerendo bella, imperium adeo magnum compararent. *Post ubi pericula virtute pepulerunt, sociis, atque amicis auxilia portarunt: et decenter his artibus Roma crevit.* Importunitatem, iniquitatem aliis tribuit Augustinus: necessitatem defendendarum rerum carissimarum, et iustitiam bellorum, et decentiam principatus parti Romanis. Sileat de iniuria Florus: [d] nisi eo verbo bellum intelligit non insolite. Sileat de Romulo, et regibus ceteris Minutius: nam probus ostensus Romulus est: et iam ceteri defendentur probi.

[a] *Bal. l. 3. lect. 3. fi. de off. præt.* [b] *Aug. 3. 4. de civ.*
[c] *Pla. apolog.* [d] *l. 19. de capt.*

---

[118] Silius Italicus, *Punica* 6. 335; 11. 517 [the speaker is Hannibal's brother Mago].
[119] Baldus, *On Digest* 1. 14. 3, fols. 54^{r} ff. [the reference is unclear].
[120] Augustine, *De civitate Dei* 3. 10.
[121] Plato, *Apologia* 18 C.
[122] [Augustine, *De civitate Dei* 3. 9.]
[123] *Digest* 49. 15. 19.

insane love of fighting"—and Hannibal, "fierce passion for the battle he wanted was driving my brother."[118] No doubt the courage of heroes, which far exceeds the common courage of men, can only be expressed by verbal excesses like these.

So this is the city's beginning, and this is the reign of Romulus—thus justly begun, led, and extended; seized by force of arms, but without wrongdoing, insofar as force and war can be without wrongdoing. Thus the interpreters of the law call the Roman empire just, for it was obtained partly by agreement, partly by the sword.[119] And the theologians and Augustine agree: "It constitutes a just defense of the Romans for so many wars undertaken and waged that it was the necessity of protecting their safety and liberty, not greed for acquiring human glory, that forced them to resist enemies who attacked them violently."[120] You are hearing about another necessity for the Roman wars and the perpetual restlessness of the Roman state than the necessity you mentioned, accuser. "Behold," you say, "another witness!"—and you say so unjustly. For it is unheard of and contrary to all good laws that the names of witnesses and accusers not be heard.[121] The wickedness of others, Augustine says, brought it about that the Romans waged wars justly—and by their just p. 126
waging of wars acquired so great an empire. "Afterwards, each time when they repelled dangers through their courage, they brought aid to their allies and friends, . . . and through these honorable means Rome grew."[122] Augustine assigns the insolence and injustice to others; to the Romans he assigns as their share the necessity of defending the most precious things, the justice of wars, and the propriety of rule. Let Florus keep quiet about wrongdoing—unless he is using that word in the sense of "war," a not unparalleled usage.[123] Let Minucius Felix be silent about Romulus and the other kings. For Romulus has been shown to be upright. And now the other kings will be defended as upright as well.

De bello Albano, Tullo rege, et sequentibus. CAP. III

Tullus sequitur. *Hic ferocior Romulo, undique materiam excitandi belli quærebat*: Sed tamen dum iniuste fecerit nihil, tu reprehendere eum non potes. [a] *Sævior ingeniis, et ad horrida promtior arma, Non scelerata tamen.* Sed tu reprehendere regem nostrum non potes: propter affectus istos ætatis, virium, avitæ gloriæ. Ut his stimulatum Tullum, idem narrat Livius. Naturæ paremus omnes. *Continuo pecoris generosi pullus in arvis Altius ingreditur, et mollia crura reponit: stare loco nescit.* A natura non datas vires frustra, intelligimus omnes: p. 127 quibus veluti stimulis amor agitatur laudum, et conscia virtus. Depredi|cata omnibus est vox Themistoclis, quemadmodum trophæa illa Miltiadis in campis Marathoniis se somnum capere non paterentur. Sexcenta sic sunt.

Sic philosophis virtus est fortitudinis, etiam heroicæ, quæ amat in periculis esse, et omnibus horribilibus, ubi fulgeat, et virescat. Aut quis ille est potens rei alicuius, qui et non optet, et non quærat occasionem ostendendæ eius facultatis suæ: quam, natura magistra, non esse sibi frustra velit? Hæc reprehendere Picenus non debuit: ne gigantum fraterculus et facere contumeliam, bellumque naturæ videretur. Reprehendere natales nec debuit Tulli. Tenetis, quæ ad natales Romuli respondebam? Etiam qui reges olim nisi pastores? Et quo alio reges nomine dicti, quam pastorum? Et unde fierent reges optimi, et vero facti sunt nisi ex pastoribus? [b] Quæ sapientes viri explicarunt? Ceterum et maiores Tullum nobilem vincunt Hostilii nobiles.

Ceterum de viri virtute videamus: et, quæ eius non putentur, ei nec in iudicium attrahantur. In patres Albanos bellum movit, Romanos resides ut moveret in arma viros? Non hoc Virgilius cecinit. Et tamen, si per iustam occasionem (huc, huc) quæsitum id est, non etiam reprehendes. Scilicet cum Iove, *nec torpere gravi passus sua regna veterno*: Et cum omnibus: qui norunt, p. 128 hanc bene regnandi esse rationem. [c] | Magnus ille accusatoris nostri auctor Cardanus in quinque caussis, quibus bellum iuste suscipitur, hanc accenset, ut milites in disciplina contineantur. [d] Ait autem Dionysius, invidisse Romanis Cluilium regem Albanorum: et, non habentem caussam iustam, aut pro-

[a] *Ovid.* 1. *Metam.* [b] *Phi. Iose. Moys. Serv.* 11. *Æne. Cl. Ale. Str.* 1. [c] *Card. enc. Ner.* [d] *Dionys.* 3.

124 [Livy 1. 22. 2, adapted].

125 Ovid, *Met.* 1. 126–7. **Translator's note:** Gentili here applies to Tullus Hostilius Ovid's words on the Bronze Age.

126 [Livy 1. 22. 2: "Cum aetas viresque, tum avita quoque gloria animum stimulabat." His grandfather had distinguished himself in the Sabine war.]

127 [Vergil, *Georgica* 3. 75–6; 84.]

128 [Plutarch, *Themistocles* 3. 4; *Regum et imperatorum apophthegmata* 185 A; Cicero, *Tusculanae disputationes* 4. 19. 44; Valerius Maximus 8. 14. ext. 1.]

129 **Translator's note:** A "little brother of giants" is a nobody, a person of unknown parents. Cf. Juvenal 4. 98: "unde fit ut malim fraterculus esse gigantis."

CHAPTER 3

On the Alban War, King Tullus, and his Successors

Tullus is next. "This man, fiercer than Romulus, used to seek an opportunity everywhere for stirring up war."[124] And yet since he did nothing unjustly, you cannot reproach him. "Fiercer in temperament and readier for frightful arms, but nonetheless not criminal."[125] But you are not able to reproach our king on account of those dispositions that derived from his youth, strength, and his grandfather's glory. The same Livy tells us that Tullus was spurred on by these things.[126] We all yield to nature. "Immediately the foal of a noble herd walks with a loftier tread in the fields and plants his supple limbs. He doesn't know how to stay in one spot."[127] We all know that nature has not given bodily powers in vain, and these serve as goads by which love of glory and a sense of one's own worth are stirred up. Familiar to all is the utterance of p. 127
Themistocles: that the trophy of Miltiades in the plains of Marathon did not let him sleep.[128] There are six hundred stories of that sort.

Thus, in the eyes of philosophers, is the virtue of courage, which loves to be in dangers and in all dreadful things, where it might shine and flourish. Or who is that man who has power over anything who would not both choose and seek an opportunity for displaying an ability that, with nature as his teacher, he would not wish to be his to no purpose? Picenus should not have criticized this, lest he appear to be a little brother of giants and making reproaches and war against nature.[129] He ought not to have reproached the origins of Tullus. Do you recall the response I was making about the origins of Romulus? Also, what kings in former days were not herdsmen? And by what other name have kings been called but that of shepherds? And from what origin could the greatest kings be made—and have in fact been made—if not from herdsmen? What have wise men set forth?[130] But in fact his ancestors, the Hostilian nobles, surpass noble Tullus in rank.

But let us see about the virtue of the man, and let us not forcibly drag those things into the investigation that are not thought to belong to him. Did he initiate war against the Alban fathers in order to stir the inactive Romans to war? This isn't what Vergil sang. And yet if this aim was sought through a justifiable occasion (*this* is what we are aiming at), you will no longer find fault. Surely you will side with Jupiter: "nor did he allow his kingdom to be sluggish in heavy lethargy."[131] And you will agree with all those others who know that this is a method of good government. That great authority of our p. 128
accuser, Cardanus, among his five causes for which war is justly undertaken includes this: in order that soldiers remain in proper discipline.[132] Moreover, Dionysius says that Cluilius, king of the Albans, resented the Romans and,

---

[130] Philo Judaeus, *De vita Mosis* II. 60; Josephus, *Antiquitates Judaicae* 2. 12; Servius, *On Aeneid* II; Clement of Alexandria, *Stromata* I.

[131] [Vergil, *Georgica* I. 124.]

[132] Cardanus, *Encomium Neronis* 18. 5, p. 50.

babilem concitandi Albanos ad bellum, curasse, fieri prædas: quod belli materia esset. Livius actas narrat invicem prædas: et negatam restitutionem ab Albanis prius. Ubi Tulli improbitas? Quod curarit callide, ut primi negarent Albani restitutionem? Id neque accusator exprimere ausus est. Nam licet liquido, caussam suam procurare meliorem, adversariorum deteriorem. Et Albani erant audiendi prius, qui rapuerant prius. Cur non restituunt primi, qui primi rapuerunt? Aut reciperent sua, qui restituere aliena negassent? Et sic igitur ipsi agnoscunt Albani a partibus suis iniustitiam et confitentur: *Ego, regem nostrum Cluilium caussam huiusce esse belli, audisse videor*: inquit Metius, Albanorum dictator: apud Livium quidem, suspectissimum accusatoris. Sed et Dionysius, (ut monui) laudatissimus accusatoris, hoc idem de Cluilio contestatur. Adfirmetur suspecti testimonium testis ab idoneiori.

Hæc itaque belli suscipiendi caussa. In autem gerendo quid est factum
p. 129 improbe a Tullo, aut crudeliter? Quid apud Livium, Dionysium, alios | huius legimus rei? Picene: fortem decet esse, et diligentem in evoluendis, et evincendis criminibus accusatorem: sed mendacem, atque falsarium (non Memmiam metuis?) esse non decet. Mendacium impudens, atque apertum ut hoc tuum est de improbissimis, et crudelissimis rationibus Tulli in bello isthoc, quas notarint historiæ, ne quidem ex parte accusati, et in patrocinio rei ferendum ducitur. Apertum mendacium: quod apertis libris apertum est.

Compositum trigeminorum certamine bellum est. Et in ea compositione mansisset, si tu dictis Albane maneres. Quæ enim de Albæ exscidio tragice traducit accusator, ea penitus vana sunt. Pœna fœdifragorum potest multo esse maior. Albam diruit Tullus, parentem quidem: sed ([a] ut solent cum coloniis esse dissidia) et imperii æmulam: quod itidem adfatetur dictator Albanus. Et ego quidem fatear, coloniam omnem oportere honore prosequi metropolim suam: sed si sibi ab ea fiat bene: quod si enim male fiat, et secedendum ab ea est. Neque enim coloniæ emittuntur, ut iis serviant, qui relinquuntur, sed ut sint pares. [b] Quæ olim contra Corinthios Corcyræi verissime. Nam pars civitatis emittentis est emissa colonia; adeoque par. [c] At *Albani parentes* (audi tuum Orosium) *ipsa ab initio Romani nominis*

[a] *Pla.* 6. *de legi.* [b] *Thucyd.* 1. [c] *Oros.* 2. *c.* 4.

[133] Dionysius of Halicarnassus 3. 2. 2.

[134] **Translator's note:** Cf. Picenus' criticism of Livy in *De armis Romanis* 1. 1, pp. 13–14. Gentili here has mangled Metius' words in Livy 1. 23. 7: "Iniurias et non redditas res ex foedere quae repetitae sint et ego regem nostrum Cluilium causam huiusce esse belli audisse videor...": "I think I have heard our king Cluilius say that the cause of this war was acts of injustice and things not handed back that were demanded in accord with the treaty."

[135] **Translator's note:** Gentili here probably draws from Valerius Maximus 3. 7. 9, who also has the wrong name (*Lex Memmia*). Gentili means actually the *Lex Remmia*, according to which calumniators were branded on the forehead. Cf. Marcian in *Digest* 48. 16. 1; see for an allusion to the branding on the forehead Cicero *Pro Sexto Roscio Amerino* 57.

[136] Plato, *Leges* 6.

[137] [Livy 1. 23. 8, where Mettius refers to *cupido imperii* as driving both sides.]

[138] Thucydides 1. 34.

not having a just or commendable cause for stirring the Albans up to war, arranged that there would be cattle-rustling expeditions, which would serve as an excuse for a war.[133] Livy recounts that booty was driven off by both Romans and Albans in turn and that the Albans were the first to refuse restitution. Wherein, then, lies the wickedness of Tullus? Was it that he cleverly contrived that the Albans would be the first to refuse restitution? Not even our accuser has dared to say this. For Tullus was clearly able to make his case out to be better—and that of his adversaries out to be worse. And the Albans, who were the first to carry off, ought to have been heard first. Why did not those who first stole first make amends? Or should those who had refused to restore other people's things recover their own? And accordingly the Albans themselves acknowledge and confess that the injustice came from their own side: "I think I have heard that our king Cluilius was the cause of this war," says Metius, dictator of the Albans—in Livy, it is true, an author highly suspected by our accuser.[134] But also Dionysius, as I have mentioned, an author very highly praised by our accuser, attests this same thing about Cluilius. The testimony of a suspect witness is strengthened by that of a more fitting witness.

So this was the cause for undertaking the war. Now, when it comes to the waging of it, what was done basely or cruelly by Tullus? What do we read about this question in Livy, Dionyius, and others? Picenus, an accuser must p. 129
be brave and diligent in setting forth and proving his charges; he ought not be a liar and a forger—don't you fear the Lex Memmia?[135] A shameless and open lie, as is this of yours claiming that Tullus' methods in that war were the basest and cruelest which history books record, is not considered tolerable even on the part of the accused in his own defense. It is an open lie, for it lies open in open books.

The war was ended by a contest of triplets. And it would have remained settled by that agreement, if you had abided by your words, Alban. For everything the accuser proclaims in high tragic style about the destruction of Alba is utterly foolish. The punishment of treaty-breakers can be much worse than that. Tullus destroyed Alba, a parent city to be sure, but (as there tend to be fallings out with colonists[136]) also a rival of Rome's rule, which the Alban dictator admits in the same place.[137] I do admit that every colony ought to treat its mother-city with honor, but only if she is well treated by her. But if she is badly treated by the mother-city, she should go so far as to secede from her. For colonies are not sent out in order to be slaves to those who are left behind, but in order that they might be equals. This is what the Corcyreans once very truly said to the Corinthians.[138] For a colony that has been sent out is a part of the state that sends it out—and to this degree equal. But (listen here to your friend Orosius) "the Alban parents persecuted the

p. 130 *germina persecuti.* Isti illi sunt [a] parentes san|guinolenti, qui recens natos abiiciunt. Isti illæ immanes feræ, quæ recens natos suos devorant. Attamen Tullus civitatem renovavit potius, et in meliorem fortunam adscivit: quam transtulit in Romanam, et multo quidem cum honore, ac iuris æqualitate. Plebem Albanam civitatis Romanæ fecit cum Romana plebe participem: patres Albanos patribus Romanis conscripsit. Et itaque non tam periisse Alba videretur, quam in suum corpus rediisse. [b] Quod et historici dicunt.

Mittit alia Tulli accusator. Nec enim videt rimulam, ubi suos figere ungues reprehensionis carptorios possit. Et sic reliquos reges (sententia nescio qua generali contra omnes lata, accepta contentus) silentio multo involuit. Sed evolvo ego: nec patiar, aut in tempus conferri, aut ad laudem sive brevitatis, sive modestæ accusationis referri, quod a mala liquido caussa est. [c] Bellum cum Fidenatibus, et Veientibus habet Tullus rursus a Romulo. Cur? Negabant illi, superesse sibi quidquam fœderis cum Romanis, mortuo Romulo. Quod et Latini respondent Anco mox de fœdere icto cum Tullo: et Tarquinio post de fœdere icto cum Anco. Et Etrusci respondent Servio de his, quæ cum Tarquinio pepigissent. Et respondent Sabini Superbo de pactis cum
p. 131 Servio. Quæ frivola cavillatio: et eo iniquior: quo frequentior, et in maiori-|bus rebus. [d] Ipsi Romani utique stare debuissent conventis Albanorum cum aliis, si alii petiissent: et obligatio est ex iure unionis civitatis Albanæ cum Romana. Cur non igitur alii stare iisdem conventis debuerint? Soloque cum Romulo fuit fœdus Veientibus, quod fuit in centum annos? Et fœdera cum regibus, non cum populo Romano contrahebantur? Aut fœdera cum Romulo rege, non cum Romano rege contrahebantur? Relegatur formula fœderum.

Bellum et Sabinis indicit Tullus: quod utrinque factæ essent iniuriæ: et res nequidquam repetitæ essent. Sed Sabini ad Feroniæ fanum, mercatu frequenti, negotiatores Romanos comprehenderunt: ad locum, qui religione habuit tutos præstare omnes: [e] in tempore, quod per summam libertatem congregare mortales solet: eos homines, quibus passim securitas, et privilegia sunt contributa. Quid hic Sabini? *Suos prius in lucum confugisse, ac Romæ*

[a] *l. ult. C. de pa. qui fi. su. dis.* [b] *Ior. de re. succ. Flor.* 1. [c] *Dionys.* 3. 4.
[d] *Decian.* 2. *cons.* 14. [e] *Alc.* 5. *cons.* 23.

---

139 Orosius 2. 4. 140 *Code*, 4. 43. 2.

141 Jordanes, *Romana* 97; Florus 1. 3. 9. [Gentili and Jordanes are quoting Florus here: "ut consanguinea civitas non perisse, sed in suum corpus redisse rursus videretur."]

142 Dionysius of Halicarnassus 3. 6.

143 Decianus, *Consilia* 2. 14.

144 **Translator's note:** See Livy 1. 24. 4 ff., where the fetial rite of treaty making is described and where it becomes clear that the fetial priest is regarded as the representative of the Roman people (*nuntius populi Romani*) rather than simply of King Tullus.

145 **Translator's note:** See for Tullus' war against the Sabines Livy 1. 30. 4 ff. Gentili is here using the language of the fetial law concerning the waging of a just war (the seeking of redress (*rerum repetitio*) after an injury (*iniuria*) has been done); see Cicero, *De republica* 2. 31 (which Gentili could not have known; *De republica* 3. 35 (which he knew from Isidore of Seville, *Etymologiae* 18. 1. 2–3; and Cicero, *De officiis* 1. 36.

146 **Translator's note:** Gentili here loosely paraphrases Livy, who also mentions the cause put forward by the Sabines for war. See Livy 1. 30. 4–5: "Hac fiducia uirium Tullus Sabinis bellum indicit, genti ea tempestate secundum Etruscos opulentissimae uiris armisque. Utrimque iniuriae factae ac res nequiquam

first shoots of the Roman name from the beginning."[139] These are those bloodthirsty parents who cast out their freshly born offspring.[140] These are p. 130 those monstrous beasts who eat their freshly born offspring. But Tullus, on the contrary, restored and brought to a better destiny that city which he transferred to the Roman state with much honor and equality before the law. He made the common people of Alba partners with the Roman populace in the Roman state, and he enrolled the Alban Fathers into the Roman Senate. And so Alba seemed not so much to have perished as to have been reunited with its own body—a fact that even the historians mention.[141]

The accuser passes over the rest of Tullus' reign, for he does not see a fissure where he might be able to fix his grasping talons of reproach. Similarly, he wraps the other kings in a great silence, content with having accepted one general judgment of some sort brought in against all of them. But I, for my part, am expanding on this point, and I will not endure what manifestly derives from a bad case to be postponed or else be made to redound to the speaker's credit either for brevity or for a temperate accusation. Tullus has a war with the Fidenates and with the Veiians reprising that of the time of Romulus.[142] Why? Those peoples denied that, once Romulus was dead, there was any longer anything left of a treaty with the Romans. And the Latins soon give the same answer to Ancus about the treaty struck with Tullus—and to Tarquin after that, about the treaty struck with Ancus. And the Etruscans give the same answer to Servius about the treaty they had agreed upon with Tarquin. And the Sabines answer Tarquinius Superbus thus about their agreements with Servius. What frivolous sophistry, and all the more wicked for being more frequent and in matters of great importance. p. 131
The Romans themselves should surely have abided by agreements made by the Albans with other peoples, if any other peoples had sought such agreements, and the obligation arises from the binding nature of the union of the Alban state with the Roman.[143] Why, then, would not others have been bound to abide by those same agreements? Was it only with Romulus that the people of Veii had a treaty—a treaty which was for one hundred years? And were the treaties contracted with the kings themselves, and not with the Roman people? Or were the treaties with Romulus the king rather than with the Roman king? Let the formula of the treaties be read over again.[144]

Tullus also declares war against the Sabines because there were wrongs done on both sides, and things seized were sought back in vain.[145] But the Sabines seized Roman merchants at the shrine of Feronia, at a crowded festival fair,[146] at a place which ought to have insured the safety of all through religious sanctions, and at a time when people are accustomed to gather together with the fullest freedom,[147] and the men seized were those to whom security and privilege are granted everywhere. What did the Sabines say here?

---

erant repetitae. [5] Tullus ad Feroniae fanum mercatu frequenti negotiatores Romanos comprehensos querebatur, Sabini suos prius in lucum confugisse ac Romae retentos. Hae causae belli ferebantur."

[147] Alciatus, *Consilia* 5. 23, col. 510.

retentos. De re transacta ante bis quadraginta annos, hoc est, de bis præscripta, perque longissimarum bina tempora præscriptionum, respondent. Etiam postquam Tatius in urbem convenit. Etiam postquam Numa omnium circa finitimorum animos fœderibus, ac societate vinxisset. Et hæc Tullus.

Sequitur iactantior Ancus. Qui Latinis despectus, Numæ nepos: id est, deses
p. 132 quasi ut avus intra sa|cella, et aras acturus regnum. *Incursionem faciunt in agrum Romanum: et repetentibus res Romanis superbe responsum reddunt. Sed medium erat Anco ingenium, et Numæ, et Romuli memor*. Et itaque iactantior: qui unus duorum præstantissimorum regum gemina virtute fulgebat belli, et pacis: [a] aut vir sane popularis, et qui favorem amaret populi: ubi laus hæc prima regis istius est. [b] Etiam iactantia sui non vituperetur, quæ sæpe necessaria: ut hic, cum vindicanda est nostra a calumniis existimatio. Verumenimvero Ancus iam non vituperatur ab accusatore: sed laudatur: qui, iure invento fæciali, iniquitatem decessorum suorum damnaverit. Et hic dicitur a Servio honorato testimonium. Quem et ego quidem honorem bonum, et honoratum Grammaticum. [c] At quis mihi aurum Servii colliget tot inter sordes interspersas, et dicat, Servius hic est?

At ostendimus nos, nullum illatum a Romanis bellum hactenus non iustissime. At vero Lactantii verba non moror. Afer ille, non a Firmo Piceno, ut auctor nescio quis de Piceno nuperus putat. Ostendemus et reliqua (quod contra istum sit) bella Romanorum iusta. Interim Afer: et Afrum item qui se præstantior incomparabiliter, contra habet, Augustinum. Non audistis? Noli
p. 133 illud ridere Africæ. [d] Ille Servius sic deprehensus alibi gratificari huic suæ | genti. [e] Sic Afri dicunt Africam decus terrarum.

Audivimus nunc tres caussas, cur bellum Ancus Latinis fecerit, sui despectum, fœderum reiectionem, rapinas. Quæ singulæ iustæ. Et quod Latini negabant, nihil sibi cum Romano imperio, etsi sibi fuisset cum Albano, sane iniustum erat perspicue, sane iniustum. [f] Nam aut unita civitas Albana erat

[a] *Serv. 6. Æn.* [b] *Plut. que. q. p. se lau. Card. 3. de sap.*
[c] *Mag. 1. Misc. 2.* [d] *Iuni. Tert. de pal. c. 1.* [e] *Sext. Vict.* [f] *Eug. 1. cons. 43.*

148 [Livy 1. 30. 5.]
149 [Livy 1. 32. 3–4.]
150 Servius, *On Aeneid* 6.
151 Plutarch, *De se ipsum citra invidiam laudando* 539E; Cardanus, *De sapientia* 3.
152 Hieronymus Magius [Girolamo Maggi], *Variarum Lectionum, seu Miscellaneorum libri IIII*, Venetiis, Ex officina Iordani Zileti, 1564, 1. 2, fols. 6v–8.
153 [Cf. *De armis Romanis* 1. 3, pp. 40–1.]
154 Junius on Tertullian, *De pallio* 1.
155 Aurelius Victor, *Caesares* 40. 19.

That "earlier the Romans had detained in Rome Sabines who had taken refuge in the grove."[148] They offer a response about a matter done eighty years earlier, that is, about a matter which had been objected to twice already, and through two periods of the very remotest objections. They do this even after Tatius made an agreement with the city. They do this even after Numa had bound the hearts of neighboring peoples with treaties and fellowship. So these, then, are the deeds of Tullus.

"Next comes the more boastful Ancus." The grandson of Numa, he was despised by the Latins—that is, as a sluggish man who would govern the kingdom amid shrines and altars like his grandfather. "They raid Roman p. 132
territory, and when the Romans seek restitution they give a haughty answer. But the character of Ancus was balanced, and he kept both Numa and Romulus in mind as models."[149] And so he was "more boastful," for in his one person he shone forth with the double excellence in peace and war shown by two most distinguished kings—or as a man who was decidedly a man of the people and who loved the favor of the people, since the people's favor was that king's principal distinction.[150] Moreover, boasting is not to be blamed, for it is often necessary—as it is right now, when our reputation needs to be defended against slanders.[151] But in actual fact Ancus is not censured by our accuser, but praised as one who, upon the invention of the fetial law, condemned the injustice of his predecessors. And here the accuser adds a testimony of the honored Servius—and I myself certainly would honor him as a good and honored grammarian. But who would gather together for me the gold of Servius amidst all the junk which has been scattered in among his writings and tell me: "*This* is Servius"?[152]

But we have shown that no war up to this point was declared by the Romans without the fullest justice on their side. And indeed I care nothing for the words of Lactantius. That author is an African, not from Firmum in Picenum, as a certain author from Picenum recently supposed.[153] We shall show that also the other wars of the Romans were just—which may contradict what Lactantius claims. But for now, let us note that this man is an African—and has at the same time an African of incomparably superior prestige to contradict him: Augustine. Haven't you heard that? Don't laugh at that Africa business. The famous Servius is discovered elsewhere being partial to his own people of Africa.[154] In the same way, Africans call Africa p. 133
the "glory of the lands."[155]

We have now heard three causes why Ancus made war against the Latins: their contempt for him; their rejection of the treaties; the cattle rustlings. All of these are in themselves legitimate excuses. And the fact that the Latins denied that they had any involvement with Roman rule, even though they did have some involvement with Alban rule—that was manifestly unjust, thoroughly unjust. For either the Alban state was joined and subordinate to the

Romanæ, et subdita; atque quæ omnia erant civitatis Albanæ, transierunt in Romanam: maxime quando et exstincta Albana erat: aut duæ hæ civitates erant simul unitæ: et Albanæ igitur adhuc stanti cur non paretur, ut prius? Vere tamen exstincta hæc erat, in Romanam translata tota funditus.

Dicam definitiones iuris hic captas? Si paterfamilias arrogatur, omnes, qui ei subsunt, veniunt simul in potestatem arrogatoris. Capellæ, et beneficia Ecclesiæ, quæ unitur, transeunt in potestatem, et qualitatem Ecclesiæ, cui uniuntur. Si evincitur Ecclesia, cui fit unio, etiam unita evincitur, &c. Et sic bellorum (ut dico) iustæ caussæ. Bellatum civiliter, et more antiquo miti: ait Dionysius. Finitum bellum sollemni more Romano, victis in urbem adsumtis, et collocatis. Atque hæc Ancus.

Vis, et Tarquinios reges? Prisco bellum a Sabinis illatum prius, et deductum ad portas urbis, quam, non dico, res essent repetitæ, et ipsum indictum,
p. 134 sed ne intellectum qui|dem esset. Etiam Latinis tulere adversum nos auxilia. Et itaque cum Sabinis bellatum. Bellatum cum Latinis: qui fœderibus cum decessore ictis abnuebant persistere. Bellatum cum Etruscis: qui se contra steterant cum Latinis. Hæc Prisci.

[a] Servii bellum memoratur cum Etruscis gestum: qui nihil sibi cum Servii imperio; nihil cum societate; nihil cum amicitia esse dicebant: quæ cum Prisco pepigissent.

Sic et Superbus iusta movit arma in Sabinos: qui, sollemni hoc sophismate, post Servii mortem detrectabant pacta cum rege, et Romano populo. Quamquam istum regem ego non tuear: quem populus semper est detestatus. Sed dicendum sit tamen, movisse illum iusta arma in Pomptinos: qui legatis nostris res repetentibus responderunt superbe: hoc est per facinus, et scelus ingens: [b] ut superbia apud maiores sic accipitur: et ut sic Tarquinius hic est Superbus cognominatus. Movit in Gabinos, et Volscos: qui contra se pro Pomptinis arma tulerunt. Quid ais fraudem in Gabinos malam? Fraus in hostes est bona. Minime Romanam dixisses cum Livio: et vicisses non magnanimam, non heroicam: sed nec vinceres propterea imbrobatam gentibus, aut aliter iniustam. Ergo is quoque *nec, ut iniustus in pace rex, ita dux*

[a] *Dionys.* 4. [b] *Serv. Aen.* 12.

---

156 Marcus Antonius Eugenius Perusinus [Marco Antonio Eugenio], *Consilia* 1. 43 [Perusiae, Apud Petrum Paulum Orlandium, 1588].
157 [Gentili is quoting Vergil, *Aeneis* 6. 817.]
158 Dionysius of Halicarnassus 4. 27. 2.
159 Servius, *On Aeneid* 11.
160 [Livy 1. 53. 4: *minime arte Romana.*]

Roman state and all the things that belonged to the Alban state passed over to the Roman, especially when the Alban state was extinguished, or else these two states were united from the first and, accordingly, if the Alban state was still standing why not still obey it as before?[156] But in actual fact, the Alban state was abolished and utterly transferred to the Roman state.

Shall I state here the definitions taken from the law? If a father of a family is adopted, then everyone who is under his authority passes into the power of the adopter. Chapels and benefices of a church which is joined to another pass over into the power and nature of the church to which they are joined. Thus if a church which undergoes a union is under an obligation, then the united church is likewise under an obligation, etc. And so these are just causes for wars, as I say. War was waged in a civil fashion and in the ancient, gentle manner, says Dionysius. The war was concluded through the solemn Roman custom, with the defeated adopted and settled in the city. And so these are the deeds of Ancus.

Do you want to see the Tarquinian kings also?[157] A war was initiated by the Sabines against Tarquinius Priscus and brought right up to the gates of the city—I won't say simply before reparations were demanded and the war itself was declared, but even before the war was known about. They even brought aid p. 134
to the Latins against us. And so there was war with the Sabines and war with the Latins, who denied that the treaty struck with Tarquin's predecessor was still valid. And there was war with the Etruscans, who took their stand against us alongside the Latins. These, then, are the deeds of Tarquinius Priscus.

There is record of a war of Servius Tullius waged against the Etruscans, who claimed that what they had agreed with Tarquinius Priscus had nothing to do with any rule of Servius over them, or alliance or friendship of his with them.[158]

In the same way Tarquinius Superbus initiated a just war against the Sabines, who, following this hoary old bit of cunning, rejected their agreements with the king and people of Rome after the death of Servius. And yet I, for one, would not defend that king, whom the people always hated. But let it nonetheless be admitted that he initiated a just war against the Pomptines, who, when our ambassadors sought restitution of goods from them, responded with insolence *(superbe)*—that is, by means of wickedness and great villainy, as insolence *(superbia)* is defined among our ancestors—and as this very Tarquin is given the cognomen Superbus.[159] He also initiated hostilities against the Gabinians and the Volscians, who bore arms against him on behalf of the Pomptines. Why do you say that the deception used against the Gabinians was wicked? Deception against enemies is good. You would follow Livy in calling this "scarcely Roman,"[160] and you would triumphantly show that it was not great-hearted, not heroic; but you wouldn't for all that succeed in showing that it was something disapproved among the nations generally or otherwise unjust. Therefore Livy himself says: "But while the king was unjust in peace, he was not similarly bad as a leader in war. In

p. 135 *belli pravus fuit: quin ea arte æquasset superiores reges, ni degeneratum | in aliis huic quoque decori obfuisset*. Audin' quale tuum argumentum a civilibus gestis ad externa?

Ais, Romulum senatorum manibus discerptum: *manavit enim hæc quoque, sed perobscura fama*: inquit Livius. Quæ valida probatio est accusatoris, maxime accedente convicio Maximi: quod et ab eadem est fama. Et quisquam mortalium credat, agi ad illum modum cum Romulo potuisse, vel si terræ misceri cælum contigisset, qui trecentis stipatus semper militibus studiosissimis cingebatur? Ridet adversarius, sublimem raptum procella, et translatum in cælum. Atque ego de cælo etiam rideo. Sed procella cur raptus non fuerit?

Id affirmat Plutarchus, et aliis quidem exemplis allatis. [a] Id magicum factum affirmant alii: an vero hostis iniqui magicum? an factum dæmonis, qui novum excitare idolum voluerit? an etiam ipsiusmet Romuli? cui aut philosophi illius fuerit mens, qui in fornacibus Ætnæ induere opinionem voluit divinitatis; aut etiam mens Alexandri, qui in fluentis Babyloniæ sibi idem destinarat: nihil hoc ad iustitiam, quam hominum quærimus. Si sibi Romulus magnus, qui sibi civitati suæ animos facere voluit, sapiens, patriæ amans. Si Romulo dæmon maleficus: quis vi maiori obsisteret? Si maleficus hostis, et hostis quoque est iniustitia: quæ in genero isto cum est frequentior, hic quoque fuerit verisimilior.

p. 136 Tullus magicis item, procuratis male, periisse narratur constantius. [b] Aræ apud maiores non incendebantur: sed ignem divinum eliciebant (hic Iovis illius Elicii) precibus: hæ male conceptæ mortem cum igne eliciebant. Atque sic facere dæmones soliti: ut sunt æmulatores Dei veri: [c] qui filios Aharonis, sacra sua non rite tractantes, immisso a se igne interfecit. Et illum interfecit, qui notanti arcæ manum admovit imprudenter. [d]*Scilicet in superis etiam fortuna luenda est. Nec veniam, læso numine, casus habet. Omnis et in magnos culpa deos scelus est*. Sic rectius, quam illic, *At bene si quæras fortunæ crimen in illo, Non scelus invenies, quod enim scelus error habebat*? Sic est de Tullo. Tui facessat hinc testimonium Zonaræ. Ancus autem si insidiis periit, an illico

[a] *Bod*. 2. *dem*. 4. [b] *Serv*. 11. *Æn*.
[c] *Lev*. 10. 2. *Sam*. 6. [d] *Ovid*. 2. *Trist*. 1. et 1. *de Po*. 11. 7. *Meta*. 3.

161 [Livy 1. 53. 1.]
162 [Livy 1. 16. 4.]
163 [Valerius Maximus 5. 3. 1.]
164 [Plutarch, *Romulus* 27–8.]
165 Jean Bodin, *De la démonomanie des sorciers* 2. 4 [Paris, Chez Iacques du Puys, 1580].
166 [See Diogenes Laertius 8. 69.]
167 Servius, *On Aeneid* 11.
168 Leviticus 10: 1–2; 2 Samuel 6: 6.
169 Ovid, *Tristia* 2. 107–8; *Epistulae ex Ponto* 1. 6. 26. [The second quotation is usually taken as a question, with "an" for Gentili's "et."]
170 Ovid, *Metamorphoses* 3. 141–2. [Like the lines from the *Tristia* above, this refers to Actaeon.]

fact, he would have equaled the earlier kings in this art had not his degeneracy in other things obscured this source of glory as well."[161] Do you see how false p. 135
an assumption you are making about dealings with foreign powers on the basis of things done at home?

You say that Romulus was torn apart by the hands of the senators. "For this report, though highly doubtful, made its way around," says Livy.[162] What a strong proof this is of the accuser, especially when the slander of Valerius Maximus is added, which is derived from the same rumor![163] And what mortal would believe that Romulus could have been treated in this manner, even if it had happened that the sky was confounded with the earth in a storm, when he was always surrounded with three hundred of the most attentive guards? The adversary finds it funny that he was snatched off by a storm and carried off into heaven. But I too laugh about the heaven part. But why could he not have been snatched away by a storm? Plutarch attests this, adducing other examples of the same thing.[164]

Others claim that this was a magical deed.[165] But was it an act of magic by an unjust enemy? Or was it a deed of a demon, who wished to set up a new idol? Or was it an act of magic of Romulus himself? If so, he had had the same intention as that famous philosopher [Empedocles] who hoped to don the reputation of divinity in the furnaces of Etna[166]—or even the intention of Alexander, who aimed at the same thing in the rivers of Babylon. This has no bearing on the justice that we seek of men. If great Romulus did this to himself, wishing to give encouragement to his city, he was wise and patriotic. If an evil demon did it to him, who could stand against that greater power? If it was an evil enemy, the injustice belongs to the enemy—and since injustice is rather common in this sort of thing, in this case too it would be the more plausible.

Likewise Tullus Hostilius is consistently said to have perished through p. 136
magical rites that were bungled. The altars were not usually being lit up among our ancestors but they used to elicit divine fire from them (this was the fire of the famous Jupiter Elicius) through prayers.[167] When these prayers were improperly composed, they elicited death along with the fire. But the demons too are accustomed to act thus, just as they are imitators of the true God, who killed with fire sent forth from him the sons of Aaron when they were not handling their ritual objects properly. And he killed that man who unwisely moved his hand to the tottering Ark.[168] "No doubt among the gods even bad luck must be atoned for, nor does mischance offer an excuse when a god's power has been injured....Every fault against the great gods is a crime."[169] This is better than the following: "But if you seek it out well, you will find no wicked deed but the crime of Fortune; for what crime did a simple mistake commit?"[170] This was the case of Tullus. Away with the testimony of your Zonaras! Moreover, if Ancus died through a plot, did the

insidiæ a Tarquinio exstiterunt? De insidiis præstat nobis (fateor) aliquod argumentum Plutarchus: neque tamen aut expressum eius de Anco est testimonium, aut de Tarquinio ullam præbet coniecturam.

Et Tarquinius cur vituperetur, si regnum, nemini debitum, at patens omnibus, affectat a populo, hoc est a domino? Et curat, se, non impuberem Anci prolem, præfici regem bellicofæ, et iactatæ tum civitati? Cur iste, cur Servius regni audiant invasores? *Servius tanto eiusdem consensu populi electus,*
p. 137 *quanto haud quisquam alius ante rex declaratus est: et voluntate pa|trum a principio statim regnavit.* Huic proles regia Prisci non obiicietur: quæ regnare etiam fuisset dignior. [a] Nam et populi beneficium nec est dignitati cuiusquam obstrictum: [b] et nec filius, neposve Prisci Superbus fuit: sed aut filius, aut nepos fratris, qui Collatiæ in præsidio derelictus.

Superbus vere regni invasor: et quem ferre populus nequiit: et cuius unius superbia fuit caussa, ut ipsa quoque regia dignitas tolleretur. Quid hic arrodit Orosius? Quid ad te, quid hic, aut ille de re velit facere sua? Regnum populi erat. Regnum habere populus noluit. Clamat anus Sicula, se vereri progeniem patribus vitiosiorem. Et hoc quoque probat Picenus argumento, reges omnes improbos exstitisse, quod statum ipsum regium passus diutius non est populus. Et hoc quoque sic torquet extra civitatem, quia non sic sint habitus animi, ut vestes variabiles facile, et momento.

At boni ostensi sunt omnes. Quid argutamur? *At libertatis originem inde magis, quia annuum imperium consulare factum est, quam quod diminutum quicquam sit ex regia potestate, numeres: omnia iura, omnia insignia primi consules tenuere.*

Et hæc infantia populi Romani est, innocentissima. Desine, tu accusator, tragica scelera, parricidia infanda clamitare. Non hæc Pelopis regna. Non hic
p. 138 crimen per ducentos potes notare annos. Hæc infantia populi Ro|mani: [c] cum is, veluti in cunis Hercules angues novercæ aggressores robusta strangulavit, stravitque manu, sic vicinos illos invidissimos, inquietissimos, etiam Albanos, non patres amplius, at sævissimos vitricos, fregit, domuit, adegit sub imperium; docuit, esse quietos, et sibi obtemperare melioribus.

[a] *Cic. pro Mur.* [b] *Vall. iud. Liv.* [c] *Serv.* 8. *Æn.*

---

171 **Translator's note:** The words Gentili presents here as a quotation are an expansion of a conflation of two passages from Livy: 1. 46. 2 and 1. 41. 6.

172 Cicero, *Pro Murena.* **Translator's note:** Gentili is probably alluding to the part of the speech that deals with the consular election of 63 (*Mur.* 49–53), where the Roman people in the assembly voted for Murena in the face of threats by Catiline, who was of patrician family.

173 Laurentius Valla [Lorenzo Valla], *Disputatio ad Alphonsum Regem, duo Tarquinii, Lucius ac Aruns, Prisci Tarquinii filiine an nepotes fuerint, adversus Livium*, in *T. Livii Patavini historiarum ab urbe condita libri, qui supersunt, omnes, cum notis integris Laur. Vallae et al.*, vol. 15, Stutgardiae, 1827, pp. 287–95, esp. p. 293.

174 **Translator's note:** Gentili is referring to a passage in Valerius Maximus 6. 3. ext. 2. While other Syracusans were praying for the death of the tyrant Dionysius, an old woman prayed that he outlive her, on the grounds that his successor would probably prove worse.

175 [Livy 2. 1. 7.] 176 Servius, *On Aeneid* 8.

plot come into being through Tarquin? I grant that Plutarch offers us some indication about a plot, but neither is his testimony clearly about Ancus nor does he offer any reasonable inference about Tarquin.

And why criticize Tarquin if he strives to obtain from the people, which was master, a rule that was owed to no one else and open to all? And does he take steps that he—and not the not yet fully grown sons of Ancus—be appointed king over a state that was warlike and at that time in a disturbed condition? Why should he, why should Servius Tullius tolerate usurpers of the kingdom? "Servius was elected by so great a consensus of that same people as scarcely any man had been proclaimed king before, and he ruled right from the start with the good will of the senators."[171] The royal children p. 137
of Tarquinius Priscus, who would have been even more worthy to rule, shall not be a matter of reproach against him. For the favor of the people is not under any obligation to the dignity of anyone.[172] Nor was Tarquinius Superbus the son or grandson of Priscus, but either the son or grandson of his brother, who was left behind in the fortress of Collatia.[173]

Superbus was truly a usurper of the kingdom, and one whom the people were unable to bear. And the overbearing pride of this one single man was the reason that the royal dignity itself was done away with. What does Orosius nibble at here? And what does it matter to you what this or that man would wish to do about his own possession? The kingship belonged to the people. The people didn't wish to have a kingship. An old woman from Sicily shouts out that she fears an offspring more wicked than his ancestors.[174] And Picenus demonstrates this also with the argument that all kings have been wicked because the people no longer endured the very institution of king. And he also twists this wickedness to apply outside the state on the grounds that habits of mind are not to be changed as easily and instantly as clothes.

But all of the kings have been shown to have been good. Why should we chatter on? "You may count the beginning of liberty more from the fact that the consular power was made to last for a year than because there was anything taken away from the regal power. The first consuls held in their power all the laws, all the insignia of office."[175]

And so this infancy of the Roman people was most innocent. Accuser, p. 138
cease denouncing crimes of the tragic stage, unspeakable acts of parricide. This isn't the kingdom of Pelops. You cannot censure a single crime here for two hundred years. This is the infancy of the Roman people. Just as Hercules in the cradle strangled and killed with his strong hand the attacking snakes of his stepmother, so the Roman people shattered, subdued, and reduced to its rule those most ill-willed and troublesome neighbors—even the Albans, fathers no longer, but most savage stepfathers—and taught them to be peaceful and to obey their superiors.[176]

Bruti, Scævola, Africanus, alii.
CAP. IV

Hinc verius, et certius agitur de gestis populi Romani: quippe iam liberi. Sed liberatori Bruto statim obloquitur accusator. Obiectat inhonoram simulationem fatuitatis, proditionem in cognatum regem, perfidiam in collegam innocentem. Nominat autem mihi Socratem: qui oratione, sibi a Lysia composita, uti noluit. [a] Sed tamen nec licebat Athenis, alterum alteri patrocinari: adeoque nec fraudem istam facere legi, et alterius uti alterum oratione. [b] At ad dissimulationem dicam Ulyssem? qui mentitus est insaniam: dicam Metonem? dicam Solonem? [c] dicam, qui finxit stultitiam multo luculentius, Davidem? *Stultitiam simulare loco, sapientia summa est.* [d] Duplex est sapientia: ut scribunt, qui scribunt de sapientia: et qui sapientissimos hic illos appellant, Ulyssem, Solonem. Neque vero par Socratis caussa, et Bruti est: ut oratio
p. 139 quoque ostendit adversarii. Ille enim anteactam vitam bene multam in-| famasset, et sæpius traditam abolesset doctrinam de contemptu mortis huius: et vir auctoritatis summæ exemplum edidisset omnibus periculosissimum. [e] Non hac nostra (Eleazarus inquiebat Macchabæicus) ætate dignum, et canicie, simulare: exemplum relinquere aliis ignobile: et meæ maculam senectuti comparare abominandam. Is aiebat, quod et tu argumentaris, Picene, propter paululam istam, et momentaneam vitam non oportere leges Dei deserere: qui iudex nobis æternus est.

Ceterum neque Bruti factum, quale Eleazari, erat: neque nobis defendendi Romani sunt ad Dei legem: qua et Romani condemnantur, et Græci, et barbari. Laxius hoc iudicium datur. Et Brutus igitur in ipso ætatis ingressu magis habuit de futuro, quam de præterito cogitare. [f] Venit autem mihi in memoriam Cato Uticensis: qui per mortem quidem sibi fugam a servitio fecit:

[a] *Quinct.* 2. *c.* 16. [b] *Plut. Alc. et co. So. et Popl. Iust.* 2. [c] 1. *Sam.* 21.
[d] *Card.* 3. *de sap. Cic.* 1. *de off.* [e] 2. *Mac.* 6. [f] *Dio.* 43.

---

177 Quintilian 2. 15. 30. **Translator's note:** Far from saying that this practice was forbidden to the Athenians, Quintilian indicates that it was a common practice that made Socrates' refusal to use Lysias' speech all the more admirable.

178 **Translator's note:** The lost *Cypria* of the Epic Cycle had Odysseus feign madness to avoid joining the expedition against Troy. The astronomer Meton is said to have similarly feigned madness in order to evade serving in the Athenian expedition against Sicily: Aelian, *Historical Miscellany* 13. 12; Plutarch *Nicias* 13. 7–8, *Alcibiades* 17. 5–6. Solon, on the other hand, is said to have feigned madness in order to advocate for a war against Salamis: Plutarch, *Solon* 8.

179 1 Samuel 21.

180 [*Dicta Catonis* 2. 18.]

181 Cicero, *De officiis* 1. 107–9; Cardanus, *De sapientia* 3.

182 2 Maccabees 6: 24–8.

CHAPTER 4
The Brutuses, Scaevola, Scipio Africanus, etc.

From here on we are more truly and firmly concerned with the deeds of the Roman people, who were now of course free. But right from the start the accuser speaks ill of Brutus the Liberator. He accuses him of disgraceful simulation of simplemindedness, treason against a king who was in addition to that his relative, and perfidy against an innocent colleague. Moreover he mentions Socrates, who chose not to make use of a speech Lysias had written for him. But Athenians were not permitted to advocate for one another; nor could they get round the law by letting one person make use of a speech composed by another.[177] As for the dissimulation, shall I mention Ulysses, who faked insanity? Shall I mention Meton? Shall I mention Solon?[178] Shall I mention one who faked stupidity much more splendidly: David?[179] "To play the fool at the right time is the highest wisdom."[180] Wisdom is of a double nature, as those say who write about wisdom and who in this regard call those men—Ulysses, Solon—very wise.[181] Nor are the cases of Socrates and Brutus in fact similar, as even the speech of the adversary reveals. For Socrates would have dishonored his long life well lived and would have p. 139
destroyed the teaching he had often given about the contempt for this death, and a man of the greatest authority would thus have furnished a most dangerous model for us all. "It does not suit our years," Eleazar Maccabee used to say, "and our white hairs to dissimulate and to leave to others a base example and to acquire for my old age a loathsome defilement."[182] He used to say that which you also argue, Picenus: for the sake of a paltry and brief life one ought not desert the laws of God, who is our eternal judge.

But what Brutus did wasn't like what Eleazar did either, nor should we defend the Romans by recourse to the law of God, according to which the Romans, the Greeks, and the barbarians stand condemned. Let this judgment be rendered a bit more liberally. Brutus, then, at the very beginning of his life had to think more about the future than the past. Moreover, Cato of Utica comes to my mind, he who through death made for himself an escape

filio tamen, et aliis servitutem subire suasit, et in meliora se servare tempora reipublicæ. Neque enim alii, ut ipse, infracta semper usi libertate essent: sed cesserint temporibus sæpe, et tempestatibus: aut in experimentum nullum antea venerint. Quæ et M. Tullius pro se, pro aliis, qui verbis efferebant Catonis facinus in cælum, nulli imitabantur. Ad sectam Stoicam, et perso-
p. 140 nam Catonis, adque personam Socratis hæc pertinent facta. [a] Et ne nescias | tamen, Picene, ipse etiam Cato deseruit aliquando proposita sua, sive vincente iuniorem illum infirmitate humana, sive quia nihil a pertinacia sua commodi videret publici, solum suum incommodum. Etiam natus, eductus Cato in civitate libera: at Brutus in serva, sub tyranno. Ut impar sit semper a Catone, et similibus ad Brutum ratio. Brutus et in patriæ commodum simulavit: et per commodam mox occasionem iuvandæ patriæ eam mox fatuitatis simulationem fortiter posuit. Semper cogitavit de commodo patriæ: quod res omnes gestæ sequentes ostenderunt luculenter.

Qui mihi osculum terræ latum criminaris? Non illud necessarium, ne prævenissent Tarquinii? Non necessarium, ut novum regnum, consulare suavius, ipse induceret? Etiamne perfidiam fidelissimo patriæ vindici obiectare? Id vero neque iusti est, neque vehementis accusatoris, sed absurdi, et impotentissimi calumniatoris. Nam de tyranno quid dicam? Nullum est ius, quod quemquam arceat a pernicie ipsius: [b] ut pleni sunt omnes omnium auctorum ea de re libri. Et de avunculo quid respondeam? Exsuisse necessitudinem istam, et abiecisse avunculi nomen avunculum prius: qui Bruti fratrem occiderat.

Neque Brutus alter, huius progenies, certe imitator, aut vituperatur hic, aut
p. 141 vituperari potest. Siquidem nec est verum, Cæ|sari eum exstitisse ingratum, cui debebat nihil: ut hoc Seneca censet: de quo auctore retulit tam multa verba accusator. In ius dandi beneficii iniuria venerat Cæsar: ait Seneca. [c] Et hoc beneficium est latronum, commemorare posse, iis se dedisse vitam, quibus non ademerunt. Imprudentiæ damnat Seneca Brutum, et alius non nemo hodie. Belle sane post exitum. Sed si recenti adhuc tyrannide, et nullis ei comparatis subsidiis, ac munimentis tempus eiusdem oppugnandæ, atque tollendæ non erat: an firmato post successore Octavio idem fuisset? cum aut

[a] *Dio*. 38. [b] *Savon*. 10. *epit. eth*. 23. [c] *Cic. phi*. 2.

183 Dio Cassius 43. 10. 5.

184 Hieronymus Savonarola [Girolamo Savonarola], *Compendium totius philosophiae, tam naturalis, quam moralis*, Venetiis, Apud Iuntas, 1542, 10. 23, pp. 588–90 [cf. also Savonarola's *Treatise on the Rule and Government of the City of Florence*, in Anne Borelli et al. (eds.), *Selected Writings of Girolamo Savonarola: Religion and Politics, 1490–1498* (New Haven and London: Yale University Press, 2006), 186 f.].

185 [Seneca, *De beneficiis* 2. 20.]

186 Cicero, *Orationes Philippicae* 2. 5.

from servitude, but nevertheless urged his son and others to undergo servitude and to preserve themselves for better times for the state.[183] For unlike himself, the others had never experienced undefiled liberty but often yielded to times and circumstances or had never before come to the test. Cicero did not imitate Cato's model for himself, nor did the others who lauded Cato's deed to the skies in words. These deeds have a bearing on the Stoic sect and on the character of Cato—and that of Socrates. And just so you know, p. 140
Picenus: even Cato himself abandoned his resolutions on occasion, either because human frailty overcame him in his younger days, or because he saw that no public good but only his own inconvenience would come from his obstinacy. Also, Cato was born and brought up in a free city, but Brutus in a servile one, under a tyrant. So it would be an improper method to always judge Brutus by the standard of Cato and similar people. Brutus both engaged in a pretence for the good of his country and soon through a suitable opportunity of helping his country he boldly set aside his pretence of feeblemindedness. He always thought about the good of his country, something which all the actions he subsequently performed made abundantly clear.

Why do you complain of Brutus' kissing of the earth to me? Was that not necessary lest the sons of Tarquin preempt him? Was it not necessary so that he might bring in a new regime, the more agreeable one of the consuls? And do you even go so far as to charge the most faithful avenger of his country with faithlessness? That is the move not of a fair or even of an over-eager accuser, but of a ridiculous and most out of control calumniator. For what should I say about the tyrant? For there is no law that would hinder anyone from doing him harm, as all the books are full of all the authorities on this matter.[184] And what should I answer about the fact that Tarquin was his uncle? His uncle had laid aside that family relationship and had cast off the name of uncle first, for he had killed Brutus's brother.

Nor is the other Brutus, this man's descendant and, indeed, his imitator, rightly censured here, nor *can* he be censured. For indeed it is not true that he p. 141
was ungrateful to Caesar, for he owed him nothing, as Seneca judges this matter—an author whom the accuser so frequently quotes. Caesar intruded upon the right of doing favors by doing wrong, says Seneca.[185] And this is the favor of brigands: to be able to claim that one has given life to those from whom one has not taken it away.[186] Seneca accuses Brutus of imprudence, and some still do so today. That is fine to say after his death. But if that was not the time for attacking and doing away with the tyranny, when it was still a recent thing and no supports and defenses had yet been gotten together for it, would it have been the time to do so later on, when his successor Octavian

superfuisset nemo, qui aut vidisset libertatem, aut servitio non insuevisset? Viden', Caligula occiso nec potuisse libertatem restitui? Sed et post crudum hoc servitium Cæsaris, Octavii longas fraudes, Tyberii libidines, Caligulæ furores eduxerint pavitantem, et stolidum hominem Claudium ad fastigia dominationis. Verum si iudicium istud iudicandum fuisset, cum puer esset Octavius, et pugnabant inter se Iuliani: aut cum obsessa Italia a Sexto, Oriens totus ad usque littora maris superi tenebatur a Bruto potenter: aliam dixissemus sententiam semper in eum diem, qui postremus Bruto, et [a] improspere (non imprudenter) repetitæ libertati fuit. [b] Sed iniquissima hæc est ratio iudicare ab exitu.

p. 142 Sed iniustitiæ (quæ propria modo agitur caussa) damnatur | Brutus: qui optimam, et necessariam reipublicæ formam subvertit: et sustulit principem, in quem iuravit. De optima tamen forma unde probatur? [c] Est quidem monarchica ceteris dignior: sed non propterea melior est, et semper aptior. Aut etiam, quod de regio statu disputatur, id de tyrannico, qui erat Cæsaris, et qui est omnium deterrimus, fiet? Aut quæ audiuntur aliquando de simplici regio supra simplicem optimatum, eadem supra utrumque mixtum et populi, qui Romanus, et qui est omnium optimus, vera erunt?

Etiam unde illa necessitas monarchiæ probatur? ut credere ita possimus, optimam hanc exstitisse pro illorum temporum occasione: et non tam interisse civitatem, quam renatam in melius. Immo enim imperium illud amplissimum, diffusum per varias, et feroces gentes plurimas, rectoribus indigebat plurimis, et diversissimis. Quid Q. Catulus, M. Cicero, alii eiuscemodi viri optimi, et præstantissimi artium pacis in bellicosis provinciis valeant? Quid Marius, quid ipse Cæsar, alii alieni studiis pacis in procurationibus pacatis, et otiosis? Sed et arduum semper, et subiectum fortunæ, nec unius mentis moles, regendi cuncta onus: et plures facilius munia reipublicæ sociatis laboribus exsequuntur. Ut ita pro magnitudine eius imperii, forte infideliter,
p. 143 at digne Tyberius disserebat. Ostendunt sequen | tia tempora veritatem

[a] *Tac. ann.* 1. [b] *Plin.* 5. *Ep. ult. Plut. Cra.* [c] *Picc.* 10. *ci. ph.* 11.

187 Tacitus, *Annales* 1. 4.

188 Pliny the Younger, *Epistulae* 5; 9. 7; Plutarch, *Crassus* (end).

189 Piccolomineus [Francesco Piccolomini], *Universa philosophia de moribus*, Francofurti, Ex Officina Nicolai Hoffmanni, 1611, pp. 903–6 (Level 10, ch. 11).

190 [Cf. Polybius 6; Cicero, *De legibus* 3. 12, where Cicero refers to the mixed constitution praised by Scipio in Cicero, *De republica* 1. 69 and 2. 65 (a work Gentili cannot have known).]

191 [Tacitus, *Annales* 1. 12.]

was established in rule and when there was nobody still alive who had either seen liberty or had not grown accustomed to servitude? Don't you see that when Caligula was killed it was not possible to restore liberty? But after the unripe servitude of Caesar, the long deceptions of Octavian, the debaucheries of Tiberius, and the mad rages of Caligula, they would raise even the trembling and stupid Claudius to the heights of rule. But if that issue had been decided when Octavian was still a boy and the Julian party was fighting among itself, or when Italy was attacked by Sextus Pompey and the whole of the East was held with strength by Brutus all the way up to the Adriatic Sea, then we would invariably utter a different opinion about that day which proved the last for Brutus and also for a liberty that was sought back not imprudently, just unluckily.[187] But this is a most unjust method, to make a judgment based on the outcome.[188]

But Brutus is also found guilty of injustice—a charge which almost argues its own defense. He is accused of overthrowing the best and most indispens- p. 142
able form of government and of doing away with a prince to whom he had sworn an oath. But how has this been shown to be the best form of government? The monarchical form is indeed more dignified than the others, but it is not for that reason better or always more suitable.[189] Or will that which is maintained with regard to the position of a king prove true of the position of a tyrant, which is what Caesar's position was—and which is in fact the worst of all? Or will those things which one sometimes hears about the superiority of unmixed monarchy over unmixed aristocracy hold true also of unmixed monarchy over a mixture of both monarchy and aristocracy with democracy—which is the Roman system, and which is the best of all?[190]

Next, on what basis is that supposed necessity of monarchy demonstrated in such a way that we might believe that it was the best thing for the circumstances of those times and that the republic did not so much perish as become reborn into something better? After all, that vast empire, extended through very many diverse and savage peoples, required very many and very different people to guide it. What would have been the use of Quintus Catulus, Marcus Cicero, and other most excellent men of this sort and most distinguished in the arts of peace, in the warlike provinces? What would have been the use of Marius, Caesar himself, and others foreign to the pursuits of peace, in provinces that were pacified and lazy? The burden of ruling everything is always difficult and subject to luck and not a burden for one mind; and several people more easily pursue with their joint labors the tasks of a state. This is what Tiberius said in the Senate worthily, though probably disingenuously, in view of the vastness of his empire.[191] The ages that followed demonstrate the truth of his speech, when emperors were very p. 143

orationis: cum cogerentur sæpissime imperatores adsciscere sibi collegas imperii: qui rem regerent suam, non servi procurarent unius domini utilitatem. Et sic illud imperium partitum sæpe in plures fuit. Tantum vera potest necessitas supraque naturam regni: quod (et vulgo dicitur) non capit duos.

Sic est, sic in imperio Europæ, Africæ, Asiæ. Ut si princeps pede premat Asiam, iam Europa assurgat, et Africa, quod vides, sedentibus Constantinopoli imperatoribus. Ut, cum ruptis obicibus, et aggeribus hinc, atque inde, inundet aliqua fluvius, necesse est: dum illi ubique obstruere nequit agricola: ita imperio illi factum cernis per inundationes varias barbarorum, frustra excurrentibus principibus in diversa terrarum, impotentibus ad omnes partes simul stare, et obsistere contra.

Non mihi unas Asiaticas gentes amplissimas, et regnatas unius imperio diutissime quisquam commemoret. [a] Molliores enim illæ, et ut facie, ita moribus ubique sibi similiores. At sola Europa, imperii Romani pars, quantam habet dissimilitudinem? quantam ubique difficultatem? Non mihi asserat Dion, popularem statum, evectum ad imperium magnum, recte esse non posse. Neque enim magnitudo perdit, sed pravi mores perdunt formam p. 144 reipublicæ. Nihil dicis de ratione, quam nominas, | Dion, pro assertione tua. Nihil de experientia dicis. Respublica Carthaginensis, et Romana stetere diu. Stetere diutius, quam minores aliæ. Aspice ad Græculas tuas. Me tamen decet esse brevem. Adi ad Aristotelem, qui unus docet omnes: [b] et qui respondet tibi, immo in maioribus civitatibus non facile aliam, quam popularem posse esse regnandi formam.

Tu autem accusator quid agis? Ais mox tyrannum Cæsarem. Ius autem iurandum tyranno præstitum obligat? Ubi iustitia? Hæc est tribuere cuique suum. [c] Sed latroni scelestissimo non debetur, quod illi nunc promittitur iuramento. Ubi iudicium? Abest mens tyrannum expavescentibus: et itaque iure legitimo omnia rescinduntur, iurataque, quæ sub tyrannide gesta sint. Ubi veritas, reliqua iurisiurandi comes? sine quibus nec est iusiurandum, sed periurium, adeoque nec observandum. Tyrannum dicere principem, sanctum, patrem patriæ id genus aliis nominibus, quæ metus congessit in Cæsarem, id vero ab omni vero alienissimum est. Non pudet, fœdi Cæsariani mancipii, ac fugitivi, Valerii Maximi verba pro Cæsaris principatu recitasse? Valeat homo iste; audenter dico, valeat: valeat sive cum [d] parvitate, quam ipsemet suam accusat, sive cum pravitate, quam hic cernimus suam ad unum omnes.

[a] *Hipp. de aer. aq.* [b] *Arist. 3. polit. Picc. ci. ph.* 13. [c] *l.* 31. *depo.* [d] *Val. Max. prin.*

192 [Seneca, *Thyestes* 444.] 193 Hippocrates, *De aere, aquis, locis.*
194 [Dio Cassius 52. 15–16.]
195 Aristotle, *Politica* 3. 10, 1286b8–14 [cf. *Politica* 4. 5, 1293a1–12]; Piccolomineus, *Universa philosophia de moribus*, p. 912 (Level 10, ch. 13).
196 [See *Digest* 1. 1. 10 = *Institutes* 1.1.pr.]
197 *Digest* 16. 3. 31 [on deposits made by thieves and on the duties of the depositee towards them].
198 Valerius Maximus, preface.

often forced to adopt colleagues in rule for themselves, men who were to rule their own territory, not just as servants look after the interest of one lord. And thus the empire was often divided among several men. So much power does actual necessity have, even beyond the nature of rule, which (as it is commonly said) does not hold two chiefs.[192]

Thus it is in the empire embracing Europe, Africa, and Asia, so that if the prince sets foot in Asia, then Europe and Africa rise up in rebellion, as you see happened when the emperors were established in Constantinople. Just as when banks and bulwarks are broken it must be that a river floods in from this direction and that, while the farmer is helpless to withstand it anywhere, so you see it happen in an empire through the repeated inundations of barbarians, when the emperors vainly run off into different directions, powerless to take a stand and put up resistance in all areas at once.

Now, don't let anyone mention to me a few Asian peoples who were of vast extent and ruled for a very long time by the rule of one person. For those people were softer and everywhere similar to one another not only in appearance but also in customs.[193] But take just Europe alone, one part of the Roman Empire, how much diversity does it have! And how much trouble it offers everywhere! Don't let Dio Cassius assure me that a democratic state which is exalted to imperial rule cannot be in good condition. It is not size but bad morals that destroy the structure of a state. You say nothing about the reason you propose, Dio, on behalf of your assertion.[194] You say nothing p. 144
about practical knowledge. The Carthaginian and Roman states lasted for a long time. They stood longer than other smaller states. Look at those little Greeks of yours. But I need to be brief here. Go to Aristotle, one man who teaches everyone. He replies to you that it is precisely in the larger states that the form of government cannot easily be other than democratic.[195]

But you, accuser, what are you up to? You soon call Caesar a tyrant. But is an oath offered to a tyrant binding? Where is the justice here? Justice is to assign to each his own.[196] But that which is now promised on oath to a very wicked brigand is not owed to him later on.[197] Where is the power of judgment here? Those who fear a tyrant lack rationality, and thus everything done and sworn under a tyranny is annulled by a legitimate law. And where is truth, the other companion of oath-taking? (For without these companions—justice, good judgment, truth—there is not oath-taking but the making of false oaths, and that is not to be adhered to.) To call a tyrant a prince, holy, father of this country, and other titles of that sort, which fear heaped upon Caesar—that is indeed utterly remote from the truth. Aren't you ashamed to repeat the words spoken in favor of Caesar's principate of that base Caesarian slave and fugitive Valerius Maximus? Let that man be off, I boldly declare, let him be off either with his insignificance [*parvitas*], which he himself accuses himself of, or rather with his depravity [*pravitas*], which we all unanimously discern in him here.[198]

p. 145 Valeat hoc loco, vir alioqui vere maximus, Dion: [a] | qui, item verius tyrannos, sic scripsit adversus Brutum: pro quo Bruto scripserit Plutarchus, multo maximus: [b] An non etiam ille Stoicus, vim veritus tyrannidis, sic carpit generosos istos libertatis ultores, Seneca? Valeat Etruscus poeta, sane valeat: qui, in ius pervadens pontificis, nec Brutum solum aliosve tales, sed et (nefas Gibellini hominis) ipsos pontifices pro arbitrio trudit ad tartara. Fremant omnes licet, [c]*deorum est immortalium beneficio, et munere datum huic reipublicæ Brutorum genus, et nomen ad libertatem populi Romani vel constituendam, vel recuperandam.* Fremant omnes licet, testimonium hoc verissimum est. Sed non fremunt omnes. [d] Etiam viri summi hac stant nobiscum: et duos hos probant Brutos: unum, quod tyrannum, alterum, quod hostem perdiderit. Etiam hi viri summi theologi sunt. Quamquam extra theologiam hæc est quæstio. Ut non ferendus sit adversarius noster, qui obiectat theologos.

Cur vero et perfidiam priori Bruto obiectat? Neque enim a Tarquinio, sed a populo, qui regumque tempore detulit magistratus, tenebat Brutus suum. Et itaque, quod a populo accepit, id pro eo populo exercuit fidei plenus, non perfidus. Quid si aut tenuisset a rege? [e] Traianus ipse præfecto, quem urbi
p. 146 constituebat, dum tradit insigne potestatis pugionem, sic addit, ut eo fer|ro pro se præfectus uteretur, si etiam se videret imperantem iuste: si autem, idem contra se stringeret. Scilicet salus populi lex suprema: cuius populi possessio et regnum est, et magistratus omnis: non est populus possessio regis, aut magistratus. Aut quid hic conquirimus magistratus? [f] Etiam a privato tolli tyrannus potest, (audi proiectam eius caussam) etiam veneficio, proditione.

Etiamne collegæ perfidus? Aut Augustinus quomodo innocentem censuit Collatinum, et virum probum? [g] qui, patriæ, ac libertatis proditores iusto affici supplicio non ferebat: et qui, bona tyrannis reddenda esse, censuerat. [h] Hæc iuris non sunt. Sed fuerit de reddendis bonis, ut Dionysius credit,

[a] *Xiph. Cæs.* [b] *Mont. 2. ess.* 10.
[c] *Cic. phi.* 4. [d] *Sot. 2. de iu. q.* 1. *a.* 3. et *lib.* 5. *q.* 1. *a.* 3.
[e] *Sex. Vict.* [f] *Cov. 2. de sp. c.* 3. §. 4.
[g] *Dionys.* 5. *Plut. Popl.* [h] *l.* 5. *C. ad leg. Iu. ma.*

---

[199] Johannes Xiphilinus, *Epitome Dionis Cassii*, on Caesar. **Translator's note:** Gentili probably also has Dio Cassius 48. 1. 1 in mind.

[200] Montaigne, *Essays* 2. 10. **Translator's note:** Montaigne says there, "Il paroit en Seneque qu'il preste un peu à la tyrannie des Empereurs de son temps, car je tiens pour certain que c'est d'un jugement forcé qu'il condamne la cause de ces genereux meurtriers de Caesar; Plutarque est libre par tout." (Michel Eyquem de Montaigne, *Les Essais*, Paris, Pléiade, 2007, p. 455.)

[201] Cicero, *Orationes Philippicae* 4. 7.

[202] Domingo de Soto, *De iustitia et iure* 2, q. 1. a. 3; 5, q. 1. a. 3.

[203] Aurelius Victor, *Caesares* 13.

[204] [Cicero, *De legibus* 3. 8, describing the law that should hold for the highest magistrates.]

[205] Diego Covarruvias, *De sponsalibus et matrimoniis* 3. 4 [in *Opera omnia*, Venetiis, Apud Gasparem Bindonum sumptibus sociorum, 1588].

[206] Dionysius of Halicarnassus 5; Plutarch, *Publicola* 3. 1.

[207] *Code* 9. 8. 5.

And in this matter let us also bid farewell to a man who is in other respects a major author, Dio Cassius, who writes against Brutus what he with more p. 145 truth writes against tyrants, while Plutarch, by far the greatest authority, writes on Brutus' behalf.[199] Does not even that famous Stoic Seneca, through fear of the violence of tyranny, disparage those noble avengers of liberty?[200] Let the Tuscan poet [Dante] be off—indeed, farewell to him, a man who usurps the right of the pope and arbitrarily drives down to Hell not only Brutus and others of that sort but even (the crime of a Ghibelline) the popes themselves. Though everyone may grumble, "it was through the favor and gift of the immortal gods that the family and name of the Bruti were given for establishing or for restoring the liberty of the Roman people."[201] Though everyone may grumble, this testimony of Cicero's is very true. But not everyone in fact does grumble. Even very distinguished men stand here with us and praise these two Bruti, one because he destroyed a tyrant, the other because he destroyed an enemy.[202] These men are even first-rate theologians—even though this question lies outside theology. So our adversary, who casts theologians in our teeth, would be intolerable here.

Why, indeed, does he charge the earlier Brutus with perfidy? Brutus did not hold his magistracy from Tarquin but from the people, who even in the time of the kings assigned magistracies. And so that which he received from the people he exercised on the people's behalf full of loyalty, not perfidiously. What if he *had* held it from the king? Trajan himself, when he handed over the dagger which was a symbol of power to the prefect whom he was installing for the city, added that the prefect should use this weapon to p. 146 protect him if he saw him ruling justly; if not, he should unsheathe it against him.[203] The highest law is the safety of the people[204]—and the supreme power and every magistracy is the possession of this people; the people are not the possession of the king or magistrate. But why do we search out magistrates here? Even by a private citizen a tyrant can be killed (hear the accuser's case utterly rejected) even by poisoning or betrayal.[205]

Was he even faithless to his colleague? Just how did Augustine decide that Collatinus was innocent and an upright man? He did not endure that just punishment be inflicted upon betrayers of their country and of liberty, and he judged that the tyrants be given back their goods.[206] These actions were not lawful.[207] But even if one granted that his advice about the return of goods was worthy, as Dionysius believes, was his order about not punishing evil-

honestum consilium: etiam de maleficis non puniendis fuit imperium eius honestum? Quod si in factum istud intuitus esset et M. Tullius, et Livius, et Augustinus, non in solam occasionem illam nominis: non scripsisset primus, non fuisse admodum cum honestate coniunctum exsilium Collatini: non secundus, excessisse isthic modum illos libertatis amatores: non tertius, etiam virum bonum Collatinum fuisse.

Tu mihi, Picene, iudica. Non solum nomen intulit civitati terrorem. [a]*Tantum ob nomen, et genus regium*: inquit Florus. Factum illud plusquam regium eximere perduelles meritis pœnis. Quod non ausus Tullus
p. 147 rex in be|nemerenti (scitis) Horatio, et in delicto longe minimo. Illud factum perculit civitatem.

Quod refertque Livius, *nescire Tarquinios privatos vivere*. Hoc est nomen, quod civitati non placuit. Non ipse displicuit sonus nominis, et litterarum, sed familia illa. Hoc est nomen invisum. Odiosus populo Collatinus propter cognationem: ut inquit Plutarchus. Manserunt in civitate alii eiusdem nominis, sed non (puto) eiusdem familiæ. [b] Meminit non multo post Livius L. Tarquinii magistri equitum: alii post nominant Tarquinios alios. Quid vero dicam levissimas occasiones, per quas evecti ad regnum sunt plurimi? [c]*Regillani nomen a regno: sit igitur rex Regillanus*: sic per iocos, et lusus nominis Regillanus quidem imperator effectus: Non hæc timuisset populus qui videbat perspicue, teneri regni cupiditate quamplurimos, regum captos amore etiam cognatos Collatini Vitellios, etiam filios Bruti. Hæc res est. Illa infelicitatis Brutorum nihil ad rem: quæ in abdito sunt consiliorum Dei.

Sed liber iam populus: et oppressis internis hostibus: ecce subit Porsennæ bellum pro eadem retinenda libertate iustissimum. In quo sunt tamen defendendæ mihi insidiæ Scevolæ. Defendo. [d]*Suprema pericula semper dant veniam culpæ*. Supremum periculum urbis scimus. Licitæ illæ insidiæ in tyrannum:
p. 148 ergo et in socium | tyranni. [e] Nec enim his solis, qui occiderunt parentes, sed et consciis, et adiutoribus quoquo modo, pœna est parricidii constituta. Licitæ illæ insidiæ etiam in hostem iustum quid ni, si licet, hostem interficere, et per insidias? Aspice omnes historias, ubique structas insidias, captos insidiis videris. Defendendum est etiam mendacium Scevolæ. Defendo.

Nego, Scevolam mentitum de aliis coniuratis: [f] et auctorem do Milesium Aristidem.

[a] *Flor.* 1. [b] *Liv.* 3. Tarquitii *tamen ait Urs. Sall. Cat.* [c] *Treb. Poll. tyr.*
[d] *Claud.* 2. *Eutrop.* [e] *l.* 6. 7. *de parricid.* [f] *Plut. coll. Ro. et Gr.*

---

208 Florus 1. 9. 3. 209 [Livy 2. 2. 3]

210 Livy 3. 27, but Fulvius Ursinus on Sallust's *Bellum Catilinae* says "Tarquitius." [So do modern editions of Livy.] **Translator's note:** Master of the Horse was the title of the dictator's second in command; in this case Cincinnatus was dictator.

211 Trebellius Pollio [one of the *Scriptores Historiae Augustae*], *Tyranni triginta*.

212 Claudian, *In Eutropium* 2.

213 *Digest* 48. 9. 6–7.

doers respectable? But if Cicero, Livy, and Augustine had looked more closely at that act and not at solely that familiar pretext of his name [of Tarquin], Cicero would not have written that the exile of Collatinus was not precisely in conformity with propriety, nor would Livy have said that those lovers of liberty went beyond the bounds in this matter, nor will Augustine have said that Collatinus was a good man.

You be the judge for me, Picenus. It wasn't the name alone that inspired terror in the state. Florus says "simply on account of his name and his royal family."[208] To exempt public enemies from their merited punishment is a deed that exceeds even royal prerogative. It was something that King Tullus did not dare against the richly deserving (as you know) Horatius, and in so p. 147
doing was guilty of a fault much less serious. Collatinus' deed struck at the state.

And there is what Livy wrote: "the Tarquins didn't know how to live as private citizens."[209] This is that name that displeased the state. It was not the sound of the name or of its letters that displeased; it was that family itself. *This* was the hated name. Collatinus was hateful to the people because of that family relationship, as Plutarch says. There remained others of that name in the state, but not (I think) of the same family. Not long afterwards Livy mentions Lucius Tarquinius, a Master of the Horse;[210] others mention other Tarquins later on. Why should I mention the trivial occasions through which very many were raised to rule? "The name of Regillanus was from 'kingship'; therefore Regillanus became king." Thus, through jests and playings upon his name a certain Regillanus was made king.[211] Wouldn't the people have feared this when they saw clearly that very many people were possessed of a lust for rule, and that even the Vitellii, relatives of Collatinus, were seized by a love of kings—and even the sons of Brutus were? This is how the matter stands. All that about the misfortune of the family of Brutus is irrelevant. These things are hidden among the plans of God.

But the people were now free and when internal enemies were troubling them, behold, the war against Porsenna arises, a most just war fought to retain that very same freedom. And it is in the context of this war that the plot of Scaevola needs to be defended by me. And I do defend it. "The most extreme dangers always give an excuse for crime."[212] We know the extreme danger of the city at that time. That plot was permissible against a tyrant; hence they were permissible against a tyrant's associate as well. For the p. 148
punishment of parricide is established not only against those who kill their parents but also against those who are confidants or helpers in any way at all.[213] Even against a just enemy a plot is permissible—and why not, if it is permitted to kill an enemy, even through an ambush? Look at all the histories, where you will have seen plots laid everywhere and people captured by plots. Must even the lie of Scaevola be defended? I do defend it.

I deny that Scaevola lied about other conspirators, and as an authority

Nego, non licitum fallere mendacio hostem: non dolus adversus hostem est bonus: et mendacium dolus est. Nec potuit Scevola rationem ullam habere meriti in se a Porsenna collati: cum publica staret hostilitas, et pene oppressa patria teneretur. Privata gratia privato debebatur beneficio: quæ nihil de publica tolleret caritate; nihil Scevolæ, militi patriæ, imminueret de eo debito, quo patriæ tum maxime obstrictus salutem procurare eiusdem cunctis viribus et manus, et ingenii habuit. Audin', quam breviter, quam est responsum veriter?

Et sic reliqua sexcenta sunt, quæ bonus tacet accusator, paria istis alia crimina Romanorum. Sexcenta? An sexaginta? An sex saltem? Ne sex quidem notare alia potuit, quæ carperet. Nam, quæ potuit, protulit, etiam hæc inanissima. Audite. Fuerit calliditas, fuerit versutia Martii, qua Perseus
p. 149 rex capitur: necdum fuit aliud tamen, | quam in hostem dolus: et in eum quidem hostem, qui perfidus, qui fœdera, cum patre inita, secum renovata, abruperat: [a]*quem per omnia clandestina grassari scelera latrociniorum, ac veneficiorum cernebant.* Quid ais accusator, habitum Martium suis impostorem turpem? Tu vero splendide mendax. Inducias ille annuit petenti Perseo in magnam gratiam: et pacis spem addidit. Num hoc turpe, et iniustum, citra conventionem ullam hosti verba dedisse, et illusisse? Hoc et Africani est crimen.

[b] Scilicet neque perfidus Siphax, ac dirus, qui cum primis Scipionibus in Hispania amicitiam pactus, cum senatu Romæ repactus, et pactus tertium cum isto Africano in Africa, ne flocci fecit. Quid mox, Picene, declamitas, et maria, et terras, et totam cies naturam rerum? Ecce tibi responsum hic est. Neque primus abrupit fœdera Africanus, qui hostem Siphaci periculosissimum vehebat secum in Africam: nam ipse ante illud tempus Siphax adfinitatem, et amicitiam cum Pœnis contraxerat. Etiam miles Masinissa magis, quam fœderatus fuit Scipionis, et Romanorum: quod tanto est minus reprehensioni obnoxium. At si civitatem meam tueri tantum cupiam, non hic clara Siphacis paret iniustitia, et accusatoris nostri: qui velint, per unum hominem
p. 150 rumpi fœdera populorum? Cur non petit rex a Romanis, si Scipio Masi-| nissam publico consilio duceret?

[a] *Liv.* 42. [b] *Liv.* 27. 28.

---

[214] Pseudo-Plutarch, *Parallela Graeca et Romana* 305 F–306 A [where the bogus Aristides of Miletus is cited as claiming that Scaevola had 400 fellow conspirators waiting nearby].

[215] Livy 42. 18. 1.

[216] Livy 27. 28.

I offer Aristides of Miletus.[214] I deny that it is not permissible to deceive an enemy with a lie; I claim that a deceit against an enemy is good, and a lie is a deceit. Nor could Scaevola have taken account of a benefit conferred on him by Porsenna, when a state of public hostility existed and his country was held virtually under siege. His private gratitude was owed to a private act of kindness, which could have taken nothing away from his love of his country and which would in no way diminish for Scaevola, a soldier of his country, that duty which at that moment most of all put him under an obligation to his country and meant that he had to attend to the safety of that country with all his powers of bodily strength and mind. Do you hear how succinctly, how truly the answer was given?

And so it is with the other "six hundred" crimes of the Romans similar to these, which our good accuser is silent about. Six hundred? Or is it sixty? Or just six? Not even six others could he make note of to criticize. For he laid out all he could—even these most empty charges. Listen. He says there was the cleverness, the cunning of Marcius, by which king Perseus was captured. And yet this was not yet anything more than trickery against an enemy—and p. 149
indeed against an enemy who was perfidious, who had broken a treaty which had been entered upon with his father and renewed with himself, a man "whom they perceived was attacking them through all the clandestine crimes of brigands and poisoners."[215] Why do you say, accuser, that Marcius was considered a base deceiver even among his own people? *You* are certainly splendidly mendacious. That man granted a truce to Perseus when he requested it as a great favor—and he added the hope of a formal peace. Was it base and unjust and against any convention to deceive and delude an enemy? This was also the crime of Scipio Africanus.

I suppose Syphax was neither perfidious nor dangerous—he who, after having made a pact of friendship with the first Scipios in Spain, then reaffirmed it with the Senate, and then made an agreement with Scipio in Africa, cared not a fig for all this.[216] Why do you proceed to launch into a declamation, Picenus, and stir up seas and lands and the whole nature of things? Behold: here is your answer. Africanus did not take the initiative in breaking the treaty when he carried off with him into Africa a man [Masinissa] who was a very dangerous enemy to Syphax, for Syphax had previously contracted a marriage tie and friendship with the Carthaginians. Besides, Masinissa was more a soldier than an ally of Scipio and the Romans, which makes this all the less liable to criticism. But if I simply wished to defend my country, would not the injustice of Syphax—and of our accuser—be clearly evident here, for they would wish that treaties between peoples be broken on account of a single individual? Why doesn't the king petition the Romans if Scipio was in fact bringing in Masinissa on p. 150
public authority?

Verum defendi hic ipsum quoque Scipionem. A quo nec poscat Pœnus Romanas artes, ipse utens Punicis. Lucro deputent, et gratiæ, si quid de magnanimitate Scipionis accipiunt vaferrimi hostes, non poscant veluti debitum. Non cum Latino, aut simili hoste alio res est: qui aperta virtute bellum gerat. Cum Græca calliditate, cum versutia Punica res est. Cum Cretensibus (nescis?) Cretissandum. Nesciebant illi certe seniores nostri: qui improbare Martii artificia visi sunt. Sed tamen hoc constitutissimum est, tales teneri oportere, et consuesse rationes bellandi, quales ipsi sunt hostes: mites cum mitibus, sævas cum sævis, apertas cum ingenuis, subdolas cum dolosis. Hoc est iuris præceptum naturæ, et omnium populorum, ac civitatum, suum cuique reddere. De his vero iam satis.

In præstigiis Fabii, in perfidia Anitii difficultas obiecta nobis paullo maior videbatur. Et est tamen multo minor. Age quid de Fabio? Nego factum. [a] Et Livius, et Appianus ita rem narrant aliter, ut stare narratio Valerii simul non possit. [b] Sane plura is tradit, quæ cum aliis scriptoribus pluribus non consentiunt: ut id magni critici ad ipsum Valerium adnotarunt. [c] Et, mirifice mendacem factum hunc auctorem a sciolis, et librariis, aiunt. [d] Et fabulosa
p. 151 censent eius, quæ testimonium non | illic inveniunt, ubi, si vera essent, invenire facile potuissent. Scilicet rhapsodiæ sunt eius. Tu autem id notes præterea mihi, non esse ab istis scriptoribus veritatem petendam, qui proposuerunt sibi, non historiam scribere, sed exempla colligere, quibus, veluti per expressa operibus monumenta virtutis, ac vitiorum, homines aut provocarentur magis, aut magis deterrerentur. Istis scriptoribus veritas quærenda non fuit. Nam et ipsæ fabulæ faciunt, quod propositum istis scriptoribus: et ea est ratio exemplorum ubique, ut veritatem nullibi polliceantur. Is est noster Valerius, dictorum, ac factorum memorabilium amaxarius: et qui nos, novus quidam docendi magister, ducere per tritam solo bonorum viam, abducere a contraria velit, etiam ut fiat ([e] sic filius Scaligeri magni) sententiarum affectator ineptus. At hic idem Valerius narrationem istam, quæ in

[a] *Liv. 38. App. Syr.*
[b] *Lips. ann. Val.*
[c] *Pigh. ann. Val.*
[d] *Glar. ann. Val.*
[e] *Scal. catal. Virg.*

---

[217] Livy 38[. 39]; Appian, *Syriaca.*

[218] Justus Lipsius, Notes on Valerius Maximus, in Stephanus Vinandus Pighius, *Valerii Maximi dictorum factorumque memorabilium libri IX, accedunt in fine eiusdem Annotationes: et Breves notae Iusti Lipsi*, Lugduni Batavorum, Ex officina Plantiniana, Apud Franciscum Raphelengium, 1594 [Lipsius' notes at the end, after Pighius', on pp. 83 ff.].

[219] Stephanus Vinandus Pighius, notes on Valerius Maximus, in Pighius, *Valerii Maximi dictorum factorumque memorabilium libri IX*, Antverpiae, Ex officina Christophori Plantini, 1574 [see e.g. Pighius' remark in his dedicatory epistle, p. 9].

[220] Heinrich Loritz [Henricus Loritus Glareanus], notes on Valerius Maximus [in his edition of Valerius Maximus, *Valerii Maximi de factorum dictionumque memorabilium exemplis libri novem*, Basileae, per Henricum Petri, 1562].

But I have here made a defense of Scipio himself as well. Let not a Carthaginian expect the methods of a Roman when he is himself employing the methods of a Carthaginian. If our wiliest enemies receive any gift from the magnanimity of Scipio, let them ascribe it to profit or indulgence; let them not demand it as though it were something they deserved. This business is not being carried on with a Latin enemy or someone like that, who would wage war with open valor. The business is being carried on with Greek cunning and Punic wiliness. With Cretans—don't you know?—one must act like a Cretan. Those ancestors of ours who seemed to find fault with the cleverness of Marcius certainly did not know this. Nonetheless, this principle holds firmly fixed: such methods of warfare ought to be maintained and considered customary as correspond to the nature of the enemy: gentle methods with gentle enemies, savage with the savage, open with the noble, cunning with the deceitful. This is the precept of the law of nature and of all peoples and states: to render to each his own. But this is really enough about all this.

When it comes to the tricks of Fabius and the perfidy of Anicius, a rather larger difficulty seems to be cast in our path. And yet it proves in truth to be a much smaller one. Come now, what of Fabius? I say it didn't happen. Both Livy and Appian relate the matter so differently that the account of Valerius Maximus could not stand alongside them.[217] Indeed Valerius hands on many things which do not jibe with most other authors—a fact which important critics accuse him of.[218] And they say that this author was made remarkably unreliable by incompetent scholars and copyists.[219] And they judge that those things of his are fanciful which find no support in those places where, if they were true, they would most easily find support.[220] No doubt p. 151
they are his rhapsodies. You yourself, however, would point out to me that the truth is not to be sought from those writers who set themselves the task not of writing history but of gathering exempla by which men might be either be more inspired or more deterred as though through memorials of virtue or vices expressed in deeds. The truth should not have been sought from writers of that sort. For even false stories on their own achieve what those writers intended; and this is the method of exempla everywhere, that they nowhere promise the truth. This is what our Valerius is, a conveyer of memorable

manibus est nobis, sic narrat, quemadmodum exponi omne incertum, et vulgi fabulosum solet: *eumdem, ferunt, cum a rege Antiocho, quem bello superaverat*, &c. Et bello etiam superavit Antiochum iste Fabius? Haeccine, fidei infirmissimæ, incertissimæ, decuit huc advocari? Sed etiam M. Tullius, vir proculdubio Romanæ omnis antiquitatis scientissimus. [a]*Ne noster quidem probandus est: si verum est, Q. Fabium Labeonem, seu quem alium* (*nihil enim*
p. 152 *præter audi|tum habeo*) &c. Nihil in universa historia est vanius.

Anicius superest. Quid reprehenditur? Gentium regem, venientem publica sua ad se fide, supplicem retinet, in triumphum ducit. At immo dixeris non regem, regno exsutum, et quem debitum sibi victum dedi Romani poscere undecunque valebant. Si publica venit ipse fide cum iure suo, non ut maius consequeretur ius: sed ut uteretur, quod erat reliquum spontaneæ deditionis: et neque vi captus, neque invitus deditus censeretur. Et sic supplex venit, non nescius sui iuris. Et sic vitæ parcitur supplicis: et retinetur tamen, et triumphatur: qui peiora promeritus erat. Peiora Illyrium promeritum erat: in quod tantum deprædatione sævitum est. An non parsum illis est urbibus, quæ civibus vacuari, ruinis affligi poterant per ius belli? Si venia pollicita eis est argentum dantibus: ecce præstita etiam venia est: vitæ, ædificia conservata sunt. Præter argentum, nolle se aliud quicquam, non dixit Anicius. Alia iam sua erant, quæ exposita oculis, et capta erant. Argentum petit, quod occultum esse valebat, et nec captum igitur; nec suum. Sic est ius, sic teneas, accusator, bona, urbem, vitas fuisse iam populi Romani: et retenta bona, relicta reliqua in veniam. Sic nostri cives inculpabiles. Et sic igitur, per accusatoris argumentationem, civitas nostra inculpata.

[a] *Cic.* 1. *de off.*

---

[221] **Translator's note:** I cannot locate the noun *amaxarius*. I am assuming that it is cognate with Greek *amaxa*, wagon.

[222] Joseph Scaliger, *Catalecta Virgilii*, in *Pub. Virgilii Maronis Appendix, Cum supplemento multorum antehac nunquam excusorum Poëmatum veterum Poëtarum*, Lugduni Batavorum, Ex officina Plantiniana, Apud Franciscum Raphelengium, 1595, p. 248.

[223] Cicero, *De officiis* 1. 33.

sayings and deeds,[221] one who as some new master of teaching would wish to lead us along the path good men have trodden into the soil and lead us away from the opposite path, even if in so doing he might become (as the son of the great Scaliger observes) an inept pursuer of commonplaces.[222] But this same Valerius relates that narrative that we are currently dealing with in the same way that every uncertain and fabulous story of the common people tends to be expressed: "they say that the same man, when he should have taken half the ships from the king whom he had overcome in battle, etc." And did that Fabius even in fact overcome Antiochus in battle? Should these things, of the weakest and most uncertain trustworthiness, be defended by recourse to this? But even Cicero, a man who was without a doubt the most learned of all of Roman antiquity, wrote: "But not even our countryman is to be commended, if it is true that Quintus Fabius Labeo—or someone else (for I have nothing beyond what I've heard), etc."[223] Nothing in all of history is more insubstan- p. 152
tial than this.

There remains Anicius. What is held against him? When king Gentius came to him under a promise of impunity, he arrested the suppliant and led him in a triumph. Why, you would go so far as to say that the Romans were not able to demand that a king who was stripped of rule and who, vanquished, was forfeit to them be handed over from wherever he was. If he himself came on his own authority under a promise of impunity—not in order that he might pursue his own case, but so that he might make use of whatever was left to him from a willing surrender—he would neither be considered someone captured by force nor someone who surrendered unwillingly. And thus it was that he came as a suppliant, not unaware of what was due to him. And so the life of the suppliant is spared—and yet he is nonetheless detained and led in triumph—he who deserved worse. Illyria itself, against which such harshness was shown through pillaging, deserved worse. But were not those cities spared which could have been emptied of citizens and afflicted with destruction in accord with the law of war? If forgiveness was promised to those cities that gave money, behold: the forgiveness *was* indeed offered to them: lives and buildings were spared. Anicius did not say that he did not wish anything besides money. The other things, which were exposed to eyesight and captured, were already his. He sought money, which could be hidden away and therefore had not been captured and was not yet his. Thus is the law (of war), and thus you would have to affirm, accuser, that possessions, city, lives belonged to the Romans, and that the remaining things were left to the Illyrians as an act of kindness. Thus our citizens were not blameworthy. And thus, therefore, in accord with our accuser's own argument, our state remains blameless.

p. 153

Romani bellis invicti.

CAP. V

Sed et argumentatur mox acute, dum contendit, victos Romanos bellis sæpe: victos illo regio, de quo dicebamus, Posennæ. Victi olim a Tatio: qui regemque se, et Sabinos suos in urbem intulit: et de Romanis Quirites fecit. Bella ratio, per quam victores alii omnes evadant, qui tracti in urbem populi sunt. Hæc est victoria, qua tracti Sabini Romam sunt: spoliatum nomen Sabinum tot millibus fortissimorum civium est: non solum retentæ mulieres raptæ, quæ belli caussa exstiterunt. Cetera ex æquo fuere. Ut sic vicerit Tatius post artes dolosas, furtum arcis, lenocinium, et perfidiam cum puella, et impietatem in deos. Regem se Tatius, et Sabinos suos intulit in urbem: quam et ædificavit scilicet: neque enim Sabinis data casula Romanorum est. Qui et rex erat scilicet: et secum inferret, quos regnaret: quique iure societatis æquissimo in consortium communis regni a Romulo propterea exciperetur, consulente urbi suæ, verissimo patre patriæ. Hæc est victoria: ut, qui urbem subvertere voluissent, res sibi raptas recipere tanto cum apparatu venissent, ii urbem ampliorem efficiant et res illic suas esse, et ipsos se velint.

Nam, quod addit de mutato nomine, quid? [a] Certe hæc lex victoriæ
p. 154 est, ut in nomen victoris vi|ctus transeat, in sermonem, in habitum. Certe dignioris partis hæc est lex, ut eius serventur hæc omnia. *Pro Latio obtestor, pro maiestate tuorum, Ne vetus indigenas nomen mutare Latinos, Neu Troas fieri iubeas, Teucrosque vocari, Aut vocem mutare viros, aut vertere vestes.* [b] Sed Romani a Romulo, Quirites a Quirino appellantur. Silete Grammatici. Roma audit ubique, et ubique Romani: [c] non, ut Messana est, sed sunt Mamertini. Aut quid si Quirites in urbe sunt a tuis Curibus?

[a] *Serv.* 12. *Æn.* [b] *Inst. tit.* 2. *Ovid. Fa.* 2. *Cic.* 1. *de leg. Flor.* 1. [c] *Str.* 6.

---

224 Servius, *On Aeneid* 12.
225 [Juno to Jupiter, Vergil, *Aeneis* 12. 820, 823–5.]
226 *Institutes* 1. 2. 2; Ovid, *Fasti* 2; Cicero, *De legibus* 1; Florus 1. 1. 18.
227 Strabo 6. 2. 3.

CHAPTER 5 p. 153

The Romans Undefeated in Wars

But he soon proceeds to make an ingenious argument when he contends that the Romans were often defeated in wars—and were defeated in that war of Porsenna's over the kingship about which we were speaking. He claims also that they were once upon a time defeated by Tatius, who forced upon the city both himself as king and also his Sabines—and made Quirites out of the Romans. This is a pretty method through which all others who are led forth against a people's city might emerge as victors. This is the victory by which the Sabines were drawn to Rome: that the Sabine name was stripped from so many thousands of very brave citizens—and not just that the abducted women, who were the cause of the war, were retained. In other matters, they were on an equal footing. So this is how Tatius triumphed after deceptive wiles, the underhanded seizure of the citadel, the pandering and perfidy with a girl, and the impiety against the gods. Tatius with his Sabines attacked as king a city that he then built up, to be sure—and not a single hut of the Romans was given to the Sabines. Yes, he was indeed a king and would bring with him those he was to rule, and he would be received by Romulus therefore into an association of joint rule through the very just law of fellowship—Romulus thus looking after the interests of his own city as the truest father of his country. This is the actual victory: that those who wished to overthrow the city and came with such military preparations in order to recover things that had been stolen from them now would make the city larger and would wish their own state and themselves to be located here.

For what does he add about the altered name—what? Indeed this is the law of victory, that the defeated pass over into the name, the language, and p. 154 the clothing of the victor.[224] To be sure, this is the law of the more worthy side, that all these aspects of it be preserved. "On behalf of Latium I beseech you, on behalf of the majesty of your people, . . . may you not order the native Latins to change their old name or become Trojans and be called Teucrians, or that the men change their language or their clothes."[225] But the Romans were named from Romulus, the Quirites from Quirinus.[226] Be silent, you grammarians. The city is called Rome everywhere, and everywhere it is the Romans. It is not like Messana, where the people are in fact Mamertines.[227] Or what if the Quirites in the city are in fact named from your Cures, and the

et auctoritati unius id conceditur Dionysii, non tantum Festi Grammatici? Tantulum redditum pro aliis nunquam efficere Sabinos victores potest. Etsi eidem tuo credimus Servio, ecce, data Sabinis civitas citra suffragii ius est. Audi: etiam Sabini a Romulo dicti: ut idem tibi notat Servius.

Vicit mox Porsenna. *Nec non Tarquinium eiectum Porsenna iubebat accipere: ingentique urbem obsidione premebat, Æneadæ in ferrum pro libertate ruebant.* Atque cum omnibus malis, quæ tum illata Romanis sunt, retenta libertas est tamen, et receptus Tarquinius non est: de quibus duobus contendebatur. *Iactatum in conditionibus nequidquam de Tarquiniis in regnum restituendis: magis quia id ipse negare nequiverit Tarquiniis, quam quod negatum iri sibi ab Romanis ignoraret*: inquit Livius. Et sic igitur dicis (ut dicitur) caussa datum
p. 155 honori regis | iudicium in caussa tyrannorum. Et de dato iudicio sic Dionysius scripserit. Datum iudicium regi fuerit, sed extra hanc partem restitutionis tyrannorum. Ut sic decet, scriptores scriptoribus concordes facere. Datum iudicium regi fuerit liberum: sed non tamen (id certum) ut pro libitu, et libidine constitueret, at cognosceret, et iuste definiret. Libertas non est licentia: iure cogitur. Atque ad ius rem referre Romani audenter valuere, conscii iustitiæ suæ, iniustitiæ tyrannorum: tuti vel ab iniqua sententia: cum et obsistere exsecutioni eius sic possent, ut tutabantur se antea adversus professam vim. Hæc fuit deditio urbis. Quid autem? Retinuerunt libertatem mei. Pulsus abiit tyrannus. Et, qui pro tyranno steterat, iudex pro Romanis sententiam tulit. Itaque Romani victi.

[a] Laudat Plutarchus, iudicationem regi datam: sic enim conciliaverit illum Poplicola, ad cuius iudicium provocaret. Respondet Plutarchus de agri parte ademta: quemadmodum pro eo castra regis opulentissima, omni commeatu instructissima, adeoque multo commodissima urbi famelicæ sint accepta. Et tamen quid si nec acceptum aliquid pro agro fuit? libertas certe retenta est: quæ una utrinque petebatur: libertas est parta: quæ inæstimabilis res est semper. *Non bene pro toto libertas venditur auro.* Sed et ferrum ademtum
p. 156 nobis? Sed et li | bertas retenta nobis: ut hoc iterum dicam, atque iterum,

[a] *Plut. Popl.*

228 [Vergil, *Aeneis* 8. 646–8.]
229 [Livy 2. 13.]
230 Plutarch, *Publicola* 18.
231 [Proverbial.]

matter is yielded to the authority of one man, Dionysius, and not so much to Festus the grammarian? A little pittance handed back instead of everything else could never make the Sabines the victors. Even if we trust that same Servius of yours, behold: citizenship was given to the Sabines without the right to vote. Listen: even the Sabines were named by Romulus, as the same Servius mentions to you.

Soon Porsena conquered. "Also Porsenna ordered them to take back Tarquin who had been expelled, and he pressed the city with a massive siege; the descendants of Aeneas were rushing on the sword for the sake of liberty."[228] And yet, despite all the evils which were then brought upon Rome, nonetheless liberty was preserved, and Tarquin was not taken back—which were the two issues being fought over. "In the proposals was a fruitless statement about the need to restore the Tarquins to power—more because he himself was unable to refuse this to the Tarquins than because he was unaware that this would be refused him by the Romans," says Livy.[229] And so thus it was solely for the sake of appearances (as the saying goes) that judgment in the case of the tyrants was granted to the king's dignity. And this p. 155
is what Dionysius meant about the assigning of judgment. The judgment would have been entrusted to the king—but *not* about this matter of the restoration of the tyrants. How proper it is to make writers agree with each other in this way. Unrestrained jurisdiction was given to the king, but nevertheless not (this is certain) so that he might make a decision in accord with his whim or desire, but so that he might justly decide and apportion. Liberty is not license; it is constrained by law. And the Romans had the power to boldly refer the matter to law, conscious as they were of their own justice and of the injustice of the tyrants. They were even safe from an unjust verdict, since they would have had the power to obstruct its execution, just as they were previously defending themselves against open force. This, then, was the surrender of the city! What's that? My people retained their liberty. The tyrant, driven off, went away. And he who had stood up for the tyrant brought in a verdict as judge on behalf of the Romans. And so the Romans were "defeated"!

Plutarch praises the granting of jurisdiction to the king, for in this way Publicola won over that man to whose judgement he was appealing.[230] And Plutarch offers this answer about the territory taken away: in exchange for it the Romans received the extremely rich camp of the king, most fully furnished with all sorts of provisions—and moreover most useful for a starving city. And yet what if there had been nothing at all received in exchange for the territory? They certainly retained their liberty, which is the one thing that is sought everywhere; liberty was obtained, which is always a thing beyond price. "Liberty is not properly sold for any amount of gold."[231] But was iron also taken from us? But we kept our liberty, that I might mention again and p. 156

quod caput est quæstionis: adeoque dicendum est semper. Non igitur vicit Porsenna, qui iussum suum non perfecit: etsi nos dedimus nonnihil honori regis potentissimi, atque vicissim liberalissimi.

Vicit Brennus? Et scelere Romanorum petiti Galli? Scilicet illic quoque vituperabimur, ubi laudem ampliter meriti sumus. Fabios namque illos dedendos senatus censuit, et collegium fæcialium: quorum hæc notio erat. Plebi quid feceris, quæ ubique gentium est eadem bellua multorum capitum, aut sine capite verius ullo. De victoria vero Gallorum notet mihi cum eodem Polybio adversarius noster, quod et coacti Galli abire Roma, infestantibus Venetis regionem ipsorum: et sic recuperarint Romani patriæ libertatem. Et hoc Picenus capiat, qui alterum ibidem cepit, abiisse incolumes Gallos, non fuisse a Camillo cæsos. Namque illa nunc quæstio magis est, si victi Romani a Gallis sunt. Ecce, Polybii testimonio, quo et utitur accusator, victi non sunt. Etiam Capitolium occupaverunt, testimonio Tertulliani, Lucani, Silii? [a] Non illud scripserit Tertullianus. Occupare, et Capere est opprimere, et obsidione premere. Est, quod Livius, quod Virgilius, *Galli per dumos aderant, arcemque*
p. 157 *tenebant*. Quod Lucanus ait de perusto. id minus est: iactis fa|cibus id fieri potest. Et tu de Tacito dicis, quale illud incendium fuerit ad rem nihili. Quid nunc de tuo Orosio? Neque enim negamus nos extrema illa mala obsessorum: sed, illic finitum esse bellum, negamus.

Quid mihi de Polyeno? Nescis, hominem Macedonem; hoc est, Romanorum (ut semel utar constituto iure tuo) hostem? Non vides, eum scriptorem stratagematum, non historiæ; hoc est, non de veritate factorum sollicitum, quam de numero qualium exemplorum? quæ vera, nec ne sint, non curare ulli consueverunt. Minus is est, quam testis. At etiam suspectus est: ignobilis est: contrarius aliis est accusatoris testibus maioribus, et accusatoris disputationi: qui, reduces Gallos, et in Galliam aurum avectum Romanum contendit: contendit testimoniis, contendit ratione de ista incolumitate Gallorum Picenogallus. An potuit latere, Sangenesium suum a provincialibus Gallis esse? Sed figurata ipsius ratio adversus Camilli inopiam ecce hic quanta est: [b]*Conon exsulans Cypri, omni alia ope destitutus, excepto corpore, et ingenio, ausus contra Lacedæmonios principes terræ, ac maris: et vicit: et a viro tam abiecto mutatus Græciæ status est*. Sic Isocrates. Addam autem mox plura. Nam (ut nunc sum)

[a] *Iun. no. Tert.* [b] *Isocr. or. ad Phil.* sed vide Iusti. 6.

---

232 **Translator's note:** Quintus Fabius Ambustus and two of his brothers or relatives were sent to negotiate the withdrawal of the Gauls from Italy in 391, but instead led an attack upon them. According to Diodorus Siculus (14. 113. 4 ff.), when the Gauls demanded that they be handed over, the Senate at first agreed to do so, but their decision was overridden by a popular vote engineered by father of one of them, a tribune with consular power. Livy's account (5. 35. 4 ff.) does not mention the Senate's vote.

233 Junius's notes on Tertullian.

234 [Vergil, *Aeneis* 8. 657.]

235 **Translator's note:** Perhaps the reference is to *Annales* 11. 23, where the Gauls' seizure of the Capitol is mentioned, with no mention of a fire. But there is no reference to Tacitus in the corresponding passage in 1. 5.

236 **Translator's note:** Alberico Gentili's birthplace.

237 Isocrates, *Ad Philippum* 63–4. But see Justin 6. 1–5.

again that which is the principal matter under discussion—and it needs to be mentioned forever. So Porsenna, who did not bring to pass the orders he gave, did not win, even though we did make a certain concession to the honor of this king who was very powerful and, in turn, very generous.

Did Brennus win? And were the Gauls attacked by the crime of the Romans? Indeed we are slandered here too where we have richly merited praise. For the Senate ordered that those Fabii be handed over, along with the college of fetiales, whose idea this was.[232] What would you do to the common people, who are in every nation the same beast of many heads—or, more accurately, without any head at all? As for the supposed victory of the Gauls, let our adversary observe with Polybius that the Gauls were forced to withdraw from Rome when the Veneti harassed their own land, and thus the Romans recovered the liberty of their fatherland. And let Picenus grasp this, he who grasped something quite different from Polybius: i.e. that the Gauls went away intact and were not slaughtered by Camillus. For the question now is, rather, if the Romans were defeated by the Gauls. Behold, on the testimony of Polybius, which our accuser also is making use of, they were *not* defeated. Yet did they occupy the Capitol, according to the testimony of Tertullian, Lucan, and Silius Italicus? Tertullian did not write this.[233] To occupy and seize is to overpower and oppress with a siege. What happened is what Livy and Vergil wrote: "The Gauls showed up through the bushes and were reaching the citadel."[234] As for what Lucan says about the seat of Tarpeia being burned, that is even less important: it could have p. 157
happened from tossed firebrands. And even you mention with regard to Tacitus how that fire was of no importance for the matter.[235] What now are we to make of your Orosius? For we don't deny those extreme misfortunes of the besieged, but we do deny that the war was brought to an end there.

Why do you tell me of Polyaenus? Are you unaware that the man was a Macedonian, that is (if I may employ just this once your own settled custom) an enemy of the Romans? Do you not see that he was a writer of military stratagems, not of history; that is, a man less concerned with the truth of actions than with amassing the kind of exempla which nobody has cared if they be true or false? He is less than an authority. He is not to be trusted, is unworthy, is in contradiction with the majority of the accuser's other authorities and even the accuser's own contention, for the accuser argues that the Gauls were brought back safe and sound and that the Roman gold was carried off into Gaul. With both testimonies and arguments this Picene Gaul insists upon the safe return of the Gauls. Or could it not be obvious that his San Ginesio[236] was formed from Gallic provincials? But behold here just how impressive is his contrived argument against Camillus' lack of resources: "Conon, as an exile in Cyprus, bereft of any other resources except for his body and his wit, made an attempt against the Spartans, the rulers of the land and the sea, and defeated them, and so by one so abject the situation of Greece was transformed." Thus Isocrates.[237] But I will soon add other

annuo Gallorum omnem incolumitatem accusatori: ubi ille tamen non videat p. 158 Romanos bello victos, sed præliis afflictos, | sed ambustos, sed spoliatos quasi a latronibus. Etiam Græciam, etiam Asiam, et sacratissima templa illi vexarunt, qui Romam.

Quid tamen vetera ista (ait accusator) conquirimus? Nos, nos Piceni, ducibus Asculanis meis, amantissimis illis patriæ meæ, amantissimis familiæ, nos in summo Romani imperii fastigio Romanos vicimus. Etiam Sangenesiates vos, vos Sangenesiates, vos, qui post ferme decies centum annos exstitistis? Et quibus ea summa laus sit in isto genere, quod in medio positi potentium, ac nobilium populorum, Camerinatum, Tollentinatum, Firmanorum, tenere cum omnibus dignum valuistis locum, etiam de Firmanis trophæa erigere, et splendida ad omnem posteritatem constituere monumenta. Sed vos, vos Piceni, Asculanis ducibus. Id bene ducibus, Piceni capite, colonia nostra nobilissima. Audi tamen, colonia: [a] et ita scilicet Florus, Italiam tum contra matrem, ac parentem suam consurrexisse. [b] Et ita scilicet non modo extra Italiam nostræ erant coloniæ, sexaginta in Africa sola, et in Gallia simul et Hispania totidem, et plurimæ in orbe reliquo ita, ut dixerit Seneca, *Ubicunque vicit Romanus habitat*: sed in Italia ipsa habuimus centum quinquaginta.

Sed de victoria Italicorum non testis producitur, sed tantum ratiuncula. p. 159 Atque illam nec probes: quæ male confusis temporibus consuitur. | Neque enim civitas nostra deferebatur Italicis tum vincentibus, at victis: versa re Italica, atque eversa. Feliciter Cæsar pugnaverat contra Samnites: hos Sylla iterum, atque iterum expugnaverat hos alii vicerant acie, duce orbarant nobilissimo. Idem Sylla Hirpinos domuerat. Marius Marsos fuderat, et Marrucinorum prætorem occiderat. Plotius Umbros vicerat. Pompeius Vestinos, et Pelignos acceperat in deditionem: et tuos fuderat Picenos, atque obsederat, et omnia flammis, ferroque populatus, non prius finem cædium fecit, quam Asculi eversione manibus tot exercituum nostrorum, direptarumque urbium fidelissimarum parentaret. Cæsi erant legati Italici, et dux auctor belli eius Popedius. Et, cum hæc ita se habebant, delata Italicis civitas est.

Sic populus Romanus victis aliis eam tribuit civitatem: qui certum agnoscerent beneficium, non autem aliquid arrogarent virtuti suæ: et itaque faciliores in obsequium civitatis nostræ semper manerent. Hoc vere arcanum eius imperii: et quidem iustum pro eo, quod Romanæ excellenti virtuti debebatur.

[a] *Flor.* 3. [b] *Paterc.* 2 *Lips.* 1. *de mach. Rom.* 9.

---

238 Florus 3. 18. 5.

239 Velleius Paterculus 2. 7. 7 [see also the catalogue of Roman colonies in Italy in 1. 14–15]; Justus Lipsius, *Admiranda, sive De magnitudine Romana libri quattuor* 1. 6, Antverpiae, Ex Officina Plantiniana, Apud Ioannem Moretum, 1598, p. 31 [Lipsius cites Velleius Paterculus 2. 7. 7].

240 **Translator's note:** The reference appears to be not to the famous Julius Caesar but his older relative Lucius Julius Caesar, who scored a major victory over the Samnite Papius Mutilus in the Social War.

241 **Translator's note:** The reference is, of course, not to Pompey the Great, but to his father, Cn. Pompeius Strabo.

242 **Translator's note:** The phrase *arcanum imperii* here is an allusion to Tacitus, *Historiae* 1. 4, where the "secret of empire" was that rulers could be made elsewhere than in the city of Rome.

things. For I grant, for now, the safe and sound return of the Gauls, while he, for his part, should nevertheless not ascertain that the Romans were defeated in a war but were harassed in battles, scorched, despoiled as though by p. 158
brigands. Those Gauls who harassed Rome even harried Greece, even Asia, and most holy temples.

"But why do I collect those ancient doings," says the accuser. "We, we Picenes, with my own Asculans as leaders, those men most devoted to my country and to my family, defeated the Romans in war at the very height of the Roman empire." Do you mean even you men of San Ginesio, you San Ginesians who came into existence almost a thousand years later? These were men whose greatest claim to fame in that race was that, located in the midst of powerful and noble peoples, the Camerinates, the Tollentinates, the Firmani, you had the power to hold a worthy place with all the others and even to raise a trophy over the people of Firmum [Fermo] and set up splendid monuments for all of posterity. But you, you Picenes, with the Asculans as leaders... That's right: they were the leaders, the capital of Picenum, and our own most noble colony. But just listen to that: a colony—and hear also Florus, who writes that Italy then rose up against its own mother and parent.[238] And so our colonies did not only lie outside of Italy—sixty in Africa alone, and in Gaul and Spain together the same number, and very many in the rest of the world, just as Seneca said: "Wherever the Roman has conquered, there does he dwell." But in Italy herself also we had 150 colonies.[239]

But no authority is produced for the victory of the Italians, only a little bit of paltry argumentation. But you should not approve of that argumentation, which is stitched together from different periods which are badly mixed up. Our citizenship was not bestowed upon the Italians then when they were p. 159
victorious but when they were defeated and when the affairs of Italy were turned upside down. Caesar had fought with success against the Samnites,[240] Sulla had repeatedly defeated them, and others had defeated them in the line of battle and deprived them of their most noble leader. The same Sulla subdued the Hirpini. Marius routed the Marsians and killed the praetor of the Marrucini. Plotius defeated the Umbrians. Pompey accepted the surrender of the Vestini and the Peligni and routed and besieged your own Picenes and after having devastated everything with fire and sword did not put an end to the slaughter until, by the demolition of Asculum, he avenged the souls of so many of our armies and our cities which had been laid waste.[241] The Italian legates and the leader and initiator of that war, Popedius, were slaughtered. And it was when matters stood thus that citizenship was bestowed upon the Italians.

In the same way the Roman people have bestowed citizenship upon other defeated peoples as well, who acknowledged our own manifest kindness but did not ascribe anything to their own excellence, and therefore always remained more easily in obedience to our state. This was the true secret of that empire,[242] and it was indeed a just one, in that it was owing to

[a] Sic senatus agros dedit lege Gracchi: propter quam tamen et Gracchus occidebatur, et ipse obnitendo legi senatus adiit ad discrimen ultimum. Sapienter (ait Valerius tuus) auctorem seditionis, et seditionis caussam ita
p. 160 sustulit. Etiam hic sapienter | meritis data civitas nunc subiectis, quæ antea superbis denegabatur. Neque enim iustitia caussæ est satis, nisi eadem iusteque proponitur. Ut cum indignus vir quidam id proponeret, quod foret civitati suæ utilissimum, non antea exceptum fuit tamen, quam mutata persona proponentis idem consuleret alius.

Atque sic Italici, et Piceni, et Asculani vincunt: cæsi, dediti, capti deleti. [b] Sit ille Picenorum sane honor, quod non ante resumsit senatus laticlavia, aut magistratus insignia dignitatum ob victorias alias de Italicis partas, quam ipsi fusi Piceni fuerint. Sit ille honor Asculanis, quod non ante captum Asculum censuerint mei, victores se esse. At victores se dicere Piceni non audeant. [c] Sacrum genus Piceni sunt. Quid crudo se mendacio maculent? Nec tu, accusator noster, novus [d] *Equitius Firmo Piceno monstrum veniens.* Admiror, Picenum, non Volscum rebellem, non Samnitem efferum, non alium hostem nostrum implacabilem, sed admiror, Picenum suscepisse istam, et quidem tanta cum libidine, accusationem Romanorum: admiror Asculanensem maxime. Tanta enim, extra hoc bellum funestissimum, fuit Romanis, et Picenis coniunctio semper, Asculanisque, ut soli omnium isti non esse Romæ peregrini viderentur,[e] atque videri vellent. [f] Laudati præ ceteris sunt Romæ,
p. 161 honestissimarum, ac no|bilissimarum familiarum nomine, eloquentissimorum extra urbem oratorum. Quid tantum nobis contumeliarum, et conviciorum rependitur? Asculani, vestram fidem hunc, delicium vestrum, iam compescite.

Ecce enim Parthosque facit Romanorum victores. [g] Intulerunt illi quidem cladem nobis sub Crasso: sed mala fraude, manifesta perfidia. Afflixerunt nec aliter Antonii copias: contra quas fluminibus quoque veneno infectis pugnarunt: et fugiendo pugnarunt: nam conserta manu victi semper abierunt. [h] *Variisque Antonius, armis Victor ab Auroræ populis.* Quid sibi Volscus voluit

[a] *Val.* 7. *c.* 2. [b] *Oros.* 5. *c.* 17. [c] *Cato orig.*
[d] *Val.* 9. *c.* 15. [e] *Cic. pro Syll.*
[f] *Cic. Bru.* [g] *App. Parth. Ant. Dio.* 40.
[h] *Virg.* 8. *ubi Serv.*

---

[243] Valerius Maximus 7. 2. 6b.
[244] Orosius 5. 17.
[245] Cato, *Origines* 43 [the reference is unclear].
[246] Valerius Maximus 9. 15. 1.
[247] Cicero, *Pro Sulla* 8.
[248] Cicero, *Brutus* 169.
[249] Vergil, *Aeneis* 8. 685–6, and Servius *ad loc.*

exceptional Roman excellence. Similarly, the Senate granted agricultural lands through the law of Gracchus, a law on account of which nonetheless Gracchus himself was killed, and the Senate approached the most extreme danger in striving against the law. Thus it shrewdly (says your Valerius Maximus) did away with both the initiator of sedition and the cause for sedition.[243] Even in this case citizenship was wisely given to those who p. 160 merited it as subjects, while it was earlier denied them when they were insolent. Nor is the justice of a cause sufficient, unless its manner of being proposed is likewise just. Thus, when some unworthy man would propose something that would be very useful for his state, it was nonetheless not accepted until, when the role of proposer had been altered, some other man would give the same advice.

And so this is how the Italians, Picenes, and Asculans triumph: by being slaughtered, forced to surrender, captured, destroyed. Let that indeed be the glory of the Picenes, that the Senate did not don again the purple stripes or the insignia of the ranks of magistracy, despite other victories obtained from the Italians, until the Picenes themselves were routed.[244] Let this be an honor to the Asculans that my people did not consider themselves victors until Asculum was captured. But let not the Picenes dare to call themselves the victors. The Picenes are a sacred race.[245] Why would they sully themselves with a crass lie? Are not you, our accuser, a new "Equitius, a monster coming out of Picene Fermo"?[246] I am amazed that a Picene, not a rebellious Volscian or a wild Samnite or some other implacable enemy of ours, but a *Picene* has taken up this accusation against the Romans, and indeed with such gusto—and I am especially amazed that it is an *Asculan*. For, apart from this most disastrous war, there was always such a close connection between the Romans and the Picenes and Asculans that they alone of all peoples did not seem to be foreigners when at Rome and did not wish to seem so.[247] They were praised at Rome beyond all others for the fame of their very respectable and noble families and for producing the most eloquent orators outside of the p. 161 city itself.[248] Why are we being repaid with so many slanders and insults? Asculans, for heaven's sake restrain this man, this darling of yours.

For behold he even makes the Parthians out to be victors over the Romans. Those people did in fact inflict a slaughter upon us when Crassus was commander, but it was through a wicked deception, through manifest perfidy. And in a similar fashion they harassed the forces of Antony—and fought against them even with rivers infected with poison and by keeping on the run—for when battle was joined they always came away defeated. "And Antony with diverse arms, victor over the peoples of the East."[249] What was

Trogus, qui tantum potuit efferre barbaros illos? An maiores ulcisci suos, toties cæsos, captos, sub iugum missos? [a] Cæsi Parthi mox a Cassio, Crassi quæstore: etiam et Osaces cæsus Parthorum dux: et a Domitio contra eosdem bellatum prospere: et repensam Crassi cladem in Pacori clade regis, sive filii regis. [b] Augusto Armeniam vindicanti cesserunt facile: et signa militaria, quæ Crasso, et Antonio ademissent, reddiderunt: obsides insuper obtulerunt ultro, et tradiderunt. [c]*Etiam Parthi hoc tempore subdidere colla*: verissime Strabo: [d]*fortes illi, sed nomine magis, quam re ipsa: ut bellandi eorum ratio ostendit*: quod Dio, qui late de armis, et aliis eius gentis tradit. [e] Et itaque
p. 162 Livius iustissime, *Levissimi ex Græcis contra Romanum | nomen Parthorum gloriæ favent*. Levissimus hic Volscus, immo Gallus Vocontius, commentus est caussam belli contra Ætolos suscepti pro Acarnensibus: commentus Corinthi, et Græciæ exscidii caussam: commentus de libertate Iudæis tributa: commentus de insidiis in Annibalem: et in laudem eius ducis profusus: aversus Romanis semper: et occasionem nullam unquam oblitus, ubi notare nos potuit. Hic vir, hic est, qui scribit, populos Scythicos intactos, et formidatos nostris fuisse. Cæcus homo ab invidia: [f] qui non viderit, Scytharum multos exercitus fusos vel ab uno Pompeio, et totum fere domitum Septentrionem. Ita vero Parthi Romanorum victores semper.

Sed hic mihi Ventidius deprædicatur victor: qui ex agro Piceno vir, et Asculanus. Ego autem nec invideo. Non invidet populus Romanus. Quod si velim tamen, Ventidium istum possum Piceno, et Asculo incertum facere, Etruriæ vindicare. Sed nolo imitari accusatorem: et de tenui coniectura, de auctore uno aliquo contra liquidam veritatem, et contra certissima testimonia depugnare. [g] Ventidium Picenum, Asculanum scimus. Immo scimus Romanum: ut alii innumeri, qui alibi nati, Romani facti et reges, et consules sunt. [h]*Religiosa patet peregrinæ curia laudi. Nec putat externos, quos decet esse suos.*
p. 163 Senator Romanus Ventidius, tribu|nus plebis, prætor, pontifex, consul. Ecce, in quantas ille dignitates evectus in mea patria. Mortuus etiam funeratus publice. Quæ nobis dicenda sunt civitatis, et spectanda facta: non etiam ratio poscenda petulantiæ, vitiive alterius, sive poetarum, sive aliorum: non quid Plancus dixerit, aliusve: qui contrariarum aliquando partium Ventidio exstiterunt.

[a] *Iust.* 42. 43. *Dio.* 49. *Liv.* 108. 112. 128. *Suid.* [b] *Liv.* 139. *Eutr.* 7. *Suet. Aug.*
[c] *Str.* 6. [d] *Dio.* 40. *Virg.* 3. *Geo.* [e] *Liv.* 9. [f] *Flor.* 3. *c.* 5.
[g] *Pater.* 2. *Val.* 6. *c.* 9. *Dio.* 43. *Gell.* 15. *c.* 4. *Plin.* 7. *c.* 43. [h] *Numet.* 1. *itin.*

---

250 Justin 42. 4. 5; Dio Cassius 40. 28–9; Livy, *Periochae* 108. 112. 128; *Suda*, ed. Adler, pi, 30.
251 Livy 139; Eutropius 7; Suetonius *Augustus* 21.
252 Strabo 6. 4. 2. 253 Dio Cassius 40. 14. 4; Vergil, *Georgica* 3. 31.
254 Livy 9. 18. 6. 255 Florus 3. 5. 27–31.
256 Velleius Paterculus 2; Valerius Maximus 6. 9; Dio Cassius 43. 51. 4; Aulus Gellius 15. 4; Pliny the Elder 7. 43.
257 Rutilius Namatianus, *De reditu suo* 1. 13–14.

Pompeius Trogus, a Volscian, aiming at when he brought himself to so exalt those barbarians? Was he trying to avenge his ancestors, who were so often cut down, captured, sent under the yoke? The Parthians were soon slaughtered by Cassius, Crassus' quaestor, and even Osaces, the leader of the Parthians, was killed. And war was successfully waged against them by Domitius, and the slaughter of Crassus was repaid by the slaughter of King Pacorus—or, rather, the king's son.[250] They easily yielded to Augustus when he was avenging Armenia, and they gave back the military standards which they had taken from Crassus and Antony, and in addition offered and handed over hostages of their own accord.[251] "Even the Parthians at this time bent their necks"—so Strabo very accurately wrote.[252] "Those brave men, but more from reputation than from actual fact, as their method of making war showed"—so wrote Dio Cassius, who passes on a lot of material about the arms and other matters of that people.[253] Hence Livy, too, most justly wrote: "The most unreliable of the Greeks show favor to the glory of p. 162
the Parthians in opposition to the reputation of the Romans."[254] This most unreliable Volscian [Pompeius Trogus], or, rather, Vocontian Gaul, lied about the reason for the war undertaken against the Aetolians on behalf of the Acananians; he lied about the reason for the destruction of Corinth and Greece; he lied about the freedom bestowed upon the Jews; he lied about the snares laid against Hannibal, and he was profuse in praise of that leader; he was always hostile to the Romans and never passed up an opportunity in which he was able to criticize us. This man, this one it is, who writes that the Scythians were untouched by our people—and a source of fear for them. The man was blind from envy, for he did not see that many armies of the Scythians were routed even by one man alone, Pompey, and that the whole of the north was subdued.[255] So this is actually how the Parthians were always victors over the Romans!

But at this point Ventidius is proclaimed to me as a victor, a man from the Picene territory and an Asculan. And in fact I don't look upon him with ill will. Nor does the Roman people look upon him with ill will. And yet if I wished I could make that Ventidius a doubtful citizen for Picenum and Asculum and claim him for Etruria instead. But I don't want to imitate my accuser and on the basis of a slender conjecture and of some one particular author to fight against clear truth and the most reliable testimonies. We know that Ventidius was a Picene and from Asculum.[256] Or, rather, we know he was a *Roman*, just as countless others who were born elsewhere became Romans and were kings and consuls. "The holy Senate House is open to foreign excellence; and it does not consider foreigners those who are fittingly her own."[257] Ventidius was a Roman senator, a tribune of the plebs, a praetor, p. 163
a pontifex, a consul. Behold, to how many dignified positions he was elevated in my country. And when he died he was even given a public funeral. We ought to speak of and look upon these actions of the Roman state, not seek out some reason for the opprobrium or reproach either of poets or others, nor what Plancius or someone else said, people who once belonged to factions opposed to Ventidius.

Iustitia Romanorum in fœderibus.
CAP. VI

Ab his autem victoriis de populo Romano partis accedit Picenogallus ad accusandum fraudes nostras in fœderibus malas. Et quærit de cæde Gallorum contra fœdus a Camillo patrata. [a] Atque ita nec audivit de suo saltem Floro, per insolentiam ad iniqua pondera additum adhuc gladium, et superbum verbum, *væ victis*. In quo ipsi Galli primi ruperunt fœdus. Sed neque sine Camillo, qui Romæ erant, potuere cum Gallis pacisci: ut nec potest corpus sine capite functiones ullas obire. Quæ ista accusatio est? Et caput rursus nec quidquam faciet absque corpore reliquo. Non hic decipiuntur Galli, non alii. [b]*Qui cum alio contrahit, vel est, vel debet esse non ignarus conditionis eius: aut sibi imputet*: inquit lex. Sibi Galli imputent, si obsidio suo iam fatigati recessum sic venditarunt, nec de qualitate emtorum quæsiere: qui, se ut
p. 164 potu|issent redimere, Camillo tamen præscribere non potuerunt. [c] Etiam qui cum alio contrahit, videtur respectu illius qualitatis contrahere. Quid pallii revolutio? [d] quæ et licita. Non dicitur iuste, impuberis contractum non valere, a quo abfuit tutor? et non valere contractum sæpe tutoris, ubi pupillus defuit? Sic sexcenta.

Quicquid erat Romæ: ais accusator, quod ego rapio. Nam Romæ quid erat? Ais, vix mille hominum. Minima igitur pars Romanæ civitatis. Et igitur, quod gestum cum ea est, aut maiorem partem non obligavit, aut nec ipsam quidem convenientem. [e] Nam hoc ius est, ut actus minoris partis universitatis neque obliget istam: quasi sic actumque fuerit, ut non aliter, quam veluti universitas obligaretur. [f] Vocandi sunt absentes, in arduis præsertim negotiis: et qui præsertim absunt ex iusta caussa: aut nec ipsi præsentes obligantur: certe non obligantur absentes. Arduissimum illud negotium quis neget? quis, non abfuisse Romanos alios ex iustissima caussa?

[a] *Flor.* 1. [b] *l.* 19. *de reg. iu.* [c] *Alc.* 2. *cons.* 3.
[d] *l.* 8. *de inoff. re. ubi gl.* [e] *Alc.* 1. *cons.* 4. [f] *Bar. alii l. omnes populi.*

---

258 Florus 1. 13. 17 [cf. Livy 5. 48].

259 *Digest* 50. 17. 19. **Translator's note:** The words *aut sibi imputet*, however, are not taken from Ulpianus but seem to have been added by Gentili himself to strengthen his point; Ulpianus goes on to make a much narrower point about the law of estates.

260 Alciatus, *Consilia* 2. 3, col. 137 [Alciati makes a narrower point about entering into a legal agreement with an heir: "qui contrahit cum haerede videtur respectu illius qualitatis contrahere"].

261 *Digest* 5. 2. 8; see the *Glossa ordinaria* on this passage.

262 [Cf. *Institutes* 1. 21. pr.–2.]

263 Alciatus, *Consilia* 1. 4, col. 21.

264 Bartolus of Sassoferrato, and others, *On Digest* 1. 1. 9, fol. 10^{r} [*In primam Digesti veteris partem*, in *Opera omnia*, tomus primus, Venetiis, Sexta Editio Iuntarum, 1590].

CHAPTER 6
The Justice of the Romans in Treaties

Now from these victories obtained by the Roman people the Picene Gaul moves on to lodging an accusation against our wicked deceptions in treaty-making. And he complains about the slaughter of the Gauls which Camillus perpetrated in violation of the treaty. And so he hasn't even heard from his own Florus, at least, of the sword that was insolently added to make the weights unequal and the proud utterance "Woe to the conquered" (*Vae victis*).[258] In this, the Gauls themselves were the first to break the treaty. Nor were those who were present at Rome able to make a pact with the Gauls in the absence of Camillus—just as a body cannot undertake any functions without a head. What is that accusation? Nor on the other hand will a head do anything without the rest of the body. The Gauls are not deceived here, nor are other peoples.

"He who will make an agreement with another person either is or ought to be not unaware of that person's condition; otherwise, he would lay the blame at his own door," says the law.[259] The Gauls would lay the blame at their own door if they offered their withdrawal for sale in this way, when they were already wearied with their siege, and did not inquire as to the state of the buyers—who, if they were able to ransom themselves, were nonetheless p. 164
unable to prescribe for Camillus. Furthermore, he who makes an agreement with another party seems to make the agreement in full consideration of that person's quality.[260] What "turning of the cloak inside out" here? Only one that is perfectly licit.[261] Is it not justly said that a contract with a ward from which the guardian is absent is invalid?[262] And that often the contract with a guardian is invalid if the ward is absent? There are 600 cases of this sort.

"Whatever was at Rome," you say, accuser—which I seize upon. For what *was* at Rome? You say, scarcely a thousand men. That is to say, a very small part of the Roman state. And therefore what was arranged with that small part not only did not bind the larger part but didn't even bind the part which made the agreement. For this is the law: that the act of a lesser part of the whole wouldn't bind even that part—as it would have done had action been taken in such a way as to obligate the entire community.[263] Those who are absent need to be summoned, especially in difficult matters of business—especially those who are absent for good reason. Otherwise, not even those present are bound—and those absent are certainly not bound.[264] Who would deny that that was the most difficult business imaginable? Who would deny that the other Romans were absent for an extremely just reason?

Etiam Corsi huc? [a] Qui neque cum consule, sed cum legato fœdus inierunt. Neque par est ratio Romanorum ducum, et aliorum, sed differentia multa per illam clausulam extremi pacti, *Ita id ratum fore, si populus censuisset.* Quæ enim brevicula accusatoris interrogatio est, nihil hic movet, ubi audimus p. 165 cum exceptione illa initum fœdus: sed aliam quæ | stionem movet. Et ei respondemus tamen, Romanos ne tum quidem obligatos futuros, nisi adprobassent fœdus. Quo enim iure procurator obstringit dominum ultra mandatum? [b] Silentio adprobasse non intelliguntur, ea postquam posita clausula est, *Ita id ratum fore*: quæ si posita clausula non esset, potuit silentium populi inducendæ ratihabitioni satis videri. [c] *Nihil interest, facto, vel silentio ratum habuerint.* [d] Silentio et quasi convenitur. Et scientia, et patientia diuturna decennii, negligentia dolus, præsumtus aliter consensus satis vel silentis. [e] Etiam filius exheredatus, si tacet, agnovisse patris censetur iudicium: et ius suum naturæ remisisse. [f] Romani præterea contradixerunt illico his, quæ pepigerunt duces sui. Viden', Picene, differentias? Quid enim illud, si non publico tacito fuit Asdrubalis fœdus observatum? Et ego enim replicarim, quid si publico tacito observatum fuit? Hoc mecum historiæ dicunt. Hoc ostendunt historiæ. Annibal autem sero huic ratihabitioni turbandæ advenit.

At inquis, si pactiones ducum tuorum Romanos non tenent, cur integra ab iisdem omnia non servantur, atque restituuntur? Et vero aliquid esse videtur, quod postulas. Sed a quibus facienda est restitutio? Transvolas ad Samnites. Quid ni igitur et Samnites restituant missionem exercitus nostri sub iugum? p. 166 probra, | elusiones? vulnera inermium, et cædes? [g] *Id enim est integrum, quod ita esset, ut fuisset.* [h] Atque si facta fieri infecta nequeunt: ut Phocylides, Theognis, Simonides, veteres cecinere poetæ, et in leges retulit Tryphoninus iurisconsultus: id quid ad nos? *Restitutio ita facienda est, ut unusquisque in integrum ius suum recipiat.*

Et itaque restituere pro sua parte non potenti nec sane restituitur. [i] Non restituitur aut minori annis, si plena non est et a parte sua restitutio: ut hic a Samnitum parte esse non potest. [j] Non restituitur aut minor, qui locupletior

[a] *Zonara.* [b] *l.* 65. *de leg.* 1. *Ceph. cons.* 272. [c] *Pau.* 1. *sen.* 9. *l.* 51. *loca. Alc.* 8. *cons.* 39.
[d] *Ceph. cons.* 647. *Bal. l.* 32. *de leg. Alc. eo. Dec.* 3. *cons.* 92. [e] *l.* 16. *de inoff. te.*
[f] *Amm.* 25. *P. Diac.* 11. [g] *Hirt. de be. Alex.* [h] *l.* 22. *de capt.* [i] *l.* 27. *de min.*
[j] *l.* 34. *de min.*

---

[265] Zonaras 8. 18. 7–8. [The lieutenant in question was M. Claudius Clineas, for whom no title is preserved; he was at most a *praefectus* appointed by the consul, or a military tribune.]

[266] [Livy 21. 19. 3.] [267] *Digest* 30. 65; Cephalus, *Consilia* 272.

[268] *Digest* 19. 2. 51. pr.; Alciatus *Consilia* 8. 39, col. 1157.

[269] Cephalus, *Consilia* 647; Baldus, *On Digest* 1. 3. 32, fol. 20[v]; Alciatus, *Consilia* 8. 39, col. 1157 [cf. 8. 29, col. 1133]; Decianus, *Consilia* 3. 92, fol. 215[r].

[270] *Digest* 5. 2. 16.

[271] Ammianus Marcellinus 25. 9. 11; Paulus Diaconus, *Historia Romana* 11 [the reference is unclear; *Historia Romana* 4. 17 would suit Gentili's argument].

[272] Hirtius, *De bello Alexandrino* 35. 2.

[273] *Digest* 49. 15. 22. **Translator's note:** Gentili here probably rather means Tryphoninus, *Digest* 49. 15. 12. 2: "Facti autem causae infectae nulla constitutione fieri possunt."

[274] [*Digest* 4. 4. 24. 4.] [275] *Digest* 4. 4. 27.

Do even the Corsicans come in here—the ones who entered upon a treaty not with a consul but with a lieutenant?[265] The procedure of Roman generals and that of others are not alike, but there is a considerable difference made by that little clause at the end of the pact: "It shall be valid if the people should so decide."[266] For that "brief bit of questioning" of the accuser alters nothing here, when we hear that the treaty was entered upon with that qualification, but he goes on to ask another question. Nevertheless we reply to him: the p. 165
Romans were not going to be obligated even then, unless they had approved the treaty. For by what law does a deputy obligate his lord when he goes beyond his commission? They are not understood to have given assent through silence after that little clause ("It shall be valid if . . . "); if that little clause had not been added, the silence of the people would have seemed sufficient for ratification.[267] "It makes no difference whether they have ratified it by action or by silence."[268] "By silence" there is almost an agreement.[269] And just as when a man is silent one can presume his knowledge of something, or a ten-year period of his daily endurance of something, or his negligence, or his deceitfulness, so too, in another way, can the assent of a silent man be sufficiently presumed. Even a disinherited son, if he is silent, is believed to have acknowledged his father's judgment and to have surrendered his own natural right.[270] Moreover, the Romans have immediately contradicted those things their own generals agreed to.[271] Do you see the distinctions here, Picenus? For if the treaty of Hasdrubal was not observed through a public silence, then what was it? And I would reply, what if it *was* observed through public silence? The histories agree with me on this. The histories show this. But Hannibal later came to throw this ratification into confusion.

But you say, "If the pacts of your generals don't obligate the Romans, why don't they preserve and restore everything to its original state?" And indeed there would seem to be something in what you demand. But by whom must restitution be made? You pass quickly over to the Samnites. Why, then, do not the Samnites make good the sending of our army under the yoke, the insults, the mockings, the woundings of the unarmed, the slaughters? "For p. 166
that is in its original state [*integra*] which is as it had been earlier."[272] And if things that have been done cannot be undone, as the old poets Phocylides, Theognis, and Simonides have sung, and as Tryphonius the jurist has applied to laws, what is that to us?[273] "Restitution has to be made in such a manner that each individual gets back his own right in its original condition."[274]

Accordingly, there is no true restitution to someone who does not himself have the power to make restitution with his own best efforts. Nor is there restitution to someone who is a minor, if the restitution is not made in full and with one's best efforts—just as in this case it cannot happen even with the best efforts of the Samnites.[275] Nor is a minor restored to his original

effectus sit: ut hic locupletiores effecti Samnites sunt, satiati calamitatibus hostium. Et hoc enim lucrum est, hosti fecisse male. [a] Non restituitur minor delinquens: ut hic deliquere Samnites: qui adversus suum fœdus probra, vulnera, mortes intulerunt, non contenti armis, vestibus, bonis aliis Romanorum. Quid agetis Samnites? Isthæc ultima, viliaque restituetis? Sed prima illa, et præcipua an vultis? [b] an potestis?

[c] Neque purgatio moræ admittitur, ubi impossibile est, rem reponere in statum pristinum. Vos igitur non restituitis. Vos fœdus illico abrupistis vestrum. [d] At etiam non dati obsides vobis sunt sexcenti? dediti consules, et sponsores reliqui? Et his igitur omnibus contenti esse debetis. Non enim
p. 167 populus Romanus vobis promisit, et veluti fideiussores, ac pi|gnora dedit obsides, et sponsores: quo casu accusare eius infidelitatem possetis, etiam obsidibus, et fideiussoribus in manu exsistentibus vestra. Sed aliqui promiserunt, Romanum populum habiturum ratum, et iidem in hanc suam promissionem tradidere obsides, et se devinxerunt, quod nihil ad populum. Obsides, promissores relinquuntur Samnitibus. Ubi notetur populus? Deditur Samnitibus Postumius, alii deduntur, qui polliciti, futuros se in potestate Samnitum. Si reliquus id pactus esset exercitus: et eum populus non dederet: etiam reprehendere posses populum. Ceterum illud stat certissimum, ut Gallis antea, ita Samnitibus nunc fœdera servari nullo modo oportuisse, qui fœdera non servarunt.

Atque ita de populo: quem tuemur. Nec tamen aut illa Postumii dediti ludibria sunt: ut Picene, credis: ille enim, aut se confecturum fœdus promisit, aut dedititium futurum Samnitum: quæ conventio et ex parte istorum stat: qui, habituros eum dedititium, simul stipulati intelligentur. Et ergo illorum erat Postumius. Hæc tamen ad rem nihil. Stratagema hominis fuerit ad animandos suos. Stratagema iustum est. Dico, neque fuisse quidquam fœderis eius? [e] Aristides utique scripsit, immo cæsas in illis angustiis legiones Romanas, et ipsum Postumium. Dico, Romanorum æquitatem in omnibus
p. 168 his con | tractibus fœderum? Ætolos sane deceptos se verbo uno existimantes restituerunt in integrum.

Sed satisfactum Samnitibus est: et Samnitum patronis. Et defensio hic est, non laudatio Romanorum.

[a] *l. 9. de min.* [b] *Dec. cons.* 73. [c] *Alc.* 8. *cons.* 4.
[d] *Gell.* 17. *c.* 2. *P. D.* 2. [e] *Plut. coll. R. et G.*

---

276 *Digest* 4. 4. 34. 277 *Digest* 4. 4. 9. 2.

278 Decius, *Consilia* 73, fol. 64^{r} [*Consiliorum pars prima*, Lugduni, 1550].

279 Alciatus, *Consilia* 8. 4, col. 1033. **Translator's note:** "Purgation of delay" (*purgatio morae*) in Roman law occurs when someone has failed to meet an obligation on the agreed-upon day, thus falling into default (*mora*), but subsequently attempts to make good the default.

280 Aulus Gellius 17. 2; Paulus Diaconus, *Historia Romana* 2. 9.

281 Ps.-Plutarch, *Parallela Graeca et Romana* 306 c. **Translator's note:** The Aristides in question was the bogus Aristides of Miletus, in the third book of his supposed *Italian Histories*.

condition when he has been made richer[276]—as here the Samnites were made richer, having been sated by the disasters of their enemies. For this, too, is a kind of profit: to have done ill to one's enemy. Nor is a minor who does wrong restored to his original condition[277]—as here the Samnites did wrong, for against their treaty they inflicted insults, wounds, and deaths, not content with the arms, clothes, and other goods of the Romans. What shall you do, Samnites? Will you restore those latter, trivial things? Or do you wish to restore the former, important things? Or are you even able to?[278]

Nor is a purging of the failure to discharge a legal duty on demand (*purgatio morae*) allowed in a case where it is impossible to replace a thing to its pristine state.[279] So you do not restore it to its original state. Rather, you have forthwith broken your own agreement. And yet were not 600 hostages given to you?[280] Were not consuls and other bondsmen given? Therefore, you ought to be content with all these. For the Roman people did not make a promise to you, nor did it give you hostages and bondsmen as sureties and p. 167
pledges as it were—had that been the case, you would indeed have been able to accuse them of injustice, even while hostages and bondsmen were in your power. But others promised that the Roman people would ratify this, and these are the ones who handed over hostages in confirmation of this promise of theirs and obligated themselves—which has no bearing on the people as a whole. Hostages and sureties are left behind with the Samnites. Where would the people be censured here? Postumius was handed over to the Samnites; others were handed over—and they promised that they would remain in the power of the Samnites. If the rest of the army had agreed to this, and the people had not handed him over, you would indeed be able to reproach the people. But this stands fixed: that as with the Gauls earlier, so with the Samnites now, treaties ought in no way be observed, for they themselves did not observe treaties.

So much for the people, whose cause I am defending. Nor was that matter of the handing over of Postumius a mockery, as you believe, Picenus. For he promised that he would either arrange a treaty or he would be surrendered to the Samnites—which agreement stands firm also on their side, for when they will have him as a surrendered captive they will know that they themselves are at the same time under an obligation. And therefore Postumius was theirs. But this is irrelevant. The man's stratagem was aimed at putting heart into his men. The stratagem is justified. But I ask, was there anything to that treaty at all? Aristides, in fact, wrote that the Roman legions were cut down in those defiles—and Postumius himself among them.[281] Do I proclaim the justice of the Romans in all these transactions of treaty-making? Indeed, judging that p. 168
they had deceived the Aetolians in the case of just one word, they made restitution to the original situation.

But justice has now been rendered to the Samnites and their supporters. And this is a defense, not an encomium of the Romans.

Caussæ belli Samnitici, et aliorum Italiæ.
CAP. VII

Videamus igitur caussam belli Samnitici, et aliorum per Italiam: quæ gesta sunt post primum a libera civitate, et pro libertate confectum: a quo in Samniticum, hac digressione de Romanis victis, et de Romanis perfidis, quasi saltu aliquo magno transiliit accusator. Decet enim adfirmare gravissimorum virorum testimonium: qui, arma nunquam, nisi iustis de causis, sumta a Romanis, tradunt.

[a] Bellum contra Auruncos fuit: ad quos oppida Romanorum, coloniæ Latinæ defecerunt, Pomœtia, et Cora. [b] Contra Latinos bellum susceptum: *qui æmulatione, et invidia Tarquinios asserebant: ut populus, qui foris dominabatur, saltem domi serviret.* Contra Volscos itum: qui auxilia comparaverunt, quæ Latinis mitterent: et contra eosdem non stantes paci petitæ, et impetratæ, at Hernicosque, et vicinas alias gentes in societatem belli concientes, bellatum rursus: Rursus contra Auruncos: qui agrum bello amissum extorquere Romanis volebant, et in fines Romanos cum exercitu festinabant.

p. 169 [c] Bellum | cum Æquis tum fuit: qui Auruncis, et Volscis se iunxerant. Non tibi iustæ bellorum caussæ istæ videntur? defensionis suarum rerum? defensionis sui? et sive defensionis, sive vindicationis adversum eos, qui non induerunt modo hostilem animum, sed aperuerunt etiam iunctis cum hoste consiliis, eique armis, et auxiliis comparatis? [d] Bellum, quod iidem Volsci, ducente exsule Romano, intulerunt, quam habuit caussam? nempe, quod agrum bello captum reddere Romani noluerunt. Et cum Hernicis ita bellatum, qui Volscis se adiunxerunt, et in Romanos arma moverunt. Qui negabant sibi cum Romanis fœdus, ictum cum Tarquinio. Qui negarunt dedere prædatores Romani agri. Horum rebelliones vicinorum assiduæ, et quotidianæ sic exercuerunt sine intermissione per annos amplius ducentos populum nostrum.

Fuit bellum contra Veientes: qui Romanis res repetentibus non satis pro iure faciunt. [e] Et contra alios mox Etruscos: qui cum Veientibus fuere: qui et

[a] *Liv.* 2. [b] *Flor.* 1. [c] *Diony.* 8.
[d] *Dionys.* 8. [e] *Dion.* 9. 10. *Liv.* 4.

---

282 Livy 2. 16. 8–9.
283 Florus 1. 11. 1.
284 Dionysius of Halicarnassus 8. 16. 3.
285 Dionysius of Halicarnassus 8. 1. 2.

CHAPTER 7
The Cause of the Samnite War and of Other Wars of Italy

Let us examine, then, the cause of the Samnite War and of others throughout Italy which were waged after the first war that was brought to completion by the free state and on behalf of its freedom—from which our accuser has as if by a great leap jumped to the Samnite War in this digression of his about the Romans in defeat and the Romans as perfidious. For it is fitting to affirm the testimony of the most serious men, who record that the Romans never took up arms except in just causes.

There was a war against the Aurunci, to whom towns of the Romans, Latin colonies, Pometia and Cora, defected.[282] War was undertaken against the Latins, "who through rivalry and ill will were defending the cause of the Tarquinii, so that the people who were holding sway abroad would at least be under subjection at home."[283] An attack was made on the Volscians, who prepared auxiliaries to send to the Latins, and when they did not abide by the peace which they had sought and procured, but stirred up the Hernicians and other neighboring peoples into a war alliance, war was waged against them again. War was also waged against the Aurunci again, who wished to wrest from the Romans land which they had lost in the earlier war, and who were bursting into the Roman boundaries with an army.

Next there was a war with the Aequi, who had allied themselves with the p. 169
Aurunci and Volscians.[284] Do not these reasons for war seem just to you: defense of one's own things, or self-defense, or defensive or punitive measures against those who have not only taken on a hostile attitude but have even manifested it by joining plans with an enemy and having furnished arms and auxiliaries to him? The war which these same Volscians waged, with a Roman exile as leader—what cause did it have?[285] Indeed, it was that the Romans did not wish to hand back territory captured in war. And war was waged with the Hernicians in the same way, for they allied themselves with the Volscians and moved their arms against the Romans. They denied that the treaty which had been struck with Tarquin was in effect for them with the Romans as well. They said they wouldn't hand over plunderers of Roman soil. The constant and daily rebellions of these neighbors wore out our people without a break for more than two hundred years.

There was a war against the people of Veii, who did not meet the demands for redress made by the Romans in conformity with the (fetial) law. And soon there was war against the other Etruscans who were with the people of Veii

quietos Veientes concitarunt in Romanos denuo. Veientes hostes anniversarii: donec rapti funditus, deletique fuerunt. Fidenas, Romanam coloniam occuparunt: legatos Romanos per extremum scelus interfecerunt: et idem scelus abominandum, cædem hominum sanctissimorum, iterum minitantur.
p. 170 Fera pectora: quibus toties par|sum: quibus seditione laborantibus intestina, itaque deprecantibus bellum, tributæ induciæ. Immanissimam barbariem reliquorum Etruscorum: [a] qui urbis, iam quadringentesimum annum vicinæ, oppressæ ab hoste inusitato, inauditoque, adeo nihil miserti sunt, ut in agrum Romanum eo tempore facerent incursiones, plenique prædæ Veios etiam, præsidium, et spem ultimam Romani nominis, cuperent oppugnare. Sic Romanæ clementiæ, longæ in Veientes patientiæ, liberalitati incredibili cum Faleriis pueris, curæ rerum Clusinorum usque ad ruinas nostrarum, repensum a cognatis istorum est. [b] Sed et iidem Etrusci mox concitant bellum maius, concitis pervicacissimis hostibus Volscis, aliisque: ut ne respirandi quidem momentum haberemus a Gallica tum vix repulsa clade suprema.

[c] Tum et Latini animos tollunt: qui tamen centum annorum pace sic nobis obnoxii, ut ne quidem ad defensionem tractare arma iniussu nostro valerent: sed tum, contemtu urbis incensæ ius civitatis, partem imperii, ac magistratuum poscebant pari imperio. His et Sabini se iunxerant, fœderum, et adfinitatum ipsi quoque immemores. Latinis bellum faciunt iidem Etrusci: atque adeo faciunt nobis, quibus Latini obnoxii erant: ut dixi: et Volscos illos,
p. 171 et Æquos nostros hostes æternos, sibi socios addunt, atque alios, | qui magnis semper votis adversus civitatis nostræ incolumitatem ferebantur. Antea nec reddiderant Romanis res: nec milites dederunt, in angustiis summis, quos dare ex fœdere tenebantur.

[d] Caussa hæc raptarum rerum, nec redditarum, caussa belli rursum in Hernicos, Tyburtes, Tarquinienses, Privernates, Veliternos, Cærites. Tyburtes hoc amplius præstitere se hostes, quod Romanis militibus, a bello Hernico redeuntibus, portas occluserint. Tarquinienses immane facinus ausi, Romanos trecentos amplius, bello captos, quasi pecudes, immolarunt. Pri-

[a] *Liv.* 5. [b] *Liv.* 6.
[c] *Flor.* 1. [d] *Liv.* 7.

---

[286] Dionysius of Halicarnassus 9. 18; Livy 4. 58 [Livy does not really support Gentili's claim].
[287] Livy 5. 45. 4. [Gentili's language is largely taken over directly from Livy here.]
[288] Florus 1. 14. 1–3; 1. 15. 1–3.

and who freshly stirred up those peaceful people of Veii against the Romans.[286] Every year the people of Veii were enemies, until they were seized from the ground up and destroyed. They occupied Fidenae, a Roman colony, killed Roman ambassadors in a extreme act of wickedness—and threatened to perform for a second time the same abominable crime, the murder of men protected by the most holy sanctions. Savage souls—men who had been spared so often; men to whom truces were granted when they were suffering under p. 170
internal discord and were begging off war. Oh, the most monstrous barbarity of the other Etruscans, who, so far from pitying a city which had been their neighbor for 400 years, now, when it was being attacked by an outlandish and unheard-of enemy [the Gauls], they chose that moment to make incursions into Roman territory and laden with booty even wanted to besiege Veii, the citadel and last hope of the Roman name. Thus was Roman clemency, her long patience towards the people of Veii, her incredible generosity with the Falerian children, and her care for the affairs of Clusium, even to the point of the ruin of our own affairs, repaid by their kin.[287] But these same Etruscans soon stirred up a greater war, having stirred up our most wicked Volscian enemies and others as well, so that we might not catch our breath even for a moment after the recent Gallic calamity which at that time had just been beaten back.

Then the Latins were encouraged too—people who for a hundred years of peace were so subservient to us that they didn't have the power to take up arms in their own defense without our orders; but at this time, through contempt for a city which had been burned, they demanded the right of citizenship, a portion of rule, and a share on equal terms in magistracies. The Sabines as well had allied themselves to them, they themselves likewise forgetful of treaties and bonds by marriage.[288] And the same Etruscans made war upon the Latins—and upon us as well, to whom the Latins were subservient, as I have said; and they added to their side those Volscians and Aequi, our eternal enemies, and others as well, who were swept along by the great vows that p. 171
they always made against the safety of our state. Earlier, they had failed to make restitution of property to the Romans, nor did they in the most extreme crises send the soldiers whom they were by treaty obligated to send.

This motive of things seized and not restored was in turn the cause of war against the Hernici, the Tiburtes, the Tarquinians, the Privernates, the Veliterni, and the people of Caere. The Tiburtes showed themselves even more hostile by the fact that they shut their gates to Roman soldiers when they were returning from the Hernician war. The Tarquinians dared a monstrous crime when they slaughtered over 300 Romans captured in war,

vernates, Veliterni incursione repentina vastant agrum nobis, in alia, et difficillima bella occupatis Cæritibus, qui et in bello Tarquiniensibus contra nos socii fuere, bellum remissum statim, et induciæ datæ in annos centum: sic remunerantes mei hospitium vestalibus, et sacerdotibus nostris habitum Cære: *ut maleficii potius, quam beneficii immemores essent*: inquit Livius. Hæc virtus, hæc, quam nullibi in terris, nisi Romæ repereris.

Undique et vitia alia, et crimen ingratitudinis experta Roma. Quis crederet, et Faliscos futuros hostes? At cum Tarquiniensibus iuventus eorum militavit: et qui Falerios victi perfugerant, ii redditi nobis non sunt. Quis crederet, adhuc Volscos futuros hostes, toties victos, cæsos, captos, sub iugum missos?
p. 172 Ferocior ad rebel|landum, quam ad bellandum gens (ut ait Livius) Latium circumit, et tentat universum, et in nos proritat. [a] Obstupescit idem auctor, unde his sic afflictis vires suffecerint, et milites. Ego sane obstupesco, unde animi fuerint adeo immites, et feri, ut perire maluerint millies, quam sub præstantioribus conservari.

At nunc de iustitia potissimum disputamus: et gradatim venimus ad Samnites. Invenimus vero nihil, in quo non iustitia, et virtus omnis Romanorum eluceat. Bellum porro pro Campanis contra Samnites suscipi a Romanis oportuisse, quid vetat? Movet duas rationes Picenus, alteram, quod ipsi Romanimet, suscipi non oportuisse existimarunt in Sidicinorum caussa pari: alteram, quod hostes fœderatorum victos, iam iam capiendos, Romani capere defendendos contra fœderatos non debuerunt. [b] Respondeo, *nec concedi quidem posse, ut amicis nostris accusantibus non etiam alienissimos defendamus, et ut adversariis amicorum nostrorum de iure consulentibus non respondeamus*.

Sed et quod de fera inducit vulnerata, immo nihil valere hic habet. Et immo ipse renarrem diversam plerorumqe sententiam: quæ et recepta probato iure Iustiniani est: laudata est laudato iure. Nego autem, contrariam Trebatii adfirmatam moribus. Et de his fuit docendum accusatori. [c] Nam est
p. 173 verius, non esse necesse, ut | interpreti iuris dicenti de consuetudine testimonium credatur. Immo enim neque credetur pluribus: non certe testantibus adeo indefinite.[d] Apagete doctores (ait Alciatus) consuetudinarii: ordinariis

[a] *Liv. 6.* [b] *Cic. pro Mure.* [c] *Ias. l.* 42. *de legi. Ceph. cons.* 299. *Alc.* 5. 24. 39.
[d] *Alc.* 5. *cons.* 25.

289 [Livy 7. 20. 8.]
290 [Cf. Livy 7. 16. 2.]
291 Livy 6. 12. 2.
292 Cicero, *Pro Murena* 8.
293 Jason Maynus [Giasone del Mayno], *On Digest* 1. 3. 32 [*In Primam Digesti Veteris Partem Commentaria*, Venetiis, Apud Iuntas, 1579, fol. 19ᵛ f.]; Cephalus, *Consilia* 299; Alciatus, *Consilia* 5. 24, col. 512; 5. 39, col. 541.

like cattle. The Privernates and the Veliterni lay waste to our territory in a sudden incursion at a time when we were occupied by other very difficult wars. For the people of Caere, who were themselves allies in war to the Tarquinians against us, the war was immediately suspended and a hundred-year truce was granted; thus my people paid back the hospitality which was shown our vestals and priests at Caere: "so that they might prove more willing to forget an injury than an act of kindness," as Livy put it.[289] *This* is a virtue you will find nowhere on earth but in Rome.

Everywhere Rome experienced, in addition to other wrongs, the crime of ingratitude. Who would believe that the Faliscans would become enemies? But their youth served in arms alongside the people of Tarquinia, and our men who had fled in defeat to the Falerii were not returned to us.[290] Who would believe that the Volscians would still become our enemies, after they had been so many times beaten, cut down, captured, and sent under the yoke? A people more savage in rebelling than in waging war (as Livy says), they go p. 172
all around Latium and make trial of the whole region and incite it against us. The same author was amazed as to whence these peoples who had been so afflicted could still derive resources and soldiers.[291] I myself certainly am amazed as to where they got spirits so savage and wild that they would prefer to perish a thousand times over rather than be saved under their superiors.

But now it is chiefly about justice that we are disputing, and so by steps we have arrived at the Samnites. In fact we find nothing in which the justice and utter virtue of the Romans does not shine forth. Moreover, who denies that the Romans ought to have undertaken war against the Samnites on behalf of the Campanians? Picenus advances two arguments. One is that even the Romans themselves judged that they ought not to have gotten involved in the cause of the Sidicini. The other is that the Romans ought not to have taken on as allies to be defended people who were the enemies of allies and were on the very verge of being captured. I answer that: "it cannot be allowed that we be forbidden to defend even utter strangers when our friends are accusing them, and that we may not respond to the enemies of our friends when they justly seek our help."[292]

But what he brings up with regard to a wounded animal has absolutely no validity here. And indeed I could myself list many a contrary judgment of a large number of people which has been received when the law of Justinian has been approved and has been praised when that law has been praised. But I deny that the dissenting opinion of Trebatius has been affirmed by custom. Our accuser needs to be taught about these matters as well. For it is very true that there is no necessity to trust an interpreter of the law who utters p. 173
testimony concerning custom.[293] For indeed one does not even trust many—no, indeed—who offer testimony that is so very indefinite. Away with the doctors of customary law, says Alciatus; let us stand firm with the

stemus, et iuri certo. Minus autem nunc est necesse eidem credere interpreti de iure dicenti, et neque legem, neque rationem, neque auctoritatem afferenti. Magnus sit Galliæ iurisconsultus Cuiacius: et Gallia causidicos doceat facunda Britannos. Non tamen magnus est ille iurisconsultus: certe non adeo magnus, qui et sedeat inter Romanos iurisconsultos, ac Cæsares, inter Trebatios, Caios, Iustinianos, Fridericos: et iudicet quasi Pythius Apollo absque verbo uno addito, quo sententia abs se lata pro parte numeri minoris, minoris auctoritatis, minoris dignitatis, hoc est pro Trebatio, et Friderico, vel tenuiter subornetur. Cephalus hoc tentat. Conficit rationes, per quas defendi posse Trebatii videatur opinio. Sed eæ ut vulgaribus quibusdam innituntur enunciatis, levissimi prorsus sunt momenti. Pro actu est potentia proxima actui: et id genus aliæ. Quibus quis non respondeat absque ulla aut difficultate, aut mora? [a]*Actus actum, potentia potentiam proprie significat*, &c. Sed neque confisus his Cephalus est: neque his est immoratus accusator. Ad sententiam p. 174 omnium iurisconsultorum uterque transvolant. | Quam et sic esse contendunt: ut, si certum sit, effugere feram non posse, fera immo adiudicari debeat vulneranti, et persequenti. Qua de interpretatione si litem moveo, eam quoque ostendam non bonam. At quæro, si certitudinem valeant istam explicare. Nam evaserunt nobis sæpe animalia mortifice vulnerata, et iam moribunda, atque morientia. Quæro ad ipsam rem nostram, si certitudo hæc ostendi in bello possit. [b]*Multa cadunt inter calicem, supremaque labra.* Quod bellica fors valde probat. [c] Ea plerumque anceps: et magnus numerus a paucissimis, et potentiores ab imbecillioribus sæpe sunt superati. [d]*Multa dies in bello conficit unus. Et rursus multæ fortunæ forte recumbunt. Haudquaquam quemque semper fortuna secuta est*: inquiebat pater Ennius. Et plurima sunt huius generis apud omnes. [e]*Mars sæpe spoliantem iam, et exsultantem perculit ab abiecto*: ait Cicero. [f]*Parvæ occasiones magnos motus, et mutationes habent*: Demosthenes. [g]*Sæpe usu venit, ut qui maiores copias haberent ab imbecillioribus vincerentur: et qui urbem obsederant, ab obsessis interirent*: Isocrates. [h]*Multi iam parta victoria maximis cladibus affecti sunt*: tuus, Picenæ, Polyenus: [i]*Sæpe minor manus, dum metuit, maiorem præ contemtu parum instructam profligavit*: Thucydides.

[a] *Bal. l.* 1. *C. de inst.* [b] *Heracl. de polit.* [c] *Herodi.* 8.
[d] *Macr.* 6. *Sat.* 2. [e] *Cic. pro Milo.* [f] *Demosth. Leptin.*
[g] *Isocr. Archid.* [h] *Polye.* 3. [i] *Thucyd.* 2.

294 Alciatus, *Consilia* 5. 25, cols. 512 f. 295 Baldus, *On Code* 4. 25. 1.

296 Heraclides Lembus, *De politiis, sive rerumpublicarum descriptiones*, p. 270, in *Aeliani de varia historia libri XIIII*, Basileae, Ex officina I. Oporini, 1548, pp. 261–80. [These are fragments of excerpts of Aristotle's constitutions of Greek city-states, which were published in Gentili's day in Latin under the title *De politiis*. The Latin form of the proverb cited can also be found in Erasmus' *Adagia*; the Greek is from an epigram by Palladas in the *Greek Anthology* 10. 32.]

297 Herodian 8. 3. 5. 298 Macrobius, *Saturnalia* 6. 2. 16.

299 Cicero, *Pro Milone* 21. 300 Demosthenes, *In Leptinem* 162.

301 Isocrates, *Archidamus* 40. 302 Polyaenus, *Strategemata* 3. 9. 2.

303 Thucydides 2. 11. 4.

regular doctors and with fixed law.[294] But it is now even less necessary to put trust in that interpreter speaking about the law who affirms neither law nor reason nor authority. Let it be granted that Cujas is a great jurist of France, and granted that eloquent France might teach British lawyers. Nonetheless, that doesn't make him a great jurist—certainly not so great as to sit among the Roman jurists, among the emperors, and people like Trebatius, Gaius, Justinian, and Frederick; and that he might pass judgment like Pythian Apollo and without a single word being added by which an opinion delivered by him might be even tenuously suborned on behalf of a party of inferior weight, inferior authority, inferior dignity—that is, on behalf of Trebatius and Frederick. So Cephalus treats of this matter. He has put together reasonings by which the opinion of Trebatius might seem to be able to be defended. But since these reasonings rest upon certain vulgar presuppositions, they are of thoroughly trivial weight. "A power is very close to an act"—and other things of that sort. Who would not respond to these claims without any difficulty or delay? "An act signifies an act; a power properly signifies a power," etc.[295] But Cephalus does not even rely on these things, nor did the accuser linger over them. Both take refuge in the opinion of all the jurists— p. 174
which they claim is as follows: that, if it be certain that the beast cannot escape, it ought to be assigned to the one who wounded and went in pursuit of it. But if I take issue with that opinion, I shall show that it, too, is no good.

But I ask if they have the power to establish that purported certainty. For often animals that have been mortally wounded and are already dying have been able to escape us. And in particular reference to our actual subject, I ask if this certitude could be shown in a war. "Many a slip between cup and lip."[296] This is something the luck of war proves true. This luck is more often than not uncertain, and a great multitude has often been overcome by a very few, and the more powerful by the weaker.[297] "A single day in a war has brought about many things. And many fortunes sink back again by chance. Scarcely ever has good luck pursued the same man forever," as father Ennius said.[298] And there are many reflections of this sort among all the authors. "Mars often strikes down by the hand of the fallen the man who is already despoiling his foe and exulting over him," says Cicero.[299] "Small occasions have major changes and transformations," said Demosthenes.[300] "It often happens in practice that those who have superior forces are defeated by those who are weaker. And those who have besieged a city have perished at the hands of the besieged."[301] "Many have been struck with the greatest disasters at the very moment when victory has been obtained"—that's your Polyaenus, Picenus.[302] "Often an inferior force, under the influence of fear, has overthrown a larger force which has been laxly drawn up out of contempt"—Thucydides.[303]

p. 175 Etiam nec solutam, at bene instructam dicimus quoque. Nescimus telum | vehementissimum, necessitas, et desperatio? *Sæpe desperatio præstat, quod nequit virtus.* Nescimus, *Una salus victis, nullam sperare salutem?* [a] Sane sic desperatio, non illa deiecta quidem, et vilis, sed quæ furorem animis addit, et rabiem, et tenax propositum inulti non moriendi. [b]

Nobilis ille locus apud Trogum est: ubi Crotoniensium centum viginti millia quindecim millibus Locrensium acie superantur. Qui paucitatem suam circumspicientes, omissa spe victoriæ, in destinatam mortem conspirant: tantusque ardor ex desperatione singulos cepit, ut victores se putarent, si non inulti morerentur. Sed dum mori honeste quærunt, feliciter vicerunt. Nec alia caussa victoriæ fuit, quam quod desperaverunt. Et id genus plurima sunt exempla. Illic apud Trogum et de his ipsis Crotoniensibus est: qui post cladem istam, et consecutum otium pauci magno, et victori exercitui alteri fortiter restiterunt. *Tantum virtutis paupertas adversus insolentes divitias habet: tantoque insperata interdum sperata victoria certior est.*

Cum desperatis istis, præceptum militare sic est, non pugnare. [c] Hoc illud Scipionis cum Numantinis: qui destinata morte in prælium ruerent, *Intellectum ab imperatore consilium: itaque non est permissa pugna morituris.* Præceptum alterum militare est, spem istis præbere aliquam: quos vincere
p. 176 prœlioque velis. Quid | nunc dicimus et exempla huius fortunæ variantis? Primo Punico bello num floruit res Punica magis, quam cum victi illi et prælio, et bello sunt? Aut de secundo quid recitem? [d]*Propius exitio fuerunt, qui vicere: et si quis conferat damna utriusque, similior victo videbitur populus, qui vicit.* [e] Atque Scipio generaliter, idem quod de Lucilio recitabas, Picene, *Magnis omnibus bellis victi vicimus.* Atque sic Dionysius, pressus obsidione a Pœnis, suis invisus, tamen vicit, quod Isocrates notat. [f] Atque sic ille alter de eodem quasi nido, cum tueri iam nequiret mœnia sua, obsidet obsessorum suorum muros: et itidem vincit. [g] Sic Dion de eodem, instructus navi una prævaluit tyranno potentissimo. Sic exsul Thrasybulus sexaginta comitatus viris contra vim, atque imperium potuit Lacedæmoniorum. Sexcenta hæc sunt.

[a] *Iacch. probl.* 65. *Bal. l. i.* C. *de eunuch.*
[b] *Iustin.* 20. [c] *Flor.* 2. [d] *Liv.* 21. *Flo.* 2.
[e] *Liv.* 26. [f] *Iustin.* 22. [g] *Plut. de vi. be. Ath.*

---

304 [Vergil, *Aeneis* 2. 354.]

305 Leonardus Jacchinus [Leonardo Giachini], *Quaestionum naturalium libellus*, Lugduni, Apud Seb. Gryphium, 1540, pp. 30 f.; Baldus, *On Code* 4. 42. 1.

306 Justin 20. **Translator's note:** Justin 20. 3; 20. 5. The Crotoniates' victory was against Dionysius of Syracuse.

307 Florus 2. 18. 12 f.

308 Livy 21. 1. 2; Florus 2. 6. 1.

309 Livy 26. 41. 9.

310 Justin 22. 4. 1–2.

311 *Plut. de vi. be. Ath.* **Translator's note:** Plutarch, *De gloria Atheniensium*; however, there is no reference to Dion in this essay. What must be meant instead is Plutarch, *Dion* 22.

We would add that sometimes an inferior band also overthrows one that is not lax, but well drawn up. Don't we know that necessity and desperation are p. 175 the mightiest weapons? "Often desperation furnishes what courage cannot do." Don't we know that "there is one salvation for the defeated: not to hope for any salvation."[304] Indeed, this is true desperation—not that downcast and base one, indeed, but that which adds rage to our spirits and a kind of madness and a firm determination not to die unavenged.[305]

That is a fine passage in Pompeius Trogus, where 120,000 Crotoniates are overcome in battle by 15,000 Locrians, who looking about at their small numbers, having lost all hope of victory, join together for a death they have chosen; and such ardor arising from desperation seized each one that they fancied themselves victors if they should not die unavenged. But when they sought to die honorably, they had the luck to win a victory. Nor was there any other cause of victory than that they had lost all hope. And there are very many examples of this sort of thing. And right there in that passage of Trogus we read about those same Crotoniates: that after that slaughter and the peace that followed, a few of them held out against another great and victorious army. "So much courage does poverty possess against insolent riches; and so much more certain, sometimes, is an unhoped-for victory than one that has been expected."[306]

It's a military maxim not to fight with those who are desperate. The story of Scipio and the Numantines shows this: when they were rushing into battle having settled upon death, "their plan was grasped by the commander; accordingly, he refused to give battle to those who were determined to die."[307] It is another military maxim to offer some hope to those whom you wish to defeat in war. Why do we now mention examples of this shifting p. 176 fortune? In the First Punic War did the Carthaginians' affairs flourish more than when they were defeated both in battle and in the war? Or why should I mention the Second Punic War? "Those who triumphed were the ones who were closest to destruction; and if anyone were to compare the losses of each side, the people who won will be seen to be similar to the defeated."[308] And Scipio might generally say what you recited from the poet Lucilius, Picenus: "Having been defeated in all our great wars, we have emerged victorious."[309] And thus Dionysius, besieged by the Carthaginians, hated by his own people, nonetheless triumphed, as Isocrates notes. And thus that other one [Agathocles], from the same nest as it were, when he was not able to protect his own walls, besieges the walls of his besiegers and in like manner triumphs.[310] Thus Dion, from the same place, outfitted with but one ship, prevailed over a very powerful tyrant.[311] Thus the exile Thrasybulus, accompanied by sixty men, prevailed against the power and empire of the Spartans. There are 600 examples of this sort.

Monstra in bello fiunt magis, maioraque, quam in ulla parte naturæ. *Num capti potuere capi? num incensa cremavit Troia viros?* Mitte, accusator, tuum iam capiendos. Quæro etiam, si alios advocare Campani non potuissent iisdem conditionibus: qui se tutari a Samnitibus potuissent? Defuissent Etrusci consanguinei, vicini Græci, Pœni avari. Quanta igitur spes illa Samnitum erat: quibus de mediis rapta faucibus præda intelligatur? [a] Neque
p. 177 enim inspicitur, aut consideratur, quod speratur, et fieri potest, nisi certum | hoc idem sit, et infallibile: ut idem scribit Cephalus.

Atque audis, accusator, valide, et varie responsum esse rationi tuæ posteriori. Simul et intelligis, opinor, hinc infirmitatem prioris. Nam si potuerunt Romani ferre Campanis auxilia, etiam Sidicinis potuissent iure. Iure inquam: ut de iure disputatio nostra est. Etenim concedam tibi, noluisse meos Sidicinis opitulari. Ultima tamen non solum necessitate horum erat extorta deditio: sed et sera fuit. Seram deditionem aspernantur patres: nam petitum iam, et impetratum per Samnites, ut sibi ab Romanis belli ius liberum adversus Sidicinos foret. Ita, quem hic sequeris, Livius. At cape, quod tibi fateor aliud. Tantæ non fuerunt Sidicinorum opes, quantæ Campanorum. Sed num tu putas, bellum sic suscipi oportere pro aliis, ut nihil cogitemus pro nobis ipsis? Primum, non tenemur esse aliis auxilio, si hinc nobis creetur periculum. Deinde, piscari aureo hamo, stultum est. Aliis tamen et fuere auxilio mei, Fabretanis, Lucanis contra eosdem Samnites, nostris dedititiis. Hoc mihi notes verbum. Ut enim Florus scribit, erat quidem fœdus cum utrisque, cum Samnitibus, et Campanis. *Sed hoc Campani sanctius, et prius, omnium suorum deditione, fecerunt.*

An tibi iam respondi ad omnia de Samnitico bello? An illud adhuc super-
p. 178 est unum de interesse, et damnis | Samnitum: quæ debeant Romani semper, etsi a Campanis suscipiendis abstinere non debuissent? Sed huic parti respondetur brevissime: sic ius esse adversus eum, qui alteri capiendas intercipit feras: adversus eum, qui alteri capiendos intercipit prædones. Nullum enim tuetur ius feras, nullum prædones. Sed Campanos tuetur belli ius, et

[a] *Ceph. cons.* 3.

---

312 [Vergil, *Aeneis* 7. 295–6: Juno's frustration over the survival of the Trojan exiles.]
313 Cephalus, *Consilia* 3.
314 [Livy 8. 2.]
315 **Translator's note:** According to Suetonius (Aug. 25 ad fin.) this was a saying of Augustus, the idea being that one tends to lose a lot of hooks when one fishes, so to fish with a golden hook would mean to risk more than any fish one might catch is worth.
316 [Florus 1. 16. 2.]

Amazing things occur in war with greater frequency and magnitude than in any other part of nature. "Couldn't captured men stay captured? Couldn't burned Troy have burned its men?"[312] Give up, accuser, your rant about people [the Campanians] "already on the verge of being captured." I even ask this: if the Campanians could not summon in others under the same terms, then how could they have protected themselves against the Samnites? Their kin the Etruscans, their neighbors the Greeks, the avaricious Carthaginians all let them down. Therefore, however great was the hope of the Samnites, whose should be judged the prey that was snatched from their jaws? For that which is hoped for and which may happen is not actually looked at and examined unless this same thing is absolutely certain and infallible, as the p. 177
same Cephalus writes.[313]

And so you hear, accuser, that your later argument has been powerfully and diversely answered. At the same time, you grasp from this, I believe, the weakness of your earlier argument. For if the Romans were able to bring aid to the Campanians, they were as a matter of law able to bring aid to the Sidicini as well. As a matter of law, I say—for our dispute is about law. And yet I will grant to you that my people did not wish to aid the Sidicini. But their surrender was not only extorted from them at their most extreme moment of crisis; it also came late. The senators rejected a tardy surrender; for the Samnites had already requested and been granted that they be allowed by the Romans a free right of war against the Sidicini. Thus writes Livy, whom you are following.[314] But grasp another thing I admit to you. The wealth of the Sidicini was not as great as that of the Campanians. But surely you don't suppose that a war should be undertaken for others in such a way that we give no thought to ourselves? In the first place, we are not bound to be of aid to others if danger is to be created for us from this. Next, it is stupid to go fishing with a gold hook.[315] Nonetheless, my people came to the aid of the Fabretani and the Lucanians, who had capitulated to us, against the Samnites. You should note my words here. For as Florus writes, there was a treaty with both the Samnites and the Campanians: "But the Campanians made their treaty holier and more of a priority through the handing over of everything that was theirs."[316]

Have I responded to you with regard to all the points about the Samnite War? Or is there still that question of the advantage and losses of the Samnites, p. 178
which the Romans supposedly always are responsible for, even if it is true that they ought not have abstained from taking on the cause of the Campanians? But let there be just a very brief response to this section of the brief: that this is how the law stands with regard to one who intercepts an animal which was going to be captured by someone else, or one who intercepts brigands who were going to be captured by someone else. For no law protects animals; no law protects brigands. But the law of war does protect the Campanians, as do the

ratio concertationis: ut, victi sententiis, non tenentur ad isthæc tamen, si qua caussa eis exstitit concertandi. Exstitit Campanis iustissima, timor nefarii Samnitum latrocinii.

Atque sic fuit bellum Samniticum, non pro nobis, sed, quod est speciosius, pro sociis nostris. Postea cum illis bellatum adhuc, cum quibus ante toties: cum Latinis, Etruscis, Umbris, Volscis: toties infidis omnibus, atque rebellibus: [a] qui neque bellum, neque pacem pati possent: nec ante quieti, quam expugnati, in deditionem accepti per singulas urbes, et omnino subacti fuissent. Subactos inquam? pro merito cuiusque accepti singuli: et multis civitas elargita. Nam tuis istis Samnitibus quid fecissemus? [b] Fœdera nobis ruperunt sexies: rabie, furore, sacrilegiis, humanis hostiis in exitium nostræ urbis agitati, post annos quinquaginta, post triumphos viginti quatuor semper superbi.

Bella et cum aliis per contagionem Samnitici exstitere: cum Marsis,
p. 179 Pelignis, Satricanis, Vestinis, Ausonibus. Miror de Ausonibus | dictum in accusatione. [c] Immo enim ipse sic scribit Livius, *Quia ducibus absentibus impetus est factus, nullus modus cædibus fuit: deletaque Ausonum gens, vix certo defectionis crimine, perinde ac si internecino bello certasset.* Siccine mutilare etiam testimonia: cum nec fabulas deceat contaminare? Miror, et Calabriam inductam Græci testimonio. [d] An enim verum non est, receptum fuisse Pyrrhum a Calabris? Græcos istos infestasse classibus mare ad usque Tyberis ostia? Cum istis gentibus ad Palæpolim bellum gestum? Per istos a Tarento Romanis abstractos socios Apulos, et Lucanos? Istos crudelissimis Romanorum hostibus favisse Samnitibus? In pace et amicitia desævisse in Romanam classem? Barbarice affecisse contumeliis Romanam legationem?

At iam memoravimus, quod fugit accusator, Italicas gentes omnes: quæ Romanorum armis oppressæ sunt: et gentium iniustitiam, Romanorum ubique iustitiam patefecimus. Quæ eius populi veluti adolescentia fuit: cum

[a] *Liv.* 8. [b] *Ior. de re. su. P. Dia.* 2. *Flor.* 1.
[c] *Liv.* 9. [d] *Liv.* 7. 8. *P. Dia.* 2. *Flor.* 1.

---

[317] **Translator's note:** Gentili's language here is adapted from Florus 1. 16. 1: "Precibus deinde Campaniae motus non pro se, sed eo speciosius pro sociis Samnitas invadit."

[318] Livy 8. 13. 2.

[319] Livy 9. 25. 9. [The "accuser" had omitted the reference to the absence of the generals.]

[320] Livy 7. 8; Paulus Diaconus, *Historia Romana* 2. 11; Florus 1. 18. 6.

rules of the debate: so that, though they may be defeated by legal opinions, they are nevertheless not bound to those conclusions if they have any ground at all for their contention. And the Campanians had the most just ground of all: fear of the wicked brigandage of the Samnites.

And so thus was the Samnite War, one not undertaken on our own behalf, but—something much more respectable—on behalf of our allies.[317] Afterwards war was still waged against those against whom it had been waged so many times: the Latins, the Etruscans, the Umbrians, the Volscians; peoples who had proved themselves faithless and rebellious so often; who could endure neither war nor peace;[318] nor were they ever peaceful until they were utterly beaten down, received into capitulation city by city, and utterly subdued. Subdued, did I say? Individuals of each city were received as a favor, and citizenship was bestowed upon many of them. For what did we do to those Samnites of yours? They broke treaties with us six times over; driven on to the destruction of our city by madness, rage, acts of sacrilege, human sacrifices, they remained insolent after fifty years, after twenty-four triumphs celebrated over them.

Through contagion with the Samnite War, there came about wars with other peoples: with the Marsians, with the Paelignians, with the Satricani, the Vestini, the Ausones. I am amazed at what has been said in the accusation about the Ausones. For the fact is that it is thus that Livy writes: "Given the p. 179 fact that the attack was made in the absence of the generals, there was no moderation to the slaughters; and the people of the Ausones were destroyed, not at all through any certain charge of disloyalty, but just as if they had contended in a murderous war."[319] Is it fitting to mutilate historical testimony in this way, when it wouldn't even be proper to stitch stories together? I am also amazed that Calabria was dragged in on the testimony of a Greek (Zonaras). For is it not in fact true that Pyrrhus was received by the Calabrians?[320] Not true that those Greeks infested the sea with their fleets right up to the mouth of the Tiber? Not true that we had to wage war on those peoples at Palaepolis? Not true that through this people's agency Rome's Apulian and Lucanian allies were taken away from her by Tarentum? Not true that those people favored the Samnites, the Romans' cruelest enemies? Not true that in time of peace and friendship they raged against a Roman fleet? Not true that they harassed in a savage way with insults a Roman embassy?

But now we have made mention of all the Italian peoples (something the accuser avoided doing) who were overwhelmed by Roman arms—and we have laid bare in every instance the injustice of those peoples and the justice of the Romans. This was, as it were, the adolescence of that people, when it

flore virtutis exarsit: [a] et Italiam, post quingentesimum a conditione urbis annum, *lacessentibus assidue usquequaque finitimis*, tot distractam in principatus, et respublicas discordantes coegit tamquam ex variis elementis in corpus unum sub se capite præstantissimo. Nisi tu feros Samnitas caput malueris, aut
p. 180 superbos Campanos, aut Etruscos, | aut alios similes, aut Picenos tuos, et Asculum, et Corfinium. [b] Mei *victis nihil præter iniuriæ licentiam eripiebant.* Meos dico veteres illos, de quibus nunc sermo est. Et id sane dico, Romano teste: sed idoneo: qui de Romanis postumis pari fide, *perinde quasi iniuriam facere, id esset imperio uti.* Nunc igitur a patriis non calamitatibus, sed felicitatibus, alio convertatur oratio: ubi provinciæ factæ, et gentes stipendiariæ, vectigales, et tributariæ sunt.

De bellis Punicis.
CAP. VIII

In Siciliam quæ caussa devexit arma Romana? *Cum viderent opulentissimam in proximo prædam, quodammodo Italiæ suæ abscissam, et quasi revulsam, cupiditate eius iungendæ, et ad continentem suum revocandæ exarserunt. Sed ecce, ultro ipsis viam pandentibus fatis, nec occasio defuit: cum de Pœnorum impotentia fœderata Siciliæ civitas Messana quereretur.* Ita Florus: quem tu, more tuo, mutilum exhibuisti. Exarserunt cupiditate etiam prædæ opulentæ: sed naturali alia adhuc cupiditate, restituendi suo corpori avulsum membrum.

Sed ecce, Florus ait, *nec occasio defuit.* Sit iusta adquirendi caussa, voluntatem nemo vituperaverit. [c] Et quamquam Cyro, et Alexandro datum crimini fuit desiderium istud imperii proferendi: iustitia tamen sine odio est. [d] Non tu de magistris tuis didicisti, bellum pro gloria, et imperio iustum iure gentium
p. 181 esse? et | iustum sic fuisse Romanorum imperium, quod ita crevit? Etiam ad iustam, et rectam dominationem iustum esse bellum didicisses. [e] Huc addidisses, Siciliam istam patriam Cyclopum, nutricem tyrannorum, captivam

[a] *Flor.* 1. 2. [b] *Sallust. Catil.*
[c] *Procop.* 2. *Pers.* [d] *Castr. rep. l.* 5. *de iu. et vi.*
[e] *Oros.* 2. *c.* 14. *Iust.* 4.

---

321 Florus 1. 9. 6.
322 Sallust, *Bellum Catilinae* 12. 4.
323 [Sallust, *Bellum Catilinae* 12. 5.]
324 [Florus 2. 2. 2–3. The quotation from Florus which Gentili offers here is, while fuller than that offered by the "Accusator," likewise truncated.]
325 Procopius, *De bello Persico* 2. 2. 15.
326 Castrensis [Paolo de Castro], *On Digest* 1. 1. 5, fol. 4v.

blazed forth in the bloom of excellence, and after five hundred years from the founding of the city, "when its neighbors were constantly and on every occasion attacking it,"[321] it forced Italy, once torn apart into discordant chiefdoms and states, as though from various distinct elements, into one body under itself as its most excellent head. Unless you would prefer the savage Samnites as the head—or the insolent Campanians, or the Etruscans, p. 180
or others of the sort—or your own Picenes, and Asculum and Corfinium. My people "took nothing from the defeated but their license to do wrong."[322] By "my people" I mean those of ancient times, about whom our discussion is. And indeed I say this with the help of a Roman witness, but a suitable one, one who said with equal trustworthiness of the later Romans that "they make use of empire just as though it were synonymous with wrongdoing."[323] Now, therefore, let the discussion be turned in another direction, away from these—not disasters—but glory days of our ancestors, to the time when provinces were created and peoples were made subject to tributes, taxes, and imposts.

CHAPTER 8
On the Punic Wars

What reason carried Roman arms to Sicily? "Since they saw a very rich prize lying very nearby, which seemed to have been somehow cut off and torn away from their own Italy, they became inflamed with a desire of reattaching it and of summoning it back to their own continent. And lo and behold, the Fates themselves of their own accord opened up a way, nor did an opportunity fail to be at hand, when the city of Messana, allied to Rome, complained of the savagery of the Carthaginians." So Florus, whom you, in your customary way, have reproduced in truncated form.[324] Indeed, they were inflamed by desire for a rich prize, but also by an additional natural desire, that of restoring to their body a limb which had been torn away.

"And lo and behold," says Florus, "nor did an opportunity fail to be at hand." Provided that the reason for acquisition is just, no one will have censured the intention to acquire. And though for Cyrus and Alexander a desire for extending their empires was a matter of reproach, nonetheless justice is alien to ill will.[325] Have you not learned from your teachers that war for glory and empire is just by the law of nations?[326] And that the empire p. 181
of the Romans was thus just because it grew in that way? You would also have learned that a war directed at just and upright domination is just. You would have added to this land that Sicily which was home of the Cyclopes, nurse of

servorum: ubi carnibus hominum primi, cruciatibus medii, mortibus postremi pascebantur. Hanc Siciliam, prædam omnium, armorum externorum semper præmium, Romani non cupiissent a tot monstris, calamitatibusque liberare, et veteri capiti sociare? Et neque tamen se dum commovent. *Sed ecce nec occasio defuit: de Pœnorum impotentia fœderata civitas queritur.* Itaque [a]*Mamertinorum sociorum periculum iusta nobis, ac pia induit arma*: ut ait Scipio. Iusta sane, ac pia: nec quisquam negaverit. At de Floro excipis, speciem quidem istam fuisse iuvandi socios, re autem prædam sollicitasse. Quo de interiori sensu animi disputandum tamen nobis non est. Aperta caussa belli iusta est. Populus autem auxilia Mamertinis decrevit: ut ut sine auctoritate senatus. Ut id est, quod Polybius ait. [b] Nam Livius, etiam a senatu decreta, etsi per contentiones, et dissensiones, narrat. [c] Decreta auxilia et contra Hieronem, et contra Pœnos.

Quid amplius? Decerni non debuerunt flagitiosissimis viris? Scilicet ad nos pertineat, iusti, an iniusti sint, qui nostræ civitatis non sunt. Et opem non
p. 182 ferimus afflictis commu | ni potius iure humanitatis, quam ullo eorum merito singulari. Et hic non etiam occurrebatur impotentiæ Carthaginensium? quos crescere, et quidem vicinos nobis, non expediebat. [d] An tu domi occlusus agis, si ædes vicini ignis ceperit? An tu ignoras, perire nostram nobis utilitatem, qui non respicimus ad vicini? Sic Deus colligare invicem omnes voluit, et hanc rebus hominum imponere necessitatem, ut in proximi utilitate alterius etiam esset colligata, et mundus ita constitutus esset universus: neque enim homines aliter commodum proximi accurassent: et hoc tamen non tam Deus voluit, quam ut ratione humanitatis benevoli omnibus, atque benefici simus. Quæ suo illo ore disserit Chrysostomus aureo.

Sic decreta semper bene auxilia Mamertinis. Sed nec mittebantur decreta auxilia? Sed neque constituta dies erat: intra quam missa esse oporteret. Et res istæ arduæ exercituum comparandorum, classium instruendarum, in civitate tum nec concordi satis, dictæ factæ esse non potuerunt. Hoc est imperii nostri arcanum, quod tu tibi ingeniose fingis, accusator. Nos notemus, quod si ita exarsissent cupidine prædæ Romani mei, utique nec controvertissent de sumendo bellum, nec cunctati essent in apparando, nec lente adeo ad istam
p. 183 cupitam prædandam movissent gradum. Aut qui ardent etiam de|liberare, et torpere valent?

[a] *Liv.* 30. [b] *Liv.* 16. [c] *Plin.* 16. *c.* 29.
[d] *Chrysost.* 1. *Cor. Hom.* 25.

---

[327] Orosius 2. 14; Justin 4. 2.
[328] Livy 30. 31. 4.
[329] Livy, *Periochae* 16.
[330] Pliny 16. 29.
[331] **Translator's note:** Given the context, I take this as a rhetorical question, though it is not marked as such in either edition.
[332] John Chrysostom, *Homily* on 1 Corinthians 11:1.

tyrants, captive of slaves, where the first inhabitants were nourished on the flesh of men, their successors on tortures, the most recent inhabitants on slaughters.[327] Would not the Romans have wished to free this Sicily, the prey of all, ever the prize of foreign arms, from so many monsters and disasters and rejoin it to its ancient head? And yet at the same time they were not bestirring themselves to do this. "And lo and behold, nor did an opportunity fail to be at hand, when the city of Messana, allied to Rome, complained of the savagery of the Carthaginians." Accordingly: "The peril of our allies the Mamertines causes us to don just and pious arms," as Scipio said.[328] "Just and pious" indeed; nor would anyone deny it. But you understand Florus to be saying that while there was indeed the pretext of aiding allies, in actual fact a prize tempted them. But we cannot have a dispute about the inner feelings of a soul. The open cause for the war is just. The Roman people, moreover, decreed aid for the Mamertines, albeit without the authority of the Senate. So Polybius has it. For Livy tells of decrees of the Senate, although passed through disagreements and dissensions.[329] Aid was decreed both against Hieron and against the Carthaginians.[330]

What more? Is it that aid ought not to have been decreed for men of great wickedness? As if it really concerned us whether those who are not part of our state are just or unjust! And do we not bring aid to the afflicted through the p. 182
common law of humanity rather than for any particular merit they may happen to possess?[331] And in this case were we not also opposing the savagery of the Carthaginians? It was not in our best interests that they grow in power—especially since they were our neighbors. Or do you stay shut up in your own house when fire has seized upon your neighbor's house? Or are you unaware that we lose our own profit if we do not pay attention to that of our neighbor?[332] Thus God wished to bring us all together and to place this necessity upon human affairs: that one person's profit might be bound up with that of his neighbor; and the entire world is thus constituted; for men would not otherwise pay attention to what profits his neighbor—and yet it was not so much God who wished this as it is by virtue of the reason of our shared humanity that we might be well-wishers and benefactors of all. This is what Chrysostom treats of with that golden mouth of his.

Thus aid was always properly decreed for the Mamertines. But was the aid that was decreed not being sent? But the day by which it ought to have been sent was not determined. And that difficult business of preparing armies and outfitting fleets, once decreed, could not be carried out in a state that was at that time not sufficiently in agreement with itself. This is that "secret of empire" which you, accuser, cleverly imagine for yourself. Let us observe that if my Romans had really been so inflamed by lust for a prize they would certainly not have been disputing among themselves about undertaking the war, nor would they have been tardy in preparing for it, nor would they have so slowly set steps in motion for snatching that prize they had longed for. Or do those who are aflame have the self-possession to deliberate and be sluggish? p. 183

At Picenus disputat contra Polybium: et, non licuisse, ait, Romanis in eas Siciliæ partes navigare, quæ Pœnis parebant: itaque nec Messanam, quæ iam Pœnis parebat. Belle. [a] Ipsi Pœni sic fœdus violarunt primi: qui auxilio Mamertinis venerunt. Et sic epitome Liviana. Quid enim Pœnis cum sociis, ac fœderatis Romanis erat? Non dubium est, quin fœdera ita fuerint, ut neque Romani navigarent in partes Pœnorum, neque in partes Romanorum Pœni. Aut si isti Siciliam totam occupassent, Romani tota exclusi Siciliæ navigatione exstitissent? Etiam ut amittere illic socios facile possent? Etiam ut metuenda Pœnorum potentia, et vicinitas posset ita augeri, nobis cis fretum religatis? Immo, *Iberum Pœnus ne transito.*

Sed instat accusator, contenditque, discedere debuisse Messana meos, quemadmodum et Carthaginenses discesserunt. Et magnam, et manifestam æquitatem hanc, ait. Cur tamen istud? Improbos Mamertini se, levesque præbuere nobis: qui nostris non exspectatis auxiliis, quæ petierant, et impetrarant, ad Carthaginenses transierunt: ad quos neque transire poterant, quin societatis, ac amicitiæ nostræ ius non violarent; addendo se illis, qui sibi per fœdera iungi nequibant. Fidere Mamertinis postea non potuimus. Fidere illic
p. 184 Pœnis postea non potuimus. [b] Quid? et non | ante etiam fœdus nobis violatum a Pœnis fuit: qui contra nos auxilio Tarentinis fuerunt? Et, cum arguerentur mali eius facinoris, labem periurio accumulaverunt? Tui hæc dicunt testes, Picene.

Sed hic et de Sardinia, hic et de Corsica: altera, quod extorta Pœnis iniquissime: et in id omnes consentire scriptores: altera, quod nec intelligitur, cur subacta sit. Et sic sane de Sardinia Livius, et pleno Polybius ore. Ego autem, quod licet per accusatorem, a scriptoribus istis quæsierim unum, si Carthaginenses ipsi, [c] qui viri acuti fuisse perhibentur, conquesti eam iniquitatem sunt unquam: etiam post quam inferre bellum Romanis sunt ausi? Verisimiliter itaque caussa illic nulla erat: aut ipsi vidissent melius, quam fecerit Livius: qui censet, querelam afferri istam iustam oportuisse.

Age, audi, accusator, aliud. Si duobus his testibus opponere ego quatuor possum, tu quid dices? [d] Sardiniam ego non extortam per fraudem, sed concessam per fœdus cum Lutatio ictum adfirmo, testibus Dione, Diacono tuo, item Orosio, et Sex. Victore. Quod si facit semper non nihil numerus

[a] *Liv.* 14. [b] *Liv.* 14. *ubi Sigon. P. Diac.* 2. *Oros.* 4.
[c] *Cic. acad.* 2. [d] *Dio. ecl. de lega. Dia.* 3. *Oros.* 4. *c.* 12.

---

333 Livy, *Periochae* 14. [Livy is, however, writing about the Tarentines here, as Gentili must know given his next reference, especially given Sigonio's comments referred to therein.]

334 Livy, *Periochae* 14, on which see Sigonius, *Scholia in Livium* [Sigonio, *Opera omnia*, Tomus III, Mediolani, 1733, col. 756]; Paulus Diaconus, *Historia Romana* 2. 14; Orosius 4. 5. 2.

335 Cicero, *Academica* 2. 31. 98.

336 Dio Cassius, *Excerpta de legationibus* [in Fulvio Orsini, *Selecta de legationibus*, Antverpiae, Ex officina Christophori Plantini, 1582, p. 378 (= Dio Cassius frag. 46)]; Paulus Diaconus, *Historia Romana* 3. 2; Orosius 4. 12. 1–4 [cf. 4. 11. 1–3]. [The reference to Sextus Victor is to Ps.-Aurelius Victor, *De viris illustribus urbis Romae* 41. 2.]

But Picenus takes issue with Polybius and says that it was not allowable for the Romans to sail to those parts of Sicily which were subject to the Carthaginians—and thus not to Messana, which was then subject to the Carthaginians. Nicely argued! By this reasoning, the Carthaginians themselves were the first to violate the treaty, for they came to Sicily in aid of the Mamertines. Thus the epitome of Livy.[333] For what business had the Carthaginians with those who were allied and leagued with the Romans? It is not in doubt that the agreements were that neither the Romans should sail to the areas of the Carthaginians nor the Carthaginians to the areas of the Romans. But if those Carthaginians had occupied the whole of Sicily, would the Romans have been shut out of all sailing in Sicily? Would this mean that they would easily abandon their allies there? Would this mean that the feared power and closeness of the Carthaginians could thus be increased, with us held back on this side of the strait? "Let the Carthaginian not cross the Ebro."

But the accuser insists and contends that my people ought to have withdrawn from Messana, just as the Carthaginians also withdrew. He says this was great and manifest fairness. Why, however, was that fair? The Mamertines showed themselves base and fickle to us, for, not having waited for our aid which they had sought and obtained, they went over to the Carthaginians, to whom they could not go over without violating our right of alliance and friendship, by joining themselves to those who were forbidden to be joined to them through treaties. After that we could not trust the Mamertines. After that we could not trust the Carthaginians over there. What? And was not the treaty even earlier violated for us by the Carthaginians, who aided p. 184
the Tarentines against us?[334] And when they were accused of that wicked crime, they augmented their disgrace with perjury. Your own authorities say this, Picenus.

But then you bring up Sardinia and Corsica and claim that the former was wrested from the Carthaginians most unjustly—and that all the authors are agreed on this—and that it is not known why the latter was subjugated. And yes, it is true that Livy and Polybius write thus about Sardinia at great length. But I would like to ask, by way of the accuser, one thing of those writers: did the Carthaginians, who are said to have been very shrewd men,[335] ever complain of that injustice, even after they dared to wage war on the Romans? It is plausible, then, that they had no case there, or they themselves would have seen it better than Livy could make it out to be, he who judges that that just complaint *ought* to have been lodged.

Come, now, accuser, listen to something else: what will you say if I am able to oppose four writers to those two? I affirm that Sardinia was not extorted through fraud but conceded through the treaty struck with Lutatius, and the authorities for this are Dio Cassius, your friend Paulus Diaconus, as well as Orosius and Sextus Victor.[336] But if it is always the case that the number of

testium: et illuc vergere habet sententia, ubi tantulum vergit probatio: nos vincimus. Maiores sunt illi sane testes, quam Diaconus, Orosius, Victor. Dionem non dixero. Sed isti tuique sunt; et valere supra unum Livium
p. 185 possunt, dum Polybius, et Dion ex | æquo certant. Vincimus tanto certius, quanto unus dici isthinc Polybius testis meretur: de quo plane hausit hic, ut facere Livius solet. Unus est testis, cum plurimi de uno habent, quod dicunt. Neque referri ratio ista valet in Orosium, Diaconum, Victorem: quos saltuatim magis concerpsisse narrationes suas videmus. Vincimus extra controversiam, postquam stat et verisimilitudo in istam partem, inverisimilitudo in alteram.

Recitemus nunc testimonia. *Sicilia, Sardinia, cæteræ insulæ concessæ a Pœnis in fœdere Lutatiano.* Hoc testes nunc mei. Etiam recitem, quæ Dion paullo distinctius habet. Rebellavit Sardinia auctoribus Pœnis: itaque illatum eis bellum est. Sed et data pax post multas legationes, et oratione quidem Hannonis, minimi legatorum. Cum enim facerent Romani apparatum belli: et Carthaginensibus, finitimo bello distentis, nihil moderati responderent: missus post Hanno est, iuvenis libertatis miræ dicendi: qui aliaque plura, et hoc dixit, dedisse se Siciliam, et Sardiniam, quibus non duraturas ad aliquod tempus inducias, sed amicitiam perpetuam redemissent: atque eas igitur reddendas insulas esse, si colere pacem noluissemus. Hæc illi alii, et Dion.

Num vero tempora nos confundimus, et varia in unum facta involuimus?
p. 186 Sane, si fœdere Lutatiano tradita Sardinia est, illud primum | tempus est omnium. Et si rebellavit Sardinia, certe et tradita fuerat. Et hic tamen habet, quod respondeat accusator: traditam quidem, at inter Africæ motum, post Lutatii fœdus: [a] nam et alii scribunt, et in laudibus Romanorum, quemadmodum adiuti sint Pœni milite, et commeatu: quæ hostibus Pœnorum, illis mercenariis, occlusa fuerint: et quemadmodum recepti non sunt, qui desciscere ad Romanos volebant, Uticenses, et Sardi. Age, relinquamus rem dubiam in ea scriptorum varietate. In re dubia accusator non vincet. Nos laudes istas arripimus Romanorum: [b] quas et alii ad cælum ferunt: et hoc addunt, ab ista clementia, et humanitate meorum factum, ut ipsi nos postea in negotia inciderimus.

[a] *Cor. Ne. Amil.* [b] *Polyb.* 3. *App. Pun. Zona.* 2.

[337] [Dio Cassius 12, epitome.]
[338] Cornelius Nepos, *Hamilcar* 2.

witnesses carries some weight, and that opinion should lean in the direction where assent leans even just a little, then we win here. True, those authorities [Livy and Polybius] are greater than Paulus Diaconus, Orosius, and Victor—I won't pronounce on Dio. But those are often your authorities as well, and they are able to have more validity than Livy alone, while Polybius and Dio strive on an equal footing. We win all the more decisively in that Polybius p. 185
deserves to be mentioned here as the sole authority, for Livy, as was his wont, was clearly deriving his account from him. It is but one source if several have taken what they say from one authority. And yet that reasoning cannot be applied to Orosius, Paulus Diaconus, or Aurelius Victor, who we see have desultorily plucked their accounts from here and there. We win beyond any contradiction, after it is clear that plausibility stands on one side and implausibility stands on the other.

Let us now read out the testimony: "Sicily, Sardinia, and the other islands were conceded by the Carthaginians in the treaty with Lutatius." This my witnesses now attest to. I would even read out what Dio records a bit more clearly. Sardinia rebelled at the instigation of the Carthaginians, and so war was waged against them. But after a number of embassies peace was granted at last through the speech of Hanno, the least important of the ambassadors. For when the Romans were making preparations for war and the Carthaginians were distracted by a war with their neighbors, the Romans made a harsh answer to them. Subsequently Hanno was sent to them, a young man endowed with a remarkable boldness of speech. He said a number of things, but in particular this: that they had given up Sicily and Sardinia in order to buy with them not truces which were going to last for a certain time, but perpetual friendship; and so if we were unwilling to keep the peace we should give back those islands.[337] This is what those other writers record as well as Dio.

But have we confused the periods and collapsed various doings into one? Well, it is certain that if Sardinia was handed over by the treaty of Lutatius, that p. 186
period came first of all. And if Sardinia rebelled, then clearly it had already been handed over. But here the accuser has a response: it was indeed handed over, but in the midst of disturbance in Africa, after the treaty of Lutatius. For others, too, write (and in praise of the Romans) how the Carthaginians were helped by Roman soldiers and supplies, which were cut off by the enemies of the Carthaginians, those former mercenaries of theirs, and how those who wished to defect to the Romans (the people of Utica and Sardinia) were not accepted.[338] But come, let us leave a disputed question like this to the varied accounts of the writers. The accuser will not win in a matter that is so doubtful. Instead, we seize upon those praises of the Romans which others bear to the heavens; and they add this: that as a result of that mercy and humanity of my people it came about that we ourselves afterwards fell into difficulties.

Venio ad secundum tempus post fœdus Lutatii. Pœni Italos mercatores, Romanosque interficiunt, et mari mergunt. Hanc dicimus iustam caussam belli: et Sardiniæ eripiendæ, oportuni criminum loci. Esto res, ut ita narrat Appianus, homo Ægyptius, id est Libycus, et Pœnus magis, quam Romanus. Atque quod Polybius replicat, transactum de his mercatorum iniuriis iam antea exstitisse: et Romanos de transactis non habuisse movere postea controversiam: sic tibi tollitur, et Polybio: ut de captis, et carceratis mercatoribus, p. 187 et de reliquis iniuriis cognitis transactum fuerit: non etiam de necatis, et | mersis mercatoribus, et de aliis iniuriis, quæ latuere (ut ait Appianus) diu. Ad incognita, et incogitata nullam trahi conventionem, certum est. Nullæ fuerunt iniuriæ aliæ, quæ latuissent? Sed testi dicenti, Appiano, credendum est magis, quam vel neganti, Polybio.

Sic igitur, si non primo, non secundo, at hoc tertio tempore tradita Sardinia, et capta est iuste. Quamquam si hoc est, non rebellioni eius insulæ, non orationi Hannonis tempus relinquitur. Secundum Polybium his nullum est tempus quoque. Secundum alios illud esse potest, quod post Lutatium fuit. Quin igitur in tanta varietate, et obscuritate aut stamus pluribus concordibus, qui in fœdere Lutatii manent? aut in illa quiescimus ratione, quod si iniustitiam accusare nostram Pœni potuissent hic, non eam tacuissent, et prudentes satis semper, et tum moventes bellum secundum potenter? Sic Sardinia est.

De Corsica iniquius proponitur argumentum. Latet caussa viros versatissimos in historia: Ergo caussa nulla est. Atque amisso Livio, et reliquis rerum earum monumentis, ita liceat argumentari? Sed et viri illi magni tantum dicunt de caussa factæ provinciæ. [a] Sed et hoc ego dico, captam Corsicam serpente bello: et Florus hoc dicit, *serpente bello Sardinia annexa, atque Corsica*: ita descriptor Flori Iornandes. Sic sæpe. [b] Sic Appianus, *Nullum in* p. 188 | *Rhætios, aut Noricos bellum gestum privatim reperi: quamobrem cum reliquis finitimis una devictos arbitror*. Sic est iunctim mentio istarum insularum scriptoribus. [c] Pro Sardis, et Corsis defensandis Pœnos adfuisse, narrant. Sardos, et Corsos lacessisse magis, quam exercuisse Romana arma. In Sardinia contra Sardos et Corsos pugnatum. Sardos, et Corsos rebellantes

[a] *Flor.* 2. *Ior. de re suec.* [b] *App. Illyr.*
[c] *Oros.* 4. *Liv.* 17. 20. 21. *P. Dia.* 2. *Sex. Ru.*

---

339 Polybius 1. 83; 3. 28; Appian, *Punica* 1. 5; Zonaras 8. 18. 3.
340 Florus 2. 2. 15; Jordanes, *Romana* 167.
341 Appian, *Illyrica* 5. 29.

We come now to the second period after the treaty of Lutatius. The Carthaginians killed Italian and Roman merchants and threw them into the sea. This we pronounce a just cause for war and for seizing Sardinia, a suitable setting for crimes. Let the matter be as Appian tells it—Appian, an Egyptian, that is a Libyan and thus more a Carthaginian than a Roman. As for what Polybius responds—that there had already earlier been an agreement about the injuries suffered by the merchants and that the Romans could not raise a quarrel later about what had already been settled—this is reared up by you (and Polybius) so as to claim that the agreement was about captured and imprisoned merchants and other openly acknowledged wrongs done, and not about merchants who p. 187
were killed and thrown into the sea and wrongs that remained concealed for a long time (as Appian said).[339] It is certainly true that no agreement was drawn up for things not acknowledged and thought about. Were there, then, no other wrongs which lay concealed? More faith should be put in the witness who says yes—Appian—than in the one who denies it—Polybius.

So thus if not on the first occasion or on the second, at least on the third occasion Sardinia was handed over and justly seized. But if this is so, there is no time allowed for the rebellion of that island or for the speech of Hanno. According to Polybius there *was* no time for these events. According to others, it could happen, because it was right after the treaty of Lutatius. Therefore, amidst such disagreement and obscurity, why don't we stand with the majority who are in agreement, who rest with the treaty of Lutatius? Or do we rest content with that other argument, that if the Carthaginians had been able here to allege our injustice, they wouldn't have kept quiet about it, given that they were always sufficiently shrewd and at that time were powerfully setting a war in motion? Well, so much for Sardinia.

Concerning Corsica, an even more unfair argument is laid out. The reason for its acquisition eludes the men who are most versed in history; therefore, there *is* no reason. But may one argue thus when Livy has been lost, along with other records of those events? But there are major authorities who say this much, at least, about the reason for its being made a province. And this I too say: that Corsica was captured in the course of the spread of the war. Florus, too, says this: "As the war spread wider, Sardinia was annexed, and also Corsica"—thus Jordanes, the epitomator of Florus.[340] And this is how it often happens. Thus Appian: "I have discovered no war that was separately waged against the Rhaetians or the Noricans; therefore I judge that they were p. 188
defeated along with their other neighbors."[341] Similarly is joint mention made of those islands by the historians. They record that the Carthaginians were on hand to defend the Sardinians and the Corsicans. The Sardinians and the Corsicans more provoked than fully occupied the arms of the Romans. War was waged in Sardinia against both Sardinians and Corsicans. The rebellious

subactos. Sardiniam, et Corsicam a Metello victas. Et id genus alia. [a] Una scilicet ut videtur insula, ita unam utriusque incendium verisimiliter fuit. Sic insulas habemus.

Habemus Punicas etiam Hispanias. [b]*Non cum Hispanis ab initio, sed cum Pœnis in Hispania inde contagio, et series, caussaque bellorum.* Pulsi illinc secundo bello Carthaginenses sunt. Et belli huius æque bona, aut etiam melior caussa fuit. Quod omnes historici tradunt. Quid mihi in Hispanica re citas contrarium, et magnum nominas testem Macchabæicum? Non ille peritus rei Romanæ, mi homo. Uni Romanos paruisse in libera republica. Senatum Romæ fuisse trecentorum, et viginti. A Romanis captum vivum Antiochum magnum: deque regnis eius tributas Eumeni Mediam, atque Indiam. Hæc illius historici: qui ad fodinas auri Romanos tibi in Hispaniam misit.

Quid mihi de perfidia Saguntinorum in Annibalem: et de Annibalis erga p. 189 Saguntinos clementia obtru | dis? [c] De Salmatensibus illud est, quod ais: relege, et quidem sic relege: nisi velis, quicquid est contra historiam omnem, ipsamque adeo certissimam veritatem. Nam qui alii illi sunt, qui tradunt, non ab Annibale, sed a Metello Saguntinos obsessos? Unus, nescio qui commentarius pannuceus ad Iuvenalem. Quid Annibalis quoque testimonium contra Romanos? Caussa desperata tua est, Picene, et desperata ratio accusandi. Quis enim inimicitias exercentis testimonium contra inimicum protulit unquam? Nec vero tu adeo desipis, ut sic putes, futuros usquam ullos unquam, qui ab insipidis his historiis traducantur in partes. Et quæris igitur, si quid in Pœno reprehendimus nos: etsi sit ita historia Saguntina, ut scripta a Livio est? Tu dicas, accusator, quid in Romanis accusas. Nos contra veteres socios pro sociis novis, et his iniustis bellum suscipere non debuisse. Ceterum quod censes de veteribus: decipis in eo te. Non enim veteres socii tum erant Carthaginenses: qui fœdera fregerant vetera, et in novo erant Asdrubalis, pariter cum Saguntinis. Vetus illa desiit amicitia per bellum. Renovata non ea est, sed instituta nova. [d] Scilicet novum est, quod exfundatum restituitur.

Et contra hos socios pro aliis sociis, forsitan fide, forsitan merito aliquo p. 190 magno nondum notis, sed certe neque perfidia: immo pro nobis ipsis contra | Pœnorum potentiam ingruentem, non decebat bellum suscipere?

[a] *Zon.* 2. [b] *Flor.* 2. [c] *Polyc.* 7. [d] *Alex.* 5. *cons.* 34.

---

342 Orosius 4; Livy 17. 20. 21; Paulus Diaconus, *Historia Romana* 2. 20; Festus, *Breviarium rerum gestarum populi Romani* 4. 2.

343 Zonaras 8. 18. **Translator's note:** The translation offered here assumes that "unam" is a slip for "unum."

344 Florus 2. 17. 5.

345 Polyaenus, *Strategemata* 7. 48. **Translator's note:** There is a similar account in Plutarch, *Moralia, De mulierum virtutibus* 10.

346 Alexander Tartagnus, *Consilia* 5. 34, fol. 42[r].

Sardinians and Corsicans were subdued. Sardinia and Corsica were defeated by Metellus. And other things of this sort.[342] Just as they naturally seem to be one island, so the conflagration of war that overtook each of the two seemed plausibly one phenomenon.[343] And this is how we came to possess the islands.

We also possess the Carthaginian Spains. "At first the fighting was not with the Spaniards but with the Carthaginians in Spain, from whom the contagion came, and the sequence and cause of the wars."[344] The Carthaginians were driven from there in the Second Punic War. And for this there was an equally good—or even better—cause, one that all the historians narrate. Why do you, when speaking of matters in Spain, cite Maccabaeus for me as a contrary witness and one you pronounce major? My good fellow, that man was not learned in Roman history. The Romans obeyed one man in a free republic. The Roman Senate had 320 members. Antiochus the Great was captured alive by the Romans and from his kingdoms were granted to Eumenes Media and India. This is the sort of stuff you find in this "historian," the one who sent the Romans into Spain for the gold mines.

Why do you thrust upon me the perfidy of the Saguntines towards Hannibal and Hannibal's mercy towards the Saguntines? That which you say is about the p. 189 Salmatenses. Go back over it, and get it right—unless you wish to take that which is contrary to the whole historical record as the most secure truth.[345] And who, exactly, are those others who record that the Saguntines were besieged not by Hannibal but by Metellus? Just one—some tattered commentator to Juvenal. What testimony of Hannibal can you offer against the Romans? Your case is a desperate one, Picenus, and your method of accusing is desperate. For who has ever brought forth against an enemy the testimony of someone actively practicing hostility? Nor are you so stupid as to imagine that there will ever be anyone who will be converted to your position by these foolish histories. And so do you ask if we have any fault to find with the Carthaginians, even if the history of Saguntum may be as it has been written by Livy? May *you* say, accuser, what it is that you find fault with in the Romans. Is it that we ought not to have undertaken a war against old allies on behalf of new allies—and these new allies unjust to boot? But you delude yourself in what you think about the old allies. For our old allies were not then the Carthaginians, who had broken the old treaties and were now bound by the new one of Hasdrubal, together with the Saguntines. That friendship of old ceased on account of the war. That friendship was not renewed, but a new one was established. Indeed, that is new which, having been razed to the ground, is set up again.[346]

Was it not fitting to undertake a war against those former allies on behalf of new allies, who while they may not yet have been known for their loyalty or for any great merit were certainly not known for perfidy either—nay, rather, was it not fitting to undertake a war for our *own* sakes against the threatening p. 190 power of the Carthaginians?

At iniusti Saguntini. Respondeo, responsum huic argumento esse, cum de Mamertinis idem afferebatur. At quare Saguntini iniusti? Non istos hic condemnaveris, quin et Numantinos condemnes postea: de quibus Florus, *Non temere, si fateri licet, ullius caussa belli iniustior. Segidenses socios et consanguineos Romanorum manibus elapsos, exceperant, habita pro eis deprecatio nihil valuit: cum se ab omni bellorum contagione removerent*. Eadem caussa cum Annibale Saguntinorum. Et nec igitur Saguntini iniusti sunt, si Numantini tui non sunt iniusti. Non sunt Saguntini iniusti: etsi medii relicti tradiderint se Romanis totos.

Non illos nos accepimus sub servitutem: quod contra fœdus fuisset, eos se ita dare, nos eos ita accipere. Sed sua cum libertate nobis adiungebantur. At istamque negamus adiunctionem, de qua nuperus scriptor (non ille Plutarchus) exponit. Saguntum æque Pœnis amicam, in Hispanicis Appiani audimus. Cautum vero, immo cautum novo fœdere Saguntinis erat. Nec fuit Livius in isto iudicio præceps. [a] Ut enim controversum valde videri possit, si ad futura verbum extenditur: cum tamen potest prævideri futurum, tum et futurum venit: et mutuum ubi quid proponitur, ibi etiam futurum
p. 191 continetur. Ut sic, si pax facta pro se | fit, et suis sociis, hi quoque comprehendantur, qui post assumti in societatem sunt. Quæ omnia in caussa Saguntinorum omnes cernimus. [b] Et in illa diserte pro Romanis ita definit Alciatus, vere magnus iurisconsultus, et eruditus Fornerius.

[c] Etiam ea definitio iuris facit cumque ipsis verbis Livii: quod si concessa sit civitati immunitas, hæc et de futuris adoptatis civibus intelligitur: ne videatur ablata civitati facultas creandi cives. Quid si cautum sociis est, et adiectum est verbum universitatis, *omnibus*? [d] Utique et futura veniunt iam, etsi alias nec venirent. Quid si huiusmodi intercesserunt cautiones, quæ intercesserunt proculdubio: ut erant formulæ illæ longis, et anxiis compositæ carminibus semper. Cedit hic accusator: et, cedat, necesse est.

Sed illam tenet arcem, quod ita decretum fuit in ipsa urbe, ne auxilia Saguntinis summitterentur: quoniam nec fœdere comprehensi, sed liberi relicti essent. Id tamen ita non est. [e] Disputatum Romæ est, ne auxilia mitterentur statim, neve statim ad arma concurreretur: sed prius de ratione videretur, per quam Saguntinis succurri, Pœnis occurri valeret: sed prius ut

[a] *Alex*. 2. *cons*. 178. *Ias*. *l*. 76. *de V. O. Alc*. 8. *cons*. 39.
[b] *Alc*. *l*. 128. *Forn*. *l*. 158. *de V. S.*
[c] *Ceph*. *cons*. 451.
[d] *Bald*. *l*. 33. *C. de episc. et cl.*
[e] *Flor*. 2.

---

[347] Florus 2. 18. 3–4. **Translator's note:** Gentili has garbled this quotation by failing to realize that what he prints as a concluding *cum*-clause is actually the beginning of another sentence.

[348] Alexander Tartagnus, *Consilia* 2. 178; Jason Maynus [Giasone del Mayno], *On Digest* 45. 1. 76 [*In secundam Digesti novi partem commentaria*, Venetiis, Apud Iuntas, 1598, fols. 95^{v} f.]; Alciatus, *Consilia* 8. 39, col. 1158.

[349] Alciatus, *On Digest* 50. 16. 123 [in *Opera Omnia in quatuor tomos*, Tomus II, Basileae, Apud Thomam Guarinum, 1582, col. 1176]; Gulielmus Fornerius [Guillaume Fournier], *On Digest* 50. 16. 158 [*In titulum de verborum significatione commentarii*, Aurelianis, Apud Eligium Gibierium, 1584, p. 403].

[350] Baldus, *On Code* 1. 3. 33, fols. 45^{r} f.

[351] **Translator's note:** I am translating the unintelligible words "longis et anxiis compositae carminibus" as though Gentili meant to write "longis et anxie composites carminibus," which at least makes some sense.

But the Saguntines were supposedly unjust. I answer that I have already answered this argument, when the same thing was claimed about the Mamertines. But why, exactly, were the Saguntines unjust? You will not have condemned those men here without also condemning the Numantines later on, of whom Florus wrote: "If one may be allowed to confess it, one won't easily find a more unjust cause of any war. The Numantines had sheltered their allies and kinfolk the Segidenses who had slipped away from the hands of the Romans. The intercession with the Romans they attempted on their behalf had no effect, while they distanced themselves from any participation in the war."[347] The Saguntines had the same cause [of war] with Hannibal. And so it follows that the Saguntines were not unjust unless your beloved Numantines were unjust. The Saguntines were not unjust even if, when left neutral, they handed themselves entirely over to the Romans.

We did not accept them under a yoke of servitude, for it would have been against the treaty for them to give themselves in that way or for us to accept them in that way. But they were associated with us with their full liberty intact. But we deny that sort of association laid out by some recent writer (that was *not* Plutarch). In Appian's *Spanish Wars* we hear that Saguntum stayed equally friendly to the Carthaginians. The Saguntines were in fact cautious, indeed very cautious about the new treaty. Nor was Livy hasty in making that judgment. For a clause may appear deeply disputable when it is extended to future situations; but when the future can nevertheless be seen in advance, and then does come to pass, in a case where something is proposed as mutually binding, there also the future is included in the agreement.[348] For instance, if peace is made for oneself and one's allies, those people are also p. 191
included who have afterwards been taken up into an alliance. All of these things we all see in the cause put forward by the Saguntines. And in the matter of that cause Alciatus, indeed a great jurist, pronounced eloquently on behalf of the Romans, as does the erudite Fornerius.[349]

Furthermore, this clarification of the law operates in accord with the very words of Livy, to the effect that if some exemption is granted a state it is understood also to apply to citizens adopted in the future, lest it appear that a state be deprived of its ability to create citizens. What if one has been cautious with one's allies and that word indicating collectivity—"all"—has been added? Indeed the things in the future now are coming, even if they didn't come previously.[350] What if provisos of this sort have been inserted, which they surely have been—just as there were those formulae in long and carefully composed poems?[351] Here the accuser yields—and yield he must.

But he still holds out as a last resort the fact that in the city itself it was decreed not to send aid to the Saguntines, since they were not included in the treaty but were left free. But this is not so. It was argued in Rome that aid not be sent immediately and that there not be an immediate military engagement, but that first there be an examination of the rationale that would suffice for aiding the Saguntines and opposing the Carthaginians, and that first the

querelæ legitimo more exponerentur. Sic magni illi, Polybius, Livius, alii. [a] Non dubium fuit, quin violatum ab Annibale fœdus esset: qui Iberum
p. 192 traiecerit contra fœderis legem. Id ipse scribit Appianus, | nec semel. Et tamen non procurritur ad arma? retinente religione, et amore legitimi iuris, nulla perfidia, nullo malo arcano.

Et sic tenent Romani Hispaniam: in quam et societatis Saguntinæ caussa bona, et caussa violati a Carthaginensibus fœderis arma portarunt. Violarunt illi fœdus, cum Annibali permiserunt, ut cum Saguntinis, transmisso Ibero, ageret pro arbitratu: et cum legatos Romanos, qui querebantur, sic raptos, et subactos populos cis Iberum, habuere ludibrio.

Quæ in Hispania sunt postea consecuta, perfidia Celtiberorum, rebelliones continuæ omnium illic populorum, et id genus alia, ne attigit quidem accusator. Rapitur ad Numantiam: quo illum sequimur: Tu, quid Flore Annei, non Iuli Flore: tu Hispane scriptor, quid popularibus tuis quid blandiris? [b] Aut Galle, quid maledicis nobis? Certe quid rhetoricaris tu professor rhetoricæ in Gallia, et in toto hoc tuo rhetor opere? Num rebellis non erat Numantia? Num illic consilium non est initum de bello contra Romanos? Hæc Appianus. Etiam si nihil fecissent isti tui Hispani, nisi quod dicis tu: illud et iusta fuit contra ipsos caussa belli: etsi tum nec iniusta ipsorum ratio diceretur: quod stat, ut bellum utrinque sit iustum scilicet. [c] Exsciderunt Numantiam, civitatem crudelem, spirituum insolentissimorum: quos culpa
p. 193 nutrierat eorum | (fatendum id nobis est) ducum, qui a nobis missi illuc primi sunt. Stulti Numantini, qui crediderint, civitati nostræ defuturos meliores, si minus bonos illos vicissent. [d] Sed immo civitas mea Numantiam non exscidit. Scipio exscidit absque decreto populi. Neque tamen hoc dixerim, quasi exscindi Numantia non meruerit: quæ est vi capta: et easdem contra se rationes habuit a Scipione, quas a populo habebat. Nunc nos insulta, Picene. Numantia iacet, tanta illa virtus, nostræ maioris monumentum virtutis. Noluit conditionibus ullis eam se dedentem accipere Scipio: qui (Florum audi) *veram vellet, et sine exceptione victoriam.*

[a] *App. Pu. Hisp. Ann.* [b] *App. Hisp.*
[c] *Cic. 1. de off. Val. 2. 4. 7.* [d] *App. Hisp.*

---

352 Florus 2. 6. 5.

353 Appian, *Punica* 2. 6; *Iberica* 2. 10; *Hannibalica* 1. 3.

354 **Translator's note:** Florus is referred to as L. Annaeus Florus in the Codex Palatinus, and this is the name currently favored, although he is often identified with the poet P. Annius Florus. He was called Julius Florus in the Codex Bambergensis. According to the Brussels fragment, he was born in Africa, but later moved to Tarraco in Spain, then to Rome.

355 **Translator's note:** Gentili here is offering two guesses as to the ethnicity of Florus the Epitomator. First he seems to attack Florus on the assumption that he is a Spaniard, hence anti-Roman. Then he entertains the possibility that the Florus in question is a Gallic rhetorician mentioned by Quintilian, faulting him for writing like a rhetorician—neither Florus can win. See Quintilian 10. 3. 13: "Iulius Florus, in eloquentia Galliarum . . . princeps."

356 Appian, *Iberica* 13. 76.

357 **Translator's note:** See the discussion of this point in *De iure belli* 1. 6.

358 Cicero, *De officiis* 1. 35; Valerius Maximus 2. 7. 1.

Saguntines' complaints be set forth in the proper manner.[352] Thus also those great authorities Polybius and Livy, as well as others. There was no doubt that the treaty had been violated by Hannibal, who crossed the Ebro against its terms. Appian himself writes this, more than once.[353] And yet there was p. 192 no rush to arms, for religious scruple and love of due process of law held them back, no perfidiousness, no wicked secret principle.

And so thus the Romans hold Spain, into which the valid cause of the alliance with Saguntum and the cause of the treaty broken by the Carthaginians carried our arms. Those people broke the treaty when they allowed Hannibal to cross the Ebro and deal with the Saguntines as he wished, and when they made light of the seizure of the Roman ambassadors who were lodging a complaint and made light of the subjugation of the peoples this side of the Ebro.

As for what subsequently occurred in Spain—the perfidy of the Celtiberians, the constant rebellions of all the peoples there, and all that sort of thing—the accuser doesn't touch on that at all. Rather, he is hurried off to Numantia, where we shall follow him. You—not Julius Florus, but Annaeus Florus, a Spanish writer—why do you flatter your countrymen?[354] Or if you were the Gaul Julius Florus, why do you speak ill of us? Indeed, why do you rant, you professor of rhetoric in Gaul, a rhetorician in your entire work?[355] Was not Numantia in a state of rebellion? Was it not there that the plan of war against the Romans was entered upon? This is what Appian says.[356] Even if your Spaniards had done nothing more than what you yourself say, that in itself was a just cause for war against them, even though at that time their own cause could be called not unjust—for it is agreed that a war may indeed be just on both sides.[357] They destroyed Numantia, a cruel city, a city of the most insolent spirits, which were fed (it has to be confessed) by the p. 193 fault of those generals whom we first sent there.[358] Foolish Numantines, who believed that our state would be lacking better men if they defeated those inferior ones. But in fact it was not my state that destroyed Numantia. Scipio destroyed it—without a decree of the Roman people.[359] And yet I would not say that Numantia did not deserve to be destroyed. It was taken by storm, and it had the same motives against itself from Scipio that it had from the Roman people. Now scoff at us, Picenus. Numantia lies in ruins, all that valor—a monument to our own greater valor. Scipio did not wish to accept its surrender with any conditions, for he (listen to Florus here) "wanted a victory that was true and without qualifications."[360]

[359] Appian, *Iberica* 15. 98. **Translator's note:** Gentili seems to think that it would have been in the power of the *populus Romanus* to decide on the destruction of Numantia even as late as 133 BC.

[360] [Florus 2. 18. 12.]

Agite, in Africam traiiciamus: bella concludamus Punica. Urbem Carthaginem, et Punicum imperium exstinxerunt. [a] Etenim Pœni contra fœderis legem instruxerunt classem, exercitum pararunt, frequenter territarunt Masinissæ fines. Quid hic obgannit Orosius? Ecce audis caussas eius belli de Appiano, ac Floro. Quod illud Orosii argumentum? Alii volebant, Carthaginem dirui ob securitatem: alii, ad virtutem acuendam servari: Igitur caussa non ex iniuria Carthaginensium erat. Videlicet non disceptatur sæpissime, si, parcere nocentibus, expediat: et quomodo expediat, victoria uti. Expediebat, exscindi Carthaginem. Sic Cato. [b] Urbem Capuam non exscidimus: erat
p. 194 enim in ocu|lis: ut timere ab ea non oporteret. At nec timore, sed magis invidia imperii est exscisa. *Invidia magis*, non invidia tantum, sed et noxia eius temporis: quam ostendi. Et quæ noxia nobis iustam fecit exscindendi potestatem: sicut fecit invidia voluntatem. Fateor invidiam, fateor: et illo utor Cæsaris, *Invideo gloriæ tuæ, Cato, quoniam et tu invidisti meæ*. Invidimus gloriæ Carthaginis, quoniam et Carthago invidit gloriæ nostræ. Hæc illa est celebris illarum rerum publicarum æmulatio.

Alterum auctoris eiusdem ferri non potest, *Magis quia volebant Romani*. Quid enim si volebant, hoc est, velle debebant: ut accusator ais? Volebant, hoc est credebant, quia timebant? [c] Sic alibi: *Quæ etsi falsa nunciata fuissent, apud timentes tamen pro veris habebantur*. Metus iustus est, si caussa metuenda iusta est, etsi periculum nullum vere subsit. Neque tamen hoc indigemus præsidio.

Sunt enim (ut dixi) ostensæ noxiæ. Etiam si nec tantæ fuissent, quantæ mererentur per se pœnam tantam: erant veteres tamen, quæ novis his additæ merebantur tantam. [d] Et vetera delicta, etiam punita, vel condonata, faciunt, quod sequitur, delictum gravius, et in eo puniendo manum addunt: ut sic convenit inter iuris prudentes, et moribus receptum est.

[a] *Flor. 2. App. Pu.* [b] *Cic. agr. 2.* [c] *Iustin.* 31.
[d] *Cla. §. furtum. Exo.* 32. *ubi Tre. Decia.* 2. *cons.* 27.

---

361 Florus 2. 15. 4; Appian, *Punica* 11. 74.
362 [The reference is to Orosius 4. 23, discussed in the matching section of Book 1, ch. 8.]
363 Cicero, *De lege agraria* 2. 32. 88.
364 [Velleius Paterculus 1. 12. 5; cf. above, pp. 76–7.]
365 Justin 31.
366 Julius Clarus [Giulio Claro], *Receptarum sententiarum liber quintus, §. furtum* [in *Opera omnia; sive practica civilis atque criminalis, Cum doctissimis Additionibus per illustrium Iurisconsultorum*, Venetiis, Ex typographia Baretiana, 1626, p. 73; Gentili probably has the following passage by one of the learned commentators on Claro in mind: "quia furta sequentia non aggravant praecedentia: sed praecedentia aggravant sequentia"]; Exodus 32, in Immanuel Tremellius, *Testamenti veteris Biblia sacra sive libri canonici priscae Judaeorum ecclesiae a Deo traditi, Latini recens ex Hebraeo facti ab Immanuele Tremellio & Francisco Junio, accesserunt libri apocryphi, &c.*, Hanoviae, 1596, pp. 115–16; Decianus, *Consilia* 2. 27, fol. 91[r].

Come, let us cross over to Africa and conclude the Punic Wars. The Romans destroyed Carthage and the Carthaginian empire. For the Carthaginians fitted out a fleet in defiance of the terms of the treaty, and they prepared an army, and repeatedly harassed the borders of Masinissa.[361] Why does Orosius growl here? Look, you hear the causes of this war from Appian and Florus. What is that argument of Orosius?[362] "Some wished for Carthage to be destroyed for their own security; others wished it to survive as a stimulus to courage. Therefore the cause does not arise from the wrongdoing of the Carthaginians." It is not very often objected to if it should prove expedient to spare those who are in the wrong—and to make use of victory in any way that is expedient. It was expedient that Carthage be destroyed. So Cato. We did not destroy the city of Capua, for we could keep an eye on it, so that we didn't p. 194
need to be afraid of it.[363] But Carthage was destroyed not out of fear, but "more from envy of its power."[364] "More from envy"—that is, not only from envy, but also from the harm it presented at that time, as I have shown. And in being harmful to us it rendered righteous our power of destroying it, just as envy supplied the will to destroy it. I concede the ill will, I concede it—and I make use of that utterance of Caesar: "I envy your glory, Cato, since you have envied mine." We envied the glory of Carthage, since Carthage envied our glory. This is that well-known competitiveness of those great republics.

Another passage in the same author cannot be endured: "It was more because the Romans wished [to believe anything that might be said about the Carthaginians than because they maintained that these things were worthy of belief that the Senate decided to destroy Carthage.]" For what if they did wish (that is, they *should* have been wishing), as you say, accuser? Did they have the will because they had a belief: that is, because they were afraid? We read this elsewhere: "Even though the things announced happened to be false, among people in fear they were nonetheless taken for true."[365] A fear is justified if there is a just reason to be feared, even if no danger is actually present. And yet we don't need this defense.

For there were (as I have said) manifest wrongs done [by Carthage]. Even if they were not so great as to deserve in and of themselves so great a punishment, there were none the less some of long standing which, added to these new ones, did merit so great a punishment. And old offenses, even if they have been punished, or even if they have been condoned, make more serious an offense which comes later, and add force to its punishment, as is agreed by all those learned in the law, and has been accepted by custom.[366]

Nec iuvat Pœnos, quod, experti iniquos Romanos, prospicere ipsi sibi p. 195 coacti sunt. [a] Namque est | semper verum, sic in fœdus venisse, *Ne bellum in Africa, neve extra Africam iniussu populi Romani gererent*. Quod etsi durum, erat servandum tamen. [b] Durissimam ipsi Pœni viderunt usque a principio legem, cum eam dici sibi audierunt: et cum recusarunt propterea pacem abusque principio: durissimam legem, interitum civitatis, viderunt: [c] Neque enim, ut privatorum tranquillus status est tutus maxime, ita et civitatis est: quod natura, quod perpetua ostendunt exempla: etiam exemplum civitatis nostræ, ablata æmula ista Carthagine. Sed et sic coacti pacem tandem tamen accipere.

Cuius ius pactæ pacis abrumpunt Pœni iniuste, tenent Romani iuste, nec crudeliter. [d] Nec enim crudele quid efficit, qui leges sequitur. Aut num iniusti mei sunt: qui regi favent Masinissæ? Mirum, si non Carthaginensibus magis, quam regi *bono, socioque*, ut Florus ait, et omnium maxime merito de re Romana. At favent, quantum possunt: [e] id est, quantum per leges possunt: ut hæc potestas est: et ut illa altera sine iustitia omnia tum potuit Romanorum, et Masinissæ supra Carthaginenses. Vera illa potestas est, quæ regi favet: et quæ plurimis in toto iure favet sæpe caussis, et personis.

Nihil est, quod nulla sit lex, aut pactio de se non defendendo. Nam publica
p. 196 ista conventio pro certo valet: ut valetque illa se dedentis hostis, per quam | vita etiam in voluntate, et manu sit hostis: quamvis in privatorum negotiis vera ista non censeantur.

Lex summa Pœnis, ne bellum gererent. Lex ea violabatur statim, ac gererent. Lex prohibitoria prævalet. Lex prævalet, quæ violatur statim: ut hæc erat de bello non gerendo: et illa non erat defensionis, quæ moras patiebatur: namque mœnibus arietes, portis Carthaginis faces nondum admoverat Masinissa.

Aut quid dico defensionis? [f] Ipsi fuerunt Pœni, qui, occupatis bello Celtiberico Romanis, vastant Masinissæ fines eius agri, qui iudicio Romanorum iudicatus Masinissæ esse. Qui legatos Masinissæ, et in his filium, non

[a] *Liv.* 30. [b] *Dio. ecl. de legat.*
[c] *Dio.* 38. [d] *Cass.* 7. *var.* 8.
[e] *l. ult. ubi gl. de relig. l.* 15. *de cond. inst.*
[f] *App. Pun.*

---

[367] Livy 30. 37. 4.
[368] Dio Cassius, *Excerpta de legationibus* [in Fulvio Orsini, *Selecta de legationibus*, Antverpiae, Ex officina Christophori Plantini, 1582, pp. 376 f. (= Dio Cassius frag. 43. 22 f.)]. [This refers to the demand by M. Atilius Regulus in 256 BC, as part of his terms, that Carthage surrender Sardinia.]
[369] Dio Cassius 38.
[370] Cassiodorus, *Variae* 7. 8.
[371] l. ult. ubi. gl. de relig. [Gentili here most probably is referring to *Digest* 11. 7. 43, and Accursius' gloss to that passage, s.v. solet: *tamen est contraria aequitati*, "yet it is in opposition to justice"]; *Digest* 28. 7. 15.
[372] Appian, *Punica* 10. 68–70.

Nor does it do the Carthaginians any good that, having found the Romans unjust to them, they were themselves constrained to look out for their own interests. For it still remains true that this went into the treaty: "They are not to wage war in Africa, nor outside of Africa, without the consent of the Roman people."[367] This may be harsh, but it nonetheless had to be observed. The Carthaginians themselves saw this condition as harsh from the very first, when they heard it read out to them. And because they rejected peace for that reason from the very beginning, they came to see the harshest clause of all: the destruction of their city.[368] This just goes to show that, though tranquility among private citizens is an especially safe state of affairs, it is not so with a state. Both nature and countless examples show this—even the example of our own state when that rival Carthage was removed.[369] But even so the Carthaginians were forced at last to accept the peace. p. 195

But the Carthaginians broke the provision of this peace which had been agreed upon, while the Romans justly and not cruelly held to it. For he who follows the laws does nothing cruel.[370] Or were my people unjust when they favored Masinissa? I suppose it's amazing that they didn't favor the Carthaginians more than they favored a king who was "a good man and an ally," as Florus says, and the one who more than anyone else deserved well of the Roman state. But they favored him as much as they could—that is to say, as much as they could in accord with the agreements, since this is a power, while at that same time the Romans did have that other power to do whatever they chose *without* justice on behalf of Masinissa over the Carthaginians.[371] That power which favored the king was legitimate, as is that which often favors very many claims or persons in the whole body of the law.

There is nothing in the claim that there could be no law or pact without the right of self-defense. For that public agreement has an absolute validity, just as there is validity in the agreement of an enemy who surrenders and thereby his life is subject to the will and hand of his enemy, although in private transactions such things are not deemed valid. p. 196

The chief condition for the Carthaginians was that they not make war. That clause was immediately violated, and they did wage war. A prohibiting clause has superior force. Also a clause which is immediately violated has superior force, as was this one about not waging war—and that had nothing to do with self-defense, which would have allowed deferments. For Masinissa had not yet moved battering rams to the walls or firebrands to the gates of Carthage.

But why do I talk of self-defense? It was the Carthaginians themselves, at a time when the Romans were occupied by the Celtiberian War, who lay waste the borders of Masinissa, of that territory which by the decision of the Romans was assigned to Masinissa.[372] It was the Carthaginians who refused to admit the ambassadors of Masinissa, his son among them, into the city

admittunt in urbem: abeuntes territant, et tractant male. Quæ igitur Romanos admonebat iustitia, non favere regi? studere, bellum componi placide, quod susceptum contra fœdus, ac gestum a Pœnis est? Hæ sunt solidæ caussæ, et rationes pro Masinissa, pro Romanis, adversum Pœnos. Ad istas mihi respice accusator: et, quæ adiectæ sunt leviores, tu mitte mecum. Nam est satis, ac super, si per aliquas vincimus rationes. Mitte tu inania verba, et Byrsam, et casas, et cumulum, et stramen. Huc ad rationes contende.

Masinissa, locum iniuriæ ratus. Et Masinissam si concedam Pœnis iniquum, quid ad meos? quid tum? Homini iniusto meos favere non oportuisse? Sane non con|tra iustos. Sed Pœni infames etiam erant: adeoque comparatione ipsorum iustus haberi Masinissa potuerit. [a]*Etiam nocentes, viri boni, si necessarii sunt, non defendendos esse, non putant.* Etiam dicimus iniuriam bellum. [b] Etiam non semper iniuste fit iniuria: non iniuriæ species contumelia.

Perge quærere, Picene, de rationibus, quibus est bellum administratum: nam, quæ in bellum moverunt Romanos, iustissimas audis. In primo Punico laceras populum morantem Reguli reditum. Regulum laceras, legatum perfidum. Iterum populum, qui Regulum, iuste necatum, iniuste vindicat. At adverte, Picene, semel ad confectas res, non ad disputatas, et cogitatas. Neque enim ignoras, multa tractari, quæ non conficiuntur: et in tractatu nullam esse obligationem. Neque enim ignoras, esse hoc quoque tempore iurisconsultos, nec eos quidem de plebe: qui, Regulum nulla necessitate rediisse, immo etiam contra ius patriæ fecisse redeundo, affirmant audentissime. Etiam perfidia obiectatur unico illi exemplo fidei? At suscepit legationem, quam in contrarium egit. At immo missus in legationem est: quam hoc agere, vel illo modo, nihil suscepit: cedo istam restipulationem: egit autem fide in patriam maxima, et admirabili. Et ergo crudeliter necatum ab hostibus crudelissimis vindicant cives sui iustissime. Atque tantum in | primo, et nihil amplius potes?

[a] *Cic. pro Syl.*
[b] *Ter. Eun. Inst. de iniu.*

373 [Cf. 1. 8, pp. 76–9.]
374 **Translator's note:** This is the passage from Livy 34. 62 that Picenus had cited in 1. 8, on pp. 75–6.
375 Cicero, *Pro Sulla* 2. 6.
376 Terence, *Eunuchus* 59–63; *Institutes* 4. 4.pr. **Translator's note:** Gentili here contradicts directly the passage he cites from the *Institutes*, where it is said explicitly that the delict of *iniuria* consists, among other things, precisely in *contumelia* (insult or outrage), which is linked to the Greek *hubris*. The delict of *iniuria* according to Roman law created a punitive action, the private *actio iniuriarum*, aiming at a money penalty.

and terrified and maltreated them as they were going back again. What justice was it, then, that warned the Romans not to show favor to the king—and to be eager to settle peacefully a war which was undertaken and waged by the Carthaginians in contravention of the treaty? These are secure causes and reasons on behalf of Masinissa, on behalf of the Romans, against the Carthaginians. Pay attention to these for me, accuser, and join me in discarding those more trivial ones you added. For it is enough and more than enough if we win through some real arguments. Throw away those empty words: the Byrsa, the huts, the roof and the straw.[373] Direct your contention over here at the real issues.

"Masinissa, judging that he had an opportunity for doing wrong."[374] Even if I concede that Masinissa was unjust to the Carthaginians, what is that to my people? What then? Ought my people not to have shown favor to an unjust man? Indeed not against those who were themselves just. But the Carthaginians p. 197 were at that time in disgrace—so much so that Masinissa could have been considered just in comparison to them. "Good men do not think that even those who are in the wrong should not be defended, if they are bound to them by close ties."[375] We call war a wrongful act. But in fact a wrongful act does not always happen unjustly. Harsh words are not a form of wrongful act.[376]

Go on to ask, Picenus, about the methods by which war has been carried out; for you have now heard that the motives which moved the Romans to war were very just. In the First Punic War you attack the Roman populace that attempted to delay the return of Regulus. You attack Regulus himself as a perfidious ambassador. Then again you attack the people who unjustly avenged Regulus who had been justly killed. But turn your attention once and for all to things which have been accomplished, not things which have been argued and thought about. For you are surely not unaware, Picenus, that many things are considered that are not brought to completion, and there is nothing binding in the consideration. Nor are you unaware that there were jurists even back then, and they were not from the plebeian class, who very boldly affirmed that there was no necessity for Regulus to go back—indeed, they affirmed that he was acting against the law of his fatherland in returning. Will nothing short of perfidy be charged against that singular exemplum of good faith? But, it is claimed, he accepted an embassy that he then acted against. No, in fact he was sent on an embassy which he made no promise to conduct in this or that manner. I grant the force of the counter-promise [sc. to return to Carthage]. But he acted on behalf of his country with the greatest and most admirable loyalty. And thus, when he was cruelly killed by our most cruel enemies, his fellow-citizens very justly avenged him. And is that all— p. 198 and no more—that you can come up with in the First Punic War?

In secundo etiam minus? Si enim captivi remissi non sunt ad Annibalem, id, quia nec repetiti ab Annibale, sic fuit. Ostende repetitos. Nam ius non petenti nec redditur. Nam Romani contemtum Annibali ius obtrudere non debebant: et, ad se ipsos quod attinet, iustitiæ fecere satis, qui turpissimos homines notis meritis confecere.

Quid nunc in tertio? Bellum simul indicitur, et infertur. Indicitur tamen? Sed nec erat necesse, Carthaginensibus indici sollemnius: qui tributarii iam, et obnoxii illa pace non arma tangendi sub nobis erant. Æqualibus illa sollemnitas, ac ritus indictionis debetur. Et ea (sic ad Polybium, atque Varronem) servata meis, donec meis exstitere æquales: servata cum his omnibus, qui professi nostri hostes non erant. Nam Germanis, Parthis, professis hostibus cur bellum indixissemus? Cur Carthaginensibus nunc? Cur eis reddidissemus hac indictione facultatem tractandorum armorum: quibus et contra nos uterentur?

Non fuit hoc bellum. Non ad perduelles ibatur. Ultio erat de obnoxiis, et rebellibus. Iam frustrationes etiam commemorantur frustra. Idque tollitur totum Appiani verbo uno, certas nunquam dictas de pace conditiones. [a]*Spem deditionis non ademit: obsidesque imperavit*: ait ille. Obsides, id genus alia
p. 199 imperare, non est pacem dare. Sal|va igitur fides, salva Romana iustitia est. De callida forsitan ratione vafrities Punica altum silebit: neque per legem ullam belli nos eam condemnare valemus. Etiam laudare isthic valemus: per quam Pœnis consulebatur, ut neque perire valerent, neque furere furorem, iam inermes, iam arctis vinculis stricti.

Dic Picene, dic unum mihi, si, loqui proprie, et verborum proprietatem sequi, et retinere, sit vetitum? Nam civitas promittebatur libera. Et promissioni sic fiebat satis, si civitas servabatur libera: si suæ leges, si sui magistratus civitati adservabantur. De alia libertate dictum nequibat intelligi excellentiori, et de illo urbis genio magno. [b] Nam facta perpetuo sub tributo, prohibita naves habere bellicas, spoliata elephantis, vetita tractare arma, obnoxia nobis

[a] *Cic. pro le. Ma.* [b] *Gell.* 6. *c.* 3.

[377] **Translator's note:** "obnoxii" should be read here for the "obnoxia" of both editions—cf. "obnoxiis," referring to the Carthaginians further down this page.

[378] Cicero, *Pro lege Manilia* 12. 35. **Translator's note:** Cicero's reference is not, of course, to the Third Punic War, but to an embassy of Cretans to Pompey.

[379] **Translator's note:** The phrase *furere furorem*, which I have translated "give way to utter irrationality," is derived from Turnus' desperate words to Juturna at *Aeneis* 12. 680: "hunc, oro, sine me furere ante furorem."

And in the Second do you come up with even less? For if captives were not sent back to Hannibal, that was because they were not demanded back by Hannibal. Express your claims! For justice is not rendered to one who does not seek it. The Romans were under no obligation to force upon Hannibal a justice he scorned. As for what concerned themselves, they satisfied justice in that they killed very base men whose deserts were well known.

What now about the Third Punic War? The charge is that the war was simultaneously declared and unleashed. But was it even declared? It wasn't even necessary that it be formally declared against the Carthaginians, who were at that time tributaries to us and were under our power through that pact by which they were obligated not to touch weapons.[377] That standard ceremony and ritual of declaring war is something owed to equals. And that ritual (this I reply to Polybius and Varro) was maintained by my people for as long as their equals existed. It was maintained with all those who were not our professed enemies. For why would we have declared war against the Germans and the Parthians, our professed enemies? And why in this case would we have done so with the Carthaginians? Why would we have handed over to them by a declaration of war the opportunity to take up arms which they could use against us?

That wasn't a real war. We weren't advancing against formal enemies. Rather, it was punishment of those under an obligation to us and rebels. The prevarications of the Carthaginians are mentioned in vain. And that whole business of Appian, that never were any fixed peace conditions mentioned, is destroyed by one simple declaration: "He did not take away the hope of surrender, but he demanded hostages."[378] To demand hostages and other things of that sort is not the same thing as offering a peace settlement. So the p. 199
good faith and the justice of Rome are intact. Concerning shrewd dealing, perhaps Carthaginian cleverness will have the sense to preserve a deep silence. Nor are we empowered by any law of war to condemn such cleverness. We are even able to praise that cleverness through which thought was taken for the best interests of the Carthaginians, lest they have the power to perish and give way to utter irrationality now that they were impotent and bound with tight chains.[379]

Tell me, Picenus, tell me one thing: shall it be forbidden to speak accurately and to follow and retain the proper meaning of words? For the Carthaginian state was assured of its freedom. And this promise was satisfied if the state [i.e. not the city] was preserved free: if the state retained its laws and its magistracies. No pronouncement about any other supposedly more excellent liberty could be understood—even about that great tutelary deity of the city you mentioned. For when it had been laid under perpetual tribute obligations, forbidden to have warships, deprived of its elephants, forbidden to

cogitare de suo illo genio Carthago non habuit: sed hoc tantum, quod dico: et quod illa audivit, intellexitque proximo fœdere Scipionis, *ut liberi legibus suis viverent.* Salva fides, salva Romana iustitia est. Non erubescimus. Carthago deleta pessimo suo est merito: deleta Numantia: altera in meridie, altera in occidente: [a] ad notandam hostium calamitatem nostrorum, æternum testificandam victoriam nostram.

p. 200

De Græcia et Syria.
CAP. IX

Et ita vix relictum Corinthi vestigium est. [b] Procul enim a conspectu imperii, potens exsurgere, atque recreare se, vehementer erat timenda reipublicæ nostræ. Nescis, tres solum urbes in terris omnibus statutas, Capuam, Carthaginem, Corinthum, quæ potuerint imperii gravitatem sustinere, ac nomen? Ipse hic tuus Cicero an non addit, in exscidium Corinthi Romanos motos ob istam caussam, ne illa loci opportunitas adhortari aliquando ad bellum faciendum posset? Aut ignoras, tantus magister, quantus videri vis, iuris licere consulere statui suo, et securitati? Res omnes, nec timendas fortassis, sed quæ aut tenuem præbent periculi suspicionem, auferre? Etiam prospicere in tempus longissimum decet: neque expectare, donec fores, et cubicula, cubiliaque periculum pulset. [c]*Victor hoc timere potest, quod non timet.* Certa hæc imperiorum ratio est.

Nunc igitur audiendum de iustitia est: per quam Romani et huic securitati caverint, et in Corinthi exscidium venerint. [d]*Critolaus caussa belli: qui libertate a Romanis data adversus ipsos usus est*: sic Florus. De quo illud, facinus indignum, ut oppressa civitas fuerit ante, quam in numerum certorum ho-
p. 201 stium referretur. Iudicium, quod negamus. Et ante diximus de | Carthagine, non esse opus cum his sollemnia hostium observare, qui sint nobis obnoxii. Audin' ab eodem Floro, ultionem mandatam criminum Corinthiorum?

[a] *Cic. agr.* [b] *Cic. agr.* 2. *de off.* 1.
[c] *Sene. Agam.* 4. [d] *Flor.* 2.

---

380 Aulus Gellius 6. 3.

381 **Translator's note:** The quote is from Livy 24. 1. 13, but refers to the Locrians in a clause of a treaty between them and the Carthaginians.

382 Cicero, *De lege agraria* 1. 5.

383 Cicero, *De lege agraria* 2. 87; *De officiis* 1. 11. 35.

384 **Translator's note:** Here "status" is closer to state, as on p. 276, similar to *stato* in Machiavelli's *Principe*: "Tutti li stati... sono stati e sono o republiche o principati."

385 Seneca, *Agamemnon* 799.

386 Florus 2. 16. 2.

handle arms, made subject to our domination, Carthage wasn't to be thinking about that famous tutelary deity of hers,[380] but only about this thing that I mention and which she heard and understood in the following treaty of Scipio: "that they should live in freedom under their own laws."[381] The good faith and the justice of Rome are intact. We are not ashamed. Carthage was destroyed by her own basest deserts; so too Numantia was destroyed—one to Rome's south, one to her west—for the sake of making known the disaster of our enemies and of bearing eternal witness to our victory.[382]

CHAPTER 9 p. 200

On Greece and Syria

And thus there is scarcely a trace left of Corinth. At some distance out of sight of our rule, capable of rising up and recovering its strength, it was very much to be feared by our state.[383] Are you unaware that there were in all the lands only three cities established which could maintain the authority and name of an empire—Capua, Carthage, and Corinth? Does not your very own Cicero add that the Romans were driven to the destruction of Corinth for that reason, lest that city's suitable location might be able someday to urge them to make war? But are you, Picenus, unaware—such a great teacher of law as you wish to appear—that it is permitted to look out for one's own state[384] and security? Are you unaware that it is permitted to make away with all things which, while not perhaps actually to be feared, offer even some slight hint of danger? It is even fitting to look ahead into the distant future and not to wait until danger beats on one's doors, one's bedchamber, and one's very bedposts. "A victor is able to fear that which he does not fear."[385] This is a secure principle of empires.

Now therefore it is time to hear of the justice through which the Romans took care for their security and came to the destruction of Corinth. "Critolaus was the cause of the war, for he made use of the liberty which the Romans gave him against them." Thus Florus.[386] He was the source of that supposedly base crime that the city was attacked before it was placed on the official register of
enemies—a judgment which we reject. For we have earlier remarked about p. 201
Carthage that there is no need to observe the formal rules appropriate to enemies in the case of those who are under our power. Don't you hear from that same Florus the punishment ordered for the crimes of the Corinthians?

Etiam cum his sollemnia teneantur, qui legationemque violarint? Non mittitur ad eos legatio, apud quos sanctum suum legatio locum non obtinet. Et isti per se satis, et super, tanto admisso facinore plusquam hostili, in numerum certorum hostium se retulerunt. Sic mecum de scriptorum sententiis, Picene, iudica.

Illa, inquis, commemorare non attinet, quæ notant omnes gesta turpiter a Romanis ad concilium dissolvendum Achaiæ: unde Corinthus, et reliqua Græcia conflagravit. Et hoc imperii arcanum nostrum, hic, alibi, notas. Ego tamen nec contra de isto pugnem: at nego solum factum turpiter. Achæi nimis potentes propter istam conspirationem videbantur? Hic nihil turpiter: ubi circumspectator oculus tantum apparet.

Quærebant Romani caussas belli? Scilicet remedium, quo tutior suus, et firmior status evadere posset: et quod neque reprehendere potes: ut ante in Tullo respondimus. Quærunt caussas. Sine caussis non movent: ut ante etiam respondimus in Sicilia. Quærunt caussas, iustas scilicet: nam iniustæ nec sunt caussæ: et iniustas nec necesse est quærere: quæ passim sunt. Et hactenus
p. 202 itaque nec quidquam turpiter: quod tu addis | verbum narrationibus scriptorum sane (pace sit dictum tua) turpiter. [a]*Quærentibus igitur Romanis caussas belli, tempestive fortuna querelas Spartanorum obtulit: quorum agros Achæi propter mutuum odium populabantur.* Hanc sociis demere iniuriam, placuit.

Nunc ne mutire quidem audet audax accusator. Aut eo revertitur, quod *legatis occulta mandata data sunt, ut corpus Achæorum dissolverent, singulasque urbes proprii iuris facerent: quo facilius ad obsequia cogerentur?* Illum iuvo. [b] Sic Themistocles graviter castigat Lacedæmonios, quod non virtute, sed imbecillitate sociorum potentiam quærerent. Sed non iuvo tamen. Erat enim Romanorum cura eius status, et libertatis Græciæ: cuius et conditores fuerunt. Audi, ut pro eo iure verba faciant, et decretum senatus in conventu totius Græciæ legati recitent. De Agrippa rege, quod factum temporibus Claudii, tanto fuit loquendum minus quanto rex ille subditus Romanorum magis erat. Sic igitur et deleta Corinthus, ingrata civitas, et violatrix legationum.

[a] *Iusti.* 34. *Plut. Philop.* [b] *Iusti.* 2.

---

[387] Justin 34. 1; Plutarch, *Philopoemen* 13.
[388] [Also from Justin 34. 1.]
[389] Justin 2. 15.
[390] **Translator's note:** Gentili seems to be referring to T. Quinctius Flamininus' famous declaration of Greek freedom and autonomy at the Isthmus in 196 BC; see Polybius 18. 46. 5, and 18. 44.

Are the formal rules to be observed with those who go so far as to violate an embassy? A formal deputation is not sent to those among whom an embassy does not receive its proper sanction. And those men by their own action have more than sufficiently counted themselves among the number of our enemies by having committed such a more than merely hostile crime. Judge the matter with me on the basis of the opinions of the writers, Picenus.

You say that there is no need to mention the actions which everyone points out that the Romans basely took in order to dissolve the Achaean league, actions which caused Corinth and the rest of Greece to catch fire. And here and elsewhere you mark this down as our "secret of empire." But I will not take issue with you about that, but I will simply deny that we did this basely. Did the Achaeans seem to be too powerful through that conspiracy? Here is nothing done basely, if it's just that a watchful eye shows up to have a look around.

Did the Romans seek causes for war? Indeed they sought a remedy by which their state might emerge more secure and stronger—and that is something you cannot find fault with—as previously we answered in discussing Tullus Hostilius. They do seek causes. Without causes they do not move, as we have already responded earlier with respect to Sicily. They seek causes—that is to say, just ones; for unjust ones are not true causes; and in any case there is no need to seek out unjust causes, for they are everywhere you look. And to this extent, therefore, they did not act basely—which adverb you add to the narratives of the writers basely (no offense intended). "Thus, p. 202
when the Romans were seeing causes for war, fortune opportunely brought their way the complaints of the Spartans, whose fields the Achaeans were ravaging on account of their mutual hatred."[387] It pleased the Romans to free their allies of this unlawful damage.

Now the accuser doesn't even dare to mutter. Or he is turning back to these words of Justin: "Secret orders were given to the ambassadors, that they dissolve the union of the Achaeans and make the individual cities subject to their own individual laws, so that they might be more easily forced to obedience."[388] I am helping him out here. Similarly, Themistocles harshly criticized the Spartans for seeking power not through their own courage but through the weakness of their allies.[389] And yet I am not really helping him out. For the Romans' concern was that condition and liberty of Greece, whose founders they themselves were. Hear how they uttered words on behalf of Greece's rights and their ambassadors read aloud the decree of the Senate in the gathering of all of Greece.[390] As for what was done with regard to king Agrippa in the time of Claudius, the more that that king was a subject of the Romans, the less ought to be said. It was thus therefore that Corinth, an ungrateful state and a violator of embassies, was destroyed.

Quid factum in Græcia reliqua? [a]*Implorantibus Athenis auxilium contra Philippi regis iniurias: placuit senatui, opem tantis ferre supplicibus. Quippe iam gentium reges, duces, populi, nationes præsidia sibi ab hac urbe petebant.* Ut pupillo nostro, regi Ægypti: ut amicis nostris, Attalo, et Rhodiis auxilia
p. 203 ferremus: bellum de|cretum contra Philippum. Etiam hoc renotemus in caussa Achæorum: quod etsi singulari, quam dixi, ratione Spartanis, aliisque adesse Romani non habuissent, hoc tamen generali decuisset eos, illam non negligere curam. [b] Id et Adherbal dicebat, Romanis pro magnitudine imperii esse curæ debuisse ius, et iniurias omnium. Id et Plutarchus censet in eo libro, qui de fortuna est Romanorum.

Græcia igitur, petita a Philippo in servitutem, Romana arma in Græciam devocavit. Iusta an non est caussa? Etiam censet accusator iustam. In altera cavillatur, Annibalis adiuti pecuniis, auxiliisque eiusdem regis: quia desierit hæc esse caussa, cum acceptas iniurias Romani dissimularint. Atque bellorum caussis sic præscribatur, ut iniuriis privatorum? [c]*Professa perdunt odia vindictæ locum.* Et in persecutione civili verum non est: cum semper sit magistratus eodem modo potens iniurias vindicare: est verum in violenta persecutione: quam præcognitam aut vitare, aut facilius omnino sustinere valemus.

Ridiculum porro postremum est, quod venerint immo ad deprædandam Græciam mei, prædones ipsi, et a prædonibus Ætolis deducti. Quid enim? liberatam Græciam non intuemur? Suspicionibus, petitis longissime, indulgemus: et præsentia cernimus gesta contraria?

p. 204 Aut iniecta hic mentio est de latronibus | et prædonibus, ut latrocinia somniata quædam memorata commode viderentur. Scilicet laudatissimo illo legum fonte societates piraticæ adprobatæ sunt: et eius rei superest vestigium illic, ubi scribitur etiamnum, potestatem a legibus duodecim tabularum his fieri, qui eiusdem collegii sunt, pactionem sibi ferre, quam velint: legem ex lege Solonis translatam: eaque permittente prædatum ire. Etiam permittente, *dum ne quid ex publica lege corrumpant* tamen: et, ut Solon dixerat, *dum ne id publicis sanctionibus prohibeatur*. Atque prohibitum tum erat prædari, et latrocinari. Aut si prohibitum non erat: quid reprehenditur? Et videtur sane necdum prohibitum: [d] nam inquit Trogus de temporibus Tarquinii regis, et Phocensium, qui Massiliam tum condidere, piratica, latrocinium maris illis temporibus gloriæ habebatur.

[a] *Flor.* 2. *Iusti.* 30. [b] *Sallust Iug.*
[c] *Sene. Med.* 2. [d] *Iustin.* 43.

---

391 Florus 2. 7. 4–5.
392 Justin 30. 3.
393 Sallust, *Bellum Iugurthinum* 14. 16.
394 [Livy 45. 22. 6.]
395 Seneca, *Medea* 154.
396 [*Digest* 47. 22. 4.]
397 Justin 43. 3.

What was done in the rest of Greece? "When the Athenians begged for aid against the wrongs of king Philip [III], it pleased the Senate to bring aid to such suppliants as these. Indeed, now kings of peoples, leaders, peoples, and nations were begging for garrisons for themselves from this city."[391] Thus we brought aid to our ward, the king of Egypt, and to our friends Attalus and the Rhodians; and thus we decreed war against Philip.[392] Let us even note this p. 203
again in the case of the Achaeans: that even if the Romans did not have to be on hand, as I have said, against the Spartans and others on this particular pretext, it would none the less have been fitting on this general principle that they not neglect this concern. And this is what Adherbal used to say: that the rights and injuries of all ought to be of concern to the Romans because of the magnitude of their empire.[393] Plutarch is also of this opinion, in the book he wrote about the fortune of the Romans.

So "the attempted enslavement of Greece by Philip . . . summoned Roman arms into Greece."[394] Is that not a just cause? Even the accuser deems it just. He finds fault with the other cause: that of Hannibal being aided by the money and troops of the king—because this ceased to be a cause when the Romans disguised the fact that they had been wronged. But are the reasons for wars to be circumscribed in the same ways as injuries done to private citizens? "When hatred is openly expressed it loses the opportunity for vengeance."[395] Even in an ordinary civil case it is not true [that one cannot disguise one's intention to prosecute], when a magistrate would be empowered only to punish wrongs always in the same routine manner; but it is true [that dissimulation is ruled out] in a case involving acts of violence, the sort of case we are able to avoid or at least more easily endure if we can see it coming in advance.

That bit at the end is particularly silly: that my people came to despoil Greece, brigands themselves and brought in by Aetolian brigands. What is this? Are we not keeping in mind that Greece was in fact made free? Are we indulging in far-fetched suspicions and viewing hostile actions as actually present here?

But mention has been thrown in here about brigands and freebooters, so that p. 204
certain imaginary acts of brigandage might seem to be conveniently mentioned. Piratical associations were supposedly approved of by that most praiseworthy font of the laws, and there remains there a vestige of that matter, where it is even now written that from these laws of the Twelve Tables those who are members of the same association have the capacity to make any agreement for themselves that they might wish, the law being adopted from that law of Solon which likewise also permitted that one may go on expeditions of prey. Indeed it did this, with the proviso "provided they impair no part of the public law"—and, as Solon had said, "provided that this is not prohibited by public sanctions."[396] And yet it was at that time prohibited to plunder and be a brigand. Or if it was not prohibited, how is this a matter of reproach? Indeed it seems as though it was not yet prohibited, for Pompeius Trogus says of the times of King Tarquin and of the Phocaeans who at that time founded Massilia (Marseilles), that piracy and brigandage on the sea were in those days considered glorious.[397]

Et fuit tamen, et nunc est aliqua latrocinandi licentia, ac sane iusta. Reprehendisti et istam licentiam prædandi res eorum, qui non in fœdere amicitiæ nobiscum sunt: leges isthic reprehendisti, quarum te sacerdotem profiteris: quarumque alii et in parte ista iustitiam defenderunt. Sed an hostium deprædari res neque licet? Et igitur sic cape pactiones illas, quæ permittuntur, nihil corrumpentes de lege publica. De hac piratica cape
p. 205 legem fœderis Carthaginensis: si Pœni piratæ sibi de | piratica omni non timuerunt ab aliis, quam ipsi affatim, et absque ullo iusti, et iniusti discrimine exercebant.

Neque vero Alexandri, neque Demetrii verbum, neque Platonis narratio tangit Romanos hic. Trahe, accusator, omnia: nihil attrahes. De Antiatibus illi dicebant: ut de his etiam senserit Plato, et de Tyrrhenis, et Thuscis: [a] qui itidem piraticam exercuerunt a prisco ævo. Oenotria ipsa proprie Sabinorum tractus est. Si vis, tibi responsum et in hoc esse. Oenotriam solam Italiam nominare prisci. Quod tibi tui auctores, Servius, et Strabo dicunt. Nunc iudicia: nunc afferuntur senatusconsulta. Et mihi fere venit in animum, concedere aliquantulum in defensione. [b] Audi Isocratem de suis Atheniensibus, *Omnia, quæ nostræ urbi obiiciuntur, non refutabo: nam alii ne deos quidem expertes omnis peccati esse putant.* [c] Audi Livium, *Nulla est civitas, quæ non et improbos cives aliquando, et imperitam multitudinem semper habeat.* An tu putas, cælestem aliquam Hierusalem a nobis isthic defendi? et non comparatione aliarum, quæ unquam fuerint, dicere, virtute civitatem meam propagasse imperium suum in orbem terrarum?

Et defendenda nobis esse etiam vitia singulorum, [d] quæ urbibus nemo adscribit? Etiam, quæ non commissa, sed sunt omissa, defendenda? Et
p. 206 grande erit civitatis Romanæ crimen, si Antiatum, et Thuscorum | latrocinia non impedierit? Etiam si non potuerit? Neque enim aut erat ubique unum populi Romani imperium, ut id posset ubique, quod cupiisset: aut, occupatissimo in bellis, semper ea fuit facultas, noxios compescendi, et puniendi. Etiam illa defendenda sunt nobis, quæ eversa contigere republica? Etiam, quæ improbata nobis: adeoque emendata nobis fuerunt? Nam, sic fuisse iudicia illa Ardeatium et Neapolitanorum, nescit nemo. Et illud accusator

[a] *Serv.* 7. 8. 10. *Æn. Cic. Hortens.* [b] *Isocr. ep.* 2. *panat.*
[c] *Liv.* 45. [d] *Sene.* 9. *contr.* 2.

[398] [Strabo 5. 1.]
[399] Isocrates, *Epistula* 2 (first letter to Philip), 16; *Panathenaicus* 64.
[400] Livy 45. 23. 8.
[401] Seneca the Elder, *Controversiae* 9. 2. 15.

There was then—and there is even now—a certain freedom of brigandage allowed—and quite a just freedom at that. You have found fault with that license to pillage the things of those who are not in a league of friendship with us—in this you find fault with those laws whose priest you profess to be and whose justice others defend in this very point. But is it in fact not permitted to plunder the goods of enemies? For this is how you must understand those compacts which are permitted provided they do no harm to anything of the public law. Take the clause of the Carthaginian treaty as concerning this kind of piracy: unless it was that the Carthaginian pirates harbored fears for themselves arising from other p. 205
people concerning every sort of piracy which they themselves abundantly practiced, without any distinction made between the unjust and the just.

Nor in truth do the words of Alexander or Demetrius or the passage in Plato touch upon the Romans here. Bring in everything you can, accuser; you will ultimately bring in nothing at all. Those men were talking about the people of Antium (as even Plato was aware of these people), and about the Tyrrhenians and Etruscans, who likewise practiced piracy from great antiquity. Oenotria itself is, properly speaking, a region of the Sabines—if you wish there to be a response to you on this issue. "For the ancients used to call only Oenotria Italy."[398] This your authorities Servius and Strabo tell you. Now you bring in court judgments and decrees of the Senate. And it almost comes to my mind to make a small concession in making my defense. Listen to what Isocrates says about his fellow Athenians: "I shall not refute everything charged against our city; for others think that not even the gods are free of all sin."[399] Hear Livy: "There is no city which does not sometimes have wicked citizens and does not always have an ignorant multitude."[400] Or do you suppose that we are defending some Celestial Jerusalem here? And do you suppose that I am not saying that it is by comparison with other states that have ever existed that my state spread its empire into the world through its excellence? And do we have to even defend the faults of private citizens, which no one ascribes to their cities?[401]

Do we even have to defend actions that were not performed, but left undone? Will it be a major crime of the Roman state if it did not hinder the brigandage of the people of Antium or the Etruscans? Not even if they were unable to do so? p. 206
For there was not everywhere one uniform rule of the Roman people that could everywhere do as it wished; nor, when they were deeply occupied in wars, did they possess the ability to restrain and punish evildoers. Do we even have to defend those things that happened when the Republic was overthrown? Do we even have to defend those things which we did not sanction and which we therefore later corrected? For no one is unaware that those decisions taken about the Ardeates and the Neapolitans were of that sort. And the accuser himself

ipse habet verbum, *Singuli non nocent universitati. De privatis spondere, aut præstare nemo potest.* Age igitur accusator, sic mecum contende de re publica. Age, contende mecum, si voles, simpliciter etiam, non per comparationem ad alias, de virtute reipublicæ nostræ. En quantum mihi præsidium aufero! Age, ad Carthaginem usque deletam mecum contende: etiam (aggredere latum campum) usque ad deletam Corinthum: usque ad deletum Mithridatem.

Neque enim mihi es imitandus: ut quemadmodum tu laudatissima omnibus secula vituperasti, ita laudem ego sequentia, quæ omnibus vituperata sunt. [a] Ad Carthaginem usque deletam laudamur certatim ab omnibus, [b]*Hactenus populus Romanus pulcher, egregius, pius, sanctus, aureus, atque magnificus.* Defendo ego et quæ sunt postea consecuta adhuc seculo altero. Nam p. 207 *hactenus* inquit historia pro|pter seditiones domesticas, et civilia bella: quæ nobis, virtute etiamnum virentibus foris, labem domi aliquam contraxisse videntur. Et de illis nec tu obiicis, accusator, nec est mihi animus respondere. Bene uterque distinguimus: quod eadem iubet historia, *ne scelera virtutibus obstrepant.* Defendo post Carthaginem multo: ut intelligas, non metu eius civitatis bonam exstitisse civitatem meam, sed sponte sua, ac virtute vera. Cur enim, si metus Carthaginis nos fecit bonos, Carthagine deleta, metu sublato non exsistimus repente mali? Id natura rerum, atque hominum experientia deposcebat. [c] At is, qui vere bonus est, nec fiet repente malus, et quibusdam veluti gradibus ad improbitatem declinat. Age, absolvamus de Ætolis prædonibus tuis: dicturi post de Illyriis, Balearibus, Histris, Dalmatis, Liguribus. Ætolis auxilia non missum, sed speculatores rerum Macedonicarum immissum accusas, et desertum Ætolos. Vera quodam modo facta. Sed accusatio non vera. Neglectæ in Græcia res: versis animis ad movendum tandem aliquando Annibalem ex Italia, bellum transferendum in Africam. [d] Et nec ita neglectæ tamen, (eodem auctore iam tuo) quin sub tempus initæ Ætolorum pacis cum Philippo proconsul in Græciam appulisset, auxilio

[a] *Aug.* 2. *de civ.* [b] *Flor.* 2. 3.
[c] *Cic. pro Syll.* [d] *Liv.* 29.

[402] **Translator's note:** Gentili seems to want to talk exclusively about the Republican period of Roman history and does not want to defend things "when the Republic was overthrown."

[403] Augustine, *De civitate Dei* 2. 18.

[404] Florus 2. 19. 1. [E. S. Forster's Loeb Classical Library translation (Cambridge, Mass.: Harvard University Press).]

[405] [Florus 2. 19. 5.]

[406] Cicero, *Pro Sulla.*

says: "Private individuals do no harm to the whole group. Who can give an assurance or answer for what is done by private men?" Come, then, accuser, enter a debate with me about the Republic.[402] Come, if you are willing, enter into a debate with me directly about the virtue of our state, not by means of comparisons to other states. Behold, how great a defense do I deprive myself of here! Come, debate with me right up to the time of the destruction of Carthage—even (let's enter upon a broad field here) all the way to the destruction of Corinth—even to the death of Mithridates.

For I mustn't imitate your method here; for though you have found fault with the ages which others have found most praiseworthy, I mustn't praise those following ages which have been criticized by all. Right down to the destruction of Carthage we were eagerly praised by all.[403] "Up to this point the Roman people was glorious, illustrious, humane, upright, and high-minded."[404] For my part, I defend also the things that were obtained afterwards in the next period. For the historical account says "up to this point" because of the domestic discords and civil wars which seem to have p. 207
brought a certain stain upon us at home while we were still flourishing with virtue abroad. But not even you make much of an objection to these things, nor do I have the inclination to respond. We keep these matters apart properly (as the same history bids us) lest "the crimes obscure the virtues."[405] I greatly defend Rome after the destruction of Carthage so that you may understand that it was not through fear of that state that my state became good, but it was of her own accord and through true virtue. For if it was fear of Carthage that made us good, why is it that we did not suddenly become bad once that fear was removed upon the destruction of Carthage? That is, after all, what the nature of things and the experience of men would have demanded. But that man who is in truth a good man will not become bad all of a sudden, but descends to baseness through certain steps on a ladder, as it were.[406] Come, let us make an end of those Aetolian brigands of yours, since we are going to have to speak afterwards about the Illyrian, Balearic, Istrian, Dalmatian, and Ligurian pirates. You make the accusation that aid was not sent to the Aetolians, but rather that spies were sent in to watch over Macedonian affairs while the Aetolians were left to themselves. To a certain extent, the facts are true here. But the accusation is not true. Matters in Greece were neglected; the Romans' attention was focused on getting Hannibal out of Italy at last and transferring the war to Africa. And yet affairs in Greece were not so completely neglected (judging by that same authority of yours) that around the time the Aetolians entered upon a peace treaty with Philip a proconsul did not land in Greece to be on hand for the aid of the

p. 208 Ætolis futurus cum decem millibus peditum, mille equitibus, triginta | quinque rostratis navibus. Et non irati mei fuissent, quod Ætoli sic sine nostra auctoritate, et contra fœdus, pacem fecissent? Non susceperamus manu plena bellum: qui in visceribus Italiæ Annibalem habebamus. Sed tueri Ætolos voluimus tantum, et Philippi arma inhibere. [a] Itaque illis dedimus, quod debuimus, aut etiam amplius: si pro libitu modo credere Livio, modo eidem abrogare funditus fidem non velis. Contra Philippum non est visum statim tentare amplius, et contra nobile regnum Macedoniæ, viribus eius incognitis, et inexploratis. [b] Legatum missum ad Annibalem dimisimus incolumem, *non in honorem regis, sed ne dubius adhuc indubitatus hostis redderetur*. Quæ sunt consilia virorum prudentum, non turpia versutorum arcana.

Sequitur de bello cum ipsis Ætolis, gesto pro Acarnensibus. Et Livius de iniquitate Ætolorum summa explicat: neque Acarnanas hic miscet. Strabo hoc scribit, Acarnanas solos relictos liberos ob istam vetustam caussam. Sed hoc aliud est. Nam in beneficio benignitas sola pro caussa. Ad bellum faciendum desiderare aliud consuevimus. [c] Si non et Plutarchi concidit fides: et Plutarchus sane accusat Ætolorum contra Romanos avaritiam, arrogantiam, contumeliosam contumaciam. [d] Etiam tuus auctor: *Offensi Ætoli,*
p. 209 *quod non ex arbitrio eorum Macedonia quoque | adempta Philippo, et data sibi in præmium belli esset, Antiochum in Romana bella impellunt.*

Etiamne defuissent prætextus omnes Romanis contra Ætolos, mortalium nequissimos: ut ad commentum illud de Arcanensibus fuerit abeundum? Sed neque auctor tuus, Picene, bellum Ætolis factum tum dicit, aut unquam ex isto commento; legationem ex isto commento Roma ad eos missam habet. Quid tamen aut commentum dico, quasi rem nihili? Et non iusta sunt bella Græciæ pro Ionibus suscepta, veteribus Græciæ coloniis? [e] Et non est verum, quod, cum venissent post Romani Ilion, tanta utrinque lætitia omnium fuit, quanta esse post longum tempus inter parentes, et liberos solet: et quantam epitomator Iustinus explicandam latius duxit? Et non est verum, ornatam eam civitatem a meis semper, de Antiochi spoliis statim? et non ipse accusator? *Albani, memores Italicæ originis exercitum Cn. Pompeii bello Mithridatico fratres salutavere*. Et hæc igitur belli fuisset caussa iusta.

[a] *Liv.* 26. 27. 28 [b] *Iustin.* 29. [c] *Plut. Flam.* [d] *Iustin.* 30.
[e] *Iust.* 31. *l.* 17. *de excus. Liv.* 38.

---

[407] Livy 29. 12. [408] Livy 26. 27. 28.
[409] Justin 29. 4.
[410] **Translator's note:** The "ancient excuse" was that the Acarnanians, alone of the Greeks, had not participated in the Trojan War.
[411] Plutarch, *Flamininus* 8. 5; 9; 15. [412] Justin 30. 4.
[413] [Justin 28. 1–2.]
[414] Justin 31. 8; *Digest* 27. 1. 17; Livy 38. 39. 10.
[415] [Justin 42. 3. 4. Cf. Livy's diverging view, *Periochae* 101. Gentili cites the same passage also in *De armis Romanis* 1. 10.]

Aetolians with 10,000 infantry, a thousand cavalrymen, and thirty-five beaked ships.[407] And would not my people have been properly angry because p. 208 the Aetolians thus without our authority and against the treaty made peace? We were not undertaking a war with our full resources here, for we still had Hannibal in the bowels of Italy. But we simply wanted to protect the Aetolians and to inhibit the arms of Philip. And so we gave to those people what we ought to have given them—or even more than that—unless you do not wish capriciously to put faith in Livy one moment and break faith with him the next.[408] It was decided not to make a fuller attempt upon Philip and the noble kingdom of Macedonia at once, when his powers were unknown and unexamined. The embassy that had been sent to Hannibal we sent back unharmed, "not to do honor to the king, but so that someone who was so far a possible enemy might not be turned into an undoubted enemy."[409] These are the plans of prudent men, not the base "secrets" of sly men.

Next follows the account of the war with the Aetolians themselves, waged on behalf of the Acarnanians. Even Livy treats of the consummate injustice of the Aetolians—and he doesn't even bring in the Acarnanians here. Strabo writes that the Acarnanians were the only ones left free on account of that "ancient excuse."[410] But this is another matter. For in the performance of a benefaction only good will on the part of the recipient serves as a proper reason. We tend to ask something beyond that for going to war. If not, then even our faith in Plutarch collapses; and Plutarch clearly accuses the Aetolians of avarice, arrogance, and insolent obstinacy against the Romans.[411] Even your own author (Justin) wrote: "The Aetolians, annoyed that Macedonia was not, as they had wished, taken away from the king and given to them as a prize of p. 209 war, drove Antiochus into wars with the Romans."[412]

Did the Romans in fact lack any other pretexts against the Aetolians, the most wicked of men, that they had to resort to that bogus business concerning the Acarnanians? But not even your author, Picenus, says that war was waged then—or ever—on the basis of that fabrication; rather, he has an embassy sent by Rome on the basis of that fabrication.[413] But why should I call it a fabrication, as though it's a serious matter to no one? After all, were not the wars of Greece justified that were undertaken on behalf of the Ionians, the ancient colonists from Greece? And is it not true that when the Romans came to Ilium afterwards the joy of everyone on both sides was as great as it tends to be between parents and children after a long separation (and at what length Trogus' epitomator Justin has considered it appropriate to draw it out)?[414] And is it not true that that city was always beautified by my people—starting immediately after that occasion, with the spoils of Antiochus? And does not the accuser himself say: "The Albani, remembering their Italian origin, greeted the army of Gnaeus Pompey as brothers"?[415] And thus this *would* have been a just cause of war.

Nam quid etiam de belli fine est? [a]*Memineramus auxilii* contra Philippum. *Sic* victis, deditis Ætolis *ignoscere placuit.* Redi, Picene, ad historias. Non etiam de iudicio risoris inepti, apostatæ flagitiosissimi hic mihi fereris mutum C. Cæsarem, virum illa vi ingenii, illa oris facundia, illa animi præsentia, illa peritia antiquitatis.

p. 210 Ætolorum casu, aut ante oppressus | Antiochus, et in regna Orientis penetratum, in quæ etiam itum antea improbe: cum Iudæis tributa fuit libertas, a rege suo deficientibus. Ita tu quidem accusator. Cæterum Tacitus, *Tum Iudæi Macedonibus invalidis Parthis nondum adultis, et Romani procul aberant, sibi ipsi reges imposuere; qui mobilitate vulgi expulsi*, &c. Ceterum quem tu memoras regem Iudæorum? Regem Syriæ, regem? non tyrannum iniustissimum? Siccine sancta illa Macchabæorum gesta? Siccine verbum effugit de ore abominandum? Non ego hic disputo: at, quod Alexander imperator respondit, aptem hic, [b]*Iurisiurandi contempta religio satis Deum ultorem habet.* Deorum iniurias diis curæ: ut alius inquit.

Etiam hic Trogus? Qui Damasco ducit originem, ducit Iudæorum: et illic regnantes maiores, Abrahamum, Israelem facit: et Israeli filios, decem: quibus divisum regnum: et Iosephi natu minimi filium Mosen: et, istum ducem Ægyptiorum: qui propter vitiliginem pulsi, et furatum sacra Ægyptiorum, et reliquas fanaticas ineptias scribit, non Tacito, aut Plutarcho melior Iudaicarum, et religionum scriptor.

Sed belli caussa cum Antiocho quæ fuit? [c]*Europa iam dubio procul ad Romanos pertinebat: Ille Lysimachiam repetebat, ut conditam a suis maioribus.* Bellum facit parvulo regi, qui postremis patris precibus nostræ erat fidei
p. 211 traditus: et | nostram hac de re spernit legationem. Civitates iure belli nostras factas occupat: et aliam legationem nostram hac de re mittit irritam. Parat in nos bellum amplius, etiam tentatis ad societatem Carthaginensibus: et tertiam legationem nostram itidem spernit: quæ id habebat, ut contentus terminis Asiæ esset, ne nobis ingrediendi Asiam necessitatem imponeret. Etiam non accipere, sed inferre bellum constituit.

[a] *Flor.* 2. [b] *l.* 3. *C. de reb. cr.*
[c] *Flor.* 2. *Iusti.* 31. *App. Syr. Plut. Ca. ma.*

---

[416] Florus 2. 9. 3.
[417] **Translator's note:** Julian the Apostate, whose *Caesares* Picenus had appealed to. I do not understand Gentili's verb *fereris*, which he seems to be using as a 2nd pers. fut. act., when it is in fact passive.
[418] [Tacitus, *Historiae* 5. 8.]
[419] *Code* 4. 1. 2.
[420] [Tacitus, *Annales* 1. 73. 5.]
[421] [Justin 36. 2. There is no reference in Justin to Moses being king of the Egyptians.]
[422] Florus 2. 8. 7 [curiously, in quoting Florus on the Romans' right to Europe, Gentili omitted the phrase "iure belli."]; Justin 31. 1; Appian, *Syriaca* 1. 3; Plutarch, *Cato the Elder* 12.

And what about the conclusion of the war? "We remembered their former services" against Philip. "Thus it pleased us to spare" the Aetolians who had been defeated and had surrendered.[416] Return to the histories, Picenes. I trust that you are not even going to rely on the judgment of an inept scoffer, a most wicked apostate and bring me here Julius Caesar struck dumb—that man with that famous power of intellect, that eloquence of speech, that presence of mind, that knowledge of ancient history.[417]

Antiochus was reduced to dire straits by the disaster of the Aetolians (or earlier), and the Romans made inroads into the kingdoms of the East, into p. 210
which they had already intruded basely when freedom was bestowed upon the Jews, who had revolted from their king. That is how you would have it, accuser. But Tacitus writes: "At that time, when the Macedonians were weak, the Parthians not yet mature, and the Romans were far off, the Jews themselves placed kings over themselves, who were driven out by the fickleness of the people."[418] But whom do you call the king of the Jews? The king of Syria? And do you call him a king, not a most unjust tyrant? Is that how you view those holy deeds of the Macchabees? Has a loathsome word thus escaped your lips? I am not going to argue with you here, but I shall apply here what Emperor Alexander Severus replied: "When the holiness of an oath is spurned it has God as its sufficient avenger."[419] As another says: "Injuries to the gods are the gods' concern."[420]

And does Pompeius Trogus, too, have anything to say here? He traces the origin of the Jews to Damascus and makes their ancestors Abraham and Israel rulers there, as well as the ten sons of Israel, among whom the kingdom was divided, and he makes Moses the son of the youngest son, Joseph, and he makes him the king of the Egyptians, and he writes that he was driven out because of leprosy, and that he stole the sacred objects of the Egyptians—and all the rest of the fanatical nonsense—a writer no better than Tacitus or Plutarch when it comes to Jewish religious matters.[421]

But what was the cause of the war with Antiochus? "Europe now without a doubt belonged to the Romans. He was seeking back Lysimachia, on the grounds that it had been founded by his ancestors."[422] He made war with a young king who had been entrusted to our loyalty by the last wishes of his father, and he rejected an embassy of ours about this matter. He seized cities p. 211
which had become ours through the law of war, and he dismissed yet another embassy of ours on this matter. He prepared a wider war against us, having even sounded out the Carthaginians for an alliance, and in the same old way he rejected our third embassy—this one was demanding that he be satisfied with the boundaries of Asia, lest he force upon us the necessity of invading Asia. In fact, he decided not to accept a war, but to initiate one.

Sic igitur, sic in Antiochum, arma cepimus: qui elatus successibus, cognomine auctus Magni, nostris, nobisque iniurius, et terribilis insultabat. Hunc multatum dices immaniter? Non ei lex ante dicta talionis, abstineret alieno, si possidere suum vellet? [a] Non hæc est æquissima lex, ut qui concupierit, et corripuerit de alieno multum, iste multum de suo perderet?

Etiam Perseus meritus, ut non aliter audiretur a nobis, quam si se dedidisset, et de summa rerum senatui permisisset arbitrium. Hæc est iusta pœna perfidiæ, et fœderum violatorum. Si vera est, inquis, defensio Persei. Si vera est: fœdera nec violavit. Sed qui nos accusas quasi ex vera illa defensione, quam nos veram inficiamur, eam nisi probaveris veram, nec efficis quidquam cum *si vera*. Falsam vincunt historiæ. Fœdus cum patre ictum, secum renovatur, [b] itaque suum, varie temeravit, et insolenter reiecit. [c] Non debet
p. 212 sperare veniam, qui ge | minat delictum: nec ei parcitur.

Quando autem illud obtulit de satisfaciendo iniuriis? Cum exercitus iam transportati in Macedoniam essent. [d] At cessare a bello non tenemur, etsi non satisfacere nobis hostis velit. Non etiam dare pacem tenemur aut ante bellum inchoatum. Non tenemur. Non tenetur iudex indulgere furi, qui furtum restituere velit. Aut nimis esset fœdifragorum bona conditio, si sic vitare iustam læsi indignationem, et reliquam peccati pœnam valerent. Sileat mihi de peccato alius. Non peccamus, qui pœnam sumimus de sceleratis, et nocentibus. Non peccamus, si, pars cum simus, supra volumus, quam parti debeatur, quod est satisfactio.

Immo enim et iudex sumus: ut alibi nonnunquam personas has duas sustinemus, in bellis autem semper. Et iudex iuste tum dicitur puniisse, cum id effecerit, ut et ipse, qui peccavit, tale posthac non audeat quidquam, et ceteri sint ad iniuriam tardiores. Sic Cicero: quem sollemni tuo more

[a] *l.* 4. *C. fin. reg.* [b] *Decia.* 3. *cons.* 117. [c] *Bald. l.* 5. C. *de episc. audi.*
[d] *Bell.* 5. *con.* 3. *cap.* 15. *ad quem Dan.*

---

[423] *Code* 3. 39. 4.
[424] Decianus, *Consilia* 3. 117.
[425] Baldus, *On Code* 1. 4. 5, fol. 58[v] f.
[426] Robertus Bellarminus [Roberto Bellarmino], *Disputationum de Controversiis Christianae Fidei, adversus huius temporis hæreticos*, 1. 5. 3. 15 [Tomi primi volumen secundum, Quinta controversia generalis, liber 3, cap. 15], Lugduni, Apud Ioannem Pillehotte, 1609, col. 1300; Lambertus Danaeus [Lambert Daneau], *Ad Roberti Bellarmini Disputationes theologicas de rebus in religione controversis*, Genevae, Apud Ioannem Le Preux, 1596, pp. 1140 f. [Daneau, however, argues against Bellarmine here and does not support Gentili's argument.]

Thus it was, therefore, that we took up arms against Antiochus, a man who, puffed up with his successes, magnified by the title "the Great," was disastrously and terribly insulting our allies and ourselves. Will you say that he was punished in a monstrous manner? Had not the law of an eye for an eye been told to him before—to keep his hands off other people's property if he wished to keep his own? Is not this the most just law: that he who has desired and seized much from another's property should himself lose much from his own?[423]

Perseus, too, deserved to be heard by us no otherwise than if he had surrendered to us and allowed the Senate judgment over everything. This is the just punishment of treachery and of the violators of treaties. You say, "If the defense of Perseus is true." That is, if it is true, and he did not violate treaties. But you who accuse us as though on the basis of that "true" defense which we deny *is* true—unless you will have proved it true, you accomplish nothing with that "if it is true." The histories prove the defense to be false. The treaty we had struck with his father we renewed with himself; and therefore it was his own treaty that he violated in various ways and insolently rejected.[424] He who repeats his crime ought not to hope for pardon, nor is he p. 212
spared.[425]

Moreover, when, exactly, did he make that offer about making up for the wrongs he had done? When armies had already been shipped over into Macedonia. But we are not bound to cease from a war even if our enemy should wish to make amends to us.[426] We are not even bound to offer peace even before a war has been begun. We are not bound. A judge is not bound to be indulgent to a thief who wishes to restore what he has stolen. Too favorable would be the condition of treaty-breakers if they were able to avoid in this way the just indignation of the injured party and avoid the rest of the punishment for their fault. Let another man keep silent to me about faults. We are not at fault when we exact punishment from the wicked and the harmful. We are not at fault if, when we are party to a dispute, we wish something over and above what is due to a party—which is what reparations are all about.

Moreover, we are also the judge in the case; while in other situations it does sometimes happen that we play these two roles, in war we always do so. And a judge is said to have punished justly when he has brought it about that the one who has done wrong would not afterwards dare anything else of the sort and others might be slower to do injury. Thus Cicero, whom you have

truncum nobis exhibuisti: sic leges, sic interpretes de pœnis: quæ prospiciunt generaliter in futurum magis, quam de peccato præterito cogitant. Ad hæc move caussam Persei. Divortii caussa nihil ad istam. *Si pænituit eum, qui libellum tradendum divortii dedit: isque per ignorantiam mutatæ voluntatis oblatus est: durare matrimonium dicendum, nisi, pænitentia cognita, is, qui acce|pit, ipse voluit matrimonium dissolvere: tunc enim per eum, qui accepit, solvitur matrimonium.* An potes non omnia mutilare? Aut ego tamen cur moras omnes non amputo? Quid responsum Perseo a senatu est? Mitteret ad consulem, qui erat in Macedonia, si satisfacere in animo esset. Mittit Romam rursus. Sed satisfactio est inficiatio facinorum manifestorum, defensio iniustorum gloriosa, deprecatio leviuscula imprudentiæ. Mittit et ad consulem postea: plenus spei ab non magna tamen victoria: et alia non pollicetur, quam quæ præstaret Philippus pater.

De Mithridate, et Annibale.
CAP. X

Superest Mithridates. Atque in caussa eius belli significanda duo habet accusator sophismata: unum, quod civitati adscribit, quod fuit a ducibus quibusdam, ut Ariobarzanes, et Nicomedes Mithridatis infestarent fines: alterum, quod hinc ducit belli caussam primam. [a] Et ante hæc Mithridates tamen contra edictum populi Romani plurima tenebat in Europa. Hoc fuit edictum, ut Asiatici omnes reges Europa abstinerent. Et edictum iustum hoc erat. Cum illi ipsi Romani tum Europam de manu Antiochi vindicassent.

Sed etsi hoc Mithridatis peccatum non esset; defendi non potest ille tamen: [b]*qui caussam quidem belli hoc prætendebat, attrectari terminos suos a*
p. 214 *Ni|comede: ceterum elatus animis ingentibus, Asiæ totius, et si posset, Europæ cupiditate flagrabat.* [c] Ariobarzanem, amicum nostrum, ac fœderatum, regno pellit, nostro munere: etiam et Nicomedem. Quos supplices cum restituere decrevisset senatus: ille meditata iamdudum, et provisa Septentrionis totius, atque Orientis arma adversum nos suscitat. Siccine decuit, aut licuit? Si

[a] *Aup. Mitr.* [b] *Flor.* 3. [c] *Iusti.* 38.

---

427 **Translator's note:** Papinian's judgment at *Digest* 24. 2. 7. In both editions, "sed" is nonsensically printed for the *Digest*'s "si."
428 Appian, *Mithridatica* 2. 13.
429 Florus 3. 5. 3.
430 Justin 38. 3. 4.

shown us in truncated form, as is your wont, and thus too the laws and the legal experts on punishments, which generally look ahead to the future rather than be concerned with the wrongdoing which is over and done with. Shift the case of Perseus to these considerations. A case of divorce has nothing to do with his case. "If the person who has filed a petition for divorce changes his mind and it has been submitted through unawareness that his mind has been changed, it is to be said that the marriage lasts, unless he who accepted the petition, in awareness of the change of mind, wishes to dissolve the p. 213
marriage. In that case, the marriage is dissolved through the agency of the one who accepted the petition."[427] Can't you manage not to mutilate *any* text? Or, rather, why do I not instead get to the point? What was the response to Perseus from the Senate? That he should send to the consul, who was in Macedonia, if he was of a mind to make reparations. Instead, he sent to Rome again. But his "reparations" were a denial of his manifest crimes, a haughty defense of injustices, a frivolous attempt to beg off of his thoughtlessness. Afterwards he also sent a message to the consul, bursting with hope after a rather unimpressive victory, and he ended up promising no more than what his father Philip had offered.

CHAPTER 10
On Mithridates and Hannibal

There remains Mithridates. And when dealing with the cause of this war the accuser has two fallacies that need to be pointed out. One is that he ascribes to the state what really was the doing of some generals: namely, that Ariobarzanes and Nicomedes were induced to harass the borders of Mithridates. The other is that he derives from this business the first cause of the war. In fact, even before this Mithridates held a good deal in Europe in defiance of an edict of the Roman people. This was the edict that declared that all Asian kings keep their hands off of Europe.[428] And this edict was just—for the Romans themselves had liberated Europe from the hand of Antiochus.

But even if that was not a wrongdoing of Mithridates, nonetheless that man cannot be defended, "he who indeed offered this as a cause for war, that his own borders were meddled with by Nicomedes; but raised up with p. 214
overweening spirits, he was burning with desire for all of Asia and, if he had the power, Europe as well."[429] He expelled Ariobarzanes, our friend and ally, from his kingdom, a kingdom which had been our gift; and he did the same to Nicomedes.[430] When the Senate decreed that these suppliants be restored to their thrones, that man stirred up against us the arms of all the North and East, which he had long planned and made ready. Was it fitting—

iniuriam fieri sibi a Nicomede credebat: et credebat etiam, agendum sibi de ea re esse cum Romanis: cur non mittit legatos Romam, ut fecit antea in controversia alia cum huius Nicomedis patre? Cur ad Cassium, aut ad alios Romanos duces nunc mittebat: a quibus concitatas sibi præsentes turbas existimabat?

Caussas (inquit Appianus) belli ita captavit: ad quod quidem paratissimus erat. Captavit occasionem ex civilibus Romanorum dissensionibus: ut sic Sylla ei respondit: immo ipse sic professus est prius: et inde suos animavit ad bellum. Quamquam et hoc falsum, a Nicomede factum principium iniuriarum. Ipse Mithridates primus et regno, et vitæ alterius insidiatus est. Id itidem ipsi exprobrat Sylla, [a] et contestantur historici. Moverat nobis bellum Mithridates cum apparatu illo suo maximo: quo solum esse contra nos opus videbatur. Et id prudentissime disserebat Nicomedes.

p. 215 [b]*Rei qualitas agentis intentionem demonstrat.* [c]*Paulum distare* | *videtur suspectus, vereque reus.* [d]*Instat nautis fera tempestas: cum sine vento tranquilla tument.* An exspectandum erat, dum professus se hostem nobis fuisset? Et non pluris facta eius, quam verba fuerant facienda? *Quis adeo stultus, ut non ex verbis potius, quam ex factis rem censeat*? alicubi Cicero. [e] Hostes sunt, qui apparatus faciunt, ut nos oppugnent. [f] Nihil a bello aperto abfuisse Antiochum dicebamus: qui magnis cum copiis in Europam traiecerat: etsi abesset adhuc a finibus nostris longissime: nam illum quidem, etiam si in Italiam traiecisset, negaturum.

Et itaque Mithridatici belli caussa, et principium sic sunt. Media belli infamare nobis tacite, clamoso illo suo silentio, maluit adversarius, quam producere in apertum. Videlicet traducere oratione nequiit Romanas partes: facinora ei narranda Mithridatis erant, quæ barbaries nulla a se admissa audeat confiteri: nullus, quantumvis audax, et ferreæ frontis patronus colorare susciperet: nulla excusare vis linguæ posset. [g] Ut cædem centum, et quinquaginta millium civium Romanorum, una die, tota Asia, uno nuntio faciendam curarit: et domos, templa, aras, humana omnia, atque divina iura violari. [h] Nam qui isti occisi sunt? Mercatores, alii inermes negotiatores, in amicis civitatibus, cum coniugibus, liberis, infantibus, etiam servis Italici generis: et
p. 216 abiecti omnes insepulti. | Proditio hæc scelerosa, latrocinium immane, fera

[a] *Sex. Vict.* [b] *Bal. l.* 14. C. *de testam.* [c] *Aus. ephemer.* [d] *Sene. Thyest.* 5.
[e] *Dio.* 45. [f] *Liv.* 33. [g] *Plut. Syl. Flor.* 3. [h] *Val.* 9. *cap.* 2. *Cic. pro Flac.*

---

431 Ps.-Aurelius Victor, *De viris illustribus urbis Romae* 76. 1–5.
432 Baldus, *On Code* 6. 23. 14. 433 Ausonius, *Ephemeris* 3. 63–4.
434 Seneca, *Thyestes* 959–60.
435 Dio Cassius 45. 37. 1–5.
436 Livy 33. 44.
437 Plutarch, *Sulla*; Florus 3. 5. 7. [The last part of this sentence is straight from Florus.]
438 Valerius Maximus 9. 2. ext. 3; Cicero, *Pro Flacco* 2 5. **Translator's note:** Valerius speaks of eighty thousand Roman citizens.

or permitted—to act thus? If he believed that a wrong had been done him by Nicomedes, and he believed also that he needed to deal with the Romans about this matter, why did he not send ambassadors to Rome, as he had done earlier in a different dispute with the father of this same Nicomedes? Why was he now sending ambassadors to Cassius and other Roman commanders, men by whom he supposed that the present brawls had been stirred up against him?

He thus grasped at causes for a war (says Appian) for which he was already fully prepared. He grasped at an opportunity deriving from the civil dissensions of the Romans, as Sulla replied to him; in fact, he himself acknowledged this earlier, and hence he encouraged his people to go to war. And this too is false: that the beginning of the wrongdoings was the work of Nicomedes. Mithridates himself plotted first against his throne and his life. In the same way Sulla reproached him for this, and the historians confirm this.[431] Mithridates was moving a war against us with such a massive mobilization that he obviously needed only if we were to be the object. And Nicomedes very prudently laid all of this out to the Romans.

"The quality of an act shows the intention of the agent."[432] "There seems to be little distance between a suspected and an actual culprit."[433] "A wild p. 215
storm is upon the sailors, even though without wind the calm seas are swelling."[434] Or were we supposed to wait until he had openly professed himself our enemy? And were not his deeds to be taken more seriously than his words? "Who is so stupid as to judge a matter not more on the basis of words than of deeds?" as Cicero said somewhere. Enemies are those who make preparations to attack us.[435] We said that Antiochus was virtually in open war with us when he had crossed over into Europe with a large force, even though he was as yet far distant from our borders; for he would be going to deny it even if he had crossed over into Italy.[436]

And so the cause and the beginning of the Mithridatic war were thus. The central parts of the war our adversary preferred to blacken for us in silence, with that noisy silence of his, rather than bring it forth into the open. Obviously he was unable to dishonor the role of the Romans in his speech. Also he would have to tell of the crimes of Mithridates, crimes no barbaric land would ever dare to confess had been committed by it. No defender, no matter how bold and how full of steely effrontery, would undertake to whitewash it. No force of eloquent tongue could excuse it—how he arranged for the slaughter of 150,000 Roman citizens to be carried out by means of a single coordinated message in a single day in all of Asia; and how he contrived that houses, temples, altars, and all human and divine laws be violated.[437] For who were those who were killed? Merchants and other harmless businessmen, in cities friendly to them, along with their wives, children, infants, and even slaves of Italian race—and they were all cast out without burial.[438] This was a criminal betrayal, a monstrous act of brigand- p. 216

rabies, internecina crudelitas: ut late etiam Appianus exponit. Dicam, prætores deditos? legatos in vincula coniectos? nominis Romani memoriam in terris illis deletam? Et his noster fecisset adversarius satis?

Sed mihi Murenæ factum est defendendum: quod factum senatus fuit: [a] et triumphus secutus est. Ais, Picene, negasse Murenam impudenter, videre se ulla fœdera. Et tamen non ille, Picene, impudenter, sed tu una amplius latranti littera imprudenter. Neque enim Sylla, a quo percussa fœdera dicebantur, eam auctoritatem habebat fœderis ineundi, ut ante tibi de isthac potestate ducum Romanorum responsum est. Et neque servata fuerant pacta a Mithridate: qui solidam Ariobarzani Cappadociam non restituerat. Sic contentus Sylla exsecutione pactorum: non facta, non perfecta, sed ex fœdere perficienda.

Quid, quod magnum parabat rex exercitum? Adversum Bosphoranos suos rebelles subditos? Sed erat opinio, eum immo cogitare Romanos. Et a qualitate exercitus utique cogitandum sic erat. Non satis Murenæ factum tibi defendi? Aut etiam testimonio Syllæ contrario habeo respondere? Sed quid ille de facto dixisset suo? Quid tu de Asdrubale, qui fœdus servavit suum? [b] Non probat testimonium, ubi vertitur testis existimatio.

p. 217 Nunc narra senatus Roma|ni fraudem: qui Murenæ palam denunciarit aliud, et clam aliud. Quasi circumvenire hostem dolis cum factorum, tum etiam verborum non liceat. Aut quasi tyrannis Syllana senatum eo modo agere non coegerit, ut sibi assentiretur, et gestis suis assentaretur. Nunc narra Murenæ sacrilegia. Quasi sacra hostium rapere nefas fuerit: aut quasi sit quidquam sacrum sacrilego homini: aut quasi non iuste repensa hæc sint Mithridati sacrilego.

Narra nunc patientiam, et æquinimitatem regis: et persuade, si potes. Alii enim censent, Mithridatem, præteritis admonitum malis, factum prudentiorem: et timuisse nunc vim Romanam magis, quam antea fecerit; cum se ad primos quorumdam ducum motus commovit. Nunc enim receperat Sylla, quæ rex rapuerat: ceciderat regi centum, et sexaginta millia hominum: castra ceperat bina cum apparatu omni. Senserat Mithridates, quod ille a suo sinu, ac latere sibi professus est, [c]*rem invictam Romana arma.*

[a] *Cic. pro le. Ma.*
[b] *Eug.* 1. *cons.* 51. [c] *Plut. Luc. Lips. prin. de mil. Ro.*

---

439 Cicero, *Pro lege Manilia* 3. 8.

440 Marcus Antonius Eugenius Perusinus [Marco Antonio Eugenio], *Consilia* 1. 51.

441 Plutarch, *Lucullus* 26. 3; Justus Lipsius, *De militia romana libri quinque*, Antverpiae, Ex officina Plantiniana, Apud Ioannem Moretum, 1598, p. 12 [citing Plutarch]. **Translator's note:** The friend of Mithridates in question was Taxiles, whom he sent to the Armenian king Tigranes to urge him to remain on the defensive and "avoid the invincible arms of the Romans."

age, a wild madness, a murderous act of cruelty—as even Appian sets forth at length. Am I to tell of praetors who surrendered, ambassadors thrown into chains, the memory of the Roman name wiped out in those lands? And could our adversary have made amends for these acts?

But I need to defend the act of Murena—which was really the deed of the Senate, and a triumph attended upon it.[439] You say, Picenus, that Murena "impudently" denied that he had ever seen any treaties. And yet it wasn't that he, Picenus, spoke "impudently," but that you spoke—just one extra letter barking out here—*imprudently*. For the fact is that Sulla, by whom the treaty was said to have been concluded, did not possess the authority to enter upon a treaty, as we have earlier responded to you about that [limited] power of Roman commanders. Nor was the treaty observed by Mithridates, who did not restore Cappadocia intact to Ariobarzanes. Thus Sulla was content with the performance of the agreements, not as though it had been done or fully carried out, but as though it was going to be done on the basis of a formal treaty.

What of the fact that the king was preparing a great army? Was it to be against his rebellious subjects on the Bosphorus? But it was the common view that he was in fact planning to move against the Romans. And given the nature of the army, one certainly had to believe this. Have I not sufficiently defended Murena, in your view? Or do I also have to reply to the contrary testimony of Sulla? But what could that man have said about his *own* deed? What could *you* say about Hasdrubal, who observed his own treaty? Testimony is not probative when the reputation of the witness is overturned.[440]

Now tell of the deception of the Roman Senate, which openly declared one p. 217
thing to Murena in public, and something else in private. As though it were not permitted to get the better of an enemy through deceptions not only of deeds but also of words! Or as though the tyranny of Sulla would not have constrained the Senate to act in such a manner as to assent to him and assent also to his deeds. Now tell of Murena's acts of sacrilege. As though it were divinely forbidden to seize the sacred objects of enemies! Or as though a sacrilegious man like Mithridates could have anything sacred in his possession! Or as though these actions were not just recompense against the sacrilegious Mithridates!

Now tell of the patience and the even temper of the king and persuade us, if you can. For others judge that Mithridates, warned by past misfortunes, became more prudent and now showed a greater fear of Roman power than he had earlier when he took action against the first moves of certain commanders. For now Sulla had recovered what the king had seized; he had cut down 160,000 of the king's men; and he had captured two camps with all of their furnishings. Mithridates had realized what a certain intimate and bosom-friend of his declared on his behalf: that "Roman arms are a thing unbeaten."[441]

Et hæc tua illa exsecrabilia media belli huius prioris. Unum hactenus bellum, unum: et alterum est, quod sequitur: et quod cum morte Mithridatis finitum est. Immo unum est bellum et prius, et posterius: quia non senatus, populusque priori, sed Syllana vis tandem posuit finem. Et scimus tamen dici ab historicis etiam tria cum Mithridate bella. [a]*Tribus ingentibus bellis sub-*
p. 218 *a|ctus felicitate Sullæ, virtute Luculli, magnitudine Pompeii.* Sed loqui historici consueverunt cum vulgo: quod ita existimaret, novum esse bellum, quod renovatum fuerat a Murena. Modo autem, cum quæritur de re subtiliter, missa vulgi et oratione, et ratione, loquendum, sapiendumque cum prudentioribus est: qui unum evincunt bellum, quod, bis suppressum, nunquam legitime finitum fuit.

At de caussa ultimi belli cur est silentium accusatoris adeo altum? Movit hoc sine caussa Mithridates. Ita Appianus. De insidiis, de parricidiis accusatio est. Sed etiam Attilii, hominis transfugæ, et deterrimi cuiusvis facta populo nostro transcribentur? Sylla cur reprehenditur, qui Archelaum ad se illexerit? Africanus cur carpitur, qui Pœnum ducem sollicitarit? Cur Papyrius, qui legatum Tarentinum corrupit? Equidem existimavi semper, licere corrumpere arma hostium, ad se pellicere.

Et Parricidium Pompeio cur datur? [b] Non hæc parricidia in illis terris sollemnia? [c] Et bella Orientis quando absque sceleribus aut cœpta, aut terminata? Non abierim longius. Mithridatis parricidia plurima Trogo notata ignoramus? Ab ingressu regni matrem veneno interfectam ignoramus? Bellum eius cum patre, gestum pro regno, ignoramus? Armatum filium Tigranis,
p. 219 nepotem suum, contra eius patrem, generum suum, ignoramus? Phar|nacem parenti insidiatum, timentem, ne faceret sibi pater, quod fecerat reliquis filiis, quos occiderat, etiam hoc ignoramus? Quid hic simile cum Farnesii casu est? Nisi quod accusator velit pudenda facere, ubi non sunt; illic retegere, ubi tegit iam tempus, et oblivio hominum, et, quasi nec sint, facit. At Pompeii facinus est: qui alia similia patrare solitus, et hoc ipsum patrarat ante in Africa?

[a] *Flor.* 3.
[b] *Liv.* 50. 100. *Oros.* 5. *cap.* 4. *App. Mitr. Iust.* 32. 38. 42. *Val.* 9. *c.* 11. *Dio.* 36. 37. *Zosim.* 2. *Serv. Æn.* 5. *Tac.* 5. *hist.*
[c] *Oros.* 5. *c.* 4.

---

442 Florus 3. 5. 2.
443 [Appian, *Mithridatica* 10. 70; Appian, however, says that Mithridates put forward the Romans' bad faith regarding their treaty as the cause for the war.]
444 Livy, *Periochae* 50; 100; Orosius 5. 4; Appian, *Mithridatica*; Justin 32; 38; 42; Valerius Maximus 9. 11; Dio Cassius 36; 37; Zosimus 2; Servius, *On Aeneid* 5; Tacitus, *Historiae* 5. 8.
445 Orosius 5. 4.

And these are those detestable events you allude to in this first Mithridatic war. Up to this point it was just one war—just one—and it was another which followed and which ended with the death of Mithridates. But in actual fact both the earlier and the later war are one and the same war; because it was not the Senate and the people who ended the first one, but the might of Sulla at long last. And yet we know that the historians speak of even three wars with Mithridates. "He was subdued in three great wars: by the luck of Sulla, the p. 218
valor of Lucullus, and the greatness of Pompey."[442] But historians are accustomed to speak in accord with popular opinion, which judged that the war which was renewed by Murena was a new war. But when one investigates the matter carefully, having dismissed the words and reasoning of the common people, one has to speak and understand in accord with the more sensible, who demonstrate that the war was one, because, though twice suppressed, it was never legitimately brought to an end.

But why is there such a deep silence on the part of the accuser about the cause for the last war? Mithridates set this in motion without [just] cause. This is what Appian says.[443] Now, there is an accusation of a plot and of parricide. But will the deeds of the deserter Attilius and of whatever deeply wicked man you wish be ascribed to our people? Why is Sulla criticized, who lured Archelaus to come to him? Why is fault found with Scipio Africanus, who tempted the Carthaginian commander? Why is fault found with Papirius, who bribed the Tarentine ambassador? Indeed, I have always believed that it is allowable to bribe enemy forces, to lure them over to one's side.

And why is parricide ascribed to Pompey? Aren't these acts of parricide customary in those lands?[444] And when were the wars of the East ever begun or ended without crimes?[445] I would not like to go too far afield here. Are we unaware of the very many acts of parricide committed by Mithridates himself, as recorded by Pompeius Trogus? Are we not aware that at the beginning of his reign his mother was killed by poison? Are we unaware of his war with his father, waged for the kingdom? Do we not know that the son of Tigranes, Mithridates' grandson, was armed against his father, Mithridates' son-in-law? Are we even unaware of this: that Pharnaces, in fear, plotted against his father p. 219
lest his father do to him what he had done to his other sons, whom he killed? What is similar here to the case of Farnese? Unless it be that the accuser should wish to create shameful deeds where none exist, to uncover things which time has covered and which the forgetfulness of men makes as though they had not been. And was it a crime of Pompey's, who was accustomed to bring about other similar acts, and had brought about this very thing earlier in Africa?

Ne tamen, ne tu mihi civilium bellorum furores huc trahas ad iusta bella. Illud, quicquid Hiempsalis fuit in Africa, belli civilis Mariani, cuius secutus partes pater Hiempsalis, exstitit. In sua sævit viscera rabies isthæc, et sceleri ius omne tradit. At alia Pompeii quid tentas? Probari nunquam Romæ valuisse cum omni eius viri gratia, et magnitudine, nescis.

Quis etiam te furor, Picene, rapit huc, illuc, quod ais, ut nullo ordine a Septentrione nunc feraris in Africam, et ab Occidente trahereris paullo ante in Orientem?

[a] Etiam Viriati notas casum, improbatum senatui, et populo, et tribubus. Et fortassis tamen nec improbandum (audi) contra latronem. *Viriatus ex venatore latro, ex latrone subito dux*: ut scribit Florus. Etiam Hispanum hunc latronem, et per latrocinia magis grassantem, latronum more, venatorum ritu, quam per acies iustas, et artes ullas imperatorias belligerantem, is
p. 220 Hispanicus auctor, ire in cælum, iubet: tamen a duci|bus nostris, nec illis quidem melioribus *fractum, et extrema deditionis agitantem*: quod idem scribit.

Non improbaveris, quod est et cum Iugurta affectum, et quod confectum est. [b] Erat regnum illud populi Romani munus: erat in fide Romanorum, et clientela. Perfidus rebellis Iugurta erat: cui iura iusti belli, et legitimi perduellis non deberentur. Verum obiter ista accusator. Et illud obiter de præmiis per nostram civitatem non uni sceleri contributis. Vidit enim ius apertum, quod dixi, licere corrumpere arma hostium, et ad se pellicere. [c]*Omne, quod datur, aut ob rem datur, aut ob caussam: et ob rem aut turpem, aut honestam: turpem autem, aut ut dantis sit turpitudo, non accipientis: aut ut accipientis dumtaxat, non etiam dantis: aut utriusque*, ut lex ait. Scelus igitur ex parte accipientis sit in casibus accusatoris: ex parte dantis non est. *Romani semper scelerum sprevere ministros*: quæ turpitudinem haberent et partis suæ. Sic traditorem pædagogum sprevere: sic veneficum medicum: sic alios. Neque enim lædere infirmam illam licebat ætatem: neque veneficiis in bello uti.

[a] *Flo.* 2. *Val.* 9. *Oros.* 5. *Sex. Vict.* [b] *Flor.* 3.
[c] *l.* 1. *de co. eb. tu. ca.*

---

[446] Florus 2. 17. 15; Valerius Maximus 9. 6. 4; Orosius 5. 4; Ps.-Aurelius Victor, *De viris illustribus urbis Romae* 71. 1.

[447] Florus 3. 1. 3.

[448] *Digest* 12. 5. 1. pr. **Translator's note:** This is about an action which was available when money had been received for an illegal or immoral purpose, with the money being recoverable if the receiver alone was the wrongdoer. The reference would only make sense in a context where the giver was trying to recover the money with said action; in the present context, however, recovery of the bribe seems besides the point.

But I ask you not to transfer the mad acts of civil wars onto just wars. For that war, such as it was, of Hiempsal in Africa was really part of the civil war of Marius, of whose side the father of Hiempsal was an adherent. That madness of civil war rages against its own vitals and hands every law over to crime. But why do you attack the other deeds of Pompey? You seem to be unaware that they never managed to be approved at Rome, despite all the grace and greatness of that man.

Also, what madness, Picenus, carries you off now in this direction, now in that, as you put it, so that in no proper order you are carried at one moment from the North into Africa, while just before that you were carried off from the West to the East?

You even censure the killing of Viriathus, which was not approved by the Senate, the people, and the tribes.[446] And yet perhaps this act was not worthy of disapproval (hear me out!), directed as it was against a brigand. "Viriathus went from being a hunter to a brigand, and from a brigand he suddenly became a leader," as Florus writes. That Spanish author praises to the heavens even this Spanish brigand, who conducted his attacks more through acts of brigandage in the manner of true brigands, in the way hunters operate, than he waged war through proper lines of battle or any arts of true generalship—and yet this same author records that he was "shattered" by our commanders, and not even the p. 220
better ones, "and he was considering the final step of surrender."

You will not have found fault, surely, with what was done with Jugurtha and how he was finally dealt with. That kingdom of his was a gift of the Roman people; it was under the protection and clientage of the Romans.[447] Jugurtha was a disloyal rebel, to whom the laws pertaining to a just war and a legitimate enemy were not owed. But the accuser just mentions these things in passing. And similarly uttered in passing was what he said about the prizes that were awarded by our state to more than one crime. Now, he sees that it is a manifest law, as I have said, that it is permitted to bribe the forces of the enemies and to entice them over to one's side. "Everything that is given is given either for a purpose or for a consideration; and for a purpose that is either base or worthy; moreover, it is base either because there is baseness in the giver, not the receiver; or because of the baseness of the receiver only, not the giver also; or of both," as the law says.[448] Therefore let the crime in the cases mentioned by the accuser be on the part of the receiver—it is not on the part of the giver. "The Romans have always spurned the accessories of crimes"—crimes that would involve baseness on their own account. Thus they have spurned the tutor who betrays his pupil; thus they have spurned the doctor who is a poisoner; and thus others as well. For it was not permitted to do harm to children or to make use of poisons in warfare.

In Annibale manet accusator. Insidias huic summo duci per orbem terrarum universum structas conqueritur, ac pæne lamentatur eiulabundus. Sed, uno verbo, an non receptum hoc ius belli est, ut victor victum, ubicumque
p. 221 existentem, postulet sibi dedi? Ut | violatores fœderum dedantur? [a] Hoc petiit populus Romanus a principio eius belli: petiit in fine: petiit postea. Dedi sibi Annibalem petiit, hostem victum, fœderis violatorem.

[b] Adde, qui infractisque rebus pertinax reges pererravit: senex non desiit omnibus angulis contra populum Romanum bellum quærere. Iste autem faciet impune iniusta omnia: populus vero Romanus adhuc persequi ius suum nequeat? Deposcebatur a Prusia Annibal, non petebatur occidi. *Sed Annibal, re cognita, sumpto veneno, legationem morte prævenit*: Trogus ait. Etiam cædis eius petitio iusta fuisset. Nam hostis iustus iam esse desierat penitus: iam privatus: iam a suis damnatus populo nostro: nobis deditus, nobis debitus. Etiam calliditas insimularetur nostra, qui versutissimum Pœnorum [c] facere suspectum suspectis nostris, et hostibus volebamus? Aut qui sunt doli isti turpes, quibus per nos petitus ille in Africa, Asia, et Europa? [d] Si dicis consilium Flaminii, quod et Romæ vituperatum exstiterit: privatæ inimicitiæ factum dicis, laudes autem civitatis. Et semper tamen dices, si verum amas, Annibalem iuste confectum.

[e] Ego tibi non dico, non ita convenire scriptores de morte Annibalis, ut de ea aliter, atque alii, non scribant alii. Etiam ut ruina cadentis Fabii Maximi in
p. 222 quodam prælio victor ceciderit. Non detraho tibi de laude e|ius imperatoria: non de isthac laude detraham Mithridatis, aut cuiusquam alterius hostis nostri. Hæc laus nostra est: vicisse viros fortissimos quosque, et eximios omnes belli duces. At neque tu mihi ratiocineris, vinci Romanos ab Annibale potuisse: qui Annibalem victum cernis.

[a] *Liv.* 21. *Sex. Vict. Iust.* 32.
[b] *Sene.* 3. *nat. q.* [c] *Iusti.* 31.
[d] *Plut. Flam.* [e] *Paus. lib.* 8. *Plut. co. Ro. et Gr.*

---

[449] Livy 21. 10. 6; Ps.-Aurelius Victor, *De viris illustribus urbis Romae* 42–9; Justin 32. 4.
[450] Seneca, *Naturales quaestiones* 3. pref. 6.
[451] [Justin 32. 4. 8.]
[452] Justin 31. 4.
[453] Plutarch, *Flamininus* 20.
[454] Pausanius 8. 11. 11; Ps.-Plutarch, *Parallela Graeca et Romana* 4 (306 D–E). **Translator's note:** Pausanias records an odd story that Hannibal, when denied asylum by Prusias, cut his finger with his sword while leaping onto his horse—and died from the infection some days later. Pseudo-Plutarch claimed to take the silly story about Hannibal and Fabius from the *Italica* of Aristides of Miletus. Knaack declared this work an invention of Pseudo-Plutarch: *RE Suppl. I* (1903), col. 132.

The accuser lingers over the case of Hannibal. He complains about the plots laid throughout the whole world against this supreme commander, and he practically goes into wailing lamentation. But, in a word, is this not a standard law of war: that the victor demand that the vanquished be handed over to him, wherever he happens to be? And that the victor demand that p. 221
violators of treaties be handed over? This is what the Roman people demanded from the beginning of that war; and they demanded it at the end; and they demanded it afterwards as well.[449] They demanded that Hannibal be given to them as a defeated enemy and as a violator of the treaty.

Add to that the fact that, stubborn even when his affairs were shattered, he wandered through the courts of kings and though an old man did not leave off seeking war against the Roman people from every remote corner of the world.[450] That man was going to do every sort of injustice with impunity; would the Roman people truly be so unable to pursue their right? Hannibal was demanded of King Prusias; it was not demanded that he be killed. "But Hannibal, when he got wind of this, by taking poison anticipated the embassy with his death," Trogus says.[451] And yet a demand for the slaughter of that man would have been perfectly just. For he had by this time thoroughly ceased to be a legal enemy, now that he was a private citizen, and now that he had been formally consigned by his own people to the Roman people—surrendered to us, owed to us. Is *our* cleverness to be arraigned, we who wished to make that wiliest of Carthaginians distrusted by those whom we distrusted and who were our enemies?[452] But what are those base tricks by which that man was sought by our people in Africa, Asia, and Europe? If you mean the advice of Flamininus, which was censured even in Rome, you are speaking of an act of private hatred, and thus you are uttering the praises of the city itself.[453] And yet you will always say, if you love the truth, that Hannibal was justly killed.

I am not trying to tell you that there isn't such a consensus among the historians about the death of Hannibal that some do not write about it in a way that is different from the way others do. Some even claim that he when he was the victor in a certain battle he fell dead because of Fabius Maximus dropping dead upon him![454] I want you to know that I do not detract from his excellence as a commander, nor shall I detract from that same excellence p. 222
of Mithridates, or of any other enemy of ours you might name. This is our excellence: that we have defeated all the bravest men and all the exceptional leaders in war. But you should do me the favor of not supposing that the Romans could have been defeated by Hannibal when you behold Hannibal defeated.

[a] Quis at dux tantus Annibal: qui Græco eguit magistro ad vincendum? [b] Et vero sic vicerant Carthaginenses antea Regulum, accito magistro a civitate Lycurgi. Conferam nunc eius facta, et Scipionis? [c] quem sibi Annibal, et reliquis omnibus prætulit: nec ausus in comparationem vocare: ut *inter magna non poni sæpe est eximiæ cuiusdam magnitudinis argumentum*: quod ipsa ista in re dici audimus. Certe præferre Scipionem potuit Annibal sibi. Annibal vix anno Saguntum cepit, urbem omnibus undique anxiliis destitutam. Scipio cepit uno die Carthaginem, urbem multo potentiorem, et præsidiis intus, et exercitibus foris munitiorem. Quot tentat alias ille urbes frustra? Neapolim, Spoletum, Cumas, Puteolos, Nolam, [d] exiguum quoque castellum, prope Placentiam, unde, quadringentis amissis, et ipse vulneratus discessit: Quas tentat noster frustra?

Vincit Annibal primo in Italiam adventu. [e] cum in otio fuissent mei post prius bellum cum hac gente: [f] et cum bellis aliis lacessita, non exercita p. 223 Romana arma fuissent. Vincit Annibal ad | Trebiam per Sempronii ambitionem inconsultam, ad Thrasimenum per impiam Flaminii audaciam, ad Cannas per furiosam temeritatem Varronis, ubique per suas fraudes multas. [g] Ut hæc fuit Punica fortitudo semper dolis, et insidiis, et fallaciis instructa: quæ certissima circumventæ virtutis nostræ excusatio est: quoniam decepti magis, quam victi fuimus.

Sensitque sic Annibal, cum imperitis ducibus se gessisse rem, postquam Fabium adversum habuit. [h] Huic neque virtute, neque bellandi arte par fuit: qui per tot victor acies iam a Fabio cohibetur, reprimitur, spe spoliatur victoriæ ultimæ. Tantine est, quod ipse Fabio dederit verba semel? Et tot iniqua Æmilii Probi afferri huc decuit? Castra castris collata non habuit? post Cannensem pugnam non habuit in campo collata? Ubi igitur Marcelli? Ubi Neronis? Qui iste invictus, a Marcello victus, ab aliis deiectus in angulum terræ Brutiorum, et delusus a Nerone veluti puer? Certe inter alia Annibalis felicia et

[a] *Veget. proc.* 3. [b] *Liv.* 18. *Flor.* 2. [c] *Liv.* 35. *Petr.* 3. *in* 3. [d] *App. Annib.*
[e] *Veget.* 1. *c. ult.* [f] *Liv.* 21. [g] *Val.* 7. *c.* 4. [h] *Front.* 1. *c.* 8.

---

[455] Vegetius, *De re militari* 3. pr.
[456] Livy 28. 43. 19; Florus 2. 2. 23.
[457] Livy 35. 14. 5–12; Petrarca, *Invectivae contra medicum* 3.
[458] Vegetius 1. 28.
[459] Livy 21. 16. 4.
[460] Valerius Maximus 7. 4. ext. 2. [461] Frontinus, *Stratagems* 1. 8.
[462] [Cornelius Nepos 23. 5. 4. Gentili tauntingly refers to Cornelius Nepos as Aemilius Probus, a grammarian of the 5th c. This was a common ascription in his day.]

But how was Hannibal in fact such a great leader, if he needed a Greek teacher for learning how to conquer?[455] And in fact that is how the Carthaginians beat Regulus earlier, having summoned in a teacher from the city of Lycurgus [Sparta].[456] Shall I now compare his deeds with those of Scipio? Hannibal set him above himself and all the others, and he did not dare to be brought into a comparison with him, since "often it is an indication of a certain excessive greatness that one not be placed among great things."[457] This we have heard said in that very matter. Hannibal certainly *could* rank Scipio above himself! Hannibal barely managed to take Saguntum in a year, though it was a city bereft of all reinforcements in every direction. Scipio took Carthage in a single day, a much more powerful city, and one more strongly protected by garrisons within and armies without. And how many other cities did Hannibal attack in vain? Naples, Spoleto, Cumae, Puteoli, Nola, also an insignificant fortress near Piacenza, from which he finally withdrew with four hundred casualties and himself wounded. What cities did our Scipio attack in vain?

Hannibal was victorious in his first arrival in Italy, since my people had been at peace after the earlier war with this people,[458] and because Roman arms had been teased, but not fully exercised, by other wars.[459] Hannibal won at the Trebia through Sempronius' thoughtless desire for honor, at Lake p. 223
Trasimene through the impious rashness of Flaminius, at Cannae through the mad foolhardiness of Varro, and everywhere else through his own numerous deceptions. Such was Punic courage, always fitted out with tricks and ambushes and deceptions—and this is the surest excuse for the frustration of our valor, since we were more often tricked than actually defeated.[460]

After he had Fabius against him, Hannibal himself realized that he had dealt with inexperienced commanders. Hannibal was no match for Fabius either in courage or in the art of making war, for after being victorious in so many battle lines, he was now held in check, forced back, and robbed of the hope of victory in the end.[461] Is it so important that he himself tricked Fabius one single time? And was it really proper to drag in here so many unfair things written by Aemilius Probus—that Hannibal did not find camps pitched opposite to his, that after the battle of Cannae he did not find Roman camps in the field at all?[462] Where, then, was the camp of Marcellus? Where was that of Nero? How was that man undefeated, when he was in fact defeated by Marcellus, was driven out by others into a corner of the land of the Bruttians, and tricked like a child by Nero? Indeed one should count among Hannibal's other pieces of luck the fact that he was called back from

hoc est, quod revocatus ex Italia est: ubi iam consenescens aut mori abiecte, aut fugere turpiter habuisset. Ceterum in disceptationem istam laudis bellicæ me non penetro, quam nec intrare voluit accusator. De factis quibusdam disceptat Annibalis: quæ contra Livium defendit. Et de illis ego silere itidem possem: qui
p. 224 hic accusationi respondeo, non accusem. At | mos gerendus est Piceno tamen: qui hoc vult importune, ut de Annibalis iustitia bellica ipsum inter, et Livium cognoscatur. Etiam ratio huc nos ducit: qui, sententias Livii, et aliorum magnorum historicorum suscepisse defendendas, et dignitatem eorumdem contra clamores huius vindicandam, videri possumus. Defendit cædem Saguntinorum Picenus, veluti necessariam, iustamque, nec crudelem. Sed neque Livius illam non excusat. Et est tamen, quæ nec meruit excusari. Audi: qui, exscusatione non contentus, quæris laudem, et pretium feres diversissimum. [a] Alexander alicubi in Oriente cum puberes omnes, qui pugnarunt secum desperate, occidisset, et urbem solo æquasset, creditus Indis est, bellare more barbarorum, atque latronum: Quorum sapientissimorum hominum, iustissimorumque iudicium reveritus Alexander, desiit ista in posterum. Romana, quæ profers, non sunt paria.

Et de Numantinis antea responsum est. Ænnensium conceptam adversus suum præsidium rebellionem, proditionemque nec tum potuimus, nec unquam debuissemus aliter vindicare. Fraus fraude pulsa, et subiectorum hominum perfidia punita est. Quid ista ad Saguntinos? At Romani in captis urbibus etiam animalia conficiebant. Sane etiam et viros, quos obviam
p. 225 habuissent armatos. At quid ista ad puberes Sagunti iam ca|ptos?

Habes de Fabio, crudelitate, perfidia: qui Brutios cecidit Tarenti. [b] Verum in triplici facti eius narratione, itaque incerta, quæ hæc est licentia accusatoris, ut rapiat deteriorem, et nobis nocentiorem? [c] Etiam absque proditione captam urbem, adfirmare valemus. [d] Sed si errore, et obscuro noctis secuta cædes est, vacat culpa omnis. Idem si errore alio. Nam quid si (et hoc pro certo fuerit cati, cauti, celantis ducis consilium) paucissimis Romanorum, atque Brutiorum cognita erat proditio? Tum rei ignari, Romanique Brutiique reliqui miscuerint utique prælia: per quæ cædes ista infirmiorum sit consecuta.

[a] *Polic.* 4. [b] *Liv.* 27.
[c] *Plut. apo. reg. et du.* [d] *l.* 4. *C. de adult. Alc.* 7. *cons.* 21.

---

[463] Polic. 4. **Translator's note:** Gentili might mean Angelo Poliziano here. He cites bk. 4 of Politian's *Epistulae* in *De iure belli.*

[464] Livy 27. 16. 6. [The three explanations are: error; inveterate hatred against the Bruttians; an attempt to eliminate the rumor that the city had been betrayed.]

[465] Plutarch, *Regum et imperatorum apophthegmata.* [Fabius Maximus 5 (195 F).]

[466] *Code* 9. 9. 4; Alciatus, *Consilia* 7. 21. **Translator's note:** The passage from the *Code* is about the Julian law about adultery; Gentili's use of the passage is based on a more than loose analogy. Alciati's *consilium* deals with the Julian law about adultery, but cannot be said to support what Gentili says here.

Italy, where he would either have had to grow old and die or flee in disgrace. But I am not going into that contest of martial glory that the accuser himself doesn't even wish to enter. He disputes about certain of the deeds of Hannibal, which he defends against Livy. And I myself could pass over these in silence, for I am here replying to the accusation, not making an accusation of my own. But we have to humor Picenus, who importunately p. 224
wishes that Hannibal's justice in war-making be acknowledged even in the pages of Livy. Reason, too, leads us in this direction, since we appear to have taken upon ourselves the defense of the views of Livy and other great historians and to protect their reputation against the outcries of this man. Picenus defends the massacre of the Saguntines as necessary, just, and not cruel. But not even Livy fails to excuse it. And yet it is nonetheless something that did not deserve to be excused. Listen, you who are not content with its being excused, but demand praise for it—and you shall receive a reward that comes from very far away. Somewhere in the East, when Alexander killed all the adult males who had waged a desperate fight against him and leveled their city to the ground, he was believed by the Indians to fight in the manner of barbarians and brigands; and showing respect for the opinion of these very wise and just men, he left off that behavior thereafter.[463]

We have already made a reply about the people of Numantia. As for the rebellion of the people of Henna hatched against their own garrison, we were unable at that time to punish it in any other way, nor ought we ever have punished it otherwise. Deceit has been repelled by deceit; and the treachery of our subjects has been punished. What bearing does all that have on the Saguntines? So the Romans even killed animals in the cities they captured. True—and men too, whom they would have found in arms against them. But what is that to the adult males of Saguntum after they had already been captured? p. 225

You go on about Fabius, cruelty, treachery—for he cut down the Bruttians of Tarentum. But given the three explanations of this deed, all of them speculative, what right has the accuser to seize upon the worst of them and the one most hostile to us?[464] Moreover, we are even able to assert that the city was taken without having been betrayed.[465] But if a slaughter followed through mistakes and the darkness of the night, all blame is absent.[466] Likewise if it was through an error of another sort. For what if—and this would indeed suit the plan of a shrewd, cautious, secretive commander—the betrayal of the town was known to only a very few Romans and Bruttians? In that case, ignorant of the facts, the other Romans and Bruttians would have undoubtedly come to blows, through which that slaughter of the weaker men would have inevitably followed.

Quid si nec errore ullo, sed vetere in Brutios insito odio cæsi sunt? [a] Hæc secunda narratio est. Dolori iusto condonari multum oportet: immo etiam temeritati ignoscitur multum, et inconsulto calori, et iræ. [b] *Quisnam audet leges vibrato imponere ferro? Inflammata semel nescit mitescere virtus.* [c] Atque audi et de ista ira, et de nocturnis præliis verbum ducis summi, *Regi frenis nequit et ira, et ardens hostis, et victoria commissa nocti: quicquid indignum, aut ferum cuiquam videri potuit, hoc fecit dolor, tenebræque, per quas ipse se irritat furor.* Duas concedimus, et ecce defendimus narrationes. Unam tu æquissimo iure habes relinquere: Quam et tueri possemus, si duri potius adversarii tibi, p. 226 quam iusti Romanorum advocati esse vel|lemus. Nam qui isti Brutii? [d] Gens bruta, et servorum colluvies: qui lictores, tabellarii esse iussi ad ignominiam sunt postea, propter defectionem, et iniqua alia in Romanos admissa. His hominibus, rebellibus, criminosis fides, si qua data fuit, etiam servata fuisset? Legitimis hostibus, non latronibus servatur fides. Atque hæc ad primum caput iudicii sunt.

Secundum est de vi captis Vicuviis. Et per criminis relationem tuatim tuum tueris Annibalem. Male. Et Pomœtiam nominas male: quæ rebellis civitas ius hostium non merebatur. Ita tu nunquam distinguis, quod distinguendum est semper, ius hostis iusti, et rebellis. Pomœtia item dedita, cum muros iam miles scanderet: adeoque tempore iam omni deditionis elapso. [e] Urbes Epiri aut perfidas, aut obstinatiores, redactas sub potestatem, et pactas de incolumitate nihil, quid non diripuerit, afflixerit Æmilius iuste? Calliditas quid exprobatur: qua usus is est in inducendo illuc rursus milites, ut non rursus oppugnare illas haberet? Non ita sævitiam suam Annibal temperavit. Vicuviæ neque vi captæ sunt: ad quas nec ductus aries fuit, neque scalæ admotæ. Et munitum oppidum captum vi sine istis quidem tentamentis dicetur, si se dedat? Apage novam rem militarem.

[a] *l.* 38. *de adult. l.* 4. C. *eo. l.* 1. *ad Turp. Tiraq.* 1. *de pœ. moll.*
[b] *Claud.* 2. *Ruff.*
[c] *Sene. Troa.* 2.
[d] *Fest.* Brutiani. *Str.* 5. *Diod.* 16. *Gell.* 10. *c.* 3.
[e] *Liv.* 45.

[467] *Digest* 48. 5. 38; *Code* 9. 9. 4; *Digest* 48. 16. 1. 5; *Digest* 48. 19. 1.
[468] Claudian, *In Rufinum* 2. 230–1.
[469] Seneca, *Troades* 279–83.
[470] *Sexti Pompei Festi de verborum significatu*, ed. Wallace M. Lindsay, Lipsiae, 1913, s.v. Brutiani, p. 28; Strabo 5. 4. 13; Diodorus 16. 15. 1; Aulus Gellius 10. 3.

And what if they were cut down not through an error but as a result of the old ingrained hatred against the Bruttians? This is the second scenario Livy offers. Many concessions need to be made to a just anger; why, there is even considerable forgiveness for rashness and unthinking heat of passion and anger.[467] "For who would dare to impose laws upon a brandished sword? Valor when it has been set aflame does not know how to grow gentle."[468] And hear now, concerning that kind of wrath and clashes in the night, the words of a commander-in-chief (Agamemnon): "But wrath and a passionate enemy and a victory achieved at night cannot be reined in. Whatever might strike someone as unworthy or savage, that anger and the shades of darkness have brought to pass—and rage stirs itself up even more though the darkness."[469] So we have accepted and, behold, defended two of the scenarios.

If you are going to be completely fair, you have to give up the third [that the Romans killed the Bruttians to cover up the agreement]. But we would be able to defend even that, if we were to be willing to be tough adversaries for you rather than just advocates of the Romans. For who are those Bruttians, after all? A p. 226
savage people and the dregs of slaves, who afterwards were ordered to be lictors and couriers on account of their rebellion and the other wrongs they committed against the Romans.[470] Even if we had given our word to these rebellious and criminal men, would we have kept it? Word is kept with legitimate enemies, not brigands. And this is an answer to the first heading of the indictment.

Your second heading is about Victumnae, which was captured by force. And in the course of relating the charge, you defend your Hannibal in your customary manner—maliciously. And you maliciously mention Pometia as well, which as a city in open rebellion did not deserve the status accorded formal enemies. Thus you never distinguish that which ought always be distinguished: the law concerning a proper enemy, and that concerning a rebel. Also, Pometia surrendered when a soldier was already scaling its walls—and thus when any possible time for surrender had already elapsed. How was it that Aemilius Paulus did not justly tear apart and shatter the cities of Epirus which were disloyal or stubborn, after they had been brought back under his power and had not made any pacts guaranteeing their inviolability? Why do you find fault with the shrewdness he used in leading his soldiers into those cities in order that he not have to besiege them all over again? Hannibal did not soften his own savagery the way Aemilus did. Nor was Victumnae captured by force, for no battering ram was led before it, nor were scaling ladders moved up to it. And is a fortified city to be said to have been captured by force if it surrenders when not even any attempts like these have been made against it? Away with your novel contribution to the art of war!

Sed iam perge ad caput tertium. Masinissæ, atque Maharbalis pacta statuis
p. 227 pari loco. Tu aberras, | Picene, non iure tantum, sed toto etiam (quod dicitur) cælo. Nam Masinissa pactum fecit Sophonisbæ iam captæ, et servæ: cui nec ipse Scipio promittere quidquam potuisset, captæ iam, et servæ factæ populi Romani. Sic ipse Scipio ait Masinissæ verissime. Et quod modo de Æmilio dicebamus, ille nec potuisset eis oppidis parcere absque iussu senatus. [a] Maharbal eos nostros nec expugnare vi poterat facile: nec putavit pugnandum cum desperatis. Sic Appianus. Et sic Maharbal cum liberis pepigit hostibus: cum quibus pactum tenet. Et tenet pactum a Maharbale initum: quia et huius paciscendi pacti potestatem dedisse ei Annibal intelligitur: qui misit: et qui iuncta mandato, quæque sollemnia ad rem mandatam sunt, intelligi denegasse non potest. De Maharbale amplius non dico, quod et ipse sua fide Punica, pactus abitum nostris tradentibus arma, nudos ad Annibalem ducit.

Superest caput quartum. Iniustum non esse perdere hostilia: et itaque magnam, et certam esse Livii imperitiam iuris, qui Annibalem in hoc accusat avaritiæ, et crudelitatis. Et Romanos idem fecisse: qui cum Annibale condemnarentur. Sed Politorium oppidum, iam antea vacuatum habitatoribus: quos in urbem, et civitatem Ancus transtulerat. Sed nostrum diruimus: ne
p. 228 hostibus receptaculum, contra nos propugnaculum esset. Ostende | caussam, accusator, cur Annibal ita fecerit non cum suis. Nam et est certe differentia aliqua, an in nostro quid faciamus, an in hostico. Voluntas nostra est ratio omnis eius, quod facere volumus in re nostra. Sed in re hostica sunt iura, et obligationes, quibus obstringitur voluntas, ac utrinque regitur.

An enim sacraque vastare hostium licet? [b] Nam tuus Annibal Deorum *sacrilegus face miscuit arces*. Hæc summa crudelitas: quæ cæco efferuescit furore: et munimentum ex se ipsa capit. [c] Hæc Annibalis tui virtus improba. Etiam virtutem facere ille improbam potuit.

Et hæc sunt omnia, quæ narravit contra Annibalem Livius. Falso tu ais, quæ potuit ille narrare. Plurima adhuc potuit: et multo quidem acerbiora. [d] Sed malignitatem redolet historici, et animum cupidum maledicendi, curiose perquirere, atque perscribere isthæc curiosius. Maximus historicus Thucydi-

[a] *App. Annibal.* [b] *Sta.* 4. *Syl.* 6.
[c] *Sil.* 1. [d] *Plut. de Herodo. ma.*

471 **Translator's note:** This is an echo of the phrase "toto caelo errare," "to err by the whole sky," found in Macrobius, *Saturnalia* 3. 12. 10.

472 [Livy 30. 14.]

473 Appian, *Hannibalica* 10.

474 Statius, *Silvae* 4. 6. 82. **Translator's note:** The text should read: *sacrilega face miscuit arces*.

475 **Translator's note:** This sentence is adapted from Valerius Maximus 9. 2. ext. 5, on Ptolemy Physcon: "adeo caeco furore summa quaeque effervescit crudelitas, cum munimentum ex se ipsa repperit," rendered by Shackleton Bailey as: "Such is the blind madness in which the ultimate in cruelty boils over, finding its bulwark in itself," Loeb, vol. 2, p. 317.

476 Silius Italicus, *Punica* 1. 58.

477 Plutarch, *De Herodoti malignitate* 3 (855 c). [The comment about Thucydides is also adapted from this passage in Plutarch.]

But now push on ahead to the third heading of the indictment. You judge the pacts of subordinate commanders Masinissa and of Maharbal to be on an equal footing. But you not only stray from the law, Picenus, you err cosmically, p. 227 as the saying goes.[471] For Masinissa made a pact with Sophonisba when she was already captured and a slave, someone to whom not even Scipio would have been able to promise anything—since she had already been made a captive and slave of the Roman people. Thus Scipio himself said very truly to Masinissa.[472] This is what we said just now about Aemilius Paulus: he could not spare those towns without the express order of the Senate. Maharbal, on the other hand, had not been able to completely defeat by force those men of ours, nor did he think that he ought to fight it out with desperate men. So Appian.[473] And thus Maharbal made an agreement with enemies who were still free, and with such men a pact is binding. And the pact entered upon by Maharbal remained binding, because Hannibal is understood to have given to him the power of making an agreement, for he sent him out and cannot have denied that those things customarily part of a mandate were indeed joined to Maharbal's mandate. About Maharbal I shall say no more than he himself made manifest with his Punic faith when, after he had agreed upon a withdrawal and after our men handed over their weapons, he led them off unarmed to Hannibal.

There remains the fourth heading of the indictment: that it is not unjust to destroy enemy property, and so Livy displayed great and undeniable ignorance of the law when he accused Hannibal of greed and cruelty in this. Besides, the Romans did the same thing, so they would be guilty along with Hannibal. But the town of Politorium was already earlier emptied of its inhabitants, whom Ancus Marcius had transferred to his city and state. It was something of our own that we destroyed, lest it might be a refuge for our enemies and a fortress to be used against us. Show me the reason, accuser, why p. 228 Hannibal would not have acted thus with his own things. For there is definitely a difference whether we are doing something in our own territory or in that of an enemy. Our own will is the complete justification of that which we wish to do with our own things. But with an enemy's property there are laws and obligations by which our will is hampered and guided by both parties.

Now, is it even allowable to pillage the sacred objects of enemies? For your Hannibal, "sacrilegious, put to the torch the citadels" of the gods.[474] This was the ultimate in cruelty, which boiled over in blind rage and found its bulwark in itself.[475] This was the "wicked courage" of your Hannibal.[476] For he could make even courage wicked.

And these are all the things Livy reported against Hannibal—and you falsely say that they are all that he *could* report. He could tell very many things besides, and things even much more bitter. But to painstakingly make a thorough search for such things and to even more painstakingly write a full account of them smacks of malice on the part of a historian and a spirit eager to speak ill.[477] Thucydides, the greatest of historians, chose not to make a

des ne quidem flagitiosissimorum plurima perspicua peccata percensuit. [a] Qui vitas scribit, is singula notat, vel levissima: de quibus cognosci homo possit, quem veluti pingit. [b] Qui historias scribit, is (sic veteres sapientes dixere) habet alium imitari pictorem: qui, si archetypum naturæ vitiosum videt, non exprimit in pictura vitium totum.

Sed vis, Picene, alias adhuc Annibalis audire virtutes tui? [c] Aut scire
p. 229 dissimulas, quomodo tractarit ille Nuceriam, quæ dedi|ta sibi per pactum erat? Senatum in balineis conclusum æstu suffocat: populum abeuntem configit iaculis. Et Acerris quid facit? Annibal non æquus Acerris. Senatum, post fidem datam, in puteos coniectum, obruit terra. Coniicit alibi in fossas captivos: qui usum pontium præberent. Inquit Florus de aggere quodam C. Cæsaris, quem fecerit ex cadaveribus, *fœdum etiam inter barbaros.* Quid hic: ubi non cadavera, sed viventes sunt? Subiecit alios elephantis proterendos. Coegit, fratres cum fratribus, filios cum parentibus digladiari.

Ad Cannas debilitavit iacentes; ut desolati morerentur. [d]*His pernas succidit iniqua potentia Pœni.* [e] Tot millia illic captivorum variis suppliciis interfecit. Hæc humanitas ad Cannas. Hæc laudata vox; *Cæsi ad hostium sacietatem: donec Annibal diceret militi suo, Parce ferro*: ut Florus recitat: qui eadem et de Cæsare in Pharsalica pugna, *Vox ad iactationem composita, Parce civibus, cum ipse sequeretur.* Parci ferro in pugna voluit, ut in otio mox resumptis viribus occiderentur, qui occidi per defessos nequibant. Vox illa Annibalis, vox non hominis, sed belluæ Libycæ, *O formosum spectaculum!* cum fossam sanguine plenam vidisset. Hæc improba vox: non illa, quam paullo ante tu reprehenderas in Africano. Ille enim in artibus, et viribus viventium potuit, ut co-
p. 230 gnoscere multa, ita etiam oculos oble | ctare. [f] Hominibus hoc contingit, ut casus alienos intuentibus etiam ipsa misericordia sit iucunda. Nescis spectacula Tragœdiarum. Sed Annibali quis alius, præter crudelitatis, vacat in spectaculo isto locus?

[a] *Plur. Alex. et Ca. Ut.* [b] *Plut. Sert. Iose. de vi. su. Nic. Greg.* 1.
[c] *App. Pun. Val.* 9. *c.* 6. *Flor.* 2. 4. [d] *Ennius.*
[e] *P. Diac.* 5. *Sene.* 2. *de ir.* [f] *Cic.* 5. *fam.* 12.

[478] Plutarch, *Alexander* 1. 1–3 and *Cato Minor* 24. 1; 37. 5.

[479] Plutarch, *Sertorius*; Josephus, *De vita sua* 65; Nicephorus Gregoras, *Romanae, hoc est Byzantinae historiae Libri XI*, 1, fol. 4[r] [in *Corpus universae historiae praesertim Byantinae*, Lutetiae, Apud Guillielmum Chaudiere, 1567]. **Translator's note:** There is no such passage in Plutarch's life of Sertorius. Gentili might simply take this biography to exemplify what he says the biographer is supposed to do.

[480] Appian, *Punica* 9. 63; Valerius Maximus 9. 6. ext. 2; Florus 2. 4. **Translator's note:** This is a faulty reference, for Florus says nothing of Hannibal's actions at Nuceria or Acerrae.

[481] **Translator's note:** Florus 4. 2. 85. Gentili misquotes. What Florus wrote of Caesar's rampart at Munda was that it "would have been disgraceful even if used against barbarians," *foedum etiam in barbaros.*

[482] Ennius, Vahlen 274. [Ennius wrote "iniqua superbia," not "iniqua potentia."]

[483] Paulus Diaconus, *Historia Romana* 3. 10; Seneca, *De ira* 2. 5. 4.

[484] Florus 4. 2. 50. [Gentili's quotation of Florus is garbled.]

[485] [Seneca, *De ira* 2. 5. 4.]

[486] [See *De armis Romanis* 1. 8, pp. 80–1, where Lucretius 2. 5–6 is put in the mouth of Scipio: "It is sweet to view even great struggles of war, drawn up through the plain without any danger to you."]

[487] Cicero, *Epistulae ad familiares* 5. 12. 5.

thorough survey of the many obvious failings even of the most wicked men. A biographer records particular events, even the most trivial, on the basis of which one can fully get to know the man whose portrait he paints, as it were.[478] But a historian (so the ancient sages declared) has to imitate the other sort of painter, who, if he finds his model in real life flawed, does not express all of the defect in the painting.[479]

But would you like to hear, Picenus, of other excellences of your Hannibal?
Or do you pretend not to know how that man dealt with Nuceria, which p. 229
surrendered to him through a formal pact? He suffocated with heat the senate which was shut up in the public baths, and he shot with javelins the common people as they were going away.[480] And what did he do at Acerrae? Hannibal was scarcely fair to the people of Acerrae. After they surrendered, he threw their senators down wells and covered them with earth. Elsewhere he threw captives into ditches that they might serve as bridges. Florus speaks of a certain rampart that Julius Caesar made from corpses, "something that would have been disgraceful even among barbarians."[481] What about this case, though: where it wasn't corpses but living people? Hannibal threw down others to be trampled by elephants. He forced brothers to fight to the death with brothers, sons with their fathers.

After the battle of Cannae he maimed those who lay on the field, so that they might die abandoned by their people. "The wicked power of the Carthaginian cut through their hams."[482] So many thousands of captives did he kill there with various tortures.[483] This was his "humanity" at Cannae. This was the context of that lauded utterance: "They were cut down until the soldiers were sated, and Hannibal said, 'Spare the sword'," as Florus relates, who says the same thing about Caesar in the battle of Pharsalus: "He uttered as a boast the words 'Spare your fellow citizens,' when he himself was pursuing Pompey."[484] He wished to spare the sword in a battle so that soon afterwards, when his men had regained their strength after some rest, those men could be killed who could not be killed by tired men. This utterance of Hannibal was not that of a man but of a Libyan beast: "O what a beautiful sight"—when he saw a ditch full of blood.[485] *This* is a wicked utterance, not that which a while back you had reproached Scipio Africanus for.[486] For just as that man was able to learn many things, so he was able to
give his eyes pleasure in viewing the arts and powers of living men. It comes p. 230
about for men that when they look upon the misfortunes of others even their very pity becomes pleasant.[487] You apparently don't know the spectacles offered by tragedies. But for Hannibal what room was there in that spectacle for anything but cruelty?

Nunc quid memorem annos eius in Italia ultimos, et ex Italia fugam? Cum videret, non se illic mansurum diu; omnes amicos, et Brutios suos, variis falsisque criminibus afflixit. Adi ad Appianum. Et hæc tamen virtus fuit tracta a gente, utcunque aucta in homine valde fuerit. [a] Nam Carthaginenses sub navibus ponunt captos nostros: qui ita per inauditum cruciatum colliderentur. [b] Vivos defodiunt dimidiatos: quibus necandis ignem admovent. [c] De Regulo cui non dictum? Ipsis etiam Afris damnatum facinus: quod tu defendere tentabas. [d] Etiam cruci suffixere captivos. [e] Quæ in tertio patrarunt bello, ea fuerunt adeo sæva: ut ipsi a sævitia sua terrerentur.

Dicam et de fide Punica? [f] Sextum de fœdere decesserunt. Audisti. Dicam facinora singula infidelitatis? [g] Cornelium consulem primo bello captum perfide: abductum Carthaginem: necatum. Secundo bello legatos Scipionis violatos contra ius gentium.

Immo me dies deficeret, si de istorum perfidia dicere omni, aut leviter attingere velim. [h] Vere, vere Masinissa, *periuram ab origine gentem*. Vere Virgilius,
p. 231 *Tyriosque bilingues*: de quibus etiam prodide|runt historiæ. Sed dicam de perfidia huius Annibalis? Dixi, *Perfidia plus quam Punica: veri nihil: nihil sancti: nullum iusiurandum: nulla religio.* [i] Missum ex pacto, qui cum elephanto depugnaverat, abeuntem mandat interfici, *Iurisiurandi immemore captivos necat*: ut tuus ait Zonara. At neque Annibalis perfida placet enumerare. [j] *Fideique sinister:* ut ait alius. [k] Infidelissimus: ut ait tuus Orosius. Nunc tu fidem memoria: quam iste aliquando servavit. Quasi improbissimus quis esse nequeat, nisi qui agit improbe semper? Et improbi etiam proba non agant improbe? [l] Et, qui nesciunt probe facere, his non accidat, ut aliquando faciant probe?

Nunc tu mihi humanitatem concelebra Annibalis: quæ dicta Livio inhumana crudelitas: et ostensa nobis vera feritas est. Sed humanitatem concelebras in funeribus ducum nostrorum. Accusas ducum nostrorum barbariem: qui caput Asdrubalis ante stationem fratris proiecerunt. Sed oportet, te scire,

[a] *Non.* palangæ. [b] *Gell.* 3. *c.* 14. [c] *Gell.* 6. *c.* 4. *Cic. Piso. Sex. Vict.* [d] *Sil.* 18.
[e] *App. Pun.* [f] *Gell.* 10. *c.* 1. [g] *Val.* 6. *c.* 6. *Oros.* 4. *c.* 7. *Flor.* 2. *P. Dia.* 2. *Ior. de re. su.*
[h] *Sil.* 16. *Virg.* 1. *Æn.* [i] *Plin.* 8. *c.* 7. [j] *Sil.* 1.
[k] *Oros.* 4. *c.* 14. [l] *Cl. Alex. str.* 1.

---

488 Nonius Marcellus, entry on *phalangae* (wooden rollers for ships).
489 Aulus Gellius 3. 14. 19.
490 Aulus Gellius 7. 4; Cicero, *In Pisonem* 43; Ps.-Aurelius Victor, *De viris illustribus urbis Romae* 40.
491 Silius Italicus 18.
492 Appian, *Punica* 118.
493 Cato in Aulus Gellius 10. 1. 10.
494 Valerius Maximus 6. 6. 2; Orosius 4. 7; Florus 2. 2. 11; Paulus Diaconus, *Historia Romana* 2. 20; Jordanes, *Romana* 165.
495 Silius Italicus, 16. 148; Vergil, *Aeneis* 1. 661.
496 [Livy 21. 4. 9.]
497 Pliny the Elder, *Historia naturalis* 8. 18.
498 Silius Italicus 1. 56.
499 Orosius 4. 14.
500 Clement of Alexandria, *Stromata* 1.17.

Now why should I have to mention his final years in Italy—and his flight from Italy? When he saw that he was not going to remain there long, he harassed all his friends, even his dear Bruttians, with various false charges. Go check with Appian. And yet this excellence of his was derived from his race, albeit it was powerfully augmented in the man himself. For the Carthaginians placed our captives under rolled ships, and they thus were dashed to pieces though an unheard-of torture.[488] They buried men alive to the waist, and then applied fire to them to kill them.[489] Who hasn't been told the story of Regulus?[490] That crime was condemned by the Africans themselves, though you were trying to defend it. They even crucified captives.[491] The acts they perpetrated in the third war were so savage that they themselves were terrified by their own savagery.[492]

Am I to speak also about "Punic faith"? "They have departed from the treaty for the sixth time."[493] You have heard this. Shall I mention the particular instances of their faithlessness? The consul Cornelius was treacherously captured in the first war, carried off to Carthage, killed.[494] In the second war ambassadors of Scipio were violated in defiance of the law of nations.

Time would fail me if I were to wish to speak of the entirety of their treachery—or even just to touch on it lightly. Truly, truly, Masinissa called it "a people faithless from its origins." Truly Vergil spoke of "double-tongued Tyrians" about whom the historical accounts have also furnished ex- p. 231
amples.[495] But shall I speak of the treachery of this Hannibal? I have already mentioned his "worse than Punic treachery, with nothing true, nothing holy, no oath-keeping, no religious scruples."[496] When a Roman captive who had successfully fought with an elephant was released according to a prior agreement, he ordered him to be killed as he was going away.[497] "Forgetful of the oath he took, he killed captives," as even your Zonaras says. But there is no pleasure in enumerating the treacherous acts of Hannibal. "Faithless," as another author says.[498] "Profoundly untrustworthy," as your Orosius says.[499] Now go ahead and mention the trustworthiness which that fellow observed on certain occasions. As though someone couldn't be utterly wicked unless he acted basely on every occasion! And do not even base men basely perform some worthy acts? And does it not happen that those who do not know how to act worthily may yet every once in a while act worthily?[500]

After all this, go ahead and extol for me as the "humanity" of Hannibal that which was called by Livy "inhuman cruelty" and which has been shown by us to be nothing short of animal savagery. But you praise his humanity in the funeral rites he gave to our commanders, and you indict the barbarity of our leaders, who hurled the head of Hasdrubal before the post of his brother.

nec iustos fuisse hostes hos fratres nobis: pro quibus eorum civitas non respondit, publico eos consilio exscidisse Saguntum, reliquum bellum gerere. Hic erras, Picene, sæpissime. [a] Perseum, et Siphacem, utcunque reprehendas, iustos tamen hostes, publico funere, honorifico, regali extulimus. Et primo Punico bello consul Romanus Annonis ducis corpus extulit magnifice de
p. 232 suo | tabernaculo consulari. Alia temporum, alia hostium conditio alios mores postulat.

[b] Et nescis, istum Asdrubalem fallaciis malis, promissis mendacibus antea huic illusisse Neroni: qui de scelerato capite vindictam in præsentia capit? qui ait, *Non hic nemora avia fallent Pyrenes, nec promisses frustrabere vanis. Ut quondam terra fallax deprehensus Ibera, Evasti nostram mentito fœdere dextram.* Et Annibali ipsi, *Duplica nunc perfida bella.* Etiam in bellorum acerbitate nec sunt ista illico condemnanda: quæ et usurpata cernimus sine reprehensione sæpius. [c]*Curruque abscissa duorum Suspendit capita, et rorantia sanguine portat* ad aliorum terrorem Turnus. *Ptolomæus*, Macedonum rex in prælio adversus Gallos, *multis vulneribus saucius capitur: caput eius amputatum; et lanceæ fixum tota acie ad terrorem hostium circumfertur.* [d] Et Priami caput affixum conto, *iacet ingens litore truncus*: et hoc sollemne fieri viris insignibus. *In hastis præfigunt capita, et multo clamore sequuntur, Euryali, et Nisi.* [e] Caput Cyri amputatum in utrem humano sanguine repletum Tomyris coniecit, cum hac exprobatione crudelitatis, ut se sanguine satiaret, quem sitierat. [f] Capiti amputato Crassi infundunt aurum Parthi cum elogio simili, ut se auro satiaret, quod sitierat. [g] Et hic repensum quod Parthis est a Ventidio: qui
p. 233 illorum regis caput per urbes circumtu|lit. Audi. Repensum et Annibali hic est: [h]*qui nobis, memini, ad Cannas lætissimus iræ, Servili fert ora ducis suffixa veruto.* Hoc ius est sine cuiusquam indignatione iusta. [i]*Fas est, ab hoste doceri.*

[a] *Val.* 5. *c.* 1. *P. Diac.* 3. 4. [b] *Liv.* 26. *Sil.* 15. [c] *Virg.* 12. *ubi. Serv. Iusti.* 24.
[d] *Serviu. Æn.* 2. [e] *Iusti.* 1. *Herodo.* 1. [f] *Appian. Parth. Flor.* 3. [g] *Flor.* 4.
[h] *Sil.* 17. *Lips.* 4. *Poliorc.* 4. [i] *Ovid. Metam.* 4.

---

501 Valerius Maximus 5. 1. 1b, 1e, 2; Paulus Diaconus, *Historia Romana* 3. 4.
502 Livy 26. 17; Silius Italicus 15.
503 [Silius Italicus 15. 790–3.]
504 [Silius Italicus 15. 816.]
505 Vergil, *Aeneis* 12. 511–12.
506 Justin 24. 5.
507 Servius, *On Aeneid* 2. 557.
508 [Vergil, *Aeneis* 9. 465–7.]
509 Justin 1. 8; Herodotus 1. 214.
510 Appian, *Parthica*; Florus 3. 11. 11. **Translator's note:** Though Appian promised at *Bella civilia* 2. 18 to give a fuller account of the death of Crassus in his *Parthica*, it appears that he never completed that account. What Gentili consulted seems to have been a Byzantine forgery.
511 Florus 4. 9. 7.
512 Silius Italicus 17. 307–8; Justus Lipsius, *Poliorceticon* 4. 4.
513 Ovid, *Metamorphoses* 4.428.

But you need to realize that those brothers had not been for us enemies protected by the laws of war, for their own state did not vouch for them that they had destroyed Saguntum or waged the rest of the war by decision of the community. You make a lot of errors in this section, Picenus. Perseus and Siphax, however you might want to find fault with them, were at least legitimate enemies, and so we bore them forth to their graves with public, honorable, even regal funeral rites. And in the First Punic War a Roman consul carried forth from his own consular tent the body of the commander p. 232
Hanno with pomp and circumstance.[501] Different historical circumstances—and different enemies—demand different behaviors.

And do you not know that Hasdrubal had previously tricked this same Nero, who now took vengeance on his criminal head, with evil dodges and lying promises?[502] Nero said: "Not here shall the trackless forests of the Pyrenees deceive me, nor shall you cheat me with false promises, as once upon a time, when seized in the Iberian land, you deceitfully escaped our right hand with a lying treaty."[503] And to Hannibal himself he said: "Now redouble your treacherous wars."[504] Also, in the bitterness of wars those acts are not automatically to be condemned, for we see that they have rather often been practiced without criticism. Thus, Turnus, in order to strike terror into the others, "hung the severed heads of two men from his chariot and carried them along spraying blood."[505] Ptolemy, king of Macedon, in a battle against the Gauls, "was captured hurt with many wounds; his severed head, affixed to a lance, was carried around the whole battle-line in order to cause terror to the enemy.[506] And the head of Priam was affixed to a pole, while "his great body lay on the shore"[507]—and this is a customary thing to happen to distinguished men. "They fix the heads of Nisus and Euryalus on spears and follow them with much shouting."[508] Queen Tomyris cast the head of Cyrus into a leather bag full of human blood, while uttering this reproach upon his cruelty: that he might sate himself on the blood for which he had thirsted.[509] The Parthians poured gold into the severed head of Crassus with a similar utterance: that he might sate himself on the gold for which he had thirsted.[510] And this was paid back to the Parthians by Ventidius, who carried the head of their king through the cities (which had revolted).[511] Listen! p. 233
There was payback for Hannibal as well here, "who, I recall, rejoicing greatly in his wrath against us at Cannae, carried the head of Servilius fixed on a javelin."[512] This right of war goes without anyone's proper indignation. "It is allowed to be taught by one's enemy."[513]

[a] Quid tibi alia dicam capita? adolescentis Pompeii in Hispania, Romanorum in Macedonia, Pyrrhi Argis, Saulis in Syria? [b] Quid capita principum Madianitarum captorum delata ad Gedeonem? Caput Goliæ a Davide præcisum, et sulpensum longo ostentui? Caput Nicanoris, dextramque, truncata, suspensa a Macchabeo? Caput Olofernis a Iuditha? At istam iam lanienam sino. Iacent Pœni, iacet Mithridates.

Reliquum imperium, et Cæsares.
CAP. XI

Nunc reliqua Romanorum bella dicenda sunt: cum Liguribus, Histris, Dalmatis, Illyriis, Balearibus, Cretensibus, Cypriis, Britannis, Gallis, Cantabris, et si quæ sunt alia. Ut enim *bona fide adolevit* ([c] quod ait historicus) nostra civitas: ita bonaque fides eius per totam hanc iuventutem, cum subegit reliquum orbem, ostendenda a nobis est.

Atque Ligures vel Gallicos intelligit accusator, vel Italicos. Nobis contra utrosque iustæ bellorum caussæ superfuerunt. [d] Itum contra illos est: quod sociorum usque a Tarquinio rege nostrorum, Massiliensium, fidissimæ, atque
p. 234 amicissimæ civitatis, oppida Antipolim, et Nicæ|am vastarent: ut contra Allobrogas vicinos, Aruernosque itum pro Heduis est fratribus, nostram implorantibus opem. [e] Itum contra alteros Ligures est, et pugnatum annos octuaginta: quod iter nobis in Hispaniam impedirent: suis assiduis latrociniis arma nostra lacesserent. [f] Cum Histris, Carnis, Iapidibus bellum fuit: qui Ætolis se contra nos coniunxere.

[a] *Herodo.* 5. *Hirs. Hisp. Liv.* 42. 1. *Sam. ult. Iust.* 25.
[b] *Iud.* 7. 1. *Sam.* 17. *Iudit.* 13. 1. *Macc.* 7. 2. *Macc. ult.*
[c] *Flor.* 2.
[d] *Liv.* 47. 60. 61. *Flo.* 3. *Iusti.* 43.
[e] *Str.* 4. *Flor.* 2.
[f] *Flor.* 2. *Plin. P. Diac.* 3.

---

514 Herodotus 5. 114; Aulus Hirtius, *De bello Hispaniensi* 39 [this work is probably not by Hirtius]; 1 Samuel 31: 9; Justin 25.

515 Judges 7: 25; 1 Samuel 17: 51;17: 57; Judith 13: 8; 1 Maccabees 7: 47.

516 Florus 2. 1. 1. **Translator's note:** This is a perhaps intentional misreading of Florus' words "cum bona fide adolevisset," where "bona fide" has the adverbial sense of "truly," not the instrumental sense of "though good faith."

517 Livy, *Periochae* 47, 60, 61; Florus 3. 2. 3–4; Justin 43. 3.

518 Strabo 4. 6. 9–10; Florus 2. 3. 1–5.

519 Florus 2. 10. 1–3; Pliny the Elder, *Historia naturalis* 3. 18. 22; Paulus Diaconus, *Historia Romana* 3. 7.

Why should I list other heads for you? There was that of young Gnaeus Pompey in Spain, those of the Romans in Macedonia, that of Pyrrhus in Argos, that of Saul in Syria.[514] What of the heads of the captured Midianite princes which were taken to Gideon? What of the head of Goliath cut off by David and hung up for a lengthy display? What of the head and right hand of Nicanor, cut off and hung up by Maccabeus?[515] What of the head of Holofernes, cut off by Judith? But I'm letting that butcher show go now. The Carthaginians lie dead now, and so does Mithridates.

CHAPTER 11

The Rest of the Empire and the Caesars

Now the rest of the wars of the Romans have to be mentioned—wars with the Ligurians, the Istrians, the Dalmatians, the Illyrians, the Balearic Islanders, the Cretans, the Cypriotes, the Britons, the Gauls, the Cantabrians, and whatever others there are. Just as our state "came to maturity through its good faith" (as the historian says[516]), so we need to demonstrate its good faith through its young manhood, when it subdued the rest of the world.

Now, the accuser understands that the Ligurians were of two sorts: Gallic and Italian. We had an abundance of just causes for wars against both. We had to move against the Gallic Ligurians because they were pillaging the towns Antipolis and Nicaea, which belonged to the people p. 234
of Massilia, a very faithful and friendly city, who had been our allies since the days of King Tarquin—just as we had to move against their neighbors the Allobroges and the Arverni on behalf of our brothers the Aedui, who besought our aid.[517] We had to move against the other Ligurians as well and to fight them for eighty years—because they impeded our way into Spain and aroused our arms with their constant acts of brigandage.[518] There was war with the Istrians, the Carni, the Iapides, who allied with the Aetolians against us.[519]

Cum Histris etiam: qui latrocinati naves nostras fuere. Belli primi adversus Illyrios non videtur accusatori caussa iusta facinus privatorum. Et quidem non est: nisi si privata nos non compescimus, aut non ulciscimur malefacta. Nam publicum sic evadit facinus, quod est privatum. [a] Et scientia enim, et voluntas, et mandatum præsumitur domini, quando non momento delinquitur, sed iterum atque iterum pluries. Et id certum, atque exploratum est. [b] Sed et legati nostri cæsi in Illyrio fuerant iussu reginæ. [c] Bella posteriora itidem iusta cum sociis hostium, et rebellibus nostris. [d] Et propter Illyrios, postea amicos, bellatum cum Dalmatis est: qui agros Illyricos devastarunt: iniurias alias amicis aliisque nostris intulerunt acerbiores: nobis nec moderate responderunt. [e] Balearibus factum bellum est piratis: aut piratas suos non ulciscentibus. [f] *Baleares piratica rabie corruperant maria*: ut sic loquuntur historiæ.

p. 235 Sed Metelli perfidiæ, et ambitionis cur est Creta? Audio Flo|rum: *Creticum bellum, si vera volumus noscere, nos fecimus, sola vincendi nobilem insulam cupiditate. Favisse Mithridati videbatur: hoc placuit armis vindicare.* At vero si Mithridati favit: cur nos fecimus bellum? Cur sola cupido, vincendi nobilem insulam, nos armavit? Sequimur testimonium: diverso iudicio non auscultamus. Et sic cum testibus fit: qui aliud narrant, aliud iudicant: ut narrationem sequatur iudex, spernat sententiæ dictionem. Atque est testimonium sane verum. [g] Nam et ipse Dion, et Plutarchus tradunt, factum ab ea insula contra fœdera, quæ nobiscum erant. [h] Quod si Antonius, qui ante Metellum intulit arma Cretæ, vituperatus fuit: si etiam ipse Metellus ab Octavio, et Pompeio fuit argutus: neque id ad iustitiam caussæ eius belli facit: quam nunc audivimus iustam. Nihil hoc tempore iudicia civium de civibus suis nos movent: cum privatas quisque cupiditates sequerentur, et ad arma civilia præcipiti gradu decurrerent, ruerent cursu citatissimo. Mithridatem iuvere Cretenses. Hoc tene.

[a] *Decian.* 3. *cons.* 88. [b] *Oros.* 4. *c.* 13. *Liv.* 20. *Polyb.* 2. *App. Illyr. Flo.* 2. *P. Dia.* 3.
[c] *Liv.* 43. 44. *Sex. Ru. App. Illyr. Iusti.* 29. [d] *Liv.* 47. *Zon. App.*
[e] *Oros.* 5. *c.* 13. [f] *Flor.* 3. [g] *Plut. Pomp.*
[h] *Liv.* 97. *Dio.* 36. *Cic. li.* 2. 3. *Verr. ubi Manut.*

---

520 Decianus, *Consilia* 3. 88.

521 Orosius 4. 13; Livy, *Periochae* 20; Polybius 2. 8. 12; Appian, *Illyrica* 7; Florus 2. 5. 3; Paulus Diaconus, *Historia Romana* 7. 4 [cf. also 3. 2].

522 Livy 43, 44; Festus, *Breviarium rerum gestarum populi Romani* 7. 4; Appian, *Illyrica* 9, 12; Justin 29. 2.

523 Livy, *Periochae* 47; Zonaras 9. 25; Appian, *Illyrica* 11. 524 Orosius 5. 13.

525 Florus 3. 8. 2.

526 **Translator's note:** The "testimony," which Gentili also calls the "narrative," is the claim of Crete's support for Mithridates. The "opinion" is Florus' claim that the Romans were motivated only by the desire of acquiring Crete.

527 Plutarch, *Pompeius* 29.

528 Livy, *Periochae* 97; Dio Cassius 36. 1; Cicero, *In Verrem* 2. 3, with comments by Paulus Manutius [*M. Tullii Ciceronis Orationes*, vol. 1, Post Pauli Manutii, Augustae Munatianae, 1703, p. 338].

Another reason we went to war against the Istrians was that they committed acts of piracy against our ships. The crime of private persons does not strike the accuser as a just cause of the first war against the Illyrians. And indeed it is not a just cause generally—unless we have failed to restrain or punish private wrongdoings. For in this way a crime that is private becomes public. For the master's knowledge, will, and order are presumed when a fault is committed not just once, but many times, over and over.[520] And this is a certain and established fact. But in addition our ambassadors were cut down in Illyria by order of the queen.[521] The later wars there, with the allies of our enemies and rebels against us, were likewise just.[522] And it was because of the Illyrians, who afterwards became our friends, that we had to make war with the Dalmatians, who lay waste the fields of the Illyrians, inflicted even worse injuries on other friends of ours, and did not return us a temperate response.[523] War was waged against the Balearic pirates—or against those who failed to punish their own pirates.[524] "The Balearic islanders ruined the seas with their piratical madness," as the history books say.[525]

But why is Crete the result of the treachery and ambition of Metellus? I listen to Florus here: "If we wish to know the truth, we brought about p. 235 the Cretan war solely through our passionate desire to conquer that island. It appeared to support Mithridates: it suited us to punish this with arms." But if it truly supported Mithridates, do we have to ask why we made war? How was it only the passionate desire to overcome a noble island that armed us? We follow the testimony here; we do not heed the opinion that is at variance with it.[526] And thus it happens with witnesses who offer one thing as an account but offer something else as an opinion: so that the judge follows the account of the facts and rejects the expression of an opinion. And the testimony here is in fact true. For both Dio Cassius and Plutarch record that that island acted contrary to the treaty which they had with us.[527] What if Antonius, who bore arms against Crete before Metellus, was loudly criticized? What if Metellus himself was reproved by Octavius and Pompey? That has nothing to do with the justice of his cause, which we have now heard was indeed just.[528] We are not influenced here by judicial decisions made by citizens about their fellow citizens at that period when everyone was pursuing his own private desires and was rushing with headlong pace, hastening with as rapid a dash as possible to take arms against fellow citizens. The Cretans helped Mithridates. Bear this in mind.

[a] Gallos adiuvere Britanni. Neque enim disputaveris, quibus adiuverint rebus. [b] Adiuvisse auxiliis is quoque dicitur, qui vel pecuniis, vel similibus adiuverit. [c] Scio, non teneri pœna auxilii, qui tale attulerit, sine quo patrare tamen maleficium potuit. Sed an istud in istis caussis obtinet? Sed an ostenditur, in
p. 236 Bri|tannico sic fuisse, ut sine eo Galli bellare potuissent, et rebellare voluissent? Hoc tene. Quicquid, odiis in Cæsarem stimulatus, privatisque, publicisque, Cato contrarium cernat. [d] Inimici viri, licet gravissimi, et spectatissimi testimonium non auditur. Supersunt commentarii Cæsaris ipsius: veridici semper habiti. Et illi iustissimas bellorum Galliæ, et Britanniæ, et Germaniæ caussas habent. [e]*Iustissimis ex caussis* (sic historiæ aliæ) factum bellum Germanis est. Etiam iuste turbavit Cæsar quiescentem Hispaniam. [f] Neque enim (ut respondet Antonius) fidam tamen eamdem offendit: itaque nec concedendum putavit, ut sub nomine pacis adversarii moliri res novas possent.

Iam sileant inimici Cæsaris. Etiam Suetonius iam, et Plutarchus: qui, Traiani regnantis studio, non sat æqui fuerint nostro huic imperatori, patriæ Traiani domitori. Sileat: aut, quia silere Cicero nequit, non audiatur Cicero: non, qui de Cicerone hauserunt proculdubio, postremi scriptores, qui Cyprum male nobis partam adfirmant. Ubi ad Clodii factum respicitur, illic Cicero audietur? Immo potiora erunt verba Paterculi de eo rege, [g]*omnibus morum vitiis eam contumeliam meritum.*

[h] Potius erit Strabonis iudicium: [i] qui auctor laudatissimus. Et qui scribit,
p. 237 regem illum hostem declaratum: qui deliquerit in nos, et ingratum | se nobis

[a] *Cæs.* 4. *Gall.* [b] *Bar. l.* 7. *de parric.*
[c] *Decian.* 3. *cons.* 125. [d] *Cic. pro Mure.* [e] *Flor.* 3.
[f] *Dio.* 44. [g] *Paterc.* 2. [h] *Str.* 14. [i] *Sig.* 1. *de a. i. p.* 13.

---

[529] Caesar, *De bello gallico* 4. 20.

[530] Bartolus, *On Digest* 48. 9. 7, fol. 166^{r} [*In secundam Digesti novi partem commentaria*, in *Opera omnia*, tomus sextus, Venetiis, Sexta Editio Iuntarum, 1590].

[531] Decianus, *Consilia* 3. 125, fol. 271^{v}. **Translator's note:** I take the active *patrare* to be a slip for the passive *patrari*. Otherwise, one would have to understand the subject of the last clause to be not the *maleficium*, but the perpetrator thereof, the person helped by the money or similar aid.

[532] Cicero, *Pro Murena*. **Translator's note:** Gentili is presumably referring to the challenge Cicero faced in defending the unsavory Lucius Licinius Murena against a charge of electoral malpractice lodged by the famously upright Cato the Younger.

[533] Florus 3. 10. 10.

[534] Dio Cassius 44. 46.

[535] [Gentili is responding to a passage in Book 1, ch. 9, here not 1. 11.]

[536] Velleius Paterculus 2. 45. 4.

[537] Strabo 14. 6. 6.

[538] Sigonius [Carlo Sigonio], *De antiquo iure provinciarum* 1. 13, col. 524 [Sigonio, *Opera Omnia*, Tomus V, Mediolani, 1736].

Similarly, the Britons helped the Gauls.[529] For you will surely not have raised a question as to the precise nature of the help they furnished. For that person is also said to have helped "with reinforcements" who helped with money or similar things.[530] I know that one is not held liable to the penalty of providing reinforcements if his contribution was such that wrongdoing could nonetheless have been brought about without it.[531] But does that apply in these cases? Or is it established that it was thus in the case of the aid offered by the Britons—that without it the Gauls would still have been able to wage p. 236 war and would have wished to rebel? Bear this in mind—no matter what Cato might believe to the contrary, motivated as he was by his private and public grudges against Caesar. The testimony of an enemy, even if he happens to be a most impressive and prominent man, is not accepted.[532] Also, there exist the commentaries of Caesar himself, always considered a truthful man. And those commentaries contain the perfectly just causes for the wars in Gaul, Britain, and Germany. "On the basis of the perfectly just causes" (according to another work of history) the war with the Germans was waged.[533] Also justly did Caesar disturb quiet Spain. For as Antony pointed out, Caesar did not commit an offense against a loyal ally, nor did he think that it should be allowed that under the name of peace our adversaries should be able to contrive a revolution.[534]

Let the enemies of Caesar now be silent. Let even Suetonius and Plutarch be silent, who on account of their cultivation of the reigning emperor Trajan were not sufficiently fair to this commander-in-chief of ours, the man who subdued Trajan's homeland [Spain]. And let Cicero be silent—or, since Cicero could never keep silent, let him at least not be listened to—and let also those later authors who no doubt drew upon Cicero be silent, those who claim that Cyprus was wickedly acquired by us. And when it is a matter of the action of Clodius, will Cicero be listened to there?[535] Much sounder are the words of Velleius Paterculus about that king [Ptolemy of Cyprus]: "he merited this insult through all the faults of his character."[536]

Sounder will be the judgment of Strabo,[537] who was a highly praised writer,[538] and who wrote that that king was an avowed enemy of ours who had wronged us and showed himself ungrateful to us who had done him p. 237

præbuit benemerentibus. Hoc teneo. [a]*Nil homine terra peius ingrato creat*: ut verissime dixit Menander. [b] Si enim gratitudo virtus est non solum maxima, sed etiam mater virtutum omnium reliquarum: etiam ingratitudo vitium est non solum maximum, sed mater quoque vitiorum omnium reliquorum, impietatis, avaritiæ, iniustitiæ, inimicitiarum efferatissimæ feritatis. [c] Nam et bruta gratitudine censentur, et obligantur. [d] Gratitudo iustitia est. Et ego si de sacerdotibus illis iustitiæ velim aut gravitatem, aut pœnas dicere ingratitudinis: ante diem clauso componet vesper Olympo. Levis culpa in gravem evadit, et gravem promeretur pœnam, si et insit ingrati vitium. Sic igitur vel si in unum peccasset Clodium Cyprius rex, illum etiam virum nequam: semper est verum tamen, fuisse regem ingratum Romano civi, et civitati. Quoniam non cum bono cive esset, quam cum civitate coniunctus, et cive. Et qui alteri est devinctus, nunquam sane vitia creditoris obiectat, aut caussatur, ne solvat debitum.

Supersunt Cantabri. [e] Et Florus, Eutropius, ipse Orosius, qui de pusilla terra dicit, sic tradunt, Cantabros, et Astures non solum propriam libertatem tueri voluisse, verum etiam finitimorum præripere, quos et assiduis popula-
p. 238 tionibus divexassent: itaque arma in se Augusti provocasse. *Cantabria gens* | *effera: pertinax in rebellando:* ait Florus. [f] Scilicet subacta fuerat et ante Augustum. Et ita rebellis nunc erat. Habes bellorum caussas. Quid mihi nugaris de terræ perpusillo?

Habes reliquorum bellorum caussas. Quid reprehendis in bellis? Regis Aruernorum exprobras captivitatem? [g] Livius tamen, cui credendum semper est supra Valerium, inquit, quod, postquam cæsa essent Aruernorum centum viginti millia: rex ille profectus Romam fuerit ad satisfaciendum senatui: et ibi retentus sic fuerit, quia contra pacem videbatur, si fuisset remissus. In quo nihil est reprehendendum. Etiam si cum Valerio dicimus, captum perfide a Domitio, et missum Romam, et non remissum: senatus adhuc defendi factum potest: cui a ducis pactione nullum iniici vinculum potuisse, velint illi iurisconsulti, qui Consalvi Hispani factum cum Valentino duce, item et Hispani regis examinant. [h] Pactus Consalvus incolumitatem venienti ad se Valentino: et eum mittit captivum mox in Hispaniam: et, pactionibus suis antestare voluntatem regis sui, dicebat. Probant et regem, et Consalvum illi. Quos ego accusatori senatus, Domitiique obiicio. Nam et Domitius ab his defenditur: si Aruernum iussu senatus Romam misit.

[a] *Aus. epigr.* 1. 2. [b] *Cic. pro Planc.* [c] *Dec.* 1. *cons.* 25.
[d] *Bald.* 10. *de iust. l.* 2. C. *de lib. et eo. lib.* [e] *Flor.* 4. *Eutrop.* 7. [f] *Liv.* 48.
[g] *Liv.* 61. [h] *Guic.* 2. 6. *Aya.* 5. *de iu. be. c.* 6.

---

[539] *Epigrammata Bobiensia* 67. 1, ed. Wolfgang Speyer (Lipsiae, Teubner, 1963), p. 81 [cited by Gentili as by Ausonius].
[540] Cicero, *Pro Plancio* 80. [541] Decio, *Consilia* 1. 25 [the reference is unclear].
[542] Baldus, *On Digest* 1. 1. 10, fol. 15^{r}; *On Code* 6. 7. 2. **Translator's note:** The context is ingratitude shown by a manumitted slave to his patron.
[543] [Vergil, *Aeneis* 1. 374.] [544] Florus 4. 12. 47; Eutropius 7. 9. [545] Livy, *Periochae* 48.
[546] Livy, *Periochae* 61.
[547] Francesco Guicciardini, *Storia d'Italia* 6 [Venetia, Presso Gio. Antonio Bertano, 1580]; Ayala, *De iure et officiis bellicis et disciplina militari* 5. 6 [the reference is unclear; Ayala's treatise has only three books].

favors. This I hold to: "The earth creates nothing worse than an ungrateful man," as Menander said.[539] For if gratitude is not only the greatest of all virtues, but also the mother of all the other virtues, even so ingratitude is not only the greatest vice but also the mother of all the other vices: impiety, avarice, injustice, the most bestial savagery of personal enmities.[540] For even brute animals are judged and bound by their gratitude.[541] Gratitude is justice.[542] And if I should wish, basing myself on those high priests of justice, to set forth the seriousness and the punishments of ingratitude, "evening would lay the day to rest, with Olympus shut up for the night."[543] A minor fault turns into a serious one if the vice of an ingrate should be in it. So thus even if the Cyprian king wronged no one but Clodius, even that one worthless man, it still remains true that the king had been ungrateful to a Roman citizen and the Roman state. For the point was not that he would have been making an agreement with a *good* citizen but with the state and its citizen. Similarly, one who is under an obligation to someone else certainly never charges or pleads the faults of the creditor in order not to have to pay his debt.

There remain the Cantabrians. Florus, Eutropius, and even Orosius (who speaks of their "insignificant territory") record that the Cantabrians and Asturians did not only wish to protect their own liberty, but also to snatch away the liberty of their closest neighbors, whom they harassed with constant plundering raids; and thus they called forth the arms of Augustus against themselves.[544] "Cantabria was a wild tribe, stubborn in rebellion," p. 238
says Florus. Indeed, it had been subdued even before Augustus.[545] And so it was now in rebellion. There you have the causes for these wars. Why do you trifle with me about "a very small bit of territory"?

You have here the causes for all the other wars as well. What do you object to in the wars? Do you make the captivity of the king of the Arverni a matter of reproach? But Livy, who should always be trusted over Valerius Maximus, said that after 120,000 of the Arverni had been cut down the king had set out for Rome to make amends to the Senate, and he was detained there, for it seemed a threat to the peace if he should be sent back.[546] There is nothing reprehensible in this. Even if we agree with Valerius Maximus that the king was treacherously captured by Domitius and sent to Rome and not sent back, the action of the Senate could be defended insofar as no binding obligation could be cast upon it by the agreement made by the commander. This would be confirmed by those jurists who examine the action of Gonzalo Fernández of Spain with Cesare Borgia, and likewise the action of the king of Spain. Gonzalo had pledged Borgia's safety if he came to him, and then he swiftly sent him as a captive to Spain, and he said that the will of his king was superior to his own pacts.[547] Those jurists approve of the king and Gonzalo here, and I set them before the accuser of the Senate and Domitius. For Domitius also is defended by them if he sent the Arvernian to Rome on the orders of the Senate.

Nunc de bello Iugurthino: in quo moram nostram vehementer accusas. Et
p. 239 tecum Sallustius esse videtur: et ego sim: si ci|vitas a paucis improbis decepta non fuit. Et si Iugurthæ dignitas, meritaque in bello Numantino quæsita non etiam facere illam moram iustissime potuerunt: ut non contra eum illico ad arma procurreretur. [a] Etiam Sallustius monumentis insevit suis litteras Africani, quas Iugurtha post exscidium Numantinum testes ad Micipsam pertulit decoris sui. [b] Erat ille Masinissæ nepos, quemadmodum et Adherbal, et Hiempsal. Nihil enim, nihil apud Numidas, quod ex legitimo matrimonio natus non fuerit. Erat ille Micipsæ itidem filius, licet per adoptionem. Sed magno suo merito adoptionem promeritus, et partem hereditatis: [c] qui unicum Numidiæ munimentum: et virtutum avi Masinissæ unicus heres.

Quid nunc de iisdem Masinissæ nepotibus, et de nepote Hieronis, et raptis additur eorum regnis? Quasi potuerimus lædi impune a liberis, quia cari nos parentibus fuimus. Quod hoc ius novum est? Et non illi multo plurima semper tulerunt a nobis? Nam quis fuerat Masinissa? Tantum illi regnum, exsuli, rerum omnium egenti, quis comparavit? Et non Masinissæ solum, sed et aliis donavit populus Romanus regna, quæ ipse quæsiit: Eumeni in longitudinem itineris triginta dierum, decem in latitudinem. [d]*Quoties hic prælia sumsit pro sociis! quoties dono concessit amicis Regibus Ausonio quæsitas*
p. 240 *sanguine terras.* | [e] Hoc ipsum regnum Numidiæ non et pro parte datum Iubæ, filio Hiempsalis, viro de genere Masinissæ? Partem alteram Boccho datam, tu dicis. Ubi igitur Romanorum rapina?

Atque sic sunt reliqua bella, et in bellis gesta. Nam de fraudibus, quibus captus Iugurtha est, ante respondi. [f]*Fraudulentissimus regum fraude soceri sui in insidias deductus est.*

De Metellis superest respondere: qui inepte ambitiosi fuisse tibi videntur. Et quid si hoc confitemur, indulsisse civibus his suis Romanos in ista parte? Et non confitemur tamen: sed virtutem, meritum illorum tuemur: ne ista indulgentia in suos, esse notatio in alienos contendatur. Qui Macedoniam vicit, et eum ducem Macedonum, [g] qui regiam formam, regium nomen animo quoque regio implevit, et res gessit maximas: et qui regem hunc cepit,

[a] *Symm.* 4. *Ep.* 24.
[b] *Flor.* 3. [c] *Alc.* 4. *cons.* 8. 10. [d] *Claud.* 3. *Stilic.*
[e] *Dio.* 41. *Sigo. de a. i. p.* 17. [f] *Flor.* 3.
[g] *Flor.* 2. *Liv.* 49. *so.* 52. *Sigo.* 1. *de a. l. p.* 8.

---

548 Symmachus, *Epistulae* 4. 23. [Sallust, *Bellum Iugurthinum* 9. 1–2.]
549 Florus 3. 1. 3. 550 Alciatus, *Consilia* 4. 8; 4. 10, col. 418.
551 [Gentili had discussed the case of the grandson of Hieron of Syracuse in *De armis Romanis* 1. 8, pp. 74–5.]
552 Claudian, *De consulatu Stilichonis* 3. 184–6.
553 Cassius Dio 41; Sigonius, *De antiquo iure provinciarum* 1. 17, cols. 532–4 [Sigonio, *Opera Omnia*, Tomus V, Mediolani, 1736].
554 Florus 3. 1. 17.
555 [This is a response to Book 1, ch. 9.]

Now, as to the Jugurthine War, in which you vehemently accuse our delay. And Sallust seems to be on your side, and I myself would be, if the state had p. 239 not been deceived by a few wicked men—and if the worthiness of Jugurtha and the services he rendered in the Numantine war were not most justly able to create that delay, so that arms were not resorted to immediately against him. Even Sallust inserted into his chronicles a letter of Scipio which after the destruction of Numantia Jugurtha carried to Micipsa in witness to his own honor.[548] Jugurtha was a grandson of Masinissa in the same way that Adherbal and Hiempsal were.[549] Among the Numidians it meant nothing, nothing at all, that he was not born from a legitimate marriage. And he was likewise son of Micipsa, albeit by adoption. But he merited the adoption and a portion of the inheritance through his own great merit, he who was the sole bulwark of Numidia and the sole heir of the virtues of his grandfather Masinissa.[550]

What now is added about those same grandsons of Masinissa and about the grandson of Hieron and their stolen kingdoms?[551] As though we could be harmed with impunity by the children because we had been dear to the parents! What new right is this? And did not they get far more things from us than we did from them? For who had Masinissa been, after all? Who got him such a great kingdom when he was an exile, in need of everything? And not only upon Masinissa but also upon others did the Roman people bestow the kingdoms that they themselves acquired: that of Eumenes was thirty days' journey in length and ten in breadth. "How often did this man undertake battles for allies! How often did he hand over as a gift to friendly kings lands acquired with Ausonian blood"?[552] This very kingdom of Numidia—was it p. 240 not given in part to Juba, son of Hiempsal, a man of the family of Masinissa?[553] You say that another part of it was given to Bocchus. Where, then, is the robbery committed by the Romans?

And thus are the other wars—and the things done in the wars. For I have already made a reply about the deceptions by which Jugurtha was captured. "The most deceptive of kings was lured into a trap by the deception of his father-in-law."[554]

It remains to respond about the Metelli, who seem to you to have been foolishly vainglorious.[555] And what if we do concede this: that the Romans indulged their own citizens in this respect? And yet we do not concede it, but we defend the valor and merit of those men, lest that indulgence towards their own might be argued to be a black mark against others. He who conquered Macedonia and that leader of the Macedonians [the pretender Andriscus] who filled a royal appearance and a royal name with a royal spirit and performed the greatest deeds—I say, was he who defeated this king and

Macedoniam domuit, indignus Macedonici cognomento: quod Macedones raptum iniuste de se valeant lamentari? Iustum cognomentum, et triumphus iustus de Macedonia: quicquid de isto falso rege constituatur. [a] Is et Achaicus dici meruit, qui exercitus fuderat Achæorum: et ipsum Corinthum premebat obsidio, *cum ad victoriam Mummius venit,* ut ait historia. Expresse ait historia, eumdem meritum et Celtiberici cognomen: qui Contrebiam memorabili cepisset exemplo, et Vertobrigis maiori gloria pepercit.

p. 241 Non alter me|ruit appellari Numidicus? [b] qui universam Numidiam sub potestatem redegerat: Iugurtham armis, viris, pecunia spoliaverat: eumdem ad Getulos, et ad Mauros depulerat: itaque fusum, et faucium tradidit successori non tam profecto vincendum, quam vinciendum. Bellum, quia conficere prohibitus fuit, pro confecto acceptum est: [c] ut Tacitus alicubi pro Germanico scribit. Et ut sic sunt leges, et rationes. Et satis tamen, superque ad nomen capta Numidia est: etsi Iugurtha captus non est.

De Dalmatico audis Appianum? [d] Sed Livii, et Asconii testimonio refutatus hic Appianus est a Sigonio eruditissimo. Quod satis est. Audivimus de Cretico, et Balearico. Magna proles Cæcilia Metellorum: [e] qui etiam de Sardis: etiam de Thracibus triumpharunt, et uno die tres fratres. Non fato isti Romæ fiunt consules. Nævi, Campane inflatissime, sile maledictum, aut verius recanta. [f]*Malum dabunt Metelli*, ni feceris.

Ecce nec per falsa nomina raptum quid orbi est a Romanis. Nihil raptum per falsa iura testamentorum. [g] Libya testamento Ptolomæi, Asia testamento Attali transcripta est. [h]*Et ne quid tamen populus Romanus non viribus partum haberet, Asiam, Attali testamento relictam, armis ab Antiocho vindicavimus.*

Donum ea populi Romani fuit. Alia regna sic fuerunt. Et populus igitur p. 242 Romanus suum ita recipiebat a donatariis | non ingratis. Quid ille non recepisset, isti non reddidissent, si legitima proles non supererat? [i] Ita et Paphlagonia, et Comana receptæ. [j] Atque hic insuper notare decet, neque data unquam sic esse a Romanis regna, ut essent hereditaria: neque ita

[a] *Flor.* 2. [b] *Liv.* 65. *Sallust. Flo.* 3. [c] *Tac.* 2. *ann.* [d] *Sigo.* 1. *de a. i. p.* 7.
[e] *Manu. pro Sex. R. A.* [f] *Scip. Gent.* 2. *par.* 30. [g] *Str.* 13. *Iust.* 36. 38. [h] *Sex. Ruf.*
[i] *Str.* 12. [j] *App.* 3. *civ. Val.* 7. *c.* 2.

---

556 Florus 2. 14. 3; Livy, *Periochae* 49 and 52; Sigonius, *De antiquo iure provinciarum* 1.8, col. 501 [Sigonio, *Opera Omnia*, Tomus V, Mediolani, 1736].

557 Florus 2. 16. 4. 558 [Florus 2. 17. 10.]

559 Livy, *Periochae* 65; Sallust, *Bellum Iugurthinum* 80; Florus 3. 1. 10–13.

560 Tacitus, *Annales* 2. 41. 3.

561 Sigonius, *De antiquo iure provinciarum* 1. 7, col. 499 [Sigonio, *Opera Omnia*, Tomus V, Mediolani, 1736].

562 Paulus Manutius, on Cicero, *Pro Sexto Roscio Amerino* [*M. Tullii Ciceronis Orationes*, vol. 1, Post Pauli Manutii, Augustae Munatianae, 1703, pp. 38 ff.]. [But Gentili's main source here is Eutropius 4. 25, where it is claimed that *two* Metelli celebrated a triumph on the same day.]

563 Scipio Gentili, *Parerga* 2. 30. **Translator's note:** The allusion here is to a Saturnian verse directed against Naevius by the Metelli: "Dabunt malum Metelli Naevio poetae," "The Metelli will give the poet Naevius grief." The source is the same as for the line from Naevius alluded to here and quoted in Book 1, ch. 9: Ps.-Asconius on Cicero, *In Verrem* 1. 10. 29.

564 Strabo 13. 4. 2; Justin 36. 4; 39. 5. 565 Festus, *Breviarium rerum gestarum populi Romani* 10. 2.

566 **Translator's note:** This is presumably a reference to the gift of Seleucid territories awarded by the Romans to Eumenes, king of Pergamon, at the Peace of Apamea (188 BC), in recognition of his services in the war against Antiochus III.

567 Strabo 12. 3. 9; 34.

subdued Macedonia unworthy of the title "Macedonicus," as of something the Macedonians could lament was unjustly taken from them?[556] It was a justly earned title, and he celebrated a just triumph over Macedonia, no matter what may be decided with regard to that bogus king. He also deserved to be called "Achaicus," for he routed the armies of the Achaean League and besieged Corinth itself, "when Mummius came in to snatch the victory," as history records.[557] And history distinctly records that the same man was worthy of the title "Celtibericus," since he captured Contrebia, an act of exemplary fame, and spared the Vertobrigi in an act of even greater glory.[558]

Did not the other Metellus deserve to be called "Numidicus"? For he had brought all of Numidia back under our power; had despoiled Jugurtha of arms, men, and money; and had driven him off to the Gaetulians and Moors; and thus handed him over to his successor, routed and wounded, not so much to be defeated as simply to be tied up.[559] Because he was forbidden to finish the war, the war was considered to be finished, as Tacitus says somewhere about Germanicus.[560] And the laws and official registers are in accord with this. And it more than suffices for the title that Numidia was captured, even if Jugurtha was not. p. 241

And do you listen to Appian about Lucius Caecilius Metellus Dalmaticus? But here Appian has been refuted by the very learned Sigonio, on the testimony of Livy and Asconius.[561] And that suffices. We have heard about Metellus Creticus and Metellus Balearicus. Great was the offspring of the Caecillian gens of the Metelli! They even celebrated triumphs over the Sardinians and over the Thracians—three brothers on a single day.[562] It's *not* "our fate that the Metelli become consuls at Rome." Naevius, you utterly puffed-up Campanian, keep your malediction quiet—or, better, recant it. "The Metelli will punish you," if you don't.[563]

Behold, nothing belonging to a childless man was snatched away by the Romans through false names. Nothing was snatched away through the false oaths of testaments. Libya was made over to us by the testament of Ptolemy Apion of Cyrene, Asia by the testament of Attalos of Pergamon.[564] "And lest the Roman people might not acquire something through force of arms, we defended our claim to Asia, which had been left to us by the will of Attalos, by arms against Antiochus."[565]

Asia was a gift belonging to the Roman people.[566] Other kingdoms were as well. And therefore the Roman people was simply taking back its own possessions from beneficiaries who were not ungrateful. What would the Roman people not have received back, what would those kings have not rendered back to them, had not legitimate offspring survived? Similarly, the Romans received back Paphlagonia and Comana.[567] And here it is fitting to note in addition that kingdoms were never given by the Romans to be p. 242

cuiquam, Masinissa excepto, ut etiam soluta ab omni nostro imperio libertas esset. Hæc in tractatu isto nihil iustificare nobis non valent.

Quid si recepta regna sunt a regibus, qui nobis rebellarunt ingratissimi? [a] Sic utique recepta sunt alia. [b] Redeunt iure ad originem suam, redeunt ad dominum feuda, exclusis filiis, et cognatis omnibus, si in dominum peccetur. Etiam vetera sic redeunt. Et itaque nova, hereditaria redeunt magis: ut interpretes iuris exponunt. [c] Etiam, cum spoliatur bonis vasallus, aut confiscatur ob caussam aliam, domino feudum redit. Atque id contra Mithridatem, et alios est, qui populi Romani beneficia rapere de hostibus suis, et sua efficere voluerunt. Contra Mithridatem, qui, regna patri donata a Romanis, ablata sibi, conqueritur apud Trogum, facit alterum prius dictum: quod in hereditatem regna dare Romani non consueverant: [d] itaque quem modum esse beneficii sui vellent, ipsorum æstimationem fuisse. Ad hæc disceptatio accusatoris de iure regum generalis non pertingit.

p. 243 Nobis autem sic imperium orbis est. [e] Postquam in Septentrione, | et Oriente Pompeius duos nobis et viginti reges debellavit: et sequentes Cæsares provincias ultra Danubium, et Euphratem constituerunt: et postquam ad occidentem solem Oceano aquarum, ad meridiem mari arenarum C. Iulius, Augustus, Tyberius veluti finibus ipsius orbis fines nostros definierunt. [f] Quæ et alii notant.

De Romanis et Alexandro.
CAP. XII

Sed hic aliam Livio litem accusator noster intendit: et in comparationem Romanorum, atque Alexandri excurrit. Credo, novus Herculi antagonista in aliqua vult forma vincere, quas varias mutat. Fraude factum imperium Romanum, iniusta vi factum contendit, et vincitur: fortuna factum nunc ait: vincatur virtute Romana hic quoque: arenas mordeat ore: guttura premantur: cornuque cadat a fronte revulsum.

[a] *Str.* 6. 7. 11. *ult.* [b] *Bar. l.* 3. *de int. et re. Alc.* 3. *cons.* 17. 5. 11. 132. 6. 28.
[c] *Alc.* 5. *cons.* 7. [d] *l.* 191. *de reg. iu.*
[e] *Eutr.* 6. *Oros.* 6. *c.* 6. [f] *Hegesip.* 2. *c.* 9.

---

568 Appian, *Punica* 32; Valerius Maximus 7. 2.

569 Strabo 6. 7. 11.

570 Bartolus, *On Digest* 48. 22. 3, fols. 192^{r} f. [*In secundam Digesti novi partem commentaria*, in *Opera omnia*, tomus sextus, Venetiis, Sexta Editio Iuntarum, 1590]; Alciatus, *Consilia* 3. 17, col. 334; 5. 11, col. 467; 5. 132, col. 703; 6. 28, col. 830.

571 Alciatus, *Consilia* 5. 7, col. 460. 572 *Digest* 50. 17. 191. 573 Eutropius 6. 12–14; Orosius 6. 6.

574 Pseudo-Hegesippus, *Historiae* 2. 9. [*Hegesippi qui dicitur Historiae libri V*, ed. Vincenzo Ussani, Corpus Scriptorum Ecclesiasticorum Latinorum, 66 (Vienna: Hölder-Pichler-Tempsky, 1932), 154.]

hereditary possessions, nor was anyone, with the exception of Masinissa, granted a freedom that was entirely independent of every aspect of our rule.[568] Every consideration serves to pardon us in these matters regarding our treatment of these peoples.

What if we took back kingdoms from kings who had most ungratefully rebelled against us? Various other kingdoms were most certainly taken back in this way.[569] They revert by law to their origin—fiefdoms revert to their feudal lord if wrong has been done against that lord, and the children and all the relatives of the vassal are shut out.[570] Even fiefdoms long held revert in these circumstances. And therefore hereditary fiefdoms of recent standing revert even more, as the interpreters of the law set forth. Even when a vassal is despoiled of his goods, or they are confiscated for some other reason, the fiefdom reverts to the lord.[571] And therefore this stands against Mithridates and others who have wished to seize the gifts of the Roman people from their enemies and make them their own. Also, against Mithridates, who complains in the pages of Pompeius Trogus that he has been deprived of the kingdoms given to his father by the Romans, there stands the other dictum mentioned earlier: that the Romans were not in the habit of giving kingdoms for hereditary succession. Therefore, the nature of the gift they might wish to bestow was a matter of their own determination.[572] The general objection our accuser makes about the right of kings has no bearing upon these matters.

This, then, is the nature of our world empire—after Pompey utterly subdued twenty-two kings in the North and the East for us, and subsequent p. 243
Caesars established provinces beyond the Danube and Euphrates, and after Julius Caesar, Augustus, and Tiberius marked out our borders in the West with the Ocean of waters and in the South with the sea of sands, as though with the borders of the very world itself.[573] Other writers, too, make note of this.[574]

CHAPTER 12
On the Romans and Alexander

But here our accuser lodges another suit against Livy and runs off into a comparison of the Romans and Alexander. It's my belief that this new antagonist to Hercules wants to score a victory in any possible shape—and he is constantly shifting shapes. He contends that the Roman Empire was built on fraud, and on unjust force—and he's defeated right here, for he now says that it was founded on luck. But here, too, let him be defeated, this time by Roman valor. Let him chew the sands with his teeth; let him be strangled; let the horn be torn from his brow and fall to the ground.

[a] Ridet Alexandrum Annibal, in Homeri tantum castris versatum: id est, hominis cæci certe qui castra, et acies nunquam aspexerit. Merito: ut qui sic fuerit Alexander quasi nauta ex commentariis, nunquam naves ingressus sit, nunquam in tempestatibus maris versatus. Nauta etiam ex commentariis nec nautæ. [b] Et irrisit Phormionem Annibal, et delirissimum senem nuncupavit merito: qui in umbris, et otio scholarum enutritus, de sole, et pulvere bel-
p. 244 lorum dicere au | deret. Hic est ille Annibal in iudicio isto a Cicerone probatus, et in re alia omni a te, accusator, omnium temporum imperatoribus cunctis prælatus. Hic est ille Annibal, [c] qui, nulla habita Alexandri mentione apud Plutarchum, se, Scipionem, Pyrrhum dilaudat solos. At verior sit tamen fabula, in qua supereminet et Pyrrho, et Annibali Alexander: etiam verum per eam est, Alexandro supereminere Scipionem, hoc est Romanum.

Falsa sit Annibalis Lucianici criminatio de educatione Alexandri; [d] qui immo in castris et sub militia patris tyrocinii rudimenta posuerit: etiam verum illud est, paucorum eam fuisse militiam mensium; pauciorum mensium, quam anni fuerint Annibalis, Scipionis, Romanorum ceterorum, quos in ista comparatione Livius Alexandro opponit. Etiam constat, propositum Alexandro fuisse Achillem, quem imitaretur, iuvenem et audaciæ, et temeritatis plenum. [e] Rident docti viri, et prudentes Græculam in historia vanitatem: quæ, cum huc omnes ingenii sui nervos intenderet, ut eximium quemdam, et inimitabilem principem depingeret, nihil tamen aliud nobis, quam toties furiosum, sed ubique felicem, et quam Homericum Achillem illaudabilem, descripsit. [f] Sic ipse Plato in Achillem invectus sæpe, et in varia
p. 245 eius peccata, ac vitia. [g] Sic Tertullianus, Seneca, Lucanus, alii Alexandrum | felicem prædonem, feliciter temerarium, vesanum, sine virtute, aiunt.

[h] Quid dicam, conficta et ab aliis, et ab ipso Alexandro de se mendacia? Quid, omnes rerum Alexandri scriptores miracula omnia pro veritate habuisse? Hæc Strabo sic notat. Et sic Curtius protestatur, se transcribere plura, quam credere. Tradit is et de temeritate Alexandri: et quod unum hoc erat solatium suis, temeritatis eius perpetua felicitas. Hæc illa virtus Alexandri: propter quam ipse sibi præconia canit, facessere a se longe omnem fortunam iubet. Et non vides, Picene, declamatoriam illam esse scriptionem

[a] *Lucia. Scip.* [b] *Cic.* 2. *de orat.* [c] *Plut. Pyrr.* [d] *Iust.* 9. [e] *Glar. ad Cur.*
[f] *Plat. de rep.* [g] *T. de ani. S. I. de bon. L.* 10. [h] *Str.* 11. 15. *Iust.* 12.

[575] Lucian, *Scipio*. **Translator's note:** Gentili cites a non-existent *Scipio* of Lucian here. The ultimate source here is Lucian's *Dialogues of the Dead* 25, an underworld contention for primacy between Alexander and Hannibal, with Scipio casting a vote for Alexander. But Gentili's source is clearly the free adaptation of this by Giovanni Aurispa, written in 1425, which was often given the title *Scipio Romanus*. Aurispa treated the Lucianic text very freely, even adding a long speech of Scipio's in which he successfully argued before Minos for his own primacy over both the contenders. See David Cast, "Aurispa, Petrarch, and Lucian: An Aspect of Renaissance Translation," *Renaissance Quarterly*, 27 (1974), 157–73.

[576] Cicero, *De oratore* 2. 18. 75–6.

[577] Plutarch, *Pyrrhus* 8.

[578] [The reference is to the story told at Livy 35. 14.]

[579] Justin 9. 1.

[580] Plato, *Respublica* [esp. 388 A–B, 390 E–391 C].

[581] Tertullian, *De anima*; Seneca, *De beneficiis* 1; Lucan, *De bello civili* 10. **Translator's note:** There is no negative reference to Achilles in the treatise of Seneca. Nor seems there to be a reference to Achilles in bk. 10 of *De bello civili*. Gentili probably misread passages there about Achillas, a general of Ptolemy's who was assigned the task of assassinating Pompey.

[582] Strabo 11. 15; Justin 12.

Hannibal laughs at Alexander as one who spent his time [as a youth] only in the camp of Homer—that is, in the camp of a blind man who had never looked upon a camp and battle-lines.[575] And he laughs at him justly—if it is true that Alexander had been like one who became a sailor from reading treatises, but never entered a ship and never got tossed in storms at sea. One doesn't become a sailor even from the treatises of a sailor. And Hannibal made fun of Phormio and called him a very daft old man, who was brought up in the shadows and leisure of the schools but dared to speak of the sunshine and dust of wars.[576] Cicero commended Hannibal in this opin- p. 244
ion—and in every other matter you, accuser, exalt him over all the other commanders of all periods of history. This is that same Hannibal who in Plutarch, with no mention made of Alexander, praised only himself, Scipio, and Pyrrhus.[577] But a more accurate story would be that in which Alexander towers over both Pyrrhus and Hannibal—and it is also true, in accord with that story, that Scipio—that is, a Roman—towered over Alexander.[578]

But the Lucianic Hannibal's accusation about the education of Alexander would be false, given that in fact he lay down the rudiments of his military training in the camps and army of his father[579]—even though one part of the accusation is certainly true: that the months he spent in his military training were fewer than the years spent by Hannibal, Scipio, and the other Roman commanders whom Livy holds up against Alexander in that comparison. It is also agreed that Achilles, a young man full of boldness and rashness, was held up to Alexander as a model to imitate. Men of learning and good sense mock the folly of Greeklings in writing history, for when they direct all the energy of their talents to portraying an exceptional and inimitable prince, they end up describing nothing but the Achilles of Homer, who was so often full of rage, albeit always lucky, and certainly not a praiseworthy character. Thus none other than Plato often inveighs against Achilles and his manifold sins and vices.[580] Thus, too, Tertullian, Seneca, Lucan, and others say that Achilles was a lucky brigand, successfully rash, crazy, without virtue.[581] p. 245

Why should I mention the fabrications of others and of Alexander himself, drawing upon his own mendacity? Why mention that all the writers of the deeds of Alexander have taken all sorts of miracles for the truth?[582] Strabo makes note of these. And thus Quintus Curtius testifies that he is setting down more than he actually believes. He also makes note of the rashness of Alexander—and the fact that the one consolation for his people was the unbroken streak of luck that attended his rashness. This was that famous valor of Alexander: on account of this he himself acted as his own herald and bade all mere luck depart far from him. And do you not see, Picenus, that that

Plutarchi, non sententiam philosophicam? Quicquid in Alexandro erat, militis strenui erat, et manu prompti, non semper boni, certe nullo modo sapientis imperatoris. Atque si tuus Annibal laudavit Marcellum ut militem, risit ut ducem: quid alteri huic fecisset, temeritatis incomparabiliter maioris?

Vidisti hæc (non dubito) clare satis. Et itaque ad Alexandri duces, ad Alexandri exercitum mox fugis. Sed hic quoque sunt Romani superiores: qui non cedunt ducibus illis secundis, aut exercitibus, et primo vincunt imperatore. Imperatores autem sunt, qui bella vincunt. [a]*Tanti exercitus, quanti imperator.* [b]*Quales præfecti, tales, qui sub eis sunt.* Et id genus alia,
p. 246 quæ a te dicta, ab aliis, vulgo decantata. [c]Numantini, postquam vicissent nos | sæpius, cum vincerentur Scipione duce, acri excepti convicio apud suos dicuntur, ut, qui toties superassent nos gloriose, nunc a suis victis turpiter vincerentur, illi autem, esse quidem oves easdem nunc, quas vincere consuevissent, at esse pastorem alium, responderunt. [d] Et hic mihi de ducibus notes secundis in Romana militia, quemadmodum ii fuerint apud Romanos sæpe secundi duces, ac legati, qui ducatus primos ante cum laude summa, et summo cum bono reipublicæ gesserunt.

Ne vero, ne usque ad finem actionis, virtutem Romanam, altissimo de loco radiantem, velis calumniarum, et conviciorum nebulis infuscare: ut Corvinos, Torquatos, Decios, Papyrios appellare fraudulentos, necromantas, belluas, pullos minimum belluarum. Nam et Decios, quos tu necromantas nominas, et alios meos, quos tu ubique verbere flagellas linguæ, Fabritium, Curium, Camillum, Coriolanum, Cincinnatum, Fabium, Marcellum, Scipiones, Scævolam, Coclitem, alios virtuti comites addit Plutarchus tuus.

Ex his etiam in castris nostris senatus, qui primo assedissent illi duci, ut dicebam, legati, atque tribuni. Cum interim et sederent alii domi, qui incertis semper bellorum prospicerent, et absentium certis necessitatibus subvenirent? An enim in castris seritur, metitur, netur, texitur, alia civitatum exercitia
p. 247 habentur, de quibus non | minus, immo magis militi est, quam pagano, atque urbano succurrendum? Vincimus duce primo; vincimus senatu gemino. Quid cum reliquo milite? Pyrrhus dixerit. [e]*O quam facile erat, orbis imperium occupare, aut mihi Romanis militibus, aut me rege Romanis*! Isti illi sunt milites, a quibus inflicta vulnera, grandia expavit Macedonia.

[a] *Flor.* 2. [b] *Xenoph.* 8. *Cyrop.* [c] *Plut. ap. re. et du.*
[d] *Liv.* 11. 37. *Cic. pro Muræ.* [e] *Flor.* 2.

---

583 Florus 2. 18. 11.
584 Xenophon, *Cyropaideia* 8.
585 Plutarch, *Regum et imperatorum apophthegmata* 201 E.
586 Livy, *Periochae* 11; 37. 1. 10; Cicero, *Pro Murena* 9. 20.
587 **Translator's note:** A reference to a passage in Plutarch's *De fortuna Romanorum*, 317 D, where Arete advances, surrounded by these Roman heroes, while Tyche skips on ahead.
588 Florus 1. 18. 18.

work of Plutarch [*On the Fortune or Virtue of Alexander*] is a literary declamation, not a philosophical treatise? Whatever there was in Alexander was characteristic of a vigorous soldier, a man of ready hand, not always a good man, and certainly not in any way a wise commander. And if your Hannibal praised Marcellus as a soldier but mocked him as a leader, what would he have done with this other man, a man of incomparably greater rashness?

You have seen this, I don't doubt, with sufficient clarity. And that is why you quickly take refuge in Alexander's lieutenants and in his army. But here, too, the Romans are superior, for they are not inferior to Alexander in their lieutenants or their armies and still triumph through their commanders-in-chief. For it is the commanders-in-chief who win wars. "An army is only as good as its commander-in-chief."[583] "Whatever the commanders are like, so too are those who are under them."[584] And there are many other remarks of this sort, mentioned by you and by others and repeated everywhere. When the Numantines were p. 246
defeated by Scipio after having very often defeated us, their fellow Spaniards are said to have saddled them with the bitter reproach that those who had so often gloriously overcome us were now shamefully defeated by those whom they had earlier defeated. But they answered that they were indeed the same sheep now who had been accustomed to win, but now there was a different shepherd.[585] And here, concerning the secondary commanders in the Roman army, I would like you to observe how those same men often served as secondary commanders and legates who had earlier exercised principal commands with the greatest distinction and to the greatest benefit of the commonwealth.[586]

May you not indeed, not to the very end of your suit, wish to blacken with the clouds of calumnies and insults Roman valor shining forth from the highest summit, so as to call people like Corvinus, Torquatus, the Decii, and Papirius tricksters, necromancers, beasts, or the sorriest offspring of beasts. For the Decii, whom you name as necromancers, and others of my Romans whom you everywhere lash with the whip of your tongue, Fabricius, Curius, Camillus, Coriolanus, Cincinnatus, Fabius, Marcellus, the Scipios, Scaevola, Horatius Cocles, and others—all these your friend Plutarch supplies as comrades to Valor.[587]

Those who would attend upon the chief general—the legates, as I was saying, and the tribunes—would form a kind of senate in our camps. Since meanwhile back at home would there not be other senators in session who would be looking out for the perpetual uncertainties of the wars, would they also be coming to the assistance of the specific needs of those who were absent? For in the camps do we not also find sowing, reaping, spinning, weaving, and other occupations of civilized communities, by which a soldier p. 247
needs to be aided even more than a country-dweller or a city person? We conquer through the chief commander; we conquer also through that twin senate. And what about the rest of the soldiers? Pyrrhus would say: "O how easy it would have been to seize the rule of the world—either for me with Roman soldiers, or for the Romans with me as their king!"[588] These are those soldiers who inflicted the great wounds that made Macedonia tremble.

[a] Nescis arma Romana? Quid tu mihi recentiora omnia Alexandro facis? [b] Tullus rex audit nostræ militiæ artifex, et omnem militarem disciplinam, artemque bellandi condidisse? [c] Sic ostendunt hi viri sæpe, qui de ista re tota politissimos commentarios ediderunt: et ipsi tamen nec satis æqui aut genti Æneæ, aut Italæ. Nos a Pyrrho castrametationem: quam ille admiratus est nostram? De Romana acie dicam? [d] Ratio Romana instruendi aciem tribuisse Romanis dicitur victorias omnes. Et erat sane illic mirabile, ut pulsi redirent semper valentiores: cum hastati a principibus exciperentur, et a triariis utrique: atque ita in hostem irent: formidolosissima acies: cum velut victos insecuti auctos repente numero contra se cernerent. Exspectas de disciplina? At hæc illa est una, cui nulla unquam a quoquam comparatur.

Quis tibi contendit, nata omnia hæc, et perfecta simul? Hoc contendimus, perfecta fuisse omnia in Alexandri ætatem: quæ tradita a patribus Albanis, p. 248 qui ceperint antea | de Troianis experientissimis, et exercita iam per continuos annos amplius quadringentos fuerunt.

Vim respicis numerorum, et copiarum? Illa scilicet nobis defuisset: [e] cum senatui, populoque Romano ante Punica bella parerent sex equitum millia, peditum centum, et quinquaginta. [f] Nam Alexandrum accepimus ad imperium Persicum subvertendum non cum pluribus, quam duobus, et triginta millibus peditum, equitum quatuor, et quingentis profectum esse. [g] Decreta patri a Græcia scimus in idem illi meditatum bellum auxilia peditum ducenta millia, quindecim equitum: extra quam summam essent exercitus Macedoniæ, et confinis domitarum gentium barbaries. Ceterum et Romanis, præter suum robur illud proprium, ex minori Italiæ parte adversus hostem externum (adi Polybium) quinquaginta millia equitum, quingenta millia peditum adiungebantur. Anguem Lernæum clamabat Pyrrhus.

Quid spectas? Quid huc, illuc voluens oculos tacitus hæres? [h] Ne tamen, ne ex hac, quæ nunc est urbium solitudine, regionum desertitudine priscam illarum gentium expendas copiam. Ex unica Siciliæ civitate Syracusis Dionysius exercitum peditum centum viginti, equitum duodecim millium confecit. [i] Hac Alexandri ætate civitas nostra ex urbana nostra, et agresti p. 249 iuventute decem legiones scribebat: quem | postea exercitum non illæ nostræ

[a] *Macch. de ar. be.* 2. 3. [b] *Flor.* 1. [c] *Lips.* 5. *de mil.* R. *prin. et* 1. *Poliorc.* 3.
[d] *Macch. de ar. be.* 3. *Lips.* 4. *de mi. Ro.* 1. [e] *Polyb.* 2. [f] *Iusti.* 11.
[g] *Iusti.* 9. [h] *Diod.* 3. [i] *Liv.* 7.

---

[589] Machiavelli, *Arte della guerra* 2. 3. [590] Florus 1. 3. 1.

[591] Justus Lipsius, *De militia romana* 5. 1, pp. 211–13; *Poliorceticon* 1. 3.

[592] Machiavelli, *Arte della guerra* 3; Lipsius, *De militia romana* 4. 1, pp. 150 ff.

[593] Polybius 2. 24. [594] Justin 11. 6. [595] Justin 9. 5.

[596] **Translator's note:** In fact, it was Pyrrhus' deputy Kineas who, after a visit to Rome, told Pyrrhus that the Senate was "an assembly of kings" and that to fight against Roman forces would be like fighting the Lernaean Hydra: Plutarch, *Pyrrhus* 19.

[597] Diodorus Siculus 3.

Are you unaware of Roman soldiery and weaponry?[589] Why do you make out everything to be more recent than Alexander? King Tullus is said to be the originator of our way of making war and to have founded all our military discipline and art of war.[590] This is shown by those men who have published the most refined treatises on this whole art—and yet are themselves not sufficiently fair to the race of Aeneas or to the Italian race.[591] Did we learn the setting up of camps from Pyrrhus, when he admired ours? Am I to speak of our line of battle? The Roman method of setting up their line of battle is said to have given the Romans all their victories.[592] And it was indeed marvelous how they always rallied even more valiantly after a repulse; when their first line was received by their second line, and then both by their third line, and so they would advance against the enemy. It was a profoundly fear-inducing line of battle, when those who attacked them as though they were defeated suddenly would see them coming against them with an increase in numbers. Are you waiting to hear about our training? But this is the one thing to which no other system of training has ever been likened by anyone.

Who has maintained to you that all of this was born and perfected at one single moment? This alone we are arguing: that all these things were perfected by the time of Alexander. They had been handed down by the Alban fathers, who had earlier received them from the highly experienced Trojans, p. 248
and they had been practiced already for more than four hundred years without a break.

Are you thinking of the strength of our troops and forces? As if *that* would have failed us, when before the Punic Wars 6,000 cavalry and 150,000 infantry were available to the Roman Senate and people.[593] For we believe that Alexander set out to overthrow the Persian empire with not more than 32,000 infantry and 4,500 cavalry.[594] We know that reinforcements of 200,000 infantry and 15,000 cavalry were ordered by decree from Greece by his father for that same war which he had planned—and that is over and above the army of Macedonia, as well as that of the neighboring barbarian territory of conquered peoples.[595] But the Romans, too, in addition to their own crack troops, were joined by 50,000 horse and 500,000 foot (see Polybius here) levied against the external enemy from less than half the Italian peninsula. Hence Pyrrhus used to complain about a "Lernaean Hydra."[596]

Why are you gaping? Why do you stand there in perplexity, rolling your eyes now in this direction, now in that? Don't try to calculate that ancient abundance of those peoples on the basis of the modern-day emptiness of those cities and the depopulation of those regions.[597] From a single city of Sicily, Syracuse, Dionysius put together an army of 120,000 infantry and 12,000 cavalry. In the lifetime of Alexander the Great, our city used to enroll ten legions from our urban and rustic men of military age. Later on, our p. 249

sequentes vires, quas vix terrarum capiebat orbis, contractæ in unum, facile effecissent: ut notat Livius. [a] Quis crederet hodie, primo Punico bello nos amisisse septingentas, [b] non triremes, aut minores istiusmodi, quas nomine inepto itidem triremes hodie appellamus, sed quinqueremes: et prælio adhuc vicisse magno navali, quod finemque attulit toti bello?

Quis illam ad bellum secundum multitudinem ex civibus, sociisque, bello aptam, relatam in numeros? Diodorus decies centena ferme hominum millia profitetur. [c] Miracula audire credimus veterum Thebarum Ægypti opes, et Ægypti postea regis Philadelphi, et classes navium quinque millium, et alia eius generis. Verum sic Livius respondet, sic ea crescere, in quæ et laboratur. Hoc erat veteribus studium, viris, et viribus pollere. Desivimus admirari: qui intelligimus, belli tempore Romanos omnes milites exstitisse: agricolas fuisse omnes semper: nunquam mercatores, artifices, aliter servos civitatis, ineptissimos militiæ, muneribus duris, atque ingenuis. Sic Spartani aliquando, etsi essent numero pauciores, præferre se numero sociorum audebant longe maiori; quod ipsi milites essent omnes, socii milites plerique omnes non essent, sed de aliis artibus in eam tum transcripti militiam.

p. 250 Sic mei Romani. [d] Sic desine, | Patriti, admirari numeros illos nostros innumeros sic desine. Tu desine, accusator, tantis his nostris viris Alexandri vim obiectare. Viros hic dixit avunculus suus: in Asia feminas, et fortunam deprædicabat eius, quæ eum detulit illo. [e] Ut nostri item fortunam Magni ratione pari laudabat Cæsar: nacti gloriam bellicæ virtutis per populos Asianos. [f] Circa Africam, Europamque exhauserunt mei laboris plurimum: et ex his tot, ac tantis gentibus Italos magno labore post quingentesimum demum annum domuerunt. Asiam paucis præliis propter infirmitatem, ignaviamque earum gentium sub potestatem fecere. Ita Appianus. Næ cognomentum Magni amisisset apud nos Alexander, quod contra Persarum pellicum, et lixarum, et spadonum agmina quæsiisset. Quid tibi Antiochos, Tigranes, reliquos Asiæ reges, et Alexandri successores memorem victos nullo negotio? [g] Lucullus cum decem millibus peditum, mille equitum vicit prælio Tigranem, qui centum ducebat, et quinquaginta hominum millia. Et ex his cecidit centum millia, amissis suis solis quinquaginta.

[a] *Polyb.* 1. [b] *Bayf. de re. na.* [c] *Tac. ann.* 2. *Theocr. eidyl.* 17. *Athen.* 5.
[d] *Patr. Dial.* 6. *de hist.* [e] *Suet. Cæs.* 35. [f] *App. præf.* [g] *Plut. ap. reg.*

---

598 Livy 7. 25. 8–9.

599 Polybius 1; Lazarus Bayfius [Lazare de Baïf], *De re navali libellus*, Lugduni, Apud haeredes Simonis Vincentij, 1537.

600 Tacitus 2. 60; Theocritus *Idylls* 17. 95–105; Athenaeus 5. 203 D–E.

601 [Livy 7. 25. 9: "adeo in quae laboramus sola crevimus, divitias luxuriamque"; "so much have we expanded only for those things we strive for: wealth and luxury."]

602 Franciscus Patricius (Francesco Patrizi), *Della historia dieci dialoghi* 6, Venetia, Appresso Andrea Arrivabene, 1560, pp. 34–5.

603 [Livy 9. 19. 11.] 604 Suetonius, *Caesar* 35. 2. 605 Appian, *Prooemium* 6. 9.

606 Plutarch, *Regum et imperatorum apophthegmata* 203 A. **Translator's note:** In fact, both here and in his life of Lucullus, Plutarch claims that Lucullus lost only *five men.*

subsequent forces, though the whole world hardly contained them, would not, had they been gathered together, have made up an army of this size (as Livy points out).[598] Who would believe today that in the First Punic War we lost 700—not triremes, much less those smaller ships of today which we call by the foolish name of "triremes"—but quinquiremes—and yet still were victorious in a great naval battle which brought an end to the entire war?[599]

Who would believe that multitude of citizens and allies, ready for war, registered in troops, for the Second Punic War? Diodorus claims that it was almost a million men. We believe we are hearing of miracles when we hear of the wealth of Thebes of ancient Egypt and of the wealth of the later Egyptian king, Ptolemy Philadelphus, and fleets of 5,000 ships, and other things of this sort.[600] But Livy responds thus: growth is limited to what one strives for.[601] This was the pursuit of the ancients: to be strong in men and resources. We have ceased to be amazed by this when we learn that in time of war all Romans were soldiers, and that they had always been farmers, never merchants and craftsmen or other sorts of slaves of the city, utterly unsuited for military service and for tough and noble tasks. Thus the Spartans once upon a time, although they were far fewer in numbers, dared to set themselves above the far larger number of their allies, because they themselves were all soldiers, but the allies were, for the most part, not all soldiers, but were temporarily drafted into service from the other crafts.

This is what my Romans were like. Cease, then, Patricius, to be amazed at p. 250
those innumerable numbers of our troops.[602] You also cease, accuser, to throw the might of Alexander against all these men of ours. Alexander's own uncle [Alexander of Epirus] said that over here there are men, but in Asia there are women; and he praised the good luck of Alexander that had taken him over there.[603] Similarly, Julius Caesar used to praise the luck of our own "Great" [Pompey], who got his glory for martial valor thanks to Asian peoples.[604] My people expended most of their effort around Africa and Europe; and among these so numerous and great peoples they subdued the Italians only with great effort, after 510 years. But they brought Asia under their power in just a few battles, due to the weakness and indolence of those peoples. So Appian states.[605] Truly, had he been among us Alexander would have lost the title "the Great" that he won against the ranks of the Persian prostitutes, camp-followers, and eunuchs. Why should I mention to you the Antiochuses, the Tigranes, the other kings of Asia, and the successors of Alexander, whom we defeated without difficulty? Lucullus with 10,000 infantry and a thousand cavalry defeated in battle Tigranes, who was leading 150,000 men. And of these latter Lucullus cut down 100,000, while he lost only fifty of his own.[606]

Sed hic mihi M. Tullius adversatur: qui, maxima cum his bella regibus fuisse, contendit. Sed respondeo, Ciceronem inservire caussæ ad Murenæ laudem: et intelligere omnes, Ciceronis contentionem falsissimam. [a] Sed
p. 251 respondeo cum historia, *Non | aliud formidolosius fama bellum fuit. Quippe cum Persas, et Orientem, Xerxem, atque Darium cogitarent*, &c. Cogitarent Annibalem: *cuius nomen* (ut alius ait) *terribile Antiochi bellum faciebat*. Elimæos, Medos, Cadusios, et id genus alia nomina audirent, quasi infinitarum nationum: quibus sane, ut etiam opibus, armisque copiosissima est Syria. Tamen et fama tantum sic bellum formidolosum: et *nihil fuit in Antiocho speciosius, quam quod a Romanis victus est.*

Desine, accusator, Livio insultare de Perseo: qui aliquo uno prælio occiderit duo millia nostrorum peditum, et ducentos equites, et ducentos adhuc equites ceperit. Desine, pavorem illic nostrorum. Nam idem Livius ostendit, immo debellari nostros non facile potuisse: qui ordine, et certo gradu recederent; cum regii sparsi essent. Audax cœptum dicit regiorum: [b] atque audax inconsultum est, temerarium, et infelix: inquit, fidum Perseo ducem contra cœptum suasisse: ait, regiorum venientium impeditum agmen.

Quod unum malum in re militari longe est maximum, et per mille clades contestatum: [c] ipsi mox Perseo cum suo expertum maximo detrimento. Et sic igitur ad ea verba, parvo potuisse momento debellari, esse (quod sollemne historicis) de aliena potius opinione, quam sua Livii: qui in re ipsa expri-
p. 252 menda demonstrat contrarium. [d] Et sic igitur, quod scribit | alibi, *debellari momento temporis potuisse id dictu, quam re, ut pleraque, facilius.*

Desine, accusator, obiectare Pyrrhum nobis: et minutulum insuper appellare regem. [e] Qui cum totis viribus Epiri, Thessaliæ, Macedoniæ, incognitis in id tempus elephantis, mari, terra, viris, equis, et hoc novo præterea advecto ferarum terrore venerit. [f] Cui trecenta quinquaginta millia peditum, viginti equitum millia a Tarentinis tribuerentur. Desine laudes Pyrrhi. [g] Nam tu scis,

[a] *Flor.* 2. *Iusti.* 31. [b] *Serv. Æn.* 8.
[c] *Liv.* 42. [d] *Liv.* 31. [e] *Oros.* 4. *c.* 1. *Ior. de re. suc. Flor.* 1. *Iusti.* 17.
[f] *Plut. Pyrr.* [g] *P. Dia.* 2. *Sex. Vict. Flor.* 1. *Iusti.* 18.

---

607 [Cicero, *Pro Murena* 14. 31.] 608 Florus 2. 8. 2.

609 Justin 31. 1. [Hannibal was at this time in the court of Antiochus and urging him to initiate a war against the Romans.]

610 [Florus 2. 8. 4.]

611 [Livy 42. 59–60.]

612 Servius, On *Aeneid* 8. **Translator's note:** For the phrase in Livy, see 42. 59. 7, *audaci coeptu.*

613 **Translator's note:** At Livy 42. 59. 8, Gentili read "postquam agmen impeditum venientium sub signis vidit." Most modern editions follow Perizonius' emendation "peditum," "foot-soldiers," for "impeditum," "obstructed."

614 Livy 42. 59. 7.

615 Livy 31. 38. 3. **Translator's note:** Gentili's splicing of a fragment of one sentence with another has resulted in considerable awkwardness here that could be remedied only by expanding the quotation from Livy.

616 Orosius 4. 1; Jordanes, *Romana* 153; Florus 1. 18. 6; Justin 18. 1. **Translator's note:** Gentili's wording here is taken directly from Florus and Jordanes.

617 Plutarch, *Pyrrhus* 13. **Translator's note:** Plutarch presents this as an enticement by the Tarentines, not the actual figure of troops delivered.

But here Cicero opposes me: he contends that the wars with these kings were very great indeed. But I reply that Cicero was serving his brief for the reputation of Murena, and everyone knows that Cicero's contention was utterly false.[607] But I offer a response in accord with the historical record. "No other war was ever more frightening according to the rumors, for indeed p. 251
the Romans were thinking of the Persians and the East and Xerxes and Darius."[608] They were thinking of Hannibal, "whose name" (another historian records) "was making the war with Antiochus terrifying."[609] They heard of the Elimaeans, the Medes, the Cadusii, and other names of that sort, as though of nations without number, in which indeed Syria is quite abundant, as also in wealth and arms. And yet it was in rumors alone that the war was so frightening—"and nothing about Antiochus was more distinguished than the fact that he was defeated by the Romans."[610]

Desist, accuser, from taunting Livy over Perseus, who in a certain single battle slew two thousand of our foot-soldiers and two hundred cavalry, and in addition captured another two hundred cavalrymen.[611] Stop mocking the fear of our men in that battle. For that same Livy showed that in fact our men could not easily be utterly defeated, for they retreated in good order and at a fixed pace, while the king's men were scattered hither and yon. He also refers to the "bold undertaking" of the king's men, and "bold" (*audax*) here means ill-advised, rash, and unsuccessful;[612] and he said that a general trusted by Perseus argued against the undertaking, for he said that the advancing column of the king's men was obstructed.[613]

This one evil in military affairs (over-boldness) is far and away the worst, as has been proved in a thousand slaughters; and before long it became known through experience to Perseus himself, to his very great detriment. And so, therefore, with regard to those words "with just a slight push they could have been utterly defeated,"[614] they were about someone else's opinion (as is a common practice among historians), not Livy's own, who in setting forth the action itself demonstrates the precise opposite. And so, therefore, as he writes elsewhere, "to be able to be utterly defeated in a single stroke is something p. 252
that is easier in the saying than in the doing, for the most part."[615]

Stop casting Pyrrhus in our teeth, accuser, and in addition calling him a petty king. With all the forces of Epirus, Thessaly, Macedonia, and with elephants, up to that time unknown to us, he came against us by sea, by land, with infantry, with cavalry, and with this new added terror of beasts.[616] Also, the Tarentines gave him 350,000 infantry and 20,000 cavalry.[617] Cease and desist your praises of Pyrrhus. For you know that he admired our arms upon

quod primo admiratus intuitu arma nostra: quodque primo victor prælio, in quo et ipse graviter vulneratus, victum se censuit, vincendum certe et bello, si iterum vinceret eodem modo: id est, tanta cum suorum fortissimorum iactura. Etiam scis, quod *Romanos vincentes iam inusitata ante elephantorum forma stupere primo: mox cedere prælio coegit: victoresque iam nova Macedonum monstra repente vicerunt. Itaque rex callidus, intellecta virtute Romana, statim desperavit armis, seque ad dolos contulit*: &c.

Quæ sunt testimonia duorum, quos tu non recuses, Trogi, ac Flori. Desine desperationem dicere nostram: pavorem ut voles. Neque enim lapides, aut mentecapti fuerunt illi: qui humanos patiebantur affectus. *Extemplo Æneæ solvuntur frigore membra. Ingemuit.* [a] Ubique supra ceteros dolet, et gemit
p. 253 mortem amicorum Æneas, concussus animum: et per ve|rum dolorem demittit lacrimas, &c. *strepitumque exterritus hausit.* Etiam illud heroicæ fortitudinis exemplar pavet. Etiam ipse fatetur, timuisse alibi quoque, *At me tum primum sævus circumstetit horror: obstupui.* Et alibi adhuc, *Nunc omnes terrent auræ, sonus excitat omnis Suspensum, et pariter comitique, onerique timentem.* Humanos Æneas patiebatur affectus: Æneadæ patiebantur: sed affectibus non succumbebant. Apage desperationem.

[b] Fortunæ violentiam toleravere. Nescis, quæsitum. [c]*Utrumne secundis, an magis adversis staret Romana propago*? et responsum? *scilicet adversis.* [d]*Nunquam succubuit damnis, et territa nullo Vulnere: post Cannas maior, Trebiamque fremebat et, cum iam premerent: flammæ murumque feriret hostis, in extremos aciem mittebat Iberos.* Apage cum tuis tacitis senatusconsultis: quæ tum erant, cum aliquid ad silendum erat.

Apage cum tuis legationibus, et quod ex una Ciceronis occasione concludis generaliter contra omnem experientiam, ultro missam legationem signum esse timoris videri. Nego, vel missam legationem. [e] Nonnullas ex Italia ait Trogus. Tacito hoc generali sermone involuisset Romanam? [f] Arrianus diserte negat, Roma missam. [g] Immo loquor tibi verba Livii: Ne fama quidem tuus sic Magnus nobis cognoscebatur. Et hæc est sententia Livii, ut Græcorum
p. 254 de Magno hoc tuo iactan|tiam simili genere vanitatis confutaret.

[a] *Serv.* 6. *Æneid.* [b] *Sall. Catil.* [c] *Sulpitia.* [d] *Claud.* 3. *Stilic.*
[e] *Iust.* 12. [f] *Arria.* 7. [g] *P. Victor. ep. an. Pol. Arist.*

---

618 Paulus Diaconus, *Historia Romana* 2. 11–12; Aurelius Victor; Florus 1. 18. 17 f.; Justin 18. 1.

619 [The quoted words are a rather incoherent pastiche of Justin 18. 1 and Florus 1. 13. 14.]

620 [Vergil, *Aeneis* 1. 92–3.] 621 Servius, *On Aeneid* 6 [line 559].

622 [*Aeneis* 2. 559–60.]

623 [*Aeneis* 2. 728–9. This is Aeneas leaving burning Troy. The "companion" is his son Ascanius; the "burden" his father Anchises on his back.]

624 Sallust, *Bellum Catilinae* 53.

625 *Sulpiciae Conquestio* 50–1. [This poem of seventy hexameters is probably late 4th/early 5th c. AD, but was attributed to Sulpicia, a poet of the time of Domitian.]

626 Claudian, *De consulatu Stilichonis* 3. 144–7.

627 Justin 12. 13. 628 Arrian 7. 15.6.

629 Petrus Victorius [Pietro Vettori], *Commentarii in VIII libros Aristotelis de optimo statu civitatis*, Florentiae, In officina Iuntarum, Bernardi Filiorum, 1576 [the passage can be found on the fifth page of the unpaginated preface, Petrus Victorius Lectori]. [The Livy passage is 9. 18. 6.]

his first sight of them; and that when he was the victor in the first battle, in which he was himself gravely wounded, he considered himself defeated and believed that he would be defeated in the war if he were to score another victory such as this—that is, with such a loss of his own bravest men.[618] And you know this also: "that when the Romans were on the point of victory the hitherto unfamiliar sight of the elephants made them gape in astonishment at first, and soon it forced them to retreat from the battle. So the strange monsters of the Macedonians quickly defeated the victors. And so the clever king, having recognized the valor of the Romans, at once despaired of winning by force of arms and resorted to trickery."[619]

These are the testimonies of two men whom you would not reject: Pompeius Trogus and Florus. Lay off speaking of our despair—or our fear, as you would have it. For those men were not stones or madmen; they suffered normal human emotions. "Suddenly Aeneas's limbs went slack with chill. He groaned."[620] Everywhere Aeneas grieves more than others do and groans over the death of his friends, stricken in spirit, and sheds tears p. 253
through genuine grief, etc. "Terrified, he heard the shrieking."[621] Yes, even that exemplar of heroic fortitude shows fear. He even himself admits elsewhere that he too was afraid: "But then for the first time a fierce horror surrounded me. I stood dumbfounded."[622] And elsewhere too: "Now every breeze terrified me, every sound stirred me up in suspense, afraid both for my companion and my burden."[623] Aeneas used to experience human emotions; so too did the sons of Aeneas experience them; but they were not overcome by their feelings. So away with that despair!

"They have endured the violence of Fortune."[624] Are you unaware of this question: "Would the Roman race stand more firmly in favorable circumstances or adverse?" And the answer? "Adverse, of course."[625] "Never did Rome yield to her losses, nor was she terrified by any wound. Greater after Cannae and Trebia than before, she roared, and when flames were already pressing upon her walls and the enemy was beating upon them, she was sending her battle array against the most distant Iberians."[626] Away with your "silent decrees of the Senate," which took place at a time when there was something that needed to be kept secret.

Away with your argument about sending embassies: something which on the basis of one particular passage in Cicero you draw as a general conclusion quite contrary to all practical experience: namely, that an embassy sent on one's own initiative is a sign of fear. Besides, I deny that an embassy was even sent. "And some were sent from Italy," says Trogus.[627] Would he have wrapped up a Roman embassy in this inexplicit general phrase? Arrian explicitly says that no embassy was sent from Rome.[628] I state emphatically to you the words of Livy: that not even by rumor was your "Great" man known to us.[629] And this is the opinion of Livy, that he might refute the boasting of the Greeks about this "Great" man of yours with a similar kind of national vanity. p. 254

Desine rursus Annibalem, et ridicula ferre. Vincere Annibal Romanos potuit, si dominus fuisset reliqui orbis terrarum: et suorum odiis, et suæ civitatis fortuna non fuisset afflictus. Alexander itaque vincere potuit. Et non in animo tuo erubescebas, cum hæc afferres ridicula? Alexander nec trahebat secum partem orbis bello meliorem, Africam, et plurimam Europam. Noster Scipio vicit istum Annibalem, nec orbis dominus, nec expers invidia apud suos: [a] ut sic sunt Fabii Maximi, et Catonis Censorii duræ illæ adversus Scipionem orationes: et reliqua obiecta sunt impedimenta: unde et fuerit illi necesse, per privatas aut suas, aut amicorum opes plurima administrare.

Hic vir, hic est, qui et fortunam virtute vicit, et traxit ad suos. [b] Aspice puerum, aspice *dum genitor nati parma protectus abiret*, cum esset annorum vix septendecim, et pro patris defensione septem et viginti vulnera tulerit. Aspice post Cannensem diem, ut sistit adolescens fugam maiorum, et desertionem Italiæ. Aspice in Hispania iuvenem, ut cladem nostrorum exercituum, et patrui, et patris, obversus fortunæ abluit sanguine hostium: et fortunam ipsam rapiat illic, et sistat nobis stabilem, atque securam. [c] Hic vir, hic est, quem, veluti in philosophis, Socratem, in poetis Homerum, imitandum in
p. 255 ducibus, ait Hieronymus. Apa | ge cum iudicio contrario Nigri, lenti hominis, inertis, supini, levis, contemtibilis: [d] ut sic narrant, atque ostendunt de Nigro historiæ.

Quid vero nunc tibi spei superest pro Alexandri victoria? Vincimus nos ducibus, militibus, viris, armis, re alia omni. Vincimur temporibus, et coniurationibus nostrorum? *Egregiam vero laudem, et spolia ampla refertis, Tuque, puerque tuus:* qui per istam calamitatem nostram, non per ullam virtutem suam, nos vicerit. Sed et calamitatem illam *credimus? an, qui amant, ipsi sibi somnia fingunt*? Falleris. Pœni nos iuvare contra Pyrrhum voluere. Pœni iuvare valide potuissent, qui tenebant principatum Africæ, et Hispaniæ: et, te modo iudice, vincere nos, et orbem reliquum valuissent.

[a] *Liv.* 28. 29. *Plut. Ca. ce.* [b] *Serv.* 10. *Æn.*
[c] *Hieronym. ep.* 13. [d] *Herodia.* 2.

---

630 Livy 28; 29; Plutarch, *Cato the Elder* 3.

631 Servius, *On Aeneid* 10. 800. **Translator's note:** I have added the words "holding off the enemy" in order to give some sense to the Vergilian line as Gentili awkwardly incorporates it here. It is perhaps unfortunate that he has cited a line about Lausus protecting his profoundly evil father Mezentius.

632 Jerome, *Epistulae* 13.

633 Herodian 2. 7. 5; 2. 8. 9.

634 **Translator's note:** Vergil, *Aeneis* 4. 93–4, Juno is speaking to Venus, and the "boy" is Cupid. Here Gentili turns the "you" into Picenus and "your boy" into Alexander.

635 [Vergil, *Eclogae* 8. 108.]

Lay off bringing in Hannibal and silly stuff: "Hannibal could have defeated the Romans, if he had been the master of the rest of the world and had not been harassed by the hatreds of his own people and the misfortune of his city. And so Alexander could have conquered them as well." Do you not blush, at least in your own mind, when you trot out this laughable stuff? Alexander would not have brought with him the part of the world that was better at war—Africa and most of Europe. Our Scipio defeated that Hannibal, and Scipio was not master of the world, nor was he lacking ill will among his own people, as is indicated by those harsh speeches of Fabius Maximus and Cato the Censor against Scipio—and the other obstacles thrown in his path, which made it necessary for him to manage most things with private resources, either his own or those of his friends and family.[630]

This man—*this* is the one who conquered luck by valor—and so brought luck to his people. Behold the boy, behold him holding off the enemy "until the father could depart, protected by the shield of his son," when he was scarcely 17 years old and endured twenty-seven wounds in defending his father.[631] Behold how, after the battle of Cannae, the youth halted the flight of his elders and their desertion of Italy. Behold the young man in Spain, how he turned to face Fortune and washed away the disasters of our armies and of his uncle and father with the blood of the enemy—and he wrested away that same Fortune there and set it up stable and secure for us. This man, *this* is the one who Jerome says should be imitated among commanders, just as among the philosophers Socrates is to be imitated, and among the poets Homer.[632] Away with the contrary judgment of Pescennius Niger, a sluggish man, feeble, p. 255
supine, trivial, contemptible, as the histories record and show about him.[633]

What hope, honestly, is now left you for having Alexander win this contest? We triumph through our commanders, our soldiers, our men, our weapons, and every other thing. Are we to be defeated by the passage of time and by the conspiracies of our own people? "Indeed, you bring back splendid glory and ample spoils, you and that boy of yours," a youth who will have defeated us through that disaster of ours, not through any virtue of his own.[634] But do we even believe in that disaster—"or do those in love fashion dreams for themselves?"[635] You are mistaken. In fact, the Carthaginians wished to give us aid against Pyrrhus. The Carthaginians would certainly have been able to aid us, since they held dominion over Africa and Spain, and, in your opinion at least, had the power to defeat us and the rest of the world.

[a] Quid Tyriorum obiectas calamitatem? Urbs illa, et vetus, et nova, credita penitus inexpugnabilis. Scis, Babylonium regem vix potitum post tredecim annorum obsidionem. Scis, irrisui fuisse Alexandrum diu. Sed audi; festinassent magis in nostrum auxilium Pœni; qui et magis vicini eramus. Nescis imperii leges. Iuvasset nos Italia, iuvasset contra communem hostem. Dixi dilectus, dum externa vis ingruere timebatur. Unit communis metus etiam adversissima. [b] Scit Alexander tuus, Oxydracas, Mallosque, alias bellare inter
p. 256 se solitos, periculi societate inter se iunctos. Sane tamen si sic vinci tantum | potuimus, cum deserti undique, et oppugnati undique fuissemus, neque velim ego hic vincere: at cedo, manum do, herbam præbeo.

Aut etiam nos in calamitate aliqua Alexandri spem perditam retinemus? Quæ autem hominis maior calamitas propriis vitiis esse potest? O quantam hic Alexandri calamitatem! Nec solum eius temporis, cum victa Asia, extremoque Oriente subacto, cumque illum deducit ad nos Picenus, et cum nihil in illo sani, nihil sinceri fingere ingenium valet, sed temporis usque sub Aristotele præceptore, sub Philippo patre imperatore, o quantam Alexandri calamitatem! Laudas discipulum Aristotelis? [c] Unde tamen viri crudeles, et inquinatissimi, nisi ex ludo Philosophorum, et Philosophorum Dei, Socratis? Quid mihi longum disputatis accusatores Socratis? Is iuventutem corrupit: ecce, qui de sua prodeunt schola, corruptissimi sunt.

[d] Noster audit Seneca in re morali præstantissimus supraque reliquos Græcos, supraque Socratem. [e] At Nero unde manavit? [f] An tu putas, iis vixisse philosophos moribus, qui picti in ipsorum libris apparent? [g] Nam, quanta fuerit vitæ Aristotelis improbitas, habent plurium monumenta: ingratissimus, impudicissimus, audax, procax, vorax, ebriosus, veneficus hic traditur Alexandri magister. Et igitur discipulus iisdem attaminatus ecce hic vitiis.
p. 257 Tu libidinem Alexandri | excusaveris, accusator? [h] Sed infamis eius notissimus: quemadmodum et præceptor. Quare et a voluptatibus tum concessis fuerit alienior. Sic et philosophus voluit aliquando concessas capere, ne solas amare inconcessas, odisse concessas videretur. Hæc nostris illis ducibus nec per suspicionem dicentur. Iuvat hic, quod verissime fiet, Scytharum laudes supra Græcos ad Romanos meos transferre: [i] *Prorsus ut admirabile videatur,*

[a] *Tremell. Isa.* 23. [b] *Cur.* 6. [c] *Athen.* 5. [d] *Petr. ep. ad Sene.* [e] *Aus. paneg. Gra.* [f] *Card.* 5. *de sap.* [g] *Patr.* 1. *disc. perip.* [h] *Cur.* 7. [i] *Iust.* 2.

---

636 Isaiah 23, in Immanuel Tremellius, *Testamenti veteris biblia sacra sive libri canonici priscae Judaeorum ecclesiae a Deo traditi, Latini recens ex Hebraeo facti ab Immanuele Tremellio & Francisco Junio, accesserunt libri apocryphi, &c., Hanoviae*, 1596, pp. 23 f. of the *Prophetici libri omnes*.

637 Quintus Curtius 9. 4. 15. 638 Athenaeus 5.

639 **Translator's note:** Gentili puzzlingly cites here a letter of Peter to Seneca. There was an apocryphal exchange of letters between Paul and Seneca, but nowhere in that exchange does "Paul" refer to Seneca as wiser than Socrates.

640 Ausonius, *Gratiarum actio ad Gratianum* 7. 641 Cardanus, *De sapientia* 5.

642 Franciscus Patricius [Francesco Patrizi], *Discussionum Peripateticorum tomi IV* 1, Basileae, Apud P. Lecythum, 1581.

643 Quintus Curtius 6. 6. 1. **Translator's note:** I take the *concessi* of the 1770 edition to be a slip for *concessis*, which *seems* to be what is in the 1599 edition. I suspect that part of the obscurity of Gentili's phrasing here is due to the fact that he is coyly hinting at Alexander's homosexual affairs.

Why do you bring up the disaster of the Tyrians? That city, both old and new, has been believed to be profoundly resistant to sieges. You know that a Babylonian king [Nebuchadnezzar] scarcely got hold of it after a siege of thirteen years.[636] You know that Alexander was a laughing-stock there for a long time. But listen: the Carthaginians would have made more haste to help us [than the Tyrians did for the Carthaginians], since they were much closer to us. You apparently don't know the way empire works. Italy would have helped us—it would have helped us against the common foe. I have mentioned the troop levies when it was feared that a foreign power was about to attack. A common fear unites even the most hostile entities. Your Alexander knew that the Oxydracae, the Malli, and others were accustomed to be at war with each other, but they joined together through the fellowship of threatened danger.[637] And yet if we could only be defeated when we might be p. 256 deserted and assaulted from every direction, well, I wouldn't want to be the winner [in this debate]: I yield, I surrender, I throw in the towel.

But do we perhaps retain a forlorn hope in some misfortune of *Alexander's*? Well, what greater misfortune for a man can there be than his own vices? Ah, what a misfortune was Alexander's here! Ah, what a misfortune was Alexander's—not just in the period when Picenus has brought him to us, when he had conquered Asia and subdued the furthest East, a period when Picenus' talent cannot invent anything that was sane, anything that was uncorrupted in Alexander; but even in that time when he was under the tutelage of Aristotle and under that of his father Philip as commander-in-chief. You praise the pupil of Aristotle? But where have cruel and deeply corrupt men emerged from if not from the schools of the philosophers—and even of the god of philosophers, Socrates?[638] Why do you accusers of Socrates go on at such length with me? That man *did* corrupt the youth. Just look: those who step forth from his school are utterly corrupt.

Our Seneca has the reputation of being the most distinguished moral philosopher, above Socrates and above all the other Greeks.[639] But were did Nero graduate from?[640] Or do you suppose that the philosophers themselves have lived in accord with those morals that appear portrayed in their books?[641] For the records of many people record how great was the unseemliness of the life of Aristotle. It is recorded that this teacher of Alexander was utterly ungrateful, shameless, rash, stubborn, a glutton, a drunk, and a poisoner.[642] And lo and behold, this pupil of his was defiled by the very same vices.

Would you excuse the lust of Alexander, accuser? In fact, he was very p. 257 widely known to be guilty of this, just like his teacher, which is why he would be more averse to the pleasures that were then allowed.[643] For thus the philosopher himself wanted him at times to enjoy allowed pleasures, lest he seem to love only those not allowed and hate those that were allowed. These things are not said of those commanders of ours, even by suspicion. It is a pleasure here to adapt the praises of the Scythians over the Greeks to my Romans (and this would be most accurate): "It would indeed seem most

hoc Romanis dedisse naturam, quod Græci longa sapientium doctrina, præceptisque philosophorum consequi nequierunt. Tanto plus in Romanis profecit vitiorum ignoratio, quam in Gracis cognitio virtutis. Et de Romanis sane Polybius ita, Sallustius, quis non?

Quid tu captivam Scipioni obiicis, et ancillam, et iuventutem solutiorem? Eum aut non ausum videre captivam, conscium suæ incontinentiæ? aut verius retinuisse captivam, in deliciis habuisse, iniustum? Ceterum laudare in primo prudentiam decuit Scipionis, qui periculum vitare tantum, quam (in quo nec utilitas, nec necessitas) facere maluit. [a] Et sic Cyrum Plutarchus laudat. [b]*Licet quidam putent, maioris esse virtutis, præsentem contemnere voluptatem: tamen ego arbitror, securioris continentiæ esse, nescire, quod quæras:* Sic Hieronymus. [c] Et Siracides, *Averte oculum a muliere formosa: nam a pulchritudine mulieris*
p. 258 *tamquam ignis amor accenditur*, &c. *Uritque vi|dendo femina*. Cum sexcentis id genus aliis verissimis. Etiam prætorem decet non solum manus, sed et oculos abstinentes habere: ut Sophocli Pericles respondit. Dux noster continentissimus, qui ne oculis quidem libare quidquam virgini cum iniuria voluit. [d] Etiam in iure humano adulter et is quadam est significatione ex animi propositione sola, qui eius est mentis, ut occasione data alienam matremfamilias sit corrupturus. Et iniuriam fieri sibi censent honestæ mulieres, quæ non honeste aspiciantur. Quod iustum iudicium est. Nam inhonestum aliquid fingunt in eo homines, quod aspiciunt non honeste: ut honestas honestatem provocat, inhonestas inhonestatem, et quidlibet simile sui.

Nunc retentam puellam a Scipione contendas. Quo tamen teste? [e] Narrat Plutarchus, quod, cum adduxissent milites quidam Scipioni virginem formosissimam, responderit illis Scipio, gratissimum sibi futurum munus privato, sed eo non usurum se eo tempore imperatorem. *Vero, an falso, incertum: fama tamen, cum esset adolescens, haud sincera fuisse*. Sic Gellius. Addit, *Versibus quibusdam Nævii adductum videri sibi Valerium Antiatem adversus ceteros omnes scriptores de Scipionis moribus sensisse: et eam puellam captivam non redditam, sed retentam, atque in deliciis, et amoribus ab eo usurpatam*. Sic
p. 259 semel testimonia proferas integra, sic. Notes | vero, peccatum, adolescentiæ,

[a] *Plut. de aud. poe.* [b] *Hier. ep.* 7. [c] *Eccl.* 5. [d] *l.* 225. *de V. S.* [e] *Plut. apopht. reg.*

---

644 Justin 2. 2 [adapted].

645 Plutarch, *Quomodo adolescens poetas audire debeat* 31 c. **Translator's note:** The reference is to the famous story of Cyrus and Panthea in Xenophon's *Cyropaideia*.

646 Jerome, *Epistulae* 7. 647 Ecclesiasticus 9: 8.

648 **Translator's note:** Vergil, *Georgica* 3. 215–16. The subject is a cow.

649 **Translator's note:** Plutarch, *Pericles* 8. Plutarch's Pericles says "a general." I am not sure why Gentili turns this into a praetor. It is interesting that Gentili seems to overemphasize the praetors' role as military commanders.

650 *Digest* 50. 16. 225.

651 Plutarch, *Regum et imperatorum apophthegmata* 196 B. **Translator's note:** In the Greek, Scipio's is a contrary to fact condition: "I would gladly have taken her if I were a private citizen and not a general." Gentili's version seems to suggest that he is planning to accept her later.

652 Aulus Gellius 7. 8. 5–6.

remarkable that nature has given to the Romans that which the Greeks were unable to achieve through the long instruction of their wise men and the precepts of their philosophers. So much more successful was ignorance of vices among the Romans than was knowledge of virtue among the Greeks."[644] And Polybius writes thus about the Romans, as does Sallust—and everyone else.

Why do you reproach Scipio with the captive maiden, the slave girl, and his somewhat lax youth? Was it unjust of him either not to dare to look upon the captive maiden, with his own lust on his conscience, or to keep the captive and treat her as his favorite? But in the first case it would have been fitting to praise the prudence of Scipio, who preferred to avoid such a risk (in which there was no use or need) rather than to run it. And Plutarch praises Cyrus in the same way.[645] And Jerome writes: "While some may think that it is the characteristic of a greater virtue to spurn a pleasure that is available, I myself think that it is the part of a superior self-control not to know what you want in the first place."[646] And the son of Sirach says: "Turn your eyes from a beautiful woman; for from the beauty of a woman love is kindled like a fire," etc.[647] "And the female sets them burning by being looked at."[648] And there p. 258 are six hundred other very true sayings of this sort. Even a praetor ought to have not only abstinent hands but also eyes, as Pericles replied to Sophocles.[649] Our commander was a man of the greatest self-control, who did not wish even with his eyes to impair a maiden in any way at all. Even in human law a man is in a certain sense an adulterer from just the disposition of his mind if he has the intention of corrupting another man's wife should the occasion present itself.[650] And respectable women who are looked at in a way that is not respectable think that an injury is being done them. And this is a just assumption. For men imagine that there is something improper in that which they look upon improperly, for honor invites honor, and dishonor invites dishonor, and generally anything invites that which is similar to itself.

Now you also contend that Scipio kept the captive maiden. But on what authority do you rest your contention? For Plutarch relates that, when some soldiers had brought a very beautiful maiden to Scipio he replied that this was going to be a very welcome gift to him as a private man, but he was not going to make use of it while he was still the commander.[651] "Whether this is true or false is uncertain, but his reputation was scarcely spotless when he was a youth." So says Aulus Gellius.[652] And he adds: "Valerius Antias was led by certain verses of Naevius to take a position on Scipio's morals contrary to that of all the other writers; and he believed that that captive maiden was not given back, but kept and enjoyed by him among his favorites and loves." I wish once and for all that you would cite testimonies in their entirety like this. Please observe that the sinning of his youth was *uncertain*. Please observe that p. 259

incertum. [a] Notes, a Nævio, Campano, homine maledico manasse narrationem. Notes, scripsisse Antiatem, Volscum hominem, tantoque suspectiorem, quanto temporibus illis coniunctiorem. Notes, adversus ceteros omnes scriptores dici hæc de moribus Scipionis. Valerius autem Maximus nec sibi contradicit, nec quidquam dicit contra ducem nostrum.

Etenim suspicio illa videtur de ancilla: [b] et ita, *ne domitorem orbis Africani uxor impotentiæ reum ageret*: id est, ne is, qui potens tot hostium fuit, parum potuisse in se coercendo videretur. Sed et magnum sane flagitium, sive captivam in deliciis habuerit, sive aliam amaverit mulierculam. Magnum eo tempore flagitium: et Alexandri flagitio infando conferendum. Nugas istas defendimus? Siccine tu defendis flagitia Alexandri: quod et peccatum alicubi a nostris est? [c] Immo noster Commodus non sic insanus, et detestabilis est visus. Auderes ad Camilli, Curii, Fabritii, aliorum quos hic tibi Livius nominat, virtutem tuum admovere Alexandrum?

Attingam eius virtutes bellicas, et disciplinam paternæ militiæ. Reliqua ille lucretur in præsentia, quæ de Aristotele, præceptore altero, imbibit, ebrietatem, crudelitatem, alia, alia. Sobrius non peccarit: ut sic Plutarchus ait in
p. 260 declamatione secunda: dum peccaverit ebrius | sæpe. [d] Et tamen summa ingratitudo, et summa crudelitas in Parmenionem, et filios, alia, alia detestanda non iam ebrii, sed sobrii Alexandri vincuntur. Sed lucretur notas istas.

[e] Crudelitas Alexandri fuit, et sævitia immanis erga virum fortissimum Betim: cuius capti, perque spirantis talos traiici lora voluit: et iustum hostem, fortissimum, ut dico, virum religari ad currum, trahique gloriatus, Achillem imitari se, a quo genus deduceret. [f] Immanis crudelitas contra Branchidas: abominata scriptoribus: urbs diruta a fundamentis: sacri luci exscisi: etiam supplices cæsi. Quæ ista feritas? Quia maiores istorum Miletum Xerxi prodiderunt.

[g] Immanitas abominata similis in Persas. [h] Quid, quod gentem Cosseorum per venationis ludibrium delevit ad Hephæstionis inferias? [i] Fato ille functus, *dotibus* ille *formæ, pueritiæque percarus*. [j] Quid, quod ad terrorem voluit, parci

[a] *Gell.* 3. *c.* 3. [b] *Lips. ad Valer.* [c] *Athen.* 10. 12. [d] *Card.* 3. *de sap.*
[e] *Cur.* 4. [f] *Cur.* 8. [g] *Arria.* 3. [h] *Plut. Alex.* [i] *Iusti.* 12.
[j] *Cur.* 9. *Polye.* 4.

[653] Lipsius, notes on Valerius Maximus, in Stephanus Vinandus Pighius, *Valerii Maximi dictorum factorumque memorabilium libri IX, accedunt in fine eiusdem Annotationes: et Breves Notae Iusti Lipsi*, Lugduni Batavorum, Ex officina Plantiniana, Apud Franciscum Raphelengium, 1594, p. 93 [at the end, after Pighius' notes; Gentili's interpretation of Valerius' passage is taken entirely from Lipsius]. **Translator's note:** The passage in Valerius is 6. 7. 1. For "domitorem orbis Africani," Shackleton Bailey's 2000 Loeb text prints the much more plausible "domitorem orbis Africanum," "the world-conquering Africanus."

[654] Athenaeus 10. 44 f.; 12. 53.
[655] [Plutarch, *De fortuna Alexandri* 337 F.]
[656] Cardanus, *De sapientia* 3.
[657] Quintus Curtius 4. 6. 29.
[658] Quintus Curtius 7. 5. 31–5.
[659] Arrian 3. 18. 12.
[660] Plutarch, *Alexander* 72.
[661] Justin 12. 10.

the story derived from Naevius, a Campanian slanderer. Please observe that the man who wrote it up was Antias, a Volscian, and all the more untrustworthy in that he was the more in tune with those times. Please observe that these statements about the morals of Scipio were contrary to what all the other writers wrote. Moreover, Valerius Maximus neither contradicts himself, nor does he say anything against our commander.

And then there appears that innuendo about a slave woman, and so we hear: "lest his wife accuse the man who subdued the world of Africa of lack of self-control"[653]—that is, lest he who had power over so many enemies might seem to have been insufficiently able to show proper restraint over himself. Oh yes, it was surely a disgraceful act if Scipio treated a captive woman as his favorite or loved some other little woman. I'm sure that was a deeply shameful act back in those days and something to set beside the unspeakable misconduct of Alexander! Am I really defending such trifles as this? And is that how you defend the crimes of Alexander—that now and again our people, too, sinned? But not even our Commodus seemed as mad and abominable as Alexander.[654] Would you dare to bring your Alexander in to face the valor of Camillus, Curius, Fabricius, and the others whom Livy names for you here?

I shall touch upon his martial virtues and the training he received from his father's campaigning. For now, though, let him have his enjoyment of those other things that he imbibed from his other teacher, Aristotle: drunkenness, cruelty, and so on and so on. He would never have sinned when sober—so Plutarch says in his second declamation on Alexander, while he did often sin while drunk.[655] And yet it is conclusively shown that his extraordinary p. 260
ingratitude and his extraordinary cruelty to Parmenio and his sons, as well as many other detestable acts, were the acts not of an Alexander who was still drunk but of a sober Alexander.[656] But let him have his profit of those badges of infamy.

Alexander showed immense cruelty and savagery to a very brave man, Betis.[657] When he had been captured and was still alive, Alexander chose to have his heels pierced with thongs and to have this legitimate enemy and, again, very brave man tied to his chariot, while he boasted that he was imitating Achilles, from whom he traced his lineage. Savage was his cruelty to the Branchidae, and it was condemned by the historians. Their city was torn up from its foundations, its sacred groves were cut down, and even suppliants were slaughtered.[658] Why this savagery? Because the ancestors of those people betrayed Miletus to Xerxes!

He showed a similar loathsome cruelty to the Persians.[659] What of the fact that he destroyed the race of the Cossei for the pleasure of the hunt at the time of the funeral of Hephaestion?[660] For that man had died, that man who was "very dear because of the endowments of his beauty and his youth."[661] What of the fact that in order to create terror he sometimes wished no one to

aliquando nemini? [a] Quid cum pollicitus tutum præsidiariis ex urbe abitum, eos progressos aliquantulum viæ occidere fecit? Quid alia? Quid alia, quæ audivimus antea?

Quæ eius iustitia movendi bellum aut Scythis, aut Indis? [b] Scytha illi, *Tu, qui te gloriaris ad latrones persequendos venire, omnium gentium, quas adisti, latro es.* Nam quid interest, navibus pluribus, an myoparone uno infestes
p. 261 maria? Quæ audita eidem vox: et a multis laudata. Tuus iste | Alexander latro ipse maximus, et latronum fautor, et scelerum remunerator.

Latro usque ad insaniam hic fuit. Aut quid doluit, nihil sibi superfuturum, quod ageret, post victorias partas? [c] Neque enim minus est negotium regere, et conservare: ut ad istum gemitum sic respondere consueverat Augustus. Et responsum Plutarcho laudatur. [d] Difficilius, res conservare, quam parare. Sed quid hæc cogitasset ille, qui etiam, dum plures credidit vesanus mundos, nihil victoriis patris, nihil suis aut affectum conquerebatur, per quas necdum unus quæsitus mundus fuisset?

Fautor iste latronum. [e] Nescis, donasse Babylonis satrapeam Mazeo transfugæ? Armeniam Mythreni, alteri proditori? [f] Cum filio Darii fecisse de proditione parentis? Plura hæc: quæ de Philippo patre didicit Alexander; et præceptorem superavit: [g]*virtute, et vitiis patre maior:* ut inquit Trogus. Nos tamen vitia tantum vidimus.

Cedite Graii: cedite nobis Macedones. Tu, Picene, ægre ne feras, si Alexandro tuo par fiat noster Germanicus: nisi iam incipis resipiscere, et videre, quemadmodum cedere Alexander et Germanico, et aliis nostris omnibus habet. Ne addideris te mancipio Tyberiano: qui eam ignaviæ notam aspersit optimo Germanico, adulatus sævo patruo. [h] Id tibi contra Tyberium, et Velleium notarunt
p. 262 ante me alii. Fortis Germanicus | probusque: ut etiam Drusus pater. Nam neque illa distinctio recipienda est magistri (ut vocant) ab Etruria: [i] ut priores nostri duces et fortes quidem fuerint, et boni, posteriores fortes tantum. Ecce tibi fortesque, bonosque omnes, et servantes (quod quærimus) bellici iuris. Neque enim relictus ullus est indefensus, ut illaudatus: nisi alicubi forte defuimus Pompeio tantulum in re illa amplissima Mithridatica: cum oppres-

[a] *Diod.* 17. [b] *Cur.* 8. [c] *Plut. apoph. reg.* [d] *Dio.* 44. [e] *Cur.* 6.
[f] *Plut. comp. G. & Ro.* [g] *Iusti.* 9. [h] *Tac.* 1. *ann. Casa.* 4. *Suet. Ald. Lips. Vell.*
[i] *Macch.* 1. *de ar. be.*

662 Quintus Curtius 9. 5. 20; Polyaenus, *Strategemata* 4. 3. 30.

663 Diodorus 17. 84. 1–2. 664 Quintus Curtius 7. 8. 19.

665 **Translator's note:** This is based on the famous remark a captured pirate made to Alexander. Gentili's source was Augustine, *De civitate Dei* 4. 4. Augustine's source was Cicero, *De republica* 3. 24.

666 Plutarch, *Regum et imperatorum apophthegmata* 207 D. **Translator's note:** Both editions of the *De armis romanis* print "post victorias patris," "after the victories of his father," here. Even apart from the inherent absurdity, the Plutarch passage makes it clear that this is a slip for "post victorias partas."

667 Dio Cassius 44. 41. 2. 668 Quintus Curtius 5. 1. 44.

669 Pseudo-Plutarch, *Parallela Graeca et Romana* 308 C. 670 Justin 9. 8.

671 Tacitus, *Annales* 1. 33; Casaubonus [Isaac Casaubon], In *Suetonii librum IV animadversiones* [in *C. Suetonii Tranquilli opera*, ed. Frid. Aug. Wolfius, vol. 4, Lipsiae, 1802, p. 68]; Ald. [the reference is unclear]; Justus Lipsius, *Ad Velleium Paterculum animadversiones, quas recenter auxit et emendavit*, Antverpiae, Apud Ioannem Moretum, 1600, p. 35, nn. 195, 197 [commenting on Velleius Paterculus 2. 108. 1].

672 Machiavelli, *Libro dell'arte della guerra*, Libro Primo, Venetia, Per Domenico Giglio, 1554, p. 9 ["& dico, che Pompeio, & Cesare, et quasi tutti quegli Capitani, che furono a Roma dopo l'ultima guerra Carthaginese, acquistarono fama, come valenti huomini, non come buoni, et quegli, che erano vivuti avanti a loro: acquistarono gloria, come valenti, et buoni [...]."].

be spared?[662] What of the fact that after he had promised safe conduct from a city for the garrison that held it, he would order them to be killed when they had gone forth a certain distance on the road?[663] What of the other things, the things which we have heard earlier?

What was his case for making war on either the Scythians or the Indians? A Scythian said to him, "You, who boast that you come in pursuit of brigands, are yourself a brigand to all of the peoples you have gone against."[664] For what difference does it make whether you trouble the seas with many ships or with just one light pirate ship? (This was an utterance heard by the same man, and praised by many.[665]) That Alexander of yours was himself the greatest p. 261
brigand, and he was a supporter of brigands and one who rewarded crimes.

This man carried his brigandage all the way to madness. Or else why did he grieve that nothing was left for him to do after the victories he had won? For it is not less trouble to govern and maintain, as Augustus was in the habit of replying to that lament.[666] And the reply is praised by Plutarch. It is harder to maintain things than to acquire them.[667] But why would Alexander have pondered that? While in his madness he believed in the existence of several worlds, and he even complained that nothing had been achieved by the victories of his father or himself, since they had not yet acquired even one world.

That man was a sponsor of brigands. Do you not know that he gave the satrapy of Babylon to the renegade Mazaeus?[668] And that he gave Armenia to Mythrenus, another traitor? That he contrived with the son of Darius to betray his father?[669] There are many of these acts—things Alexander learned from his father Philip, and in which he surpassed his teacher: "he was greater than his father both in virtue and in vices," says Trogus.[670] We, however, see only the vices.

Yield to us, Greeks; yield to us, Macedonians. And you, Picenus, please don't take it ill that our Germanicus should become the equal of your Alexander. Or perhaps you are already beginning to recover your senses and to see how Alexander has to yield both to Germanicus and to all the rest of our generals. Do not associate yourself with a slave of Tiberius [Velleius Paterculus] who cast that brand of laziness on Germanicus in order to curry favor with his savage patron. Others before me have alerted you against Tiberius and Velleius.[671] Germanicus was brave and worthy, as p. 262
was his father Drusus as well. Nor should we accept the distinction drawn by one who is rumored to have been a Tuscan schoolmaster: that our earlier generals were indeed brave and good but the later ones were only brave.[672] Behold: they were all brave and good and (to mention what we are mainly looking for) upholders of the laws of war. Nor is there any of them left undefended, unless perhaps we have somewhere parted company with Pompey just a bit in that very extensive affair of Mithridates, when he

sisse dicitur Albanos sub fide pacti, et Phraatem. Et tamen, amplissima quia fuit illa res, veluti diluvio quodam ferri multa, necesse fuerit.

[a] Nam de Antiocho quid est? victo Tigrane rex Syriæ iste Antiochus a Lucullo appellatur, non a civitate. Pompeius regnum ademit: indignum (ut erat) iudicans, dari regem hominem Syriæ recusanti: quique annos octodecim, quibus Tigranes Syriam tenuit, in angulo Ciliciæ latuerit: nunc vero ad alieni operis præmia venerit. In re Mamertinorum non fuit necesse pro Pompeio aliquid dicere: quæ immista erat bellis civilibus: quorum natura alia, nec nostræ contentionis est. Ita nec Pompeius relictus indefensus est. Ita Magnum nos, merito magnum, habemus: immerito habent Græci suum.

Magnum quæsivit imperium Alexander. Certe. Sed, ut dixi, in Asia. [b] Ubi regna pauca, et præstantes viri pauciores: ut honor scilicet, artium nutricula,
p. 263 non | virtuti deferri sub regibus solet. [c] Sed adversus Darium ille egit, hominem novum, Codomannum quemdam, non de Cyri, aut Xerxis genere. Sed tum ille movit in Persas, cum instituta Cyri, et Persarum vetera collapsa erant. Hæc fortuna Alexandri multiplex.

Mei in Italia, per Africam, et Europam egerunt: ubi respublicæ plurimæ gentesque liberæ, obstinatissimæ in libertate tuenda, viris virtute virentibus instructissimæ. Quid mihi diuturnos loqueris labores nostros? quid Alexandri brevissima tempora? Regnum regno fuit conferendum, non regnum gestis unius regis. Regnum erat Alexandri Macedonicum ante Alexandrum natum. Illius regni viribus magnis aggressus est Orientem. Nostri a casis (ut tu dicis) ad imperium prodiere. De quibus si prodiisset Alexander, tum laudares, quod annis decem plus egisset, quam egerint nostri centies decem. Alioqui sic disputas tu, plus multo te in iure tuo civili (do tibi exemplum, quod videas facile, et amplectaris libenter) quærere nunc mense uno, quam faciat puer in mensibus centum, atque centum, itaque puero te esse præstantiorem. Agnoscis ridiculam, atque pudendam orationem?

Aut hoc dicis, plus quæsiisse imperii Alexandrum annis decem, quam nos fecerimus unquam, etiam viribus Macedoniæ pares? Sed neque nobis id
p. 264 solum agebatur, ut imperium quæ|reremus, sed etiam ut quæreremus innocente per caussas iustas, ut audisti. Alexandro hæc iustitiæ cura nulla. Dic mihi bellorum Alexandri caussas? Caussæ bellorum non semper, non

[a] *Iustin.* 40. [b] *Macch.* 2. *de ar. be.* [c] *Card.* 3. *de sap. Iusti* 12.

673 Justin 40. 2.
674 Machiavelli, *Libro dell'arte della guerra*, Libro Secondo, p. 39.
675 Cardanus, *De sapientia* 5, p. 299; Justin 10. 3.
676 [Cf. *De armis Romanis* 1. 8, pp. 78–9.]

is said to have oppressed the Albani who were under a pact and also Phraates. And yet, because that affair was so very long and drawn-out, it would be inevitable that a lot of things would have carried along in it as though by a flood.

And what of the business about Antiochus? When Tigranes was defeated, this Antiochus was named king of Syria by Lucullus, but not by the state. Pompey took the kingdom away from him, judging it unworthy (as indeed it was) that a man be given as king to Syria when Syria rejected him, and who for the eighteen years that Tigranes held Syria hid out in a corner of Cilicia, but now came to claim the prizes of another man's labor.[673] In the affair of the Mamertines it was not necessary to say anything in Pompey's defense, for that affair was mixed up with civil wars, whose nature is different from regular wars, and is not at issue here. Thus not even Pompey was left without defense. So we rightly consider him "the Great," while the Greeks wrongly consider their Alexander "the Great."

Alexander acquired a great empire. Certainly. But, as I have said, it was in Asia—where there were few kingdoms and even fewer men of distinction; for honor, which is the nurse of the arts, does not tend to be accorded to excellence p. 263 under the rule of kings.[674] Also, he was operating against Darius, a new man, a certain Codomanus, not of the line of Cyrus or Xerxes.[675] And he moved against the Persians at a time when the old institutions of Cyrus and the Persians had collapsed. This was part of Alexander's manifold good luck.

My people, on the other hand, operated in Italy, and throughout Africa and Europe, where there were a great number of free states and peoples, profoundly stubborn in the defense of their liberty and fully stocked with men flourishing with valor. Why do you speak to me of our long extended labors and of the very brief time that Alexander had? The one empire should be compared with the other, not an empire with the deeds of a single king. Alexander's kingdom was Macedonian before his birth. It was with the great forces of this kingdom that he invaded the East. Our people, on the other hand, advanced from huts (as you yourself say) to empire.[676] If Alexander had set forth from huts, then you could praise him for accomplishing more in ten years than our people did in a thousand. You might make an analogous argument (I'm giving you an example here that you could easily understand and willingly embrace) that you now earn in the practice of your civil law more in one month than a boy could do in a hundred months—and in another hundred—and so you are more distinguished than a boy. Do you see how foolish and embarrassing your speech is?

Or are you saying that Alexander acquired more of an empire in ten years than we have ever done, though we are a match for the forces of Macedon? But our activity was not solely directed at acquiring an empire, but also at p. 264 acquiring it honestly, through just causes, as you have heard. Alexander had no interest at all in justice. Tell me the causes for the wars of Alexander? Causes for wars do not show up everywhere and at all times, but they

ubique sunt, sed offerunt se per tempora. Et itaque tempora nobis effluxerunt, per quæ imperium comparavimus.

[a] Imperium si forte non ita latum, ut tu dicis Alexandri, at certe multo validius, ex tuis illis fortibus Italis, duris Germanis, bellicosis Gallis, indomitis Hispanis, invictis Britannis, nobilibus Græcis, domitoribus gentium Macedonibus, columinibus Africæ Pœnis perfectissimis, et regnis pluribus magnæ Asiæ potentissimis: id est, terris his omnibus sub utroque sole optimis, atque pulcherrimis. Hæc est amplitudo imperii vis eius, et firmitas. Quid enim, quid est imperium hodie Hispanicum? [b] etsi decuplo latius, et eo amplius post Lusitaniæ regna adiecta, hodierno Turcico imperio est? Romano olim quadruplo?

Atque sic habes, Picene, Alexandri tui, et Romanorum meorum comparationem. Nunc ad iudicem adeamus. Nam, aliquem dum exspecto Æacum, aut Catonem per tua illa ampullata, *virum sapientem, loquentem decenter, non indulgentem affectibus*, et non video nisi litteratorem quemdam, atque declamatorem, sic fugio indigni sententiam iudicis, et ad maius tribunal provoco,
p. 265 ubi caussæ istæ maiores | cognosci solent. Age, agnosce, quantum sit fiduciæ in caussa bona. Te, te acerbissimum accusatorem nostrum, facio iudicem.

Si ab ineunte ætate, sub improbo præceptore, sub improbiore parente, ad imaginem furiosi iuvenis non est educatus Alexander: et tota hæc educatio nihil potest: si ficta, si mentita plurima in adulationem Alexandri non sunt: si ille fuit imperator sapiens: si viros, arma, militiam habuit meliora nostris: si cum viris ei res fuit eximiis: sr res tractavit bellicas per iustitiam: si ornatius nostro quæsivit imperium: age, ad te nunc adeo, iudica pro Alexandro. Sed si his contraria omnia demonstrata sunt tibi: si hæc omnia, si plura Romanorum decora perpetua ostensa sunt tibi, quin ipse tu pro Romanis non iudices, caussam nullam habes.

In collatione autem fortunæ, et virtutis Alexandri quid potes aliud, si collegeris supradicta, quam constituere cum Curtio, [c] quod, etsi virtuti debuerit Alexander plurimum, plus tamen fortunæ debuit: cuius beneficio sæpius, quam virtutis magna illa gloria ipsi contigerit. At de fortuna, et virtute nostrorum: [d] *Populus Romanus tot laboribus, periculisque iactatus est, ut ad constituendum eius imperium contendisse virtus, et fortuna viderentur*. Sic et Plutarchus: *Virtute duce, comite fortuna*. [e] Sic alius, *Virtus hic convenit, et fortuna, plerumque dissidentes*.

[a] *Card. d.* 3. [b] *Bod.* 2. *de rep.* 2. et *lib.* 3. *c.* 1.
[c] *Cur.* 9. 12. [d] *Flor. prin.* [e] *Amm.* 14.

---

677 Bodinus, *De republica* 2. 2; 3. 1.
678 [This is Picenus' characterization of Apuleius in *De armis Romanis* 1. 12, pp. 116–17.]
679 Quintus Curtius 10. 5. 25–36.
680 Florus, pref. 2.
681 Ammianus Marcellinus 14. 6. 3.

present themselves under certain circumstances. And therefore the kinds of circumstances under which we have acquired our empire have at times eluded our grasp.

If perhaps our empire was not as extensive as you say Alexander's was, at least it was much stronger, being composed of those brave Italians of yours, the tough Germans, the warlike Gauls, the unconquerable Spaniards, the undefeated Britons, the noble Greeks, the Macedonian conquerors of peoples, those most perfect pillars of Africa the Carthaginians, and the many most powerful kingdoms of great Asia—that is, from all these most excellent and most beautiful lands which lie under either the rising or the setting sun. This wide extension of the empire was its strength and its stability. For what, *what* I ask you is the Spanish empire today, even if in its wide extent (all the more so now that the Portuguese territories have been added to it) it is ten times larger than the Turkish empire of today or four times larger than the ancient Roman Empire?[677]

And so, Picenus, there you have the comparison of your Alexander and my Romans. Let us now approach the judge. For while I am expecting some Aeacus or Cato when I hear your bombastic words about "a wise man, who speaks properly, not giving way to his feelings,"[678] and all I see is some scribbler or public speaker, I flee the sentence of such an unworthy judge and make an appeal to a higher court, where these more important cases tend to p. 265 be heard. Come, see what confidence I have in a good case here: for I make you the judge, *you* our bitterest accuser.

If Alexander was *not* brought up from his earliest years under a base teacher and even baser father on the model of a hot-tempered youth [Achilles], or if all this kind of upbringing had no effect; if there have *not* been many lies and fabrications to serve the adulation of Alexander; if that man was a wise general; if he had better men, arms, and soldiers than ours; if it was outstanding men with whom he had to deal; if he handled military affairs with justice; if he acquired an empire more splendid than ours—go on, I approach your bench now: find for Alexander. But if everything that is contrary to these things has been demonstrated to you; if all these things, if the greater eternal glories of the Romans have been shown to you—then you have no reason not to find for the Romans.

Moreover, in the relative assessment of the luck and the valor of Alexander, what else can you do, if you bring together the things mentioned above, than decide along with Quintus Curtius that, although Alexander did owe a great deal to his valor, he owed even more to luck, through whose favor, more often than through that of valor, that great glory that was his came his way?[679] And as for the luck and valor of our people: "The Roman people was so often tossed about by sufferings and dangers that virtue and luck seemed to be in a competition to establish their empire."[680] Thus also Plutarch: "With virtue as their guide, with fortune as their companion." And thus another author: "Here virtue and luck, usually at variance, were in agreement."[681]

p. 266

Fortuna Imperii Romani.
CAP. XIII

Nos non pudet, post virtutem civitatis nostræ fortunam admittere: quæ fortunatum simul imperium, et felicissima secula orbis confecit. [a] Non fuit primo illi magistro Alexandri Homero nota, aut nominata fortuna; quam Latinus Homerus facit etiam omnipotentem. [b] Attamen illa intelligitur divina sors, et voluntas superior quædam arcana: eo olim nomine nuncupata, cum caussæ, rationesque incognitæ eventuum essent. Cui quidem voluntati et templa fuerant erigenda multo quam virtuti iustius: vis enim mortalium virtus est. Atque tu mihi disceptationem istam refer religionum ad tempora sua: cum illi forent dii, deæque venerandi, quos civitas, et terrarum orbis universus colebat.

Mittenda hic sunt omnia, quæ veræ religionis sint. Neque enim de sapientia divina, aut etiam propria naturæ humanæ incorruptæ, sed de humana, quæ in natura isthac reperiri corrupta potest. Hanc fuisse in Romanis excellentem defendi: [c] quemadmodum et theologi ipsi faciunt, et distinguunt recte. Mittenda itaque et de diis propudiosis, et de templis, et cetera huius generis: quæ extra oleas longe lateque posita sunt. Quid tamen de templo pacis, ac fidei affers? [d] Immo enim usque a Numa harum apud nos
p. 267 exstitit templum: si Clementis Alexandrini testimonium evale|re tuo debet. Quid de templo Quietis, post tot sæcula, perditis illarum religionum monumentis, interpretaris? [e] Martis templum pacifici in oppido fuit. Quod essent aliqua extra oppidum, non ea potest fuisse ratio, quia illorum absentiam Deorum amarit civitas: [f] curatoris enim valetudinis, propulsatoris incendiorum templa, Æsculapii, atque Vulcani erant extra oppidum templa. Hæc mittamus: et de iustitia, et de reliqua virtute politica orationem peragamus.

In fine accusationis memoras malas nostras retinendi imperii artes, et malas exercendi: adeoque infelicem orbis conditionem, nobiscum hostibus, nobiscum victoribus, nobiscum rerum dominis, nobiscum semper exstitisse. Aspice, inquis, vicina urbi loca. Romanos agnosces veros Suevos. Immo,

[a] *Virg.* 8. *Æn. Macr.* 5. *sat.* 16. [b] *Cic. Phil.* 3. *Arist.* 2. *phys. Boeth. top.*
[c] *Aug.* 5. *de civ. Da. Bell.* 5. *con.* 3. *c.* 4. [d] *Cl. A. Str.* 5.
[e] *Mart. Cap. lib.* 1. [f] *Plut. probl. Ro. Serv. Æn.* 6.

[682] Vergil, *Aeneis* 8. 334; Macrobius, *Saturnalia* 5. 16.
[683] Cicero, *Orationes Philippicae* 3 [*sic*, though 13. 10, 12 seem closer]; Aristotle, *Physica* 2; Boethius, *Topica*.
[684] Augustine, *De civitate Dei* 5.12; Lambertus Danaeus, *Adversus Bellarminum* 5, controv. 3, ch. 4.
[685] **Translator's note:** Literally, "they have been placed far and wide outside the olive-trees," *extra oleas longe lateque posita sunt*. The phrase *extra oleas*, unknown in classical Latin but common in the Renaissance, was derived from Aristophanes' *Frogs* 993–5, where the reference is to passing beyond the bounds of a race-course marked by olive trees. The phrase *extra oleas* in the sense of "off-course, irrelevant" received an entry in Erasmus' *Adagia*, Chil. II, Centur. II. Prov. 10. See C. W. E. Miller, "Ne Extra Oleas," *American Journal of Philology*, 35 (1914), 456–62.
[686] Clement of Alexandria, *Stromata* 5. 1. [687] Martianus Capella 1.
[688] Plutarch, *Quaestiones Romanae* 47, 276 B; Servius, *On Aeneid*.

CHAPTER 13 p. 266

The Good Fortune of the Roman Empire

After celebrating its virtue, we are not ashamed to admit the good fortune of our state, a good fortune that has at one and the same time made the empire lucky and the ages of the world most blessed. Fortune was not mentioned or named by that first teacher of Alexander, Homer, though the Latin Homer made it out to be even "omnipotent."[682] Nonetheless it is understood to be divine luck and a certain hidden higher will, referred to by that name in earlier times because the causes and reasons of events were unknown.[683] Indeed, temples ought more justly to have been erected to this will than to virtue. For virtue is a power belonging to mortal men. But you must refer that dispute over religious rites to their own times, when those gods and goddesses were to be venerated whom the state and the entire world used to worship.

Here we should set to one side all those matters that belong to true religion. For our discussion is not about divine wisdom, or even about the wisdom proper to uncorrupted human nature, but about the human wisdom that can be found in this corrupted nature of ours. I have maintained that this wisdom was exceptional among the Romans, just as the theologians themselves do, and they make a proper distinction here.[684] Therefore the remarks about the shameful gods and the temples and other things of this sort ought to be set to one side, for they are quite out of bounds here.[685] What are you alleging about a temple of Peace (Pax) and of Trust (Fides)? Why, from the very time of Numa there has existed a temple to these among us, if the testimony of Clement of Alexandria ought to prevail against yours.[686] What p. 267
pronouncements are you making about a temple of Quiet, after so many centuries, when the monuments of those rites have perished? There was a temple of Peace-making Mars within the town.[687] The fact that there were some temples outside the town cannot be a reason to argue that the state cherished the absence of those gods. The temples of the healer of sickness and of the averter of fires, Aesculapius and Vulcan, were outside the town.[688] Let's set these things aside and go through with an oration on justice and on the rest of public virtue.

At the end of your accusation you mention our evil arts of retaining our rule and our evil arts of exercising rule, and you say that the state of the world was always so very unfortunate with us as enemies, with us as conquerors, with us as rulers of the world. Behold, you say, the regions close to the city, and you will recognize in the Romans the true Suevians. Nay rather, I say,

inquam ego, etiam aspice, et agnosces veros parentes humanitatis: ipsis humanissimis Atheniensibus humaniores: nam ut illi ex amicis pagis pluribus composuerint urbem: nostri adhuc ex hostibus in cives allectis istud fecere. De Sabinis audisti, Albanis, aliis. Felix imperium, sub quo vincentium, et victorum conditio eadem prorsus est. Aspice, inquis, remotiora, aspice Capuam. [a] Aspice, inquam ego quoque, et videbis stantem urbem, quæ multo maxime merita dirui a fundamentis: multo magis id merita, quam
p. 268 ulla alia, quam Carthago ipsa. [b] Etiam, in defectione illa fœ|dissima, Romanos, dominos, balneis includunt, ubi æstu anima interclusa fœdum in modum expirarent. Et locus ipse, a natura factus ad superbiam, arrogantiam, ferociam, hortari sic nostros potuit, cur urbem illam exscinderent. Verum cum effecissent, ut nihil esset, cur Capuam timeremus, sublata illinc (ut tu hoc unum concludis) omni imagine reipublicæ, urbem ipsam pulcherrimam non sustulerunt. Ecce, Capuam aspicimus, laudes illic nostras invenimus, æquitatem, moderationem, prudentiam: invenimus fortunam eius urbis, quæ maleficio civium cecidisset, nisi hostium manibus sustentata fuisset.

Aspiceremus Macedoniam, et Illyrium? [c] Aspicimus regna non semel rebellia: et sic relicta tamen, ut libera iugo regio per nos, neque nobis tamen subiecta essent: iussa suis legibus vivere, et libera esse: ingentibus liberata vectigalibus: dimidio exonerata tributi, quod pendebant sub regibus suis. Quæ illarum regionum felicitas? ut victæ melius duplo, immo incomparabiliter melius (si res est libertas inæstimabilis) sub hoste fuerint, quam sub civibus suis. Quæ laus munificentiæ Romanæ, benificentiæ, liberalitatis, splendoris, magnanimitatis incomparabilis. Romanos tu avaros audeas? [d] Sic et Ægypto postea, sic aliis regnis remissius semper sub Romanis fuit, quam fuisset sub regibus.

p. 269 [e] Sed Siciliæ civita | tes sic in amicitiam, fidemque recepimus, ut eodem iure essent, quo fuissent, quæ bello subactæ, earum ager, cum esset publicus populi Romani factus, tamen illis est redditus. [f] Apage os latum, quod audes, ex minoribus, decumis, et portoriis, et pastoribus illic colligere triplo amplius,

[a] *Cic. agr.* 2. [b] *Liv.* 23. [c] *Liv.* 45. [d] *Str.* 2. *ult.*
[e] *Cic. Verr.* 4. [f] *Lips.* 2. *de ma. Ro.* 2. 3.

---

[689] Cicero, *De lege agraria* 2. 32. 87–8.
[690] Livy 23. 7. 3.
[691] **Translator's note:** This sentence is fashioned from elements of Cicero, *De lege agraria* 2. 33. 91.
[692] Livy 45. 29. 4 ff.
[693] Strabo 17. 1. 12 f.
[694] Cicero, *In Verrem* 2. 3. 13 [cf. 2. 2. 90].

behold, and you will recognize in them the true parents of humane treatment, men more humane than the very humane Athenians themselves, for just as they put together their city from several friendly villages, our people did that from enemies who were adopted into the rank of citizens. You have heard of the Sabines, the Albans, and others. It is a lucky empire under which the condition of the conquerors and the conquered is utterly the same. Behold, you say, things lying further off—behold Capua. I too say behold Capua, and you will see a city still standing, which very much deserved to be torn down from its foundations, having much more merited this than any other city, even Carthage itself.[689] In that most foul revolt they even shut up the p. 268
Romans, their lords, in baths, where, their breathing blocked by the heat, they were to die in a foul manner.[690] And the very place itself, having been fashioned by nature for pride, arrogance, and fierce spirit, could urge upon our people good reasons to utterly extirpate that city. But when they had brought it about that there was no reason for us to fear Capua, the whole semblance of an independent polity having been removed from there (as you argue this one sole point), they did not destroy that very beautiful city itself.[691] Lo, we are indeed looking upon Capua, and what we discover there are our own laudable deeds: our fairness, moderation, and prudence. We also discover the good fortune of that city, which would have fallen through the evildoing of its citizens had it not been propped up by the violence of her enemies.

Are we to look upon Macedonia and Illyrium? We behold in them kingdoms which were rebellious more than once, but were nevertheless so left alone as to be freed of royal yoke by us and yet not made subject to us either; ordered to live under their own laws and be free; freed of huge tax burdens; and made exempt from half of the tribute which they used to pay when they were under their own kings.[692] What was the blessedness of those regions? It was that, upon being conquered, they were twice as well off—nay, incomparably better off (if liberty is a thing that cannot be measured)—under the power of their enemy than under the power of their own citizens. What a matchless commendation this is of Roman munificence, beneficence, liberality, magnificence, magnanimity. Would you dare call the Romans greedy? In the very same way for Egypt later on, in the very same way for other regions, life was easier under the Romans than it had been under their own kings.[693]

And the city-states of Sicily we received into our friendship and protection p. 269
in such a way that, after they were subjugated in war, they lived under the same lawcode as they had before, and their land, though it had been made public land of the Roman people, was nonetheless restored to them.[694] Away with you, big mouth, that you have the presumption to deduce there from the lesser tithes on produce and port duties and pasturage fees thrice the amount

quam ex decumis frumenti maioribus: quæ quarta millionis erant. Apage, qui a quantitate terræ Siciliæ argumentaris ad provincias alias: cum Siciliæ qualitas provinciis multo amplioribus eam æqualem efficiat, aut etiam superiorem. Apage cum tuis illis summis Ægypti, et Galliæ. Quid enim caussæ est: ut Suetonii, et Eutropii veteres libri mendam numeri habeant potius, quam Strabonis, et Diodori? Illi millionem ex Gallia capiunt. Isti ex Ægypto, Strabo septem milliones, et semissem, Diodorus circiter quatuor, capiunt tempore regum: adeoque plus multo capere nos solitos postea: et plus adhuc ex Gallia; de qua et plus caperetur, quam ex Ægypto. Audin', multo abire Diodorum a Strabone? Strabo notat talenta duodecim millia, et quingenta: Diodorus tantum supra sex millia. Atque ut hæc Diodori sint Ægyptia, id est, maiora Romanis Strabonis: [a] tamen sic est Romanum librarum septuaginta, Ægyptium autem octuaginta: abeatque nimis summa a summa. Et ergo ne
p. 270 libro Strabonis credatur, nec Diodori li|bro, tam variis. Scis, variis testibus non credi, et discordantibus. Nam cur lubet, credere Ciceroni, de quo Strabo accepit, quam ipsis quæstoribus Ægypti, de quibus accepit Diodorus? [b] Scis, credi his magis, qui magis cognovisse valent. Viden', quo tibi abeant centum illi, et quinquaginta milliones? Etiam fac magis contrarios Strabonem, et Diodorum; et imminue adhuc de summa: nam scriptores, qui talenti meminerint, solent omnes ad talentum Atticum sexaginta librarum respicere. Et itaque de eodem dixerit et Strabo, et Diodorus, et Cicero: aut cur Cicero, et Strabo retraxerint rem ad Romanum, Diodorus Ægyptiam rationem tenuerit?

Audi ab ore angusto, sed certe veriori: non quindecim milliones erant in reditibus his populi nostri. [c] Ecce, scribit Cicero, populum Romanum ex tantis vectigalibus exercitum alere vix potuisse. Et exercitum numerat sex legiones, magna equitum, ac peditum auxilia. In quæ tamen omnia non duo milliones insumebantur. [d] Adi ad tuum istum magistrum: qui legiones, equites, auxilia numerat, et stipendia partitur: nec patitur, te aut eam summam attingere: *o nostri reges*, exclamat, *quanto plus impenditis in legiunculas incompositas vestras*? Neque tamen dico, non multo supra duos milliones nobis fuisse. Sed reliqua insumebantur in alia: ut vix ista superessent in
p. 271 exercitus: | et tamen plura incommensurabiliter superfuissent, si, non dico centum quinquaginta, sed si quindecim fuissent milliones.

[a] *Serv.* 5. *Æn.* [b] *c.* 2. 35. *q.* 6. [c] *Cic. parad.* 6.
[d] *Lips. de mi. Ro. lib.* 2. *c* 5. 6. 7. *lib.* 5. *c.* 16.

695 Lipsius, *Admiranda, sive De magnitudine Romana* 2. 1–3, pp. 38 ff.
696 Servius, *On Aeneid* 5.
697 *Decretum Gratiani* C. 35 q. 6 c. 2.
698 Cicero, *Paradoxa Stoicorum* 6. 45.
699 Lipsius, *De militia Romana* 2. 5–7; 3. 16.

of that arising from the larger tithes of wheat, when in fact they were a quarter of a million.[695] Away with you, who argue from the size of the territory of Sicily to the other provinces, since the quality of Sicily makes it equal to—or even superior to—provinces of much greater size. Away with you and those sums of Egypt and Gaul. What would be the reason that the old books of Suetonius and Eutropius would have more numerical inaccuracy than those of Strabo and Diodorus? Suetonius and Eutropius accept a million from Gaul. Strabo accepts seven and a half million from Egypt, Diodorus around four, in the time of the kings; and they say that we were afterwards accustomed to receive much more; and more in addition from Gaul, from which even more was received than from Egypt. Do you hear? Diodorus is a long way off from Strabo. Strabo records 12,500 talents; Diodorus only something over 6,000. And yet even if these talents of Diodorus are Egyptian talents—i.e. more than Strabo's Roman talents—even so the Roman talent is 70 pounds,[696] while the Egyptian is 80, and the one sum would still differ too much from the other. And therefore let no faith be put in the book of Strabo, nor in that of Diodorus, so at odds are they. You p. 270
know better than to trust varying and discordant witnesses. For why is it agreeable to trust Cicero, from whom Strabo gets his information, rather than the quaestors of Egypt, from whom Diodorus gets his? You know that more faith should be put in those who have the ability to know more.[697] Don't you see how far off your 150 million are? Make Strabo and Diodorus even more at odds with each other and take even more from your total; for the writers who have mentioned a talent all tend to be referring to the Attic talent of 60 pounds. And thus Strabo, Diodorus, and Cicero would have spoken of the same thing, or why would Cicero and Strabo have referred the matter to the Roman talent, while Diodorus would have kept to the Egyptian accounting?

Hear it from a mouth that is terse, but certainly more truthful: there were not fifteen millions in these revenues of our people. Behold, writes Cicero, the Roman people was scarcely able to support an army from such great taxes.[698] And six legions, with considerable auxiliaries of horse and foot, make up an army. Nonetheless, two million were not bestowed on all of these. Go off to your teacher [Lipsius], who counts up the legions, cavalry, and auxiliaries and divides up their pay; he does not allow you to reach that figure either: "O our modern kings," he exclaims, "how much more do you expend upon your rag-tag little legions?"[699] And yet I am not saying that we did not have a lot more than two millions. But the remaining funds were spent on other things, so that scarcely those amounts were left for armies, and p. 271
yet immeasurably more would have been left over if—I won't say 150—but if there had been fifteen millions.

[a] Etiam, sexcentos milliones nobis conditos in usum belli, credam dicenti Panigarolæ? Ut auget iste aurum nobis immensum, et immensum male: ita cimminuit reliqua male, quæ tamen admiranda simul cum auro cupit ostendere. Rem bellicam nostram stetisse peditum ducentis millibus, equitum quadraginta, curruum falcatorum tribus, navium duobus, triremium mille quingentis, quinqueremibus octuaginta, paratu duplici in armamentariis, elephantis trecentis. [b] Amplius, amplius. In classibus erant centum millia militum, remigumque: alibi supra quingenta. Sed cum auro maneam.

Post Pompeii de Mithridate victoriam, octo nobis milliones et semissem fuisse, Budæus, et alii hactenus docti crediderunt. Quid contra dicitur? Ego ut dem, ex una Asia milliones duos relatos; non dederim tamen, supra sex, et semissem captos ex reliquo. [c] Nam ceterarum provinciarum vectigalia ita erant tenuia, ut ad ipsas provincias tutandas vix satis essent. Asia vero tam opima erat, et fertilis, ut et ubertate agrorum, et varietate fructuum, et magnitudine pastionis, et multitudine earum rerum, quæ exportantur, facile omnibus terris antecelleret.

p. 272 Hæ sunt solidæ rationes. Illæ levissimæ sunt in | numeris, qui tam facile, et tam varie corrumpuntur: quique per levissimam variationem notæ minutulæ, litterulæque summas immane variant. Illæ sunt declamationes, *O clementiam imperii Romani*, &c. Et vere tamen o clementiam. [d] Integra tum Gallia non tertiam præstabat partem eius, quod Galliæ pars regibus præstitit postea; ut Alciatus, ecce, scripsit verissime: non vigesimam eius, quod nunc præstat, ut vident omnes. Felix seculum illud. Forte autem nec ditius erat multo, nec multo plus poterat dominis erogare. [e] Non sunt divitiæ succedentium temporum ætati illi, vere aureæ, veteris imperii Romani conferendæ: quod idem Alciatus te docet. Aut numquid tu putas, novum istum orbem, sive novam potius istam navigationem Columbi attulisse huc ad nos plus auri, et divitiarum, quam et Troglodytica, et Indica, quæ erat olim negotiatio? Si ad tempora spectas avorum, et misera illa post direptum toties imperium nostrum, fortassis putes bene: [f] Sed certe nihil ista sunt, si respectes imperium nostrum.

[a] *Panig. conc. extr. in Pentes.* [b] *Lips. de ma. Ro. lib.* 1. *c.* 4. 5. [c] *Cic. pro le. Ma.*
[d] *Alc. l.* 27. *de V. S.* [e] *Alc.* 3. *disp* 9. [f] *Lips.* 3. *de ma. Ro.*

---

700 Francesco Panigarola, *Predica della potesta di Christo*, in *Prediche quadragesimali*, Venetia, Appresso Gio. Battista Ciotti Senese, 1599, p. 28.

701 Lipsius, *Admiranda, sive De magnitudine Romana* 1. 4–5, pp. 13–28.

702 Cicero, *Pro lege Manilia* 14.

703 Alciatus, *On Digest* 50. 16. 27 [in *Opera Omnia in quatuor tomos*, Tomus II, Basileae, Apud Thomam Guarinum, 1582, col. 1063].

704 Alciatus, *Disputationum libri IIII* 3. 9 [in *Opera Omnia in quatuor tomos*, Tomus IIII, Basileae, Apud Thomam Guarinum, 1582, cols. 215–16].

705 Lipsius, *Admiranda, sive De magnitudine Romana* 3 [4. 12, pp. 251 ff. seem most suitable].

Furthermore, shall I believe Panigarola when he says that six hundred millions were laid up by us for use in wartime?[700] Just as that fellow wrongly magnifies our supposedly measureless gold for us, so he wrongly diminishes everything else, which nevertheless he wishes to display as marvelous along with the gold. He claims that our military affairs consisted of two hundred thousand infantry, forty thousand cavalry, three thousand chariots armed with scythes, two thousand ships—fifteen hundred triremes, eighty quinqueremes, twice as much equipment in armories, three hundred elephants. More and more! In the fleets there were 100,000 soldiers and rowers; in other sources over 500,000.[701] But let me stay with the gold for now.

After Pompey's victory over Mithridates, there were eight and a half million for us—so Budé and other learned men have believed up to now. What is said against this? While I would grant that two millions were recovered from the province of Asia alone, I would not however grant that over six and a half were captured from the remaining area. For the revenues of the other provinces were so slender that they were scarcely sufficient for the protection of those provinces themselves.[702] Asia, indeed, was so wealthy and fertile that it easily surpassed all other lands in the fertility of its fields, the variety of its crops, the vast extent of its pasturage, and the multitude of the things which were exported from it.

These are reliable calculations, but those others are most untrustworthy in their numbers, which are so easily and so variably corrupted, and which p. 272
through the slightest variation of a tiny notation or one little letter cause the totals to vary immensely. There are those declamations: "O, the clemency of the Roman Empire, etc." And yet true enough: O, the clemency! In those days the whole of Gaul did not supply a third part of that which a part of Gaul provided to the kings in later times, as Alciatus, behold, most truly wrote: "not a twentieth part of that which it now offers, as all can see."[703] A blessed age was that! But perhaps it was not much wealthier than later, nor able to pay out much more to the rulers? No, the riches of succeeding ages are not to be compared with that time of the Roman Empire, a true golden age, as the same Alciatus teaches you.[704] Or do you suppose that that new world—or rather that recent voyage of Columbus—has brought here to us more gold and riches than the Ethiopian and Indian trade that existed back then? If you look to the days of our ancestors and that wretched period after our empire was so often torn asunder, perhaps you would be right. But those days are indeed nothing, if you look back on our empire.[705]

Dic, portio quota fuit imperii nostri regnum Iudææ, et Salomonis? [a] Iste quatuor milliones ex re una accipiebat: ut in sacris libris est, testibus illis incorruptissimis. Felix ergo seculum, felix imperium: cum erogabatur in
p. 273 dominos minimum, et subditi erant multo ditissimi. Tu non laudes seculo-| rum felicitatem?

Tu Romanos immites audeas? [b] qui victo Antiocho nihil ad conditiones illas addidere pacis, quas ante victoriam dixere, nisi elogium hoc verissimum, *Neque Romanos, si vincantur, animo minui, neque, si vincant, secundis rebus insolescere*: qui captas civitates in eo bello diviserunt inter socios: ipsi gloria sola contenti. In eo bello, in Philippico, in Punico, in aliis. [c] Quæ gaudia, quæ vociferationes universæ Græciæ in eo Philippico, cum vetus a nobis restitutus illic est status, et avita libertas? Qui plausus in sacro, sollemni, amplissimo conventu editi? Quid florum in homines nostros profusum: quid laudum? An tanta terrarum hilaritas seculi felicitas non fuit maxima? Tu in tanta communi lætitia gemis, distracta regna fremis. At securitati nostræ consulere nos etiam decuit. At quieti illorum populorum inquietæ prospicere eo modo oportuit. Sic et fortunati, qui sic positi, ut inquietari vix possent. Sic, sic *O fortunatos nimium, sua si bona norint.*

Aspiceremus nunc ipsum regem Persea, filios, reliquam Macedoniæ nobilitatem? Aspicimus, quod prima specie sævum, mox apparuit multitudini pro libertate sua esse factum: nam regis amici, imperare assueti, non æquæ libertatis patientes. Sic Livius quod nos dicimus. Aspicimus hos viventes omnes: qui pessimo suo merito interfici debuissent: qui per instituta gentium,
p. 274 et reli|giones manibus nostrorum debebantur, qui illo Macedonico bello cecidissent. Vixit Perseus. Vixit: hoc certum, funere honoratus: certum et hoc: sed illud incertum, quomodo mortuus: [d] nam et est traditum, sibi ipsum manum intulisse. Scilicet didicit tandem homo ignavissimus, in sua fuisse positum manu, nec teneri in custodia, nec duci antea in triumphum: [e] ut, hoc cum deprecaretur, sic audivit ab Æmilio, eius esse in potestate situm, et catenis, et spectaculo formidato se subducere: Homo ignavissimus, et abi-

[a] I. *reg.* 10. [b] *Iusti.* 31. [c] *Flor.* 2.
[d] *Zonara.* [e] *Plut. apoph. re.*

---

706 I Kings 10.
707 Justin 31. 8. 8.
708 Florus 2. 7. 13–14.
709 **Translator's note:** This is Vergil, *Georgica* 2. 458: "o fortunatos nimium, sua si bona norint," where the reference is to farmers.
710 Zonaras 9. 24.
711 Plutarch, *Regum et imperatorum apophthegmata* 198 B (cf. *Aemilius Paulus* 34. 2, 273 C).

Tell me: how large a portion of our empire was the kingdom of Judea and Solomon? That man used to receive four millions from one estate, according to the sacred writings, those most incorruptible witnesses.[706] A blessed age, therefore, and a blessed empire, when a very small amount was paid out to the rulers, and the subjects were by far the wealthiest ever known. Would you not praise the prosperity of those ages? p. 273

Would you dare to call the Romans savage? They were the ones who, after Antiochus was defeated, added nothing to those peace terms which they had announced before, unless it were these very true words of praise: "The Romans, if they were defeated, would not be diminished in spirit, nor, if they proved victorious, would they grow accustomed to favorable circumstances."[707] They were the ones who divided up the cities captured in that war among their allies, contenting themselves with the glory alone. In that war they did this, and in the Philippic War, and in the Punic, and in the others. What joys, what exclamations of all of Greece there were in that Philippic war, when their ancient status and ancestral liberty were there restored by us?[708] What bursts of applause were given forth in the sacred, solemn, vast gathering? How many flowers were showered upon our people, how many praises? Did not such rejoicing of the lands constitute the greatest prosperity of the age? But you groan amidst such great shared happiness, you rage over kingdoms pulled apart. But it was fitting for us to have a care for our own security. It was necessary to take precautions in that way for the restless peace of those peoples. Thus they were even fortunate themselves, in that they were put in such a position that they would scarcely be able to be restless. And so it was truly thus: "O too fortunate ones, if they only were aware of their good fortune."[709]

Were we supposed to be beholding that king himself, Perseus, and his sons, and the remaining nobility of Macedonia? What we in fact behold is something that seems at first sight cruel, but that soon appeared to the multitude as done for their own liberty. For the king's friends, accustomed to give orders, could not endure a just liberty. Thus says Livy, and it is the very thing that we too say. We behold all those people surviving who ought to have been killed according to their basest deserts; whose lives, through the laws and religious sanctions of the nations, should have been paid to the p. 274 shades of our men who fell in that Macedonian War. Perseus survived. He survived: that is certain, and he was later honored with a funeral. But this one thing is uncertain: just *how* he died. For it is even reported that he turned his hand upon himself.[710] No doubt this very cowardly fellow finally learned that it had been in his power neither to be held in custody nor, before that, to be led in a triumph—just as he heard from Aemilius Paulus, when he was supplicating him, that it lay in his own power to withdraw himself from the chains and from the spectacle he feared.[711] Most cowardly and abject of

ectissimus: [a] cuius ipsum victorem puderit. Quid si etiam enectus vigiliis est: sed a militibus custodibus (id siles, Picene) pertæsis custodiam longiorem? Quid? etiam credimus Mithridati: cuius illa recitas apud Sallustium verba de nece Persei?

Nunc tu audi, quis iste Perseus. [b] Subdititius Philippi filius ex ignobili femina: [c] a Philippo exheredatus: et itaque non nativitate, non hereditate verus rex. Gestione autem regni tanto minus dignus, cui ullus capto tribueretur regius honor, quanto ipse nullo nobiscum egerat regio more, at per omnia clandestina scelera, perque veneficia grassatus est. Huic ullum ius patrocinatur in re ulla? Negant scriptores de iure belli.

Et nunc igitur tu iudica si clementia singularis nostra non fuit, qui vitam immerenti, honorem indigno aliquem habuit aut hoc tantum nomine, quod
p. 275 nomen | ille regium tulerit. Mihi sane videntur mei voluisse rebus omnibus aliquid beatitatis dare, qui vanis etiam tantum attribuere nominibus. Beata tempora.

[d] Iubæ captivitatem fortunatam: qui per eam ex barbaris Numidis inter eruditissimos historicos censeatur: ut sic Plutarchus scribit. Beata illius imperii tempora: cum et calamitates beatitatem calamitosis afferrent: et ab acri prodiret dulce. Quod si filii Persei tales a natura non exstitissent, ut servi potius, quam reges essent: an non ipsi quoque, quod Iuba, digniorem vivendi conditionem arripuissent? Sed Iuba passus etiam in civilibus bellis calamitatem: de quibus hoc non esse iudicium, convenit. [e] Sed Iubæ regnum populi Romani donum, adeoque nec indignus ille contumelia, servus ingratus. *Namque memor generis Carthaginis impia proles Imminet Hesperiæ*: ut de hoc Lucanus dixerat. Sane transierunt per longa secula in hos minores, quæ odia, et inimicitiæ fuere maiorum: et sic notavi antea: [f] et sic de Samnitibus in bello civili Mariano: sic generaliter de subditis nostris aliis in pugna Pharsalica notant alii: quemadmodum sub specie partium agerent magna contentione, et Pyrrho, et Annibale atrocius, adversus nos, ut se suosque priscos illos ulciscerentur: itaque non Afrum Arnobium, non Hispanum Orosium, non
p. 276 similem alium decet obiicere nobis: et Britannos | illos tanto minus, qui nec minus linguam habuere promptam in nos illo tempore, quam manum.

[a] *Liv.* 45. *Plut. Æm.* [b] *Plut. Ara.* [c] *Liv.* 40.
[d] *Plut. Cæs.* [e] *Tac.* 4. *ann.* [f] *Dio.* 41. *Flor.* 3.

---

712 Livy 45 [Livy does not really convey this sense here]; Plutarch, *Aemilius Paulus* 26. 8–12.
713 Plutarch, *Aratus* 54. 3. 714 Livy 40. 21. 10.
715 **Translator's note:** This sentence offers an ungrammatical relative pronoun *qui* where only *quae*, with the antecedent *clementia*, seems to work.
716 Plutarch, *Caesar* 55.
717 Tacitus, *Annales* 4. 5.
718 [Lucan, *De bello civili* 8. 284–5.]
719 Florus 3. 21. 22; Dio Cassius 41. 59. 4.

men, of whom even his victor was ashamed.[712] What even if he *was* killed by sleep deprivation—though by soldier guards (this you are silent about, Picenus) who were sick of longer guard duty? What? Do we go so far as to trust Mithridates, whose words in Sallust about the death of Perseus you repeat?

Now hear from me who that Perseus was. He was a supposititious son of Philip from a base-born woman[713] and disinherited by Philip,[714] thus not a true king either by birth or by inheritance. Furthermore, by his behavior he was so much the less worthy of his kingdom than any other captive king granted royal honors, in that he never dealt with us in any royal fashion, but proceeded through every sort of secret crime and poisoning. Does any law defend this man in any of his doings? Writers on the law of war say no.

And now you be the judge if ours was not a remarkable clemency, which granted life to one who didn't deserve it and a certain honor to an unworthy man, albeit for only this reason: that he had borne the name of a king.[715] In p. 275
my view, at least, my people seems to have wished to give some degree of blessedness to all things, for they accorded even so much as this to empty titles. Blessed times!

O, the lucky captivity of Juba, who by means of it rose from the barbarous Numidians to become numbered among the most learned historians, as Plutarch writes.[716] Blessed were the times of that empire, when even disasters could bring happiness to those struck with disaster, and sweetness could come forth from bitterness. But if the sons of Perseus had not been by nature such as to be fitter slaves than kings, would not they too, like Juba, have secured a more worthy condition of life? And yet Juba underwent disaster in nothing less than a civil war, in which it is not normally fitting for such mild judgment to be passed. More striking still, Juba's kingdom was a gift of the Roman people, and so he was deserving of reproach as an ungrateful servant.[717] "For the unforgetting disloyal offspring of the Carthaginian people threatens Italy," as Lucan said about this man.[718] To be sure, the hatreds and hostilities of the ancestors passed on through long ages to the descendants, and thus I have noted earlier. And thus it was with the Samnites in the civil war of Marius, and thus others record about our subject peoples in the battle of Pharsalus: how under the pretence of party spirit they were acting against us with great zeal and more savagely than Pyrrhus and Hannibal in order to take vengeance for themselves and their ancestors.[719] Therefore neither the African Arnobius, nor the Spaniard Orosius, nor anyone else like them ought to cast reproaches upon us—and those Britons of yours least of all, who had p. 276
at that time a tongue no less ready for use against us than violence.

Et iura tamen non nego populi Romani in dilectu, in tributo, in metallis, in aliis, quæ memorat accusator. Respondent de metallis interpretes sui iuris. Respondit de tributis, et dilectibus Cerialis: *Nos iure victoriæ id solum victis addidimus, quo pacem tueremur. Nam neque quies gentium sine armis, neque arma sine stipendiis, neque stipendia sine tributis haberi queunt. Cetera in communi sita. Ipsi victi legionibus plerumque impositi præsides, provinciis rectores. Nihil separatum, aut clausum.* Sic provinciarum sanguine provinciæ victæ. Et sic tamen republica eversa: cum antea Romano milite, et socio Latino, Italicove provinciæ domarentur. Et de remigibus tamen, quod hodie sævum videtur, illud nec fuit olim aliud, quam militia maritima, et sociorum navalium itidem dilectus. Ne tu tibi somnies adfixos hos nostros remo vel captivos miseros, vel turpes maleficos.

Vastati, spoliati, deleti sunt multi? Se accusent: qui in se provocaverint arma Romana. [a]*Quæritur belli exitus, non caussa*, sane inepte. Nec enim ulla est legum culpa, si sontes afflicti sint, atque peremti. Ad causas ego te factorum retraxi: et illic vanissimus es deprehensus. Felices tamen et istos dices afflictos semper: [b] quia et pœnas luere delictorum sit semper melius,
p. 277 quam impune in deli|ctis vitam transigere: ut verissimæ sunt philosophorum traditiones. Felicissimos dixeris, nobis victoribus, dominisque, per quos victis nihil, præter facultatem malefaciendi, ablatum est. [c]*Nam quantum ferro, tantum pietate potentes Stamus. victrices temperat ira manus.*

Amicos, socios, cives voluimus nostros hostes: [d] ecce paulatim civitas data omnibus, qui in orbe Romano exstiterint: ecce Roma communis patria. O immensam civitatis Romanæ laudem! [e]*Hæc est, in gremium victos quæ sola recepit: Humanumque genus communi nomine fovet, Matris, non dominæ, ritu: civesque vocavit. Quos domuit: nexuque pio longinqua revinxit. Huius pacificis debemus moribus omnes. Quod veluti patriis regionibus utitur hospes: Quod cuncti gens una sumus.* [f]*Vivitur omnigenis in partibus haud secus: ac si Cives congenitos concludat mœnibus unis Urbs patria, atque omnes lare concilientur avito.* Hæc sunt testimonia, quæ cum ipsis consentiunt rerum experimentis. Hæc sunt testimonia fortunati imperii Romani, et Romanæ virtutis.

[a] *Sen. Her. fu.* 2. [b] *Pla. Gorg.* [c] *Prop.* 3. *eleg.* 21. [d] *Mag.* 4. *misc.* 5.
[e] *Claud.* 3. *Stilic.* [f] *Prud.* 2. *Symm.*

---

720 **Translator's note:** This is from Tacitus, *Historiae* 4. 74.

721 **Translator's note:** The phrase rendered "criminals" here is, in both the 1599 and 1770 editions, *turbes maleficos*. Either *turbes* is a mistake for *turpes*, or the whole phrase is an error for *turbas maleficas*. Either way, the clear reference is to convicted criminals. Gentili is, of course, thinking of the galleys of his own day.

722 Seneca, *Hercules furens* 407–8. **Translator's note:** The sentiment is not, of course, that of Seneca. The tyrant Lycus is the speaker.

723 Plato, *Gorgias* 472 E.

724 Propertius 3. 22. 21–2. **Translator's note:** I have adopted W. A. Camps's version of *victrices temperat ira manus*.

725 Hieronymus Maggius [Girolamo Maggi], *Variarum Lectionum, seu Miscellaneorum* 4. 5, fol. 176.

726 Claudian, *De consulatu Stilichonis* 3. 150–5 and 159.

727 Prudentius, *Contra Symmachum* 2. 610–12.

Nor do I deny the rights of the Roman people in levying troops, in gathering tribute, in extracting precious metals, and in other things that the accuser mentions. As for the precious metals, the interpreters of their own law provide an answer. As for tributes and levies, Cerialis has answered: "By the right of victory we have imposed upon the defeated only that amount by which we might be able to maintain peace. For it is impossible to have peace among peoples without arms, or arms without soldiers' pay, or soldiers' pay without tributes. Everything else has been placed in common between us. The defeated themselves have for the most part been appointed as commanders over the legions and as magistrates over the provinces. Nothing is set apart or put off limits."[720] It is in *this* way that the provinces were conquered by the blood of provinces. And it continued to be thus even after the Republic was overthrown, although earlier the provinces were conquered by the Roman soldier or by the Latin or the Italian ally. And as for the rowers, which these days seems a cruel business, in those days it was nothing other than military service on the sea and a levying of naval allies for that purpose. Don't dream that those men of ours attached to the oar were either wretched captives or criminals.[721]

Many people were ravaged, plundered, destroyed? Let them accuse themselves, in that they provoked Roman arms against themselves. "The result of a war is inquired about, not its cause"—quite foolishly.[722] For it is not the fault of the laws if the guilty are cast down and done away with. I have dragged you back to the causes of deeds, and there you have been caught out as most foolish. But you will say that those who have been cast down are always lucky, because it is always better to pay the penalty for crimes than to pass one's life amidst crimes with impunity, in accord with the truest teachings of the philosophers.[723] You p. 277
would have called them most lucky indeed with us as their victors and rulers, through whose agency nothing has been taken away from the defeated but their power to misbehave. "For we stand powerful as much through our sense of duty as through the sword. Our wrath stays its hand in victory."[724]

We have wished our enemies to be friends, allies, citizens. Behold, gradually the citizenship was given to all who lived in the Roman world.[725] Behold: Rome, the common fatherland. O the immeasurable glory of Roman citizenship! "She is the only one who has received the defeated to her bosom. And she has protected the human race with a shared name in the manner of a mother, not a ruler; and she has called citizens those whom she has subdued, and has bound together far distant regions with a bond of duty. To her peaceful ways we all owe it that the traveler makes use of regions as though they are his ancestral lands, that we are all now one people."[726] "In all sorts of lands people live just as though an ancestral city were shutting in kindred citizens within unbroken walls, and as though all were united by an ancestral household god."[727] These are testimonies that agree with the actual results of historical fact. These are testimonies of the blessed Roman Empire and of Roman virtue.

O mirificam virtutem, quæ et amat, et fovet hostes! [a] *Cum duobus ducibus de imperio in Italia decertatum est, Pyrrho, et Annibale ab altero, propter probitatem eius, non alienos animos habemus alterum propter crudelitatem eius, semper hæc civitas oderit.* Semper oderit Roma Annibalis crudelitatem: Sed virtutem
p. 278 Annibalis amarit semper: [b] cui statu|asque in medio oppido plures habuit. O mirificam fortunam orbis in tanta domini caritate, et cura! Cives voluit Roma omnes: [c] voluit de barbaris mites. Adnotabo tantum de Hispania. [d] Populus ille barbarus, ac ferus: cui propiora feris, quam hominibus fuisse dicuntur ingenia: cui in tanta seculorum serie nullus dicitur dux magnus, præter unum illum a latrocinio (hæc virtus Hispana) Viriatum: ille populus legibus nostris ad cultiorem vitæ usum traductus est: et militia nostra iam instructus triumphatores nationum, imperatores orbis dedit, Balbos, Traianos, Theodosios. Populos fortunatos nostros omnes: qui in imperio nostro non acceperunt solum, sed etiam dederunt imperatores, ipsi etiam Afri, et Syri, et Thraces, et Britanni ultimi. [e] Vicimus nos coniurationes vicinorum mortales, flammas Gallicas, Pyrrhi elephantos, opes Antiochi, Siphacis amentiam, Mithridatis pertinaciam, Annibalis dolos, Punicam perfidiam, Ligurum difficultates, Samniticam rabiem, Etruscum robur, Campanam superbiam, Hispanorum rebelliones, Cimbrorum immanitatem, Macedonum minas, paludes Germanorum, æstuaria Britannorum, deserta Africæ, culta Asiæ. Omnia virtuti Romanæ pervia patuerunt, et dederunt victa manus. Sed sic victa sunt omnia, ut victa esse profuerit, ut sceptro hoc nostro regerentur.

p. 279 [f] Audi martyris ad | deum verba, *Qui sceptra Romæ in vertice rerum locasti, sanciens, mundum Quirinali togæ servire, et armis cedere: ut discrepantum gentium mores, et observantiam, linguasque, et ingenia, et sacra unis domares legibus.* Fortuna orbis, virtus urbis. [g] Non fortuna universale nobis imperium peperit, sed virtus, disciplina, apta ad tantam rem omnia: quod Polybius contra Græcos quosdam suos et dicit audenter, et docet potenter. [h] Bonus, qui rebus interfuit, miles: bonus, qui rebus præfuit, ductor: bonus, qui summis imperatoribus adfuit, arbiter. [i] Hunc lege de republica nostra, lege

[a] *Cic. Lel.* [b] *Iov. icon. et lib.* 27. *Herodia.* 4. *Pli.* 34. *c.* 6. [c] *Stra.* 2.
[d] *Iusti. ult. Serv.* 3. *Geor. Cuia. de abig.* [e] *Petr. ep. ad Caro.* 4. *Prop.* 2. *el.* 1. et 3. *el.* 10.
[f] *Prud. Laur.* [g] *Polyb.* 1. [h] *Polyb.* 3. 4. 12. *Plut. apoph. reg.* [i] *Polyb.* 1. 2. 3. 6.

---

728 Cicero, *De amicitia* 8.28.

729 Paulus Jovius [Paolo Giovio], *icon.* [the title is unclear; the *Dialogo dell'imprese militari et amorose*, In Lyone, Appresso Guglielmo Rouillio, 1574, might be meant] and *Historiae sui temporis* 27, Tomus secundus, Lugduni, Apud Haered. Seb. Gryphii, 1561, p. 244; Herodian 4. 8. 5; Pliny 34. 6.

730 Strabo 2 [4. 1. 12 or 6. 1. 2 could be meant here].

731 Justin 44. 5. 8; Servius, *On Georgics* 3; Cuiacius [Jacques Cujas], *On Digest* 47. 14 [*Paratitla in libros quinquaginta Digestorum seu Pandectarum*, Coloniae, Apud Maternum Cholinum, 1570, p. 322 f.].

732 Petrarca, *Epistola ad Carolum IV Imp* [in Petrarca, *Epistolae de rebus familiaribus et variae*, volumen secundum, Florentiae, Typis Felicis Le Monnier, 1842, liber X, epistola 1,], p. 61; Propertius 2. 1; 3. 10.

733 Prudentius, *Peristephanon* 2. 417–24. **Translator's note:** The martyr speaking is Lawrence.

734 Polybius 1. 63. 9.

735 Polybius 3. 4. 12; Plutarch, *Regum et imperatorum apophthegmata.* **Translator's note:** No obvious passage presents itself.

O marvelous virtue, which both loves and protects enemies! "We struggled over the rule of Italy with two leaders, Pyrrhus and Hannibal; we do not have hostile feelings towards the one, thanks to his noble behavior; the other this state will always hate, thanks to his cruelty."[728] Rome will always hate the cruelty of Hannibal, but it will have always loved his virtue, and has had many statues to him in the middle of a town.[729] O the marvelous good luck of a p. 278 world in such loving care of its ruler! Rome wanted all to be citizens; it has wanted barbarians to turn into gentle peoples.[730] I shall make note only of Spain. Barbaric and wild was that people, whose minds are said to be closer to those of animals than men; for whom in such a long series of ages there is said to have been no great leader, apart from that one of a robber band (this was the Spanish virtue), Viriathus. That people was brought over by our laws to a more cultivated way of life and, trained by service in our army, produced triumphators over the nations and rulers of the world: men like Balbus, Trajan, Theodosius.[731] How fortunate were all our subject peoples, who in our empire did not only accept, but also gave us emperors—even the very Africans themselves, and the Syrians, and the Thracians, and the remotest Britons. We have overcome the deadly conspiracies of our neighbors, the flames of the Gauls, the elephants of Pyrrhus, the riches of Antiochus, the madness of Syphax, the stubbornness of Mithridates, the wiles of Hannibal, the perfidy of the Carthaginians, the refractoriness of the Ligurians, the madness of the Samnites, the toughness of the Etruscans, the pride of the Campanians, the rebellions of the Spaniards, the brutality of the Cimbri, the threats of the Macedonians, the swamps of the Germans, the estuaries of the Britons, the deserts of Africa, the sown fields of Asia.[732] The whole world lay open, allowing passage to Roman courage, and humbly yielded in defeat. But the world was defeated by us in such a manner that it was to its advantage to have been defeated, so that it could be ruled by this scepter of ours.

Listen to a martyr's words to God: "You who have placed the scepter of the p. 279 world in Rome's citadel, ordaining that the world serve the toga of Quirinus [deified Romulus] and yield to his arms, so that you might subdue to one set of laws the customs, the reverence, the languages, the minds, and the sacred rites of diverse peoples."[733] The virtue of this city is the good luck of the world. It wasn't luck that produced universal dominion for us; it was virtue, discipline, and all things suited to so great a deed—as Polybius boldly declares and powerfully teaches against some of his own Greeks.[734] He was a good soldier who was involved in important activities; he was a good leader who was in charge of public business; he was a good judge who was present with the most important generals.[735] Read this man about our state, read him

de re militari: et cernes infra civitatem nostram omnia, veluti lenta viburna infra aerias cupressus. Sed hæc virtus nostra non inhumana, non superba erat: quæ benevolentiam omnem, et bonitatem diffundere liberalissime in omnes nollet. [a]*Armorum, legumque parens, quæ fundit in omnes Imperium primique dedit cunabula iuris.* Hoc illud est ius civitatis nostræ, quod de floribus libatum Græciæ, refictum de arte Romana, exstincto imperio nostro durat adhuc, et in omnes penetrat orbis terrarum partes, etiam in eas, ad quas Romana arma non pertigerunt. Habes orbis desiderium, Picene: habes orbis delicium: qui destitutus fortuna illa beata imperii nostri: retinet tamen mordicus, et rapit
p. 280 sitiens Romanas leges: cum quibus et memoriam dulcem sibi renovet veteris | sub imperio Romano felicitatis, et horum temporum tristitiam parte aliqua admista temperet voluptatis. Illis artibus Roma crevit: istis artibus Roma stetit. Sile mihi, Picene, arcana tua; quibus illi utuntur, aut imbelles domini, aut impotentes tyranni: quorum nec leonina satis ubique pellis, et vulpina est longe propria. Ista non decent Æneadas magnos.

Heu, et ingentem Æneam, et magnanimum heroem defendemus? Etiam defendemus contra Picenum: quemadmodum et se defendit Æneas ipse contra Picenos. [b] Scimus, hos pro Turno stetisse: iste noster Picenus, ecce, antiquum sapit. Dardanium Æneam, Etruria oriundum, dixeris peregrinum? Cognato auxilia tulisse Etrusco non pateris? *Hinc Dardanus ortus: genus a quo principe nostrum. Dardanidæ duri, quæ vos a stirpe parentum Prima tulit tellus, eadem vos ubere læto Accipiet reduces: antiquam exquirite matrem:* Dardanium Æneam sane: nec Dardanum parricidam, si immo defendi sæpius ista cædes, etiam et laudari potest: adeoque nec damnata illico sit, atque accusata est. Audisti de cæde Remi: explicant de aliis iurisconsulti. Laomedontium sane, sed heroem: et nec de sanguine tamen satum Laomedontis, at cognatum tantum.

Etiam ne fictitia placent Daretis fictitii scripta? etiamne Phrisingensis, nescis cuius, chartas ineptissimas laudas? Servius ubi exsplicat postea, quæ
p. 281 fuerit Æneæ necro|mantia: perge eodem commentario legere. Sciomantiam

[a] *Clau. 3. Stilic.* [b] *Serv. 7. 8. 9. Ænai. Mess. de orig. gen. Rom.*

---

[736] **Translator's note:** This is a reference to Vergil, *Eclogae* 1. 26. Cf. Book 1. 1, pp. 1–2; the marginal reference is to Polybius 1. 2; 3. 6.

[737] Claudian, *De consulatu Stilichonis* 3. 136–7.

[738] **Translator's note:** Cf. Gentili's *De iure belli libri tres* 1. 3, p. 26 in vol. 16, pt. i of "The Classics of International Law" series, ed. James Brown Scott (Oxford, 1933).

[739] Servius, *On Aeneid* 7–9. Mess. [the reference is unclear] *De origine gentis Romanae* [13. 4–6 mentions Turnus; on the *De origine gentis Romanae*, see p. 160, n. 56 above].

[740] **Translator's note:** This is a pastiche of *Aeneis* 3. 167–8 and 94–6.

about our military affairs, and you will see that everything is inferior to our state, like pliant wayfaring trees under lofty cypresses.[736] But this excellence of ours was not inhumane, not proud, not the sort which would be unwilling to spread most liberally every sort of goodwill and benevolence. "Parent of arms and laws, who spreads empire among all peoples and offered the cradle of the beginnings of law."[737] That is the law code of our state, which, initiated from the first blossoms of Greece, reshaped by Roman art, persists to the present day even now that the empire has been extinguished and penetrates into all parts of the world, even those parts to which Roman arms did not reach.[738] Picenus, you possess what the world longs for, you possess what the world delights in—the world which, though deprived of that blessed good luck of our empire, nevertheless tenaciously hangs onto and thirstily gulps down Roman laws, with which it renews for itself the sweet memory of its ancient happiness under Roman rule and alleviates the sadness p. 280
of these times by this little bit of pleasure that has been mixed in. By those arts did Rome grow; by those arts did Rome stand firm. Do me a favor and pass over in silence, Picenus, those secret arts which unwarlike rulers or powerless tyrants make use of, men whom a lion's pelt does not suit but for whom that of a wolf is far and away more fitting. Those arts do not suit the great descendants of Aeneas.

Alas, are we going to have to defend the great and lofty-spirited Aeneas? Shall we even defend him against a Picene, just as Aeneas himself defended himself against the Piceni? We know that they took a stand on the side of Turnus. This Picenus of ours has an old-fashioned flavor to him.[739] Would you call Dardanian Aeneas, whose origins were in Etruria, a foreigner? Do you not allow his Etruscan relative to have come to his aid? "From here Dardanus was sprung, from whom first our race comes. Stout sons of Dardanus, that land which first bore you from the seed of your parents will be the same one to receive you to its fertile breast when you return: seek out your ancient mother!"[740] Yes, he is called Dardanian Aeneas, but Dardanus was not a parricide—if that murder can be defended and even praised more often than it has been—and indeed it would not have been so condemned as the accusation has it. You have heard of the death of Remus: the jurists give explanations for other such deaths. True, he is called "Laomedontian" but it's "Laomedontian *hero*" [*Laomedontius heros*], but even so he was not sprung from the seed of Laomedon, but he was only a relative.

Do you even enjoy the phony stories of phony Dares? Do you even praise the extraordinarily stupid pages of what's-his-name from Freising? Where Servius afterwards explains what the necromancy of Aeneas was, keep on p. 281

videbis innocentem. Æneam autem proditorem? [a] Et Dionysius non auditur, tantæ diligentiæ, tantæ fidei auctor Dionysius ait, refugisse Æneam in arcem: illinc infirmiores, et thesauros misisse: illum ibi restitisse Græcis diu, abiisse Græcis invitis incolumem.

Huius viri adventum in Italiam doles? [b] et nesciebas, Aborigines, genus hominum agreste, sine lege, solutum cum Troianis sic convenisse, et coaluisse, ut invidiæ fuerint vicinis mox, et incomparabilis imperii fortunatissimi iecerint fundamenta. Etiam minæ fortunatæ, de quibus tanto augustius Ilion consurrexerit: irasceris agrestibus illis tamen: et perfugas indignaris receptos. Quid? et hoc igitur tibi ius est, undique exterminare, quos irreparabilis calamitas alicunde dispulerit? Pium certe, humanum, et æquum hoc ius est tuum.

Nam quanta illa fuerit mensura agri, et qualis ager fuerit, qui tributus Troianis fuit, pudet dicere. [c] Iugera duri, atque asperrimi agri septingenta. Sed et hæc felix paupertas. [d] Paupertas, et parsimonia, et honor his habitus extulere imperium nostrum, et urbem nostram rem pulcherrimam effecerunt. [e] Illic Poplicolæ, Curii, Fabritii, Scipiones, Scauri, Menenii Attilii, reliqui: qui divites honorum, pauperes opum aliarum vixerunt. Divitiæ, et luxuria, et honor his habitus imperium nostrum perdiderunt. [f] Otium, et divitiæ
p. 282 ingruentes | miseriæ fuere: et ex iustissimo, atque optimo imperium meorum crudele, intolerandumque reddiderunt.

Sic tempora distingues cum auctoribus omnibus: et voluptates, et lascivitates desines Curibus obiectare severis. Antonii desines obiectare crudeles voces: reliqua temporum succedentium: quæ nec laudat quisquam: nec ipse defendere velim: in defensione ego moderatior tanto, qui nec iure utor concesso defendendi etiam nocentes, atque nefarios, quam tu, qui per damnatum omnibus immane nefas, tempora iustissima variis, et iniustissimis omnibus modis accusasti.

Imperium accusasti præstantiorum: quibus per omnem iustitiam, per universalem, ac sempiternam legem naturæ parere habent inferiores: [g] ut sic Philosophi generaliter docent: Dionysius in hac caussa nostra respondet. [h] Iustum Romanum imperium Augustino, Ambrosio, Hieronymo, Thomæ, aliis sanctis patribus, et magnis doctoribus visum est. [i] Iosephus, Polybius, alii

[a] *Dionys.* 1. [b] *Sallust. Catil.* [c] *Serv.* 11. *Æn.* [d] *Liv. prin.*
[e] *Val.* 4. *c.* 4. *Liv.* 46. [f] *Sallust. Catil. pr.*
[g] *Pla.* 4. *de legi. Dionys.* 1. [h] *Cov. reg. peccatum. p.* 2. § 10. *Vict. relect. Da. ad. Bell.* 5. *con.* 3. *c.* 6.
[i] *Ioseph.* 3. *be. Polyb.* 1.

---

[741] Dionysius of Halicarnassus 1. 46.
[742] Sallust, *Bellum Catilinae* 6. [743] Servius, *On Aeneid* 11.
[744] Livy, preface 11. [745] Valerius Maximus 4. 4; Livy 46 [probably faulty reference].
[746] Sallust, *Bellum Catilinae* 10. 2–6.
[747] Plato, *Leges* 4. 718 c; Dionysius of Halicarnassus 1. 5. 2.
[748] Diego Covarruvias, *Regulae peccatum, De regulis iuris libri VI*, Venetiis, Bartholomaeus Rubinus, 1569, secunda relectionis pars, §10, p. 167; Victoria [Francisco de Vitoria], *De Indis relectio posterior, sive de iure belli* 3. 7, § 56, in Relectiones XII in duos tomos diuisae, Lugduni, Apud Jacobum Boyerium, 1557, p. 422.

reading in that same commentary. You will see that the oracular consultation of the shades is innocent. Aeneas a traitor? Don't you even listen to Dionysius, an author of such diligence and trustworthiness? Dionysius reports that Aeneas took refuge in the citadel, sent out from there the weaker ones and the treasures, made a stand against the Greeks for a long time, and then went off at last unharmed, against the will of the Greeks.[741]

Do you lament the arrival of this man in Italy? Were you unaware that the original inhabitants, a savage, lawless, and unruly race of men, so came together and became united with the Trojans as to soon become a source of envy to their neighbors and to lay down the foundations of an incomparable and extremely prosperous empire?[742] Even their threats were fortunate, for from them Ilium arose again with even more majesty. But you grow angry with those rustics and are outraged that the fugitives were given a home. What? Is this, then, your idea of justice: to everywhere exterminate those whom irreparable disaster has driven out from somewhere or other? No doubt this justice of yours is pious, humane and just!

You're ashamed to say how large a measure of land, and what sort of land it was, that was assigned to the Trojans. Seven hundred acres of hard and very rugged land.[743] But even this poverty was happy. Poverty and thrift and the honor acquired by them have raised up our empire and have made our city the most beautiful thing in the world.[744] In that place were the Poplicolae, the Curii, the Fabricii, the Scipiones, the Scauri, the Menenii, the Attilii, and the rest, who lived rich in honors, but poor in other riches.[745] Wealth and luxury and the honor acquired by them have destroyed our empire. Leisure and riches were afflictions that attacked us and reduced the empire of my p. 282
people from being the best and most just to being cruel and unbearable.[746]

Thus you shall distinguish one period from another, along with all the authorities, and you will cease to accuse the severe Curii of pleasures and wantonness. You will cease to oppose the cruel words of Antonius, the relics of succeeding ages, which no one praises, nor would I myself want to defend. For in making my defense I, who do not employ the legal right that is allowed of defending even the guilty and the wicked, am so much more moderate than you who, by exploiting a monstrous crime everyone has condemned, have leveled charges against the most just ages in all sorts of shifting and extremely unjust ways.

You have leveled charges against the rule of the men of superior excellence, whom their inferiors ought to obey on account of all justice, of the universal and eternal law of nature, as the philosophers, as a whole, teach—and Dionysius speaks in defense of this case of ours as well.[747] The Roman Empire appeared just to Augustine, Ambrose, Jerome, Thomas Aquinas, and other holy fathers and great scholars.[748] Josephus, Polybius, and others

et hoc dicunt, docentque, imperium factum virtute. Virtute retentum imperium est. Scilicet et servatur res eo modo, quo quæritur. [a] Armis iustis quæsitum, legibus iustis conservatum: ut de nostro sic imperio Gothus.

[b] Tanta maiorum nostrorum virtus, ut etiam vitia potuerit posterorum
p. 283 sustentare: quod inquit Seneca: et quod est virtutis signum plus | quam humanæ: neque enim fulcrum ullum est, quod sustentare rem possit, quæ præcipiti ruina devolvatur. At illaudata tibi, laudata omnibus virtus maiorum illas ipsas ruinas vitiorum consecutorum, et præcipites in ruinam posteriores, et perire festinantes sustentat. [c] Hi nostri maiores, *hi tantum parient Latio per vulnera regnum, quod luxu, et multum mutata mente nepotes, non tamen evertisse queant.*

Sed eversum tandem est imperium: et cum reliquis omnibus mortalibus habuit finem suum. [d] Sed, quod prædictum tanto antea fuit a viris sapientibus, ecce pulsis Romanis: Romanos dico? et hos intelligo postumos, colluviem nationum, moribus exstinctis antiquis, deleta omni etiam imagine veteris populi? [e]*Nil patrium, nisi nomen, habet Romanus alumnus.* Sed ecce hoc quoque nomine depulso, hac larva, umbraque per barbaros triumphata, ecce bella omnium, omnium inter se gentium, *vicinæ ruptis inter se legibus urbes Arma ferunt, sævit toto Mars impius orbe. Ut cum carceribus sese effudere quadrigæ. Addunt se in spatia, nec quisquam retinacula tendit: Fertur equis currus, nec quisquam regit habenas.* Et hic rides Picene, orbis ridet? et, discrepare gentes moribus, legibus, linguis, sacris, animis, etiam rides? Sed, si quid mihi orbis
p. 284 facies, et omnium mortalium | ora significant, contra vicimus: et unitatem scissam animorum deplorant omnes: pietatem, liberalitatem, fidem, magnanimitatem, pacem, securitatem, æquanimitatem Romanam suspirant, et imperium Romanum: cui iusto, æquo, bono subductos se lamentantur.

FINIS

[a] *Ior. de. re. su.* [b] *Sene. de co. ad ma.* [c] *Sil.* 3.
[d] *Sall. or.* 2. *ad Cæs. Tac.* 4. *hist. Lact. de di. pro. c.* 15. *Plut. de for. Ro.* [e] *Prop.* 4. *eleg.* 1.

---

749 Josephus, *Bellum Judaicum* 3; Polybius 1.

750 **Translator's note:** Cf. Sallust, *Bellum Catilinae* 2. 4: "Nam imperium facile iis artibus retinetur quibus initio partum est."

751 Jordanes, *Romana* 3.

752 Seneca, *De consolatione ad Helviam* 10. 7. **Translator's note:** The notes in both editions mistakenly identify the source as the *De consolatione ad Marciam.*

753 Silius Italicus, *Punica* 3. 588–90.

754 [Ps.-]Sallust, *Oration to Caesar* 2; Tacitus, *Historiae* 4. 74; Lactantius, *Divinae institutiones* 7. 15. 11–12; Plutarch, *De fortuna Romanorum.*

755 Propertius 4. 1. 37.

756 **Translator's note:** Vergil, *Georgica* 1. 510–14. Gentili was apparently quoting from memory, for the last lines should read "and vainly pulling on the halter, the charioteer is borne along by the horses, and the chariot doesn't heed the reins"—"et frustra retinacula tendens / fertur equis auriga neque audit currus habenas."

also say and teach this: that the empire was created through virtue and was retained through virtue.[749] Indeed, a thing is held onto in the same manner in which it is acquired.[750] As a Goth said of our empire, it was sought out by just arms and preserved by just laws.[751]

Such was the virtue of our ancestors that it could even support the vices of later generations, as Seneca said;[752] and this is a sign of a virtue more than p. 283
human; for there is no fulcrum which could support a thing while itself tumbling down in headlong ruin. But the virtue of our ancestors, dispraised by you but praised by all others, props up the very ruins of the vices of later times and their descendants heading for ruin and in a hurry to be destroyed. These ancestors of ours, "these shall through their wounds produce for Latium such a great kingdom, which their descendants would not be able to overthrow through luxury and a greatly altered disposition."[753]

But at last the empire was overthrown, and along with all other mortal affairs it had its end. But what had been predicted so long before by wise men,[754] behold, when the Romans had been driven away—wait: *Romans*, do I say? Do I consider these last ones to be Romans, the dregs of the nations, when the old ways had been snuffed out and every aspect of the ancient people had been destroyed? "The Roman offspring has nothing ancestral but his name."[755] But behold, now that when even this name itself has been driven away, this ghost and shadow triumphed over by barbarians, behold now the wars of all, of all peoples among themselves. "Neighboring cities, the laws among them burst asunder, take arms; impious Mars rages throughout the globe; as when chariots pour out from the starting pens, they go faster each lap; nor does anyone hold the halter; the chariot is carried along by the horses, and no one guides the reins."[756] And are you laughing here, Picenus? Is the world laughing? And do you still laugh when the world's peoples differ in customs, laws, languages, sacred rites, and thoughts? But if the look of the globe and the faces of all mortal men are saying anything to me, then we have p. 284
triumphed over you, and all lament the now sundered unity of hearts and sigh for Roman piety, liberality, trustworthiness, magnanimity, peace, security, justice—and for the Roman Empire, from which, in all of its justice, fairness, and goodness, they lament that they have been withdrawn.

THE END

APPENDIX

Gentili's Dedicatory Epistle to Robert Devereux, Earl of Essex, in *De iniustitia bellica Romanorum actio*, Oxonii, Excudebat Iosephus Barnesius, 1590

Rob. Devoraxio Illusstrissimo Comiti Essexio Albericus Gentilis S.

Quae mea, illustrissime ESSEXI, voluntas sit erga te, et qui affectus animi mei in te colendo, vel hinc sentias licet, quod si vacui temporis quidquam a muneribus publicis mihi est, id omne arripioque statim, et nomini tuo consecrare protinus consuevi. Rapuit me in admirationem tui primum virtus tua: et eadem virtus spectata indies magis magisque meos ita sensus omnes in tui observantiam accendit, ut hoc unum cogitem semper, quomodo voluntatem hanc meam adprobare tibi, et largiter contestatam efficere possim. Et vero quid attinet, favorem, quo me prosecutus absentem es, memorare? Quid humanitatem, qua me semper excipere soles? Quid illud, quod ego summi beneficii loco duxi, quod filiolo meo ad sacrum fontem pater esse, et nomen tuum late inclytum communicare voluisti? Haec scilicet virtutis illius tuae opera tanto mihi acciderunt gratiora quanto attigerunt me propius, aut me verius unum contigerunt.

Sed est Actio haec nostra tibi debita, qui librosque tenes a nobis de iure belli, aut parentes huius Actionis, aut certe a quibus separari ipsa sine flagitio non potuisset. Quod ergo tua tibi virtus, quod merita in me tua, quod ius tuum a me in praesentia munusculum hoc novum sumunt, et tu, obsecro, ad te venire patiaris, et apud te esse sinas, ut, me tuum a longo tempore, tibique addictum in perpetuum esse, cerni ubique, et intelligi queat.

Nam ad munus ipsum quod spectat, si nostram dictionem huic argumento imparem vides, quod eloquenter tractari oportuisset, id tu studiis nostris condonaveris, quae in istas literas amoeniores descendunt raro, sed in aspretis Iurisprudentiae habitant. Nec ego volui sane oratoriam isthic profiteri, at notare magis censura sapientiae gesta terrarum principis populi; et recti officii, verae virtutis atque iustitiae rationes paullo vestigare diligentius; quam facere commune literarorum vulgus soleat, et scriptorum narrationes atque sententiae tradiderunt. Est nobis in censendis narrationibus maior, quam in diiudicandis sententiis difficultas. Si enim testimonia auctorum conveniunt, nobis nihil relinquitur, quo contrarium disceptemus, nisi ratio coniecturarum: quam firmam non esse satis, cum nomen monet coniecturarum, tum quod ipsarum potissimaeque nec coeteris vim meliorem sortitae sunt: si verum nos docent Aristoteles, et Quinctilianus, qui multa hominibus credibilia, et verisimilia asserunt, quae falsa sunt fre-

Alberico Gentili, to Robert Devereux, Most Illustrious Count of Essex, Greetings

The good will I have towards you, Essex, and the dispositions of my heart in cultivating you are things you can be aware of from this fact: that if I have any bit of time free from my public duties I seize upon all of it and have been in the habit of devoting it forthwith to your fame. It was your excellence that first seized me and led me to admire you; and that same excellence, once I had viewed it day after day, has more and more so inflamed all my feelings to honor you that I always have only this goal in mind: how I might establish this good will of mine to you and make it abundantly proved. And indeed, what good does it do to mention the favor with which you have attended me when I have been away from you? What good does it do to mention that kindness with which you are always accustomed to receive me? What good does it do to mention that which I regard as the highest possible favor: that you are the godfather of my little son and have wished to share with him your name made famous far and wide? Indeed, these works of that famous excellence of yours have become even more pleasing to me because they have touched me more closely—or, to put it more accurately, have fallen the lot of me alone.

But this *actio* of ours is owed to you, who have books from us on the law of war which are the parents of this *actio*, or at least works from which it could not be separated without doing wrong. Your own excellence, your services to me, and what I owe you in the present receive this new little present, and, I beg you, please allow it to come before you and to be with you, so that people may be able to everywhere see and understand that I have been yours for a long time and am drawn to you forever.

For as to the work itself, if you see that our language is not equal to this subject matter, a subject matter that ought to be handled eloquently, may you find an excuse in my areas of study, which seldom come down into these more pleasant literary genres, but live in the thickets of jurisprudence. Nor have I wished to profess the art of oratory here, but rather to brand with the criticism of wisdom the deeds of the people who ruled the world, and to search out arguments of proper duty and true virtue and justice a bit more industriously than the common herd of writers and the narrations and opinions of writers tend to do. There is a greater difficulty for us in assessing narratives than in deciding between opinions. For if the testimonies of the writers are in agreement, nothing is left for us by which we might choose a contrary position, unless it would be a method of conjectures, and this cannot be sufficiently secure, as not only the word "conjectures" warns us, but not even the most powerful of them has been allotted any superior power than the others, if Aristotle and Quintilian teach us the truth, for they assert that very often very many things that are false strike men as credible and verisimilar, while there are very many things that are true which seem profoundly

quenter; et vera esse plurima, quae incredibilia penitus videantur. Hoc in sententiis scriptorum expendendis non contingit: nam eodem sumus nos loco atque illi, aut etiam meliori, qui studio partium non imbuti, et saeculis succendentibus magis instructi ad iudicandum accedimus. Caeterum nec denegatum est nobis testimoniorum iudicium, quod ipsique rerum scriptores alius adversus alium exercere non infrequentissime solent: et rerum, iurisque auctores latissime notant argumenta, quibus testimoniorum omnium elevare fidem possimus. Socrates etiam, ut est apud Platonem, minus se testibus mille credere, quam rationi uni, sapienter, et summa cum ratione asserebat.

At vero nos in Actione hac nostra iuris praecipue tractare sententias pro munere nostro voluimus, et de iniustitia disputare, qua argui populus Romanus posse in bellicis, hoc est, in longe nobilissimis gestis suis, videtur. Id utor verbi, Comes excellentissime, quoniam Defensionem Romanorum, et disputationem huic adversariam de ipsorum iustitia bellica paratam habeo. Quam afferamque tibi, si Actionem audieris prius, et Defensione illa opus Romanis esse censueris. Vale, vir nobilissime. Oxonii, prid. natalitiorum Domini. MDXC.

unbelievable. This does not apply to the weighing of the opinions of writers, for we are in the same position that they are—or in an even better position, given that we are not imbued with party zeal, and we come to the acts of judging more instructed by succeeding ages. Furthermore, we are not denied the right to pass judgment on testimonies, for the writers of deeds are not infrequently in the habit of exercising judgment one upon another; and authors of history and law very widely make note of arguments by which we are able to diminish the trustworthiness of all sorts of testimonies. For Socrates, according to Plato, wisely and with the greatest reason declares that he put less faith in a thousand witnesses than in a single reasoning.

But indeed we in this *actio* of ours have especially wished to treat of the rulings of the law, in accord with our set task, and to make a disputation about the injustice of which the Roman people seems to be accused in its martial—that is to say, its most noble deeds. I use the word "seems," Most Excellent Earl, since I have ready a defense of the Romans and a disputation directly opposed to this one on their justice in making wars. I shall bring you this, if you will have read this *actio* first and then judge that the Romans stand in need of that defense. Farewell, most noble man. 1590.

Errata

Our Latin text was emended according to the following list and reflects the changes suggested therein.

1.1

p. 10, line 3 (p. 2, lines 24–5 1599 edn.): for *apta pinnis iurandum Iovis* read *apta pinnis ius iurandum Iovis*
p. 10, line 24 (p. 4, line 2 1599 edn.): for *quæ* read *qui*

1.2

p. 18, line 10 (p. 9, line 18 1599 edn.): for *πονερόπολιν* read *πονηρόπολιν*

1.3

p. 32, line 21 (p. 21 line 5 1599 edn.): for *quodam* read *quondam* (as in Virgil *Aen.* 6.794, but see note ad loc.)

1.8

p. 66, line 14 (p. 47, line 17 1599 edn.): for *noxia* read *noxiæ*

1.9

p. 76, lines 5–6 (p. 55, lines 2–3 1599 edn.): for *iudicium turpis in caussa* read *iudicium turpi in caussa*

1.13

p. 114, line 19 (p. 86, line 1 1599 edn.): for *opidis* read *oppidis*

2.1

p. 122, line 16 (p. 92, line 20 1599 edn.): for *ut ut nati* read *ut nati*
p. 126, line 10 (p. 96, line 1 1599 edn.): for *abblanditur* read *ablanditur*

2.2

p. 134, line 13 (p. 102, lines 19–20 1599 edn.): for *orbis totus invitamentum* read *orbis totius invitamentum*
p. 140, line 11 (p. 107, line 16 1599 edn.): for *Hæc natura* read *Hæc natura.*
p. 146, line 31 (p. 113, line 21 1599 edn.): for *alii* read *Alii*

2.4

p. 186, line 1 (p. 145, line 1 1599 ed.): for *veritus* read *verius*
p. 188, line 14 (p. 147, line 7 1599 edn.): for *Callatinus* read *Collatinus*

2.8

p. 250, line 8 (p. 198, line 12–13 1599 edn.): for *obnoxia illa pace* read *obnoxii illa pace*

2.9

p. 262, line 22 (p. 209, line 3 1599 edn.): for *prætexus omnes* read *prætextus omnes*
p. 268, line 3 (p. 212, line 27 1599 edn.): for *Sed pœnituit eum* read *Si pænituit eum*
p. 268, line 5 (p. 212, line 30 1599 edn.): for *pœnitentia* read *pænitentia*

2.10

p. 274, lines 20–21 (p. 218, line 24 1599 edn.): for *aut terminata.* read *aut terminata?*

2.12

p. 322, line 28 (p. 257, line 2 1599 edn.): for *quare* read *Quare*
p. 328, line 10 (p. 261, lines 4–5 1599 edn.): for *post victorias patris* read *post victorias partas*

2.13

p. 346, line 12 (p. 276, line 22 1599 edn.): for *turbes maleficos* read *turpes maleficos*
p. 350, line 19 (p. 280, line 14 1599 edn.): for *Hetruria* read *Etruria*
p. 350, line 20 (p. 280, line 16 1599 edn.): for *Hetruscos* read *Etrusco*

Glossary of Terms

bellum iustum: "Just war," a public war fought with just cause (*causa iusta*), as opposed to a public war fought without just cause or as opposed to civil war.

causa belli: "Cause of war." This has a strong normative undertone, as just cause (*causa iusta*) is used in Roman just-war theory as the defining feature of just war; accordingly, in Book 1, *causa belli* is often used with a skeptical undertone, translated here sometimes as "pretext," while it is used in the second book in its original Roman sense of "just cause of war."

civitas: "City-state" or "state," often used to stress the corporate entity made up of citizens; it can also be used as a synonym for "commonwealth" (*res publica*) by Gentili. Usually, however, it simply means "state" in *The Wars of the Romans*, as in 1. 8, p. 71, where the accuser says that the "state" (*civitas*) "consists of citizens and people," as opposed to the "city" (*urbs*), "which consists of houses and walls."

honestum: "That which is honorable," in the sense of virtuous and, above all, just. *Honestas*, virtue, for Cicero consists in the four cardinal virtues, chief among them justice; it also has a strong connotation of social standing. Its chief use both for Cicero and for Gentili is, however, in opposition to *utile*, "that which is useful or beneficial or expedient," that is to say *utile* is what is conducive to self-interest; adducing Cicero (*On Duties*), the accuser in Book 1 holds in a characteristic passage (*The Wars of the Romans* 1. 4, p. 41) that "nothing is *utile* which is not *honestum*". The background in classical ethics concerns the relation between morality and self-interest, where an identification of the *utile* with the *honestum* and *iustum* is attempted along the lines sketched in the quote; the aim is to show that the just at a deeper level is actually expedient.

hostis: An enemy in a public war, as opposed to a mere robber or brigand (*latro*), as in *The Wars of the Romans* 2. 10, p. 285: "Word is kept with legitimate enemies, not brigands." In *De iure belli* (1. 2, p. 18 f.) Gentili explains that the *hostis*, as opposed to the bandit, is in a sense "the equal of his opponent," which corresponds with his idea, adumbrated already by Vitoria, that occasionally "a war may indeed be just on both sides" (*The Wars of the Romans* 2. 8, p. 243); however, Gentili's point (as was Vitoria's) is merely an epistemological one, namely that since it is often doubtful on which side justice is, neither side to a war "can be called unjust"—which does not mean that there is not a fact of the matter as to where justice lies (see his discussion of the issue in *De iure belli* 1. 6).

imperium: In its original constitutional sense *imperium* means the "legitimate power of command of a Roman magistrate" exercised in war, the aftermath of war and in order to enforce the law (jurisdiction); however, in Emperor Augustus' time the term increasingly assumed the additional meaning of "territorial unit," and "empire"—the territory in which Roman magistrates exercise their power; in *The Wars of the Romans* the term is used both to mean "power" and "empire."

ius: Usually used in the sense of "law," but occasionally Gentili uses it in its subjective sense as "right," as in *The Wars of the Romans* 2. 10, p. 279: "would the Roman people truly be so unable to pursue their right (*ius suum*)?"

ius gentium: "Law of nations," a term originally used by the Roman lawyers to describe a body of law containing rules that were considered to be available in the laws of all civilized peoples. This body of law contained especially remedies given by the praetor that were available to citizens and non-citizens alike, as opposed to the remedies and rules contained in the civil law (*ius civile*), which were given by law and custom and which acknowledged only citizens as subjects. The law of nations is sometimes characterized in the Roman legal sources as identical with natural law, by virtue of its being based on natural reason (*ratio naturalis*); in Gentili it is used both in its original Roman sense as well as in the sense of a body of rules that is binding between sovereign states, i.e. in the sense of "international law," and which is equated with natural law.

ius/lex naturae: "Law of nature," used by Gentili as synonymous with *ius gentium*, that which, as opposed to positive law, is grounded in, or identical with, natural (human) reason (*ratio naturalis*) and therefore perennial and immutable. According to Cicero (*Republic* 3. 33 = Lactantius, *Divine Institutes* 6. 8. 8–9), natural law is "eternal and unchangeable," and there "will not be one law at Rome and another at Athens, one now and another later," and "we cannot be released from this law by the senate or the people"; natural law can thus not be changed by will. Gentili equates it with the "law of nations" and takes the Roman law of the *Corpus iuris* to be declaratory of it.

iustitia: "Justice," as opposed to self-interest and expediency (*utilitas*); Gentili in *The Wars of the Romans* 2. 4, p. 185 follows the tersest definition, that of Ulpian (*Digest* 1. 1. 10 = *Institutes* 1. 1. pr.), according to which "justice is to assign to each his own," a very property-centered account of justice that acknowledges both the distributive as well as the rectificatory aspect of justice. In the *Corpus iuris*, the whole passage reads "Justice is a steady and enduring will to render unto everyone his own. The basic principles of right are: to live honorably, not to harm any other person, to render each his own."

latro: "Robber" or "brigand," as opposed to an enemy (*hostis*) in a public war.

libertas: "Liberty," as opposed to slavery, servitude, or being dependent as a tributary; *libertas* can mean both the liberty of an individual as well as the liberty of a polity; for the former, see *Digest* 1. 5. 4. pr., where *libertas* is described as "one's natural power of doing what one pleases" and is the opposite of slavery (*servitus*); for the latter, see *The Wars of the Romans* 1. 8, p. 71, where the accuser contrasts "the liberty of the state" (*civitatis libertas*) with Carthage being a "tributary" (*stipendiaria*) to Rome and a "slave" (*serva*). Apart from this sense of sovereign independence and autonomy there is a further sense of *libertas* where it is used to describe republican constitutional arrangements that stand opposed to absolute monarchy (*regnum*).

metus: "Fear"; Gentili expands the concept of self-defense to include instances where "a just cause of fear" (*De iure belli* 1. 14, p. 99) can give rise to pre-emptive self-defense; see *The Wars of the Romans* 2. 9, p. 253.

necessitas: "Necessity"; an important concept in Gentili's work, helping him to construe self-defense as widely as possible and underlining the *ragion di stato* strand in his thought; e.g. in *The Wars of the Romans* 2. 2, p. 151 Rome's defender says: "That which is not allowable according to the law necessity makes allowable. Necessity has

no law, but it itself makes a law. Necessity makes that acceptable which would otherwise be unacceptable. And because of necessity one justly departs from customary measures."

rerum repetitio: "Seeking of redress," usually for the recovery of property or damages, after an injury (*iniuria*) has been done; this is one of the necessary conditions for waging a just war according to Roman just-war doctrine, and it certainly is the one that carries most moral weight; see *The Wars of the Romans* 2. 3, p. 169, where the Roman defends King Tullus thus: "Tullus also declares war against the Sabines because there were wrongs done (*iniuriae factae*) on both sides, and things seized were sought back (*res repetitae*) in vain."

res publica: "Republic," or "commonwealth"; the term can also simply mean "state," but it usually carries strong constitutional connotations and means "republic" as opposed to "monarchy". In *The Wars of the Romans* it is often used to refer to the republican period in Roman history before the erection of Augustus' Principate when Rome was still a republic; see *The Wars of the Romans* 2. 9, p. 259, where the defender seems to express a desire to limit his defense to the republican era: "Do we even have to defend those things that happened when the Republic was overthrown?" Gentili thinks of the Roman Republic as a mixed constitution in the tradition of Polybius and Cicero, which he deems the best system of all (see *The Wars of the Romans* 2. 4, p. 183).

socius, socii: "Ally, allies"; originally the term was used to describe Italian communities; after entering a treaty of alliance (*foedus*) with Rome, they had remained formally independent but were obliged to assist Rome with troops. It was also used for allies outside Italy who gradually lost their independence after concluding treaties of alliance. Both in the Roman sources and in Gentili the *socii* are important as Rome is said in Cicero's *Republic* (3. 35) to have gained its empire "through defending its allies," an idea heavily used by Gentili's defender in Book 2 of *The Wars of the Romans* (see e.g. 2. 7, p. 227).

utile: "That which is useful or beneficial or expedient," used in opposition to *honestum*, "that which is honorable or virtuous," or moral; see the entry on *honestum* above.

Benjamin Straumann

Bibliography of Postclassical Works Referred to by Gentili

This bibliography does not include classical authors and their works, nor does it include references to the *Corpus iuris civilis*, the *Corpus iuris canonicis*, or to Scripture. Where possible or advisable, we have consulted editions Gentili himself might have used.

Aemilius: Paulus Aemilius [Paolo Emili], *De rebus gestis Francorum Libri X*, Lutetiae Parisiorum, Ex officina Vascosani, 1566.

Aerodius: Petrus Aerodius [Pierre Ayrault], *Decretorum, rerumve apud diversos populos ab omni antiquitate iudicatarum, libri duo*, Parisiis, Apud Martinum Iuvenem, 1567.

Alciatus: Andrea Alciati, *Commentaria in Codicem*, in *Opera omnia in quatuor tomos*, Tomus III, Basileae, Apud Thomam Guarinum, 1582.

—— *Commentaria in digestum novum*, in *Opera omnia in quatuor tomos*, Tomus II, Basileae, Apud Thomam Guarinum, 1582.

—— *De verborum significatione, liber quartus*, in *Opera omnia in quatuor tomos*, Tomus IIII, Basileae, Apud Thomam Guarinum, 1582.

—— *Dispunctionum libri IIII*, in *Opera omnia in quatuor tomos*, Tomus IIII, Basileae, Apud Thomam Guarinum, 1582.

—— *Parergon*, in *Opera omnia in quatuor tomos*, Tomus IIII, Basileae, Apud Thomam Guarinum, 1582.

—— *Responsa libris novem digesta*, Basileae, Apud Thomam Guarinum, 1582.

Alexander Tartagnus: Alexander Tartagnus Imolensis [Alexander of Imola], *Consiliorum seu responsorum libri VII*, Venetiis, Ex Officina Iac. Antonij Somaschi, 1597.

Ayala: Balthazar Ayala, *De iure et officiis bellicis et disciplina militari libri tres*, Duaci, Ex officina Ioannis Bogardi, 1582.

Baldus: Baldus de Ubaldis, *Consiliorum, sive responsorum*, vol. 1–5, Venetiis, Apud Hieronymum Polum, 1575.

—— *In primam Digesti veteris partem commentaria*, [n.p.], 1535.

—— *Super primo, secundo, tertio Codicis commentaria*, Lugduni, 1539.

Baronius: Caesar Baronius [Cesare Baronio], *Annales ecclesiastici*, Moguntiæ, Impensis I. T. Schönwetteri, 1614.

Bartolus: Bartolus of Sassoferrato, *In primam Digesti veteris partem*, in *Opera omnia*, tomus primus, Venetiis, Sexta Editio Iuntarum, 1590.

—— *In secundam Digesti novi partem commentaria*, in *Opera omnia*, tomus sextus, Venetiis, Sexta Editio Iuntarum, 1590.

Bayfius: Lazarus Bayus [Lazare de Baïf], *De re navali libellus*, Lugduni, Apud haeredes Simonis Vincentij, 1537.

Bellarminus: Robertus Bellarminus [Roberto Bellarmino], *Disputationum de controversiis Christianae fidei, adversus huius temporis hareticos*, Lugduni, Apud Ioannem Pillehotte, 1609.

Bodinus: Ioannes Bodinus [Jean Bodin], *De la démonomanie des sorciers*, Paris, Chez Iacques du Puys, 1580.

—— *De republica libri sex*, Francofurti, Apud Ioan. Wecheli viduam, sumtib. Petri Fischeri, 1594.

Bruto: Giovanni Michele Bruto [Ioannes Michael Brutus], *De historiae laudibus, sive de certa via, et ratione, qua sunt rerum scriptores legendi*, liber I, Cracoviae, Typis A. Petricovii, 1583.

Cardanus: Hieronymus Cardanus [Girolamo Cardano], *De sapientia libri quinque: quibus omnis humanae vitae cursus vivendique ratio explicatur; Eiusdem De consolatione libri tres. His propter similitudinem argumenti, & ipsius Cardani commendationem, adiecti sunt Petri Alcyonii De exilio libri duo*, Aureliopoli, Apud Petrum & Iacobum Chouët, 1624.

—— *Encomium Neronis*, ed. Nikolaus Eberl, Frankfurt a. M., Peter Lang, 1994.

Casaubonus: Isaac Casaubon, *In Suetonii librum IV animadversiones*, in *C. Suetonii Tranquilli opera*, ed. Frid. Aug. Wolfius, vol. 4, Lipsiae, 1802.

Castelvetro: Lodovico Castelvetro, *Poetica d'Aristotele vulgarizzata et sposta*, Basilea, Stampata ad instanza di Pietro de Sedabonis, 1576.

Castrensis: Paulus Castrensis [Paolo de Castro], *Prima super Digesto veteri, commentariorum in Digestum vetus pars prima*, [Lugduni, Apud S. Gryphium,] 1531.

Cedrenus: George Cedrenus, *Historiarum compendium*, in J.-P. Migne, *Patrologia Graeca*, vol. cxxi.

Cephalus: Ioannes Cephalus [Giovanni Cefalo], *Consiliorum sive responsorum libri quinque*, Francofurti ad Moenum, Apud Ioannem Feyerabendt, impensis Sigismundi Feyerabendts, 1579.

Clarus: Julius Clarus [Giulio Claro], *Receptarum sententiarum liber quintus*, in *Opera omnia; sive practica civilis atque criminalis, cum doctissimis additionibus per illustrium iurisconsultorum*, Venetiis, Ex typographia Baretiana, 1626.

Comes: Natalis Comes [Natale Conti], *Universae historiae sui temporis libri triginta*, Venetiis, Apud Zenarum, 1581.

Cominaeus: Philippe de Comines [Philippus Cominaeus], *Mémoires*, ed. J. Blanchard, Paris, 2001.

Cotta: Catellanus Cotta, *Memoralia*, Lugduni, Apud Antonium Vincentium, 1556.

Covarruvias: Diego Covarruvias, *Regulae peccatum, De regulis iuris libri VI*, Venetiis, Bartholomaeus Rubinus, 1569.

—— *De sponsalibus et matrimoniis*, in *Opera omnia*, Venetiis, Apud Gasparem Bindonum sumptibus sociorum, 1588.

—— *Variae resolutiones ex Pontificio, Regio et Caesareo iure*, in *Opera omnia*, Venetiis, Apud Gasparem Bindonum sumptibus sociorum, 1588.

Cuiacius: Iacobus Cuiacius [Jacques Cujas], *De feudis, libri quinque*, in *Opera quae de iure fecit*, Tomus secundus, Lutetiae Parisiorum, 1617.

—— *Paratitla in libros quinquaginta Digestorum seu Pandectarum*, Coloniae, Apud Maternum Cholinum, 1570.

Curtius Junior: Franciscus Curtius Junior [Francesco Corti], *Consilia*, Venetiis, Ex officina Ioannis Baptistae Somaschi, 1575.

Danaeus: LAMBERTUS DANAEUS [LAMBERT DANEAU], *Ad Roberti Bellarmini Disputationes theologicas de rebus in religione controversis*, Genevae, Apud Ioannem Le Preux, 1596.

Dantes Aligherius: DANTE, *Divina commedia*, Venetia, 1529.

Decianus: TIBERIUS DECIANUS, *Responsa*, Venetiis, Apud Vassallinum, 1602.

Decius: PHILIPPUS DECIUS [FILIPPO DECIO], *Consiliorum pars prima*, Lugduni, 1550.

—— *Consiliorum pars quarta*, Lugduni, Apud Iacobum Giuntam, 1546.

—— *De regulis iuris*, Lugduni, Apud Nicolaum Parvum, 1539 [containing Postillae by Hieronimus Chuchalon Hispanus].

Drusius: IOHANNES DRUSIUS [JAN VAN DEN DRIESCHE], *Observationes sacrae*, Antverpiae, Excudebat Aegidius Radaeus, 1584.

Eugenius Perusinus: MARCUS ANTONIUS EUGENIUS PERUSINUS [MARCO ANTONIO EUGENIO], *Consilia*, Perusiae, Apud Petrum Paulum Orlandium, 1588.

Fornerius: GULIELMUS FORNERIUS [GUILLAUME FOURNIER], *In titulum de verborum significatione commentarii*, Aurelianis, Apud Eligium Gibierium, 1584.

Giovius: PAOLO GIOVIO [PAULUS JOVIUS], *Dialogo dell'imprese militari et amorose*, In Lyone, Appresso Guglielmo Rouillio, 1574.

—— *Historiae sui temporis*, Lugduni, Apud Haered. Seb. Gryphii, 1561.

Gregoras: NICEPHORUS GREGORAS, *Romanae, hoc est Byzantinae historiae libri XI*, in *Corpus universae historiae praesertim Byzantinae*, Lutetiae, Apud Guillielmum Chaudiere, 1567.

Guicciardinus: FRANCESCO GUICCIARDINI, *Storia d'Italia*, Venetia, Presso Gio. Antonio Bertano, 1580.

Heraclides: HERACLIDES LEMBUS, *De politiis, sive rerumpublicarum descriptiones*, in *Aeliani de varia historia libri XIIII*, Basileae, Ex officina I. Oporini, 1548, pp. 261–80.

Isernas: ANDREAS ISERNAS [ANDREA D'ISERNIA], *In usus feudorum commentaria*, Neapoli, 1571.

Jacchinus: LEONARDUS JACCHINUS [LEONARDO GIACHINI], *Quaestionum naturalium libellus*, Lugduni, Apud Seb. Gryphium, 1540.

Jason de Maino: JASON MAYNUS [GIASONE DEL MAYNO], *In primam Digesti veteris partem commentaria*, Venetiis, Apud Iuntas, 1579.

—— *In secundam Digesti novi partem commentaria*, Venetiis, Apud Iuntas, 1598.

Krantzius: ALBERTUS KRANTZIUS, *Regnorum Aquilonarium, Daniae, Sueciae, Norvagiae chronica*, Francoforti ad Moenum, 1575.

Lipsius: JUSTUS LIPSIUS, *Admiranda, sive De magnitudine Romana libri quattuor*, Antverpiae, Ex Officina Plantiniana, Apud Ioannem Moretum, 1598.

—— *Ad Velleium Paterculum animadversiones, quas recenter auxit et emendavit*, Antverpiae, Apud Ioannem Moretum, 1600.

—— *C. Velleius Paterculus cum animadversionibus I. Lipsi*, Lugduni Batavorum, Ex officina Plantiniana, Apud Franciscum Raphelengium, 1591.

—— *De magistratibus veteris populi Romani*, in *Tractatus ad historiam Romanam cognoscendam apprime utiles*, Cantabrigiae, 1592.

—— *De militia Romana libri quinque*, Antverpiae, Ex officina Plantiniana, Apud Ioannem Moretum, 1598.

—— *Poliorceticon sive de machinis libri quinque*, Antverpiae, Ex officina Plantiniana, Apud Viduam et Ioannem Moretum, 1596.

Loritus: HENRICUS LORITUS GLAREANUS [HEINRICH LORITZ], *Valerii Maximi de factorum dictionumque memorabilium exemplis libri novem*, Basileae, per Henricum Petri, 1562.

Machiavelli: Niccolò Machiavelli, *Libro dell'arte della guerra*, Venetia, Per Domenico Giglio, 1554.

Magius: Hieronymus Magius [Girolamo Maggi], *Variarum lectionum, seu liscellaneorum libri IIII*, Venetiis, Ex officina Iordani Zileti, 1564.

Manutius: Paulus Manutius [Paolo Manuzio], *M. Tullii Ciceronis epistolae ad familiares. Annotationes breves in margine adscriptae*, Coloniae Agrippinae, Apud Cholinum, 1604.

—— *M. Tullii Ciceronis Orationes*, Amstelodami, Ex Typographia P. & I. Blaeu, 1699.

—— *Scholia ad Asconium*, in *Asconius Pedianus, Explanatio in Ciceronis orationes in C. Verrem, in orationem pro C. Cornelio, in orationem contra competitores, in orationem pro M. Scauro, in orationem contra L. Pisonem, in orationem pro Milone. Scholia Pauli Manutii*, Venetiis, 1563.

Maynus: see Jason de Maino.

Melanchthon: Philippus Melanchthon [Philip Schwarzerd], *Philosophiae moralis epitomes libri duo*, Argentorati, Apud Cratonem Mylium, 1546.

Montaigne: Michel Eyquem de Montaigne, *Les Essais*, Paris, Pléiade, 2007.

Nellus: Nellus de Sancto Geminiano, *Tractatus de testibus*, in *Tractatus universi iuris*, Venetiis, [Franciscus Zilettus], 1584–6.

Orsini: see Ursinus.

Otto Frisingensis: Otto of Freising, *Chronica sive historia de duabus civitatibus*, rec. Adolfus Hofmeister, Hannoverae et Lipsiae, 1912.

Panigarola: Francesco Panigarola, *Predica della potesta di Christo*, in *Prediche quadragesimali*, Venetia, Appresso Gio. Battista Ciotti Senese, 1599.

Patricius: Franciscus Patricius [Francesco Patrizi], *Della historia diece dialoghi*, Venetia, Appresso Andrea Arrivabene, 1560.

—— *Discussionum peripateticarum tomi IV*, Basileae, Apud P. Lecythum, 1581.

Paulus Castrensis: see Castrensis.

Paulus Diaconus: Paulus Diaconus [Paulus Warnefridus, Diaconus Foroiuliensis], *Epitoma Festi*, in *Sexti Pompei Festi de verborum significatu quae supersunt cum Pauli Epitome*, ed. Wallace M. Lindsay, Lipsiae, 1913.

—— *Historia Romana*, in Sextus Aurelius Victor, *Historia de vita et moribus imperatorum Romanorum*, Paris, Simon de Colines, 1531.

Petrarca: Francesco Petrarca, *Invectivae contra medicum*, a cura di Francesco Bausi, Firenze, Le lettere, 2005.

—— *Epistolae de rebus familiaribus et variae*, volumen secundum, Florentiae, Typis Felicis Le Monnier, 1842.

Petrus Martyr: see Vermilius.

Piccolomineus: Franciscus Piccolomineus [Francesco Piccolomini], *Universa philosophia de moribus*, Francofurti, Ex Officina Nicolai Hoffmanni, 1611.

Pighius: Stephanus Vinandus Pighius, *Valerii Maximi dictorum factorumque memorabilium libri IX, accedunt in fine eiusdem Annotationes: et Breves notae Iusti Lipsi*, Lugduni Batavorum, Ex officina Plantiniana, Apud Franciscum Raphelengium, 1594.

Pontanus Romanus: Ludovicus Pontanus Romanus [Lodovico Pontano Romano], *Consilia et allegationes*, Venetiis, Bonetus Locatellus, 1500.

Pseudo-Prosper: *Liber de promissionibus et praedictionibus Dei*, in J.-P. Migne (ed.), *Patrologia Latina*, vol. li.

Savonarola: HIERONYMUS SAVONAROLA [GIROLAMO SAVONAROLA], *Compendium totius philosophiae, tam naturalis, quam moralis*, Venetiis, Apud Iuntas, 1542.

Scaliger: JOSEPH SCALIGER, *Catalecta Virgilii*, in *Pub. Virgilii Maronis Appendix, cum supplemento multorum antehac nunquam excusorum poëmatum veterum poëtarum*, Lugduni Batavorum, Ex officina Plantiniana, Apud Franciscum Raphelengium, 1595.

—— *Poetices libri septem*, [Genevae], Apud Petrum Santandreanum, 1594.

Schoppius: CASPAR SCHOPPIUS, *Verisimilium libri quatuor*, Amstelodami, Apud Judocum Pluymer, 1662.

Sigonius: CAROLUS SIGONIUS [CARLO SIGONIO], *De antiquo iure provinciarum libri tres*, in *Opera omnia*, Tomus V, Mediolani, In aedibus palatinis, 1736.

—— *Scholia in Livium*, in *Opera omnia*, Tomus III, Mediolani, 1733.

Soto: DOMINGO DE SOTO, *De iustitia et iure libri decem*, Venetiis, Apud Gratiosum Perchacinum, 1568.

Tremellius: IMMANUEL TREMELLIUS, *Testamenti veteris Biblia sacra sive libri canonici priscae Judaeorum ecclesiae a Deo traditi, Latini recens ex Hebraeo facti ab Immanuele Tremellio & Francisco Junio, accesserunt libri apocryphi, &c.*, Hanoviae, 1596.

Ursinus: FULVIUS URSINUS [FULVIO ORSINI], *Selecta de legationibus*, Antverpiae, Ex officina Christophori Plantini, 1582.

Valla: LAURENTIUS VALLA [LORENZO VALLA], *Disputatio ad Alphonsum Regem, duo Tarquinii, Lucius ac Aruns, Prisci Tarquinii filiine an nepotes fuerint, adversus Livium*, in *T. Livii Patavini historiarum ab urbe condita libri, qui supersunt, omnes, cum notis integris Laur. Vallae et al.*, vol. 15, Stutgardiae, 1827.

Vermilius: PETRUS MARTYR VERMILIUS [PIETRO MARTIRE VERMIGLI], *In librum iudicum commentarii*, Tiguri, Excudebat Christophorus Froschoverus, 1571.

Victoria: FRANCISCUS A VICTORIA [FRANCISCO DE VITORIA], *De Indis relectio posterior, sive de iure belli*, in *Relectiones XII in duos tomos divisae*, Lugduni, Apud Jacobum Boyerium, 1557.

Victorius: PETRUS VICTORIUS [PIETRO VETTORI], *Commentarii in VIII libros Aristotelis de optimo statu de civitatis*, Florentiae, In officina Iuntarum, Bernardi Filiorum, 1576.

Vitoria: see Victoria.

Xiphilinus: JOHANNES XIPHILINUS, *Epitome Dionis Cassii*, Lutetiae, 1551.

Benjamin Straumann

Index of Authors and Works Cited

References are to page numbers and footnotes indicated by *n*

General Index

References are to page numbers and footnotes indicated by *n*